Technical Sourcebook
for Apparel Designers

Technical Sourcebook for Apparel Designers

THIRD EDITION

JAEIL LEE
Seattle Pacific University

CAMILLE STEEN

FAIRCHILD BOOKS
NEW YORK · LONDON · OXFORD · NEW DELHI · SYDNEY

FAIRCHILD BOOKS
Bloomsbury Publishing Inc
1385 Broadway, New York, NY 10018, USA
50 Bedford Square, London, WC1B 3DP, UK

BLOOMSBURY, FAIRCHILD BOOKS and the Fairchild Books logo are trademarks of
Bloomsbury Publishing Plc

This edition published 2019
Reprinted 2019, 2020

Cover design by Sam Clark / By The Sky design
Cover image: Versace show, Milan Men's Fashion Week Spring/Summer 2018, June 17,
2017, Milan, Italy. © Victor VIRGILE / Gamma-Rapho / Getty Images
All illustrations by Camille Steen unless otherwise indicated

Library of Congress Cataloging-in-Publication Data
Names: Lee, Jaeil, author. | Steen, Camille, author.
Title: Technical sourcebook for apparel designers / Jaeil Lee, Seattle Pacific University,
Camille Steen.
Description: Third edition. | New York : Fairchild Books, an imprint of Bloomsbury Publishing
Inc, 2019. | Includes index.
Identifiers: LCCN 2018006929 | ISBN 9781501328404 (pbk.)
Subjects: LCSH: Clothing trade. | Fashion design. | Clothing and dress.
Classification: LCC TT497 .L44 2019 | DDC 746.9/2—dc23 LC record available at
https://lccn.loc.gov/2018006929

ISBN: PB: 978-1-5013-2840-4
           ePDF: 978-1-5013-2841-1

Typeset by Lachina
Printed and bound in the United States of America

To find out more about our authors and books visit
www.fairchildbooks.com and sign up for our newsletter.

Contents

 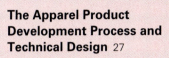
v

Extended Contents

14

Labels and Packaging 243

15

How to Measure, Size, and Grade 255

16

Fit and Fitting 279

Preface

Thanks to technology, apparel production has come to rely heavily on international industry, and specification buying has become a standard way of manufacturing apparel products. As a result, the knowledge and training related to technical design have become more important for both designers and merchandisers, and it has become a specialty in its own right, one in high demand. However, only a few apparel textbooks addressed this increasing need, covering the basic concepts sporadically. Thus, we published *Technical Sourcebook for Designers* in 2010, a comprehensive textbook dedicated solely to a holistic perspective of technical design processes.

Technical Sourcebook for Apparel Designers, 3rd Edition, is an advanced textbook completely devoted to preparing students for the growing demand in the apparel industry. It is a comprehensive compilation of technical design processes and principles in current apparel manufacturing practices. This book was written to inspire students to delve further into the commercialization process, developing designs into successful products. It provides a conceptual understanding and practical applications of the role of technical design in apparel production, including how an original design is created and communicated; how fashion trends, target markets, budgets, and construction details influence design; and finally, how products are commercialized for consumers. It presents practical guidelines for developing the skills to write concise instructions for prototypes and revisions and to conduct a fit session. This book meets the needs of courses such as apparel product development; apparel product quality evaluation; apparel design, construction, and fit; CAD (computer-aided design) for apparel design; and flats and specs for designers in the fashion industry.

This book integrates fundamental knowledge that students have gained from previous related courses in construction, pattern making, apparel design, textiles, illustration, and CAD drawing in order to provide them a holistic view of the current apparel product commercialization process. Furthermore, the book provides practical exercises that apply the current standards used by designers and other professionals in the fashion industry.

New to This Edition

As a result of its popularity since release in 2010, *Technical Sourcebook for Designers*, 2nd Edition, was published with a new Chapter 8 on sweater product development, which is one of the most popular product categories in the apparel product market. We are excited to publish this 3rd edition as the *Technical Sourcebook for Apparel Designers*, which contains more practical and updated knowledge; exercises practiced in the industry incorporated in each chapter; and more visuals—including a second color in many of the drawings—to improve readers' understanding of the subject matter. The 3rd edition contains the following updates:

- Current retailing and apparel product trends in the industry (Chapter 1).
- Expanded boxes with real-life jobs and descriptions (Chapter 1).
- Updated cost sheets and information (Chapter 3).
- More examples of supportive materials for underwear (Chapter 12).

- Increased examples of labels (Chapter 14).
- More in-depth examples of sizing and measurements (Chapter 15).
- Applicable "Study Questions" and "Check Your Understanding" sections throughout the book.
- Style Banks for Chapters 5 and 6 available in the STUDIO.
- A set of thumbnail sketches representing editable styles and pocket details in two different digital formats in the STUDIO. Appendix C features thumbnail clip art for all of these styles; the live files are available for download in the STUDIO.
- Updated Instructor's Guide includes more questions using updated examples of styles, tech packs and new added assignments, activities, discussion questions, and a test bank.

Organization of the Text

In 16 chapters, this book follows a logical progression to introduce readers to the role of technical design in apparel product commercialization. Chapter 1 describes the global nature of the modern apparel industry and the route of apparel products from producers to their target customers at the retail level. It suggests the importance of understanding technical design for designers and other industry professionals to perform their jobs effectively. Boxes featuring career profiles and job descriptions show the skills and knowledge needed for each industry profession. We also included new global trends of retailing and apparel production practices in this chapter. Chapter 2 demonstrates the understanding of technical design that apparel producers need to turn design concepts into actual garments that will appeal to the fashion sensibilities and budgets of their ultimate consumers. Chapter 3 explains the contents of the tech pack and the purposes of each item listed on each page. Costing sheets are the new adds-on to Chapter 3.

Chapters 4, 5, and 6 focus on the visual and verbal information that technical designers prepare for tech packs. Chapter 4 presents drawing conventions for technical sketches and step-by-step instructions for drawing various apparel products to scale. Chapter 5 defines technical terms related to silhouettes and design details. Garment terminology used in technical sketches is elaborated with ample examples. Styles, lines, and details used for garment shaping are identified in Chapter 6. Technical aspects of garment shaping devices are also demonstrated, with examples for effective communication in written and oral formats.

Chapters 7 through 13 discuss the reasons for design decisions, including the selection of fabrics and design details that will work well together to achieve quality commensurate with the costs of production. Chapter 7 provides practical knowledge of various fabrics and discusses layout and cutting instruction for tech packs. Chapter 8 covers one of the most important and popular product categories in apparel: sweaters. This chapter explores sweater design and manufacturing, recognizes the differences between knit and sweater apparel products, identifies the essential components of sweaters and the main types of sweater construction, and demonstrates how to create and build sketches and technical design packages. Chapters 9 and 10 identify the stitches and sewing machines for various end uses and examine practical considerations, such as whether particular seams or edge treatments are appropriate for fabric of a particular weight.

Chapter 11 provides construction-related design details such as pocket options and reinforcement stitches. Chapter 12 explains underlying fabrics and support materials used for various design details. Support materials for underwear are also included in the 3rd edition. Chapter 13 explores options for fasteners, including selection, details of each category of fasteners, and technical aspects of communicating information about them in writing and orally.

Chapters 14, 15, and 16 take the reader from the prototype in the sample size to issues related to production and marketing. Chapter 14 explains legal requirements and marketing considerations for information on labels, hang tags, and packaging. We added more examples of labels to the chapter. Chapter 15 discusses how to measure, size, and grade various product categories. A size chart with information for underwear is the new addition to Chapter 15. Evaluating and adjusting the fit of the garment, the topic of Chapter 16, demonstrates the importance of well-executed designs and clearly written tech packs and fit comments to the apparel production process.

Among the major strengths of this textbook is its extensiveness. To facilitate learning of this complex subject, each chapter begins with a set of objectives and a list of key terms, which are also defined in a comprehensive glossary at the end of the book. The text covers a variety of women's and men's product categories for different target consumers. To provide an opportunity to consider the different characteristics of product specifications and fabrications, wovens and knits are also covered.

A second strength is its real-life applications, based on the authors' hands-on knowledge, experience, and expertise. Exercises incorporating up-to-date industry standards and practices provide a practical learning experience. A fictitious company, XYZ Product Development, Inc., serves as a model to engage students in the subject matter. The book approaches the subject with the same industry tools and standards that an apparel company uses, focusing on the importance of specification for fabrics, findings, and design details. End-of-chapter study questions and activities that use industry-focused materials and terminology give students an opportunity to apply their knowledge and perfect their skills.

Third, the textbook includes ample visuals related to fabric cutting and layout, design details, flats, and examples of tech packs, to familiarize students with the apparel industry's standards for communication. Appendix A includes industry standards for seams and stitches, to which students can refer throughout the course. The technical aspects of product development are also explored, with great emphasis on the tech pack as a means of specifying the details of a design so that the prototype will fulfill the vision. Appendix B features a tech pack for a women's shirt in print, and the STUDIO includes a collection of additional tech packs for various product categories for study and reference. In this 3rd edition, the technical packages have been expanded to include one for a bra, to showcase a greater variety of those used

in the industry. Appendix C, new to the 3rd edition, includes a set of thumbnail sketches representing editable styles of various designs from various product categories. These feature 101 pockets with various design details and are a new bonus to the 3rd edition that will be incorporated into classroom learning activities. These thumbnail sketches are included in Appendix C in the book in order to provide a clear visual understanding.

The STUDIO provides a library of editable style flats in two different digital formats (Adobe Illustrator and JPEG), allowing students to engage in interactive learning. They can download and import these flats into blank tech pack documents (also found in the STUDIO) to prepare tech packs for products of their choice.

Using this textbook, students will be able, first, to obtain solid design development and related hands-on knowledge. Second, they will understand the technical design processes used in apparel firms. Third, they will gain specific knowledge and skills for technical design, such as flat sketch, measurement, sizing, fit, and grading. Fourth, they will be able to practice what they learn by using the STUDIO to create their own tech packs and will thereby become familiar with industry computer technology and terminology related to technical design. Fifth, they will be prepared to apply their understanding and skills to real-life situations when they begin their careers. Finally, this textbook will help them develop critical thinking and problem-solving skills in analyzing garments with an eye toward maximum customer acceptance.

Teaching Resources

- The Instructor's Guide includes updated course outlines, group projects, assignments, more interactive learning activities, discussion questions, a test bank, and more
- PowerPoint presentations available for each chapter

Technical Sourcebook for Fashion Designers STUDiO

Fairchild Books has a long history of excellence in textbook publishing for fashion education. Our online STUDIOS are specially developed to complement this book with rich media ancillaries that students can adapt to their visual learning styles. The *Technical Sourcebook for Apparel Designers* STUDIO features include online self-quizzes with scored results and personalized study tips and flashcards with terms/definitions to help students master concepts and improve grades. The STUDIO also includes standards for seams and stitches, examples of flats, technical packages, and a style bank with photos of apparel product examples of each design detail and style. All materials included in the STUDIO are provided in full color where applicable.

The *Technical Sourcebook for Apparel Designers* STUDIO can be accessed at www.fairchildbooks.com.

Acknowledgments

Many people have provided us assistance to complete this project, and we would like to thank them for their time, effort, and support. Jaeil Lee would like to express her thanks to her sister-like cousin, Jung Woo Nam, for her love and prayers, and especially her coauthor, Camille Steen, for her friendship and extensive technical expertise and knowledge about this project.

Camille Steen would like to thank Wanda Clarke-Morin for her read-through and suggestions; Martha Boyd for help on merchandise planning and organization charts; Ken Sandow, American and Efird; Chris Karam, principal, Chameleon PLM; Helen Sharp and Karen Mitchell for their inspiration and expertise in sweater design; and Bernie Kulisek and Ingrid Schneider for their photographic contributions. She expresses her special thanks to her husband, Phil Hyatt, for his patience and forbearance.

Both authors are grateful for the recommendations and comments of the following reviewers, selected by the publisher: Victoria Bezpalko, Mount Ida College; Helen Burbidge, De Montfort University (UK); Tameka Ellington, Kent State University; Hilary Hollingworth, University of Huddersfield (UK); Genevieve Jezick, Parsons New School; and Mary Simpson, Baylor University.

Lastly, we would like to express our appreciation of the team at Fairchild Books, who worked with us throughout the race, to Olga Kontzias and Joe Miranda, who invited us to become Fairchild authors for the first edition; Amanda Breccia, our acquisitions editor; Edie Weinberg, who guided us through the preparation of the art for the text and STUDIO; to Amy Butler, our development editor, and Claire Cooper, our production editor, who are true examples of all the hard work the Fairchild team does; and to Courtney Coffman, project manager at Lachina. Thank you.

Overview of the Industry

1

Chapter Objectives

After studying this chapter, you will be able to:

- Describe the apparel industry and its production process
- Survey apparel product categories
- Identify different professionals involved in the product development process in the industry and describe their roles
- Survey different kinds of ready-to-wear apparel companies
- Identify the role of private labels in the industry
- Survey new product development and retailing trends in the industry

---

Key Terms

agent
carry-over styles
child labor
colorist
crowd sourcing
dual distribution
globalization
graphic designer
haute couture
horizontal integration
lab dip
lead time
line plan
merchandiser

moda pronto
multi-channel retailing
national brands
omni-channel retailing
pattern maker
prêt-á-porter
private label
product lifecycle
   management
quality assurance
   professionals
ready-to-wear
rep (representative)
reshoring

retail store brand
sample maker
social responsibility
specification buying
specifications (specs)
sweatshop
tech pack
technical designer
technical package
textile designer
textile lab technician
vertical integration

Since the Industrial Revolution, the apparel industry has been one of the most important economic sectors in the world. This chapter presents a general overview of current trends in the apparel production process and the ready-to-wear apparel industry. Apparel products are also introduced based on merchandise segments, and the work of the main professionals in the industry who participate in the apparel product development process is also explored.

The Global Apparel Industry

Welcome to the global apparel industry. Considering everyone, from farm workers who grow cotton to mills that produce yarns and fabrics to companies creating designs and products for the selling floor, the apparel industry is one of the biggest economic sectors and one of the most important sources of income for many parts of the world economy. The textiles and apparel industry is one of the most powerful sources of industrial employment, providing jobs for millions of people worldwide (Kunz, Karpova, and Garner, 2016; Dickerson, 1999).

In the industry's production processes, apparel manufacturing is no longer a matter of domestic in-house production. Although simple domestic manufacturing methods exist for independent, small-scale designers, most apparel is currently produced in large-scale operations, with the manufacturing of domestically created designs outsourced.

The apparel industry is one of the most globalized businesses, with different sectors of production, marketing, and distribution channels in different regions in the world working as one unit. Simply check the labels of garments you have now. You are likely to see names of various countries in different parts of the globe. The unique characteristics of the apparel industry make it stand out as the leader in **globalization**. Globalization is a modern trend of interaction among countries, governments, and businesses, regardless of their defined borders and boundaries (Daly, 1999). Globalization enables people around the world to function together as one unified, single entity, joined by the main economic flows of goods and services, labor and people, capital, and technology (Bhagwati, 2004). Globalization unites people in the industry throughout the world to produce apparel products. Changes in procedures and processes influence all sectors of the apparel industry as a global complex.

Availability of Labor

One factor contributing to the industry's leadership role is its very labor-intensive character. For that reason, the industry's manufacturing regions have always been shifted to where lower labor costs are available for production. Throughout history, the apparel industry has boosted economic power to those less-developed countries to stimulate their economic growth.

More fashion trends can also be introduced to people who live in less-developed countries, where new fashion information was rarely available in earlier times, because they now participate in the apparel production process. We now see a trend of global fashion that is led by the globalization of the apparel production process (Dickerson, 1999).

Taiwan, China, Hong Kong, and South Korea were given the nickname "four dragons in Asia," signifying their important role in the 1980s and 1990s. The apparel industry was a point of entry for these countries moving into export-led businesses. The industry requires only simple technology (that is, simple machinery such as sewing machines), and thus has low start-up costs for the less-developed countries, which, in most cases, have ample labor forces. Also, a labor-intensive activity, such as a simple assembly process, does not require a formal education. Thus, it is easy to start a business in less-developed countries.

China, Vietnam, and Indonesia are among the most active countries producing apparel lines. China is the most influential role player in current apparel production, as exemplified by U.S. consumption of apparel products, including actual consumer consumption in the United States and imports (at the wholesale level), which increased 6.1 percent to 20.5 billion in 2005 from 2004 (American Apparel and Footwear Association, 2006). In 2005, China's textile production accounted for one-third of the world's textile supply. That year, China exported a total value of US$22.4 billion to the United States, and in 2006, its exports reached US$27.8 billion. China became the single largest source of imports of textiles and clothing for the United States during the past decades (Shen, 2008).

The United States imports most of its apparel and fashion products—more than 95 percent of its apparel and 99 percent of its shoes—from other nations (American Apparel and Footwear Association, 2009).

Availability of High Technology

The industry also requires high-technology components for apparel production processes, such as computer-aided design (CAD) programs. But the combination of low- and high-tech characteristics of systems allows companies in the highly developed countries to use high technology to design apparel products and hire contractors for the low-tech, labor-intensive production activities in less-developed countries. Usually, with the help of an **agent** who acts as a go-between, a company that designs and a factory that manufactures collaborate to produce apparel products (Bonacich et al., 1994). The agent decides which factory would be best suited to a product; negotiates prices; and helps to solve production, scheduling, and shipping issues. Technology such as websites, email, and design software enables apparel companies to conduct business globally.

Worldwide Collaboration for Global Production

Because manufacturers from many countries participate in the production process of apparel, the finished products become global products. The apparel you are wearing now may have traveled thousands of miles to come to you.

Figure 1.1 illustrates the global production process for apparel. For example, a jacket designed by an apparel company in the United States is made through a contracted agency such as Li and Fung, headquartered in Hong Kong. The fabric for the garment is woven in Thailand; the prototypes are developed in Shanghai, China; the production is done in Zucheng, China; and the finished goods are shipped to San Francisco, trucked to the distribution center in Reno, Nevada, and shipped out to individual retail stores all over the United States.

The Impact of Global Economic and Political Factors

Current issues related to political and economic factors around the globe—for example, a sluggish economy, rising fuel costs for

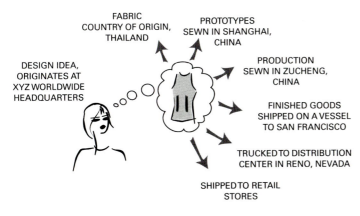

Figure 1.1 Globalization.

transportation, and limited fossil fuels for synthetic fibers and global production—also influence apparel production. Considering soaring fuel costs, one can predict that domestic manufacturing may be a better solution to cut down the total cost of future apparel production. Considering the fast-paced nature of fashion, success in the industry also requires an understanding of its manufacturing processes and trends for shortening the time between the design and the completion of final products in retail stores.

Ready-to-Wear Apparel

In early times, clothing and shoes were custom made; that is, made for an individual according to that person's own measurements. Apparel was cut, sewn, and fitted by a dressmaker or tailor, one customer and one garment at a time. There were no "sizes." The **ready-to-wear** industry started in the early nineteenth century, and mass-produced garments were introduced in the 1850s. Ready-to-wear was started for lower-class people who were not able to afford the cost of custom-made garments, and later was accepted by middle-class people. After the invention of the sewing machine by Walter Hunt (1832), Elias Howe (1845), and Isaac Singer (1846), ready-to-wear apparel could offer mass-produced products to the majority of consumers (Burns, Mullet, and Bryant, 2011). Thanks to high demand and the availability of sewing machines, more tailors who previously custom made garments worked for the ready-to-wear garment business.

With the standardization of sizes for military uniforms and less attention to individual fit issues, men's wear set a trend in the ready-to-wear apparel market, and women's wear and children's wear followed. Men's ready-to-wear was available in the mid-nineteenth century and the women's ready-to-wear industry expanded its business by the late nineteenth century. In the early twentieth century, ready-to-wear skirts and shirtwaists were available for sale in the market (Burns, Mullet, and Bryant, 2011).

Today, apparel products can be divided into two main categories based on their manufacturing practices: ready-to-wear and couture design. Ready-to-wear—**prêt-á-porter** in French and **moda pronto** in Italian—means ready to be worn, off the rack. It means customers can buy apparel products that are created based on standardization of sizes. It is different from couture design, also called **haute couture,** which means "high sewing" in French (Burns, Mullet, and Bryant, 2011). Haute couture is the design of apparel collections, in most cases produced in small quantity by high fashion designers such as Christian Dior, Chanel, and Givenchy.

Authentic haute couture collections are created by a very small group of designers, regulated by the Chambre Syndicale de la Haute Couture in France. The use of the term *haute couture* is regulated by law by the French Ministry of Industry, which ensures that the finest fabrics and most skilled technicians are employed to create these designs. In the 1950s there were more than 100 companies, or design houses, who were members of the haute couture. The organization dictates that to be a full-fledged member, a couture house must be in France, must employ at least 20 full-time people in its workshop, and must present at least 50 original designs to the press twice a year. In 2009, there were nine companies that comprised the haute couture; about twice that many participate in the couture shows, but are not full-fledged members; for example, companies in other countries, such as Valentino in Italy (O'Hara Callan and Glover, 1998). The term *couture* is bandied about with great abandon these days, but a garment that has a size tag is ready-to-wear, not couture, no matter how expensive.

Though not members of the haute couture, many designers have a structure in which their custom or high-end label is extended to include a lower-priced brand as well. Many produce custom-made apparel for their exclusive clients and sell these items in a very high price range. However, many designers extend their design influence into high-end ready-to-wear. Designers have their own house design line as well as a ready-to-wear line that is sold through department stores. A good example is Saint Laurent and its ready-to-wear line, Rive Gauche.

Categories of Ready-to-Wear Brands

There are several categories in ready-to-wear, distinguished by the relationship between the producer and the retailer.

Brands That Are Strictly Wholesale

Many brands are produced strictly for sale by the wholesale manufacturer to retail buyers. Underwear brands, including Hanes and other brands familiar to store buyers but not well known to the general public, also belong to this category. Most companies begin this way, and as their brand becomes stronger they may open their own retail store for greater visibility and promotion of their brand, even though the retail element may not be part of their primary business model.

An example is 7 For All Mankind, a brand that was mainly sold to consumers only through various retailers such as department stores and independent boutiques, but has added selected retail stores as well. Another example is Columbia Sportswear, a very successful wholesaler who also maintains a flagship store in Portland, Oregon, near its headquarters. The retail element enables the brand to display its complete line in its own environment as it was originally envisioned.

Business plans change constantly, and companies may add or subtract retail stores according to the business climate and to their marketing strategies.

Brands That Are Both Wholesale and Retail

Some brands have their own stores but also sell in other retail outlets. Some of these are **national brands**, to which consumers attach specific images, quality levels, and prices, such as Nike, Polo Ralph Lauren, and Liz Claiborne. They use **dual distribution**, which means selling their products through their own retail stores as well as to department stores that carry their

Figure 1.2 Designer Tommy Hilfiger.

brands. It means they can access more consumers through the conduit of other retail channels. Having their own stores allows the brands to showcase these products to their best advantage.

Some brands find their way into department stores through an exclusive arrangement. An example of this is Tommy Hilfiger (see Figure 1.2), who signed a contract with Macy's roughly 800 stores in the United States beginning in the fall of 2008. As part of the agreement the line was no longer carried by rival department stores such as Dillard's.

Private Label Brands Sold Through Their Own Retail Only

Companies that create their own products and distribute them exclusively through their own stores are called direct market brands or **retail store brands**. These well-known brands have exclusivity of designs and develop their own brand message, supported by their store layouts, custom fixtures, and ad campaigns. Consumers have wide recognition of their brand image. Abercrombie & Fitch, Gap, Victoria's Secret, and Anne Taylor are examples of this category.

The Gap Stores, Inc., includes Old Navy, Gap, and Banana Republic. All of their apparel is created through their own design teams and sold through their own retail stores. Although these stores are owned by The Gap Stores, Inc. (parent company), one cannot purchase the product of any of these chains in other stores of the parent company. For example, you cannot purchase Old Navy products in a Banana Republic store.

Private Label Brands Developed by Retailers

Some retailers develop **private label**, or store brands that they sell alongside their many other brands. Macy's, as a department store retailer, carries I.N.C., which is a private label created by Macy's and sold exclusively through its own department store, along with many other brands.

Nordstrom is another example of a retailer that has several of its own private label lines such as Classiques Entier, B.P., and Caslon. Nordstrom Product Group, a division of Nordstrom, creates its own private label products, and the in-house buyers purchase the styles to sell through Nordstrom stores only.

Arizona Jeans is another example of a brand that is exclusive to a retailer—JCPenney—that also carries many other brands. REI (Recreational Equipment Incorporated) carries many outdoor equipment brands in addition to developing its own branded products. The advantage of this arrangement is that in addition to building customer loyalty it also provides a measure of pricing freedom which can potentially boost the bottom line.

All of these private labels have their own design and product development teams and use **specification buying** as outlined in this book. That means that they oversee the production process, although the actual cutting and assembling process is done by their hired manufacturers. Ready-to-wear is created by mass production and sold wholesale for distribution by retail stores and department stores. Therefore, we can consider these retailers as manufacturers, although, technically, their apparel products are cut, assembled, and packaged by hired contractors who manufacture the apparel products for them.

Private Label with Retail Store Name

Some companies do not manufacture their own merchandise but rather buy their products from wholesale manufacturers and assign it their retail brand name. Forever 21 is an example of a retailer that in the past did not create products but bought from wholesalers. Recently, Forever 21 began their own private label brands, producing their own products instead of buying from other manufacturers. Forever 21 owns its own retail stores and buys the majority of their merchandise from multiple manufacturers, relabeling it with the "Forever 21" label.

Some companies sell mainly through catalogs and the Internet, but even they often have some retail stores or outlet stores. Primarily mail-order catalog companies such as Coldwater Creek, Land's End, and L.L. Bean often source products from a number of manufacturers but need to ensure that different styles will fit the same customer the same way. For example, a customer needs to be able to predict that she will be a size 10 in whatever garment she orders from a given company; this is particularly important in a mail-order company because it's not possible to try a garment on before purchase. By providing consistent sizing, companies can reduce return rates, and build loyalty and customer satisfaction. For all of these development processes, the technical design aspect is crucial.

Unbranded Products

Different from private labels, these are generic products that are created and sold to retailers and wholesalers. Such a product does not have its own brand name attached to it. It is sold and assigned its brand name according to the name of retailer or wholesaler. Branded products are sold to retail-only private labels with their own brand name and retail-only private labels under one store name and sold to the consumers.

The product development information in this book applies to any type of organization because both the processes of design and manufacturing go through similar specification steps.

Merchandise Segments

There are different ways of segmenting apparel merchandise. It is divided based on price range, on target consumers' demographic characteristics such as gender or age, and on product category.

Price Range

Wholesale price is a good indicator of ready-to-wear apparel companies as well as products. There are various product lines available based on their price range.

- *High* or *designer price zone* is the most expensive of the wholesale prices. Designers' collections such as Calvin Klein, Donna Karan, Yves Saint Laurent, and Chanel are included in this price zone. The introduction of new price ranges of designer products is an interesting phenomenon of the industry. New, high-end merchandise such as Purple Label from Ralph Lauren is a good example of a price line even more exclusive than the designer's name brand (Figure 1.3).

- *Bridge* is the category between the high or designer and better price ranges. It includes the less expensive lines of designers, but is a bit higher range than the better price lines. Two examples of designer bridge lines are cK by Calvin Klein and DKNY by Donna Karan. Other brands in this category are Ellen Tracy and Emporio Armani.

- *Better* includes national brands that are widely recognized by consumers. Tommy Hilfiger, Liz Claiborne, Jones New York, Reunion, Nike, and Nautica are examples. Store labels such as Ann Taylor, Talbot, and Banana Republic are also included in this price range.

- *Moderate* is a category including many private labels such as Guess, Levi's, and Gap (Figure 1.4).

- *Mass market or budget* is the price range for merchandise carried in discount stores such as Target and Kmart. It is the least-expensive merchandise found in the markets. Wholesalers such as Costco's Kirkland brand, Swedish apparel line H&M, and retailers' product lines such as Forever 21 are examples. Currently, mass market or budget companies such as H&M and Forever 21 have reached their heights of popularity (Figure 1.5).

Many apparel companies expand their acquisition by adding a new apparel line in various price ranges. Vera Wang, a top wedding dress designer for celebrities, expanded her business by adding a new women's ready-to-wear line at the moderate market. The Simply Vera label was introduced at Kohl's, the department store chain well known for its value-oriented products and price (Crawford, 2007). After witnessing the fall of Halston, a famous designer in the 1960s and 1970s, after he sold his line at JCPenney and lost his high-fashion image, the fashion industry is paying attention to see what comes of Wang's bold move.

Figure 1.3 **Trademarks for high-price zone brands.**

Figure 1.4 **Guess is an example of a brand in the moderate price zone.**

a   b

Figure 1.5 **Tracy Feith for Target Go International.**

Figure 1.6 **Forever 21 is an example of a brand in the mass or budget price range.**

Figure 1.7 **The design process in the past.**

Forever 21 is one of the leaders of the "fast fashion, cheap chic" trend (Figure 1.6). The clothing company has grown tremendously over the last decade since its foundation in 1984. This retail powerhouse relentlessly keeps up with trends and is widening its market to men and women, from toddlers to adults. It is known for its strategy of catering to entire families rather than focusing on teens or fashion-forward women. It also carries product categories such as women's footwear, lingerie, plus sizes, and cosmetics (La Ferla, 2007). It added more categories such as men's wear in 2006 and children's apparel in 2010. The company has also added several additional women's lines, including the plus-sized collection Faith 21 and the more envelope-pushing Twelve by Twelve, which is its most high-fashion line (Holmes, 2010).

A privately held company, Forever 21 has continuously expanded its stores under branch brands such as Forever 21, XXI Forever, Love 21, 21 Men, Heritage 1981, Faith 21, Forever 21 Girls, and Love and Beauty throughout North America, Asia, the Middle East, Europe, Mexico City, and Latin America, as well as a Korean e-commerce site (http://www.forever21.co.kr). Forever 21 interprets cheap fashion at a faster momentum—typically six weeks—than other leading fashion companies; for example, Marc Jacobs may take six months (La Ferla, 2007).

Gender and Age

Merchandise segmentation is determined by one's target consumer's demographic profile, with special attention to gender and age. Many companies own multiple brands to reach out to various ranges of consumers who are distinguished by their demographic characteristics. As previously mentioned, The Gap Stores, Inc. owns Banana Republic, Gap, and Old Navy. Each brand has its distinct price range and its unique styles geared to its own target consumers. Each brand owns its own merchandise segments based on their gender and age; for example, Old Navy caters to men's, women's, boys, girls, babies, maternity, and women's plus segments.

Based on these categories, apparel products are broadly divided into men's, women's, and children's. In the past, the women's line

was the main focus in the industry; however, over time, with men paying more attention to their style, men's fashion has been growing, and different brands based on various target consumers have come to the industry. The decision for a given brand to expand from a successful women's line into men's and children's is not taken lightly because success in one area does not guarantee success in another. A separate staff with expertise in the new area is needed to successfully bring the products to market.

Many apparel companies expand their business by adding more brands. Apparel companies find it easy to expand their business because they have their own know-how of product development and distribution channels. For example, Abercrombie & Fitch plans to add a new apparel line every two years. Abercrombie kids, Hollister, and Ruehl No. 925 are examples of brands added to the company's brand lines. The company's main idea is to cover all the customers in various demographics. The customers who grow up with abercrombie kids can move to A&F in their teens and college years, and then move to Ruehl No. 925 in their 30s when they want an age-appropriate feel of Abercrombie & Fitch for themselves.

Table 1.1 shows how the broad market segments of men's, women's, and children's wear are further segmented by age and other demographic characteristics.

Product Category

Apparel products are subcategorized based on end use. Product categories included in Table 1.1 and the following list of women's apparel product categories are not mutually exclusive.

- Outerwear: coats, jackets, vests
- Dresses
- Blouses, shirts
- Sweaters
- Skirts
- Suits and coordinates
- Knits and tees
- Swimwear
- Sportswear and active sportswear: golf wear, tennis wear, skiwear, snowboard wear, yoga wear
- Eveningwear

Table 1.1 Merchandise Segments Based on Gender, Age, and Body Type

Men's Wear	Women's Wear	Children's Wear
Men's	Missy	Infants (3, 6, 12, 18 months)
Big and tall	Women's large	Toddler (2T to 3T)
Young men's	Petite	Children's (3 to 6X)
	Tall	Boy's (8 to 18)
	Maternity	Boy's husky (8 to 18)
	Juniors	Girl's (7 to 16)
		Girl's plus (7 to 16)
		Young junior (3 to 13)

- Bridal and bridesmaid dresses
- Maternity wear
- Uniforms
- Intimate apparel (foundations): bras, girdles, and other shaping garments
- Sleepwear and loungewear
- Accessories, bags
- Shoes
- Hats, scarves, and gloves
- Socks and hosiery
- Furs
- Leathers

Generally, apparel companies specialize in one of several categories of products. An interesting current trend is the success of specialized apparel lines such as the Portland, Oregon-based swimwear company Jantzen Inc. and Victoria's Secret, a Columbus, Ohio-based brand specializing in intimate apparel as well as sleepwear and loungewear.

Professionals in Apparel Product Production and Distribution

To be successful in the industry, it is important to understand its structure, including both the manufacturing and retail sides, as well as to be up to date in knowledge of the market and product trends. Apparel products are produced by teams of creative professionals. Owing to globalization, specification buying is a current trend that is widely practiced in the industry.

Influence of the Specification Buying Process on Roles

In the past, the design process was more commonly based on in-house production (Figure 1.7). Designers designed and produced a style on a small scale, and production was more like the process for custom-made apparel. Later, the design would be produced in-house by the company's own factory. However, after mass production became the norm and ready-to-wear had come to dominate the industry, production began to be done on a mass scale in other countries.

Currently most ready-to-wear apparel producers practice specification buying. The majority of companies in the United States do not own their manufacturing facilities. This means that a company works with the agents and factories it hires to produce its apparel products; in most cases, these agents and

factories are overseas. Companies specify the production process, approve the creation of designs, and stipulate the materials and the details of designs. However, actual cut, assembly, tagging, and shipping are done by hired contractors. In this sense, on the one hand, the apparel companies are buyers who pay money to the manufacturers who manufacture the products for them, following the specifications given by the companies. On the other hand, they are manufacturers who design and dictate the product specifications. The U.S. companies are buying the products from the offshore manufacturers who make the product on the basis of designs provided by the U.S. companies, and according to those companies' own specifications such as specific design details, trims, fits/specs, grades, constructions, labels, and finishes set by the in-house design teams.

Specifications (specs) are written guidelines for a style that include all the specific information related to producing a certain garment. Because specifications are used as a tool to communicate between design teams and contractors, it is very important to write clear as well as complete specifications. The written specification is called a specification package or technical package—tech pack for short. (See Chapter 3 for more information on technical packages.)

Private label companies commonly practice specification buying in their apparel production process. The products are created based exclusively on the company's specific, established standard specifications. On this point, there are various advantages of private labels. First is the exclusivity of design (Brown and Rice, 2014) in that the designs are created by the in-house design team based on their brand image for target consumers. They carry the products only in their retail stores so they can easily create their own exclusive brand images, using advertisements, signage, and other forms of promotion. Private label companies such as Polo, Gap, Abercrombie & Fitch, and most apparel companies are included in this category.

Second, it is easy to set up or dissolve the business because it does not need the startup investment of setting up an actual manufacturing plant. The design company can easily hire contractors to fulfill its orders (Brown and Rice, 2014).

Third, the company does not need to worry about personnel issues. The workers are contracted through the hired agents or contractors, and it is not the company's direct responsibility to meet with each individual worker and union to take care of any issues (Brown and Rice, 2014). However, contracting for manufacturing can raise huge issues related to sweatshops and child labor for the brand because the U.S. public is becoming increasingly demanding of ethical labor standards in the factories that produce their clothes. Consumers are holding companies responsible for selecting manufacturers that treat their workers humanely.

A sweatshop is a working condition with very unhealthy, difficult, or hazardous situations; in most cases, workers do not have unions or collective bargaining rights to protect themselves and are often forced to work long hours for little or no pay. On April 24, 2013, the Rana Plaza garment factory building in Savar, an industrial suburb of Dhaka, the capital of Bangladesh, collapsed and killed 1,127 people. It is the deadliest disaster in the history of the garment industry. The building was constructed with substandard materials and in blatant disregard for building codes. The factory owners urged workers to return to their jobs despite evidence that the building was unsafe (Yardley, 2013).

Sweatshops also frequently engage in **child labor**. Child labor is the employment of children under an age determined by law or custom. Each country has its own standard for setting the minimum age of workers. Under the child labor laws in the United States, the minimum age to work in an establishment without parental consent is 16. More information on sweatshops and child labor can be found on the following websites:

- Fair Labor Organization: www.fairlabor.org
- Sweat Shop Watch: www.sweatshopwatch.org

Apparel companies should monitor the working conditions in manufacturing factories to avoid sweatshop and child labor issues. Most apparel companies require manufacturers to abide by the regulations regarding working conditions and labor issues spelled out in their contract. For example, Nike developed its own requirements from its past mistake of hiring children as young as ten years old to make shoes, clothing, and footballs in its Pakistani and Cambodian manufacturing facilities (www.commondreams.org/headlines01/1020-01.htm).

Horizontal Integration Versus Vertical Integration

There are two different kinds of organization in the apparel industry. One is **vertical integration**, which means that the company owns the production process facilities, and employees from management to line workers may work under one roof. There are several advantages to this kind of production: easy control of the production process because all personnel can check the process on the spot; ease of communication with everyone who is involved in the process; and the absence of need to physically move the product for the production process.

The Spanish company Zara (a producer of apparel in the moderate price zone) is a great example. The company has total control of its management (Figure 1.8) from design to production, including most of its supply chains and even distribution. Interestingly, most of the production facilities are owned by Zara and are located in Spain. Zara produces an average of 50 percent of its apparel products by dozens of company-owned factories in Spain; 26 percent is from factories elsewhere in Europe, and 24 percent is from factories in Asian countries and the other parts of the world. Zara wins over other competitors by shortening its **lead time** (the amount of time needed between creating a new design and moving it into retail stores) to two weeks using its domestic manufacturing facilities (Ferdows, Lewis, and Machuca, 2004). Only staple items, for example basic T-shirts, which stay a longer time on the shelf, are outsourced to low-wage and somewhat far areas from their company such as Asian countries and Turkey.

Considering the importance of timing in the fashion industry, other companies, which in most cases outsource to Asia and have nine months lead time, cannot compete with Zara. Creative decisions made at Zara, stemming from impromptu discussions at Inditex headquarters, occur in an open workspace slightly bigger than a soccer field. Everyone from designers and commercial staff to store managers around the world are closely connected in their manufacturing processes through electronic and telephone contact. Store managers frequently visit the corporate headquarters to consult, view samples, and help improve designs in an informal capacity. These practices result in Inditex's speedy conception and production in a two-week cycle (Kowsmann, 2016).

Figure 1.8 Zara, a leading retail brand known for its vertical integration.

The high-end apparel brand Saint John is another good example. Located on a campus in Irvine, California, the company owns all of its manufacturing facilities, from yarn producing to sewing. It is easy for all the professionals involved in the production process to communicate and check progress. Because they produce their own yarns and cut and assemble them themselves, it is possible for them to maintain quality and exclusivity.

The other type of organization is **horizontal integration**, whereby each part of the production process is owned and completed separately. This means all of the processes involved in creating materials, such as trims and fabrics, cutting, assembly, and packing, are done by different parties, and all the parties work separately in different places. It is applied to most brands, such as Ann Taylor, Abercrombie & Fitch, and Banana Republic. Disadvantages of this process are that unlike vertical integration, it is not easy to control each production process or communicate among personnel. Also, the products must physically move around, as must the employees who check the process; therefore, it may take more time to complete production. However, considering the labor-intensive nature of the apparel production, if the company can take advantage of cheaper labor from overseas manufacturers, it may be a good way to produce the products compared to domestic vertical integration. This would be a practical method for a start-up company without the high investment.

Main Professionals

Before entering the industry, it is important for prospective fashion designers to understand the roles of the three main professional groups in the production process. In the big picture, professionals are involved primarily in the distribution process, the production process, or the product development process.

Distribution Process

Retailers create private label products and set up their own design team. They then produce their own products, or hire **vendors** or **contractors**. The words *vendors* and *contractors* are used interchangeably. Vendors oversee production to ensure that the products meet the quality standards set by the design team. In the case of overseas manufacturing, the workers usually do not understand English, so bilingual agents direct the production process.

Production Process

A product coordinator's job responsibilities include coordinating production and dealing with contract information and deliveries. Product coordinators work with contractors and agents. Real-Life Job Description #1 is an example of an actual production assistant position for a medium-size private label company.

The responsibility of contractors hired by apparel companies to manufacture products is to produce those products based on the specifications set by the apparel companies. The contractors actually manage or own and manage the sewing plants. One of the biggest international contractors in the world is Youngone Corporation, which is based in Korea.

Wholesalers produce products under their own label and sell those products to retailers. Considering the retailer's or manufacturer's side, there are different positions specifically related to the design process.

Product Development Process

Merchandisers analyze the market, review the best-selling styles from the previous season, and provide direction to the design staff. In many companies they work with the designers and have a good feel for the customer and what styles will be accepted and successful. They act as a bridge between the buyers and the designers, interpreting the next season, what styles will be needed, and what colors and trends are relevant to the brand. They also ensure that the new styles offered will be what the target customers will be looking for at the price they want to pay.

Merchandisers spend time working on budget and sales data spread sheets. Communication skills and critical analysis of trends, designs, and sales data are essential for merchandisers. They monitor both the new and carry-over styles, which are styles that were popular in a previous season and are repeated in the next season, and have a feel for what is trending up or down. Based upon the sales figures and their own experience and perspective, they provide a key document each season called the line plan, which is an outline of all the styles to be produced for the season. See Table 2.1 in Chapter 2 for a sample line plan. Real-Life Job Description #2 is an example of an assistant merchandiser position for a medium-size private label company.

Apparel designers create actual styles for apparel products. They work far ahead of the delivery season based upon the lead time (the time it takes a factory to develop a style from the moment it receives the design instructions until the time the goods arrive in the retail store, usually six months to one year). Their designs are based on in-depth research of past and current trends. They often travel to get inspiration from different places and sources, including textile trade shows, before beginning a new season and creating designs with the inspiration. This position requires the ability to understand cultural diversity and interact with overseas workers. Real-Life Job Description #3 is an example of an assistant designer position for a medium-size private label company.

In large companies, the technical design department is separate from design and includes the apparel engineers who specialize in making designs into real products. The technical designer's job description includes reviewing tech packs (manuals of each style) initiated by the apparel designers' computer-aided design skills, fitting, writing fit comments, and so on. Technical designers closely direct the production process. Creativity and problem-solving skills are required to create functional as well as aesthetically pleasing garments that meet the quality standards set by the specifications. One of the most important issues, cultural sensitivity, is essential to working with manufacturers, given that most production is outsourced overseas. Understanding diverse cultures will ease work stress and avoid problems in interactions with workers in these factories. Real-Life Job Description #4 is an actual example of a job posting for a technical design assistant position in a large private label company.

The people who create graphics of apparel products, packages, labels, embroidery designs, and signage of the product are the graphic designers. Creativity and critical analysis are important for this job. An art background with an emphasis on color and design is needed for this work.

Textile designers design new fabrics for apparel products. Knowledge about various colors, design motifs, printing techniques, and fiber and fabric structure as well as CAD skills are important for a textile designer, as is a knowledge of the technology of printing. Designing textiles is an important job, especially for the men's and women's woven area. To create styles in keeping with current trends for specific target markets, it is essential to create unique textiles.

An appealing color is often the first thing that draws a customer's eye. Every season, new color influences arise and the colorist works with the forecasting companies, researches color trends, and develops storyboards to present new color direction or new ways to present carry-over colors to the design team. Colors are often given poetic names in an effort to target the market segment, and the colorist is often in charge of managing the color names. For example, rather than calling a color "dark gray," the colorist may give it the name "anthracite" to tie in with other jewel tone names within a certain seasonal palette. When the color story is set each season, requests go out for lab dips of all the fabrics in each new color. A lab dip is a small swatch of the fabric that has been dyed to match a standard (for example, Pantone colors, a widely used standardized color reproduction system created by Pantone Inc.). The colorist manages this process. Real-Life Job Description #5 is a job posting for a textile print designer and colorist position for a large private label company.

Real-Life Job Description #6 describes a raw materials developer. This person handles new fabrics, new trims, and coordination with the mills. In some companies the duties of the raw materials developer and colorist (see Real-Life Job Description #5) may be combined. In these examples they are split into two distinct positions.

If a company has its own sample room, it will include the areas of pattern maker, sample maker, and cutter. The sample department personnel will create patterns and samples for fitting and review in the technical design process. In some cases, in a smaller organization, pattern makers are also sample makers, and possibly cutters as well. The advantage of having a staff pattern maker is that the pattern and fit can be approved early in the process, saving development time. Other companies outsource the pattern-making process to the factory producing the goods. The advantage to using the factory pattern maker is that the pattern can be closely engineered to run through the factory in the smoothest way possible. If the factory is furnished with block (or basic) patterns, which the company has already fit and approved, the garment fit can be consistent. Real-Life Job Description #7 provides information about pattern makers.

After the pattern maker has created patterns, **sample makers** create the first prototype samples for style. Similar to pattern making, sample making is often one of the responsibilities of contractors. Many companies do not own their sample rooms and rely on manufacturers for sample making. **Quality assurance professionals** work in the design division and deal with the product quality issues. When received, products are inspected to make sure they meet the expectation of the tech pack. These professionals perform quality audits on incoming shipments by examining specs (that is, measurements for fit and trims). Understanding various quality issues related to products, such as garment washes, is an important part of this job. Quality assurance personnel work closely with other design teams so communication skills are vital. Real-Life Job Description #8 is an actual posting for an apparel quality assurance professional-assistant position for a medium-size private label company.

Textile lab technicians, usually part of the quality assurance department, test the fabric and textile requirements for apparel products. *Dimensional stability* is the term used to describe shrinking or stretching during washing or dry cleaning. Other important standards that must be met include tension, tenacity, crocking (color rubbing off), and color fastness to light and to washing. Evaluating how well textiles meet these standards is central to the job of this professional.

The **product line manager (PLM)** oversees the whole development process and takes full responsibility for the overall product planning assortment and the line plan creation process. Real-Life Job Description #9 shows the job description of the product line manager.

Because the Internet and electronic commerce is such a big area of selling, an **e-commerce manager** oversees the direct-to-consumer website as well as related mobile sites and social media. Collaborating closely with management, product development, sales, customer service, and information technology (IT) is key for success in this position. Real-Life Job Description #10 demonstrates a job posting for this position.

The **brand manager's** main goal is to create and develop strategic private-label brand plans that create revenue for the company through developing products that satisfy consumers' ever-changing needs and wants. The brand manager works closely with the merchandising design teams to ultimately meet their goals and establish their brand power and more sales. Real-Life Job Description #11 provides a job description for the position.

Selling Process

Larger companies show their lines to the retail buyers in a showroom. Another type of selling structure entails company representatives, either in-house (a salaried company employee) or independent (self-employed, paid by commission, usually with multiple lines), who cover a regional territory. They are known as reps (representatives). The garments are shown at regional trade shows where the retailers come to place their wholesale orders.

Introduction to the Design Department

The design department is structured in different ways, depending on the size or type of the company.

Small- to Medium-Sized Companies

In terms of what exactly a given department designs, a small company encompasses more categories. For example, in a small company, one designer may handle all categories of women's products, and another designer will handle all men's. They may also take on more than one role within the process. The designers participate in the whole process of production. At a medium-sized company, such as Union Bay, the designers may decide the colors for the season, create textile prints, style the garments, create the technical package, participate in the fit process, and complete the production process. They take care of various production processes from designing to fitting to finalizing garments. Because each company is structured in its own way, it is advantageous to have a thorough understanding of all of the processes. In a smaller company, a new, aspiring designer can get a position closer to the design department, and peripheral skills such as an understanding of technical design will help.

Large Companies

A large company splits its departments into more narrow categories, and a designer handles, for example, all missy career knits or all men's woven casual bottoms. Also, there are clear job distinctions among colorists, textile designers, creative designers, and technical designers. In a large company such as Nordstrom Product Group, each division has its own job description, and each employee deals with a clearly defined aspect of the process. Recent graduates who get their first job in a large company learn a more specific part of one production process and become an expert in one specific area. However, the job would not provide a holistic perspective of the apparel production process. The first-time employee needs additional preparation to be well rounded and avoid being limited to following one specialty throughout his or her career.

Figure 1.9 provides a detailed look at an organization chart for XYZ company's product development team, and how it relates to the company as a whole. The highlighted positions have job descriptions in Boxes 1 through 11.

Designing for Movies, Plays, and Theater

Boxes 1 through 11 provide job titles and their descriptions related to ready-to-wear apparel production. For those interested in costume design and production for film or theater, Boxes 12 and 13 showcase positions for a costume designer and costume director.

Organization Chart for XYZ Product Development

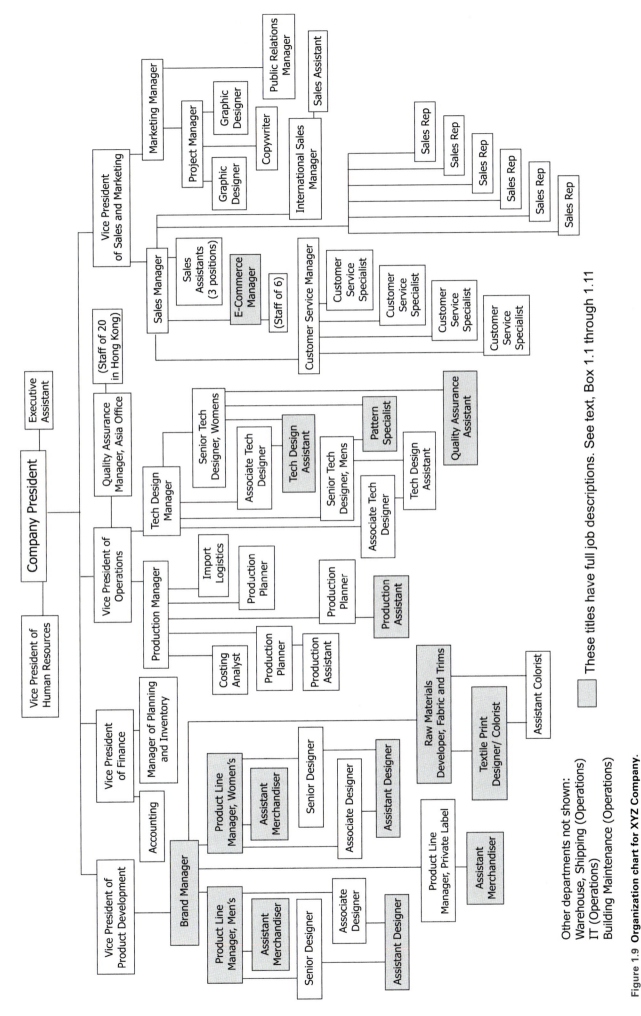

These titles have full job descriptions. See text, Box 1.1 through 1.11

Other departments not shown:
Warehouse, Shipping (Operations)
IT (Operations)
Building Maintenance (Operations)

Figure 1.9 **Organization chart for XYZ Company.**

Box 1.1 Real-Life Job Description #1

Job Title: Production Assistant
Reports to: Production Planner, various divisions

Primary Purpose: An entry-level position created to provide broad exposure to employees with an interest in production and merchandising. Employees in this position will be assigned projects and responsibilities that will allow them to learn product management processes and procedures at our company. This position is rotational and will require a minimum of two different division assignments within the first year of employment.

Major Responsibilities:

- Enter data into the computer system; maintain and coordinate production and contract information to include Stylemaster, availability file codes, contract entry and revisions, and shipping notices.
- Assist with issuing sample, fabric, and development purchase orders.
- Identify, analyze, and research production and delivery problems to maximize customer deliveries and minimize negative impact on inventory levels and product profitability. Review solutions with business product managers.
- Order and follow through on customer samples and sales reps' samples, including specification changes and quality checks as needed.
- Research, audit, and update production status including cost sheets and delivery/shipment issues, i.e., monitor work in progress (WIP) report.
- Communicate via phone, email, and/or fax on production issues to agents (international and domestic) and internal customers (allocations, customer service, shipping, and sales).
- Undertake special projects and tasks as requested by the divisions.

Qualifications:

- Minimum of one year of production scheduling, inventory control, buying experience, or other office-related experience, preferably within the apparel industry.
- Data entry experience required, including a minimum typing speed of 45 words per minute.
- Personal computer skills and proficiency in Word and Excel required. Familiarity with software applications as they relate to the apparel industry preferred.
- College degree in business, clothing, and/or textiles, or equivalent work experience preferred.
- Excellent written and oral communication skills.
- Ability to work well independently. Strong organizational skills. Ability to analyze and prioritize critical information, handle multiple tasks, and meet deadlines.
- Flexibility to adapt to business changes. Ability to work well under pressure.

Box 1.2 Real-Life Job Description #2

Job Title: Assistant Merchandiser
Reports to: Product Line Manager

Division: Apparel

Primary Purpose: To support the Merchandising Division in driving sales profitably through systems maintenance, sourcing support, sample management, and tactical execution.

Major Responsibilities:

- Weekly selling meeting preparation
- Item setup in product profile for all styles
- Mechanical proofing for items, prices, hangtags, etc.
- Photo and inline sample ordering and check-in/tagging
- Represent merchandisers when out

Key Interfaces:

- Product Line Manager
- Sourcing Manager
- Planning
- Marketing Tech Design
- Design

Qualifications:

- Merchandising degree and/or equivalent business experience
- The ability to communicate and work well in a team environment, as well as independently
- A strong knowledge of PC-based systems such as Windows, Excel, Lotus, and Word
- Prior retail business knowledge and experience preferred

Box 1.3 Real-Life Job Description #3

Job Title: Assistant Designer, Men's Wovens Product Category
Reports to: Senior Designer, Men's Collection

Primary Purpose: Assist in men's division with the design and development of the clothing line, with emphasis on the woven shirt product category.

Major Responsibilities:

- Assist and support in other product categories as needed.
- Assist the design team in color selection, styling, fabric, fit, and spec development.
- Provide input for fabric designs, coloring, prints, and technical drawings in Illustrator.
- Assist in preparing sample orders for initials and sales rep samples. Track, maintain, and execute design information, including sample orders for initials, sales rep samples, and production with accurate spec, fabric, accessory, and detail information.

- Provide accurate and complete communication and documentation of design information to international and domestic agencies.
- Maintain a strong familiarity with the men's casual target market with regard to demographics, lifestyle, fashion trends, and consumer habits.
- Travel as required, internationally and/or domestically.
- Other duties and special projects as assigned.

Qualifications:

- Bachelor's degree in fashion merchandising or apparel design, or equivalent work experience, preferably in men's contemporary market
- PC proficiency with Illustrator and Photoshop computer design programs, and Microsoft Word and Excel
- Strong technical skills in regard to fit and construction
- Excellent organizational skills and attention to detail
- Excellent written and oral communication skills
- Ability to work both collaboratively and independently; consistently self-motivated

Box 1.4 Real-Life Job Description #4

Job Title: Technical Design Assistant
Reports to: Senior Technical Designer

Primary Purpose: We are currently looking for a committed individual with a positive/energetic attitude to join our team! A successful technical design assistant is responsible for supporting fit and construction of fashion products.

Major Responsibilities:

- Assist in maintaining consistent size and fit standards, grade rules, and tolerances
- Support the maintenance of construction and quality standards
- Collaborate with technical design team to resolve fit and construction issues
- Prepare for and participating in fit sessions
- Assist in developing and maintaining complete and accurate spec packs
- Understand and interpret the designs as accurately as possible
- Work collaboratively with the brand team
- Assist with the appropriate resources on blocks and pattern development
- Utilize digital tools, Web PDM, and Microsoft Office proficiently
- Track product development against workflow dates
- Work productively with close supervision
- Develop and maintain strong partnerships with internal and external partners

Qualifications:

- Degree in pattern making, clothing and textiles, or related field
- Experience in apparel or textile industry preferred
- Experience in pattern making preferred
- Factory exposure a plus
- Excellent computer skills: Excel, Word, and Outlook

Note: This job description has been designed to indicate the general nature and level of work performed by employees within this classification. It is not designed to contain or be interpreted as a comprehensive inventory of all duties, responsibilities, and qualifications required of employees assigned to this job.

Box 1.5 Real-Life Job Description #5

Job Title: Textile Print Designer/Colorist
Reports to: Design Manager

Major Responsibilities:

- Main contact for supplies related to color and artwork
- Utilize CAD tools to create color repeats and colorways based on the print designer's direction
- Match colors by establishing color standards
- Build accurate color-ups on all artwork for production
- Evaluate lab dips and communicate clearly to achieve desired color results
- Approve strike-offs and knit-downs for print and pattern
- Keep abreast of copyright laws and new technological advancements with regard to CAD
- Work with brand team/vendors to create electronic art transfers between systems to reduce lead times
- Maintain color reference library
- Assist with color presentation materials for buy meeting
- Comment on strike-offs and bulk fabrics to ensure textile artwork is approved and executable in production
- Assist with approving knit-downs for patterns
- Comment on all bulk production colors with patterns
- Assist team with buy meeting preparation
- Take on additional responsibility as needed

Qualifications:

- Ability to follow through all news for a pattern from inception through to production
- Ability to follow through on all color-related issues for adopted color standards
- Ability to match colors; must have a high score on Farnsworth Munsell Hue Test
- Ability to approve color and layout for patterns

- Ability to create multiple colorways of textile artists' prints/patterns
- Ability to interpret art concept into finished product
- Ability to achieve deadlines established by brand calendar
- Degree in art, clothing, and textiles or related field preferred
- Broad textile media experience preferred
- Experience with CAD system scanner use
- Ability to utilize the following programs/tools: Excel, Word, and Outlook Microsoft applications, Ned Graphics, Photoshop, Illustrator, Color Test

Box 1.6 Real-Life Job Description #6

Job Title: Raw Materials Developer
Reports to: Sourcing Director

Primary Purpose: Work closely with the Product Group to provide sourcing for on-trend textiles and color direction for each season. Interface closely with Design, Merchandising, and Production.

Major Responsibilities:

Essential Functions, Fabric:

- Act as a resource for the product team, researching fabric direction.
- Coordinate textile and trim sourcing with factories and mills, including QA testing and approvals. Provide alternatives for failed trims.
- Coordinate mill communication and introductions to insure smooth development and handoff to Production.
- Coordinate color lab dips and approvals with vendors.
- Negotiate textile pricing.
- Manage all fabric testing and approval status.

Essential Functions, Color:

- Complete understanding of the science of color within a textile setting and how to evaluate it effectively, passing results of color testing a requirement
- Create and maintain textile and trim piece goods and pricing matrix in collaboration with Product Line Manager and Costing Analyst
- Develop and maintain internal physical and online textile and trim library, including documentation of current and revised fabric standard, lead time, care recommendations, and fabric minimums
- Complete and maintain accurate material adoption specs (MAS)
- As requested, attend fabric shows, research, and communicate trends to all product teams
- Coordinate tracking of textiles for initials and sales samples and provide seamless handoff to Inventory Managers and Production Planners for designated team
- Ensure invoice accuracy for all textile purchases
- Interface with Import to insure compliance with U.S. Customs

Qualifications:

- Strong knowledge of textile construction, dyeing, and finishing, including expertise in cutting-edge finishes and wet processing
- Excellent understanding of both natural and synthetic fibers, and their specific limitations
- Must have knowledge of existing textile mills and contacts
- Must be highly self-motivated and be a team player with a sense of urgency
- Must have excellent communication skills, oral and written, especially with people of diverse cultures
- Must have excellent organizational and prioritization skills, including ability to multi-task while working within a deadline structure
- Must have strong negotiating and analytical skills, including strong mathematical skills and accuracy
- Must have a good working knowledge of PC operations, Word, Excel
- Must be willing to learn product data management system as needed to fulfill job requirements
- Must evidence a professional manner and appearance as a representative of the company
- Must be willing and able to work overtime and travel when needed
- BA degree in design or a technical AA degree or equivalent; fashion design/merchandising or textile degree preferred
- Minimum five (5) years of progressive and diverse experience/practices in design and/or textile sourcing including experience in color evaluation

Box 1.7 Real-Life Job Description #7

Job Title: Pattern Maker
Reports to: Product Manager

Primary Purpose: Build and maintain pattern block library to support the development and distribution of pattern specifications with vendors

Major Responsibilities:

- Organize and manage pattern block library for specified divisions.
- Keep accurate spec details on all existing blocks, update them as needed and provide that information to technicians on a regular basis.
- Adjust existing blocks in reaction to vetted stakeholder feedback on returns or testing performance.
- Communicate with vendors about block updates and processes.
- Order fabric to create block mock ups in-house. Direct the sample maker in block garment creation.
- Update block patterns in the system to keep them current as we alter fits.
- Update block spec packs whenever block number or critical specs change.

- Make recommendations to Technical Designers and Designers about appropriate blocks to use to achieve desired fit intent.
- Manage the hardware and software needs of the digitizing and plotting equipment.
- Send and receive pattern electronically to/from vendors.
- Digitize and plot patterns as needed.
- Review vendor graded nests for adherence to company standards.
- Assist in training Technical Designers on the e-pattern system, and offer technical support as needed.

Qualifications:

- Five years of pattern making/block development and technical design experience
- Excellent written and verbal communication
- Thorough understanding of design, development, pattern making and production
- Degree or certificate in apparel or fashion design a plus

Box 1.8 Real-Life Job Description #8

Job Title: Quality Assurance Assistant
Reports to: Quality Assurance Manager

Primary Purpose: Assist with processing quality control audits on incoming production shipments, based on established standards and tolerances. Report results and help maintain accurate records of audits and libraries of reference resources at the distribution center.

Major Responsibilities:

- Compare shipment samples to a standard with regard to:
  - Color
  - Construction
  - Packaging and labeling
  - Specs
  - Workmanship
  - Fabric/materials
- Measure garments and recording specs and deviations
- Note measurements that exceed tolerances
- Identify flaws, defects, discrepancies
- Sort and re-package as needed
- Handle special projects as needed in preparation to be well rounded and avoid being limited to following one specialty throughout his or her career
- Assist in training new employees and/or temporary staff

Qualifications:

- Associate apparel degree desired
- Ability to read a spec pack
- Ability to communicate in English

- Demonstrated ability to measure accurately
  - Add and subtract
  - Convert fractions and decimals
- Superior ability to distinguish color
- Garment construction knowledge
- Fabric structure knowledge
- Attention to details and accuracy

We are full of smart, creative people. We support a work-hard, play-hard culture, and hope you are ready for the challenge. We provide excellent compensation packages, including medical/dental/vision benefits, a 401K with company match, generous clothing discounts, paid time off, and much more.

Box 1.9 Real-Life Job Description #9

Job Title: Product Line Manager
Reports to: Product Line Director

Primary Purpose: Responsible for overall category planning and the product creation process. Lead, drive, and communicate product and business strategies that meet the financial objectives, maximize profitability, and gain market share.

We are seeking a creative person with innovative ideas and a love for outdoor sports to develop and execute product line plans. The position's primary accountabilities center on bringing successful products to market in a timely and profitable manner. The position works closely with the Brand Manager, Marketing, and Sales, and is a hands-on development position requiring strong market understanding and technical capabilities.

As the Product Line Manager, you will work with key management and research and design comprehensive collections that are in line with product philosophies, and coordinate with marketing and other departments to complete projects within company timelines.

The Product Line Manager will inherently find the development of the multiple markets exciting and will look forward to broadening the product's reach even further. This opportunity is awaiting an individual who recognizes that the business is poised for growth, offering for him or her the chance to create their business legacy by applying their talents and skills.

The Product Line Manager will be responsible for domestic markets. This position reports to the Brand Manager and Vice President of Product Development.

Major Responsibilities:

- Bring market channel expertise to drive market penetration.
- Develop and execute product line plans based on company's marketing strategy and objectives.
- Create and propose comprehensive line planning recommendations.
- Actively participate with end users and attend events to gain consumer insight.
- Maintain up to date knowledge on category trends and competitive activity. Keep abreast of the market

conditions, consumer preferences, competitive products, and current trends by attending trade shows, consumer events, industry sites, visiting retailers, and social media.

- Research consumer needs, new technology, and innovation. Share findings to internal team.

- Drive ongoing product development, including recommendations on new product design, materials, market strategy, sales forecast, and price structures based on market research.

- Work with external design partners or vendors to assure that new products are developed on time and meet quality, price, and margin requirements. Develop product briefs for designers to follow, including styling, color, fabrication recommendations and prototype, production sample reviews, and testing.

- Manage the development process calendar including costing, quality evaluation, fabric trim, and color approvals.

- Coordinate and lead product development meetings.

- Develop and maintain product communication process. Manage and maintain accurate marketing product specifications and feature benefit details.

- Identify and develop annual marketing objectives and strategies consistent with annual long-term business plan strategies. Develop and manage appropriate expense budgets to support the product/marketing plan.

- Collaborate and partner with Marketing Manager in overseeing the execution of marketing materials including catalogs, advertisements, point of purchase, hang tags, and sales materials.

- Participate in sales meetings and activities as necessary to support the sales effort as well as obtaining insight on market trends and conditions. Meetings and activities include major account presentations and market shows.

- Lead presentations of new product lines to sales forces to support the sales and marketing efforts of Sales Manager to ensure continuity in the message being delivered.

Qualifications:

- Seasoned category management experience directly relevant to the categories and distribution channels

- Proven ability to lead product introductions and line extensions

- Demonstrated experience and success in building a brand

- Strong project management abilities and follow-through with great attention to detail

- Strong written, verbal, and quantitative skills

- Ability to present information effectively

- Strong problem solving and negotiation skills

- Creative thinker

- Bachelor's degree in related area

- Five to seven years of experience in product management within multisport, outdoor, running, or consumer product industry

- Strong knowledge of design and development process

- Proficiency with MS Office (Word, Excel, and PowerPoint)

- Passionate interest and active participation in related sports

- Willingness to travel

Competitive pay and benefits package includes medical, dental, LTD insurance, 401K with company match and generous holiday and vacation benefits.

Box 1.10 Real-Life Job Description #10

Job Title: E-commerce Manager
Reports to: Merchandise Manager

Primary Purpose: This position is responsible for managing our company's direct-to-consumer (D2C) website and related mobile and social initiatives. Will oversee day-to-day operations, including production and content of the website, as well as strategic planning, developing, and executing marketing initiatives, budget management, brand stewardship, performance analysis, and guiding overall workflows. This position works closely with management and cross-functional teams—Sales, Sales Ops, Creative Services, Product Development, Finance, Customer Service, and IT—and supervises the E-commerce team as well as strategic vendors and partner relationships.

Major Responsibilities:

- Oversee day-to-day management of (D2C) channel, including site functionality, site improvements, brand execution, overall product strategy/mix, customer experience, and revenue performance

- P&L responsibility, monitor budgets and forecasts and evaluate channel performance

- Identify customer segments and acquisition targets, create strategic messaging and marketing programs, and drive their development and deployment

- Ensure that all customer touch points from website to marketing communications to packaging to customer service messaging are consistent and brand appropriate

- Negotiate and manage relationships with vendors and partners for the D2C channel
- Identify and prioritize site improvements, building and presenting business cases as necessary
- Advocate usability, functionality, and customer experience best practices
- Create promotions for the D2C channel, adhering to corporate markdown schedule, writing and submitting proposals to the executive team, and communicating with appropriate internal stakeholders
- Ensure that D2C channel policies including privacy, terms and conditions, shipping, and returns and exchanges are current, accurate, and communicated appropriately
- Supervise upload of merchandise assortments for inclusion on the site, including copy and imagery

Education and Experience:

- 5+ years leading online and/or software development projects
- 5+ years leading multi-channel consumer direct marketing initiatives
- 3+ years progressive experience managing direct-to-consumer site(s)
- Demonstrated experience developing business strategies, creating marketing plans, and improving website usability and functionality
- Demonstrated ability to develop and oversee marketing, SEO, SEM, and email campaigns
- Experience driving operational efficiencies and marketing strategies through data and metrics
- Strong understanding of creative processes and online marketing and e-commerce best practices
- Proven outstanding leadership, communication, presentation, and interpersonal skills
- Excellent organizational and program management skills
- Demonstrated ability to work independently and effectively with daily time constraints in a high pressure environment
- Ability to be an effective leader of large, complex projects
- Strong writing skills
- Understands how to communicate difficult/sensitive information tactfully
- Mitigates team conflict and communication problems
- Flexible, "make-it-happen" attitude with willingness to seek out new responsibilities and opportunities for growth
- Apparel industry experience preferred
- Proficiency with Microsoft Office and Adobe CS
- Bachelors Degree or related experience required; MBA preferred

Box 1.11 Real-Life Job Description #11

Job Title: Brand Manager

Job Summary: This job contributes to the company's success by leading a team of Product Line Managers (PLMs) to achieve sales, margin, and in-stock goals for $90–$150MM in company annual sales. Develops strategic private label brand plans that support the company's corporate policies, drive financial performance, focus on the customer, and guide product line development. Directs and manages private label brand positioning, marketing, merchandising, category and collection development, and financial planning. Works collaboratively with PLMs, Design Teams, and various cross-divisional partners to ensure cohesive customer facing presentation of brands, products and stories within product development, marketing, e-commerce, direct mail, visual merchandising, and retail. Models and acts in accordance with company's guiding values and mission.

Major Responsibilities:

- Creates and implements the one-to-five-year brand plan that communicates priorities, collections, strategies, customer, and marketplace trends
- Partners with VP of Product Development to create brand and specialty shop financial goals based on corporate and brand strategic objectives and financial, market, and industry trends
- Ensures identification of key market, lifestyle, and product trends affecting the brand and their category responsibilities and develops brand and collection plans to meet market opportunities
- Creates business plan for new category development by researching sales potential, market size, assortment requirements, and relevance to the brand
- Ensures product line offerings and initial margins support brand and divisional goals
- Collaborates with PLMs to develop strategy and ensure appropriate brand positioning, collection, gender, and cross department consistency in product line execution
- Collaborates with Brand Manager to create one-to-five-year product planning direction for division and shared vision consistency across departments
- Creates and coordinates cross department collections, stories, and themes to create cohesive merchandising for seasonal product launches
- Provides content and brand priority stories across marketing programs, public affairs, and sales channels
- Ensures integrity of brand creative, positioning, and differentiation in product line management and collateral
- Creates strategy and direction for brand sales staff training and supporting materials
- Creates strategy and provides support for private label brand connection to our customers including market research, social media, and retail events

Box 1.12 Real-Life Job Description #12

Job Title: Costume Designer

Job Summary: The artist who creates the look of the clothes for a production based on collaboration with the director and costume staff.

Major Responsibilities:

- Reads script and determines the costume needs of the production
- Meets with the Director of Production to determine the concept which all artists will work within
- Researches period details, fabric availabilities, and rental possibilities
- Creates the color scheme to be used in the production
- Sketches ideas into renderings for director and actor approval, and as working drawings for costume construction team
- Determines fabrics and/or fabric modifications necessary to fulfill ideas determined on renderings
- Meets with costume shop personnel as necessary to facilitate the interpretation of the costume rendering into three-dimensional costume
- Attends rehearsals as necessary
- Attends fittings as necessary
- Meets scheduled design deadlines

Qualifications:

- Experience in script analysis for a variety of theatrical styles
- Excellent research skills
- Excellent knowledge of costume and fashion history
- Excellent knowledge of fabrics, trims and notions
- Good knowledge of basic theatrical culling and sewing
- Excellent knowledge and experience in the basic principles and elements of design
- Good drawing and painting skills with a variety of media
- Ability to work as a member of a collaborative design team
- Excellent interpersonal and communication skills
- Good time management skills
- Ability to remain calm in high stress situations

Box 1.13 Real-Life Job Description #13

Job Title: Costume Director

Job Summary: The individual responsible for the planning, development, budgeting, and control of all costume and wardrobe areas for a specific theatrical organization.

Major Responsibilities:

- Oversees the completion of all costume elements of a production to the theater's and costume designer's satisfaction
- Supervises staff in all costume/wardrobe areas including, but not limited to, workroom, crafts, dye shop, wardrobe, wig shop, and costume storage
- Determines, interviews, and hires staff for all costume/wardrobe areas
- Determines the yearly budgetary needs for all costume/wardrobe areas
- Manages budgets for all costume/wardrobe areas
- Advises and oversees the season schedule for the costume/wardrobe areas including, but not limited to, designer residency, costume staff work dates, and wardrobe staff schedule
- Determines and maintains a costume production quality of the highest standard
- Analyzes scripts and creates costume plots
- Participates in the long-range planning for the theater
- Performs other duties as assigned by the production manager or artistic director

Qualifications:

- Knowledge of and basic experience in all areas of theoretical costuming
- Knowledge of and experience in basic accounting procedures
- Demonstrated experience in personnel management
- Demonstrated experience in time management and work flow analysis
- Working knowledge of costume and fashion history including costume manufacturing history
- Working knowledge of costume materials including historical references and modern availabilities
- Working knowledge of safety standards and the implementation of same
- Excellent interpersonal and communication skills
- Excellent organizational skills

Launching a Career in Apparel Design

To be successful, it is important to find the most current information about fashion trends and the design production process. Various websites are useful for researching these topics. Professional organizations provide connections with professionals in the industry and academia. The International Textiles and Apparel Association (ITAA) is the premiere academic clothing and textiles association. ITAA sponsors a fashion design contest, awards scholarships, and provides other opportunities to learn the industry. Students in the clothing and textiles areas can also apply for Student Fashion Group International membership where members enjoy opportunities to connect with professionals in the industry and win scholarships.

For fashion trend research, Worth Global Style Network (WGSN) is one of the leading fashion forecasting websites (www.wgsn.com). This London-based online company provides free membership to students who are enrolled in a clothing and textiles program in a college. First View (http://firstview.com) and Style sight are another popular ones (https://fashionista.com/tag/stylesight), providing services through the Internet. This website is known for its cutting-edge global fashion trend research. Also, *Women's Wear Daily* (WWD) is one of the leading trade and trend publications and Business of Fashion (https://www.businessoffashion.com) is a popular online fashion news portal that provides the most up-to-date information on the fashion industry. Spoonflower (https://www.spoonflower.com) is one website students who have interests in fabric design can purchase fabrics with creative prints and also upload their created prints to produce fabric.

If LinkedIn is a business-oriented social networking service for all areas of the industry and all majors in fashion studies, students in the design area can create an online portfolio using the web platform Coroflot (http://www.coroflot.com). Many design-driven companies globally use it to recruit for their companies. Wix (http://www.wix.com) is another web platform students can utilize to create online stores, a résumé, and portfolio.

Current Trends in the Fashion Industry

Global Sourcing and Reshoring

Global sourcing and manufacturing became a norm of the industry. Global sourcing is the process of selecting the final supplies or materials used for product development including fabrics, zippers, threads, and buttons in the global supply channel. But global sourcing also means the process of selecting factories that will assemble and manufacture apparel products. As trade regulations and standards change rapidly, understanding the competitive advantages at all market levels globally has been a main focus of retailers. In order to create a successful global apparel product, it is necessary to critically and creatively analyze the past, present, and future state of supply chain sourcing opportunities utilizing strategies of competitiveness, design, distinctive content, market timing, responsiveness, reliability, and integrity.

Reshoring is the trend of bringing back manufacturing of a broad range of products to the United States (i.e., the opposite of globalization). Global sourcing pushes the manufacturing means away from U.S. soil to take advantage of cheaper labor. However, many manufacturers recently reached the conclusion that U.S. production is a smarter business decision in that U.S. manufacturing is not only price competitive, but also offers distinct strategic and logistic advantages, such as effective communication within closer time zones and with fewer language challenges. It results in a faster and smoother production process and can also shorten the product development processes, shortening the turnaround time of prototypes and sample approval (Le, 2013). Although reshoring is not a definite answer for all manufacturers, it has recently become a popular option.

Social Responsibility

Emphasizing social responsibility has become an important issue in order to make ethical and socially responsible decisions. Every step of the apparel and textile product development and retailing process requires socially responsible decision making. This includes examples such as selecting sustainable labor forces without child labor and sweatshops, growing and processing eco-friendly materials, selecting eco-packing and

marketing, and retailing products to efficiently operate and reduce emissions and carbon footprints. Social responsibility includes socially responsible supply chain management, that is, the process of socially responsible design, production, marketing, and distribution process. Tragedies at clothing factories in recent years—including a 2013 Bangladesh factory collapse due to an unstable building structure that took about 1,100 garment workers' lives—clearly brought retailers' attention to the importance of making socially responsible sourcing decisions. To solve the issues the industry currently faces, all participants, such as retailers, manufacturers, and consumers, should take responsibility to increase the safety of workers.

Crowd Sourcing

Product development used to be solely the domain of the design and product development teams within a company. However, crowd sourcing is a new way of creating products by soliciting contributions from people who are not related to the company rather than from traditional employees or suppliers. Internet technology has made it possible for companies to solicit ideas from the online community. In the fashion industry, there have been several popular websites; for example, www.designcrowd.com asks for consumers' direct participation in designing and creating products like T-shirts.

Omni-Channel Retailing

Omni-channel retailing is a new trend in fashion retailing. "Omni" means "all" in Latin and "channel" means a route of distribution and retailing of products. Omni-channel retailing is a strategy combining the consumer experience of online and offline together, centered on providing customers with a seamless and satisfying retail experience.

Omni-channel is different from multi-channel—in multi-channel retailing, sellers exist separately and operate separately. Some examples are pure online sellers (such as own-branded online stores), third-party online marketplaces (e.g., eBay, Amazon, Zulily), mobile stores, comparison sites (e.g., Shopzilla), general retailers selling via brick-and-mortar stores, or one or more of the above.

In contrast, omni-channel is a retailer selling through incorporating all or some of the above channels together to provide a combined experience of selling. An example is "click-and-collect," which means customers use an online shopping experience to view the product and then go to a brick-and-mortar store to purchase and collect the product. A second example is "in-store purchased and home delivered," which is when a customer reviews the products and makes a purchase in a brick-and-mortar store, but has the product delivered to their door.

Zara's new retailing strategy, "Bigger bricks and more clicks," demonstrates a successful story of incorporating omni-channel strategy into their retailing practices (Kowsmann, 2017). Zara recently opened a new flagship store in its hometown of La Coruna, Spain, with over 54,000 square feet and five stories. This clearly demonstrates its new winning strategy of retailing ahead of its rivals (e.g., Neiman Marcus). Inditex believes this is the right direction to fully integrate the brick-and-mortar store and online experiences. Zara began closing smaller stores and setting up larger stores instead. These newer megastores will showcase its full collections of numerous trendy styles. Zara's expectation that it would drive more consumers to visit the stores to see a greater number of products and ultimately buy more proved to be right (Kowsmann, 2017). Inditex's net profit jumped 10 percent in 2016, while its sales hit a record of 23.31 billion euros (US$24.72 billion), according to figures released in March 2017. That momentum continued into 2017, with 13 percent growth in store and online sales in constant current terms over a six-week period. Sales of Inditex increased at least 8 percent more in the first six weeks of the 2017 fiscal year after opening the stores (Kowsmann, 2017).

Closing of Brick-and-Mortar Stores

The revolution of the digital world brought dramatic changes in fashion retailing. Easy access to the Internet through personal computers and mobile devices has shifted consumers away from spending at brick-and-mortar stores. Recently, Macy's has announced it will close 63 stores; Sears, 15; The Limited, 250; BCBG Max Azria, 120; Guess 60; American Apparel, 104; Abercrombie & Fitch, 60; and JCPenney, up to 140 (Helmore, 2017).

It is not the end of the story. There is no exception based on price point, with stores at both ends of the price spectrum preparing to close their doors. The long-time dominant shoe chain Payless Inc. filed for bankruptcy and announced plans to shut down 400 stores. Ralph Lauren Corp. is a new victim of the retail trend (Rupp, Coleman-Lochner, and Turner, 2017). It will close its flagship Fifth Avenue Polo store—a symbol of old-fashioned luxury that no longer resonates with today's shoppers. Shoppers are used to discounts and are less likely to seek out old-fashioned luxury brands (Wong, 2017).

Teen-apparel retailer Rue21 Inc. is another casualty. It currently has about 1,000 stores, which are preparing to file for bankruptcy. Bloomberg Intelligence reported they are not sure how many malls can reinvent themselves (Rupp, Coleman-Lochner, and Turner, 2017). Table 1.2 demonstrates the clear closing increase in 2017.

The rapid change of the retailing landscape may cause more than 10 percent of U.S. retail space, or nearly 1 billion square feet, to close, according to data provided to Bloomberg by CoStar Group. It will also be taking a toll on jobs. According to Labor Department figures released in April 2017, retailers cut around 30,000 positions in March (Rupp, Coleman-Lochner, and Turner, 2017).

One the contrary, Amazon, the Seattle-based online retailer, announced 53 percent e-commerce sales growth in 2016, according to EMarketer Inc. (Rupp, Coleman-Lochner, and Turner, 2017). The company is now the world's fifth most valuable listed company (C.H. 2017). Amazon launched seven fashion brands while ramping up hiring for its own clothing line. Amazon has been increasingly spending more on fashion, scooping up online fashion stores like Shopbop, MyHabit, and East Dane. Last year, it sponsored New York Men's Fashion Week for the first time (Kim, 2016). Fashion is a relatively high-margin business and it could contribute to Amazon's profitability.

With the rest of the industry sharing the remaining 47 percent (as Amazon accounts for 53 percent of e-commerce sale growth), some fashion retailers are trying to survive by re-emerging as e-commerce brands, such as Kenneth Cole Productions and Bebe Stores Inc. (Rupp, Coleman-Lochner, and Turner, 2017).

The key is creating the right experience, whether it's online or off. Retailers should "refocus on customers" (Rupp, Coleman-Lochner, and Turner, 2017). Brick-and-mortar stores will exist in the future as people are social and they would like to have a place to share ideas and be entertained. However, there will be fewer (Synchrony Financial Report, March 18, 2017).

New Consumerism: Transparency

Consumers are more educated than ever, and they are reassessing their priorities in their fashion purchase behavior. One strong characteristic consumers focus on is the "transparency" of the retailer. Consumers are keen on the environmental issues

Table 1.2 Record Closings of U.S. Retail Stores in 2017

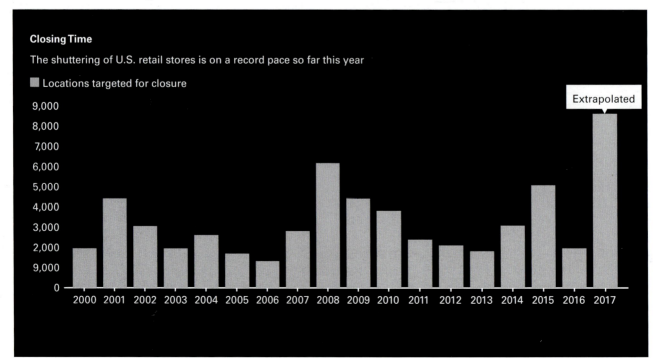

Closing Time

The shuttering of U.S. retail stores is on a record pace so far this year

■ Locations targeted for closure

of manufacturing and the working conditions of workers. Consumers clearly respond to retailers with transparent business practices. Some retailers, for example Reformation, a Los Angeles-based private label brand, focus on sustainable design and manufacturing processes to attain success (Hoang, 2016).

Transparency is one important factor that is not an option, but rather is an expectation of consumers, says Reformation founder Yael Aflalo. Revealing business practices brings more engagement with customers in a new way, opening up more conversation and creating more stories, which is far different from traditional global conglomerates that kept such information under wraps (Hoang, 2016).

Sharing business practices also allows for a company like Everlane, a direct-to-consumer fashion brand rooted in "radical transparency," to become a leading fashion retailer (Kansara, 2016). Michael Preysman started his fashion brand for today's digital world, where e-commerce and social media help to remove high-cost intermediaries and allow retailers to sell directly to consumers online, keeping margins high and prices low. The brand embraces "radical transparency," revealing the cost breakdown for every aspect of the production process, including figures for materials, hardware, labor, duties, and transport, alongside Everlane's retail price (marked up 2 to 3x cost) and the traditional retail price (marked up 5 to 6x the cost). Everlane has no stores, no advertising, and no discounts. It does not have seasonal collections. They introduce products one by one. As Preysman mentioned in the interview (Kansara, 2016), they are focused on the idea of trying to create the best products possible, one at a time. Figure 1.10 shows their cost segmentation of their best-selling women's linen shirt.

Technological Advancements in Product Development

The apparel industry and consumer market is competitive. Consumers expect higher levels of innovation, greater selection, and better quality, for increasingly less cost. As a result, companies

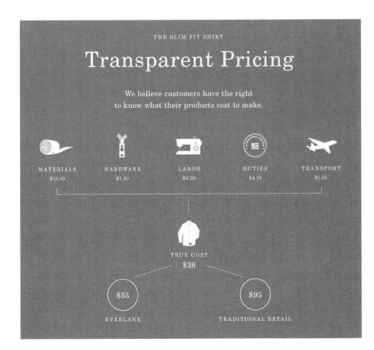

Figure 1.10 Cost segmentation of Everlane's best-selling women's linen shirt.

put increasing pressure on their product teams to improve margins and cut costs, while reducing lead times. At the same time, an increasing number of products are developed globally in partnership with suppliers, and government requirements on material content, testing, disposal, and recycling continues to increase.

The development of technology accelerates the current trends of the fast fashion phenomenon. Technology examples include design development software programs such as **product lifecycle management** and its sub-program product data management, and 3D virtual fitting programs such as Optitex and Clo.

Product Lifecycle Management

More and more companies are adopting product lifecycle management systems to help them better manage the entire lifecycle of products from concept through design, development, sourcing, and manufacturing. Product lifecycle management systems provide infrastructure for more streamlined, collaborative, and faster product innovation with fewer errors, reduced time to market, and reduced product cost. They also allow global product teams increased visibility and transparency to shared data, schedules, and product information in real time.

Product lifecycle management systems are comprehensive software tools that can become the backbone of a company's entire product development process. Merchandisers can create seasonal calendars and line plans. Designers and developers can create tech packs including design details, bill of materials and measurements, and manage sample orders and sample reviews with vendors. Materials developers can manage lab dips, strike-offs, materials quality requirements, and materials testing. Sourcing and production teams can manage cost sheets and production schedules with vendors and factories to ensure orders are delivered on time. Product lifecycle management systems can also be integrated with other corporate systems including merchandising, purchase order, and fulfillment systems for seamless corporate data sharing and decision making.

A variety of product lifecycle management companies have surfaced over the past 5 to 10 years to help meet the needs of the market. These include systems that can sometimes be costly even for the largest apparel companies, including PTC (FlexPLM), Gerber Technology (YuniquePLM), and niche providers including Lectra PLM (fashion focused) and Texbase, Inc. (materials focused). More recent entries in the market, including ChameleonPLM, offer robust yet affordable product lifecycle management solutions using cloud-based software as a service technology.

3D Virtual Fitting programs

Optitex (http://www.optitex.com) and Clo (http://www.clo3d.com) are the virtual fit simulation programs recently adopted in the apparel product development process (Figure 1.11). Both programs create 3D virtual prototyping, real-life sample fitting, and virtual fabric simulations. They can save lead time dramatically as designers can create prototype samples and then view and edit them in one place, reducing the time of sending patterns back and forth to manufacturers. As a result, the product can become available to the market quickly.

In addition, 3D-created fit model avatars can be modified with wide flexibility of changes in fit. 3D simulations can also make the product easily fit by modifying design details, for example,

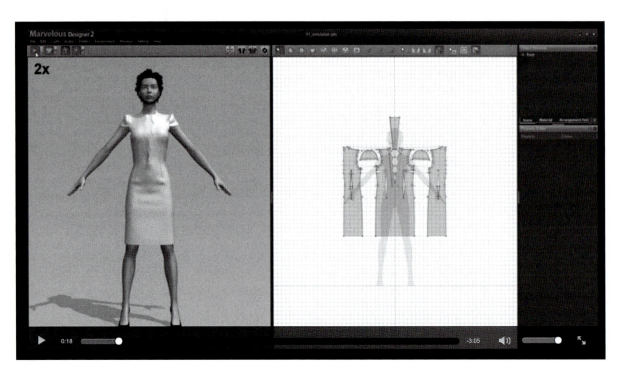

Figure 1.11 **CLO 3D: Apparel CAD and 3D simulation software.**

changing the sizes of trims such as buttons, zippers, and rivets. It can also adjust seam finishes such as adding topstitchings as well as design elements such as adding pleats, facing, and interlinings.

Although 3D software programs have some shortcomings—such as the challenge of accurately creating the stretchability of different knit fittings on the body—it is an innovative approach that can bring tremendous outcomes in apparel product development by accelerating production accurately and cost effectively

Sustainability and Fashion

Consumers are more conscious of and sensitive to the environmental impact and sustainability issues of fashion than ever before. Recent trends show companies creating products targeting this growing number of consumers. Thanks to the advancement of technology, many products using upcycle and recycle practices are in the news. Adidas, a Portland-based athletic wear company, is leading the trend. Adidas released the first mass-produced ocean plastic shoe, "UltraBOOST Uncaged Parley running shoe," created using plastic waste retrieved by clean-up operations in the Maldives (95 percent) and recycled polyester (5 percent). Each of the 7,000 pairs created is made with eleven plastic bottles. Parts of the shoe, such as laces, heel cap bases, heel webbing, heel lining, and the sock liner cover, are also made with recycled materials. Freitag, shown in Figure 1.12, is another company using upcycled truck tarps and transforming them into highly functional and uniquely styled bags.

Figure 1.12 **Freitag products and advertisement.**

Adidas also created the world's first performance shoes from "future craft bio-fabric" made from bio-steel fiber, which deconstructs within a day and a half after the introduction of a particular enzyme. They are an alternative to harmfully toxic plastic materials that are being thrown into the garbage and sitting in landfills for indefinite periods of time before breaking down. The biodegradable shoes are made by a biotechnology firm called AMSilk. The materials of the top part of the shoes are made from the same silky materials that spiders produce for their webs. Only the soles of the shoes will not be biodegradable. Adidas displayed the shoes in 2016, and they will be available to consumers in 2018 (Aamir, 2017).

Wearables

Innovation in wearable technology has become a new trend in the fashion industry. Fashionable Google Glass and smart watches are examples. Smart watches that monitor wearers' steps, sleep patterns, heart rate, and other bio information are steadily becoming the norm for modern consumers. High performance base layers (https://www.liveathos.com/athletes) or sports bras and jogging tops that monitor and transfer extensive muscle and heart rate data to computerized gadgets such as smartphones are not just for special athletes or patients. They have become a fashionable as well as functional item for many consumers.

Levi's partnered with Google to create new practical functions for wearables via Bluetooth. Google's project the Jacquard Initiative started out of its Advanced Technology and Projects (ATAP) group and provides a great future for many fashion inventions. "Jacquard makes it possible to weave touch and gesture interactivity into any textiles using standard, industrial looms," according to Google (Sherman, 2017). Google representative Ivan Poupyrev noted to Business of Fashion, "on the same loom you can create millions of shapes, colors, and patterns—which bridges the gap between technologies and aesthtics . . . Everyday objects such as clothes and furniture can be transformed into interactive surfaces" (Sherman, 2017).

The first product of the collaboration, the Levi's commuter trucker jacket embedded with Jacquard by Google, became available in stores as of September 2017 with a price tag of $350. It is a machine-washable denim jacket that allows a wearer to control a mobile device through a patch of fabric on the left-hand sleeve cut. A dongle (known as the "Jacquard Tag") is hooked into the sleeve and allows connectivity between the sleeve and the device. Via an interactive haptic motor by hand touch and LED lights, the wearer can receive alerts for phone calls, play or pause a song, check the weather, or consult maps to plan a commute (Sherman, 2017).

Summary

This chapter presented an overview of the apparel industry and its product development process. Various categories of ready-to-wear apparel products based on their relationship between manufacturers and retailers were surveyed. Various private label brands were categorized with examples, and current trends in the industry were explored. Merchandise segments based on price range, gender, and age were described. The main professionals who take important roles in the apparel production process and distribution were explored, with actual examples of job postings from the industry providing a preview of the real world of the industry. New trends of retailing and the fashion industry were provided.

Useful Websites

Professional Organizations

- International Textile and Apparel Association: www.itaaonline.org
- American Association of Family and Consumer Sciences: www.aafcs.org
- American Association of Textile Chemists and Colorists: www.aatcc.org
- The Fashion Group International, Inc.: http://newyork.fgi.org/index.php

Other Links

- Worth Global Style Network (WGSN): www.wgsn.com
- Daily News Record (DNR): www.dnrnews.com
- Fashion.net: www.fashion.net
- Fashion Center—New York City
- First View.com: http://firstview.com
- Just Style: www.just-style.com
- Women's Wear Daily (WWD): www.wwd.com
- ApparelSearch.com: www.apparelsearch.com
- Fabric University: www.fabriclink.com/university/index.cfm
- Fiber World
- Business of Fashion: https://www.businessoffashion.com
- Spoon Flower: https://www.spoonflower.com
- Coroflot: http://www.coroflot.com
- Wix: http://www.wix.com
- Promostyl: http://www.promostyl.com/en
- Fashion Trend Forecast: https://fashionista.com/tag/stylesight

Study Questions

1. Visit two women's wear apparel company websites to compare the product categories for each company. List the names of the companies, their price ranges, and the product categories they offer. Are there any differences in product categories? If so, why do you think they are different?

2. Find one related news article from *The New York Times* on apparel production and the industry. (Note: The Thursday Styles section and daily Business section are where you are likely to find such articles.) The article can be about anything that directly or indirectly influences the industry and its future; for example, the stock market, export and import, or global warming. What is the topic of the article? Why is the topic related to the apparel industry? How might it influence the future of the apparel production process? Please print the article and attach it to your written homework.

3. Visit two retailers that serve the same age and gender target consumers, but are positioned in two different price ranges. List the name of each brand and its web address. List the target consumer profile and price range. Select two similar garments sold by both retailers. Examine the product characteristics.

What influences the difference in the prices? Consider fabric costs, findings costs, and labor costs. Check where each garment was made, and try out your assumption about why the labor cost may or may not be a factor in the retail price. What other factors do you find?

4. Select one garment. Examine it and list three features that you, as a manufacturer or retailer, would be willing to sacrifice to reduce costs. Choose three features that you, as a consumer, would be willing to sacrifice to reduce the price. Are the features you chose as a manufacturer or retailer the same as those you chose as a consumer? What accounts for the similarities and differences?

5. What are some current trends on the horizon for fashion retailing? How do those trends affect apparel product development processes?

Check Your Understanding

1. What is ready-to-wear? What is couture?

2. Why is globalization necessary for the apparel industry?

3. What is your forecast for the future of apparel manufacturing?

4. What are the advantages and disadvantages of globalization for the apparel industry?

5. What is the role of the technical designer in the apparel design process?

References

Aamir, S. (March 30, 2017). "Adidas Unveils World's First Biodegradable Shoes That Can Be Dissolved in 36 Hours." *I4U NEWS*. Retrieved April 5, 2017, from https://www.i4u.com/2017/03/121871/adidas-unveils-worlds-first-biodegradable-shoes-can-be-dissolved-36-hours.

American Apparel and Footwear Association. (June 2006). 2005 Annual Report. Retrieved January 7, 2008, from www.apparelandfootwear.org/UserFiles/File/Statistics/trends2005.pdf.

American Apparel and Footwear Association. 2009. Trends: An Annual Statistical Analysis of the U.S. Apparel and Footwear Industries. Arlington, VA: American Apparel and Footwear Association.

Barbaro, M. 2007. "Macy's and Hilfiger Strike Exclusive Deal." *New York Times*, October 26, 2007.

Bhagwati, J. 2004. *In Defense of Globalization*. Oxford, New York: Oxford University Press.

Boggan, S. 2001. "'We Blew It': Nike Admits to Mistakes Over Child Labor." Common Dreams.org News Center. www.commondreams.org/headlines01/1020-01.htm.

Bonacich, E., et al. 1994. The garment industry in the restructuring global economy (ed.). In *Global Production: The Apparel Industry in the Pacific Rim*. Edited by Edna Bonacich, Lucie Cheng, Norma Chinchilla, Nora Hamilton, and Paul Ong. Philadelphia: Temple University Press, pp. 3–18.

Brown, P., and Rice, J. 2014. *Ready to Wear Apparel Analysis* (4th ed.). Upper Saddle River, New Jersey: Prentice Hall.

Burns, L. D., Mullet, K. K., and Bryant, N. O. 2011. *The Business of Fashion* (4th ed.). New York: Fairchild Publications.

C.H. (April 3, 2017). "Why Investors Are So Keen on Amazon." *The Economist*. Retrieved April 25, 2017, from http://www.economist.com/blogs/economist-explains/2017/04/economist-explains.

Crawford, Z. 2007. "Critical Shopper, You Won't Believe Who I Saw at Kohl's." *The New York Times*, September 20, 2007. www.nytimes.com/2007/09/20/fashion/20CRITIC.html.

Daly, H. 1999. Globalization versus internationalization—some implications. *Ecological Economics 31*: 31–37.

Dickerson, K. 1999. *Textiles and Apparel in the Global Economy* (3rd ed.). Upper Saddle River, New Jersey: Prentice Hall.

Ferdows, K., Lewis, M. A., and Machuca, J. A. D. (2004). Rapid-Fire Fulfillment, *Harvard Business Review 82(11)*. Retrieved April 21, 2018, from https://hbr.org/2004/11/rapid-fire-fulfillment.

Helmore, E. (March 26, 2017). "'People aren't spending': Stores close doors in 'oversaturated' US retail market." *The Guardian*. Retrieved April 5, 2017, from https://www.theguardian.com/us-news/2017/mar/26/us-retail-stores-market-macys-sears.

Hoang, L. (September 29, 2016). "The 10 Commandments of New Consumerism." *Business of Fashion*. Retrieved April 26, 2017, from https://www.businessoffashion.com/articles/intelligence/the-10-commandments-of-new-consumerism.

Holmes, E. "Forever 21 Pursues Big-Store Branding." *The New York Times*, June 24, 2010.

Kansara, V. A. (March 21, 2016). "Michael Preysman on Iterating Everlane and 'Fixing' Fashion Retail." *Business of Fashion*. Retrieved April 24, 2017, from https://www.businessoffashion.com/articles/founder-stories/michael-preysman-on-iterating-everlane-and-fixing-fashion-retail.

Kim, Y. 2017. "Amazon Quietly Launched Seven Fashion Brands While Ramping Up Hiring for Its Own Clothing Line." *Business Insider*. Retrieved April 25, 2017, from http://www.businessinsider.com/amazon-owns-7-private-label-fashion-brands-2016-2.

Kowsmann, P. (December 6, 2016). "Fast Fashion: How a Zara Coat Went from Design to Fifth Avenue in 25 Days." *The Wall Street Journal*. Retrieved April 29, 2017, from https://www.wsj.com/articles/fast-fashion-how-a-zara-coat-went-from-design-to-fifth-avenue-in-25-days-1481020203.

Kowsmann, P. (March 16, 2017). "Zara's New Focus: Bigger Bricks, More Clicks." *The Wall Street Journal*. Retrieved April 29, 2017, https://www.wsj.com/articles/zara-parent-inditex-profit-up-as-sales-hit-record-high-1489562814.

Kunz, G., Karpova, E., and Garner, B. M. (2016). *Going Global: The Textile and Apparel Industry* (3rd ed.). New York: Fairchild Publications.

La Ferla, R. 2007. "Faster Fashion, Cheaper Chic." *The New York Times*. May 10, 2007.

Le, K. (March 27, 2013). "Reshoring, Bringing Manufacturing Jobs Back to the United States." *(TC)² Technology Communicator*. Retrieved March 9, 2014, from http://www.tc2.com/ newsletter/2013/032713.html.

Levy, M., and Weitz, B. A. 2007. *Retailing Management* (6th ed.). Boston: McGraw-Hill/Irwin.

MarEx. (November 29, 2016). "Adidas Releases First Mass-Produced Ocean Plastic Shoe." *Maritime Executive*. Retrieved March 10, 2017, from http://maritime-executive.com/article/adidas-releases-first-mass-produced-ocean-plastic-shoe.

O'Hara Callan, G., and Glover, C. (1998). *The Thames and Hudson Dictionary of Fashion and Fashion Designers.* New York: Thames and Hudson.

Rupp, L., Coleman-Lochner, L., and Turner, N. (April 7, 2017). "America's Retailers Are Closing Stores Faster Than Ever." *Bloomberg*. Retrieved April 25, 2017, from https://www.bloomberg.com/news/articles/2017-04-07/stores-are-closing-at-a-record-pace-as-amazon-chews-up-retailers

Shen, D. 2008. What's happening in China's textile and clothing industries? *Clothing and Textiles Research Journal*, 26(3), 220–222.

Sherman, L. (March 22, 2017). "Will Consumers Want Levi's New 'Wearable Tech' Jacket?" *Business of Fashion*. Retrieved April 20, 2017, from https://www.businessoffashion.com/articles/digital-scorecard/will-consumers-want-levis-new-wearable-tech-jacket.

Synchrony Financial Report. (March 18, 2017). "The Future of Retail: Insight and Influences Shaping Retail Innovation." *Synchrony*

Financial Report. Retrieved April 29, 2017, from http://newsroom.synchronyfinancial.com/document-library/future-retail-0.

Wong, S. (April 4, 2017). "Ralph Lauren Is Latest Fashion Victim in New Era for Retailers." *Bloomberg*. Retrieved April 25, 2017, from https://www.businessoffashion.com/articles/news-analysis/ralph-lauren-is-latest-fashion-victim-in-new-era-for-retailers.

Yardley, J. (May 22, 2013). Report on deadly factory collapse in Bangladesh finds widespread blame, *New York Times*. Retrieved April 22, 2018, from https://www.nytimes.com/2013/05/23/world/asia/report-on-bangladesh-building-collapse-finds-widespread-blame.html.

The Apparel Product Development Process and Technical Design

2

Chapter Objectives

After studying this chapter, you will be able to:

- Identify the apparel design calendar
- Examine the related production processes in the apparel design calendar
- Understand the various steps of producing samples
- Define technical design
- Understand the application of the principles of technical design as it relates to styling techniques

Key Terms

color story
colorways
commercialization process
concept board
construction details
development window
FOB (free on board)
findings
forecast companies

landed price
line plan
preproduction sample
prototype samples
sample evaluation
    comments
silhouette
size set sample
stock-keeping unit (SKU)

style number
technical flat
tolerance
top of production sample
    (TOP)
trade show
vendor manual

In the scope of this book, *product development* refers to the creation of new apparel products for production. Various stages are involved in the creation of each new garment, from the initial idea to its completion and delivery, and each stage has its own unique steps. This chapter provides opportunities to look at each step of the apparel product development process. As we move more into the production process, samples at each stage are explored.

Design Development

The first stage of creating new apparel products is the process of design development. The design development calendar is often short and crowded. Most women's apparel categories have at least four—and possibly as many as six—seasons. Each season is often split into multiple deliveries so that fresh merchandise can appear in the stores every month or so. Designers are often finishing one season, developing another, and planning a third simultaneously, so the ability to multitask is one of the main keys to success for designers.

The Role of Designer

The **team** nature of apparel development cannot be emphasized enough. Who are the team members? See the organization chart in Figure 1.9 on page 11. Initial direction for designing comes from a senior person, the design director, product line manager (PLM), or senior designer. The job of designer is one of constant and creative problem-solving. A new design will be successful if it fits the customer well, hits the target price, and fits into the line as a whole. The designer's job is to create wonderful designs that fit into important parameters. Some of the key parameters are listed in Figure 2.1.

Most designers begin their careers in a supporting role, such as assistant designer. This involves developing an understanding for the calendar and deadlines, a sense of urgency, and a willingness to do what the job requires. Various routine tasks—such as approving labels and communicating details to the agent or factories—are likely to be part of the mix. Most jobs include important but unexciting tasks, and apparel design is no different.

On the other hand, every day is different, and the atmosphere is very dynamic. In addition, as in sports, being part of a successful team is very rewarding.

The Role of Product Line Manager

The PLM is responsible for overall category planning and the product creation process. Another common name for this job would be category manager, and different organizations have different titles and slightly different duties. But for all, the job is to lead the design team, create product and business strategies to meet the financial goals each season, and gain market share. At the beginning of the season, the PLM will prepare a preliminary framework from which to develop ideas that are appropriate for the company. After research is completed, a spreadsheet known as the **line plan** is prepared as a list of all the styles and projected prices required for the season, including any carry-over styles. The line plan is also a sales plan, with an estimate of the sales volume of each item projected.

Table 2.1 shows the tasks involved and who is mainly responsible. Many tasks are collaborations among many departments.

Target Market

The apparel company has a good idea of its target customer based on his or her sales history, and the better it can provide for its customer, the more successful it will be. In the past, customers were more dictated to by the apparel brand and advertising, but younger consumers rely more on word-of-mouth, online reviews, and the advice of their friends.

Four other guidelines that are keys to the apparel company's understanding of their customers are listed in the following sections.

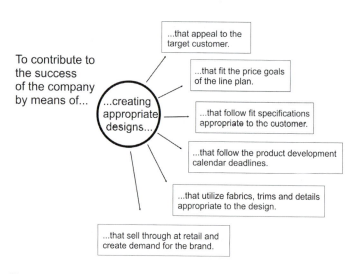

Figure 2.1 The role of designer.

Table 2.1   Tasks of Each Product Development Professional

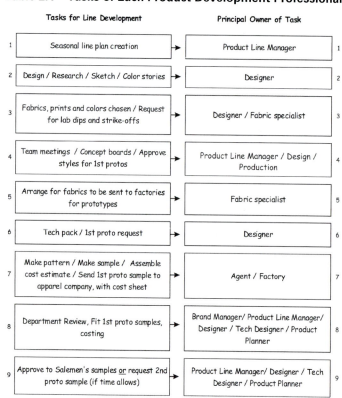

Tasks for Line Development	Principal Owner of Task
1 Seasonal line plan creation	Product Line Manager 1
2 Design / Research / Sketch / Color stories	Designer 2
3 Fabrics, prints and colors chosen / Request for lab dips and strike-offs	Designer / Fabric specialist 3
4 Team meetings / Concept boards / Approve styles for 1st protos	Product Line Manager / Design / Production 4
5 Arrange for fabrics to be sent to factories for prototypes	Fabric specialist 5
6 Tech pack / 1st proto request	Designer 6
7 Make pattern / Make sample / Assemble cost estimate / Send 1st proto sample to apparel company, with cost sheet	Agent / Factory 7
8 Department Review, Fit 1st proto samples, costing	Brand Manager/ Product Line Manager/ Designer / Tech Designer / Product Planner 8
9 Approve to Salemen's samples <u>or</u> request 2nd proto sample (if time allows)	Product Line Manager/ Designer / Tech Designer / Product Planner 9

Target Consumers' Age, Size Range, and Gender

Consumers' age, size range, and gender are important factors to consider and are all related to each other. Size range particularly requires a different approach to styling. For example, fit and styling for teens is quite different from fit and styling for men and women in their 50s. Gender is also an important factor. Fit for women has different considerations than fit for men, with certain areas of the body emphasized or de-emphasized. For example, a men's tailored shirt is usually baggier than a women's tailored shirt because women generally prefer a more body-conscious fit. In any apparel item, it is important to understand the customers' expectations of fit.

It is imperative to create apparel products that are functional, comfortable, and flattering for the intended customers, whatever their age or sizing range. When an age range becomes part of the brand identity, any deviations from it should be done with caution.

Several companies have been known to court a younger, hipper customer only to leave their existing customers behind. A move toward another target customer can be successful, but it usually needs the support of another brand name, a new marketing campaign that includes a new brand image to connect with the new customer, and probably an additional product development team. Abercrombie & Fitch is an example of a brand that managed this shift successfully. For many years, it specialized in upper-class safari and hunting wear, and then moved its target market to young teens and 20s. But lately, they have shifted again to a more classic fashion customer and new store layouts. Fashion retailing is about newness and novelty, and as the customer "ages out" of a concept, they will cease to shop that brand.

Price Range

Each company has certain price parameters to which buyers look. Consumers have an idea of the product characteristics of each company, as well as its price. For example, a lower-end company would not be successful with a higher-end garment no matter how wonderful because that is not what its customers, the buyers, expect. In addition, to maximize one's profit, the lower end of the market will have higher volumes, and the styles must appeal to a broader segment of the mass market. For this type of brand, very specialized trends catering to a small number of ultra-high-fashion consumers will not be appropriate. At the same time, designers and merchandisers should develop items in the right price range, and with stair-step increments (also called price tiering) that support the different prices. For example, in the line plan in Table 2.2, skirt 1 has a wholesale price of $34 and skirt 2 has a wholesale price of $56.75. The reason for such a difference must be obvious to the buyer. All the items must fall within the target price range set for the product line.

Target Consumers' Lifestyles

Each target consumer group has a different lifestyle for which the designers create their products. If the target consumer's lifestyle is casual, a very sporty or comfortable style of garment will be well understood by the buyers, but formal suits and dress pants will not. In addition, a garment that must be dry cleaned or ironed after each washing may be considered too much trouble for a customer concerned with "easy care." An unmarried consumer will often follow trends more closely, and may have more discretionary dollars to dedicate to fashion apparel. A family with young children will have more of their clothing budget going to outfit their kids. A university student can dress largely however

Table 2.2   XYZ Missy Career Line Plan, Spring 20XX, Alfresco

Item (new or carry-over)	fabric	colorways	size scale	projected units	F.O.B.	landed cost (w/duty, shipping)	wholesale	sugg. retail	Ext Wholesale Cost
skirt 1, A-line (C/O)	stretch twill " "	lavendrine bamboo black	2-16 " "	2600	$12.75	$17.00	$34.00	$68.00	$88,400.00
skirt 2, cigarette (new)	silk jersey " "	honeycomb white black	2-16 " "	1850	$23.41	$31.21	$56.75	$113.50	$104,987.50
skirt 3, sarong (new)	dot print	print-multi	xs-xl	900	$22.05	$29.40	$49.00	$98.00	$44,100.00
Dress 1 (C/O)	crepe "	bamboo black	2-16	3100	$18.56	$24.75	$49.50	$99.00	$153,450.00
pant 1 (new)	crepe "	honeycomb black	2-16 "	2900	$21.14	$28.19	$51.25	$102.50	$148,625.00
jacket 1 (C/O)	stretch twill " "	lavendrine white bamboo	2-16 " "	2200	$26.33	$35.10	$67.50	$135.00	$148,500.00
jacket 2 (new)	crepe "	black honeycomb	2-16 "	1200	$30.73	$40.98	$74.50	$149.00	$89,400.00
top 1, tie blouse (C/O)	voile print "	honeycomb lipstick	xs-xl "	1250	$12.68	$16.91	$29.15	$58.30	$36,437.50
top 2, halter sweater (C/O)	large gauge " "	lipstick honeycomb black	xs-xl " "	1800	$13.46	$17.94	$34.50	$69.00	$62,100.00
top 3 knit tank (C/O)	silk jersey " " " "	light lipstick light honeycomb white light lavendrine light bamboo black	xs-xl " " " " "	4000	$12.56	$16.74	$31.00	$62.00	$124,000.00
						total wholesale dollars			$1,000,000.00

he or she likes, but upon entering the job market, they will need to conform to the level of dress at their new place of employment. A very active person, one who rides a mountain bike, hikes, or does snow sports each weekend, often adopts casual clothing with stretch characteristics and performance styling such as flatlock seaming and with durability cues such as reinforced areas. A successful company will understand the lifestyle-related issues of its consumers so that it can approach them effectively.

Image

Consumers' lifestyle is closely related to a company's brand image. Traditional garments can be high end or low end, and at the other end of the style scale, so can fashion garments. The general character of the garments must clearly conform to the brand image, aside from questions of price. A successful company creates its own consistent brand image, which appeals to its customer. The product should conform to what people expect in terms of a "look" from that company, from fashion-forward on one end of the spectrum to conservative on the other. The apparel company Tommy Bahama created a fictitious person, Mr. Tommy Bahama, to create the company image and the company continuously educated customers about who he is (including how he spends his time and leisure) and what he wears.

Often a person's desire for upward mobility will move them to adopt the styles and brands of their target lifestyle. Brand image plays an integral part to reach and educate a certain target consumer, encouraging them to adopt the lifestyle the brand portrays by wearing its products.

Tools for Designing

Forecast companies are organizations that specialize in researching colors and trends and creating books that predict the direction of fashion from 18 to 24 months in advance. Forecast companies are often hired to give presentations about upcoming influences. An apparel company may also have an in-house trend director to assist in interpreting the current fashion direction. These companies also have an in-house library of newspapers, magazines, and trend reports, as well as fabric swatches, buttons, and trims for inspiration. The plan will be discussed with the design staff, and the influences that are fitting for the company will be defined. The line plan is a key document for each season.

Designing for the Target Market

Based on the information gathered from various sources of inspiration, designers begin the design process. Every season, there are many influences on fashion. Research, research, and research! A lot of research on the current trends comes from the street, television, runways, magazines, news, movies, music videos, and other sources. For example, young men's apparel direction is often influenced by famous athletes. Sports stars, skateboarding, and snowboarding have had a big influence on fashion, as has hip-hop music. However, it is important to understand each company's unique target market and its product characteristics. Each company caters to a particular consumer and market segment, so not every trend is right for every line. For example, adding a smart phone pocket for outerwear is something designers would consider for target customers in a younger age bracket rather than for target customers in an older age bracket.

Basic Season Outline

A **line** is a group of related products. How is a line developed? By the process of trend research and market analysis with input from people on the team and from others within the industry. The following is an example of some typical milestones in the process of developing a line for XYZ Product Development, Inc., the fictitious company for which we will be developing products throughout the rest of the book.

This line is part of the Missy Career Division for Spring 20XX, and is called "Alfresco." Our target customer for this line is female missy size range, 25 to 45 years old, and a working professional who buys in the mid-price range (better to moderate). Styling is classic, and semi-fitted styles sell well for this line. Let's walk through the steps together to understand how the creation process moves forward. A number of steps proceed more or less in tandem, with touch points for the principal developers, depending on the working style of the company.

Market Research

The merchandiser reviews trends, analyzes sales, and comes up with the line plan. It is based on the budget for the department, and on projected sales, as in the example in Table 2.2. The design team gathers information from forecasting companies such as Promostyl, which combines both color and trend information.

The Color Story

An early step in the product development process is developing a color story. Designers and colorists select colors for the upcoming season, with input from color forecasting companies, which develop colors one to two years in advance. A color forecast consists of sets of fabric swatches, color chips, or yarns arranged into color groups or color stories. The **color story** is a palette of related colors that follow a theme.

The forecast companies create seasonal books and sell them to people in industries for which color trends matter. Clients of color forecasters include automobile manufacturers, interior designers, cosmetic companies, and furniture designers in addition to apparel companies. The Color Association of the United States in New York and the Color Committee in New York are some examples. These color forecasters use sources of colors from magazines to designers' color choices in Europe to fashion innovators' color choices to consumer's color preferences by sales data to determine the directions of future color palettes (Burns, Mullet, and Bryant, 2011).

After a set of colors that complement each other is selected, names are assigned for the colors according to the themes of the season, and to the sophistication level of the customer. For example, one company may call a color rust and another may call that same color iron oxide. Children's wear color names are often whimsical and playful, menswear may be more automotive or equipment-related, and so on. The identical shade of green could be named kelly green, emerald, leaf, parrot, or grassy knoll, depending on the line, and apple may be green in one line but red in another. It just depends on the season's themes and on what may appeal most to the buyers.

Alfresco means "taking place in the open air," so the theme for Spring 20XX in our example has a springtime feeling—fresh, feminine, and floral. The color names are lipstick, bamboo, lavendrine, honeycomb, black, and white. This palette is a mix of classic and fashion colors; lavendrine, bamboo, and honeycomb are new fashion colors this season, black and white are carried every season with occasional variations, and the fashion color lipstick is a carry-over color, which was a great success last season and is being repeated. The garments offered last season in lipstick really "sold in" (were picked up by the buyers) and the color also had high "sell through" at the retail level. The name "lipstick" doesn't quite follow the Alfresco theme, but because the color is popular with the buyers, and changing the name may confuse the fabric mill, it stays. The popularity of colors run from previous seasons is closely tracked by the company to follow whether they are trending up or trending down.

Prints

Another step is developing print designs for fabrics. These are developed for the season by in-house fabric designers, or bought from independent companies (e.g., Patricia Nugent Textiles) that specialize in fashion prints. Some apparel markets, such as swimwear, use many prints each season, and some, such as outerwear, use relatively few. There are in-house fabric and print designers in a large company, but in small- or medium-size companies, developing prints may be the designers' responsibility. In developing the prints for the spring Alfresco line, the staff researched many ideas, some of which fit the target customer whereas many did not. Some of the many color and print directions forecast for the season were white on black, antique tropicals, scarf prints, retro florals, stylized polka dots, border prints, paisley, graphic foulards, trellis, texture prints, batik-type, digital prints, geometric dots, stenciled motifs, watercolor effects, and logo prints.

Fabrics

Developing various fabrics is a key step, and identifying trends in fabrics is an important element in planning the new line. Designers and merchandisers may attend international fabric trade shows such as Interstoff in Germany or Premier Vision in Paris, where a great deal of fabric, trend, and color information is presented. Another source of information is sales representatives (fabric reps) who work for textile mills and visit the design department with fabric swatches. There are also textile trade magazines, trade newspapers such as *Women's Wear Daily* and *DNR*, and trend reports. Designers also have personal files of tear sheets—photographs taken from magazines—which they collect continuously to use for inspiration, and they also draw from their own style notebooks (see Chapter 4).

Certain fabrics in a season may be developed either as an *exclusive*, meaning a custom weave or print ordered from the textile mill, or as existing fabrics (called *running fabrics*). If a fabric is not a running fabric, the planners must factor extra time into the production schedule. For an exclusive print that no other company is buying, a careful calculation must be made of how many yards of that print will actually sell, because the printing house will have a minimum order, for example, 3,000 yards. The fabrics are selected by designers and merchandisers, who, after their study of the market direction, select new fabrics that will blend with repeat fabrics, appeal to the target customer, and fit within the target price.

Trend information for fabrics, in addition to identifying specific fabrics, also points to the general direction of the look for the season with descriptive information such as two-tone effects, silky hand, tactile qualities, and sanded surfaces. Interestingly, knits and wovens are different in their properties, and often follow different trends.

Some of the knit directions highlighted in the trend information for the Spring 20XX season are pointelle and pointelle borders, silk jersey, wide ribs and rib textures, matte jersey, cut-and-sew sweater knits, and drop-needle stripes. Some examples of general trends forecasted for woven fabrics for Spring 20XX are delicate shine, gauzy transparency, lighter suitings, and smooth surfaces.

More specific information on woven fabric direction highlights pearlized shantung, tattersall check, yarn-dye stripes, floral stripes, openwork stripes, crepe, voile and printed voile, chiffon, washed linen, linen/cotton blends, stretch linen, workwear casuals, "denim" linen, hand-woven looks, and deck-chair canvas stripes. The fabrics chosen for the Alfresco line appear on the line plan in Table 2.2.

Silhouettes

The fourth step is outlining the silhouettes for the season. Silhouette refers to the general shape of the garment; specifically, it means what part is tight, what is loose, what part of the body is covered, and what part is uncovered.

Trend reports are often targeted to specific market segments, such as active, which gets direction from sports; young men's, with direction from music and street trends; and so on. Trend report books have sketches showing what shapes are directional and often include photographs of retail window displays from popular fashion-forward stores around the world, and street trends in key places such as Tokyo, Barcelona, and Saint Tropez, as well as the capital cities of the United States and Europe.

For women's wear, the trends and silhouettes often begin in high fashion and filter down slowly, depending on what is acceptable to the target customer. For example, if a trend appears in Paris or London for jackets with very fitted waists, that is not a style appropriate for every customer; however, after a season or two, if that look takes hold, a jacket may be developed with vertical seaming that gives the effect of a fitted waist without being overly slim-fitting.

Each women's product category—for example, tops, bottoms, dresses, and outerwear—has its unique silhouettes. The forecast information for women's Spring 20XX silhouettes targets general themes such as dress-up, clean lines, obvious construction, sixties-inspired, Spanish flamenco, ladylike and playful, and asymmetric details. General trend directions for women's product categories are as follows:

- *Skirts*: gypsy skirt, flip and flare, pencil skirt, dirndl, petal skirt, pleat details
- *Pants*: side closures, riding pant, knee pant for evening, Hollywood waistband, slim trouser with sports detailing, diagonal seaming
- *Blouses*: the new romantic blouse, ribbon details, tie closures, sleeve volume and details
- *Dresses*: the chiffon dress, very long or very short lengths, romantic details, sheer layers, draped bodice, and collar details
- *Suits and jackets*: the pajama jacket, the big blazer, the little jacket, mismatched suit, the short jacket over a long skirt
- *Details*: military, pleats and tucks, frog closures, tie neck, high necks, cowl neck, contrast buttons, structured seaming, concealed closures, newest metallic is copper

What is a person to make of all this sometimes contradictory information? Certain unfamiliar terms may be included that must be researched, and ultimately many of the trends will never be right for XYZ Career. But some will work next year, when the customer is ready for them, and some can be used right now to add a fresh direction to the Spring 20XX Alfresco line. Figure 2.2 shows the ones chosen as right for this customer and season. Figure 2.3 shows the line approved for development.

Concept Board

Based on the direction meeting, designers will prepare their ideas for presentation, making use of their research and their own feelings about the season. If they have ideas other than what is on the preliminary line outline prepared by the merchandiser, this is the time to present them, because some extra styles are needed and a certain percentage of the ideas presented will be dropped or modified.

Designers' presentations will often be in the form of **concept boards** or focus boards, which are presentation boards upon which are mounted sketches, swatches, and other inspirations for the season. Foam-core board is popular for this purpose because it is both lightweight and rigid. Figure 2.2 shows an example of a preliminary concept board. This style of board includes fashion illustrations and colors, and may include inspiration photographs, swatches of fabric, prints or painted mock-ups of prints, and samples of trims such as buttons and stitching details. It does not have all the details represented or all the styles, but it has the ones that are directional.

The merchandise manager will review the concept boards and use them to discuss the proposed designs with the designers. Individual designs will be decided upon, based on the previous season's selling patterns and on trends going forward. The use here of swatches and **findings**—that is, all the smaller items, other than the fabric, that are used for sewing and garment construction, such as the proposed buttons, and a sample of the stitching details—helps to sell the idea and shows that the designer has taken steps beyond just a sketch and toward problem-solving all the related elements of these designs. The concept board helps communicate the intent of the design group and speeds communication. It also shows how garments are intended to coordinate as well as other strategies of successful styling.

Presentations

Presentations are an important part of the designer's job, and concept boards are a vital tool used as a springboard for discussing the upcoming line development. Early in the development season, the designer will present ideas to the merchandiser, and will have many subsequent meetings, both formal and informal, as the season progresses. Learning to talk about one's ideas is an important skill, as is a familiarity with fashion and garment terminology. Part of the presentation is to

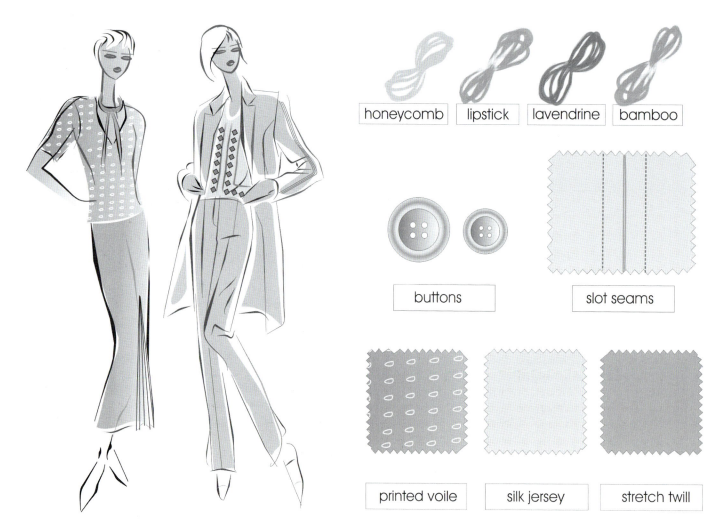

Figure 2.2 Concept board for Spring 20XX Alfresco line.

honeycomb   lipstick   lavendrine   bamboo

buttons   slot seams

printed voile   silk jersey   stretch twill

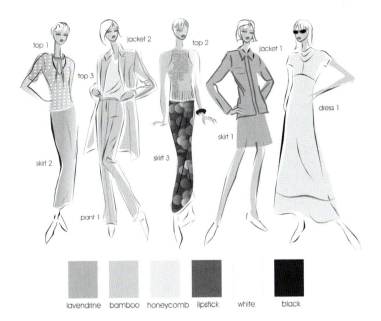

a l f r e s c o

top 1
jacket 2
top 3
top 2
jacket 1
dress 1
skirt 1
skirt 2
skirt 3
pant 1

lavendrine   bamboo   honeycomb   lipstick   white   black

Figure 2.3 **Completed Alfresco line.**

discuss the designs being proposed in terms of current trends, and how they fit into the company and appeal to the target customer.

There is always a learning curve for a new designer in considering his or her design as a product, rather than in a more personal way. Hearing an associate criticize a favorite creation requires some adjustment, but such comments should be considered as constructive attempts to maximize the effectiveness of the line as a whole. If a particular style is in some way an outlier in cost, does not apply to the target customer, or would not be accepted by the buyer, then it will need to be revisited. Even two great designs in the exact price point are not always desirable because they may split sales. For example, placing 5,000 units of each would not be as good as 10,000 units of one consolidated style, since greater volume will provide a price break.

Each design needs a reason to be and a logical place in the line plan. If the design concept is not clearly communicated to the PLM, a certain design may not be accepted for the season. The other team members in the production process also need to clearly understand the designs and what is desired, and the designers, in turn, need to understand the challenges of the production staff to avoid delays or quality problems.

Figure 2.3, the completed Alfresco line, shows this particular merchandise group completed. Some changes were made to help the items sell in higher volume and fit in with each other. For example, the skirt in Figure 2.2 has pleat detailing at the hem, but the final fabric chosen is a knit, which does not take crisp pleating in the way that was planned. Figure 2.3, skirt 2, shows the final style without pleats. The slot seam detail in jacket 2 has been revised to triple-needle topstitching because slot seams don't work well on a curve, and a tailored sleeve is curved. That also led to triple-needle topstitching at the waist of pant 1, which ties the two items together visually. The top shown under jacket 2 was originally planned as a scarf print (a type of border print), but it was deemed too busy and not versatile enough. Instead, the colors will be based on the jacket and pants, but lighter coordinating pastels because few people would be interested in a head-to-toe matching outfit.

Line Plan

The line plan is the puzzle needing completion, and the designs are the puzzle pieces. The styles all need to fit together to encourage multiple sales and successfully complete the plan.

Overview of Line Plan

The line plan is developed in tandem with the styles. Each season has only so many openings for new styles, and a great deal of strategic thinking goes into the offerings. Table 2.2 is a (somewhat simplified) line plan for the Alfresco line. A line plan could be considered as one large riddle with many smaller riddles inside. The answer to the large riddle is already known: the $1,000,000.00 sales goal for this season. The smaller riddles are: How many? What designs? How many colors, and which colors for each? At this point, the quantities outlined by the PLM are based on a best-guess estimate.

The total of all of the prospective items must add up to the budget of $1,000,000.00, which represents how much must be sold to pay for the company expenses and overhead and to make a profit. Of course, if more is sold, the profit for the season will be greater. But if, for example, twice as much is sold as planned, it may be difficult to finance because it far exceeds the budget, and more money will be needed to purchase the goods. Predictability of the sales outcomes is an important challenge for the PLM.

The line plan has a certain number of tops and bottoms, presented in a calculated way to maximize the sales volume. An example from Table 2.2 shows jacket 2, a new style in crepe, paired with pant 1, in the same fabric and with similar detailing, offered in the same colors. That encourages the shopper to buy both items and make an outfit.

The line plan illustrates various merchandising and selling strategies, and follows certain principles proven in the sales history of the XYZ Missy Career, such as the fact that there are often fewer colors offered in bottom styles because people prefer neutral and darker colors for bottoms; that white jackets sell well in the spring, and that spring tank styles do well in every color.

There are many costs to each garment, all of which need to be captured to maintain profitability. The line plan breaks the costs into different components. The original price quoted by the agent will be the **FOB** price, which stands for free on board. If the garment price is quoted as, for example, FOB Shanghai, the garment factory quotes the price of a garment to the nearest port (in this case, Shanghai), so the price quote includes fabric, cutting, sewing, finishing, folding and bagging, boxing, and sending the goods to the port for shipping. It does not include ocean freight, duty, and transportation to the destination warehouse, which need to be calculated separately. The price with all of those costs included is called the **landed price**.

One last change was made to the line after the line plan in Table 2.2 was handed out, but before the tech packs were begun. The plan in Table 2.2 shows sarong skirt 3 with projected units of 900, which is not sufficient to use up the 3,000-yard minimum of the custom dot print. In addition, based on sales history, fewer people will purchase a print skirt than a print top. So the decision was made to move those units into a tank top using the dot print, to complement the halter sweater tank (top 2) and solid knit tank (top 3).

SKU and Line Plan

Another tracking method for the line plan is based on the SKU count. **SKU** stands for stock-keeping unit, and is calculated by multiplying the **colorways** (color combinations in the same garment) offered times the size scale. For example, the first item in the line plan, skirt 1, is offered in eight sizes (2, 4, 6, 8, 10, 12, 14, and 16) times three colorways (lavendrine, bamboo, and black) for a total SKU count of 24.

For line planning purposes, a simpler definition of SKU is used, just "item multiplied by colors offered," excluding the sizing information, which in this case is three SKUs. After a certain point (different for different companies), if a SKU is added, such as one extra color, another one must be dropped to avoid having too many SKUs and diluting the line.

The line plan is an important framework within the **commercialization process**, in which a concept is turned into an actual product. All the styles need to fit into it so the company can avoid offering too many or too few items. After the concept boards are signed off on, the designers turn their attention to the technical design aspects of each item, and to creating tech packs in the race for producing apparel products.

Technical Design in the Design Process

Technical design is an important element of the commercialization process. It involves analyzing designs and design details, creating and editing CAD sketches for accuracy, understanding how the garment should fit, working with the factory to communicate precisely what is wanted, confirming all the details, and acting as the last pair of eyes on the tech pack before it's sent out for production.

The discipline of technical design is key to the product development process. It is often a specialty on its own, but apparel designers need to speak the same language as the technical designers with whom they collaborate and know how to get what they want on a technical level; otherwise, their designs may not actually work. In any given week (or perhaps just one very busy day), a designer may ponder issues such as:

- Should I use flatlock or top-and-bottom coverstitch at the armhole?

- How many inches wide should the leg opening of this pant be?

- Should this top get bust darts or yoke gathers? How many gathers will equal a dart?

- How can this high-fashion runway look be adapted to be flattering for average-height people?

- What is a good but inexpensive substitute for $100/yard Italian wool doubleface?

- Do I know what my boss means when she asks me to design a "Spencer jacket with passementerie trim, and leg-o-mutton sleeves"? Do I know how to find out?

- And the eternal question, do I have time to request another prototype?

In brief, the technical design aspect of the product development process can be defined as:

- Creating the blueprint of apparel products; that is, proportionally correct sketches including front and back views and details

- Assigning the correct measurements appropriate to the fabric and the design

- Including the construction details that achieve the look and price

- Evaluating the **prototype samples**; that is, the first actual garments provided according to the instructions in the tech pack, analyzing the garment fit, and following up as needed

- Communicating clearly with the factory about revisions and corrections

Developing the concept and look of the design is the beginning step, and the next step is to make all the instructions for reproducing it. That is essentially what a tech pack is, and it enables manufacturers in the factories, perhaps on the other side of the world, to reproduce the intended design properly.

The knowledge of the technical side of design will enable one to work through design projects efficiently, to have a firm grasp of what makes a style successful, and to have designs be adopted into a line with as few prototypes as possible. Because most of the production process is executed by hired overseas manufacturers, the tech pack should be simple, precise, and accurately written for effective communication. (See Chapter 3 for more information about the tech pack.) At this stage of product development, the tech packs are prepared to send out, so that the first prototype samples can be developed and reviewed.

Developing Samples

After the tech pack is prepared and sent out to the agent, the first sample is developed and returned to the design team. One of the responsibilities of the agent, who acts as the middleman for a number of manufacturers, is to return the completed samples within the contracted time period, generally within two to three weeks. In most cases, the manufacturers are overseas, and they send their products by express mail or courier services, such as FedEx.

Information on the Sample Tag

Each stage of product development has samples with a different name and purpose, and when any new sample arrives, it is carefully dated, measured, and tracked. Some companies assign a special identification number, and some track samples with bar codes. To create quality apparel products, it is necessary to review samples in each stage of the apparel production process, from first prototypes (called protos) through to the final production sample. Therefore, it is very important to keep an accurate record of each sample, designating each development stage. Figure 2.4 shows an actual sample tag for XYZ Product Development, Inc., and illustrates the wealth of identifying information on the card.

The following information should be noted by the factory, and will be attached securely to the garment:

- *Date when sent*. The receipt date should also be noted by the person processing the sample.

- *ID #*. A number unique to this individual garment, used for evaluations and for records.

- *Style number*. The **style number** incorporates much important information, and is the way that tech packs are filed in the computer. For that reason, the name and description alone are not enough information. The first part of the example here is of a "smart" style number; MWT stands for Missy Woven Top. Other tech pack systems assign numbers on a strictly sequential basis, such as the last part of the number, 1770.

- *Status*. Where the sample is in the development process. There may eventually be multiple versions of the style, each with

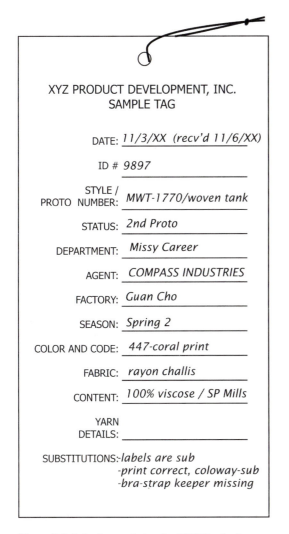

Figure 2.4 Actual sample tag for XYZ Product Development, Inc.

slightly different measurement specs or details, so it is crucial to keep them identified and differentiated. The status will have been assigned in the last set of comments. For example, the status of the sample in Figure 2.4 is the second proto. The previous sample was the first proto, and if approved to go ahead, the next sample set will be the sales samples.

- *Department name and product category.* Men's casual, women's career, girl's sleepwear, and boy's outerwear are examples of departments. Each department is divided into product categories such as woven top, sweaters, and so on, and not every department runs every category.

- *Agent and factory names.* Every agent may represent numerous factories in various countries, so the factory name is important. In addition, certain factories specialize in certain operations, so the factory name will help confirm that the style has been assigned to the most appropriate factory.

- *Selling season* (Spring 1, Summer, Back to School, Holiday, and so on). It is important to note the season, so the **development window**—the time frame for style development this season—is obvious. This also helps to distinguish between carry-over styles.

- *Color and code.* Colors and shades evolve from season to season, and that must be documented by the color code.

- *Fabric and content.* The fabric and fabric content should be noted. Fabric supplier and dyer are often noted. For sweaters, the yarn information is key.

- *Yarn details.* In the case of sweaters, weight per dozen needs to be specified as a standard way of assuring the final product quality for sweaters. The tag in Figure 2.4 shows a woven garment, so this area is blank.

- *Substitutions.* If the correct findings are not yet available at the time of the sample making, information on the tag can make clear that their absence is not an oversight of the factory. This spares the need for mentioning it in an email. It is important to stress to the factory to note all substitutions on the sample card.

Kinds of Samples

The following is one model of the life of a prototype, and all the sample versions it may go through throughout the commercialization process, until it is finally produced, shipped to the stores, and sold. First comes a wonderful idea, which begs to be developed.

First Prototype

After the idea has been presented (see Figure 2.5) and is chosen for development, it is translated into a tech pack similar to the one in Figure 2.6 and sent to the factory to be made into a sample. Sometimes the correct fabric is not yet available, especially in the case of a customization like an exclusive print. In that case, a substitute fabric with a similar weight and drape may be used for this initial stage of production for a first prototype sample.

The sketch on the tech pack in Figure 2.6 is in quite a different drawing style (called a **technical flat**) from that of the fashion illustration. We will look more at sketch styles and their differences and usage in Chapter 4. Figure 2.6 shows the initial request for a first prototype. It shows the first page of the multipage tech pack.

The factory receives the tech pack and then develops the first proto sample (see Figure 2.7). The style is a sleeveless blouse in the Alfresco dot print, which is replacing skirt 3 on the line plan in Figure 2.3. The back view details for this new style are the same as the front, four vertical darts in Figure 2.7. The neckline closure is a back neck button with self-fabric loop. It is fitted through the waist and also has a zipper closure at the left side seam.

It is the factory's responsibility to return the first prototype sample within two or three weeks. When the first proto arrives, it is measured and reviewed for fit and quality, usually within a short time frame of two to three days. During the fit session, the garment is evaluated by the product development team (e.g., designers, technical designers, and merchandisers) to determine how it fits into the line as a whole, whether it will appeal to the target customer, and whether it will sell well at the intended price.

Figure 2.5 It begins with an idea.

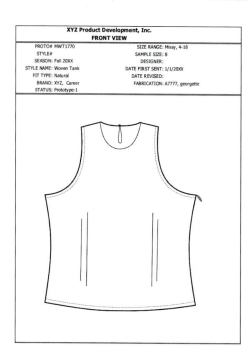

XYZ Product Development, Inc.	
FRONT VIEW	
PROTO# MWT1770	SIZE RANGE: Missy, 4-18
STYLE#	SAMPLE SIZE: 8
SEASON: Fall 20XX	DESIGNER:
STYLE NAME: Woven Tank	DATE FIRST SENT: 1/1/20XX
FIT TYPE: Natural	DATE REVISED:
BRAND: XYZ, Career	FABRICATION: A7777, georgette
STATUS: Prototype-1	

Figure 2.6 Tech pack for the tank top, first proto.

Figure 2.7 First proto sample, available fabric.

The garment fit is checked with the help of a dress form or fit model, and all the elements are reviewed. Dress forms are often used to check the general fit of the garment at this stage. However, using a live fit model is very important to finalize a fit and make sure the garment is comfortable and functional (see Chapter 16).

In this example, a number of developments occurred that required some revisions before the style could be confirmed for the XYZ Missy Career line. The garment was not achieving the target price in the line plan, so the team identified some areas in which the price could be reduced. These include changing from vertical darts (four front and four back) to two bust darts only, and changing the overall dimensions so that the garment could be slipped on over the head, eliminating the side zipper, center back neck closure, and button. In addition, the neck and armholes will be finished with bias binding, rather than a facing, reducing the fabric usage. These changes allow it to remain in the line. All these changes reduce the labor costs of sewing.

All the necessary changes are incorporated into the existing tech pack, and the revised version with written **sample evaluation comments** (simplified to "comments") on the first proto sample are sent to the factory to request a second proto sample (see

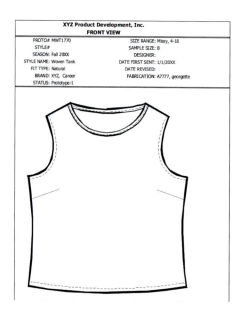

XYZ Product Development, Inc.	
FRONT VIEW	
PROTO# MWT1770	SIZE RANGE: Missy, 4-18
STYLE#	SAMPLE SIZE: 8
SEASON: Fall 20XX	DESIGNER:
STYLE NAME: Woven Tank	DATE FIRST SENT: 1/1/20XX
FIT TYPE: Natural	DATE REVISED:
BRAND: XYZ, Career	FABRICATION: A7777, georgette
STATUS: Prototype-1	

Figure 2.8 Revised tech pack requesting second proto.

Figure 2.8). Comments are all the notes, instructions, revisions, and updates on a sample, including fit history, that are added to the tech pack before the next sample is requested.

Communicating clearly with the manufacturing partners requires a methodical approach, which will help them understand the issues and revisions needed. Companies have a **vendor manual**, which is sent to all agents. It is an agreement of standards for different departments, and covers shipping, fair labor practices, quality audits, and other issues. For the product development area, it includes sewing standards and terminology, abbreviations, samples of key documents, instructions on how to measure, and other important tools of communication (see Chapter 15 for how to measure guidelines). It is one of the important jobs of the agent to make sure all the factories understand and comply.

Second Prototype

The second proto will be made up in the (now available) correct fabric, the dot print, in the correct colorway, according to the revised tech pack. The garment measurements have also been revised, reflecting the fact that the garment fit type will be "relaxed" rather than "slim," and can be slipped on over the head. (See Chapter 15 for more information on fit types.)

The second proto (see Figure 2.9) arrives and goes through the same measuring and checking process as the first proto. Because it was executed with good planning, good proofing, good communication, and a good set of measurements, the resulting style is approved to sales samples (see Figure 2.10).

Sales Samples

Depending on how many salespeople represent the line, enough sales samples (see Figure 2.10) will be produced to give one to each, plus some extras for the house line. In this way, valuable information is gathered about the new line, the less successful styles are culled before production, and the orders for production are compiled based on actual sales projections rather than guesswork. And because the style has been in a mini-production (sales sample production in Figure 2.10), the manufacturer has an opportunity to test the construction methods.

Figure 2.9 **Second proto sample.**

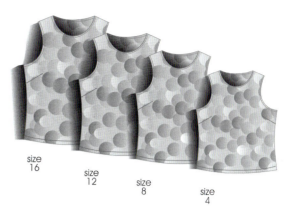

Figure 2.11 **Size set samples.**

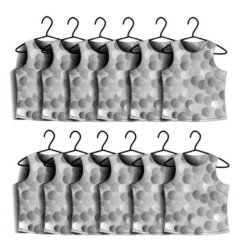

Figure 2.10 **Sales samples.**

Bought Style

When the style has been shown at trade shows or chosen by the buyers, and the sales can be projected, it moves into bought or adopted status, meaning it will be produced. If the technical design department is a separate entity, after a hand-off meeting with design, the responsibility for preparing the style for production will pass to technical design. If there is not a separate department, designers will review **construction details**, that is, specific information about how each area of garments is sewn and assembled. Designers will also review all other details (including trim, labels, and so on), check the sample specs, and do everything else needed to ensure the garment's smooth progress through production. Purchase orders will be placed by the production department. At this time size set samples are requested by the company (see Figure 2.11).

Size Set Samples

Up to now the samples have all been in the sample size, a size generally near the middle of the size range, which for women may be a size M or a 7 or 8, and for men an L chest for tops or 34 waist for bottoms. After the style is approved for selling and all the fit details are correct, **size set samples** (see Figure 2.11) are requested. The graded set of samples (4, 6, 8, 10, 12, 14, and 16 for women), or a representative set such as 4, 8, 12, 16 (see Figure 2.11), is produced, and is fit on models and reviewed to ensure that the sizing and all the details are in proportion for all sizes. The more slim-fitting the style is, the more important this step is. The grade rules govern the difference among sizes at various areas of a

pattern piece. Each company has its own standards, but there may often be exceptions to the rules for certain details. For example, patch pockets at the chest would generally be the same for all sizes, but patch pockets at the bottom of a jacket may need to increase in size for size 14 and 16 to remain in proportion. Because that is a visual decision, it is best reviewed on an actual sample. At that point, it can be determined whether that pocket should be larger for the larger sizes. If so, it would require a grade rule, the precise difference between sizes for pocket height and width.

Preproduction Sample (Red-Tag Sample)

The factory sends the sample, called the **preproduction sample**, to the apparel company. This sample (see Figure 2.12) should be sewn in the actual factory doing the production, and should be correct in all the fabric, trims, garment details, folding, packaging, hang-tags, and so on. (The term *preproduction* is sometimes used to mean everything that happens before production, but is used much more narrowly here to refer to the one sample just previous to production.) Only very small corrections can be made at this point. If approved, the sample can be red tagged, and the manufacturer will start production.

Top of Production or Shipment Sample

The red-tag sample will be used by the quality assurance (QA) department to compare to the next sample, the **TOP (top of production)** sample, which is a small sampling of the first garments coming off the production line. The QA department will measure and check the TOP sample, compare it to the preproduction (red-tag) sample, and decide whether the shipment is approved to ship. The two types of samples should be alike in every detail. Figure 2.13 shows the garment folded and packed

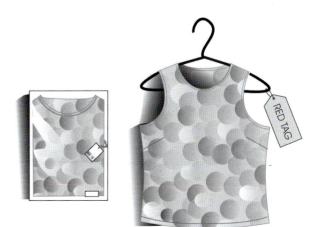

Figure 2.12 **Preproduction sample (red-tag sample).**

Figure 2.13 Shipment sample (TOP) packaged and approved to ship.

into a plastic bag as it will be for shipping, with the correct bar-code sticker at the lower left corner (wearer's perspective), and the hangtag visible for scanning. The QA department is guided by the fully corrected and updated tech pack, together with fabric- and color-approved swatches and approved trims for comparison. The QA department is also guided in its review by the **tolerances**, the amount that the garment can be off specification, larger or smaller, and still be accepted. The design department is no longer directly involved, unless a problem arises about which the QA department needs to be advised. At this stage, production is almost completed, so no changes for the style can be made.

Sample Lead Times

Companies have different sample lead times, also called turn times or turnaround times. These are the amount of time between stages of the product development process. Table 2.3 is an example for XYZ Product Development Company. The lead times represented are from the day the tech packs are sent to the day of exit from the company. Because this company sends and receives from both domestic and overseas sources, the lead times for both are differently given. You can also see from Table 2.3 that certain garment categories require more development time. These styles should be prioritized to make sure that all the styles can be ready by the meeting date. It is also important to determine and add on the transit time, because samples coming from overseas can sometimes be subject to delays in shipping and inspections by U.S. Customs.

When a bulk production shipment is imported into the United States, they are subject to certain regulations. Samples, on the other hand, have special rules that allow them to enter in a more

streamlined way. There are two types of sample shipments: (1) marked and (2) mutilated.

A *marked* sample has the word "sample" stamped or written on the inside in indelible ink, in letters at least 1-inch high. A *mutilated sample* is one that has a 2-inch hole cut into it or the word "sample" written indelibly on the outside. Both of these methods seem like the waste of a perfectly good garment, but it is done to prevent the importation of garments as samples to then be re-sold in violation of customs regulations. If the samples need to be received with no marks or damage, for example to show to buyers, they can be imported as *quota samples*, subject to other rules regulated by U.S. Customs. This method of importing requires a longer lead time, and for that reason, samples for development are usually marked or mutilated. Samples made domestically need no such considerations.

The Apparel Production Process

The development process for apparel depends on whether the apparel company sells its designs to outside companies through sales representatives or produces goods for its own internal buyers. Some differences occur between these two situations.

Companies Selling Through Sales Representatives

Figure 2.14 shows a timeline for companies that have reps who show their styles at a trade show, common for medium or smaller-sized companies. A sales meeting is held, usually at the company headquarters. The reps are introduced to the line, and have an opportunity to give their feedback, based upon what they know about their customers. Some items may drop out at this point. For example, if there are two knit tops—equally salable and priced the same—that will appeal to the same customer, they will compete with each other and split the sales. It would be better to drop one and consolidate the sales into the remaining one. The sales reps provide valuable input on this type of consideration.

If, at the sales meeting, too large a percentage of styles are dropped or considered "wrong," it would point to a weakness in the planning or merchandising. There is only so much time to develop styles, and it is important to get it right and accurately predict the needs of the buyer, and target customer.

The more conservative the customer base, the easier it is to predict the next season because the changes from season to season are smaller and more subtle. For markets that are more fashion- and novelty-driven, such as the juniors market, the risk of not having the hottest style in the right color, fabric, fit, and price is high. The financial rewards for timing every element perfectly are also high.

The season culminates in the national trade show, where each company shows its new apparel line from a booth. **Trade shows** are a place to showcase the newest products and enables companies to promote to prospective buyers under one roof. Trade shows are sponsored by apparel marts, promotional companies, and/or trade associations. The sales reps attend, meet with their customers to review their orders, show them the line again, and present other colors and whatever updates and revisions may have occurred.

An example of a major national trade show would be the Men's Apparel Guild in California (MAGIC) show. Another is the

Table 2.3 XYZ Product Development, Inc. Lead Times for Sample Development

Product category	Source	Weeks for first proto	Weeks for second proto
Knit tops	Overseas	4	2
	Domestic	3	2
Bottoms	Overseas	5	3
	Domestic	3	2
Jackets/ Outerwear	Overseas	7	5
	Domestic	4	3
Sweaters	Overseas	10	7
	Domestic	7	4

DEVELOPMENT STAGES OF ONE SAMPLE

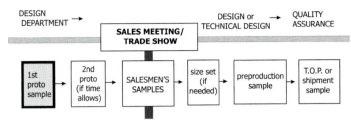

Figure 2.14 **Developmental stage for samples with sales representatives.**

DEVELOPMENT STAGES OF ONE SAMPLE

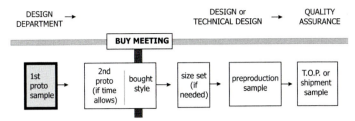

Figure 2.15 **Companies developing products for in-house labels.**

Outdoor Retailer (OR) show, held in Salt Lake City, for outdoor activities (such as hiking, climbing, and mountain biking) apparel and hardware companies. The trade shows are places where the buyers review orders, look for new lines, attend promotional events like fashion shows put on by the trade show association, and other events such as contests and celebrity appearances. These shows give companies the opportunity to promote their products to buyers in a more exciting way than just presenting the garments on a hanger. These shows are to the trade only, and are not open to the general public.

These companies typically employ sales representatives who cover local territories. One example of a territory may be Pennsylvania, New Jersey, Maryland, northern Virginia, and Washington, D.C. The sales rep is responsible for traveling in the territory, introducing the new lines to his or her retailers each season, explaining the features and benefits, dealing with problems with shipments, and keeping the retailers happy.

Reps may be paid by the company as employees, or they may be independent reps who earn a commission on everything sold in their territory. Each season, the reps are provided with their own line that they show to retailers prior to the trade show. So, each style is produced in a small production, one sample per rep, plus extras for the trade show and other promotional uses, or for editorial purposes to send to magazines for write ups. The benefits of attending trade shows are many, from meeting customers, to seeing what competitors are doing, to getting ideas about where the market is headed.

Companies Developing Products for House Labels

Figure 2.15 shows an example of an apparel company with in-house buyers who do the buying for each new season. They develop products for in-house labels such as specification buying. In this case, no sales samples are needed. In general, these are large-sized companies, such as Abercrombie & Fitch, Gap, and Polo, that have merchandisers who make their buying decisions, as do department store private label brands. When styles are bought by in-house company buyers, they are added to the production schedule and go through the same steps as any other company (size set, preproduction, and TOP). Larger company buyers who know their market and can afford the risk can skip the steps of sales samples and attending trade shows.

Summary

In this chapter, we presented an overview of the apparel product development process in the apparel industry based on the relationship between manufacturers and retailers. We also reviewed job responsibilities of professionals involved in the apparel production process and organizational structure in a company. Design development process starting from a line development for a season was discussed with practical examples used in the fashion industry. The importance of technical design and technical designers' role in the apparel design and product development processes were examined to provide a clear understanding of the apparel production process. Finally, developmental stages for samples in the apparel production processes based on the differences of retail companies were also reviewed and compared to provide an overview of the differences in apparel production processes.

Study Questions

1. What are the important factors to take into consideration for design development? Why is each important? What is a design? What went into the development of one of the garments you are wearing now?

2. Name the sample stages in sequential order for a company with sales reps (i.e., proto, sales sample, size set samples, preproduction, production). Name the stages for a company doing in-house labels.

3. Explain the process of a developing line plan for apparel products.

4. What are the influences from the forecast that were utilized for the Alfresco line Figure 2.3 (print, fabrics, and silhouette)?

5. What is a concept board and how it is used? What information is included on a concept board?

6. Refer to Appendix C: Thumbnail Clip Art, dress categories, found in the *Technical Sourcebook for Apparel Designers* STUDIO. Give an example of price tiering by selecting four related dress designs. What makes each design important to the seasonal outline? What would make appropriate price steps?

Check Your Understanding

1. Why is understanding target consumers important in developing lines?

2. Explain the various information used for samples in the apparel production process.

3. Design a Spencer jacket with passementerie trim and leg-o-mutton sleeves.

Reference

Burns, L. D., K. K. Mullet, and N. O. Bryant. 2011. *The Business of Fashion: Designing, Manufacturing, and Marketing* (4th ed.). New York: Fairchild Publications.

All About the Technical Package

Chapter Objectives

After studying this chapter, you will be able to:

- Prepare a detailed technical package for garment production
- Identify the information needed for product development

Key Terms

alpha sizing	numeric sizing	strikeoff
bartack	points of measure (POM)	style number
colorway	sample evaluation	style summary
dyed to match (DTM)	comments	vendor manual
grade rules	sample status	wet-processing
handloom	stitches per inch (SPI)	

The document used throughout the process of apparel development is the *technical package*, or tech pack. This document is known by other names in different companies, such as *specification pack* (or spec pack), *style file*, or *dossier*. We will use the term *tech pack* from now on, but whatever the name, it is the package of information sent to the manufacturer that covers every detail for the development of the prototypes.

Functions of the Tech Pack

As the primary means of communication between the brand's designers and the manufacturing company, the tech pack provides the following information:

- Identification of construction methods
- Specific fabrics, findings, and trims details
- Colorways of each style
- Fit specs and grade rules
- Labels, hangtags, and information about their attachment to the garment
- Packaging information

Creating the technical package is the next step in the commercialization process, and allows the manufacturer to provide an accurate cost estimate and correct sample. It is a document of the exact standards for the production of an item. It is also a contract, in which the agent agrees to provide goods as specified in the tech pack at a certain price. (That is why the garment maker is sometimes called the contractor.) Therefore, any issue that affects the cost or the quality of the garment must be decided by the product development team at a very early stage, and outlined clearly from the beginning to make sure the price quoted is accurate.

Components of the Tech Pack

Although each company in the industry uses its own format, generally the tech pack pages are laid out as follows.

- Front view
- Back view
- Detail views
- Sample spec/points of measure
- Grade page
- Bill of materials
- Construction methods
- Labels and packaging
- Fit history, sample evaluation comments

We will use a familiar garment as our example, a pair of men's jeans. The five-pocket blue jean is an enduring traditional silhouette that has been popular for many decades since Levi Strauss patented the application of rivets on men's denim work pants in 1873. Jeans are a good example of a classic category, the challenge of which is best described by the merchandiser's mantra, "The same, but different." The designer is often called upon to change an existing style just slightly, to make it fresh for the next season. Often, the most obvious change for a pair of jeans is the decoration on the back pockets. Finishes and processing can vary as well, and may include overdyes, bleaches, and enzyme washes, steps done to finished garments known as **wet-processing**.

Other recent incarnations for jean styles have included (in no particular order) low-rise, high-rise, bell-bottom, pegged, baggy, skin-tight, stretch, pleated, and cuffed. In the example here, the details follow a traditional pair of men's Levi's with the addition of a seam in the front panel at thigh level. The other standard jean details and construction methods are hand-pockets with rivets, seven belt loops, zipper fly with jean-tack button, right-hand coin pocket with rivets, true felled seams at the back yoke, rise, and inseams, and the waistband set with a folder and joined by chainstitch.

Style Summary

At the top of each page is a **style summary** (see Figure 3.1), which has important identifying information, including **style number**, season, fabric, size information, the date the style was first begun, fit type, the date it was last revised, and the **sample status**, or stage of development. It appears identically on all of the tech pack pages.

- *Proto number.* SWB1778 is the temporary number assigned to this style for the development process (see Figure 3.1a). In this case, SWB stands for Sport (the division label) Woven Bottom, and 1778 is strictly a sequential number given to this style. Style numbers can also contain a gender element, but in this case because the Sport Division for XYZ Product Development is men's only, there is no need to specify that.

XYZ Product Development, Inc.		
FRONT VIEW		
A. PROTO# SWB1778	H.	SIZE RANGE: Mens 30-42
B. STYLE#	I.	SAMPLE SIZE: 34 / 32
C. SEASON: Fall 20XX	J.	DESIGNER: Monica Smith
D. NAME: Mens Woven Pant	K. DATE FIRST SENT: 1/2/20XX	
E. FIT TYPE: Standard 5-pocket jean	L.	DATE REVISED:
F. BRAND: XYZ, Sport	M.	FABRICATION: 11 oz denim
G. STATUS: Prototype-1		

Figure 3.1 **Style summary information.**

- *Style number.* When the item is officially chosen for production, a style number is assigned and the factory is informed of the new numbers (see Figure 3.1b). At this early stage, there is not yet a style number, only a proto number. The style number will be added after the style is bought and before production. Other product development systems keep the same style number throughout the life of the garment, whether it is produced or not.

- *Season.* This refers to the season this style will reach the retail floor, fall of 20XX, usually three to six months from the beginning of development (see Figure 3.1c). There is always a great deal of pressure to work "closer to the season" and get goods to the retail store more quickly, and high fashion styles with a shorter "shelf life" are sometimes produced within a few weeks.

- *Style name.* This can be straightforward, or can designate a merchandise group (see Figure 3.1d). The merchandise groups for a missy line may have names such as "Plush Velvet," "Opposites Attract," "Melange," or whatever title the merchandise department deems appropriate for the season.

- *Fit type.* Fit type is chosen by the designer or merchandiser, and refers to the general silhouette desired and what pattern or block to use to begin the style (see Figure 3.1e). This one says "standard 5-pocket jean," and it refers to the standard measurements for XYZ Product Development, Inc., not an industry standard, given that there is no standard shared by all companies. It is important to become familiar with how much ease is allowed for different styles, according to the standards of the company. The more consistent and flattering the fit, the more customer loyalty is built.

- *Brand.* Companies often have different divisions and sell to different customers under a variety of labels (see Figure 3.1f).

- *Status.* The garment will undergo different changes at different points, and the status will explain where in the process it is (see Figure 3.1g). A brand new style will go out as Prototype-1.

- *Size Range.* The projected size range is important information that can affect the costing, and will need to match the grading (see Figure 3.1h). In addition, there may be some sales history that would lead the buyer to avoid some sizes, for example, the smallest and the largest sizes (waist sizes 30 and 42), if the item is not considered to be high volume enough. In addition, it is decided from the beginning whether the style is to be offered in S-M-L (called **alpha sizing**) or 30–42 (called **numeric sizing**).

- *Sample size.* The sample size is set by the company and remains the same each season within each brand (see Figure 3.1i). For this men's style, the sample size is 34/32, which is a 34-inch waist and 32-inch inseam. It would not be efficient for the sample size to change, for example missy samples to be size 8 one season and size 6 or 10 the next, because all the sample patterns are based on a certain set.

- *Designer.* The originator of the spec pack puts his or her name here to signal the factory to whom to direct their follow-up questions and emails (see Figure 3.1j).

- *Date first sent.* This shows the date that the factory first received the spec and helps to track its progress (see Figure 3.1k).

- *Date revised.* This will signal to the factory that there are revisions and that they need to note all the new information (see Figure 3.1l).

- *Fabrication.* This is for reference and also helps to interpret the sketch (Figure 3.1m).

Front and Back Views

The front view (see Figure 3.2) is a proportionately correct technical flat of the front of the garment, including topstitching and other details such as buttons and so on. Similarly, the back view (see Figure 3.3) is a proportionately correct technical flat of the back, including topstitching details. A side view is included if needed.

Companies generally reserve the front and back pages for a clean sketch with a minimum of notations. This gives the factory a place to make its notes and add translations. Additional detail sketches with notes and callouts are shown on subsequent pages.

Details View

All of the detail measurements, garment stitching, and close-up sketches needed to define the construction, and quality details are shown in the details view (see Figure 3.4). If additional pages are needed, they can be added here (see Figure 3.5). A very complicated style could have six or seven detail pages. The abbreviations used are CF for center front, CB for center back, and BT for **bartack**, a common type of reinforcement stitching used in areas of stress where extra strength is needed. Pockets and other details need to have their *dimensions*, *stitch details*, and exact *placement* on the garment specified.

Points of Measure for Samples

Figure 3.6 shows the sample's finished measurements, which will direct the fit of the product. For the first prototypes, only the sample size will be produced—in this case, size 34 waist. Graded measurements for each size will be added later, when the size set samples are requested.

Figure 3.6 includes an illustration for reference of where to measure each **point of measure**, or **POM** (see Chapter 4 for further discussion of POMs). Most companies outline their methods of how to measure in a separate company manual, with descriptions of how each spec is measured. The girth measurements here are full circumference or full measure, which is used for most woven products. The points of measure are generally arranged in the sequence in which they will be measured, from top to bottom of the garment. (More information on how to measure is found in Chapter 15.)

If a detail has more than one way to define it, it is extremely important to be specific. A good example is the rise measurement, and whether it is measured to the waistband seam (bottom of waistband) or to the top of the waistband. The rise is not very forgiving, and anything very far past tolerance will not be comfortable. A pant as far off specification as an entire waistband width (front and back) will be entirely unwearable. It is important to be concise about the points of measure and, to avoid confusion, not to revise them after development begins. The more the POMs are standardized the easier it is for the factory to avoid mistakes.

Tolerance refers to the allowable amount of difference between spec and actual sample. Note that there is both a plus tolerance and a minus tolerance, and the allowances are not always the same. The prototypes will be measured and the measurements compared to see whether they are within tolerance.

STYLE SUMMARY AREA

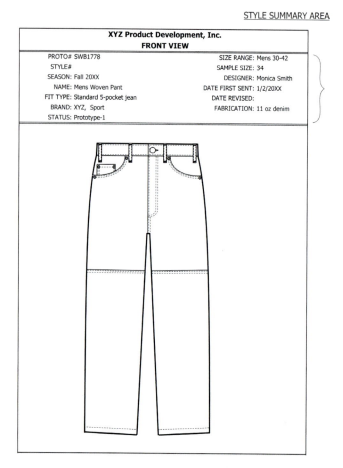

XYZ Product Development, Inc.
FRONT VIEW

PROTO# SWB1778   SIZE RANGE: Mens 30-42
STYLE#   SAMPLE SIZE: 34
SEASON: Fall 20XX   DESIGNER: Monica Smith
NAME: Mens Woven Pant   DATE FIRST SENT: 1/2/20XX
FIT TYPE: Standard 5-pocket jean   DATE REVISED:
BRAND: XYZ, Sport   FABRICATION: 11 oz denim
STATUS: Prototype-1

Figure 3.2 Technical package, front view.

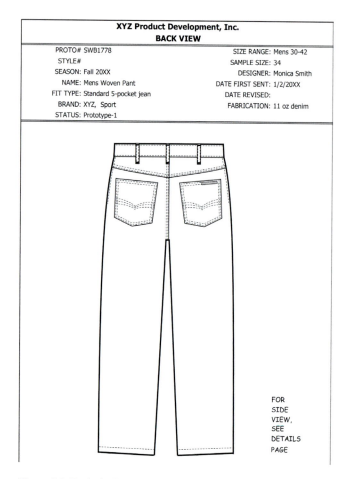

XYZ Product Development, Inc.
BACK VIEW

PROTO# SWB1778   SIZE RANGE: Mens 30-42
STYLE#   SAMPLE SIZE: 34
SEASON: Fall 20XX   DESIGNER: Monica Smith
NAME: Mens Woven Pant   DATE FIRST SENT: 1/2/20XX
FIT TYPE: Standard 5-pocket jean   DATE REVISED:
BRAND: XYZ, Sport   FABRICATION: 11 oz denim
STATUS: Prototype-1

FOR SIDE VIEW, SEE DETAILS PAGE

Figure 3.3 Technical package, back view.

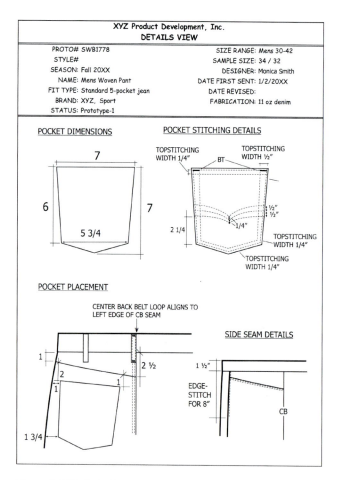

XYZ Product Development, Inc.
DETAILS VIEW

PROTO# SWB1778   SIZE RANGE: Mens 30-42
STYLE#   SAMPLE SIZE: 34 / 32
SEASON: Fall 20XX   DESIGNER: Monica Smith
NAME: Mens Woven Pant   DATE FIRST SENT: 1/2/20XX
FIT TYPE: Standard 5-pocket jean   DATE REVISED:
BRAND: XYZ, Sport   FABRICATION: 11 oz denim
STATUS: Prototype-1

POCKET DIMENSIONS

POCKET STITCHING DETAILS

POCKET PLACEMENT

SIDE SEAM DETAILS

Figure 3.4 Technical package, details view, one.

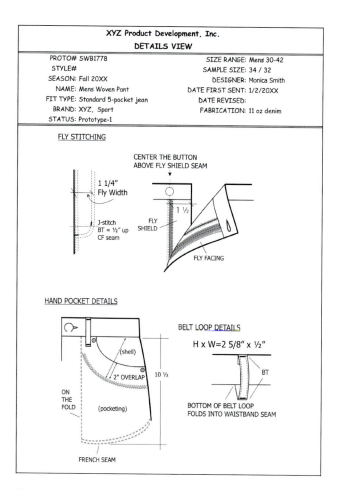

XYZ Product Development, Inc.
DETAILS VIEW

PROTO# SWB1778   SIZE RANGE: Mens 30-42
STYLE#   SAMPLE SIZE: 34 / 32
SEASON: Fall 20XX   DESIGNER: Monica Smith
NAME: Mens Woven Pant   DATE FIRST SENT: 1/2/20XX
FIT TYPE: Standard 5-pocket jean   DATE REVISED:
BRAND: XYZ, Sport   FABRICATION: 11 oz denim
STATUS: Prototype-1

FLY STITCHING

HAND POCKET DETAILS

BELT LOOP DETAILS

Figure 3.5 Technical package, details view, two.

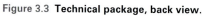

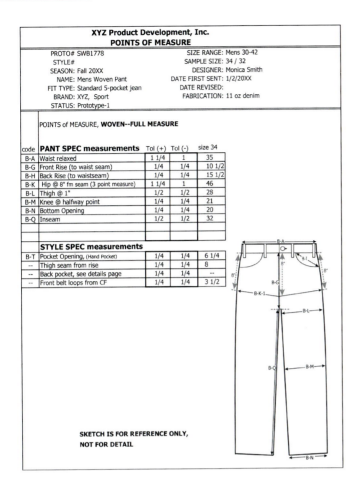

XYZ Product Development, Inc.
POINTS OF MEASURE

PROTO# SWB1778	SIZE RANGE: Mens 30-42
STYLE#	SAMPLE SIZE: 34 / 32
SEASON: Fall 20XX	DESIGNER: Monica Smith
NAME: Mens Woven Pant	DATE FIRST SENT: 1/2/20XX
FIT TYPE: Standard 5-pocket jean	DATE REVISED:
BRAND: XYZ, Sport	FABRICATION: 11 oz denim
STATUS: Prototype-1	

POINTS of MEASURE, **WOVEN--FULL MEASURE**

code	PANT SPEC measurements	Tol (+)	Tol (-)	size 34
B-A	Waist relaxed	1 1/4	1	35
B-G	Front Rise (to waist seam)	1/4	1/4	10 1/2
B-H	Back Rise (to waistseam)	1/4	1/4	15 1/2
B-K	Hip @ 8" fm seam (3 point measure)	1 1/4	1	46
B-L	Thigh @ 1"	1/2	1/2	28
B-M	Knee @ halfway point	1/4	1/4	21
B-N	Bottom Opening	1/4	1/4	20
B-Q	Inseam	1/2	1/2	32

code	STYLE SPEC measurements			
B-T	Pocket Opening, (Hand Pocket)	1/4	1/4	6 1/4
--	Thigh seam from rise	1/4	1/4	8
--	Back pocket, see details page	1/4	1/4	--
--	Front belt loops from CF	1/4	1/4	3 1/2

SKETCH IS FOR REFERENCE ONLY,
NOT FOR DETAIL

Figure 3.6 Technical package, points of measure (POM) page.

Grade Rules

The page for **grade rules** (see Figure 3.7) defines the precise way in which to convert the sample size into all the other sizes bought by the buyer, in order to produce the size runs. The grade rules are also needed so that the factory can cost the item. For instance, if the size range is only 4 through 14 instead of 4 through 18, that will represent a savings in fabric that will affect the overall cost of production.

This example is set up to compare each size with the sample size (not with the preceding size). The tolerance figures appear again in the third and fourth column. As noted previously, the plus and minus tolerances may be different. For example, in the case of the waist, the plus tolerance is $1\frac{1}{4}$ inch and the minus tolerance is 1 inch; sometimes, as on pant styles, too small is worse than too big.

The tolerance for a small detail, such as waistband height, is small ($\frac{1}{8}$ inch). More than $\frac{1}{8}$ inch off spec and the waistband will begin to look out of proportion. The tolerance for circumference measurements is generally one half of the grade, so if the grade between sizes is 1 inch, the tolerance is typically $\frac{1}{2}$ inch.

Every company has different size ranges and grade rules according to its target consumers. Not all points of measure get graded, for example, waistband height. The height of the waistband is a style point and is the same for all sizes, so it does not receive a grade.

XYZ Product Development, Inc.
GRADE PAGE

PROTO# SWB1778	SIZE RANGE: Mens 30-42
STYLE#	SAMPLE SIZE: 34 / 32
SEASON: Fall 20XX	DESIGNER: Monica Smith
NAME: Mens Woven Pant	DATE FIRST SENT: 1/2/20XX
FIT TYPE: Standard 5-pocket jean	DATE REVISED:
BRAND: XYZ, Sport	FABRICATION: 11 oz denim
STATUS: Prototype-1	

POINTS of MEASURE, **WOVEN--Specs and tolerances are FULL MEASURE**

code	PANT SPEC measurements	Tol (+)	Tol (-)	30	32	34	36	38	40	42
B-A	Waist relaxed	1 1/4	1	-4	-2		+2	+4	+6	+8
B-G	Front Rise (to waist seam)	1/4	1/4	- 1/2	- 1/4		+1/4	+1/2	+3/4	+1
B-H	Back Rise (to waistseam)	1/4	1/4	- 1/2	- 1/4		+1/4	+1/2	+3/4	+1
B-K	Hip @ 8" fm seam (3 point measure)	1 1/4	1	-4	-2		+2	+4	+6	+8
B-L	Thigh @ 1"	1/2	1/2	-2	-1		+1	+2	+3	+4
B-M	Knee @ halfway point	1/4	1/4	-1	- 1/2		1/2	+1	1 1/2	+2
B-N	Bottom Opening	1/4	1/4	- 1/2	- 1/4		+1/4	+1/2	+3/4	+1
B-Q	Inseam	1/2	1/2	0	0		0	0	0	0
	STYLE SPEC measurements									
B-T	Pocket Opening, straight (Hand Pocket)	1/4	1/4	0	0		0	0	0	0
--	Thigh seam from rise	1/4	1/4	0	0		0	0	0	0
--	Back pocket, see details page	1/4	1/4	--	--		--	--	--	--
--	Front belt loops from CF	1/4	1/4	- 1/4	- 1/8		+1/8	+1/4	+3/8	+1/2

Figure 3.7 Technical package, grade page with grade rules.

XYZ Product Development, Inc.
GRADE PAGE

PROTO# SWB1778
STYLE#
SEASON: Fall 20XX
NAME: Mens Woven Pant
FIT TYPE: Standard 5-pocket jean
BRAND: XYZ, Sport
STATUS: Prototype-1

SIZE RANGE: Mens 30-42
SAMPLE SIZE: 34 / 32
DESIGNER: Monica Smith
DATE FIRST SENT: 1/2/20XX
DATE REVISED:
FABRICATION: 11 oz denim

POINTS of MEASURE, **WOVEN--Specs and tolerances are FULL MEASURE**

code	PANT SPEC measurements	Tol (+)	Tol (-)	30	32	34	36	38	40	42
B-A	Waist relaxed	1 1/4	1	31	33	35	37	39	41	43
B-G	Front Rise (to waist seam)	1/4	1/4	10	10 1/4	10 1/2	10 3/4	11	11 1/4	11 1/2
B-H	Back Rise (to waistseam)	1/4	1/4	15	15 1/4	15 1/2	15 3/4	16	16 1/4	16 1/2
B-K	Hip @ 8" fm seam (3 point measure)	1 1/4	1	42	44	46	48	50	52	54
B-L	Thigh @ 1"	1/2	1/2	26	27	28	29	30	31	32
B-M	Knee @ halfway point	1/4	1/4	21	21 1/2	22	22 1/2	23	23 1/2	24
B-N	Bottom Opening	1/4	1/4	19 1/2	19 3/4	20	20 1/4	20 1/2	20 3/4	21
B-Q	Inseam	1/2	1/2	32	32	32	32	32	32	32
	STYLE SPEC measurements									
B-T	Pocket Opening, straight (Hand Pocket)	1/4	1/4	6 1/4	6 1/4	6 1/4	6 1/4	6 1/4	6 1/4	6 1/4
--	Thigh seam from rise	1/4	1/4	8	8	8	8	8	8	8
--	Back pocket, see details page	1/4	1/4	--	--	--	--	--	--	--
--	Front belt loops from CF	1/4	1/4	3 1/4	3 3/8	3 1/2	3 5/8	3 3/4	3 7/8	4

Figure 3.8 **Grade page, populated.**

Figure 3.8 shows the grade page with all the numbers included, following the grade rules in Figure 3.7. Most grade pages are set up to automatically calculate the correct figures. When the sample size figures are dropped in, the page automatically populates. POM codes accompany areas needing measurement. Some points of measure have no code because they are specific to this style. The inseam, 32, is the same for all sizes, common for Regular size. Some jeans are available in many lengths, but because the unit projection for this style is small (2,000 units) it can support only one inseam length. A larger volume style could be offered in three inseam lengths, for example, short (30-inch inseam), regular (32-inch inseam), and tall (34-inch inseam).

Bill of Materials

The bill of materials (BOM; see Figure 3.9) is used to determine what components to order for one unit. All of the construction components, the fabric, and findings (everything on a garment that is not fabric) appear on the bill of materials page. The main fabric is listed first, then lining or other fabrics where appropriate. All of the remaining roll goods are listed next. The fabrics do not have a quantity listed here because the fabric calculation is part of the costing process, based on the fabric width, which is handled between the factory and the production department. Because this page describes what is used for one garment unit, the thread quantity is also not included; it is another of the costs calculated by the factory. The thread quality, however, is very important, as is having the fabric weight and thread weight compatible. In

this example, heavier thread (tex 90) is often used as a decorative accent, or as reinforcement (as on a pair of jeans). For other styles, such as joining stretch fabrics, special stretch threads are used. This affects the costing, so it needs to be noted on the BOM. The non-garment components, such as the hangtags and shipping bags, are equally important and can be seen on the labels and packaging page. Together they make up the cost of materials.

The BOM also calls out information on the individual **colorways** offered. Garment colorways are the breakdown of which component is what color for all the trims. Here, the black wash gets silver topstitching, and the dark denim gets bronze topstitching; both get a copper button and rivets. (The term *colorway* is also used to describe color combinations for plaid and print fabrics, as in Figures 3.15 and 3.16 at the end of this chapter.) The acronym **DTM** means **dyed to match** and is often used to describe color matching, as for the thread color. Buttons and other trims can also be specified DTM.

Construction Details

On the construction page (Figure 3.10), instructions on hems, seams, and stitches are included to help the manufacturer put the garments together to meet the quality standards. Specific **stitches per inch (SPI)** are included also. As noted, 11, plus or minus 1, means that 10 SPI, 11 SPI, or 12 SPI is acceptable. The +/– designation is the tolerance. (More information on details of stitches, seams, and construction appears in Chapters 4 and

XYZ Product Development, Inc.
Bill Of Materials

PROTO# SWB1778
STYLE#
SEASON: Fall 20XX
NAME: Mens Woven Pant
FIT TYPE: Standard 5-pocket jean
BRAND: XYZ, Sport
STATUS: Prototype-1

SIZE RANGE: Mens 30-42
SAMPLE SIZE: 34 / 32
DESIGNER: Monica Smith
DATE FIRST SENT: 1/2/20XX
DATE REVISED:
FABRICATION: 11 oz denim

ITEM / description	CONTENT	PLACEMENT	SUPPLIER	WIDTH / WEIGHT / SIZE	FINISH	QTY
Indigo denim, 32/2x32/2, 116x62	100% COTTON	body	Luen Mills UFTD-9702	58" cuttable, 11.4 oz	garment laundered, 60 min.	--
Pocketing	65 polyester 35 cotton, 45dx45d, 110x76	HAND POCKETS	K. Obrien Company	58"	pre-shrunk	--
interfacing, non-woven fusible	100% poly	waistband, fly	PCC	style 246	--	--
Zipper	4YGC , brass teeth	CF fly	YKK Tokyo	6 1/2"	See below	1
Button, Jean Tack	--	CF waistband	Schneider Button, style w345t	27L, shank height=1/4"	Copper C-21	1
rivet	--	hand pkts x 2, coin pkt x 2	Zupan Trims	9mm	Copper C-21	6
thread-DTM body	100% spun polyester	join & overlock	A & E	tex 30	--	--
thread-DTM LABEL	100% spun polyester	back pocket	A & E	tex 30	--	--
thread-CONTRAST	100% spun polyester	topstitch	A & E	tex 90	--	--

COLORWAY SUMMARY

color #	main body color	zipper tape	zipper finish	topstitching	
477	wash black--enzyme	580	antique brass	A-448	
344B	dark denim--enzyme	560	golden brass	R-783	

Figure 3.9 **Technical package, bill of materials (BOM).**

5.) Figure 3.10 is shown with no abbreviations; Figure 3.11 is a more typical version with many notations abbreviated to save space. The top section, cutting information, concerns matching patterns, plaids, and one-way fabrics. (More information on fabric matching can be found in Chapter 7.)

Every company has a certain set of abbreviations that it uses for different operations. A full set of abbreviations and their definitions are given in each company's **vendor manual**.

Labels and Packaging

Labels and tags are important selling tools, and important elements of the total cost of the garment. Labels for many different factories are often sourced from a central supplier for color and quality consistency. Specific information related to the type and sizes of labels, including placement and sewing instructions, are included on the labels and packaging page (see Figure 3.12), as well as instructions on folding. All label

and hangtag information is together on the labels page. Folding instructions often appear in a separate manual, but they are included here for reference. That is why the pant shown here is not this specific jean style—it is a generic pant sketch taken from the XYZ Folding Instructions Manual.

Fit History

The last pages of the tech pack are the fit history (Figure 3.13) and **sample evaluation comments** (Figure 3.14). Most of the tech pack pages do not change during the sampling process, except to update items or clarify details. In contrast, the fit history and sample evaluation comments (which we call the comments page) is updated for each new version.

Because this tech pack represents a request for a new style, there is not yet any history. The fit history page is used to record the measurements of each subsequent sample. It will compare the actual prototype measurements against the spec

XYZ Product Development, Inc.
CONSTRUCTION PAGE

PROTO# SWB1778	SIZE RANGE: Mens 30-42
STYLE#	SAMPLE SIZE: 34 / 32
SEASON: Fall 20XX	DESIGNER: Monica Smith
NAME: Mens Woven Pant	DATE FIRST SENT: 1/2/20XX
FIT TYPE: Standard 5-pocket jean	DATE REVISED:
BRAND: XYZ, Sport	FABRICATION: 11 oz denim
STATUS: Prototype-1	

Cutting information: 1 way, lengthwise

Match Horizontal: NA

Match Vertical: NA

Match, other: NA

Stitches per inch (SPI) 11 +/- 1 for joining, 8 +/- 1 for topstitching

AREA	DESCRIPTION	JOIN STITCH	SEAM FINISH	TOPSTITCH	INTER- LINING
back yoke, back rise, inseams	join & topstitch	flatfell	flatfell	flatfell	--
front rise, below fly	join & topstitch	single-needle lock	flat fell	two needle lock (to match flatfell)	--
side seams	join	5-thread safety	5-thread safety	1/16 (partial)	--
waistband	folder-attached	two-needle chain	--	1/16	fusible
waistband	ends	single-needle lock	--	1/16	--
belt loops	form & finish	1/4" two-needle bottom coverstitch			--
Bartacks	see detail sketches	--	--	--	--
coin pkt, set	see detail sketches	single-needle lock	--	1/16-1/4	--
coin pkt	hem	single-needle chain	clean finish	at 1/2"	--
hand pocket, side front	palm side, shell to pkt bag	1/4" two-needle top-and-bottom coverstitch		--	--
hand pocket bag	French seam across bottom	single-needle lock	--	1/4"	--
bottom opening	hem	single-needle lock	clean finish	at 1/2"	--
CLOSURES					
button, waistband	jean-tack	riveted	--		--
buttonhole	Buttonhole, keyhole	--	--	--	--
fly, J-stitching	--	single-needle lock	--	2 rows, 1/4"	--
fly shield edge	--	--	3-thread overlock	--	--
fly facing edge	CF edge, topstitch	single-needle lock	--	1/16	FUSIBLE

Figure 3.10 Technical package, construction page, no abbreviations.

XYZ Product Development, Inc.
CONSTRUCTION PAGE

PROTO# SWB1778	SIZE RANGE: Mens 30-42
STYLE#	SAMPLE SIZE: 34 / 32
SEASON: Fall 20XX	DESIGNER: Monica Smith
NAME: Mens Woven Pant	DATE FIRST SENT: 1/2/20XX
FIT TYPE: Standard 5-pocket jean	DATE REVISED:
BRAND: XYZ, Sport	FABRICATION: 11 oz denim
STATUS: Prototype-1	

Cutting information: 1 way, lengthwise

Match Horizontal: NA

Match Vertical: NA

Match, other: NA

Stitches per inch (SPI) 11 +/- 1 for joining, 8 +/- 1 for topstitching

AREA	DESCRIPTION	JOIN STITCH	SEAM FINISH	TOPSTITCH	INTER-LINING
back yoke, back rise, inseams	join & TS	FF	FF	FF	--
front rise	join & TS	SN-L	flat fell	2N-L (to match FF)	--
side seams	join	5Tsafe	5Tsafe	1/16 (partial)	--
waistband	folder-attached	2N-C		1/16	fusible
waistband	ends	SN-L		1/16	--
belt loops	form & finish	1/4" 2N-BTTM CvS			--
Bartacks	see detail sketches	--	--	--	--
coin pkt, set		SN-L		1/16-1/4	--
coin pkt	hem	SN-C	clean finish	at 1/2"	--
hand pocket, side front	palm side, shell to pkt bag	1/4" 2N-T&B-CvS		--	--
hand pocket bag	French seam across bottom	SN-L	--	1/4"	--
bottom opening	hem	SN-L	clean finish	at 1/2"	--
CLOSURES					
button	jean-tack	riveted	--	--	--
buttonhole	BH-keyh	--	--	--	--
fly, J-stitching	topstitching	SN-L	--	2 rows, 1/4"	--
fly shield edge		--	3T-OL	--	--
fly facing edge,	CF edge	SN-L		1/16	FUSIBLE

Figure 3.11 Technical package, construction page, with abbreviations.

XYZ Product Development, Inc.
Labels and Packaging

PROTO# SWB1778	SIZE RANGE: Mens 30-42
STYLE#	SAMPLE SIZE: 34 / 32
SEASON: Fall 20XX	DESIGNER: Monica Smith
NAME: Mens Woven Pant	DATE FIRST SENT: 1/2/20XX
FIT TYPE: Standard 5-pocket jean	DATE REVISED:
BRAND: XYZ, Sport	FABRICATION: 11 oz denim
STATUS: Prototype-1	

ITEM / description	SKETCH	PLACEMENT	SUPPLIER	WIDTH / WEIGHT / SIZE	FINISH / description	QTY
woven loop label, #IDS15	#1 BELOW	inside CB waistband	Standard Label, factory sourced	standard size	permanent	1
woven endfold label, #IDS14	#2 BELOW	right back pocket	Standard Label, factory sourced	standard size	permanent	1
COO label (country of origin)	#1 BELOW	inside CB waistband	Standard Label, factory sourced	standard size	permanent	1
care content	#1 BELOW	inside CB waistband	factory sourced	to fit, see label manual	permanent	1
hang tag-sport	#3 BELOW	--	Phimpela Label Company	see label manual	removeable	1
barcode stickers	#3 BELOW	one polybag, one hangtag	Nakanishi Coding Systems	see label manual	adhesive back	2
retail ticket	#3 BELOW	standard placement, see label manual	Nakanishi Coding Systems	see label manual	removeable	1
safety pin--with string, for hangtags	#3 BELOW	see manual for placement	factory sourced	see sample sent	brass	1
poly bag, (Flatpack)	#3 BELOW	--	factory sourced	H X W = 18 X 13	self stick, closes at bottom	1

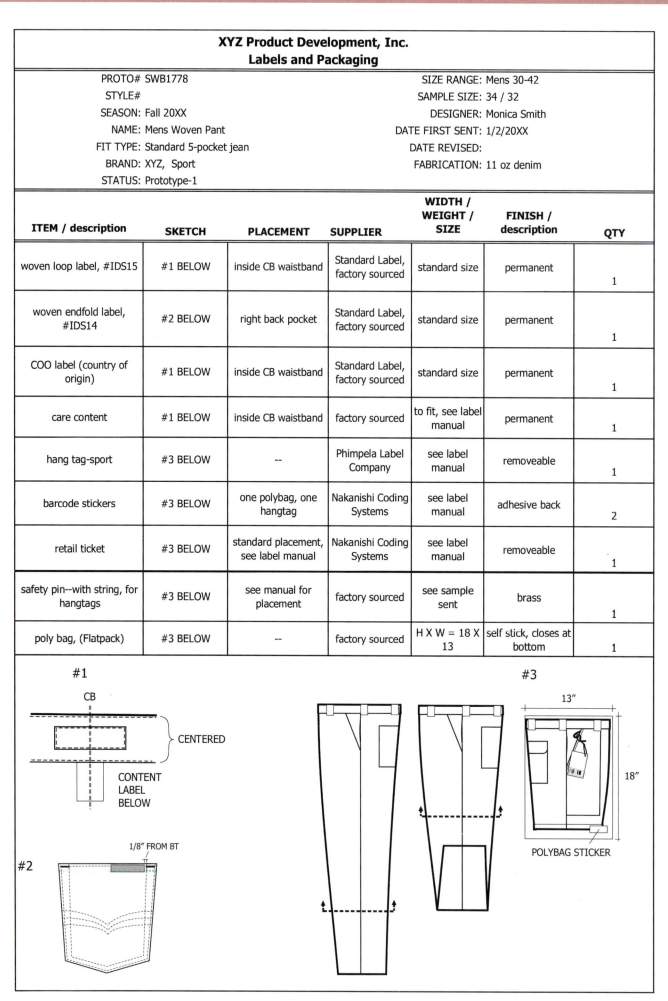

Figure 3.12 Technical package, label and packaging page.

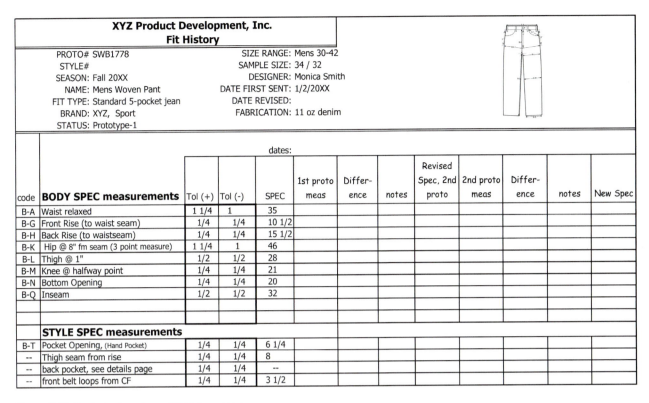

		dates:											
code	**BODY SPEC measurements**	Tol (+)	Tol (−)	SPEC	1st proto meas	Differ-ence	notes	Revised Spec, 2nd proto	2nd proto meas	Differ-ence	notes	New Spec
B-A	Waist relaxed	1 1/4	1	35								
B-G	Front Rise (to waist seam)	1/4	1/4	10 1/2								
B-H	Back Rise (to waistseam)	1/4	1/4	15 1/2								
B-K	Hip @ 8" fm seam (3 point measure)	1 1/4	1	46								
B-L	Thigh @ 1"	1/2	1/2	28								
B-M	Knee @ halfway point	1/4	1/4	21								
B-N	Bottom Opening	1/4	1/4	20								
B-Q	Inseam	1/2	1/2	32								
	STYLE SPEC measurements											
B-T	Pocket Opening, (Hand Pocket)	1/4	1/4	6 1/4								
--	Thigh seam from rise	1/4	1/4	8								
--	back pocket, see details page	1/4	1/4	--								
--	front belt loops from CF	1/4	1/4	3 1/2								

Figure 3.13 Technical package, fit history page.

to determine whether it is on spec or off spec for each point of measure. (See Chapter 16 for a discussion of the evaluation of the prototype based on how well the factory followed the tech pack instructions.)

Sample Evaluation Comments

The sample evaluation comments page (Figure 3.14) is the place to add notes, record changes, confirm details, and make revisions, if necessary. The comments will be carefully read by the factory and used to make the next sample. The latest sample information is added at the top of the page. This example has a brief space for each status, from first prototype to production sample, but the actual comments could be a few pages long depending on the development. This example represents the fewest samples there would usually ever be.

Specifications for Special Fabric Development

Many fabrics are chosen from the standard available styles, but sometimes special fabrics are developed. When a special print or plaid is run, it has its own specification sheet that lays out which color goes where for each colorway. For example, Figure 3.15 shows a yarn-dyed plaid for menswear. This example is being developed in three colorways (colorway A, B, and C). Each colorway consists of five shades woven together into the plaid design shown in the color breakdown. The location for each of the colors is also given.

The exact shade of each of the colors is called the standard. The standards will also be sent off with the yarn dye request. Standards can be swatches, paint chips, or Pantone swatches, such as those furnished by the color forecast services. The mill will make small, specially dyed, and woven swatches known as **handlooms** and send them to the designer for approval.

Printing is the process of transferring patterns to fabric in one or more of a variety of methods. To specify a special custom print for development, a process similar to that for yarn dyes is followed. The full-size original artwork, often hand painted, is sent to the print mill along with the color standards. A form such as Figure 3.16 is included to indicate the location of each color in the colorways.

The mill will produce special large swatches (about half a yard or so) in each colorway; these are called **strikeoffs**. This example has five colors in each colorway and is being developed in two colorways.

Custom prints and yarn dyes require considerable extra lead time to develop. They usually also require a higher minimum order quantity than standard running fabrics. However, they provide a unique way to tie together the seasonal color story, and to differentiate a company's styles from those of its competitors.

The costing process is a crucial part of product development, and the factory producing it sends a cost sheet with the first prototype. If the style does not "cost in" (if the FOB price is too high and does not meet the goals of the Line Plan), then that style will be re-examined. Some solutions are:

- Simplify the cut-and-sew requirements of the style (revise the pattern)
- Remove trims, or replace with less expensive ones (revise the BOM)
- Negotiate with the fabric mill for lower fabric costs
- Send the style to another factory for costing

Figure 3.17 is an example of a typical costing sheet. Note that all costs must be captured, even the carton and packing tape. Since it is preliminary, not all the costs are fully broken down. Great care will be taken in the future to make sure that all the revisions are re-costed accurately.

XYZ Product Development, Inc.

Sample Evaluation Comments

PROTO# SWB1778	SIZE RANGE: Mens 30-42
STYLE#	SAMPLE SIZE: 34 / 32
SEASON: Fall 20XX	DESIGNER: Monica Smith
NAME: Mens Woven Pant	DATE FIRST SENT: 1/2/20XX
FIT TYPE: Standard 5-pocket jean	DATE REVISED:
BRAND: XYZ, Sport	FABRICATION: 11 oz denim
STATUS: Prototype-1	

Date	
SAMPLE TYPE / ID#	preproduction
STATUS	**Approved to production**

Detail review

Date	
SAMPLE TYPE / ID#	size set
STATUS	**Approved to preproduction, use production quality fabic and trims**

Detail review

Date	
SAMPLE TYPE / ID#	sales sample
STATUS	**Approved to size set, send 32-40**

Detail review

Date	
SAMPLE TYPE / ID#	Prototype-1
STATUS	**Approved to Sales Samples, send pattern tracing**

Detail review

DATE	
SAMPLE STATUS	request for 1st prototype

Figure 3.14 **Sample evaluation comments.**

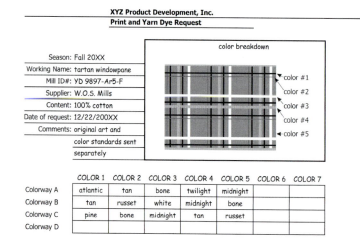

XYZ Product Development, Inc.

Print and Yarn Dye Request

	color breakdown
Season: Fall 20XX	
Working Name: tartan windowpane	color #1
Mill ID#: YD 9897-Ar5-F	color #2
Supplier: W.O.S. Mills	color #3
Content: 100% cotton	color #4
Date of request: 12/22/200XX	color #5
Comments: original art and	
color standards sent	
separately	

	COLOR 1	COLOR 2	COLOR 3	COLOR 4	COLOR 5	COLOR 6	COLOR 7
Colorway A	atlantic	tan	bone	twilight	midnight		
Colorway B	tan	russet	white	midnight	bone		
Colorway C	pine	bone	midnight	tan	russet		
Colorway D							

Figure 3.15 **Yarn dye request sheet.**

XYZ Product Development, Inc.

Print and Yarn Dye Request

	color breakdown
Season: Fall 20XX	
Working Name: rose floral	color #1 FLOWER PETAL
Mill ID#: sil-18777	color #2 FLOWER OUTLINE
Supplier: RA Myers	color #3 LEAF
Content: 100% cotton	color #4 LEAF OUTLINE
Date of request: 12/22/200XX	color #5 GROUND
Comments: original art and	
color standards sent	
separately	

	COLOR 1	COLOR 2	COLOR 3	COLOR 4	COLOR 5	COLOR 6	COLOR 7
Colorway A	blush	lipstick	leaf	pine	white		
Colorway B	lipstick	lavendrine	bamboo	willow	storm		
Colorway C							

Figure 3.16 **Print request sheet.**

pant   3refig 3.17 XYZ cost sheet for pant.xlsx

XYZ Product Development PRELIMINARY COSTING SHEET

COLOR KEY		ABBREVIATIONS	
GREEN = Apparel Co. info		C of O	Country of Origin
YELLOW = Factory info		CIF	
PEACH=FORMULAS		REV	Revised

PROTO #	W1618	SEASON	Spring 20xx
STYLE #		DESIGNER	
MERCH. CATEGORY	WOMENS PANTS	TECH DESIGN	
DESCRIPTION	W's Stretch Millennial Pant	PROD PLANNER	
DATE	5-Nov-12	FACTORY	BRIGHT SUN
1st proto cost	$15.82	LOCATION	CHINA
2nd cost			
Final cost			
REV DATE			

FABRICS

ITEM #	DESCRIPTION	Mill	LOCATION ON GARMENT	WIDTH/ SIZE	MARKER USAGE	%ALLOW, SZ & WST	USAGE, YARDS	COST STATUS	COST $/YARD	CIF	EXTEN.
FVF2429QD	86% Polyester 14% Spandex 4-way Stretch	Everest	body	52"	1.716	8%	1.853	FOB	$2.60		$4.82
#9177	100% Nylon Wicking+UV	Li Peng	inner waistband, fly	57"	0.280	8%	0.302	FOB	$2.10		$0.64
#22703	100% Polyester Chain Mesh	Fiberred	pocket bag	60"	0.100	8%	0.108	FOB	$0.60		$0.06
TOTAL FABRICS											**$5.52**

TRIMS

		C of O	USE	SIZE	QTY	%ALLOW	QTY	COST STATUS	$/ITEM		
P1025	knitted paper interlining	Freudenberg	waistband, upper fly	39"	0.32	5.00%	0.34		$0.40		$0.13
B71-EFB080-M15	AG707 (01) jean tack button	Unitex	center front	6"	2.00	5.00%	2.10		$0.08		$0.17
EXRT-MR741	rivet	LLL	hand pocket@side seam	9.5mm	2.00	5.00%	2.10		$0.04		$0.08
#3C DA	twill 1-way close-end DA auto-lock	YKK	center fly	-	1.00	5.00%	1.05		$0.13		$0.14
#3 MGTH	3YF twill 1-way close-end GS6 semi-lock	YKK	hand pocket	-	1.00	5.00%	1.05		$0.41		$0.43
LT029F13	woven main label	BW	center back waistband	-	1.00	5.00%	1.05		$0.04		$0.04
CT133F13	3/8" twill logo tape	BW	inside right hand pocket	-	0.25	5.00%	0.26		$0.34		$0.09
CO-WPN	care content label	BW	below main label	-	1.00	5.00%	1.05		$0.07		$0.07
WC-001	wash care label	BW	behind care label	-	1.00	5.00%	1.05		$0.05		$0.05
LT021	1"x3/4" factory ID label	factory	underneath of wash care label	-	1.00	5.00%	1.05		$0.05		$0.05
EXO-S11	main hangtag with string	BW	refer spec file	-	1.00	5.00%	1.05		$0.08		$0.08
TBD	style/fabric specific tag	BW	refer spec file	-	1.00	5.00%	1.05		$0.10		$0.10
polybag	polybag	factory	-	-	1.00	5.00%	1.05		$0.25		$0.26
sticker	upc/polybag sticker	factory	hangtag/polybag	-	2.00	5.00%	2.10		$0.03		$0.06
thread	thread	Coats	garments	-	1.00	5.00%	1.05		$0.50		$0.53
Packaging (carton/swift tag/carton tape/safety pin/plastic clip/tissue paper/ misc.)											$0.50
TOTAL TRIMS											**$2.79**

COMMENTS			
11/02/12 : initial costing base on 1st protos, not a final price			

TOTAL MATERIALS	$8.31
CHARGES, FABRICS	
CHARGES, TRIMS	
SPECIAL TREATMENT	
$ CMT $/MIN:	
PROFIT & OH @	
QUOTA CHARGE	
F O B	**$15.82**

Figure 3.17 Costing sheet.

Summary

In sum, a tech pack as a document of exact standards is an essential tool for apparel production. Designers should clearly communicate the details of design in a written tech pack with carefully rendered technical drawings. Understanding the details of tech packs is the key to successful production.

Study Questions

1. What is a tech pack? List all the people who use it and explain how it is used by each.

2. Look at the measurements on the points of measure page (Figure 3.6). Which measurements are considered girth (circumference) measurements?

3. Find a pair of men's size 34 Levi's and compare them to the jeans in the tech pack in this chapter. Review each page. How are they the same and how are they different?

4. Find size 40 on the grade page (see Figure 3.8) and look at the line "waist relaxed." How much larger is size 40 than size 38? Than size 36? Than the 34 sample size? How much larger is it than size 32?

5. What is tolerance, and how does it help to ensure quality? What is the tolerance for thighs on men's jeans? Why are the tolerances of thigh and waistband height so different?

6. What is the dominant color for each colorway in Figure 3.16?

Check Your Understanding

1. Why is the tech pack used in the apparel production process?

2. What is the main information included in a tech pack?

3. Why is understanding target consumers important in developing lines?

4. Explain the various stages of samples in the apparel production process.

5. Using the costing sheet in Figure 3.17, what could be done to revise the style and reduce costs, while retaining the essential character of the design?

   a. What could be done to simplify the cut-and-sew requirements of the style (revise the pattern)?

   b. What could be done to reduce trim costs?

6. Refer to Figure 3.11. Please spell out the below abbreviations.

   a. FF

   b. SN-L

   c. 2N-L

   d. 1/4" 2N-T&B-Cvs

4

Developing Technical Sketches

Chapter Objectives

After studying this chapter, you will be able to:

- Develop an inspiration workbook
- Understand the different styles of sketches
- Explore the typical personal design process
- Understand drawing conventions of technical sketches
- Understand how to draw a flat sketch to scale
- Survey terminology related to technical sketches
- Understand how to draw detail sketches

Key Terms

callout
croquis
drawing conventions
drawn to scale

fashion sketch (fashion illustration)
flat (technical flat, or tech sketch)
float (portfolio flat)

high point shoulder (HPS)
personal sketch
technical flat
trueing
wearer's right

Every day, designers work with a variety of sketches and flats as part of the design process. Starting from fast pencil sketches to proportionally correct technical flats, designers learn to clearly communicate their design ideas and inspirations to other members of the product development team to create functional as well as aesthetically pleasing apparel products in a timely manner. As lead times for the production of fashion products speed up, fast sketching skills are one of the most needed competencies in the industry. Because of the prevalence of globalization in apparel production, it is also important to communicate design ideas to professionals in other countries. Sketching is a universally understood language, so an understanding of the different types of sketches is necessary for effectively communicating design.

The Family of Sketches for Fashion Design

The process of designing and developing a new style involves many different creative drawing processes. These can be divided into drawing for inspiration, drawing for presentation, and drawing for specification (the type of drawings that appear in the tech pack).

Drawing for Inspiration: Personal Sketches

Personal sketches are included in the category of drawing for inspiration. Usually personal sketches are hand sketches. Designers keep a journal or inspiration notebook of their ideas, and it is one of the most important tools for creativity. This notebook contains collected photos and sketches that are keys to design inspiration. It is not necessarily a collection of completed

designs, but is rather a place to compile thoughts, details, elements, influences, assorted random visual notes, and anything else that may prove useful. Figure 4.1 shows an example of a page from a personal notebook, with color ideas, front and back views, and shape directions.

For their personal idea books, designers have their own shorthand for noting styles and details. Notation styles are unique to each person; some designers work on the computer, others use hand-drawn sketches. Sketchbooks can be in any medium that helps ideas to flow freely and enables the designer to recall memorable details. Personal sketchbooks can run the gamut from notebooks not meant to be seen by anyone other than their creator, to open sketchbooks with figure drawings, ideas, photographs, caricatures, and tear sheets. These can be part collage, part travelogue, and part diary. Museums, movies, art books, and magazines are constant sources of new ideas and directions that can be recorded in personal sketches for later use.

When applying for a creative design position, a personal inspiration notebook is often requested at the interview, along with other portfolio items, sample presentation boards, and so on. The notebook serves as an important window into the designer's creative process.

Drawing for Presentation: Fashion Sketches and Floats

Two different kinds of drawing are included in the category of drawing for presentation. One is fashion sketches, and the other is floats. **Fashion sketches** are figure drawings used for formal presentations and have a number of important functions. Fashion sketches are also called fashion illustrations. They give a sense of attitude, who the customer is, what market segment is being appealed to, how the items are merchandised into groups, and what seasonal themes are being followed.

Presentation sketches also help an aspiring designer land a first job in the design department, by means of his or her portfolio. There are many excellent books on developing a portfolio, but keep in mind three key points you want your portfolio to communicate:

1. You have the skills required, including technical sketches and detail sketches that demonstrate an understanding of the process.
2. You have *lots* of ideas, so include multiple styles for each category.
3. You understand how to merchandise; present garments in groups that support each other and create outfits.

Figure 4.2 shows an example of a group of fashion sketches showing one smaller merchandise group, which we will call "A day at the beach." The sketch shows offerings for spring/summer, or "holiday," on figures and with accessories, jewelry, hairstyles, and so on, appropriate to the target customer (in this case, the type who wears high heels at the beach). These drawings are then organized onto presentation boards (see Figure 4.2).

A second type of presentation sketch is called a float (sometimes known as a portfolio flat). A **float** is a simplified fashion drawing without a figure, also used for focus boards and selling. Floats are used to add additional information to a design group because it is not practical to show every garment on a figure. These drawings can show colors, patterns, texture, and garment drape, and they are all drawn to the same scale. The set of floats in Figure 4.3

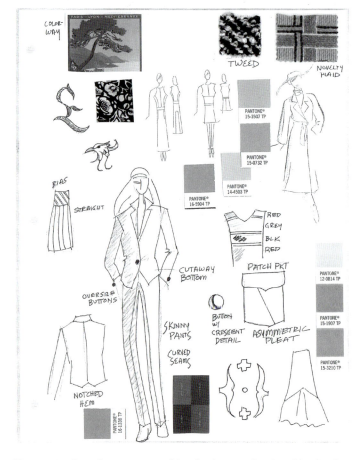

Figure 4.1   **Page from a personal inspiration notebook or idea book.**

Figure 4.2 Fashion sketch, "A day at the beach."

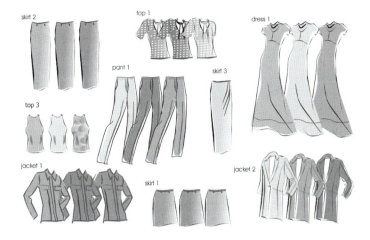

Figure 4.3 Example of floats for the Alfresco line.

would be used to support the presentation of the Alfresco line in Chapter 2 (see Figure 2.3), and act as an illustrated line plan.

Floats provide backup for the fashion sketches. They can help the buyer visualize the color stories and how they may set up on their floor for selling after the goods are delivered. They show what tops go with what bottoms, and they encourage multiple sales. They show that the designer has thought through the merchandising issues and understands the concerns of the buyers because good coordination of items is a key for increasing sales volume. Customers may come to the store to purchase a single item such as pants, and if the line is attractive they may end up buying matching items, such as tops and accessories to go with the pants. By having the coordinated pieces communicated clearly through the flats, the observer can come to a quick understanding of what is being proposed.

Floats and illustrations are often developed with the help of a sort of master sketch called a **croquis**. To speed the drawing process, a croquis, or basic silhouette, can be used to show different design details. Another method for hand drawing uses tracing paper laid on top of the master.

Because multiple color versions are presented in the floats in Figure 4.3, the process would clearly be speeded by the use of a master figure for each style. The process is similar whether done on a CAD system or by hand. The use of a CAD program allows the designer to save different sets of croquis, which can be colored in the shades from the color story, and can have the prints and plaids represented to scale. Croquis are also useful for the design process itself and help the designer concentrate on the garment design rather than the figure proportions. From a set of croquis, including the front and back view, figures or common garment-only shapes can be developed and then multiple copies printed

for future use. A set of blanks of this type can also be part of a personal idea book for quick notes while doing style research.

Figure 4.4 shows another presentation board that displays a men's outwear group. This shows the sketches mounted onto a hinged board, as they may be to present to buyers for a buy meeting.

The figure demonstrates again how fashion sketches and floats are used together. The floats support the large figure on the left, which is used to show the attitude and the customer, along with the accessories of gloves, boots, and snowboard, and displays the garments as they would be used together. At bottom right is the color story that supports the seasonal theme. This group is simplified for the purpose of illustration. An actual group would include 10 to 12 items or more, representing various price strategies, similar to the line plan in Chapter 2.

As illustrated, floats can be drawn in a variety of styles, some suggesting a figure inside and some not. The float is created to communicate information to the buyer. Figure 4.5 gives us an assortment of floats in different styles.

Different types of floats can be used on presentation boards. They are used to show colors (see Figures 4.5c and 4.5d), textures (see Figure 4.5c), patterns (see Figure 4.5d), and other elements of

Figure 4.4 Example of floats: snowboard group.

Figure 4.5 Floats used to show color, texture, and detail.

movement, proportion, and attitude. Figures 4.5f and 4.5g are two different ways of showing the same style. Figure 4.5f shows the garment as if on an active body (sometimes called the "invisible man" style), and Figure 4.5g shows the same pant in a different style of float, one that is more flat but still dimensional, and that includes callouts. **Callouts** are written references that clarify the details shown, such as the zip-off leg or cargo pocket.

Drawing for Specification: Flats or Technical Sketches

Flats are two-dimensional technical drawings used for specification. All the examples of flats in this book were prepared by means of drawing program software. Three of the more popular are Adobe Illustrator, CorelDRAW, and Micrografx Designer to make a full tech pack. A simple program such as Excel can be used for the tabular information in tech packs, and there are many **product data management (PDM)** systems, such as Gerber PDM and Lectra, that are used as publishing programs for tech packs, usually linked with a drawing program to import and export sketches. Web-based systems (Web-PDM systems) are becoming more popular as well. Considering frequent design detail changes, these systems allow a factory on the other side of the world to see the latest version of the tech pack information via the Web; thus, the designers do not need to send out updated tech packs. The advantage to making tech sketches using a computer program is that the drawings are easy to revise and store, and the tools make it easy to enlarge the drawings for details, create mirror images for back views, draw to scale, produce consistent sketches, develop electronic croquis and transmit sketches via the Web or email. It is certainly possible to draw tech sketches by hand and make them part of an electronic tech pack through the scanning process, but the industry is rapidly going toward electronic files for all communications, and a tech sketch created on a computer saves steps.

The term *computer aided design* (CAD) is a general term that is used in many contexts. Very sophisticated CAD programs help designers to visualize a design or a print fabric draped onto a three-dimensional figure. These software programs also have many other wonderful features. Some companies visualize a time when buyers will select products from virtual samples, viewed on a computer screen. It is important to remember, however, that even if such a way of doing business ever becomes commonplace, a tech pack with technical sketches and all the written information will still be needed to get the goods manufactured and delivered.

Let's assume that a meeting with your product line manager and product development team was a great success based on your presentation drawings and concept boards. Many of your styles were chosen for development, and now the presentation ideas need to be drawn in detail for tech packs and sent off for first protos, as explained in Chapters 2 and 3.

The type of drawing used for this purpose is called a **technical flat**. A flat is a specialized drawing, rather like a blueprint. It is drawn to scale and includes sewing and construction information, like the jeans examples in Chapter 3. In this type of drawing, the notions of how a garment may appear while worn are not strictly relevant. Because it has no three-dimensional sense of the garment while on a body, the technical flat makes the garment look short and wide. In fact, it looks like a garment laid flat onto a table. The proportions have much more in common with a flat pattern than with a fashion sketch.

The drawing is detail-specific, precise, literal in proportion, and is the next step in explaining the design for making a pattern and sewing a prototype. After being approved for development, each style will be translated into tech packs. The first step will be to make a set of drawings—technical flats—with front view (see Figure 3.2), back view (see Figure 3.3), and details (see Figures 3.4 and 3.5).

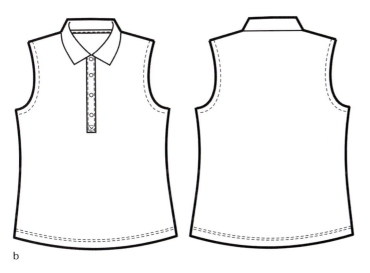

b

Figure 4.6 **Float and technical flats: women's sleeveless top.**

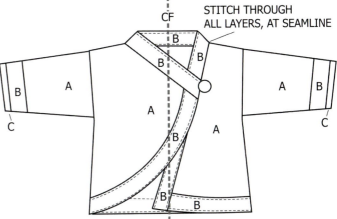

b

Figure 4.7 **Comparison of a float and a flat.**

Compare Figures 4.6a and 4.6b. Figure 4.6a would appeal to a buyer or customer, and Figure 4.6b would be used in the tech pack to request a garment prototype. Figure 4.6b does not need to show the fabric texture or print unless it is part of the pattern-making process, such as confirming a stripe direction. In that case it can be added as a detail sketch.

Figure 4.7 is another example of a float compared to a technical flat. The float in Figure 4.7a represents the fabric placements, and provides a feeling for the drape and proportion of the finished garment. It leaves many unanswered questions, however. What exactly is going on at the armhole? Is it a dolman or kimono sleeve? How many different fabrics are being used, and where? The contrast solid trim at the cuff, is that binding? Piecing? Appliqué? Is the garment lined? Unlined? It is clearly asymmetric, but how, exactly? Because these features affect the cost, specifications, and construction, it is the designer's job to work through the answers to these questions by the time the tech pack is produced and before a prototype can be ordered.

The questions raised by Figure 4.7a are answered by Figure 4.7b. We see that it has a square, drop-shoulder sleeve, that three fabrics are used on the outside (marked A, B, and C), and that the narrow trim at the cuff is indeed a pieced section, given that

there is no topstitching to indicate binding or appliqué. We see that the construction is consistent with a lined garment, perimeter joined and topstitched all around the outside edge, and that the topstitching around the band (shell B) is sewn through the lining at the bottom edge, inside. Because the center line is drawn (and notated CF for center front), we can see the shape of the right and left panels and how they come together. We can see that the collar is two layers and is clean-finished to the inside. Additional details will be called out elsewhere, but these are important questions for which the patternmaker must have answers in order to proceed with development.

Figure 4.8 shows two views of the same cap sleeve blouse of woven fabric. In Figure 4.8a, the blouse is on a mannequin, so we see it in three dimensions. Figure 4.8b shows the same garment laid flat on a table, in preparation for measuring. It looks quite different, and not the way we are accustomed to seeing it. Yet Figure 4.8b is almost the perfect proportions of a technical sketch.

Figure 4.9 compares the same flattened garment and a technical sketch of the same style. The tech sketch reveals various details that the photo does not, such as how many rows of gathers are needed, and so on. The tech sketch shapes are similar to pattern shapes and help to guide the further development of the style.

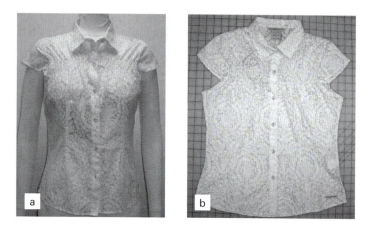

Figure 4.8 **Garment shown on mannequin (a) and flat (b).**

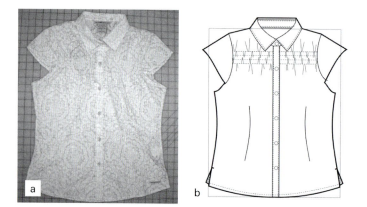

Figure 4.9 **Flat garment (a) and flat sketch (b).**

Understanding the Terminology of Garments

To develop technical sketches, it is essential to understand the terminology used for apparel products. The globalization of production demands the use of standard terminology to communicate to all professionals from various countries in the apparel production team.

Whenever apparel detail positions are given in the tech pack, right or left side is based on the wearer's perspective. It means that when a sketch of a garment is labeled right side, it is on the person's right but on the viewer's left. It is understood to be the standard and does not need to be routinely labeled except on detail sketches or in instances where it may not be clear.

In reviewing the techniques used for making a technical flat, we will want to define the principal areas and where they are found on the garment with some common abbreviations. We will review the general terminology of a tank top, long-sleeve shirt, and pants before sketching each of the three types of garment.

High point shoulder (HPS) is the anchor point for most tops, such as jackets, shirts, and dresses. In specifying garment dimensions, it is important to begin with a measurement that is constant for different garment styles. For length, neckline comparisons, and many other specs, that point is high point shoulder.

To define high point shoulder, it is helpful to consider the pattern because HPS is the point at which a pattern will fold when the side seams are lined up. Figure 4.10a shows the pattern with the shoulder seams attached, and Figure 4.10b shows where it would

fold when the side seams are lined up. It is important to note that HPS is not the same as the shoulder seam. Comparing Figures 4.10b and 4.10c, Figure 4.10b has the shoulder seam $1/2$-inch forward. In Figure 4.10c the HPS is actually part of the raglan sleeve, yet the HPS position is the same. Figure 4.10d has a much wider neck and different neck shape, but HPS is still the point where the pattern—and garment—fold. Garments often have the shoulder forward for fit or style reasons, and some styles, such as raglan sleeves, have no shoulder seam at all. But the method for finding high point shoulder remains the same.

HPS varies slightly based on design details. Figure 4.11 shows more examples of high point shoulder based on design details. In Figures 4.11a through 4.11c, HPS is at the neck seam. In Figure 4.11d, where there is no seam, HPS is at the edge.

Drawing Conventions of Technical Sketches

Technical flats have certain visual standards that help the viewer understand what is being communicated. It is important that these elements remain constant from flat to flat. Every company has certain standardized ways, or **drawing conventions**, for drawing different elements such as seams, topstitching, and so on. That makes the drawings and the details easy to understand. Drawing conventions for showing standard details vary slightly from company to company. We will be utilizing the drawing conventions for XYZ Product Development, Inc. in the next sections. The first elements discussed are fonts and line weights.

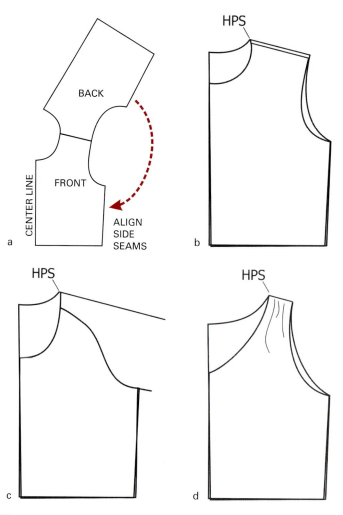

Figure 4.10 **HPS for basic tops.**

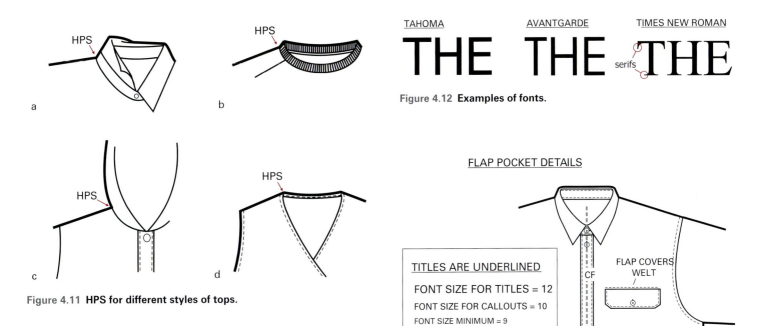

Figure 4.11 **HPS for different styles of tops.**

Figure 4.12 **Examples of fonts.**

Fonts

The type style used for the technical drawing notes and callouts remains constant for all technical flats and is known as the *font*. The font chosen should be simple and easy to read. The font used for the drawings throughout this book is called Tahoma. It has the advantage of appearing slightly bolder, and is easier to read when reduced to smaller font sizes. Other popular fonts are Arial and Avant Garde. It is best to choose a sans serif style, meaning "without serif" (*serifs* are the small bars at the end of each letter stroke). For that reason, Times New Roman would not be a good choice. Whatever font is chosen should be used for all drawings. Figure 4.12 compares some font styles. Note that all the lettering used for the drawings is in ALL CAPS, that is, all capital letters.

Figure 4.13 shows further details where different font sizes are used. The font size for most callouts is 10 point, and the minimum size is 9 point. It is important not to have the font too

Figure 4.13 **Font sizes for XYZ Product Development, Inc.**

small because it may limit the readability when the file is sent electronically. The titles for sketches and details are underlined as in Figure 4.13. The font size for titles is 12 point.

Line Weights

By assigning certain standardized line thicknesses—called line weights—to be used for the garment outline, edges, and details, the garment sketch can be assessed more easily by the viewer. Figure 4.14 provides information about different line weights. Various line weights are used consistently for the drawings to facilitate the viewers' understanding. For example, the outside line is 2-point solid. Different line weights are used to describe

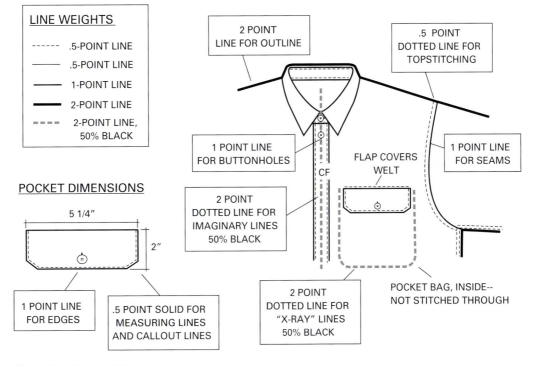

Figure 4.14 **Line weights.**

different details. Topstitching, which is stitching visible on the outside, is indicated by dotted lines in 0.5-point weight.

The line that connects the **callout** (which is a label, description, or explanation of a feature) to the area of note is called a callout line. Solid lines in 0.5-point weight are used for callout lines, which have their own line weight to avoid confusion with other details. It is important to avoid very thin lines (smaller than 0.5) because they may not be visible when sending the file electronically. The seams, where two panels are sewn together, and other edge details (like the pocket flap) are indicated in 1-point lines, and the overall garment outline in 2-point solid. A 2-point dotted line in gray (a specific shade called 50 percent black) is used to indicate an imaginary line, such as where to measure, or the center line, as in Figure 4.14. That same style is also used to show X-ray views such as the pocket bag shape, which is actually seen only on the inside. It is not to be confused with topstitching. Information used here for explaining the drawing method that is not part of the drawing is boxed.

Drawing to Scale of Technical Sketches (Flats)

Remember that a technical flat is **drawn to scale**, that is, it's a visual representation of the actual garment measurements. A drawing in 1:8 scale, like most tech sketches, is one-eighth of the actual size. For example, a 1-inch long line would represent a length of 8 inches.

Technical flats are typically drawn in 1:8 scale for adults' clothing and 1:4 for children's clothing. Figure 4.15 shows why drawing an infant's or a child's flat at 1:8 scale would make it too small for the drawing to be useful. The version shown in 1:4 scale is easier to understand. Figure 4.15 shows proportionally correct sketches of a women's and a children's jacket. The women's jacket chest is 40

inches full circumference in full scale, 20 inches across the front, side seam to side seam, so it is 2.5 inches in the drawing at 1:8 scale.

Although drawings should initially be to scale for accuracy, it is not necessary to mark the scale on the drawing because the finished garment size will be clear from the spec figures noted on the points of measure page of the tech pack. If the drawing is revised in size at all, for example to fit onto a spec page, it is no longer to the original scale. So to put it another way, a technical flat starts out drawn to scale. Thereafter, it may be increased to 1:7 or shrunk to 1:12376 (or any other size), and it retains the same proportions.

Drawing to scale has other uses as well. It helps the design process and is especially helpful in checking proportions of details such as patch pockets. If a pocket looks too tall and narrow in the drawing, it will probably look the same on the garment. Smaller items such as tabs, pocket flaps, or labels can actually be drawn in 1:1 (actual size) scale, printed, cut out, and reviewed for proportion on a real garment.

Figures 4.16a and 4.16b show examples of flaps that are rather out of proportion with the pocket. By using the scale functions of your CAD drawing program, or by drawing on graph paper, you can see how the finished pocket will look and then specify those measurements, as in Figure 4.16c. Of course, a person may actually prefer the proportions of Figure 4.16a or 4.16b. If so, the same principal would hold true, and the measurements can be taken from them. The points of measure shown in Figure 4.16c are the ones needed to specify a simple patch pocket and flap. Approaching the drawing that way, it is possible to set up guidelines in the drawing program and follow the specifications quite literally. Drawing programs have special tools and rulers to help.

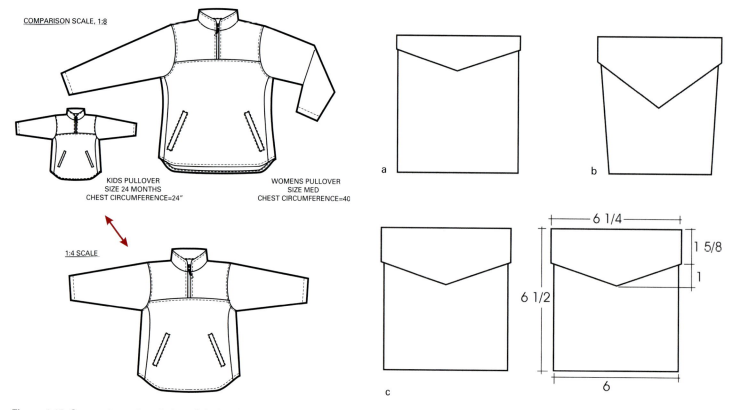

Figure 4.15 **Comparison of scale for adults' and children's sketches.**

Figure 4.16 **Drawing pockets to scale.**

Drawing Garments to Scale, Step by Step

To develop proportionally correct technical sketches, an understanding of each step is important. Each product category has unique aspects. Let's walk through each step to develop some basic apparel items together. Three apparel products—a women's tank top, a men's long-sleeved shirt, and a pair of women's pants—are selected for the drawing practices in this chapter.

Drawing a Women's Tank Top

Our first example is a very simple garment, a women's tank top, but the principles are the same for any top style. Because the technical flat is a visual interpretation of the garment specs (measurements), by definition, we need the measurements in order to proceed. The measurement tables given are examples of the specs found on the points of measure page. Before we start to draw a tank top to scale, let's review some common abbreviations. Abbreviations used in tech sketches are illustrated in Figure 4.17 and include:

- HPS = high point shoulder (see Figure 4.10)
- FND = front neck drop, defines the lowest point of the front neck
- BND = back neck drop, defines the lowest point of the back neck
- CF = center front, center line in front
- CB = center back, center line in back

Marking the points of measure is somewhat like drawing points on a graph; each one has both a vertical and a horizontal position. Each area of the drawing represents two points of measure, one

for height and one for width. An example is the combination of shoulder drop, a height measurement, and shoulder point-to-point width measurement. Both are needed to locate point 3 in Figure 4.18. Drawing the tank top is as easy as plotting these points of measure and then connecting the points. To ensure that the drawing is symmetrical, we will draw the right half and then mirror the drawing.

Before beginning to draw, review a garment top (knit or woven, any style or size) and identify center front and all the points of measure. Figure 4.18 maps out where two points make up each point of measure, and each pair is numbered to indicate the order of the drawing. In Figure 4.18 points 1 through 7 will be drawn first, and point 8, back neck drop at CB, will be added last. High point shoulder is the reference for many points of measure. Any measurement described as drop (as in "armhole drop") is squared from high point shoulder. The most common drops are shown in Figure 4.19.

Start Drawing

Begin a new page in the draw program (see Figure 4.20). Set up the page at 1:8 scale and then draw a rectangle as a guide. This rectangle will serve as the height and width of the garment.

Figure 4.21 provides the measurement specs for this garment. The chest measurement ($18^{1}/_{2}$ inches) determines the width of

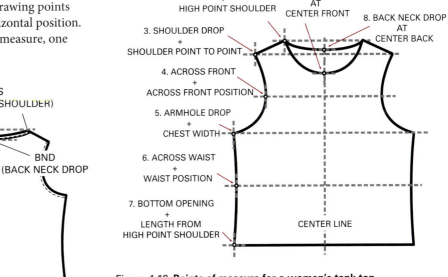

Figure 4.18 **Points of measure for a women's tank top.**

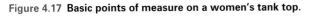

Figure 4.17 **Basic points of measure on a women's tank top.**

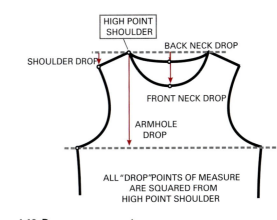

Figure 4.19 **Drop measurements.**

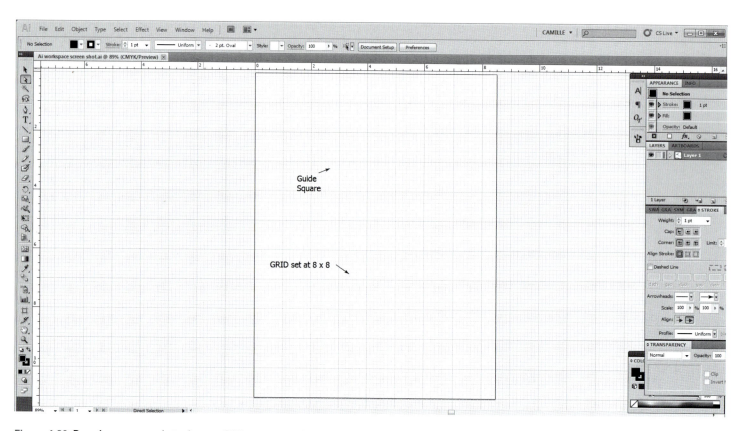

Figure 4.20 **Drawing a women's tank top—CAD screen work space.**

POINTS of MEASURE	Spec	right side, from centerpoint
Shoulder Point to Point	15	7 1/2
Shoulder Drop	1 3/8	
Front Mid Armhole	13	6 1/2
Back Mid Armhole	14	
Armhole Drop from HPS	8 1/2	
Chest Width	**18 1/2**	9 1/4
Waist Width	17 1/2	8 3/4
Waist position fm HPS	15 1/2	
Bottom Opening	18 1/2	9 1/4
Front Length fm HPS	**23**	
Back Length fm HPS	24	
Front Neck Drop, to edge	5	
Back Neck Drop, to edge	1	
Neck Width, edge to edge	8	4

width = 18½

length= 23

CENTER LINE

Figure 4.21 **Establishing the guide square.**

the rectangle and front length from HPS (23 inches) determines the length of the garment, so the rectangle is drawn 18¹/₂ × 23 inches. The vertical guideline is positioned at the exact middle of the square, and the horizontal guideline is at the top of the square. The guide square is not part of the finished drawing. When the sketch is completed, the guide square will be deleted, or if the drawing program allows, it can be drawn on a separate layer.

Starting at the center of the square (center front) with a guideline as in Figure 4.20, we will draw the right side. As always, when we say the right side, it means the **wearer's right** side. The measurement specs for drawing just the right side have been calculated and appear in the table in Figure 4.21 in the right side from center point column. The specs we are using for the guide square are in boldface.

Figure 4.22 provides a visual preview of all the measurements separated into horizontal and vertical, to help you understand what is measured and how. This is a list of the points of measure positions and of the actual measurements we will use to make our technical flat, so it's helpful to have it to review while going through the drawing steps. Because we are drawing only the right half of the garment, the horizontal measurements are for one half. When that is completed, we will mirror the drawing, which will make it perfectly symmetrical.

Step 1: Find the first point, front neck drop at center, 5 inches down. Find the right HPS on the guide square, 4 inches to your left from the center. Figure 4.23 shows neck width at HPS, 4. Draw a line connecting the two, and curve it. This is the neckline, right side shown in Figure 4.23, Step 2. The

HORIZONTAL MEASUREMENTS   VERTICAL MEASUREMENTS

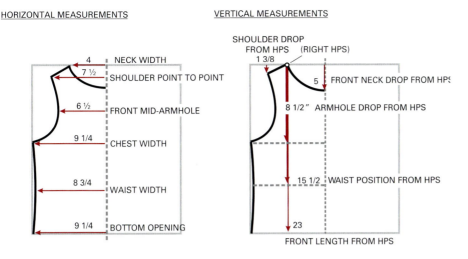

Figure 4.22 Measurements, horizontal and vertical.

points of measure are indicated with a small circle for reference, but this is not part of the finished technical flat.

Step 2: Mark the point where the shoulder drop, which is 1³/₈ inches, as noted in the spec table, and shoulder point-to-point (half) intersect. Draw a line between the two points. This is the shoulder.

Step 3: Draw a line from the shoulder to the armhole drop position at 8¹/₂ inches down. It intersects with the guide square in Figure 4.24.

Step 4: Draw the next line segment straight down the guide square to the bottom corner (see Figure 4.24).

Step 5: Finish the last line segment by returning to the center line.

Step 6: Curve the armhole according to the spec of front mid-armhole (6¹/₂ inches). Then curve in the side seam line slightly at the waist section (see Figure 4.25). The waistline position, where waist width is determined, is located 15¹/₂ inches down from HPS. Waist width is curved in following the spec of waist width (8³/₄ inches). Last, add the back neck drop, 1 inch down (see Figure 4.25, step 6).

Step 7: As shown in Figure 4.26, check that the shoulder at armhole and the shoulder at neck are reasonably square, the same way that a pattern is trued. **Trueing** is the process of smoothing the line connections and transitions of a pattern to achieve a functional and aesthetically pleasing garment. Technical flats should be trued in the same way, to guide the pattern maker in developing the style. The drawing in Figure 4.27 shows the method for checking the shoulder, neck, and armhole shapes with a square. Trueing should be done before the sketch is mirrored. Mirror the right side to create the left side (see Figure 4.26). It will fit into the guide square perfectly.

Step 8: Remove the guide square and center guideline (see Figure 4.26). The torso is complete.

Step 9: After the proportionally correct flat is developed, details should be checked and stitching added to complete the flat. Line weights are checked according to the standard drawing conventions laid out in Figure 4.14. The outline is 2 point, and a 1-point line weight is used for internal lines. In this case, the front neckline and back neck binding edge are 1 point. Topstitching at the neck, armholes, and bottom opening is added with 0.5-point dotted line. The front view is complete.

Step 10: The next step is creating the back view. Make a copy of the garment front view

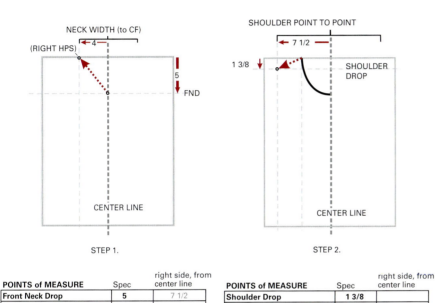

POINTS of MEASURE	Spec	right side, from center line
Front Neck Drop	5	7 1/2
Neck Width at HPS	8	4

POINTS of MEASURE	Spec	right side, from center line
Shoulder Drop	1 3/8	
Shoulder Point to Point	15	7 1/2

Figure 4.23 Drawing the neck line and shoulder, Steps 1 and 2.

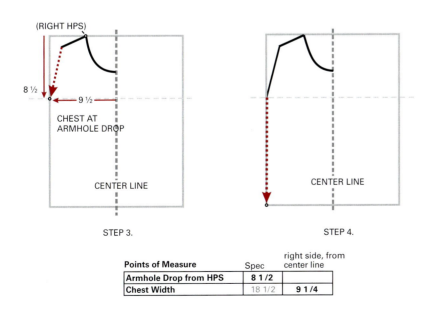

Points of Measure	Spec	right side, from center line
Armhole Drop from HPS	8 1/2	
Chest Width	18 1/2	9 1/4

Figure 4.24 Drawing the armhole, Steps 3 and 4.

and remove the front neckline detail (one solid line, one stitching line). For the back neckline, remove the lower solid line of the front neck, leaving just the outline at the back neck and one stitching line. The back view is complete. The drawings are ready to be put into the tech pack and represent the sample size measurements from the points of measure page. The drawings for any type of garment will always be drawn in the sample size, whether men's, women's, or children's.

Step 11: Once a flat is produced, it can be used for any other garment with the same proportions. This style, a sleeveless blouse, has darts, side vents, and a stitched-through facing. The details are shown on the wearer's right side only, as a reminder that they will be mirrored, rather than re-drawn. The buttons go directly at center front, so they are placed into the sketch last.

Hand Drawing to Scale

A perfectly good scale drawing can be hand drawn using graph paper (see Figure 4.28). The method for hand drawing is essentially the same and begins with graph paper at 1:8 scale. It is easy to make graph paper with the drawing program, which should have the page filled with 1/8-inch squares. One square represents 1 inch.

Draw a guide square onto the graph paper, counting out the measurements 23 squares long and 18$\frac{1}{2}$ squares wide. The width will be 9$\frac{1}{2}$ squares each side of the center line (see Figure 4.28a). Then place tracing paper over the grid paper and proceed to draw in just the same way as Figure 4.23, Steps 1 and 2. Figure 4.28b is a close-up view of the drawing in progress. Draw the right side, then the left side, and all the steps through Step 11. For the first time through, drawing the preliminary shape in pencil is advised and then the final version in ink.

There are some other interesting things to consider related to drawing flats. Points of measure should employ only the measurements needed without creating possible contradictions. Although it may seem that every possible measurement has been noted,

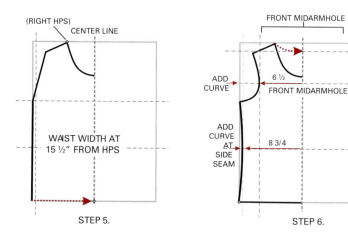

STEP 5.   STEP 6.

POINTS of MEASURE	Spec	right side, from center line
Front Mid Armhole	13	6 1/2
Waist Width	17 1/2	8 3/4
Waist position fm HPS	15 1/2	
Bottom Opening	18 1/2	9 1/4
Back Neck Drop	1	

Figure 4.25 Completing half, Steps 5 and 6.

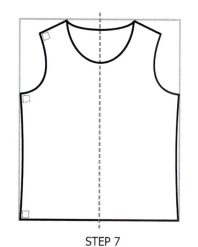

STEP 7   STEP 8

Figure 4.26 Torso completed, Steps 7 and 8.

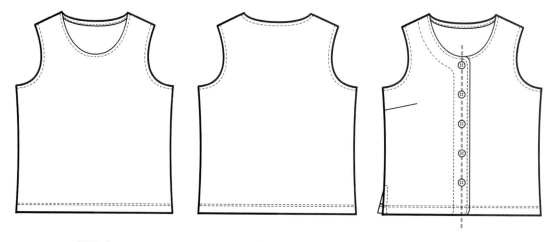

STEP 9   STEP 10   STEP 11

Figure 4.27 Finishing details, Steps 9 through 11.

PAGE SET-UP

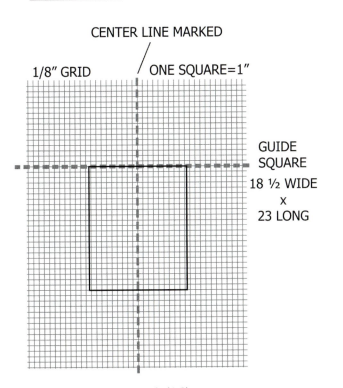

CLOSE-UP DETAIL

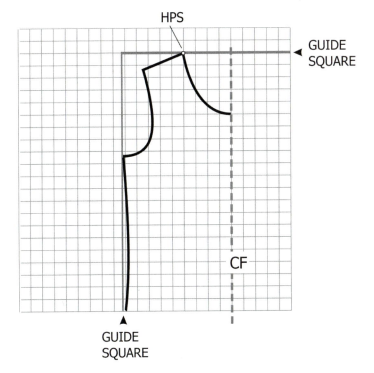

Figure 4.28 Hand drawing to scale (1:8).

there are some measurements that are not specified, for example, the side seam length (see Figure 4.29). Side seam length is not a standard point of measure, but if it needs to be calculated for some reason (such as a trim detail at the side seam), it can be. For this style it would be the length from HPS (23 inches) minus the armhole drop 8^1/$_2$ inches (see Figure 4.29).

The same principle holds true for many other places as well. Another one is the shoulder width (strap width). It is governed by the shoulder point to point and neck width. It is the amount left over, so to speak, so to actually specify that particular point can lead to potentially conflicting information; therefore, it is not included in the points of measure. For this style—in which the strap width is an important style point and must be a certain specific width—it is included in choosing two of the three

possible measurements. But for most styles, shoulder point to point and neck width are more important, and the shoulder width is not usually given. In Figure 4.29, the strap width is shoulder point to point minus neck width divided by 2. Review Figure 4.29 and then calculate the measurement of the distance noted by the question marks to make sure that it is drawn correctly.

Drawing a Men's Long-Sleeved Knit Shirt

The points of measure shown on the men's knit long-sleeve shirt are the same as on the women's tank top, with the addition of sleeve measurements (see Figure 4.30). Of course, the actual garment measurements are different because it's a men's size large, which is a much larger garment.

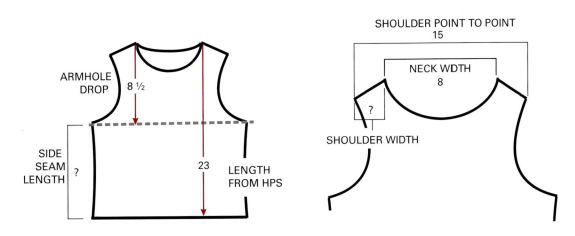

Figure 4.29 Avoiding contradictions.

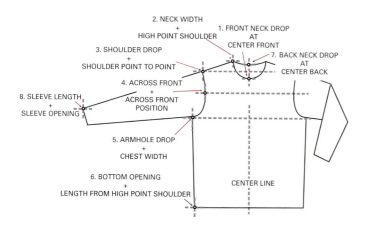

Figure 4.30 Points of measure for a men's long-sleeved knit shirt.

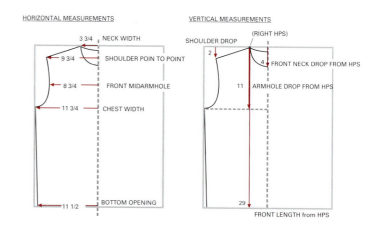

Figure 4.31 Measurements, horizontal and vertical, men's shirt.

Use Figure 4.32 to start the draft. Again, the right-hand side measurements have been calculated beforehand in the right side from center point column. Make a guide square for the length and width, again at 1:8 scale. For width, use the widest point, which is the chest (not the bottom opening). The order of drawing is the same as for the women's tank top, counter-clockwise on the right side, from neck to bottom.

Start Drawing

As with the women's top, begin by drawing a guide square at 1:8 scale, 23 inches wide by 29 inches long. That represents the chest width and the garment length. Review which measurements are horizontal and which are vertical. Figure 4.31 is a recap which lays out each direction, so have it handy when drawing.

Step 1: Set up the horizontal guidelines for front neck drop and neck width. Identify the HPS position. Draw the front neckline according to the spec (see Figure 4.32).

Step 2: Set up the guides for shoulder point to point, and shoulder drop. Draw the line segment, which is the shoulder seam (see Figure 4.32).

Step 3: When the shoulder seam is in place, continue on to the armhole.

Step 4: Draw the side seam and the bottom edge, ending at the center line. Note that for this style, the bottom tapers in slightly (the chest measurement is bigger than the bottom opening), which is typical for a men's knit style.

Step 5: Draw a back neck line (see Steps 3 through 5 in Figure 4.33).

Step 6: Mirror the image. Remove the guide square, but leave the center line, which will be used to position the sleeve (see Figure 4.34).

Step 7: For drawing the right sleeve, Figure 4.35a shows how to make a horizontal sleeve guideline to be the length of the sleeve (the point of measure to follow is the center back sleeve length). To save space, the drawings are partial in this illustration. It should extend horizontally out from the center line, touching HPS. Rotate the line along HPS until it rests flush with the shoulder (see Figure 4.35b). Then delete the section that is overlapping the shoulder. This line is the top edge of the sleeve. Add the 3³/₄ inches in sleeve opening (see

POINTS OF MEASURE	Spec	right side, from center point
Shoulder Point to Point	19 1/2	**9 3/4**
Shoulder Drop	**2**	
Front Mid Armhole	17 1/2	8 3/4
Back Mid Armhole	18 1/2	
Armhole Drop from HPS	11	
Chest Width	**23 1/2**	11 3/4
Waist	23	
Waist position fm HPS	18	
Bottom Opening	23	11 1/2
Front Length fm HPS	**29**	
Back Length fm HPS	29	
Center Back Sleeve Length	35	
Bicept @ 1" fm Seam	8 1/2	
Sleeve Opening	3 3/4	
Front Neck Drop, to seam	**4**	
Back Neck Drop, to seam	3/4	
Neck Width, seam to seam	7 1/2	**3 3/4**

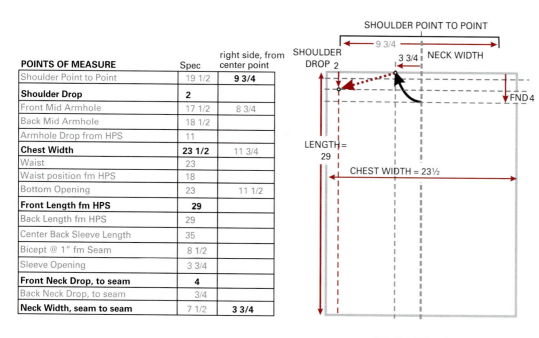

Figure 4.32 Drawing a men's long-sleeved shirt: Steps 1 and 2.

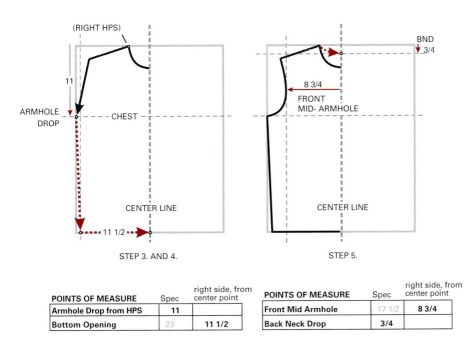

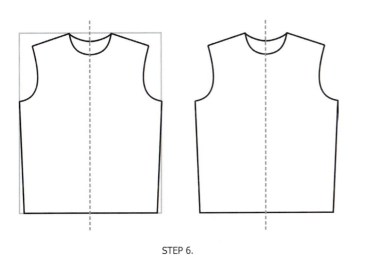

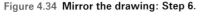

STEP 3. AND 4.   STEP 5.

POINTS OF MEASURE	Spec	right side, from center point
Armhole Drop from HPS	11	
Bottom Opening	23	11 1/2

POINTS OF MEASURE	Spec	right side, from center point
Front Mid Armhole	17 1/2	8 3/4
Back Neck Drop		3/4

Figure 4.33 Drawing a men's long-sleeved shirt: Steps 3 through 5.

STEP 6.

Figure 4.34 Mirror the drawing: Step 6.

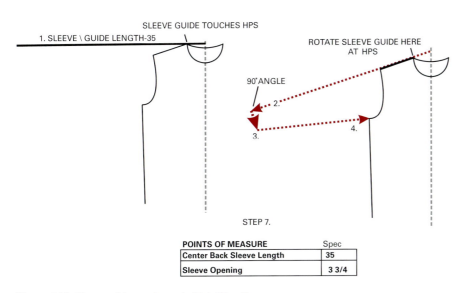

STEP 7.

POINTS OF MEASURE	Spec
Center Back Sleeve Length	35
Sleeve Opening	3 3/4

Figure 4.35 Sleeve of long-sleeved shirt: Step 7.

Figure 4.35b). Make sure it is a 90-degree angle. Finish the sleeve at the undersleeve edge, connecting it to the body. When connecting point 3 to point 4, there are no measurements to follow (see Figure 4.35b).

Step 8: Figure 4.36a shows adding a mirror image of the left sleeve at elbow level, and then rotating it as in Figure 4.36b. That is so the sleeve end will not overlap the side seam. The sleeve can be rotated a bit more or less; the precise amount is not important. Figure 4.36c shows where to add the last fold line at the elbow level, and Figure 4.36d shows which line segments to remove so that the final drawing will look like Figure 4.36e.

Step 9: Add the neck trim and style details, and the drawing for a men's long-sleeved knit shirt, front view, is complete (see Figure 4.37).

Step 10: The back view is drawn by making a mirror image of the front, so the wearer's left sleeve is still the one that is bent (see Figure 4.38).The sleeve direction is easily revised by moving two lines, as in the detail. The front collar is removed, leaving the back collar. And that completes the back view.

Drawing Pants

Even before preparing to draw pants, one must be familiar with the terminology used to convey information about the garment in the tech pack. The designer can then begin the preparation and actual drawing.

Terminology

The parts of a pant have certain terms to describe the seams and details. Figure 4.39 shows the terminology we will use to make the next drawing, a pair of men's jeans. Look at a pair of jeans and identify all the areas.

Before Beginning

Pants have certain areas that would appear distorted if the garment were drawn strictly to scale. Because of the nature of a pant shape, the actual width of the thigh would have to be shown overlapped, which would serve no visual purpose. Figure 4.40a shows a women's pant in size 8 with the measurements given.

Figure 4.40b is modified somewhat, and strikes a balance between the measurements and the appearance. The front rise is 1 inch longer than spec, and the thigh is blended. The same principle holds true for men's and children's pants, and the same modification is used.

Because of the shape of a pant, it will not fit into a guide box in the same way as a top. Instead, begin by setting up a file in 1:8 scale, and establish a center line guide. (It will be a guide from the

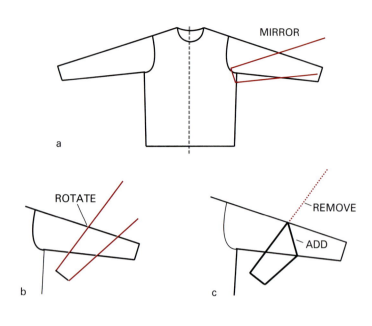

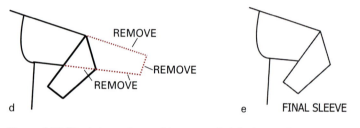

a

ROTATE

b

REMOVE
ADD

c

REMOVE
REMOVE
REMOVE

d

FINAL SLEEVE

e

Figure 4.36 Men's long-sleeve shirt, wearer's left sleeve: Step 8.

drawing program, not a part of the drawing.) The pant we will draw is a men's jean style, size 34/32 (34 waist, 32 inseam).

Start Drawing

Figures 4.41 and 4.42 illustrate step by step how to draw the pants front.

Step 1: Draw a rectangle to represent the waistband, following the specifications in Figure 4.41 for waist width slightly, as it is squared to the inseam (17^3/$_4$ inches), and waistband height (1^1/$_2$ inches). Following the measurement for front rise, plus 1 inch, add the rise seam.

Step 2: Draw the inseam, following the spec (32 inches).

Step 3: Add the bottom opening (9^3/$_4$ inches). It can angle up slightly, as it is squared to the inseam.

Step 4: The outseam is next. There is no spec for it, and it connects back at the waistband edge.

Step 5: Curve the outseam slightly at the hip area, and then mirror the finished pant leg. This is the basic silhouette (see Figure 4.42). Make a copy and save it to use for the back view.

Step 6: Add the right hand pocket details: pocket with topstitching, coin pocket, rivets, and belt loops. Add the inseam and bottom opening topstitching (see Figure 4.42).

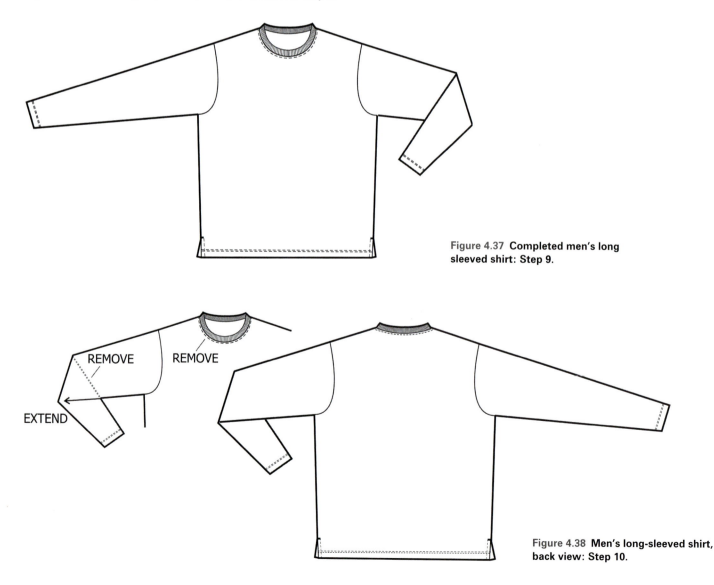

Figure 4.37 Completed men's long sleeved shirt: Step 9.

REMOVE   REMOVE

EXTEND

Figure 4.38 Men's long-sleeved shirt, back view: Step 10.

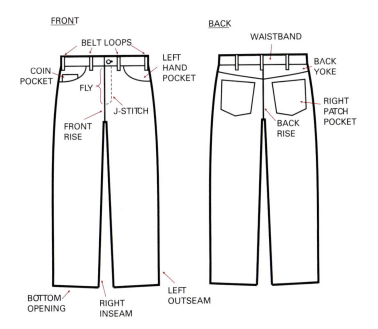

FRONT

BELT LOOPS

COIN
POCKET

FLY

LEFT
HAND
POCKET

J-STITCH

FRONT
RISE

BOTTOM
OPENING

RIGHT
INSEAM

LEFT
OUTSEAM

BACK

WAISTBAND

BACK
YOKE

RIGHT
PATCH
POCKET

BACK
RISE

Figure 4.39 Terminology of pants.

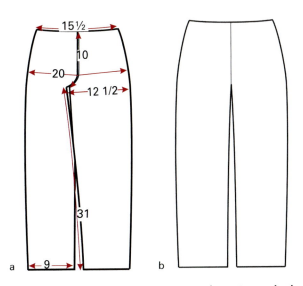

15½

10

20

12 1/2

31

a   9   b

Figure 4.40 Basic measurements, women's pant, sample size 8.

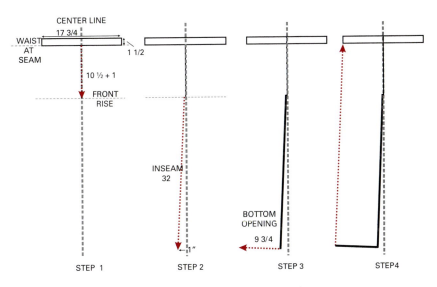

CENTER LINE
17 3/4

WAIST
AT
SEAM

1 1/2

10 ½ + 1

FRONT
RISE

INSEAM
32

BOTTOM
OPENING
9 3/4

1"

STEP 1   STEP 2   STEP 3   STEP4

Figure 4.41 Drawing a pair of pants to scale: Steps 1 through 4.

Step 7: In Figure 4.42, mirror the details (removing the extra coin pocket). Add fly J-stitch, waistband topstitching, and the rest of the details. The pant sketch, front view, is complete.

Step 8: The back view does not have a great many of the points of measure on the spec page because they are easier to illustrate than to describe. Step 8 is drawing the basic silhouette, as in Step 5 (see Figure 4.43).

Step 9: Add the back details as in Figure 4.43, which, for this style, are the yoke, patch pockets, and belt loops. The actual pocket placements, dimensions, and details will be added on the details page, which we will develop next.

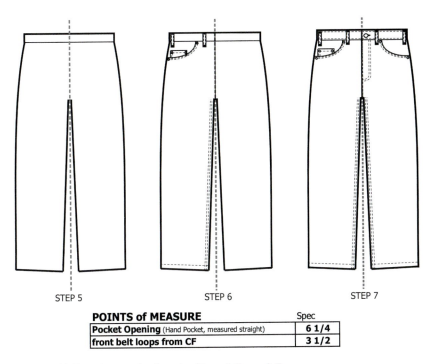

STEP 5   STEP 6   STEP 7

POINTS of MEASURE	Spec
Pocket Opening (Hand Pocket, measured straight)	6 1/4
front belt loops from CF	3 1/2

Figure 4.42 Drawing a pair of pants: Steps 5 through 7.

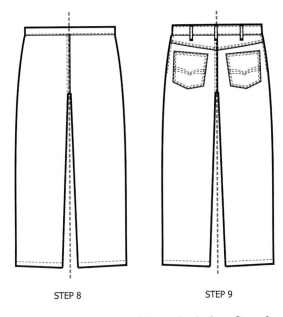

STEP 8   STEP 9

Figure 4.43 A pair of men's jeans, back view: Steps 8 and 9.

Drawing Detail Sketches

Detail drawings accompany the front and back view. They are called *tech sketches*, a term that makes them sound a bit tentative, but they are actually very exact and detailed. Tech sketches are necessary for dimension, stitch details, and placement, construction, and other features to ensure that each style will have a good prototype returned, and that company quality standards are followed.

The line weights for details follow the same rules as for the other garment drawings, with the outside outlines of the garment in 2-point, seams in 1-point, and so on. The jeans flat we just completed has the basic pocket shapes shown, but there is other information still to be specified.

Start Drawing

Fly Detail: Figure 4.44 shows the fly details. Figure 4.44a reveals the stitching dimensions for the fly, and the bartack placements. Figure 4.44b has a view with the zipper open and shows other information about the zipper-set and button placement.

Pockets and Belt Loops: Figure 4.45 gives details of the hand pocket depth and construction, and shows the side front piece with a 2-inch overlap (palm side), so the white pocketing won't pull out and show when the wearer has to fish something out of the pocket. Figure 4.45b has information on the belt loops and their dimensions and construction. You will notice that the waistband topstitching is missing from Figure 4.45a and b.

These drawings represent standard detail drawings, which many companies use to specify details that are the same for many garment styles. This type of drawing is simplified to show what they need, and no more. Figure 4.45b is about the belt loops, so details and topstitching pertaining to it are included, and other details are not. That way the detail sketch can be used in conjunction with waistbands that have single edge-stitch, double-needle topstitching, or no waistband topstitching at all. Detail drawings are a balance between too much information and not enough, and care must be taken to avoid contradictions with other sketches.

Pocket Placement and Side Seam: Figure 4.46 shows the back view and the pocket placement details. In Figure 4.46a, the CB belt loop is not centered over the seam, but is lined up slightly to the left to line up to the back rise topstitching, which gives it the appearance of being centered. The patch pocket at the top edge does not parallel the back yoke seam exactly, but is set at an angle, as is traditional for most jeans. Pockets are generally centered within the back pant panel, but in this case there are a lot of odd angles, so it can't be left open for interpretation. Figure 4.46b shows another traditional jeans detail, the partial topstitching of the side seam. The side seam and center back are marked because there are so few other details for orientation.

Back Pocket Dimension and Stitching: Because jeans are typically traditional in styling, the back patch pockets of a pair of jeans often have the most distinctive styling of the garment. Figure 4.47a shows the overall dimensions of the pocket, and Figure 4.47b provides all the stitching information. Details of topstitching width are not usually

FLY STITCHING

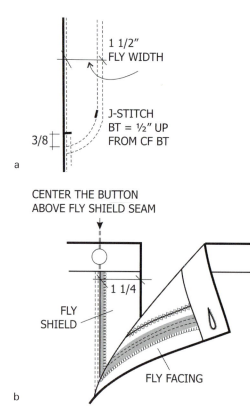

Figure 4.44 Detail sketches: fly detail.

HAND POCKET DETAILS

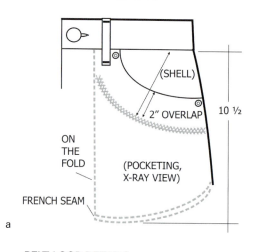

BELT LOOP DETAILS

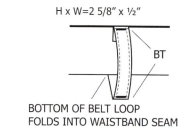

Figure 4.45 Details: pockets and belt loops.

POCKET PLACEMENT

CENTER BACK BELT LOOP ALIGNS TO
LEFT EDGE OF CB SEAM

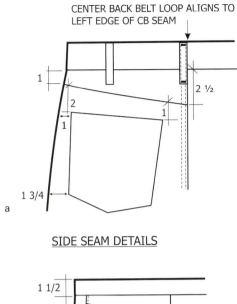

a

SIDE SEAM DETAILS

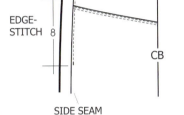

EDGE-
STITCH 8

CB

b   SIDE SEAM

Figure 4.46 Pocket placement (a) and side seam (b).

called out in the sketch, but it is added in this case because the width varies along the side, from $^1/_4$-inch at the side bottom to $^1/_2$-inch at side top. Again, use of the scale function in the drawing program can help to design the appearance of pockets, tabs, and other small details.

Other Details in Drawing Flats

Side Views

Because of the nature of the front and back views, garment side construction or details may not be clear. If so, a side view should be added. The edge of the drawing is often the seamline, but it may also be a fold. For example, see the pant in Figure 4.46a. Like most pants, the left edge of the waistband is a fold, but the left edge of the body is a seam (the outseam). Figure 4.48a shows a standard blouse, and Figure 4.48b shows which parts of the outline are seams and which are folded edges. The shoulder seams are slightly forward, which is a common standard, so the edge is a fold. Because the side seams end with a slit, it is clear that the side edges are indeed seams.

The blouse in Figure 4.49 is less clear. The side edge could be a side seam, a forward seam, or a side panel. In this case, the back view would provide additional information about whether it is a forward seam or a side panel, but it can't be ruled out whether a seam at the side seam is required, so that must be specified. The skirt in Figure 4.49b is probably a four-gore skirt without side seams, but because the edge could also be a side seam, it must be specified. The skirt is shown with a contour waistband, which often has no side seam, but for design or pattern matching reasons, it may. That also needs to be made clear.

POCKET DIMENSIONS

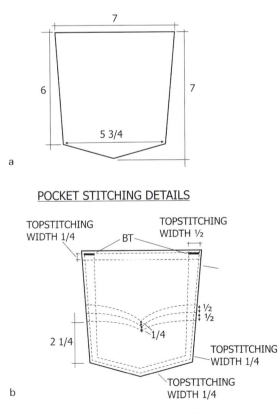

a

POCKET STITCHING DETAILS

TOPSTITCHING
WIDTH 1/4

TOPSTITCHING
WIDTH ½

BT

½
½

1/4

2 1/4

TOPSTITCHING
WIDTH 1/4

b

TOPSTITCHING
WIDTH 1/4

Figure 4.47 Details—pocket dimensions and stitching.

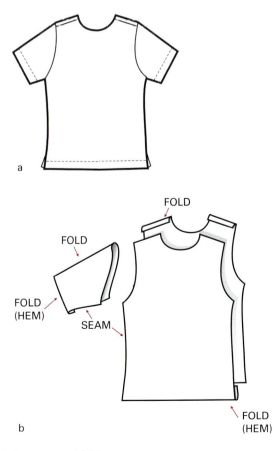

a

FOLD

FOLD

FOLD

FOLD
(HEM)

SEAM

b

FOLD
(HEM)

Figure 4.48 Seams and folds.

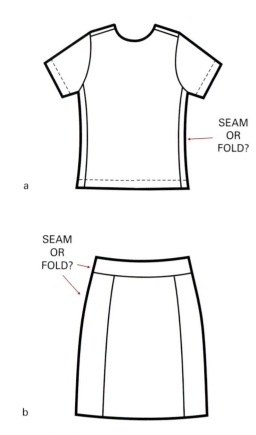

Figure 4.49 Specify seams or folds.

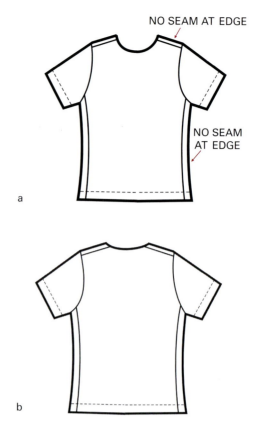

Figure 4.50 Specify no seam.

Figure 4.50 shows both the front and back views of the blouse, and we see that the back view details echo the front for this style. Figure 4.50 calls out clearly that there is no side seam or shoulder seam, and shows the way that would be notated. We see that the blouse seam at the shoulder is not just a forward shoulder, but a narrow panel.

Imaginary Positions

If there is no actual side seam, but a detail is to be positioned there, the term *imaginary side seam* is used (see Figure 4.51). The side view here is added to show that there is no seam, and to provide the welt pocket position.

Common types of stitches are also represented in a standard way. We looked at topstitching before in Figure 4.14 in the section on line weights. Other finishes are shown in Figure 4.52, including coverstitch, binding, and multi-needle. Many stitches look different on the top from the way they do on the bottom, so the sketch will identify how it looks on the outside of the garment, and additional information can be found in the tech pack on the construction page. We will learn more about the construction methods represented by these stitches in Chapter 9. (There is also a list of stitches in Appendix A.)

Figure 4.52 shows various stitch details. A coverstitch is a useful and popular finish used mainly on knits. A common place to find

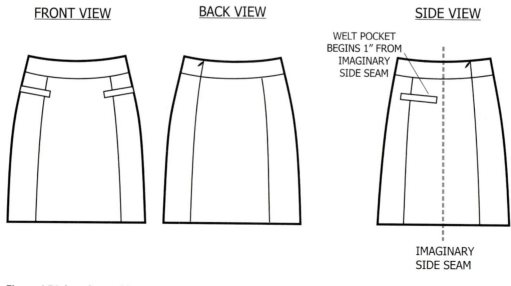

Figure 4.51 Imaginary side seam.

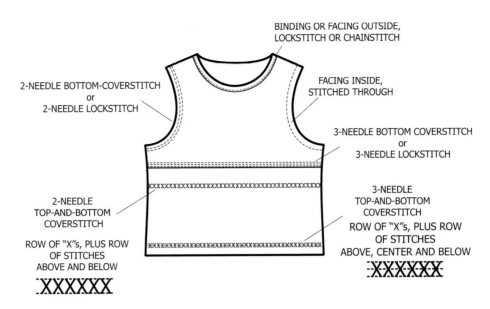

BINDING OR FACING OUTSIDE,
LOCKSTITCH OR CHAINSTITCH

2-NEEDLE BOTTOM-COVERSTITCH
or
2-NEEDLE LOCKSTITCH

FACING INSIDE,
STITCHED THROUGH

3-NEEDLE BOTTOM COVERSTITCH
or
3-NEEDLE LOCKSTITCH

2-NEEDLE
TOP-AND-BOTTOM
COVERSTITCH

ROW OF "X"s, PLUS ROW
OF STITCHES
ABOVE AND BELOW

3-NEEDLE
TOP-AND-BOTTOM
COVERSTITCH
ROW OF "X"s, PLUS ROW
OF STITCHES
ABOVE, CENTER AND BELOW

Figure 4.52 Stitch details.

it is as a hemming method for T-shirts, at the sleeve and bottom openings.

Figure 4.53a shows how to note the wrong side of the fabric; for example, in a detail sketch with a standard shade of gray. Figure 4.53b is a detail sketch of the construction of a back yoke with multiple seam allowances shown. It also shows the method for indicating a break in the illustration, where space does not allow the entire panel to show.

Figure 4.54a is a sketch of gathers as may be found at the front of a shirt or the waist of a full skirt. The cuff section also shows the method for indicating the direction a tuck opens. This notation is

used to distinguish a tuck detail from a seam or dart. Figure 4.54b shows the method and line weight for drawing rib trims, and also for showing fully fashioned marks, a method of shaping sweaters.

Because they are on the inside of a garment, pocket bags are often shown with a sort of X-ray line that is used to indicate their position or size as if the viewer could see through the outer layers of fabric. Figure 4.55a calls out the pocket depth. Figure 4.55b shows a patch pocket under another patch pocket, as may be used for a travel or security pocket. Figure 4.55c includes the terminology for each of the two layers of fabric that form a pocket bag for situations in which the two layers of pocket need to be

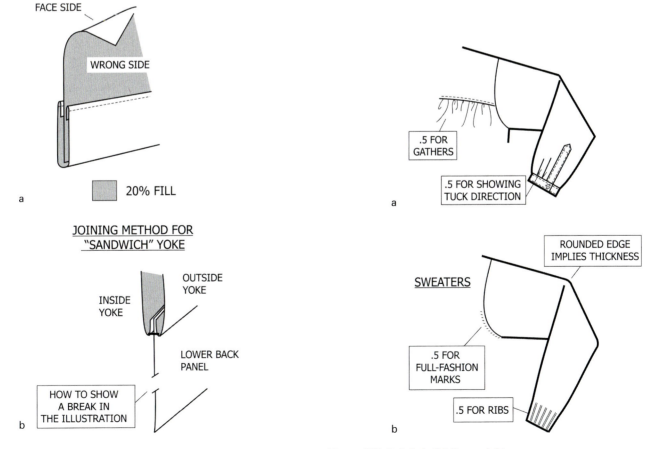

FACE SIDE

WRONG SIDE

20% FILL

a

JOINING METHOD FOR
"SANDWICH" YOKE

INSIDE
YOKE

OUTSIDE
YOKE

LOWER BACK
PANEL

HOW TO SHOW
A BREAK IN
THE ILLUSTRATION

b

Figure 4.53 Inside views.

.5 FOR
GATHERS

.5 FOR SHOWING
TUCK DIRECTION

a

SWEATERS

ROUNDED EDGE
IMPLIES THICKNESS

.5 FOR
FULL-FASHION
MARKS

.5 FOR RIBS

b

Figure 4.54 Details in 0.5 line weight.

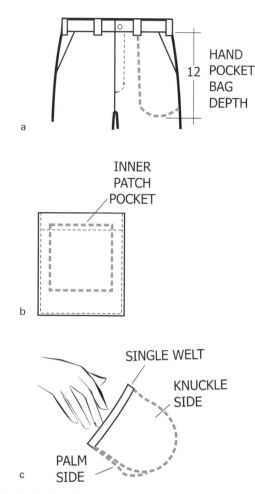

a

INNER
PATCH
POCKET

b

SINGLE WELT

KNUCKLE
SIDE

PALM
SIDE

c

Figure 4.55 **Pocket details, X-ray.**

distinguished from each other. The palm side is the bag closest to the body; the knuckle side is to the back of the hand. These pocket examples are not actually visible from the outside.

Summary

Developing flats requires precision and accuracy. Paying attention to details of apparel products may not be an easy task at first, but when one becomes familiar with knowledge about stitches, seams, specs, and other elements of apparel products, the task will be a fun experience. Technical design requires the creative aspects of designing as well as paying attention to detail, critical thinking skills, and problem solving.

Study Questions

1. Lay a woven blouse, a sweater, and a pair of shorts flat onto a table, and photograph each of them from directly above. Next, photograph the same garments on a body or dress form. Compare the two photographs. How do they differ? How are the differences reflected in sketching flats for each product category? Note that flats are exact replicas of the garment that are proportionally correct.

2. Select one simple tank top in your wardrobe. Measure the garment followed by the basic measurements (refer to Figure 4.21 to get basic measurements). Draw a flat sketch of the selected garment to scale (scale 1:8) with correct stitch detail. If a CAD program is not available, draw the sketch in pencil. Make sure to check the proportion of your drawing. The sketch should be proportionally correct.

3. Draw a pocket in actual size (scale 1:1) for your tank top or for another garment. Cut it out and pin it onto the sample shirt or other garment, and confirm the position by trying it on and checking the appearance in the mirror. Adjust the size, position, and details as needed, and redraw. Then add the pocket detail to your tech sketch, sizing it to 1:8, and positioning in the same way as the sample. Be sure to include dimensions, stitch details, and placement.

4. Select one simple pair of jeans from your closet. Measure the garment followed by the measurements in Figure 4.40. Draw a flat sketch of the selected garment to scale (scale 1:8) with correct stitch detail. If a CAD program is not available, draw the sketch in pencil. Make sure to check the proportion of your drawing. The sketch should be proportionally correct.

5. Compare the overall proportions of the women's tank and men's shirt.
   a. If the men's shirt were simply sized down, could the same style be offered for a women's shirt?
   b. How could it be modified to be more stylish?
   c. What points of measure would change, and what would they change to?
   d. How could the women's tank top specifications be changed to be suitable for a man's tank top garment?

6. Develop a set of croquis for designing swimwear. Make front and back views for a women's set, a men's set, and a children's set (three- to five-year-olds). Draw two styles for each.

7. (If CAD system is available only.) Draw a gathered skirt with waistband. Use the correct line weights for the outline, interior seams, and gathers. Find a welt pocket (such as on a blazer). Identify the palm side and knuckle side pocket bag. Why would the designer need to call out palm side and knuckle side?

8. Refer to the *Technical Sourcebook for Apparel Designers* STUDIO.
   a. Choose Pant #1: Bell Bottoms from Appendix C and design a back view using patch pockets from 101 pockets included. Note: Please keep the same line weight for the sketch.
   b. Repeat the exercise with Skirt # 3: Kilt from Appendix C and design a back view. Note: Please keep the same line weight for the sketch.
   c. Repeat the exercise with Shirt #4: Tie Blouse from Appendix C and design a back view. Note: Please keep the same line weight for the sketch.
   d. Repeat the exercise with the selection of a jacket you choose from Appendix C and design a back view. Note: Please keep the same line weight for the sketch.

Check Your Understanding

1. What is a technical sketch?
2. How are floats and technical flats different? How are they similar?
3. What are the basic measurements used for a T-shirt?
4. What are the basic measurements used for a pair of pants (body measurements compared to style measurements)?
5. Define these terms:
   a. CB
   b. FND
   c. BND
   d. HPS
   e. CF

Technical Design Terms for Silhouettes and Design Details

Chapter Objectives

After studying this chapter, you will be able to:

- Define various technical terms related to silhouettes and design details
- Demonstrate various silhouettes and design details
- Communicate the silhouettes and design details using written and oral technical terminology
- Identify fashion trends by analyzing silhouettes and design features
- Apply various design features in the creative design process

---

Key Terms

active pant
armscye (or
   armseye)
baby doll dress
bell bottoms
bell sleeve
bertha collar
boat neck
bodice
bow collar
break point
caftan
cascade collar
cheongsam
Chinese collar
coatdress
convertible collar
cuff
culotte

cut-and-sew
dhoti
dirndl skirt
dolman sleeve
drawstring pant
gathered flared skirt
gaucho
gored skirt
gorge
gypsy (peasant) skirt
harem pants
hobble skirt
hourglass
J-stitch
jodhpurs
jonny collar
Juliet sleeve
jumper
kilt

kimono sleeve
knickers
Mandarin collar
mock turtle
overalls
palazzo pants
pant
paperbag waist
peasant dress
peasant skirt
pegged pant
pegged skirt
pilgrim collar
polo dress
pouf skirt
princess-seamed
   dress
princess seaming
raglan sleeve

saddle sleeve
safari dress
sailor collar
sarong skirt
set-in sleeve
shawl collar
shirtwaist
silhouette
sleeve cap
slipdress
sundress
surplice
tent dress
trapeze dress
trouser style
trumpet skirt
tunic dress
wing collar
zoot suit

This chapter provides information on terminology related to apparel design, and enables you to clearly communicate and understand silhouettes and design details. Silhouettes in a variety of garment categories with various design details are also covered. In each section of design details, technical aspects of each part are also added to provide a better understanding of the applications and how they relate to technical design.

Garment Terminology

Designers use certain terms in the design of a garment as well as in communicating style, fit, and revision information. Parts of a garment may have different names in different countries or regions, but the important principle is to designate one term and use it consistently in communication among the members of the production team, whether those members are in the office or in a factory thousands of miles away. In the specification process, from tech packs through the sampling process and fit comments, mastering the technical terminology is a must.

Some basic terminology for a knit top and pair of pants was introduced in Chapter 4, as related to developing technical flats. This section includes additional terms for pants, as well as technical terms of other garment categories: woven shirts, dresses, jackets, pants, and hats.

Terminology of a Shirt

A shirt is a top, usually with sleeves and a collar. A men's or women's dress shirt generally has two different types of placket: a front button placket and sleeve plackets at each cuff. (A **cuff** is a band attached to the bottom of a sleeve or leg.) Figure 5.1 shows a shirt with a back yoke, below which a device for ease is often added, in this case, pleats. A woman's blouse would use the same terminology for the same features.

The use of a collar band helps the collar to stand automatically and shapes it smoothly around the neck. A dress shirt like the one in Figure 5.1 often has a short, wide sleeve cap, which allows for ease of movement. In Figure 5.1, front closures follow the rule of left front on top for men's styles and right front on top for women's styles. Another way to remember is right-over for women's, left-over for men's. Suits and coats follow the same rule.

The *topcollar* is sometimes known as the *upper collar*, but since those two terms refer to the same part of the garment, we will avoid having two terms and will use the term *topcollar*. As with most shirts and many other styles, the shoulder seam is slightly forward.

Terminology of a Dress

A dress is a woman's single garment that covers the torso and legs. The **bodice** is the portion of a woman's garment between the shoulders and the waist (see Figure 5.2); the part below the waist is called the skirt. Both examples in Figure 5.2 have yokes, which are horizontal seams used for style and fitting. Figure 5.2a has a hip yoke and Figure 5.2b has a yoke at the bodice. Both also have gores, vertical panels used for shaping. The bodice in Figure 5.2b has **princess seaming**, is fitted with seams rather than darts, and has no waistline seam. The seams extend from the bodice to the hemline and create a slenderizing silhouette.

As called out in Figure 5.2b, the **sleeve cap** is the area above the bicep. In this sketch, it is much higher and narrower than on the shirt style (see Figure 5.1). The armhole seam is called the **armscye** (or **armseye**). Figure 5.2b also features triangular inserts called *godets*, which add width to the bottom of an otherwise very fitted shape skirt.

Terminology of a Jacket

Tailored clothing has many traditional elements that center around the collar and lapel details. There are many small proportions that make a large impact. Figure 5.3a shows a jacket with a peaked lapel and princess seaming.

In terms of technical sketching, note that the center of the button is positioned at center front and is also where the lapels come together. The **break point** is the place where the lapel folds back from the edge of the garment. The classic tailored jacket has no seam at the actual side position; rather, one panel extends across the side seam. This is a more expensive construction, but results in a smooth fit. As noted in Chapter 4, since the observer of this drawing cannot tell if there is a seam at the side, that information would need to be noted on the technical flat.

The bottom back vent is used to provide ease for sitting, and the sleeve vent at one time in history buttoned open to form a placket that could be rolled up. That is rarely seen anymore, and the sleeve vent and buttons are now decorative. In Figure 5.3b, the back vent is at the center back of the jacket; an alternate placement can sometimes be found with two vents, one each at the bottom of the back princess seams. Lapel terms are specified in Figure 5.3c.

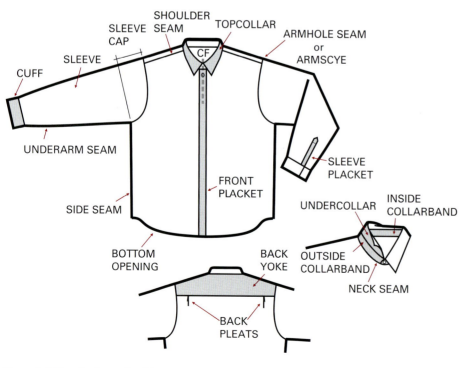

Figure 5.1 Terminology of a shirt.

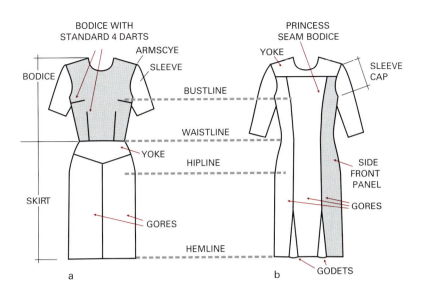

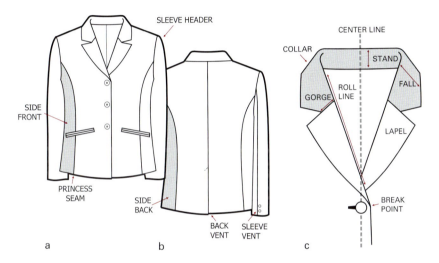

Figure 5.2 Dress terminology.

Figure 5.3 Jacket terminology.

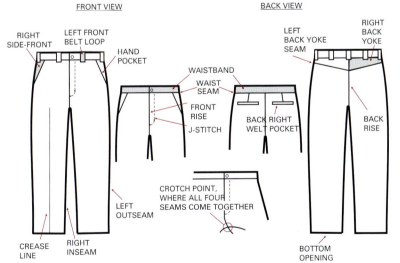

Figure 5.4 Pant terminology.

Terminology of Pants

Figure 5.4 shows a pair of pants, as well as the terms for the seams and panels. The same terms are used for men's, women's, and children's pants. We will use these terms when describing treatments and details.

A **pant** typically consists of four panels—two fronts and two backs. Notice that the long vertical seams have special names—*inseam* and *outseam*. The front opening is called the fly and is finished with a type of topstitching called a **J-stitch** because of its shape (Figures 5.4a and 5.4b). Men's pants have the fly opening on the right. Women's styles can have it on the left or right because they sometimes follow the "men's way," but men's pants never have the fly sewn the "women's way."

Tailored pants usually have a crease line pressed in. Casual pants do not (see Figure 5.4a). A crease line in a technical flat is rendered in 0.5-point line weight to distinguish it from a seam. Hand pockets come in different styles. The style shown in Figures 5.4a and 5.4b is called a slash pocket (quarter top pocket).

Terminology of Hats

There are many different styles of hats, from traditional felt hats to knit caps and berets. Figure 5.5 shows examples of **cut-and-sew** hats, which are produced with flat patterns, laid out, cut, and then joined on sewing machines.

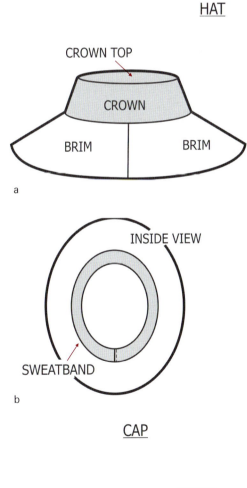

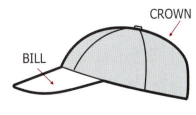

Figure 5.5 Cut-and-sew hat and cap.

Silhouettes

The **silhouette** of a garment refers to the outline or shape. Another way to think of it, as noted previously, is this: where the garment is fitted, and where it's loose; where the body is covered, and where it's uncovered. Silhouette change is an important element in the way styles evolve and in the sense of the new. Men's silhouettes change much more slowly than women's, but change nonetheless. By comparison, women's fashion silhouettes often change quickly, and with far greater shifts from high to low and loose to fitted.

Shifting trends in fashion influence the silhouette constantly, but certain shapes return time and again. High fashion silhouettes are more exaggerated in shape, and as a new silhouette makes its way through different markets, it is adapted and simplified, as appropriate to each market segment.

With a few notable exceptions, the waist has been the focus of women's dress throughout the centuries, and the waist position remains one of the key elements of women's silhouettes. Figure 5.6 shows dress shapes, but a similar pendulum shift occurs for waist position on pants and other categories. In this chapter, silhouettes for dresses, skirts, and pants are specified, and the pant and skirt silhouettes based on length are also noted.

Silhouette Changes by Waist Position

Various names are used to specify silhouettes. Women's basic dress silhouettes are determined based on waist position and the fit of the dress on the body (see Figure 5.6).

- *Sheath*: Figures 5.6a and 5.6b have a waist at the natural position, the first with an actual waist seam and the second with waist shaping through darts. Figure 5.6a comes into popularity when an **hourglass** shape is popular, with a slimmer waist and fuller bust and hip. This example has a pegged hem in which the hemline is narrower than the hipline, which further emphasizes the curve of the hip.
- *Empire*: This dress has a seam or style line under the bustline (see Figure 5.6c).
- *High waist*: This is a transitional waist position, when the waistline is trending upward (see Figure 5.6d).
- *Dropped waist*: Often with a fitted bodice, a dropped waist is also used for girls' dresses without fitting at the waistline (see Figure 5.5e).
- *Chemise*: This is a straight style with no waist definition (see Figure 5.6f).

Classic Dress Silhouettes Defined by Shape

A number of the more classic silhouettes can be defined by shape alone, with or without consideration of the other styling details (see Figure 5.7). For example, a trapeze dress with short or long sleeves is still called a trapeze dress. Any of these styles could have a variety of sleeves or collars and still have the same silhouette name. The exception is the jumper, which is sleeveless and intended to be layered over another garment.

A **tent dress** is an exaggerated A-line-shape dress introduced by Cristobal Balenciaga as a coat, and used for dresses and coats in the 1950s. A **trapeze dress** is a knee-length full-tent-shape dress that was introduced by Yves St. Laurent in 1958. The style is an unfitted dress made with narrow shoulders that gradually widens to a very wide hem. Although both styles are technically different, they are similar, as seen in Figure 5.7a, to a pyramid-shaped dress with a wide bottom.

Here are a few more classic dress silhouettes:

- A **tunic dress** (see Figure 5.7b) is a two-piece dress with a separate narrow skirt or a one-piece dress with a similar look.
- A **jumper** is a sleeveless garment, generally worn with a sleeved blouse, shirt, or sweater (see Figure 5.7c). It can have any body shape.
- A **princess-seamed dress** (see Figure 5.7d) is fitted through vertical seams rather than darts, and generally without a waistline seam.
- A **baby doll dress** (see Figure 5.7e) is a short dress or top style with pleats or gathers hanging from a yoke, for girls or women. The term refers to styles used for children's and infants' clothes in the early twentieth century.
- The **surplice** (see Figure 5.7f) is also called a wrap dress, usually with overlapping layers, often with gathers at the side seam. The same look can also be achieved without the underlay.

Dress Silhouettes Changed by Design Detail

In addition, there are certain other classic shapes that come and go in style, but versions of which have come back time and again. These styles are not defined just by shape, but by detail as well. The first three drawings in Figure 5.8 are from western dress traditions; the last three are from other cultures.

The **shirtwaist** (see Figure 5.8a) is based on a classic tailored shirt with many similar details such as a collar with collar band, cuffs,

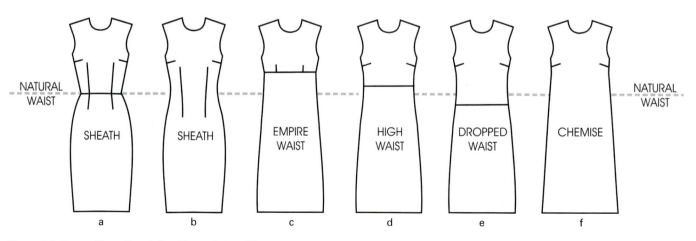

Figure 5.6 Dress silhouettes defined by waist position.

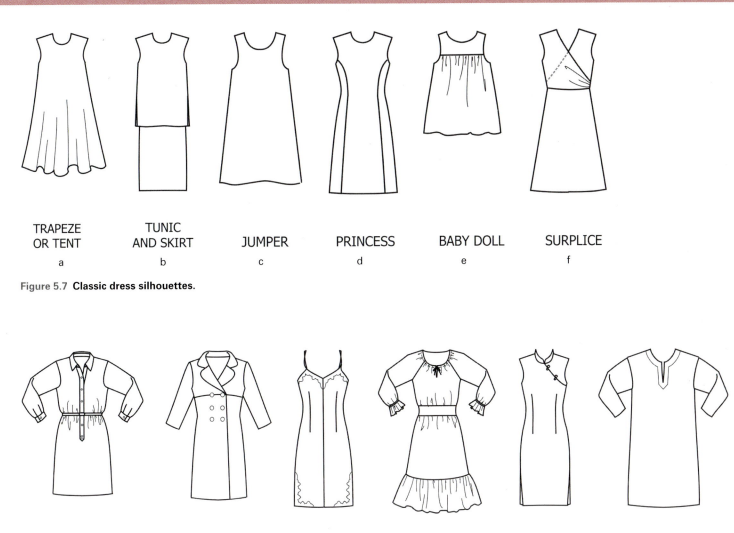

TRAPEZE OR TENT	TUNIC AND SKIRT	JUMPER	PRINCESS	BABY DOLL	SURPLICE
a	b	c	d	e	f

Figure 5.7 **Classic dress silhouettes.**

SHIRTWAIST	COATDRESS	SLIPDRESS	PEASANT	CHEONGSAM	CAFTAN
a	b	c	d	e	f

Figure 5.8 **Silhouettes by design details.**

and front placket. It is usually made from woven fabric and is often belted. A related style is the **polo dress**, a casual knit style based on a polo shirt, with a collar similar to the one in Figure 5.34 on p. 94.

The **coatdress** (see Figure 5.8b) is often double breasted, and versions of it have other details borrowed from a coat or trench coat (epaulets, belt, and so on). The **slipdress** style (see Figure 5.8c) is for evening wear and borrows details from lingerie, such as spaghetti straps, lace trim, and lightweight, silky fabric. It is often cut on the bias. Other classic dress styles include the **safari dress**, a style after an African bush jacket with a belt and multiple patch pockets, made popular by Yves Saint Laurent, and the **sundress**, a sleeveless style with a full skirt often worn with matching short-sleeved jacket.

The **peasant dress** (see Figure 5.8d) has a gathered neckline and raglan sleeves ending in a ruffle. The skirt shown here has one ruffle at the bottom, but this style often features multiple tiers as in the three-tiered skirt. The **cheongsam** (see Figure 5.8e) is a slim garment, originally Chinese, with a Mandarin collar, side closure, and slit skirt. The **caftan** (see Figure 5.8f) is a long, loose-fitting garment with embroidered trim at the neckline. It sometimes comes into fashion for men also, as a casual loungewear garment.

Skirt Silhouette Defined by Shape and Design Detail

A skirt is a cylindrical garment that covers the body from the waist down. Some cultures have skirt-like garments for men, such as the *kilt* in Scotland, and a wrap garment in the South Sea Islands called the *lava lava*. But a skirt is a quintessentially feminine garment in Western culture. The bottom of a dress is also called the skirt. In any case, the skirt is an important element in a silhouette, whether or not it is attached to a bodice.

Skirt silhouettes follow whatever aspect of the body happens to be in focus at the time. If a small waist and fuller hips are being emphasized, the pegged, dirndl, and gathered shapes become popular with their characteristic fullness at the hipline. Figures 5.9 through 5.11 show various skirt silhouettes.

The *basic straight skirt* (see Figure 5.9a) has a slim fit, a straight waistband at the natural waist, and front and back darts. The *wrap skirt* (see Figure 5.9b) is adjustable in a way that makes it easy to fit different sizes. The **kilt** (see Figure 5.9c) is a pleated garment derived from a traditional Scottish skirt worn by men. The **gored skirt** (see Figure 5.9d) trades the waist darts for flare. Gored skirts also come in 4, 6, 8, 10, 12, and other numbers of gores, and are a classic style. The *jean skirt* (see Figure 5.9e) often uses a heavier

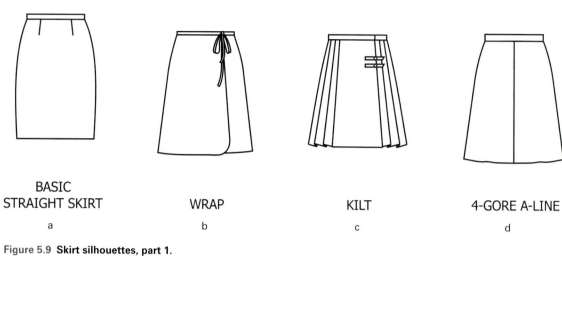
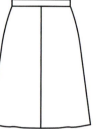

BASIC
STRAIGHT SKIRT

a

WRAP

b

KILT

c

4-GORE A-LINE

d

JEAN SKIRT

e

Figure 5.9 Skirt silhouettes, part 1.

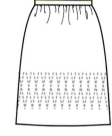

SARONG

a

DIRNDL

b

PEGGED

c

POUF

d

A-LINE
CULOTTE

e

Figure 5.10 Skirt silhouettes part 2.

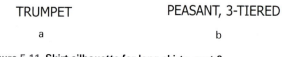

TRUMPET

a

PEASANT, 3-TIERED

b

HOBBLE SKIRT

c

FLARED AND GATHERED
FROM
SCALLOPED YOKE

d

Figure 5.11 Skirt silhouette for long skirts, part 3.

bottom-weight fabric of denim and, in that case, is cut slim. A style in a lighter-weight denim could have more flare at the bottom opening.

The **sarong skirt** (see Figure 5.10a), also called a *pareo*, is derived from a simple style that wraps and ties; modern sarong styles are adaptations that usually give an asymmetrical look with soft draping, but without needing to be adjusted. **Dirndl skirts** (see Figure 5.10b) are straight skirts with ease or gathers going into a straight waistband. They are adaptable for border design fabrics. The origin of this style comes from the Tyrolean peasant costume (Calasibetta and Tortora, 2003). The hipline of a **pegged skirt** (see Figure 5.10c) is wider than the bottom opening, and generally needs a slit or vent at the bottom to facilitate movement. The **pouf skirt** (see Figure 5.10d) is a type of exaggerated silhouette generally reserved for evening and special occasions because it's not always easy to sit in.

The **culotte** (see Figure 5.10e) is a type of bifurcated skirt that is a comfortable blend of skirt and pant; a longer version is called a gaucho (see Figure 5.15d). As with many garment styles, the culotte has an interesting history. It was originally developed when the bicycle came into popular use, and a divided skirt was needed for that activity. It would have been a full-length version at that time, of course, but it is an early example of a sports activity influencing fashion.

Figure 5.11 shows the silhouettes of four long skirts. Because long skirts have been worn for many centuries, they have a lot of drama and history associated with them. Longer skirts sometimes come into style for daywear, in lengths as long as midi or ballerina, but for practical reasons, full-length skirts are reserved for special occasion wear.

The **trumpet skirt** (see Figure 5.11a) also works well as a ballerina length. As it gets longer, the flare needs to start at around the same distance at the knee so there is enough width provided for walking. The **peasant** or **gypsy skirt** (see Figure 5.11b) is a long skirt with gathered tiers, as is seen in the rural costumes worn in many countries, especially Eastern Europe. This style comes into vogue when simplicity and back-to-the-land nostalgia is popular, as in the 1970s.

The **hobble skirt** (see Figure 5.11c), introduced in the pre-World War I era, is cut and draped in such a way as to narrow at the ankles. The original version was so restrictive at the bottom opening that it allowed only the smallest steps to be taken. Modern adaptations have a slit to allow for ease in walking. The **gathered flared skirt** (see Figure 5.11d) is a type generally attributed to Christian Dior and was made popular after World War II. Skirts from that era often used 15 or more yards of fabric over a stiff underskirt to increase the volume even more. This abundance of fabric was a reaction to the restrictions imposed during the war years by many women who tried to express their freedom.

Silhouettes Based on the Length of the Garment

The length of a garment is a key part of any silhouette. Figures 5.12a and 5.12b show the main lengths of skirts (including dresses), pants, and what they are called. The lengths and the names for them change frequently as new ideas and shapes come into the marketplace. For that reason, many classic lengths have several names.

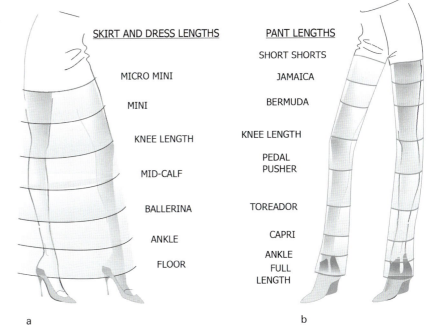

Figure 5.12 Silhouette based on length.

For decades, skirt lengths were an important part of the current look, and a certain length was either right or wrong; a change in hemline was front-page news, with an occasional street protest against a new length, as happened with the arrival of Dior's New Look Collection in 1947. Lengths are less controversial these days, and often cycle from high to low more quickly than in the past.

Pant Silhouettes Defined by Shape and Design Detail

A pant is a bifurcated (in two parts) garment, one for each leg. An early version of women's pants was the bloomer, a very full, long pant gathered in at the ankle, introduced by Amelia Bloomer in the nineteenth century. Women wearing pants at all was controversial in Western cultures for quite a few centuries, and even recently, pants were worn mostly by the daring and impervious, such as film stars—Marlene Dietrich and Katharine Hepburn come to mind. Pants were popular throughout the 1930s after being adopted by film stars and were worn in manufacturing plants during World War II (Calasibetta and Tortora, 2003). In the past few decades, pants have become a wardrobe staple; quite a shift from the 1960s when restaurants would not allow women wearing pants to enter.

Denim styles are worn by all sizes and shapes of women. **Bell bottoms** (Figure 5.13a) are pants that flare from the knee down, and were popular in the 1960s. The style is adapted from a traditional navy uniform.

The **drawstring pant** (see Figure 5.13b) is a popular style, and a version of it is often seen in sleepwear. It is comfortable and easy to fit many body types because of its adjustable waist. This one has a shortened inseam. The **active pant** (see Figure 5.13c) and similar styles are used for running and bicycling. Zippers on the bottom allow the wearer to pull them off and on over shoes.

The **trouser style** (see Figure 5.13d) has a high waistband and a relaxed fit. The Hollywood waistband has no waist seam. A greatly exaggerated version is the pant of a **zoot suit**, a style made

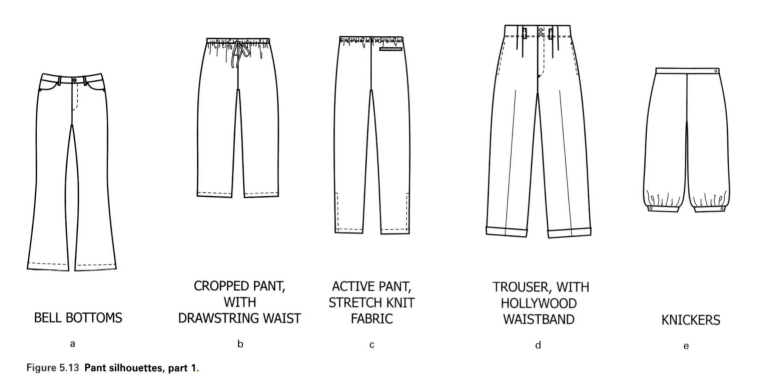

BELL BOTTOMS

a

CROPPED PANT,
WITH
DRAWSTRING WAIST

b

ACTIVE PANT,
STRETCH KNIT
FABRIC

c

TROUSER, WITH
HOLLYWOOD
WAISTBAND

d

KNICKERS

e

Figure 5.13 **Pant silhouettes, part 1.**

popular by working class young people in the United States in the 1940s, originating in Los Angeles. **Knickers** (see Figure 5.13e) were introduced as country wear in the 1860s and were often seen as a part of a man's golfing outfit in the late nineteenth and early twentieth centuries. Loose gathers with a buckled band at the knee characterizes this style (Calasibetta and Tortora, 2003).

Overalls (see Figure 5.14a) are derived from the workwear of farmers, but are also seen in women's wear because of their comfort and loose-fitting waistline. A bib top and suspender straps are attached to the body. Figure 5.14b shows **pegged pants**. Pegged refers to a silhouette with fullness at the top and a tapered bottom. A skirt can also have a pegged shape. A high gathered waist on pants (and skirts) is called a **paperbag waist** (see Figure

5.14c) because of the appearance of the gathers. **Palazzo pants** (see Figure 5.14d) are a kind of wide, soft divided skirt, or culotte, popular in the late 1960s and early 1970s (Calasibetta and Tortora, 2003).

A number of pant silhouettes are versions (or at least fanciful versions) of pants worn in other cultures (see Figure 5.15). The **harem pant** (see Figure 5.15a) is associated with belly dancing and beautiful genies in a bottle. **Jodhpurs** (see Figure 5.15b), worn in and around the city in India for which they are named, are a pant adapted for horseback riding. The **dhoti** (pronounced doe' tee) (see Figure 5.15c) is an ethnic style of draped pant, also from India. It has come to refer to a type of pant with a low draped rise and may be gathered at the waist and have tight legs

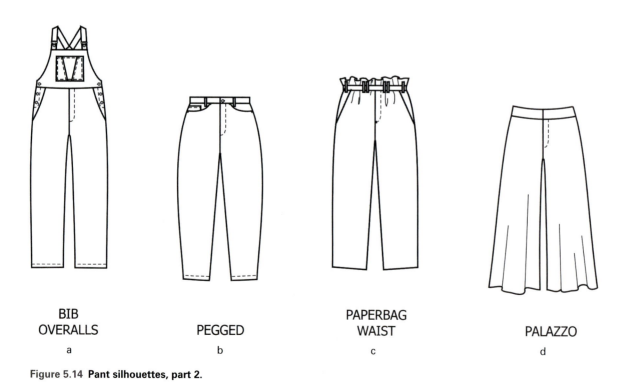

BIB
OVERALLS

a

PEGGED

b

PAPERBAG
WAIST

c

PALAZZO

d

Figure 5.14 **Pant silhouettes, part 2.**

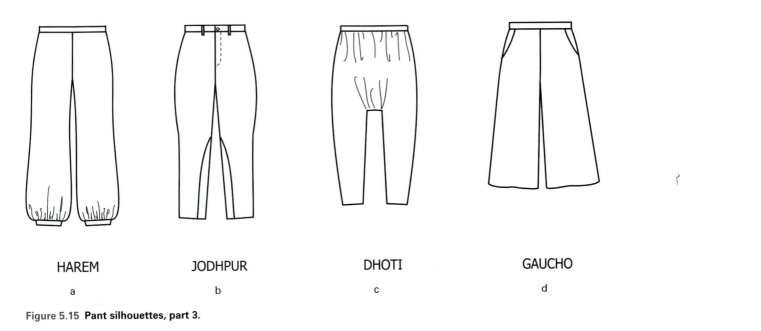

HAREM	JODHPUR	DHOTI	GAUCHO
a	b	c	d

Figure 5.15 **Pant silhouettes, part 3.**

(Calasibetta and Tortora, 2003). The **gaucho** (see Figure 5.15d) is named after a pant from South America, worn in the Pampas region by horsemen there known as gauchos. They are usually women's calf-length pants that are typically worn with boots, with no bare leg showing.

The women's underwear category has many forms. The most traditional bottoms style, the full-cut brief, is shown in Figure 5.16a. This sketch shows the garment made from a fabric with moderate stretch, as suggested by the gathers in the waistband. Figure 5.16b, the high-cut brief, is nearly as high in the rise, but far higher in terms of the leg opening. Figures 5.16c through 5.16e are various styles of underwear that appeal to different customers in the marketplace; the sketches have no gathers at the waistband, suggesting a very stretchy fabric and a tighter fit. The thong (Figure 5.15f) was developed to wear under tighter pants for a smooth look and to avoid any show-through. It has no back panel at all, just a narrow strip up the back that connects with the waist elastic.

The brassiere (commonly known as a bra) is a fairly recent garment, dating from the early 1900s (Callan, 1998). Contemporary bras are designed for more or less support, depending on the activity, and have different ways to help them fit different body shapes. Most bras have certain features in common, outlined in Figure 5.17.

The standard bra, shown in Figure 15.18a, is a familiar one to most women and sometimes has added padding. Figure 15.18b has an "underwire," a type of curved boning, under the cups. The sports bra (Figure 15.18c) comes in many configurations and is designed to be lightweight, absorb moisture, have the straps fit firmly and not slip off, and provide firm support in high activity sports, even for larger cup sizes. The longline bra (Figure 15.18d) provides a smoother shape across the back and is worn under knit fabrics. The strapless bra was developed to wear under dresses that are strapless, or have very thin straps. It often has some boning to help keep it in place. The sleep bra

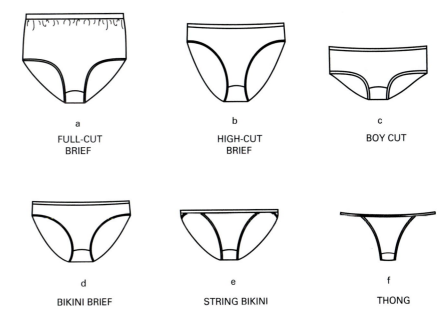

a	b	c
FULL-CUT BRIEF	HIGH-CUT BRIEF	BOY CUT
d	e	f
BIKINI BRIEF	STRING BIKINI	THONG

Figure 5.16 **Women's underwear silhouettes.**

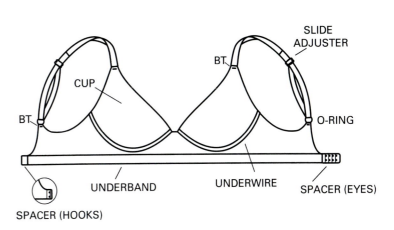

Figure 5.17 **Parts of a bra.**

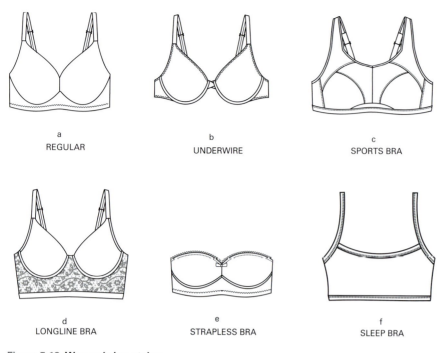

Figure 5.18 Women's bra styles.

(Figure 15.18f) has minimal support and is designed for casual wearing at home.

In general, bras are constructed of specialty fabrics, often knits that have a very soft surface. In a molded bra, the rounded cup shape is achieved through a heat process, rather than through darts or seams.

Design Details

Sleeves, cuffs, neck shape, and collars are the design details related to the silhouettes of garments.

Sleeves and Cuffs

Sleeve shapes follow the general silhouette of the garment. The main sleeve classifications, based on armhole shape, are set-in and cut-in-one, which includes the dolman or kimono sleeve and raglan or saddle variations.

Any one style of sleeve is best suited for a certain range of issues, and all present certain trade-offs. A set-in sleeve provides a smooth tailored appearance, but a more limited range of motion. A dolman sleeve has great comfort properties, but is best when used with a certain range of lighter weight fabrics. It is important to study sleeve properties so the best fabrics and shapes can be specified for the greatest appearance and comfort.

Set-In Sleeves with Various Caps

The **set-in sleeve** is the basic standard and the one that appears on the sloper. It is attached to the body of the garment around the arm socket and has the potential to be the most slim-fitting while retaining freedom of motion. The function and comfort of the set-in sleeve is achieved by the balance of many points of measure. We will study more about that in Chapter 16.

All other sleeve styles are developed from the set-in. Figure 5.19 shows three different set-in sleeves, each with different cap heights. A high cap (see Figure 5.19a) provides a smooth fit, as on a tailored jacket, but the trade-off is that when one lifts one's arms, the jacket tends to rise also. The medium cap (see Figure 5.19b) is shorter and has more "lift" for raising the arms up or forward without raising the jacket. The sleeve with no cap (see Figure 5.19c) generally requires a dropped shoulder, low armhole, and a lighter fabric that will drape softly around the underarm.

The short sleeve examples seen in Figure 5.20 are set-in, although most have other variations. Short sleeves have associations with younger styling, and are used for girls' styles as well. Set-in sleeves with long lengths have variations as well (see Figure 5.21). The *tailored sleeve* (see Figure 5.21a) is found on a semi-fitted or relaxed shirtdress or men's or women's shirt. The *gathered* (see Figure 5.21b) and *bishop sleeves* (see Figure 5.21c) are women's variations on the tailored sleeve, although the bishop may be used for a man's stage costume.

The **bell sleeve** (see Figure 5.21d) is flared between the elbow area and the bottom opening. Another name is *angel sleeve*. The *leg-o'-mutton sleeve* (see Figure 5.21e) is usually seen in conjunction with a fitted waist and flared skirt. The **Juliet sleeve** (see Figure

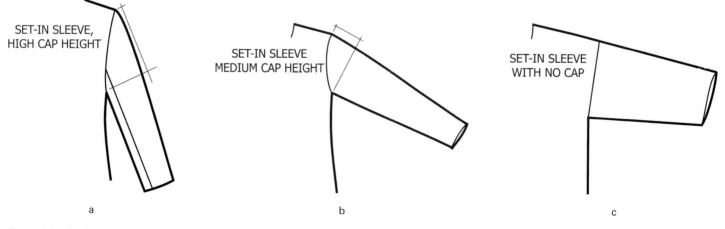

Figure 5.19 Set-in sleeves with various caps.

FRONT VIEW, LEFT SLEEVE

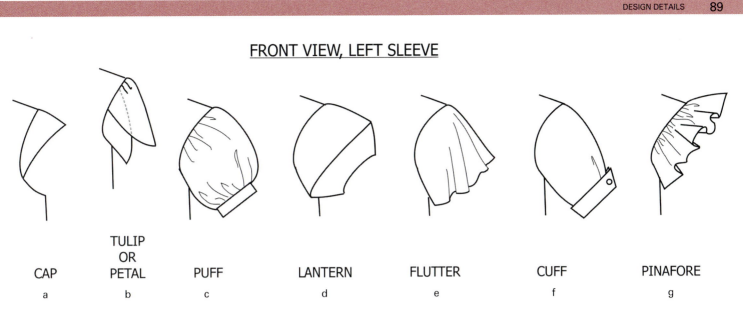

CAP	TULIP OR PETAL	PUFF	LANTERN	FLUTTER	CUFF	PINAFORE
a	b	c	d	e	f	g

Figure 5.20 Set-in sleeve variations for short sleeves.

SIDE BACK VIEW, RIGHT SLEEVE

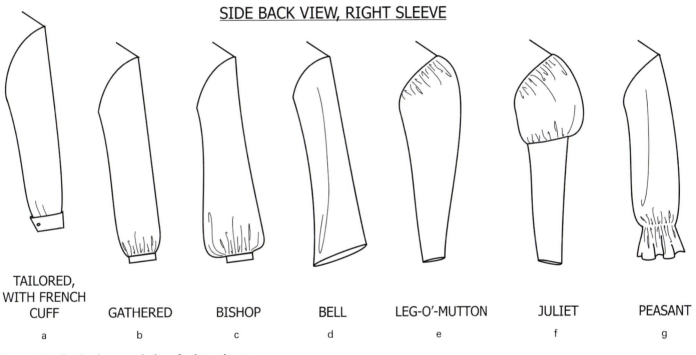

TAILORED, WITH FRENCH CUFF	GATHERED	BISHOP	BELL	LEG-O'-MUTTON	JULIET	PEASANT
a	b	c	d	e	f	g

Figure 5.21 Set-in sleeve variations for long sleeves.

5.21f) is a variation with a slimmer fit through the elbow. It has a long sleeve with a puffed top, which is fitted onto the lower arm; it is named after the title character in the play *Romeo and Juliet* (Calasibetta and Tortora, 2003). The *peasant sleeve* (see Figure 5.21g) has a straight cut with the excess gathered at the wrist.

Outerwear sleeves often feature a cuff cinch of some type to help avoid heat loss through the sleeve opening (see Figure 5.22). That is true of the first four examples in Figures 5.22a through 5.22d. The styles in Figures 5.22e and 5.22f are meant to fit over another bulky garment, such as a suit, so the sleeve opening is more generous and not adjustable.

Raglan Sleeves

The second type of sleeve is the raglan sleeve. The **raglan sleeve** (and its close cousin, the saddle sleeve) is cut partly in-one with

the body and ends at the neckline. A very simple shape, it has a straight underarm-to-neckline seam (see Figure 5.23a). This is the type of sleeve that would be found on an ethnic shirt such as the peasant sleeve in Figure 5.21g, and requires a soft fabric.

A more fitted style has a curved shape at the underarm-to-neckline seam (see Figure 5.23b), which allows for excess fabric to be eliminated. It also has a dart at the shoulder for shaping. This version, with a lower armhole, works well for a raincoat or men's overcoat. The last version, the **saddle sleeve** (see Figure 5.23c), is in between Figures 5.23a and 5.23b in fit and has a narrow shape at the top.

Kimono and Dolman Sleeves

The last type of sleeve is the **kimono sleeve** (see Figure 5.24a). It is cut-in-one with the bodice. Sometimes a gusset is required to

SIDE BACK VIEW, RIGHT SLEEVE

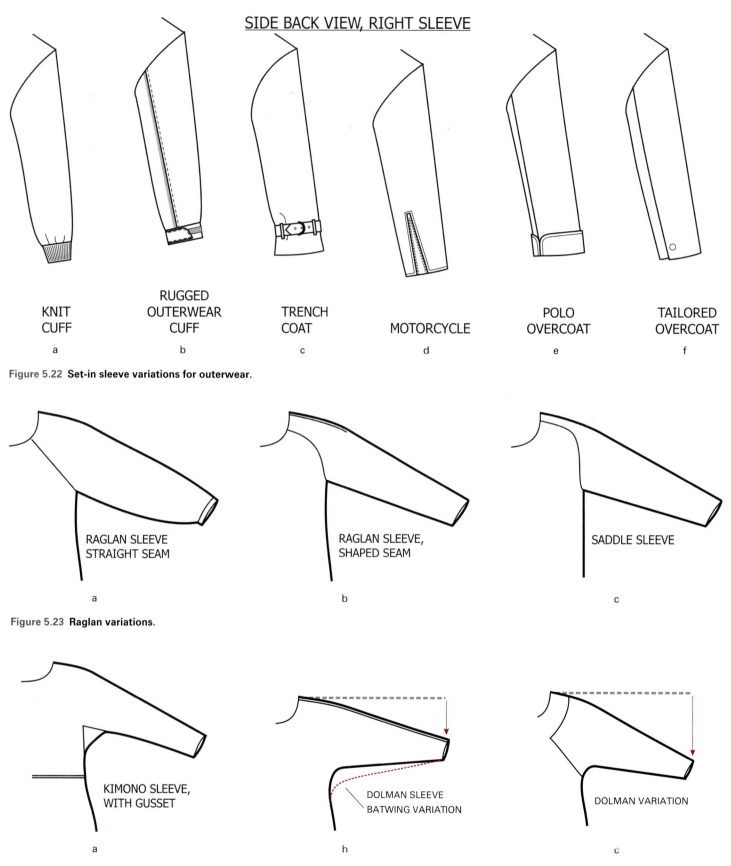

KNIT CUFF	RUGGED OUTERWEAR CUFF	TRENCH COAT	MOTORCYCLE	POLO OVERCOAT	TAILORED OVERCOAT
a	b	c	d	e	f

Figure 5.22 Set-in sleeve variations for outerwear.

RAGLAN SLEEVE STRAIGHT SEAM	RAGLAN SLEEVE, SHAPED SEAM	SADDLE SLEEVE
a	b	c

Figure 5.23 Raglan variations.

KIMONO SLEEVE, WITH GUSSET	DOLMAN SLEEVE BATWING VARIATION	DOLMAN VARIATION
a	b	c

Figure 5.24 Kimono or dolman sleeve.

achieve a classic fit. A gusset is a small diamond-shaped insert at the underarm, added to introduce lift and more freedom of movement. This type of sleeve was extremely popular in the 1950s and 1960s when garment shoulders were soft and unpadded. Ironically, an actual Japanese kimono does not have this style of sleeve, but rather a set-in drop shoulder style, as in Figure 5.16c.

The **dolman sleeve** (also called a batwing sleeve) is a variation on the kimono sleeve, but with no gusset. The dolman (see Figure 5.24b), with no armhole seam at all, is fitted at the wrist. This sleeve is not easy to place onto a marker and uses a lot of fabric. A variation with an even deeper armhole is called a batwing. Designed with a seam down the arm, it has a lot of design possibilities, especially with directional fabrics such as stripes because a miter is created there.

With the dolman sleeve, there is a lot of freedom regarding where to place the seams, as seen in the dolman variation (see Figure 5.24c). The angle of the sleeve is very important, based on the exact fabric being proposed. The dolman sleeve (see Figure 5.24b) has a straighter angle than the dolman variation (see Figure 5.24c) and will end up with more fabric at the underarm when the wearer's arm is lowered. Dolman sleeves are adaptable to different fabric weights, but the sleeve shown in Figure 5.24c will have less bulk at the underarm. The trade-off is that there will be less freedom to lift the arm.

Necklines

Necklines are one of the most important design features that determine the style of the garment. There are many neckline variations, and this section features just a few of them.

Shapes of Necklines

Figure 5.25 shows the most common necklines:

- *Square neck*: Any square shape from narrow to wide, shallow to deep (see Figure 5.25a).

- *Crew neck*: Usually finished with ribbed trim and sits at the base of the neck. Also the style of neck on a standard T-shirt. Must be in a knit fabric to allow for stretching over the head (see Figure 5.25b).
- *Keyhole neckline*: Includes a type of closure and can be used as a back opening as well (see Figure 5.25c).

Figure 5.26 shows more necklines:

- *V-neckline*: Includes wide variations of styles based on the depth and width of the neck shape (see Figure 5.26a).
- *Scoop neckline*: Compared to crew neck, it is a low-curved neckline. A great many variations are possible based on the exact dimensions (see Figure 5.26b).
- *Sweetheart neckline*: Low neckline with a heart shape at the center front; a popular neckline in the 1940s (see Figure 5.26c).

Figure 5.27 shows examples of more necklines:

- *Ballet neckline*: A wide, round shape; a common style for a dance leotard (see Figure 5.27a).
- *Bateau neckline* (also called boat neck): A high, wide shape adapted from a French sailors' sweater (see Figure 5.27b).
- *Cowl neckline*: One or more folds introduced into the neck shape (see Figure 5.27c). May be high or low, and may also be used as a back detail. Cowls work best when cut on the true bias, or on soft and drapable fabrics.

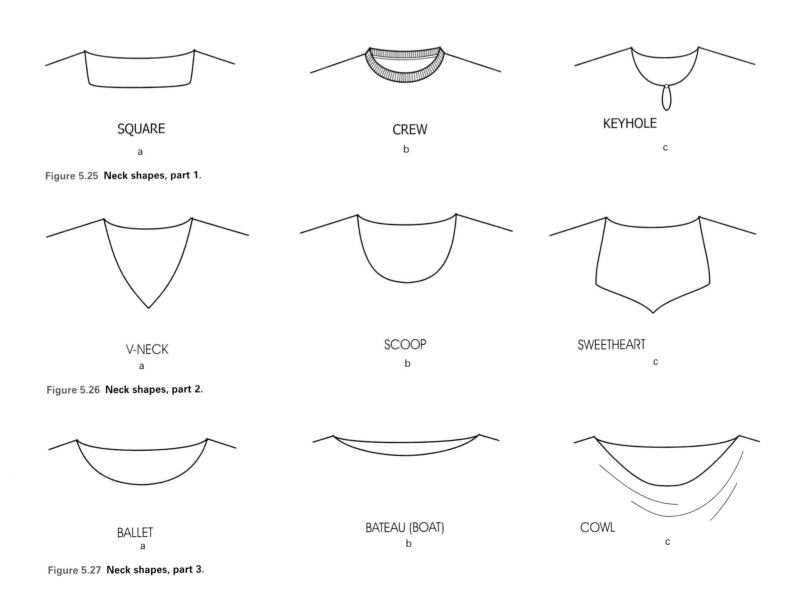

SQUARE
a

CREW
b

KEYHOLE
c

Figure 5.25 Neck shapes, part 1.

V-NECK
a

SCOOP
b

SWEETHEART
c

Figure 5.26 Neck shapes, part 2.

BALLET
a

BATEAU (BOAT)
b

COWL
c

Figure 5.27 Neck shapes, part 3.

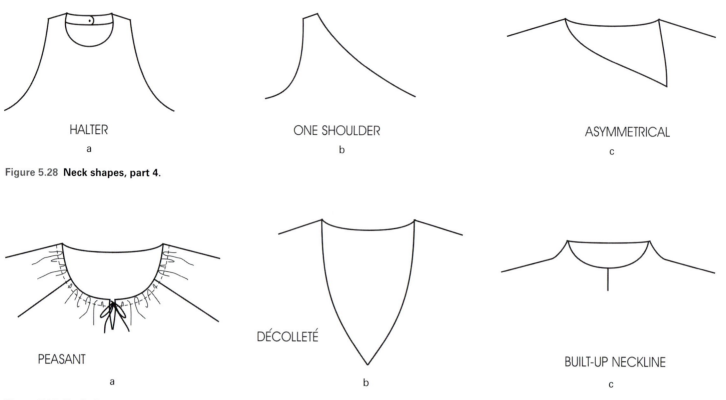

HALTER
a

ONE SHOULDER
b

ASYMMETRICAL
c

Figure 5.28 Neck shapes, part 4.

PEASANT
a

DÉCOLLETÉ
b

BUILT-UP NECKLINE
c

Figure 5.29 Neck shapes, part 5.

Figure 5.28 shows more styles of necklines:

- *Halter neckline*: Designed to bare the shoulders and upper back by sharply reducing the shoulder line (see Figure 5.28a). It is usually fastened at the back neck.
- *One shoulder neckline*: Often has gathers or other elements of dart shaping (see Figure 5.28b).
- *Asymmetrical neckline*: Any of a number of novelty shapes where the left half is shaped differently from the right (see Figure 5.28c).

Figure 5.29 shows more variations of neck shape:

- *Peasant neckline*: The neck edge is gathered and is used in conjunction with a raglan sleeve (see Figure 5.29a).
- *Décolleté neckline*: Any style of low-cut, revealing neckline (see Figure 5.29b). This shows a low, curved V, but sweetheart and other shapes are used as well.
- *Built-up neckline* (also called *funnel*): Extends above the base of the neck (see Figure 5.29c). It must include accommodations

for the neck as it sits forward. The version here has a center front seam for that purpose.

Technical Aspect of Neck Design

The specific measurements of a neck shape are of primary importance to the style. Figure 5.30 shows a typical set of measurements that would be used for a jewel neck, a simple style designed to sit right at the base of the neck. The sketch includes the way the measurements would be written in the tech pack for a sample size 8, medium for women's wear.

The *front neck drop* is important for comfort and should not sit too high, especially for a woven fabric. A knit fabric has a little more leeway, but still has to feel comfortable at the throat. The *back neck drop* should create a smooth shape around the high point shoulder (HPS). Here, the neck width is narrow, so the back neck drop is fairly high.

A narrow *neck width* is part of what gives the jewel neck its characteristic shape. If it became too wide, it would no longer be a

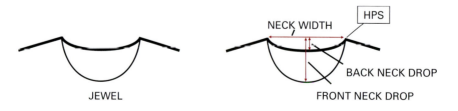

NECK WIDTH

HPS

BACK NECK DROP

FRONT NECK DROP

JEWEL

POINTS of MEASURE	Tol (+)	Tol (-)	size 8
Front Neck Drop, HPS to edge	1/4	1/4	3
Back Neck Drop, HPS to edge	1/4	1/4	1
Neck Width, edge to edge	1/4	1/4	6

Figure 5.30 Specs for typical jewel neckline.

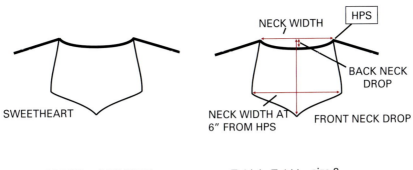

POINTS to MEASURE	Tol (+)	Tol (-)	size 8
Front Neck Drop, HPS to edge	1/4	1/4	10 1/4
Back Neck Drop, HPS to edge	1/4	1/4	3/4
Neck Width, edge to edge	1/4	1/4	6 1/2
Neck Width, AT 6" from HPS	1/4	1/4	10

Figure 5.31 **Specs for sweetheart neckline.**

jewel neck. The measurements for a typical jewel neckline appear below the sketches, just as they would appear in the tech pack. Notice that the measurements are from HPS. There is no closure shown, but this style of neck in a woven fabric would require a placket, zipper, or other method for getting it on over the head. A knit fabric may be able to be pulled over the head, but that would have to be tested on a sample in the actual fabric and would require a fabric with a lot of stretch.

When the neck style has more shaping involved, such as a sweetheart neckline, additional points of measure can be added to achieve the desired look (see Figure 5.31). In this case, the first three are the standard measurements, the same as in the jewel neck, and the fourth one, neck width at 6 inches from HPS, is the one that defines this as a sweetheart neckline. Notice that the 6 inches referred to is the *position from HPS*, and not the width. Another way to say it would be, "Neckline is 10 inches wide at a point 6 inch down from HPS."

Collars

A collar is a band or construction that finishes off the neck edge of a garment and provides many options for styling. It can be permanently attached or removable. In outerwear styles, the collar is important for protection from wind and water.

Collar Styles

Figures 5.32 through 5.36 show a selection of commonly seen collar shapes. Some are more useful for knit styles, and Figure

5.32 shows three examples: polo (see Figure 5.32a), mock turtle (see Figure 5.32b), and Henley (see Figure 5.32c). The *polo* style is seen here with a "flat knit" collar, often used for golf wear. This version of the style is not cut and sewn, but is actually a single layer of knit, ordered separately from the fabric. The **mock turtle** (or *mock neck*) is a close-fitting collar, usually knit, but sometimes in woven fabric (see Figure 5.32b). The Henley is a finished binding that ends in a button placement (see Figure 5.32c). It is often used for long underwear styles for men, women, and children.

The *tailored shirt collar* is an important style in men's shirts (see Figure 5.33). The collar has two parts when sewn: a *collarband* (also called *collar stand*) and the *collar*. The exact length of the collarband, which encircles the neck, is very important; in fact, men purchase shirts according to this measurement, rather than a chest measurement. How is that possible? It is because the collar and cuffs are the only places on a shirt where the garment fits close to the body, and the other measurements are developed proportionately to the neck girth.

Women's sizing methods do not have any such equivalent, and a dress size cannot be selected by a woman's neck measurement. There are too many other more important fit points (bust, waist, and hip) and too many other styling variations to make a measurement such as neck size meaningful.

The **convertible collar** seen in Figures 5.33b and 5.33c has no stand and has more or less roll, depending on the collar pattern. The straighter the neck edge of the collar pattern, the greater the

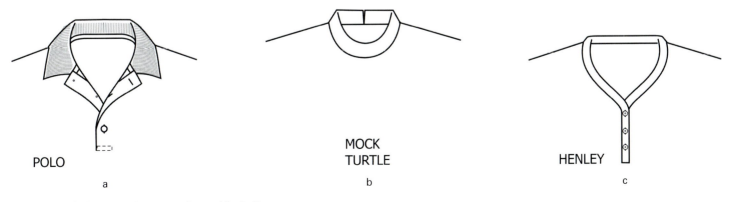

POLO

a

MOCK TURTLE

b

HENLEY

c

Figure 5.32 **Collars, part 1, commonly used for knits.**

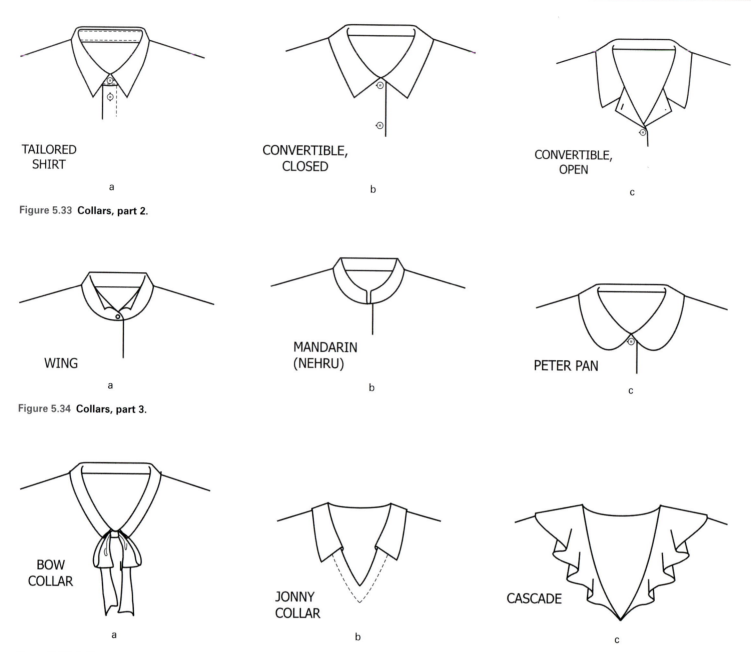

TAILORED
SHIRT
a

CONVERTIBLE,
CLOSED
b

CONVERTIBLE,
OPEN
c

Figure 5.33 Collars, part 2.

WING
a

MANDARIN
(NEHRU)
b

PETER PAN
c

Figure 5.34 Collars, part 3.

BOW
COLLAR
a

JONNY
COLLAR
b

CASCADE
c

Figure 5.35 Collars, part 4.

stand, and the more curved the neck edge, the flatter the collar will lie. It is also called a *pajama collar* or *Hawaiian shirt collar*. The *Peter Pan collar* (Figure 5.34c) is developed exactly the same as the convertible (see Figure 5.33b), except that a different shape is given at the outer edge (rounded instead of pointed).

The wing collar (see Figure 5.34a) has certain technical similarities with the Mandarin collar in that the collar pattern is very straight. The **wing collar** is a high, stiff, tailored shirt, or blouse collar with spread points turning down in front, a style worn by Eton College upperclassmen and sometimes worn for daytime formal wear in the late nineteenth and early twentieth centuries.

A **Mandarin collar**, also called a **Chinese collar** or **Nehru collar** (see Figure 5.34b), is a standing band collar, the front edges of which do not quite meet at center front. Nehru collars, named for the late Indian prime minister, were briefly popular on men's suits in the 1960s.

The **bow collar** (see Figure 5.35a) has many variations for length and width, and its success depends on a soft fabric. It has

extended ends sewn to the neckline with the stand-up band. The style was introduced in the 1920s and has often been popular since. The **jonny collar** (also called *Italian collar*) is a very simple way to attach a collar to a neckline (see Figure 5.35b). The collar is sewn between the body and a facing. The facing is then turned to the inside. The **cascade collar** is a type of circular ruffle attached at the neck seam, which has many variations and sometimes reaches to the waistline (see Figure 5.35c).

The **bertha collar** is a type of oversize collar, round at the outside edge, sometimes made of lace (see Figure 5.36a). A variation called a **pilgrim collar** is open at the front. It can be made in an oversize version, extending past the armscye, and would then be called a *cape collar*. The **sailor collar** (see Figure 5.36b) is used for children's styles, school uniforms, and costumes. It comes into style for women every so often when a schoolgirl look is desired. The **shawl collar** (see Figure 5.36c) is a two-piece collar without separate lapels. It is a versatile shape because the collar follows the front opening of the garment. It can be narrow or wide, and the crossover point can be high or low. Figure 5.40 shows additional shawl collar variations.

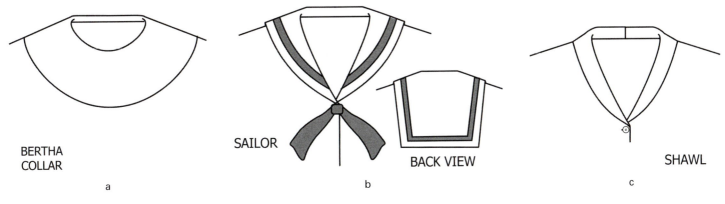

BERTHA
COLLAR

a

SAILOR

BACK VIEW

b

SHAWL

c

Figure 5.36 Collars, part 5.

Technical Aspects of Collar Design

The method for specifying the neck dimensions for collars involves the same three points of measure as for necklines, with one difference for a men's tailored shirt that has *collarband length* rather than neck width. As noted earlier in this chapter, men's dress shirts are actually sized by the collar measurement; a traditional dress shirt sizing would be given as 16$^{1}/_{2}$, 34 (neck size, sleeve length). Figure 5.37 shows specific points of measure for a women's size 8 shirt collar with no collarband, as it would appear in the tech pack.

Tailored Collars

Tailored collars have many subtle variations and specialized terms and points of measure related to the collar details. The lapel width and shape, the position of the **gorge**, which is a seam where the collar meets the lapel in tailored garments, and many other points create harmony on a tailored garment, and a small variation makes a big difference. Figure 5.38 shows some of the more common lapel configurations.

Review the terminology in Figure 5.39 and then locate all the points of measure below on an actual garment. To find the actual HPS, the collar would be first flipped up. Three additional standard points of measure are not shown in the diagram: back neck drop, center back collar height, and neck width. More information on points of measure and how to measure can be found in Chapter 15.

Shawl Collars

Figure 5.40 shows variations of shawl collars. Shawl collars involve much less sewing and labor than tailored collars. Because the outer edge is faced, there is a great deal of freedom in the choice of collar shape. Figure 5.40d shows a shaped shawl style that mimics a tailored lapel, although it requires careful clipping and pressing. The distinguishing characteristic of a shawl collar is a center back seam. The *revere collar* (see Figure 5.40e) is not technically a shawl, but has a similar appearance from the front.

POINTS of MEASURE	Tol (+)	Tol (-)	neck size 16 1/2
Front Neck Drop, fm HPS	1/4	1/4	4
Back Neck Drop, fm HPS	1/4	1/4	1/2
Collarband Length, button to end of buttonhole	1/4	1/4	16 1/2
Collar Spread	1/4	1/4	3 1/2
Center Back Collar Height	1/8	1/8	3
Collar Point	1/8	1/8	2 3/4

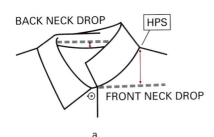

BACK NECK DROP   HPS

FRONT NECK DROP

a

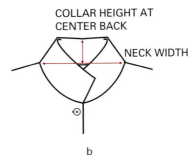

COLLAR HEIGHT AT
CENTER BACK

NECK WIDTH

b

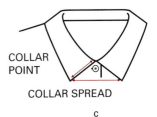

COLLAR
POINT

COLLAR SPREAD

c

Figure 5.37 Specifying collars.

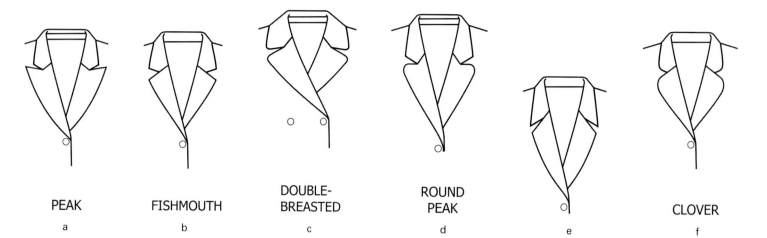

PEAK	FISHMOUTH	DOUBLE-BREASTED	ROUND PEAK		CLOVER
a	b	c	d	e	f

Figure 5.38 **Lapel styles.**

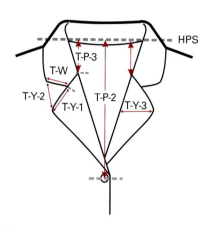

code	POINTS of MEASURE	Tol (+)	Tol (-)	size 8
T-P-2	Front neck drop, HPS top button	1/4	1/4	11
T-P-3	Gorge position	1/4	1/4	3
T-W	Collar Point	1/4	1/4	1 3/8
T-Y-1	Lapel point	1/8	1/8	2 1/4
T-Y-2	Lapel point to collar point	1/4	1/4	1 3/4
T-Y-3	Lapel Width	1/4	1/4	4 1/4

Figure 5.39 **Points of measure for tailored collars.**

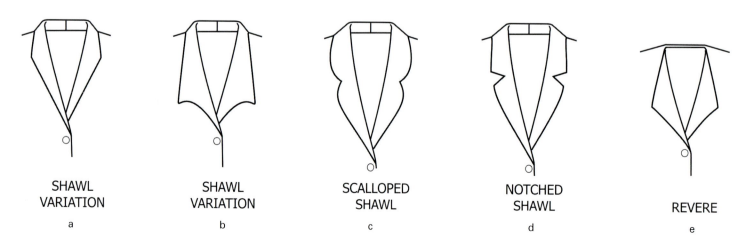

SHAWL VARIATION	SHAWL VARIATION	SCALLOPED SHAWL	NOTCHED SHAWL	REVERE
a	b	c	d	e

Figure 5.40 **Shawl collar variations.**

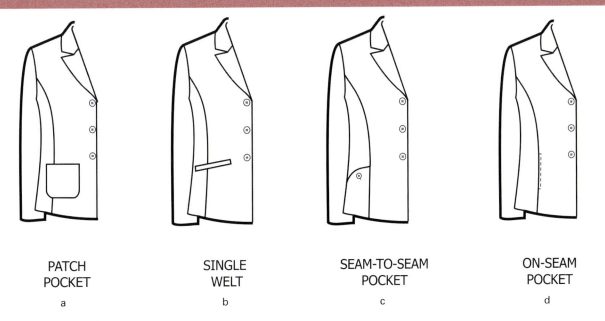

PATCH POCKET	SINGLE WELT	SEAM-TO-SEAM POCKET	ON-SEAM POCKET
a	b	c	d

Figure 5.41 **Pocket types.**

Pockets

Pockets are an important component for apparel design. The four types of pockets (see Figure 5.41) are patch pockets, welt pockets, seam-to-seam pockets, and on-seam pockets, and they can be combined. Many more pockets and pocket construction details can be found in Chapter 11.

Summary

As we explored in this chapter, silhouettes and design details are used in apparel design to create a unique and fashionable product. Using the correct terminology in written and oral communication to specify each of these silhouettes and design details is essential for delivering the designed results. The styles presented here are just a brief sampling of all the ones that have been developed over the years.

Study Questions

1. Select your favorite pair of denim jeans. Label the different parts of your jeans with the terminology used for jeans in drawing.

2. Select one shirt from your wardrobe. Label the different parts of your shirt with the terminology used for shirts in drawing. Bring one tailored jacket from your wardrobe. Work in a group of two in your class. Using tailored jacket terminology, name the parts of your and your partner's jackets. Are any key terms missing? Check against Figure 5.3.

3. How can you specify the measurements of a tailored jacket? Create a spec page for a tailored jacket.

4. Select one of your favorite necklines or collar styles for women's wear for a target market of women in their 30s to 50s. Create a spec page for the neckline or collar.

5. What are the current fashion trends of dress silhouette by waist position? Visit your favorite Internet retailer and print out one representative style. Write your ideas about the current fashion trends of the waist position.

6. What are the current fashion trends of silhouettes based on length? Visit your favorite Internet retailer and print out one representative style. Write your explanation about the current fashion trends.

7. What is the current fashion trend for sleeve types? Visit your favorite Internet retailer and print out one representative style. Write your explanation about the current fashion trends.

8. What is the current trend for neck shape? Visit your favorite Internet retailer and print out one representative style. Write your explanation about the current fashion trends.

9. Design and specify five different necklines for a woman's casual T-shirt.

10. What are the three main types of sleeve shape? How are they different? What are the specs used for each sleeve type? Why are they different?

11. Refer to the *Technical Sourcebook for Apparel Designers STUDIO*. Select the neckline from #12: Caftan and put it onto #11: Cheongsam body. What are the five points of measure needed for the new style?

Check Your Understanding

1. List and define the terminology used to design pants.

2. List and define the terminology used to design shirts.

3. Compare the specs used for crew neck and V-neck.

4. Identify six classic dress silhouettes in drawing and explain the differences for each.

5. Identify six different dress silhouettes by waist position in drawing and explain the differences for each.

References

Calasibetta, C. M., and P. Tortora. 2003. *The Fairchild Dictionary of Fashion* (3rd ed.). New York: Fairchild Books.

Callan, G. O. and O'Hara G. 1986. *The Encyclopedia of Fashion* (1st Ed.). Reed Business Information, Inc.

Styles, Lines, and Details for Shape and Fit

Chapter Objectives

After studying this chapter, you will be able to:

- Identify various styles, lines, and details used for shaping
- Communicate various styles, lines, and details orally and in writing
- Explore various garment shaping devices and how they are specified in the technical package
- Examine fashion trends in analyzing design features related to the body shape and fit
- Apply various design features in the creative designing process

---

Key Terms

accordion pleating	French darts	pleat depth
box pleats	gathering	pleats
casing	gathering ratio	princess seam
cluster pleats	godet	shirring
crystal pleats	gores	slit
dart	gusset	sunburst pleating
dart depth	inverted pleats	tailored knot
dart folding	knife pleats	tuck depth
dart length	lacing	tucks
drawcord	miter	vent
easing	pin tucks	yoke

This chapter provides information on various styles, line, and design details related to the shape and fit of the garment. It explores darts and dart substitutes with example sketches. Also demonstrated are the types of specifications needed to achieve the required shapes.

Garment Shaping Devices: Darts and Others

Fabric is two dimensional, yet the human body is three dimensional; therefore, important devices have been developed throughout the years to create garments that adapt fabric to the body shape. Different shaping devices are used in apparel making to incorporate and enhance the shape of the body and provide an appealing fit for each body type.

A major shaping device is a dart, which is used near the area of waist, hip, and bust to incorporate the contour of the body. Other shaping devices are called *dart equivalents*, *dart replacements*, or *dart substitutes*, terms that are used interchangeably. Shaping devices used in garment production include the following:

- Darts
- Tucks
- Pleats
- Gathers
- Easing
- Elastic
- Drawcord
- Lacing
- Princess seam
- Gores
- Yoke
- Godet
- Gusset
- Slit or vent

Darts

A **dart** is a method used to take up excess fabric to incorporate the shape of the body. It consists of a fold of fabric doubled back on itself, and tapered to a point, which allows the garment to fit more closely to the curved shapes of the body. It is a useful and popular fitting device, and has many variations.

Single- and Double-Pointed Darts

A single-pointed dart, positioned at the bust and waist, is somewhat triangular in shape. A double-pointed dart has more of an elongated diamond shape (see Figure 6.1).

To add additional fitting at the waist, a double-pointed dart (also called a *diamond dart*) can be used as well. However, it is important to note that the depth of a double-pointed dart cannot be as great as a single-pointed dart because after a certain point, it would require clipping to avoid distortion. Clipping is usually not recommended because there is no way to finish the raw edge created by the clip, and it is prone to raveling. Double-pointed darts are almost always vertical, and the fold of a vertical dart is placed toward the center of the garment, either center front or center back.

An important construction detail on darts is at the end where it is stitched off. One must take care to avoid having the end stitching break, which could cause the dart point to unravel, and yet this area is difficult to backstitch. So the dart is stitched very close to the edge for the last few stitches and then 1 inch of thread is left (see Figure 6.1a). The thread should not be clipped closely here, or the result will be seam failure at the dart point (see Figures 6.1b and 6.1c). The **tailored knot**, tied at the dart point, is used to provide good apparel quality.

Technical Aspects of Dart Design

Many terms are used to describe darts. Figure 6.1a shows the main terms used to specify the measurements in the tech pack: *dart depth* and *dart length*. **Dart depth** is measured at the seam line (not at the cut edge) and the **dart length** is measured from

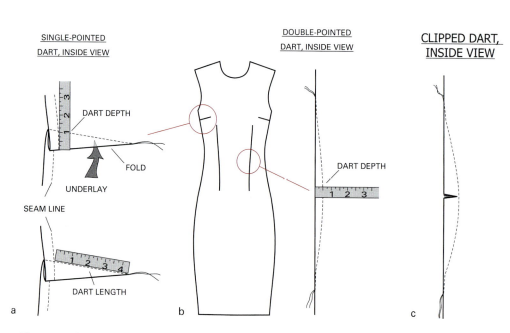

Figure 6.1 Single- and double-pointed darts.

the seam to the point of the dart (see Figure 6.1a). The most common place for the dart to begin is at a seam, as in the single-pointed bust dart (see Figure 6.1a). The underlay is the part underneath, and the fold of a horizontal dart is usually down, as shown. **Dart folding** is one detail that requires special attention from the designer. All the vertical darts, such as waist, neck, and hip darts, should be folded toward the center front and center back. On the other hand, horizontal darts, such as bust darts, should be folded toward the bottom of the garment.

How darts are used changes according to the current silhouette, and designers can incorporate different darts to achieve different shapes. Figure 6.2 shows the fit comparison between a sheath dress with a waist seam and one without. The waist seam, as in Figure 6.2a, allows for a very tightly fitted waist and uses a large waist dart. The use of double-pointed darts in Figure 6.2c creates a more blended transition between the bodice and skirt areas whereas Figure 6.2b shows the comparison of both Figures 6.2a and 6.2c. Figure 6.2a shows a method that may be used to exaggerate a small waist and the curve of the hip when such a look is in style. This was a popular look in the 1950s and 1960s, and will undoubtedly be popular again.

Tucks

Tucks are the take-up of fabric by stitching through parallel folds, usually evenly spaced. Tucks are used to create a controlled amount of fullness. They add to creation costs because they require extra labor to sew and press them. Figure 6.3a shows the fullness controlled through the waist and released above and below. Figure 6.3b has the fullness released into the sleeve cap area and Figure 6.3c has more and deeper tucks, creating a fuller skirt as more fabric is released. Tucks are not pressed below the stitching, which, as you will see, distinguishes them from pleats.

Pin Tucks

Pin tucks are very narrow tucks, $1/8$ inch or less. They can be used as dart substitutes for shaping or as decorative devices. Pin tucks are often used as inserts. Single pin tucks can also be used on pants to create a permanent crease line. The horizontal tucks in Figure 6.4a have no shaping effect; they are used as a texture emphasis. If the style is intended to be fitted, other dart shaping can be added, such as the bust dart seen here at the armhole line. Figure 6.4b shows the tucks radiating along different angles, which works if the tucks are short and are used as a shaping device to incorporate the contour of the bust. Figure 6.4c shows the pin tucks used for dart shaping so the garment does not need an extra bust dart. In Figures 6.4b and 6.4c, note that the tucks capture the fullness above or below, and release it into the bust area.

Technical Aspects of Tuck Design

Designers need to clearly specify design details and specifications of tucks, including position, length, and depth. Figure 6.4d and

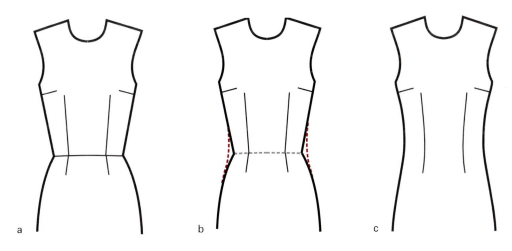

Figure 6.2 Variations of fit with and without a waist seam.

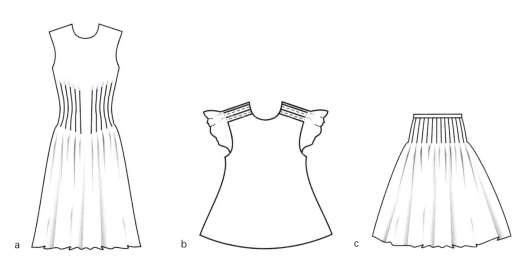

Figure 6.3 Tucks in various areas.

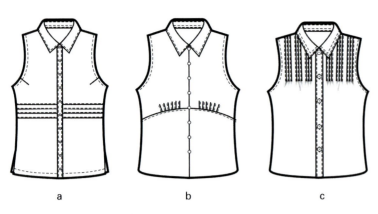

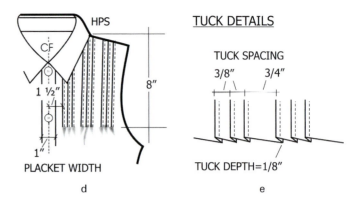

Figure 6.4 **Pin tuck variations.**

6.4e show how tucks are formed, their position on the garment, and how they would be specified on the detail page of a tech pack. **Tuck depth** (which in this case is $^1/_8$ inch) means the total folding of the tuck, measured on the face side of the completed garment.

To specify the first tuck placement, the center front is used as a standard anchor line, and the first tuck is placed $1^1/_2$ inches away from the center front. Because tucks are placed symmetrically on both sides (wearer's left and right side; see Figure 6.4c), the placement is given from center front (Figure 6.4d). The tucks are spaced $^3/_8$ inch apart within the set of three, and each set is placed $^3/_4$ inch away from the next set (see Figure 6.4e). Figure 6.4c shows a total of three sets of tucks placed on each side for a total of six sets for the garment.

The total length of tuck is specified as "All tucks end at 8" from HPS." In sum, the specs related to the styles are given as in Table 6.1. Even a simple arrangement such as in Figure 6.4c requires that all the tuck details be stated to ensure that the prototype will return exactly as desired. Clearly, a detail sketch can provide a lot of information with few words. It is an important part of the process to creatively and effectively communicate the design details with all the professionals involved in production of the garments.

Pleats

Pleats are any of various folds of fabric that are formed by doubling the fabric back on itself, fixed at one end by pressing, stitching, or anchoring in a seam, and released at the other. They are used at the waist and shoulder, across the back, and at the hipline for fitting. They can be used elsewhere for detail. All-around pleats, or pleat insertions, are a common shaping device for skirts. Pleats are useful and attractive, and some variation of the pleated skirt is always in style. The following types of pleats are explored in this section of the chapter:

- Knife pleats
- Box pleats and inverted pleats
- Cluster pleats
- Mechanically engineered pleats (accordion, crystal, sunburst)
- Shaped pleats (straight, contoured, tapered)
- Pleats with design details (side, action, style, kick pleats)

Technical Aspects of Pleat Design

Creating pleats in garment construction needs careful instruction. To clearly communicate design details of pleats it is first essential

Table 6.1   **Specs for Tucks Shown in Figure 6.4c**

Tuck Specs	Measurements
Tuck depth	$^1/_8$"
Tuck length from HPS	8"
1st tuck position from CF	$1^1/_2$"
Distance b/n tucks w/in the set	$^3/_8$"
Distance b/n sets	$^3/_4$"

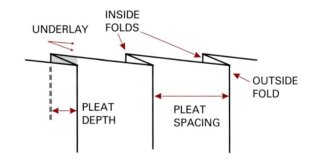

Figure 6.5 **Pleat terminology.**

to understand the terminology used in specifying pleat details. Figure 6.5 illustrates several terms used in specifying pleats. **Pleat depth** is the distance from the outside fold to the inside fold. *Pleat spacing* is the distance between one pleat and the next on the outside. These are the two key distances in specifying the pleat in technical design terms and will be noted on the tech pack in a sketch (see Figure 6.5).

Pleats can be placed in various areas. Figure 6.6 shows some standard uses of pleats for men's and women's woven shirts. Figure 6.6a shows how to specify the pleat depth and position for a cuff pleat. Pleats are also used at the back yoke to provide ease in movement (see Figures 6.6b and 6.6c). Figure 6.6b shows a close-up of the method for drawing the pleat depth. In this case, the exact position is not specified because it is understood that the detail is at center back.

Types of Pleats

Pleats are often used to form an entire skirt and are laid out in different arrangements. This section describes different types of pleats and how they are measured.

CUFF PLEAT DETAILS

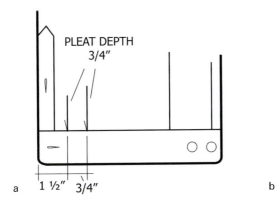

Figure 6.6 Pleat details in cuff and back yoke.

Knife Pleats

Single pleats turned in the same direction are called *flat pleats* or *side pleats*. Figure 6.7a shows this type, which is often seen in traditional kilts. When this type of one-direction pleat is 1 inch or narrower, it is called a **knife pleat**. This type of pleat is not suitable for stretchy, bulky, or napped fabrics with which it is hard to achieve a crisp press; rather it's best suited for woven fabrics that can take a sharp press.

Box Pleats and Inverted Pleats

Figure 6.6 illustrates **inverted pleats** and **box pleats**, in which the pleats are evenly spaced and pressed in alternate directions. The reverse side of inverted pleats is similar to box pleats. Inverted pleats are reversed so that the fullness is turned inward. Another definition of an inverted pleat is one in which the folds of fabric meet each other at a central point on the face side of the garment.

Figure 6.6.c shows a single inverted pleat. Note that the structure and dimensions of the pleat are the same, whether it is box side out (box pleat) or box side on the wrong side (inverted pleat).

Cluster Pleats

Figure 6.7c shows a type of double pleat formation known as **cluster pleats**, which means pleats are arranged in groups. It is usually made by a combination of a large box pleat and several small knife pleats on either side (Calasibetta and Tortora, 2003). Because of the extra care and precision involved in this type of pleat, it is considered a quality indicator and is more costly to construct than less complex types.

Mechanically Engineered Pleats

Other types of narrow pleats are formed with special equipment and are heat-set permanently.

- **Accordion pleating** creates a narrow pleat that fits close to the body, similar to the musical instrument (see Figure 6.8a). The panels are cut to a predetermined length, and the bottom opening edge is hemmed prior to pleating.

- Figure 6.8b shows a technique called **sunburst pleating** in which the pleats widen from one edge to the other, meaning pleats are smaller at the top but larger at the bottom hem. This type of pleating creates a full silhouette without bulk at the top edge and works well for lightweight fabrics, especially synthetic fibers and those that can be heat-set permanently. Cut panels are set with an industrial pleating machine; this technique can be used for an entire garment, as an insert (see Figure 6.8c), an edge ruffle, or a sleeve. As with accordion pleats, the panel is hemmed before pleating.

- Similar to but narrower than accordion pleats, **crystal pleats** are a series of very narrow, parallel pleats, used when a slim straight silhouette is desired. They can also be used on flounces and ruffles and can be set into a partial length of fabric, such as a border, to create a novelty effect. The panel can be hemmed before or after pleating; if the panel is hemmed after pleating, it creates a ruffled effect at the hemmed edge. The unhemmed edge is controlled by a facing or style line (see Figure 6.8c).

Designers' Choices of Pleats

Given the various pleats available, designers must carefully select the right pleats to complement the styles of their apparel products.

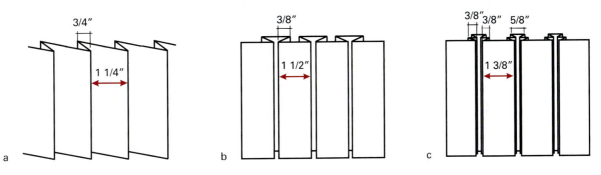

Figure 6.7 Knife (a), box (b), and cluster (c) pleats.

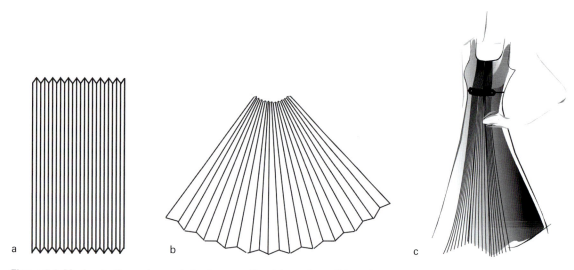

Figure 6.8 **Mechanically engineered pleats: accordion (a), sunburst (b), and crystal (c).**

Pleat Shapes

The shape of pleats can be characterized as straight, contoured, or tapered.

- *Straight pleats*: Pleats can be used without shaping in which the pleats have the same width from top to bottom (see Figure 6.9a). In this skirt, they are attached to a hip yoke, which provides all the shaping.

- *Contoured pleats*: Figure 6.9b shows the pleats transitioning into darts at the hipline. The dart shaping is added to the underlay, from hip to waist, as needed. Here, the examples are contoured inverted pleats and the shaping is transferred to the seams, at the dart areas at side front and side back. For a style with many pleats, the dart depth amount is divided among the pleats.

- *Tapered pleats*: The pleats can also taper to create flare. Figure 6.9c shows a separate underlay panel added, narrow at the waistline (or hip) and wider at the bottom. Sunburst pleats (see Figure 6.8b) are also considered tapered pleats.

Placement Variations for Design Detail

Side pleats, action pleats, style pleats, and kick pleats are placement options that vary the design detail of a garment.

- *Side pleats* are single pleats used to create extra room for movement. The most common location is at the back yoke of a men's shirt (see Figure 6.10a).

- *Action pleats* usually extend into a seam (Figure 6.10b). This style is used for jackets and helps to create a slim fit that still is not too tight across the back. A common place to see this detail is at the back of a leather motorcycle jacket.

- *Style pleats* (see Figure 6.10c) take a different approach, in which a style detail also incorporates a comfortable fit across the back through the addition of multiple pleats.

- A *kick pleat* is a special pleat used at the bottom of a straight skirt to allow ease in walking. It is placed at knee level or slightly below (see Figure 6.11) and is usually a single flat pleat or one knife pleat (Calasibetta and Tortora, 2003). As with many functional details, kick pleats can be integrated into the garment in other ways as well. Figure 6.12 shows three of the many possible methods in which the function of the kick pleat is also part of the styling.

Fabric Estimate for Pleats

Pleats use a significant amount of fabric compared to an unpleated garment. The formula for all-around pleats is

The total width = (twice the underlay depth) × (the number of pleats) + (the hip circumference) + 2 inches of ease

In planning a pleated garment, if price is an issue, less fabric can be used by decreasing the underlay depth; however, if it becomes too small, it can look skimpy. As with most elements of design, a balance must be reached between cost and details.

 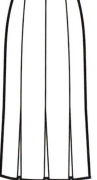 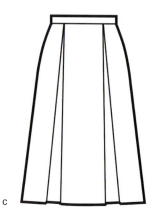

Figure 6.9 **Shaped pleats: straight (a), contoured (b), or tapered (c).**

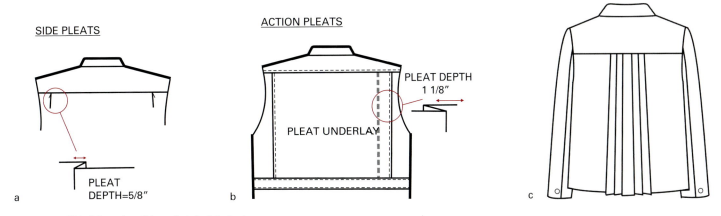

SIDE PLEATS

ACTION PLEATS

PLEAT DEPTH
1 1/8″

PLEAT UNDERLAY

PLEAT
DEPTH=5/8″

a   b   c

Figure 6.10 Side (a), action (b), and style (c) pleats.

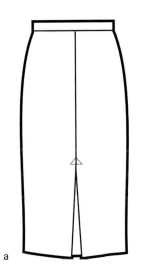

BOX PLEAT

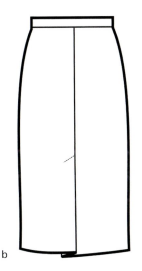

OVERLAY PLEAT

a   b

Figure 6.11 Kick pleats for a skirt.

Gathers

Gathering is the control of a predetermined amount of fullness drawn up to correspond to a smaller adjoining seam line or measurement. Examples of its use are on skirts, sleeve cuffs, and details, and it can also be used as dart shaping. A second type of gathering occurs when extended elastic is sewn to fabric; gathers

are formed when the elastic relaxes. Figure 6.13 shows a few examples of gathered applications. Gathers are a very popular and useful detail with many applications.

Figure 6.13a shows how some of the gathers at center front form a dart substitute (those around the bustline), but are simply decorative lower down on the bodice. The gathered insertion in Figure 6.13b is purely decorative, so other bust shaping must be employed if the garment is intended to have a fitted shape. In this case, the style has bust darts. Figure 6.13c shows how the gathers act as a dart substitute, incorporating the contoured shape of bust, and Figure 6.13d shows how the gathers are used to shape the cuff and provide flare to the sleeve silhouette.

Technical Aspects of Specifying Gathers

The technical aspects of gathers need to be considered to successfully communicate the details of the design desired. The main information concerning gathers that the designer needs to determine is the **gathering ratio**, which is another way of saying "how much gathering." As we learned in the definition of gathers, the fullness on one side of a seam is gathered into the smaller side on the other. So, in Figure 6.13c for example, it must be decided how many gathers are needed in the upper bodice to achieve the look desired. A common place to begin is 1:1.5, or 11/2 times as much fabric for the gathered section as for the flat section. More or less fabric can be introduced as needed. Because the answer is a visual one, the best way to decide the correct ratio is to work with the actual fabric, or something close, and simulate gathers until it looks right.

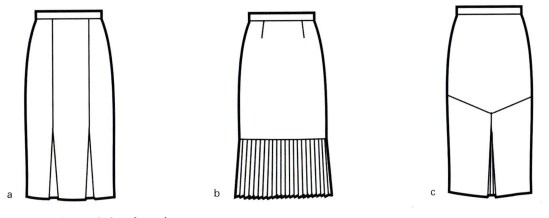

a   b   c

Figure 6.12 Kick pleat variations for style.

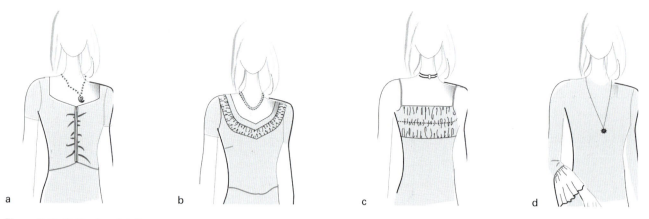

Figure 6.13 Gathering details.

Figure 6.14 shows a little girls' blouse with a gathered ruffle at the top of a patch pocket. The ruffle trim dimensions are given, along with the gathering ratio and ruffle height. In this case, let's come up with the actual length of ruffle panel. With the information in Figure 6.14, how long will the ruffle be cut before it's gathered?

$3\frac{1}{2}$ inches (total pocket width) $\times 1\frac{1}{2}$ (ratio) $\times 5\frac{1}{4}$ inches

The fabric for the ruffle needs to be $5\frac{1}{4}$ inches long, not including the hem at the ends.

Various fabrics have different properties when it comes to gathering. A lighter-weight fabric can handle more gathers, and a heavier-weight style, fewer. Too few gathers will look skimpy; too many will puff outward and add too much bulk. A crisp woven fabric will require different handling from a softer fabric, and gathers too far apart may require another row of control stitching (see Figure 6.13c), centered between the top and bottom in order to create a natural, balanced gather. Lightweight fabrics such as jersey work well for gathering detail.

Application of Gathering

Gathers are often controlled by elastic or a drawcord (also called a *drawstring*) with **casing**, which is a tunnel of fabric. Figure 6.15a shows bust shaping created with elastic stitched directly onto the garment. In the figure, the detail position shown here as beginning 10 inches from high point shoulder (HPS)—as well as the gathering amount, expressed as "relaxed" and "extended"— should be noted because they determine the look and placement of the gathering and affect the fit and fabric usage for the style.

Figure 6.15b is a pull-on pant style; there is no fly front or other waist opening. In this case, to be functional, the waist extended measurement must be large enough to accommodate the hips as the garment is pulled up. Because this detail is a simple and inexpensive way to style a pant, there is sometimes a temptation to use it for a casual woven bottom-weight fabric. Unless the current silhouette allows, however, it can easily get too puffy directly below the waist, which is not always a desirable silhouette for the wearer. This style of waist works best with lightweight fabric, especially ones with some stretch. It is good for summer jogging shorts and pajama bottoms. Figure 6.15c shows a kind of gathering made with elastic thread, an effect called **shirring**. Shirring can also be done with thread or cord. This detail is used for the waist, cuffs, and, of course, for that indispensable garment, the tube top.

In some cases fabric is manufactured with the elastic already in place, for example a full-length skirt style meant to have an elasticized yoke. Note that in all cases when specifying elastics, the relaxed (36 inches in Figure 6.15c) and extended (42 inches in Figure 6.15c) measurements must be provided.

Easing

Easing is a shaping method similar to gathering, but is very subtle and has no visible folds. It can accommodate small darts, but not large ones. It is used to join two seam lines of slightly different lengths, and can be used in place of darting to create a smooth appearance. Figure 6.16 shows a garment where the back

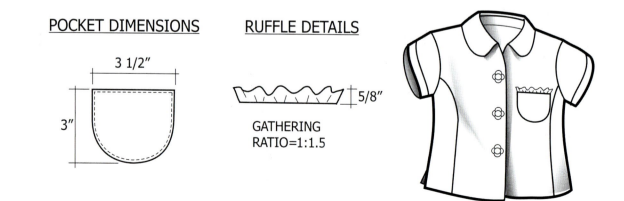

POCKET DIMENSIONS
3 1/2"
3"

RUFFLE DETAILS
5/8"
GATHERING
RATIO=1:1.5

Figure 6.14 Gathering ratio for trim.

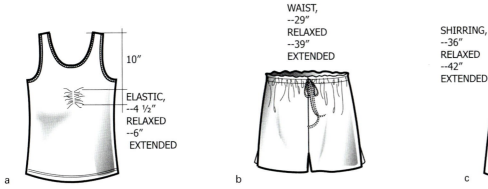

Figure 6.15 **Applications for gathering.**

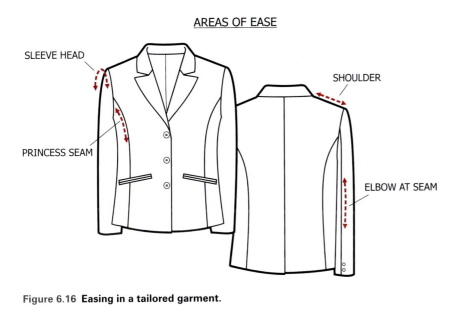

Figure 6.16 **Easing in a tailored garment.**

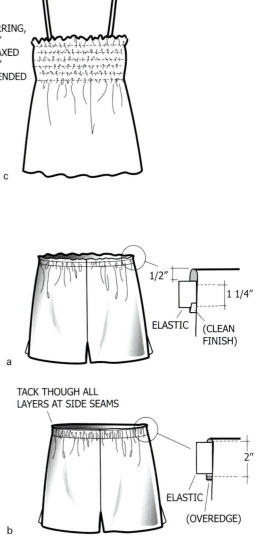

Figure 6.17 **Elastic casing details.**

shoulder seam is longer, and is eased imperceptibly into the front seam while sewing. Usually a sleeve has 1/2 inch total ease evenly distributed in the area of the sleeve head on the armhole line. It takes sewing and pressing skills, and works best with a fabric such as wool. It is employed in the making of tailored garments, in the areas shown in Figure 6.16.

Elastic

An elastic band can be used as a shaping device for gathering at various parts of a garment, such as at the bust and waist (see Figure 6.17). Figures 6.15a and 6.15c show elastic thread directly attached to the body to create a shape. An elastic band can be directly attached to the waist of a garment or to the bottom of a bra, and elastic binding is used to finish the edges of knit garments, such as armholes. In many cases, the band is not showing on the face side of the garment, but elastic can be used as a trim as well, as it is often on lingerie.

Elastic can also be inserted into a casing. The garment in Figure 6.17a is sewn in such a way as to create a ruffle at the upper edge; the second method is a smooth fold at the top (see Figure 6.17b). The same method is used for a cuff. Elastic creates an easy and cost-effective way to shape the garment for various sizes and effects.

Drawcords

A **drawcord** is a string inserted inside the casing of garments where shaping is needed, such as at the waistline, sleeve hem, and neckline. A drawcord can also be used at the waist and provides another measure of adjustability for a garment. Some garments have elastic and a drawcord for maximum comfort. Other areas for drawcords are sweatshirt hoods and other casual styles. Edge casings are usually formed by folding down an extension of the edge itself and then stitching it in place to form the tunnel (see Figure 6.17b).

One special precaution is that drawstrings are not used on children's clothing because they can catch onto objects and lead to serious injury. The risk of entanglement with drawstrings, especially on a hood where it could cause choking, dictates that elastic or other closure method be used instead, such as hook-and-loop.

Lacing

Lacing is a closure similar to the common method for shoes, in which a cord is threaded through finished holes (grommets, loops, or buttonholes). To draw up the closure, the lacing is pulled and tied at the top (see Figure 6.18a). This style can have a rustic or Western look to it, or in another application, a corset feeling.

LACING DETAILS

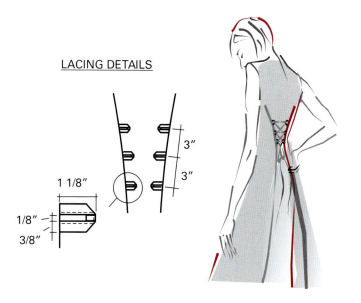

Figure 6.18 Lacing.

Lacing for a fitting device or dart equivalent (see Figure 6.18b) is a type of lacing that uses fabric loops, and the detail sketch shows how the details are specified. Because it requires two hands to manipulate, lacing is not practical as a working cuff closure, although it can be used as a decorative detail.

Seam Shaping

A *seam* is the joining together, by means of stitches, of two or more pieces of material. Seams can be curved or straight. Shaped seams are an important method for taking away extra fabric to conform to the body contours. Seams can be used for fitting, for decorative purposes, or both. There are additional shaping devices—the ones created by modifying structural lines of apparel products—which serve to shape a garment at the seams:

- Princess seams
- Gores
- Yoke
- Godets
- Gussets
- Slits
- Vents

Princess Seam

A **princess seam** is a type of shaped seam; it can include both waist and bust dart shaping. It avoids the "dart end" because it is a seam and, therefore, gives a sleek look and can be very fitted. It is also used for tailored jackets, as in Figure 6.16. Figure 6.29a shows a variation with a straight, rather than the typical curved seam.

Gores

Gores are vertical divisions within a garment, usually tapered panels seamed together for shaping. Skirts are frequently gored, the gores acting as seam shaping in place of darts. Gathers, flare, or other shaping can be combined with gores (see Figure 6.19).

Yoke

A **yoke** is a panel with a horizontal seam and is used for shaping, style, or both. On pants, a yoke helps to create a fitted shape without the use of darts, and most jeans have a back yoke (see Figure 6.20a). Figure 6.20b shows a yoke with no shaping function; it is positioned for style and for construction reasons, giving the zipper a place to terminate. Figure 6.20c has a decorative two-piece yoke with a shaped bottom, and is cut so that the stripes form a **miter** (lines in patterns or stripes that meet in a V shape at a seamline at center back).

In specifying yokes, the position and shape are the key elements needed. Figure 6.20a shows a jeans-style back yoke, noting the yoke height desired at side seams and center back is sufficient, and the yoke seam itself is a straight line. Figure 6.20b shows the yoke seam position from HPS is all that needs specifying.

In a complicated yoke (see Figure 6.20c), the detail sketch in Figure 6.21 provides the additional measurements of yoke height at center back (6 inches), yoke height at armhole ($4^{1}/_{4}$ inches), yoke drop at points ($1^{3}/_{4}$ inches), details of curves (one is curved $^{3}/_{4}$ inch the other $^{1}/_{2}$ inch), and the angle of the miter (45 degrees).

Godet

A **godet** is a triangular piece of fabric usually set into the hem of a garment to help facilitate the movement of the wearer or to add fullness to the silhouette. Figure 6.22a shows the godet set into a seam for support, and used this way, it is similar to a kick pleat. Figure 6.22b shows a godet within a godet, and Figure 6.22c shows godets cut on the bias in a shape called scarf points. This would work well with a sheer fabric that is strong enough to support the sharp point at the top of the godet. Figure 6.22d shows a way to avoid the upper point for lightweight fabrics.

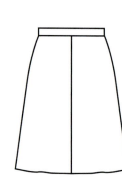

4-GORE
A-LINE

6-GORE
WITH GATHERS

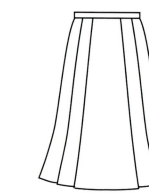

10-GORE
TRUMPET FLARE

Figure 6.19 Gored skirts.

Figure 6.20 Front and back yokes.

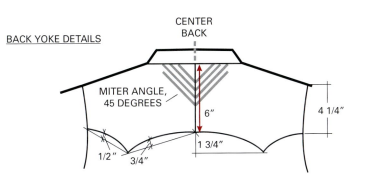

Figure 6.21 Specifying yoke details for the mitered yoke in Figure 6.20.

The features that need to be specified for godets are:

- Position (how far down they start from the top)
- Length
- Width across the bottom of the godet
- Shape, if the edges are other than a straight line

Gusset

A **gusset** is a diamond, triangular, or sometimes tapering piece of cloth, designed to ease restriction in an armhole or crotch. It is often inserted into a slashed opening as a kind of inset corner, such as in a kimono (see Figure 6.23). This one is shown cut on the bias to provide maximum shaping.

Gussets are also used in the crotch of pants or long underwear to add comfort, and to move the seam bulk away from the crotch point (see Figure 6.24). The use of a gusset in pants is more common in men's than women's clothing (see Figure 6.24).

Slit and Vent

Both a **slit** and a **vent** are long, straight openings used to provide easy movement for the wearer. The difference between the two is that a slit has the edges touching, and a vent has an underlay (Figure 6.25).

Designers' Choice of Various Shaping Devices

The many shaping devices we have explored so far show that various options are available for designers to create unique and functional apparel products. Figures 6.26 through 6.29 show some examples of the many ways that designers can use various devices to shape the silhouettes of the garments they design.

The designs in the following figures present various scenarios, using various shaping devices for the bodices. The garment in Figure 6.26a has all its shaping provided without darts, using just side seam shaping combined with gathers at the waist and shoulders. It has certain details in common with the ancient Greek garment, the chiton.

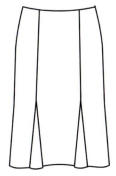

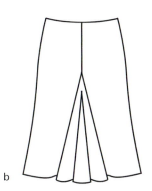

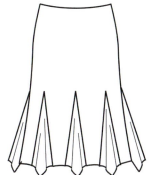

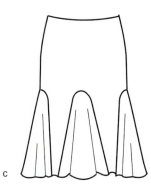

Figure 6.22 Godets.

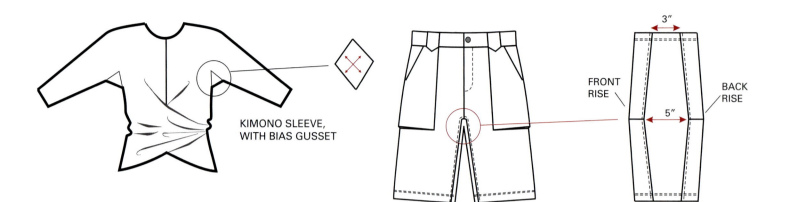

Figure 6.23 Gusset in kimono sleeve.

Figure 6.24 Gusset in pants.

VENTS

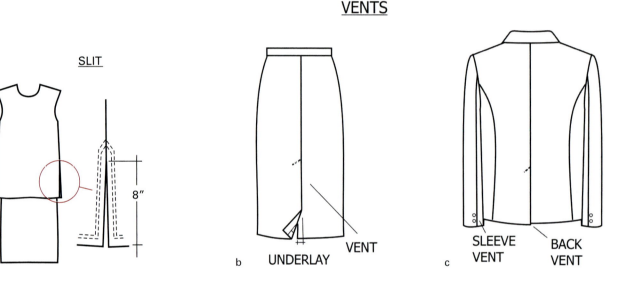

Figure 6.25 Slit and vent.

Figure 6.26b shows a waist seam and darts, similar to the basic bodice for garment pattern making. It would be possible to fit this shape very close to the body. It provides a slim, clean look with echoes of the cheongsam (see Figure 5.8e in Chapter 5) for professional dressing or formal styles.

Figure 6.26c shows dart shaping as gathers at the center front bodice. The shaping would be well adapted to being formed with elastic, and this style would tend to fit most any bust shape. The additional gathers to the right and left of the center front are for control and style, not for fit.

Figure 6.27a shows fit through the use of multiple pin tucks that extend above and below the waistline. The pin tucks are used as a dart equivalent for bust and waist to fit the contour of the body. Figure 6.27b shows gathers below the bust area and below the waist seam. The gathers on this style would not be set with elastic (except as a sewing aid) because they end at the seam. The inserted midriff panel provides shaping for the bust and waist, and could also be cut on the bias (that is, with patterns placed

not on the length grain or cross grain but on a bias direction) for additional contouring.

Figure 6.27c shows gathers above the bustline (elastic shirring, in this case). This style has a minimum of silhouette shaping, and would fit loosely through the body, as would be desirable in a nightgown or loungewear.

Figure 6.28a shows a close fit at the under-bust seamline, but requires darts as well to achieve the slimmer fit desired. Figure 6.28b shows the type of crossover styling of a surplice (or *wrap*), in which the right and left side cross over each other. Surplice styling has many variations, and the asymmetrical effect is a flattering one. The main challenge for this style is to prevent the bodice from gapping at center front, when the crossover takes place *below* the bustline as it is here. Other variations place the crossover *above* the bustline.

Figure 6.28c shows the dart shaping shared between two different bodice seams. The design lines are shaped to accommodate a smooth fit through the bust and waist.

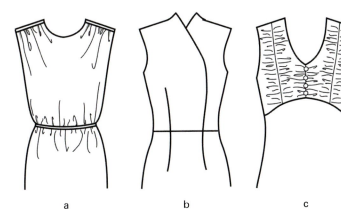

Figure 6.26 **Shaping devices, part 1.**

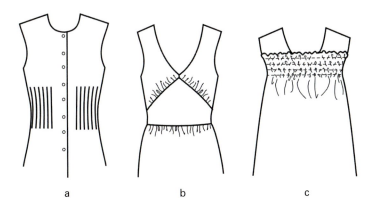

Figure 6.27 **Shaping devices, part 2.**

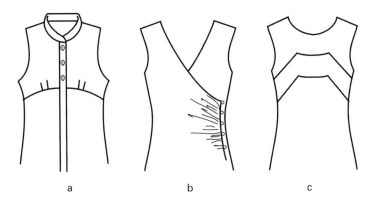

Figure 6.28 **Shaping devices, part 3.**

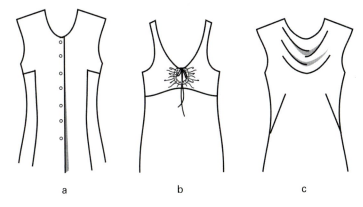

Figure 6.29 **Shaping devices, part 4.**

Figure 6.29a shows a type of princess seam set with an inset (square) corner. Figure 6.29b shows the dart shaping essentially the same as Figure 6.14a, but the tie closure provides a more customizable fit. Figure 6.29c shows two shaping methods: one by means of a cowl neckline, and the other through long diagonal darts, known as **French darts**, starting at the side seam near the waistline.

Summary

The choice of shaping should be made according to the target consumers' functional and aesthetic needs, trends, and costs, among many other factors. Designers' creativity, as well as their clear understanding of their target customer, combined with solid foundational knowledge about apparel production (construction, materials, notions, and so on) are necessary to make the best choice of shaping devices.

Study Questions

1. Design a women's top targeting consumers in their 20s to 40s. Use two different dart substitutes and explain why you chose these shaping devices.

2. Design a women's top with darts. Create a spec sheet for the darts.

3. Suggest the two most popular dart equivalents, and explain your rationale.

4. Design a gather for a cuff as shown in Figure 6.13d, and one for a ruffle trim as shown in Figure 6.14. Draw it and specify placement and gathering ratio. Make a sample.

5. What are the specs used for pleats?

6. Refer to Figure 6.4b. What can you suggest to replace with other dart equivalents? List at least three.

7. Refer to the *Technical Sourcebook for Apparel Designers* STUDIO. Select Sleeve #2 Tulip and Neckline #6 Sweetheart to Dress #17 Aline Sheath. Then, add a table of point of measure specifying the new style.

Check Your Understanding

1. List various dart substitutes.

2. Why are dart substitutes used?

3. What are mechanically engineered pleats?

4. Why is ease needed? Where is it placed?

5. What are the three pieces of information needed to specify a dart or tuck?

6. List and describe various types of pleats.

7. Design a garment using each type of pleat.

Reference

Calasibetta, C. M., and P. Tortora. 2003. *The Fairchild Dictionary of Fashion* (3rd ed.). New York: Fairchild Books.

Fabrics and Cutting

7

Chapter Objectives

After studying this chapter, you will be able to:

- Identify the structure of fabric
- Describe the differences and similarities between wovens and knits
- Demonstrate the differences in cutting instructions based on fabrics and patterns
- Identify the importance of fabric selection for each garment panel regarding its design detail
- Explore cutting and usage of fabric from a technical design perspective

---

Key Terms

basket weave	interlock	selvedge
bottom weight	jacquard	skewed
bowed	knits	tenter
courses	lay-up	tentering process
crosswise grain	lengthwise grain	top weight
dobby	linking	torqued
engineered prints	marker	true bias
fabric layout	one-way direction	twill weave
fallout	piece-dyed fabric	wales
garment bias	pile	warp
gauge	plain weave	warp knitting
greige	repeat	weft
hand	running style	weft knits
hanger	satin weave	woven
herringbone twill	Schiffli lace	yarn dyes

This chapter explores the importance of fabric and its usage for apparel products and reviews the two principal kinds of fabrics—knit and woven—and the various cutting instructions for each fabric related to its various design details and end use. The technical design perspective of design and cut details and the effect of cutting instructions on the quality of apparel products are also examined.

Fabrics

Fabric quality is a major indication of apparel quality. Every fabric has its own unique properties; different guidelines apply when working with various fabrics, so the fabric needs to be carefully chosen. For example, a crisp fabric will not produce a flowing garment, and silk linen is not suitable for inexpensive, casual bottoms. Fabrics need to be chosen according to whatever will translate into a garment with the intended look, and at the intended price. A design can be stunning on paper, and when it is produced in a fabric for which it's best suited will be equally stunning as a garment.

In addition, many fabrics require special cutting instructions and treatments. The plan for cutting has important implications for the finished garment appearance, quality standards, and cost. These issues should be specified and discussed up front, and confirmed when the tech pack is issued. Designers should consider the technical issues related to fabric selection with an eye toward the production process to foresee any potential issues.

Hand

Hand is the term that refers to the feel of the fabric when it is handled. This term is used to describe the properties of a textile, which can help determine how it will make up into a garment. It is somewhat subjective, and experience will help to develop one's judgment about whether the hand of a given fabric will be appropriate for a given style. Whether a proposed fabric is thin and delicate or thick and bulky affects the suitability for its use on a particular garment design.

When new fabrics are proposed to a designer or merchandiser, a fabric sales representative will present examples in the form of a **hanger** or *hand sample* (see Figure 7.1), swatches of fabric roughly 9 inches by 12 inches. Figure 7.1a shows a hanger with additional smaller color swatches available for sampling. This is

often the case with fabric that is a **running style**, meaning not necessarily new and not exclusive, but successful and readily available. If the fabric is a larger scale print design, a larger swatch is often presented to show the pattern scale and repeat (see Figure 7.1b). Hanger swatches give the design staff the opportunity to observe many characteristics of the fabric and judge the suitability for appearance, weight, drape, pliability, depth of color, stretch qualities, wrinkling, and other important issues. Fabric hangers of interest are often collected and hung together to make a fabric library in design companies. The header cardboard at the top has important information about the content, the fabric width, and other details.

Fibers have a major influence on the hand, sometimes at a microscopic level, such as the size and twist of the yarns and other elements of the yarn structure. Fiber content is a key element as well. Certain fibers, such as cotton, have qualities that are universally understood, and a fabric may be described as having a "cottony" hand, meaning dry and comfortable, whether it contains cotton or not. Fabric structure and thread count will affect the pliability and opaqueness, and whether the hand is firm or soft, compact or spongy. Other descriptive terms for hand (in no particular order) are crisp, smooth, supple, delicate, papery, harsh, lofty, clammy, loose, boardy, flimsy, dry, sheer, drapey, fluid, clingy, stiff, firm, springy, and velvety. By testing the hand and feeling the hanger swatch, handling the fabric, grabbing and releasing it, and observing the fabric's reaction to movement, a great deal can be ascertained about its suitability for a proposed garment.

Yarn Size

The threads that make up fabrics are known as *yarns*. Yarn size has a big impact on the finished fabric. Fabrics constructed with heavier yarns tend to be rougher and make the fabric stiffer, but more durable and less prone to wrinkling than finer yarns. Woven fabrics with lighter vertical yarn and heavier horizontal yarns tend to be stiff or crisp in the direction of the heavy yarns. A fabric with a structure such as shown in Figure 7.2c may make a great pair of slim pants, but if it is made into a skirt, the horizontal stiffness should be taken into account. This fabric would be a good choice if a lot of volume is desired, but not if the skirt is intended to drape in soft folds.

Knits and Wovens

There are two major textile categories for fabrics: knit and woven. Most people have no idea whether a given fabric is knit or woven, but for apparel design, the distinction between the two is fundamental, and often designers will specialize in one or the other throughout their careers. A familiarity with both is valuable.

A **woven** is defined as fabric formed with **warp** yarns (also called *ends*) that are attached to harnesses lengthwise, and **weft** yarns (also called *filling*, *picks*, or *crosswise grain*). To form the fabric, these yarns are wound onto bobbins and then interwoven crosswise on a loom by the use of a shuttle.

Woven Fabric

Woven fabrics generally have a tighter and more rigid construction than knits. The most common woven construction is plain weave; other variations are twill weave and satin weave.

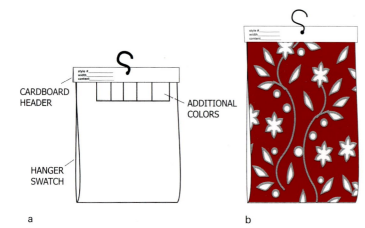

a   b

Figure 7.1 Fabric hanger swatches.

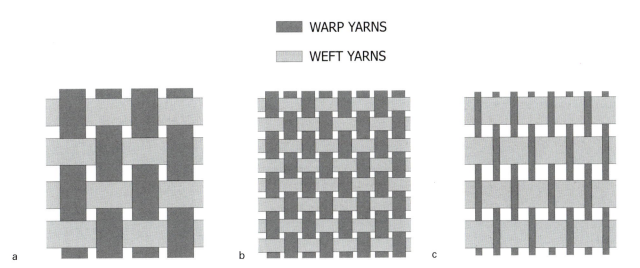

Figure 7.2 **Variations of plain weave.**

Plain Weave

Plain weave consists of the warp and weft that are aligned and form a simple crisscross pattern (see Figure 7.2). Each weft thread goes over one warp thread and under the next repeatedly. Plain weave creates a checkerboard-like appearance (Kadolph, 2007). A common example of a plain weave item is a bed sheet, which has the characteristic firmness and strength of a close plain weave fabric. Plain weave has the greatest tendency to wrinkle and to require ironing. Two common fabrics in plain weave are chambray and poplin.

Comparing Figures 7.2a and 7.2b, the warp and weft in Figure 7.2a are much heavier than in Figure 7.2b, but for each example the yarns are balanced between warp and weft, as would be seen in common plain weave fabrics such as broadcloth, muslin, or voile. Other names for plain weave are *tabby weave* or *taffeta weave*.

Figure 7.2c shows a fabric such as poplin, in which the filling yarns are heavier than the warp yarns, a construction also known as a *rib weave*. Plain weave fabrics can vary widely in appearance based on the size and look of the warp and weft yarns. They can be woven with novelty yarns such as bouclé, tweed, or metallic. Plain weave fabrics are also used as a basis for prints and embroidery. The weight of plain weave fabrics ranges from the sheerest georgette to camel-hair fabric used for overcoats, and even heavier weights for industrial uses. Plain weave has a variation called **basket weave** in which two warp threads are woven over two weft threads. It is sometimes called a *mat* (matte) weave because it is used in floor matting. Fabric is woven by two or more yarns as one and the weave is described as the number of warp x the number of weft. For example, 4 × 4 means four warp and four weft yarns are used in weaving (Humphries, 2009).

Twill Weave

Figure 7.3a shows a twill weave where the yarns interlace in a step-like formation. **Twill weave** looks like a pattern of diagonal parallel ribs. It consists of weft threads passing over one warp thread and then under two or more warp threads repeatedly, which creates the diagonal pattern on the surface. Because this type of fabric has more yarns packed into a given area, it is very durable, and the *floats* (the skipped yarns) make the fabric pliable and comfortable. Other characteristics are good wrinkle recovery,

durable wear, and often a distinct difference between face side and wrong side. Some examples of fabric in a twill weave are denim, gabardine, and chino.

A variation of twill weave is the herringbone twill, in which a different effect is achieved with the warp and weft in different colors. **Herringbone twill** has lines of wales reversing at regular intervals. It resembles the backbone of a fish (herring), thus the name. Herringbone is good for suits and coats (Humphries, 2009).

Satin Weave

In **satin weaves** (see Figure 7. 3b), the filling yarn passes under, or skips, many warp yarns. This creates the characteristic smooth

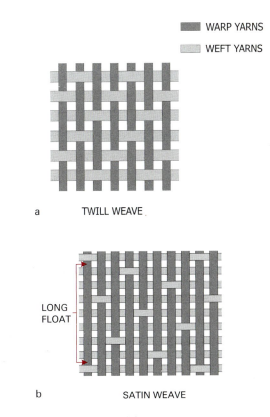

Figure 7.3 **Twill (a) and satin (b) weaves.**

luster, and drapeability of satin fabrics. The longer, unattached floats are prone to snagging and abrasion, making this fabric less durable. A common construction is five-end repeat, meaning over four yarns and under one. Figure 7.3b shows an eight-end repeat with even longer floats. This would increase the drape but decrease the durability.

Jacquard

Jacquard is produced with an attachment to the loom that enables it to produce complicated patterns such as brocade and raised effects such as matelassé. Other patterned fabrics produced on the jacquard loom are damask and tapestry.

Dobby

Dobby is a small geometric patterned weave produced with a special attachment to the loom called a dobby attachment. Examples of patterns are birdseye, nail head, and honeycomb.

Pile

Pile surface fabrics such as velvet are made on a double-action shuttle loom on which two layers of fabric are woven at the same time and then slit apart. Another common pile fabric is corduroy. Pile fabrics have an up and a down direction. In the up direction, the color appears darker and deeper, and in the down direction the color is lighter and duller. We will look at this further later in the chapter because it is taken into account when a garment is cut.

Pile surfaces may be formed with a W formation looped around three yarns, or a V formation with the pile looped around one yarn. The W is more durable and considered a higher quality (see Figure 7.4). By pulling off a few fibers at the edge a swatch of velvet or corduroy, it is easy to determine whether the pile formation is V or W. The less-expensive V is far more common.

Pile fabrics are also used for their thermal qualities because they are effective at trapping air and holding in body heat for insulation purposes. Other fabrics with pile structure are fake fur and fleece used for outerwear.

Woven Fabric and Its Terminology

Figure 7.5 identifies the main terms for woven fabrics. The enlarged view shows the selvedge edge of a plain weave.

Lengthwise Grain

The warp yarns are attached to the loom before weaving begins. The weft yarns are woven crosswise back and forth over and under the warp yarns to form the fabric. The selvedge edges are the finished edges. The **lengthwise grain** is formed by the warp yarns, which may be many yards long (50 yards is an example of one roll of fabric). Technically, they need to be strong enough to handle the tension of the loom during the warping process. Later, when the finished fabric is taken off the loom, it relaxes. If it relaxes too much, especially after washing, the result will be

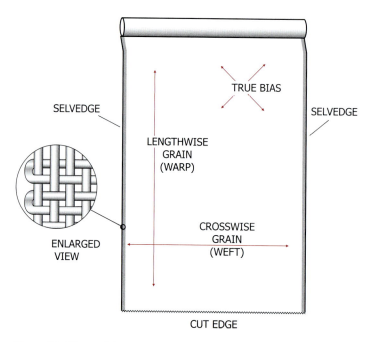

Figure 7.5 Woven fabric and its terminology.

excessive lengthwise shrinkage. This is why garments tend to shrink more lengthwise than crosswise. The lengthwise grain of a fabric is less stretchy and more suitable for areas of the garment that need stabilizing, such as the waistband of a skirt or the back yoke of a men's shirt. The major pieces of garments are generally cut lengthwise. This makes the garment better able to maintain its shape over time.

Selvedge

The **selvedge** edge (see Figure 7.5) is the self edge of the fabric, which is lengthwise in the direction of the warp, formed as the weft is interlaced with the warp during weaving. The selvedge can be made with heavier yarns for strength; the fabric is carried through various processes on a **tenter** frame, secured at the edges with pins that form tenter holes. The set of tiny holes can be observed within the selvedge on most woven fabrics, and they usually poke through toward the face side because fabric is carried face up in the processing. The **tentering process** is used for pulling out wrinkles, shrinking and stretching, straightening the grain, and other finishing applications. If done incorrectly, it will result in pulling the fabric off-grain, also known as *skewing* (see Figure 7.8). Knit goods have a similar problem called *torqueing*.

Fabric in the state just after weaving is called **greige** goods (or gray goods). It has not yet been dyed, bleached, or had any finishes applied. Fabric selected for which greige is available (already woven) will shorten the manufacturing process considerably and is an important consideration in planning garment deliveries.

A garment cut off-grain tends to pull in the direction of the lengthwise grain. For example, on a pant with a flared bottom, if the panels are not cut along the straight of the grain (or if one leg does not match the other) the pant legs will not flare equally, but may poke out too far at the inseam or outseam, or the seams may twist to the front or back.

Because cutting pieces off-grain may result in fabric savings for the manufacturer, there may be a price savings incentive for them to do so. Whether it creates an unacceptable appearance will depend on the garment, price point, the type of fabric, and the

W-PILE FORMATION   V-PILE FORMATION

Figure 7.4 W pile and V pile.

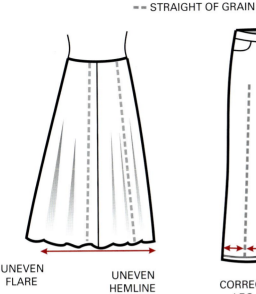
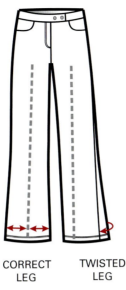

- - STRAIGHT OF GRAIN

UNEVEN
FLARE

UNEVEN
HEMLINE

CORRECT
LEG

TWISTED
LEG

Figure 7.6 Garments cut off-grain.

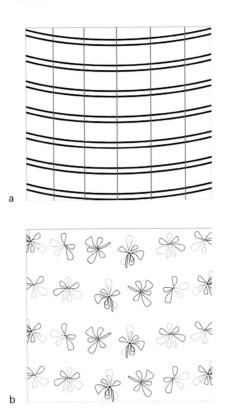

Figure 7.7 Bowed fabric.

overall length of the garment. The longer the garment, the more pronounced the effect will be. A slim-fitting short skirt in a tweed fabric would be able to take more off-grain than would a sheath dress, long coat, or gabardine pants. Grainline is an important quality indicator. Figure 7.6 shows a skirt that has its left and right panels cut on different grains. The right side (wearer's right) flares out more, and the left side drapes down more. Either of these may be the desired effect, but of course they must match within the same garment. In the pant example, the right leg has the grain correctly placed in the center of the panel. The left leg is cut off-grain and will twist and flare unevenly.

Crosswise Grain

The **crosswise grain** yarns (other terms are crossgrain, weft, fill, and width) are the ones that are interwoven into the warp. There are sometimes important situations in which a garment may be cut on the crosswise, such as for pattern placement, and sometimes for drape (especially if the fill yarns are heavier than the warp yarns). It may increase the fabric usage and is not considered as durable as the lengthwise grain.

The crosswise grain should be at exactly right angles to the lengthwise grain. If it is not, the fabric is said to be off-grain, or **bowed** (see Figure 7.7), which means "fabric grain distortion in which crosswise yarns are across the fabric" (Brown and Rice, 2001), **skewed**, or **torqued**, which is another "fabric grain distortion in woven fabrics when crosswise yarns slant from one selvedge to the other" (Brown and Rice, 2001). Figure 7.8 shows fabric that is skewed, and the defect could cause problems with the stripe. Figure 7.7b has the same amount of bow, but would probably pass unnoticed because of the print. If the fabric relaxes back to being on grain after laundering, however, it may become twisted and unsightly.

The fabric in Figure 7.8 is distorted, like the bowed fabric, but in such a way that one edge is different from the other. This occurs during processing when one selvedge feeds through the machine faster than the other. A garment made of skewed fabric, like bowed fabric, will experience difficulty in matching patterns and quality problems after laundering. Whether cut lengthwise or

FABRIC SKEW

Figure 7.8 Fabric skew.

crosswise, the garment pieces need to be placed on the straight-of-grain, unless there are design reasons to cut them otherwise.

Figure 7.9 shows some examples of standard grain direction. The lengthwise grain (standard grain direction) is stronger and more stable than the crosswise grain. The crosswise grain is less sturdy but more stretchy. The back yoke and cuff of a men's shirt (see Figure 7.9a) are usually cut with the warp sewn horizontally to keep the fabric from stretching, and the other pieces are cut as shown in the figure.

The women's skirt (see Figure 7.9b) also has the waistband cut with the lengthwise grain to prevent stretching. The pocket facing (the small piece to the garment left) in Figure 7.9b is cut on the lengthwise grain to help stabilize the hand pocket edge, which is on the bias. The side front piece follows the grain of the skirt.

Bias

In a strict sense, any direction on a woven fabric that is not straight-of-grain is *bias*. It would not be correct to refer to the

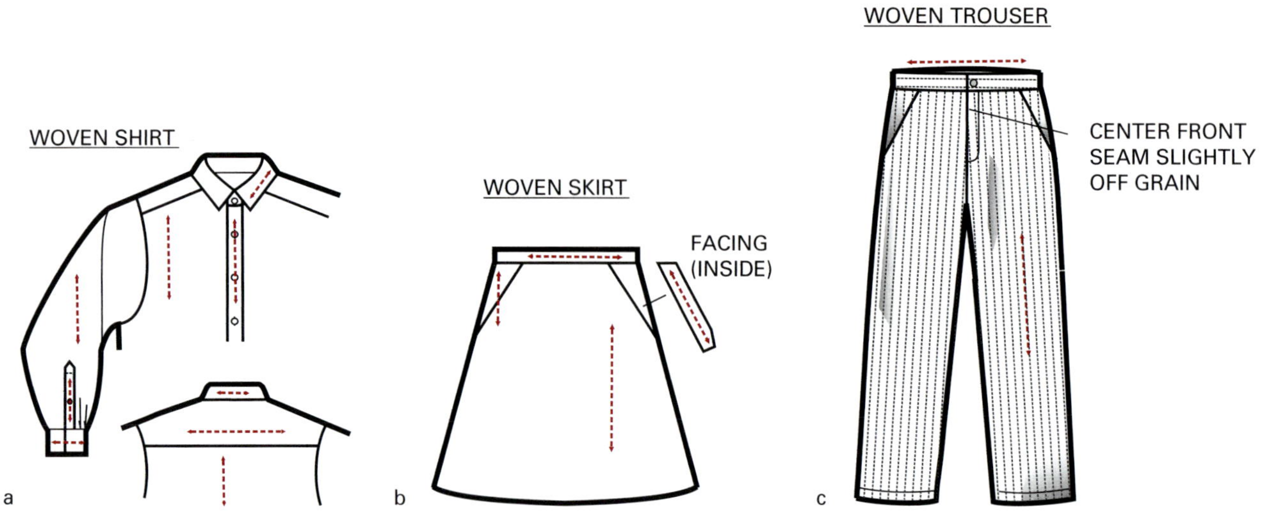

WOVEN TROUSER

WOVEN SHIRT

WOVEN SKIRT

FACING
(INSIDE)

CENTER FRONT
SEAM SLIGHTLY
OFF GRAIN

a   b   c

Figure 7.9 Standard fabric layouts and grainline.

"bias grain" because that is a contradiction in terms. Bias can be used for all or part of a garment, and has a multitude of useful applications.

True bias is a 45-degree angle to the lengthwise or crosswise grain (see Figure 7.5) and is the direction of maximum stretchability. Cutting a garment on the true bias creates a symmetrical drape. Bias adds a distinctive molded shape to a garment, and a garment cut entirely on the bias does not need intricate design lines, curved seams, and excessive detail. For an all-bias garment, the styling works especially well when it is kept simple, and in fabrics where the warp and fill yarns are balanced in size.

Plackets cut on the bias, or other areas where a long bias edge joins to a non-stretchy section, present a challenge to construct. A two-piece pattern style, such as a bias A-line skirt, must have the center line on the true bias in order to hang evenly.

Not all fabrics are suitable for bias cutting. Fabrics such as loosely woven types with slick yarns that will "slip" would not be suitable for all-bias garments because they will sag. Bias is not often used for pants, and very slim-fitting garments could become stretched out at areas that require flexing, such as the knee or elbow on fabric not woven tightly enough.

Bias is also used effectively for partial areas of a garment. For a pant, the front fly is cut slightly off grain to take advantage of the stretch of the **garment bias** (an angle of bias other than 45 degrees), which will help the edge to lie smoothly (see Figure 7.10).

Figure 7.11 also shows examples of bias cut for each part of garments. All of the detail areas in Figure 7.11 use the true bias, a

BIAS AT CENTER FRONT

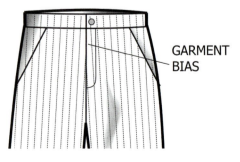

GARMENT
BIAS

Figure 7.10 Bias cut for center front seam.

45-degree angle. Details such as an inset cowl neckline in Figure 7.11a are perfectly suited to the bias cut. Figure 7.11b shows a bias waist insert, set off by contrast bias piping. Figure 7.11c shows a bias ruffle attached to the bottom of a girls' dress and bias cuffs and facing as trim elements. The dress itself is not bias.

Bias can be used for details and finishing (see Figure 7.12). Figure 7.12a has a bias finish at the neckline as well as outlining the keyhole detail. Figure 7.12b shows bias binding used to finish the side seam edges and bottom opening on a casual pant. It also uses bias as a decorative stripe detail element. (More information about bias on edge finishes is in Chapter 10.)

Fabric Weight: Woven Fabric Selection Indicator

Weight is a significant factor when selecting fabric for a certain design. Weight is also a significant cost factor because the heavier the fabric, the more fibers used to construct it, and thus the higher the cost per yard. Fabric weight is also a choice for aesthetic reasons and needs to be chosen according to the design. For example, a very heavy fabric will not take a lot of gathers or draping as well as a light fabric. A light fabric cannot achieve the volume or provide the insulation that a heavy fabric can.

Fabric that is heavy enough for pants is called **bottom weight**, and lightweight blouse or shirt fabric is known as **top weight**. Dress styles are usually made of top weight fabric, although a style cut close to the body can often be achieved in a bottom weight. Table 7.1 provides a comparison of various examples of fabrics, their weights, and their common descriptions.

Silk fabric has a unit of weight known as *momme* (4.33 g/m^2). A higher momme designates a heavier fabric composed of either heavier yarns or a closer weave. Fabric weights are generally expressed as grams per square meter (g/m^2) or ounces per square yard (oz/yd^2, or oz/sqy). Depending on the mill and the country of origin, the unit of measure could be grams per *linear* meter, or ounces per *linear* yard.

Knits

A **knit** is a fabric formed by interlooping adjacent yarns. Knit, in this context, does not include sweaters, but rather cut-and-sew knits such as that used for children's wear, T-shirts, and many other categories. The basic structure of many knit fabrics provides

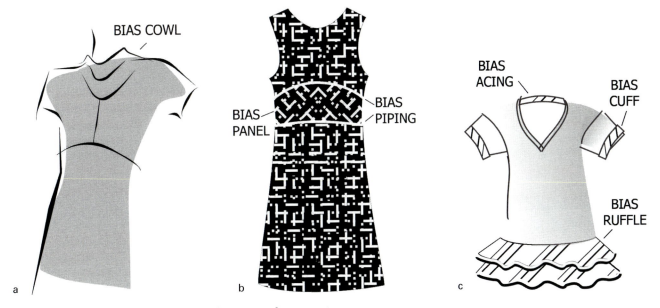

Figure 7.11 Application of bias cut for various parts of a garment.

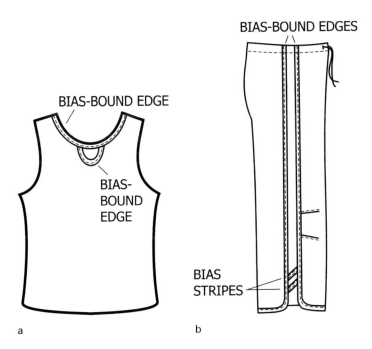

Figure 7.12 Bias for trim.

a measure of stretchability not available in wovens. Knit fabrics are comfortable and popular for everything from infants' wear to activewear T-shirts to eveningwear. The two primary types of knit fabrics are weft knits and warp knits.

Weft Knits

Weft knits are similar to the loop structure of a sweater. The yarns are applied horizontally by use of a fixed bed of latch hook needles—either a flat bed that produces flat fabric, or a circular bed that produces tubular fabric, subsequently cut open to lie flat for cutting into garments. Common knit constructions are jersey, ribbed knits, and interlock. T-shirt fabric is an example of a weft knit.

Knits have a wide range of appearance and construction, and the density of the fabric depends on the yarns, the needles per inch (called the **gauge**), and the tension. Gauge varies in technical definition based on different machines, for example, 1 inch for flat weft machines and $1^1/2$ inch for weft knits and tricot (Humphries, 2009). Knits used for apparel range in weight and appearance from boiled wool to shiny, skin-tight spandex. There are also cut-and-sew knits that have the look of a sweater. However, actual sweaters follow different construction techniques, such as **linking**, which are created by the use of a specific knitting machine called a *linker*.

Warp Knits

Warp knitting is performed with a variety of machines in which the yarn zigzags along the length of the fabric. This type of knit is resistant to runs. The types of fabric produced by warp knit machines include tricot, common in lingerie; raschel, which has little stretch and is bulkier; and Milanese, which is stronger, smoother, and more expensive than tricot.

Characteristics of Knits

Knits don't technically have a "grain," but still follow similar rules in terms of cutting direction. Knit fabric often has a lot of inherent stretch, but does not have the properties of *additional* drape and stretch when cut at a 45-degree angle (bias) as a woven

Table 7.1   Fabric Weight Comparisons

	Gram Weight	Ounces Weight	Example
Sheer fabric	Up to 50 gm/m²	Up to $1/2$ oz/sq yd	Sheer, curtains, chiffon
Light fabric	50–150 gm/m²	1.5 to 4.5 oz/sq yd	Batiste, shirting, lining, top weights
Medium fabric	150–300 gm/m²	4.5 to 9 oz/sq yd	Denim, suiting, bottom weights
Medium-heavy fabric	300–600 gm/m²	9 to 18 oz/sq yd	Canvas, coating
Heavy fabric	600 gm/m² and higher	18 oz/sq yd and higher	Upholstery

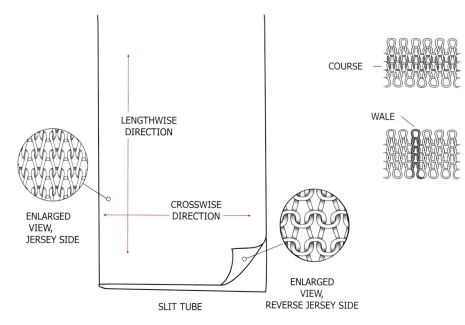

Figure 7.13 Fabric terminology for weft knit and jersey construction.

does when cut on the bias. In fact, a knit does not have a bias. Knits have an intrinsic degree of comfort based on the stretch, which allows for both a close fit and ease of movement. Knits vary significantly in the amount and direction of stretch, which affect the design and the fit characteristics a great deal. Knit fabrics are often less durable and more prone to shrinking and stretching than wovens. They are also less opaque.

Jersey has a number of characteristics in common with a hand-knit sweater except that the yarns are much finer. Similar to a sweater, the stitch itself is the same as what would be called a *stockinette stitch*, with its characteristic flatter face side and more textured purl side. It also has the same tendency to curl to the back, and a broken or "dropped" stitch will develop into a run, or ladder. The horizontal rows of stitches are called **courses**, and the vertical rows are called **wales** (see Figure 7.13). Knitting machines produce either flat or tubular fabric. Tubular goods are slit open after being knitted so that they can be laid out flat.

Some garments such as T-shirts actually use the tubular goods as originally knitted, and such items have no side seams. This saves on labor, but it is a specialized operation because there must be separate knitting machines to accommodate each chest size. Moreover, the chest, waist, and hip are the same dimension, so there is no accommodation for waist fitting as would be desirable for most women's garments.

A factory has to understand how to handle knits, because their qualities differ from those of wovens. In the spreading and cutting process, care must be taken to avoid stretching the fabric as it's laid out on the cutting table, or it will relax back to its original dimensions after the pieces are cut apart. This could result in the garment being too small or short. An experienced factory may compensate by letting the fabric relax overnight, or by not cutting too many layers high. Different fabrics may have different qualities that may affect their cutting characteristics, and a factory experienced in knits will know how to assess these factors.

Rib Knits

A vertical high–low effect is created by alternate jersey and reverse jersey stitches for *rib knits*. This forms a lengthwise rib and adds a

crosswise stretchability. Comparing it to a sweater again, a 1 × 1 rib is the same as the famous "knit one, purl one" in hand knitting. Figure 7.14 illustrates how a rib knit can mold to the body. A ribbed fabric shapes itself to the body in a very comfortable and, if cut that way, close-fitting manner. This is used for sleepwear, children's clothing, and many other categories. Because of its thickness, rib knit is also a good insulator and is used for warmth in long underwear, leggings, and other thermal garments. Rib knits trap more air within the structure, providing more insulation and warmth.

Rib knits make a comfortable body fabric and are also quite useful as trim and bindings to finish edges. They have more elasticity (stretchability) than the jersey structure. Figure 7.14a shows a body fabric that is knit in a 3 × 1 specification, which gives it a wider rib effect, and the edge binding uses a 1 × 1 rib, seen in the detail sketch. The detail sketch for Figure 7.14b shows striped 2 × 2 rib knit used as trim for collar, cuffs, and bottom edge. The inset magnifies the 2 × 2 rib of the cuff. Any number of rib configurations can be specified; for example, a sweater or ribbed shirt may have a rib specification of 1 × 2 × 1 × 2 × 1 × 2 × 3 × 2 × 3 × 2 × 3 × 2. This creates a pattern that is repeated across the garment.

A rib construction requires somewhat more yarn, but also adds an extra stretch quality to the construction and can use a smaller girth spec, which would improve the yield. For example, if the typical bust spec for a jersey T-shirt is 18 inches (half measure), the bust spec for a rib-knit shirt could be 17 inches or less, depending on the specific fabric.

Double Knits

Double knit is a weft knit process that produces a double-constructed fabric with good stability. Double knit will not sag

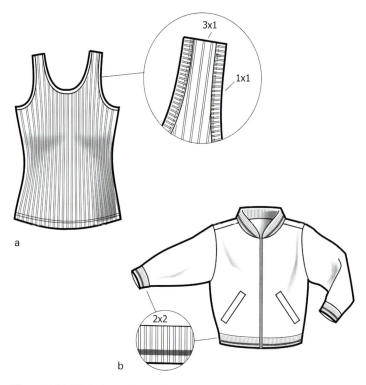

Figure 7.14 Rib knits and application.

or stretch out, thus making it popular for knit bottoms. It has the same appearance on the face and back, a characteristic known as *double-face*. It does not curl at the cut edge and is easy to handle on the sewing floor.

Interlock

Interlock is a weft knit fabric consisting of two separate 1 × 1 rib fabrics interknitted to form one cloth. Interlock, a common style of knit, has the same appearance front and back, and is reversible. It has a smooth surface and stretches in the lengthwise and, to a limited degree, crosswise direction. It is heavier, more stable, not as stretchy as jersey, and makes high-quality shirts, dresses, and coordinates. A heavier version of interlock would be suitable for knit pants. Because it does not stretch as much, it does not work well as self-binding. Figure 7.14a shows a shirt that would not be able to fit as closely if it were constructed in interlock as compared to a rib-knit, nor would the binding trim be able to shape itself around the curves of the neck and armhole. On the other hand, interlock would work well for a dress or a light jacket, something that 1 × 1 rib may not. When selecting a fabric for a new design, it is important to understand its strengths and limitations.

Quality Issues Related to Knit Fabric

In woven fabric, *torque* is caused in the finishing process. Knits (and sweaters) have a problem with the same name as torque, but of different origin. In knits it causes one side seam to twist forward and the other to rotate toward the back (see Figure 7.15). Companies establish an allowance or tolerance for this problem, based on location, so a large amount of torque, more than an inch or two, would not be acceptable.

Fabric Layout

A crucial element included in the tech pack is the cutting instructions to the factories. These instructions should include any special considerations that will be needed to achieve the quality appearance intended. The technicians at the factory will plan the arrangement of the pattern pieces on the fabric. Careful thought will be given for the best and most economical

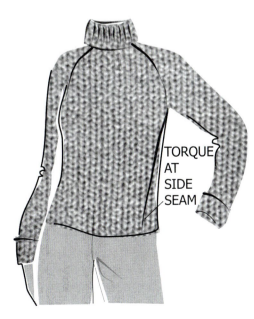

Figure 7.15 Torque in a knit garment.

use of fabric to furnish a reasonable cost. Later, when preparing for actual production, the same plan will be followed when markers are made. Plain fabrics in a solid color can have a very straightforward layout, in which a pattern can be laid out with the top of the pattern pieces either up or down. Other fabrics need more consideration: plaids, patterns larger than a certain size, certain twills, and brushed or napped fabrics.

Making Markers

When the garment factory prepares to cut out the fabric for a given style, a **marker** (a layer of paper with all the pieces drawn onto it in the most efficient arrangement possible) is prepared. A tight marker is one with very little waste, and smaller pieces are arranged to fit around the larger ones like a puzzle. The fabric in between the pattern pieces, which ends up as scrap, is called **fallout**.

Creating a tight marker with a minimum of fallout is an important process for a factory, and an amount of fallout between 10 and 15 percent is about average. A savings in fabric of even 1 percent, when multiplied over thousands of yards, is significant. For that reason, some pattern pieces may be allowed to overlap slightly on the marker, and some smaller pieces that don't show may be tilted slightly off-grain. But the straight of grain must be followed for all the principal visible pieces, and the marker still has to preserve margins at the edges in case the fabric width varies from ply to ply as the fabric is being spread. Fabric can vary in width as much as 1 inch, and the width is often given, for example, as 56 inches to 57 inches. The marker, of course, has to be made to accommodate the narrowest width.

In the past the pattern pieces were hand-traced onto special paper called marker paper, but markers are increasingly produced with a computer system; for example, AccuMark or Pattern Design System (PDS) by Gerber Garment Technology, which has the ability to make duplicates, keep records, and simplify the process itself by working in miniature rather than by manipulating full-size pattern pieces.

Figure 7.16 shows how the finished marker is laid onto a stack of fabric (also called a lay-up) in preparation for cutting a style (in this case, a jacket). The straight of grain of each pattern piece is laid along the warp and parallels the selvedge. A separate **lay-up** (plies of fabric rolled out to be cut) and marker is prepared for each type of fabric, such as lining, underlining, and interfacing.

Plaid and Pattern Matching

An important quality indicator is plaid matching or, in the case of print, pattern matching. Very small checks or florals may not require matching, although each situation must be examined. But larger ones on better-quality garments do need to be matched. The highest-quality garments will have pattern matching at all the seams; because additional fabric is required to accomplish this and extra skill needed to sew it, it does affect the cost and has to be specified at the costing stage, when the first tech pack is sent out.

Matching Even Plaids

Plaid is a woven fabric made with different colors of yarn on the loom. Plaid fabrics are also known in the industry as **yarn dyes** because the yarns are dyed before they go onto the loom for weaving (in contrast to **piece-dyed fabric**, which is woven first as greige goods and then dyed). Some plaids are actually printed onto the fabric, but these are not usually of the same quality as yarn dyes, and the chance of skewing would make it very hard to match the plaids.

Generally, plaids are rectangular rather than square with the pattern taller than it is wide, creating a more flattering proportion. The plaid design and plaid matching are important quality indicators. If the **repeat**—the basic pattern that is repeated many times—is very small or subtle, such as a small check, the matching instructions are less critical, or even unnecessary. But for a large or dominant plaid, the fabric is the driver of the design, and the details should be chosen to blend with the fabric. Figure 7.17 shows a suit jacket where many details are matched both vertically and horizontally. This is an example of an even plaid in which the plaid elements are mirror images, right-to-left (whether they are mirror image top-to-bottom is less critical). Additional fabric is required to accomplish this, based on the dimensions of the repeat.

Another consideration in choosing plaids is to consider whether the plaid is even or uneven. Figure 7.17 also shows an example of the cutting instructions which have different considerations for this particular plaid jacket. This appears on the construction page of the tech pack; notice that the horizontal and vertical matching instructions are called out separately.

Plaid matching requires a much higher skill level in sewing as well. Not every factory will be set up to handle plaid matching, so the assignment will be given to one that specializes in it. Figure 7.17 shows a complete list for all the matching points.

Matching Uneven Plaids

In Figure 7.18, the fabric is an uneven plaid. The garment is usually designed so that the pattern goes around the body in one direction. It is possible to use this type of fabric, even with a jacket and lapels, but it requires more planning to make use of the dominant elements to achieve visual balance. The layout is planned in a **one-way direction**, meaning that the tops of the pattern pieces will all be placed "head up."

Other garments with simpler shapes, such as a gathered skirt, can use uneven plaids without much special consideration. In any case, the matching instructions will be carefully spelled out in the tech pack to inform the factory how to cut the goods. Plaid matching can become very elaborate, and the more important it is to the design, the more crucial it is to spell it out carefully.

Cutting Instructions

Figure 7.19 shows a layout with the pattern pieces one way head up as they would need to be for the print example in Figure 7.24a or the plaid example in Figure 7.18. This layout requires approximately 15 percent more fabric than a two-way layout. Because

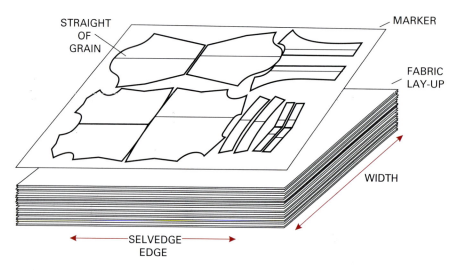

Figure 7.16 Marker and lay-up.

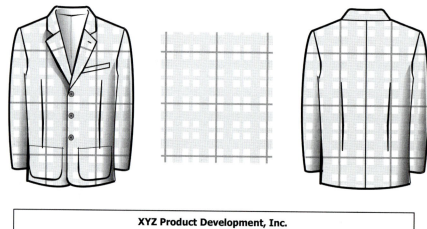

XYZ Product Development, Inc. CONSTRUCTION PAGE
Cutting information: no nap, cut 2 way, lengthwise
MATCH HORIZONTAL—across front, sleeves match body, lapels, patch pockets, side seams, across back
MATCH VERTICAL—breast pocket welt, patch pockets, topcollar at center back

Figure 7.17 Matching even plaids.

XYZ Product Development, Inc. CONSTRUCTION PAGE
Cutting information: no nap, 1 way, lengthwise
MATCH HORIZONTAL—across front, sleeves match body, lapels, side seams, across back, welt pockets
MATCH VERTICAL— welt pockets, topcollar at center back

Figure 7.18 Matching uneven plaids.

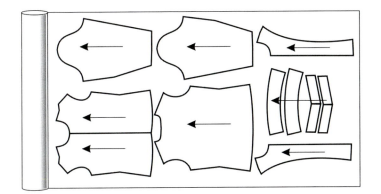
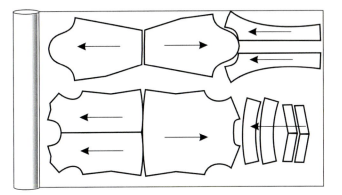

Figure 7.19 **Pattern pieces cut one way, head up.**

matching the direction creates a significant cost difference, it needs to be included in the costing process.

Figure 7.20 compares two actual mini-markers of the type the apparel company factory might request from the factory if they had a question. Figure 7.20a represents the plaid version of a garment and uses significantly more fabric than Figure 7.20b, the solid version of the same style. The more expensive the fabric is per yard, the greater the price difference between plaid and solid. The larger the plaid, the more yardage is required to match.

One other thing that will affect the cost are the designated matching points. For example, some apparel companies match across the side seams (which will cost more) and some do not. This will be decided early on and is an important design decision. On a garment like this (men's windbreaker) standard matching points might be "horizontally across front," "across design lines," and "sleeves match each other." The plaid version also has some bias elements, which require additional yardage.

Since these two examples are actual markers, it is interesting to see the economy with which these are laid out. It is remarkable to see how little fabric is wasted. That is a very important feature of most electronic pattern-making programs. Cutting the fabric in a two-way direction would be possible if no consideration of matching is needed, such as for a solid color fabric or fabric with small or unidirectional patterns (see Figure 7.20). Less fallout means a tighter marker, which is more cost effective.

Matching Plaids for Some Areas of Garments

Areas of some plaid garments, such as the cuff plackets and center front placket, require special consideration for matching.

Cuff Placket

The cuff placket on men's woven shirts is another common matching area. Figure 7.21 shows three different matching configurations. Figure 7.21a shows a sleeve placket without matching. Some plaids may look better than others, but this is not considered a high-quality construction. Figure 7.21b is matched horizontally, but not vertically. This is the most common method. On very-high-quality construction, the placket may be matched vertically as well, as in Figure 7.21c. For a different effect, the placket may be placed on the bias (Figure 7.21d) and does not need to be matched while cutting or sewing.

Center Front Placket

Figure 7.22 illustrates matching at the center front placket. The placket in Figure 7.22a is seamed, which creates an additional

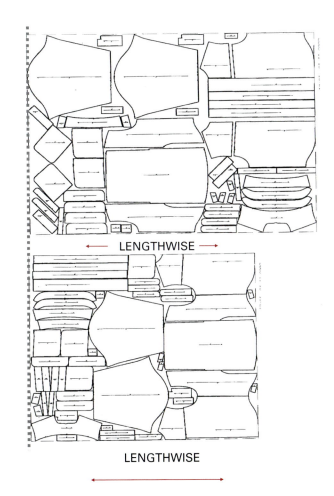

LENGTHWISE

LENGTHWISE

Figure 7.20 **Pattern pieces cut two way.**

matching point (or, in this case, a potential nonmatching point). Figure 7.22b has a topstitched placket, which requires no additional matching. It also has the dominant stripe positioned at center front, which gives the shirt a neat and balanced look. The instructions for the plackets (Figure 7.22) are given below the sketch. (For the purpose of illustrating, we will assume there are no unseen matching points, such as the cuff placket.)

Technical Design Aspects of Cutting

In addition to matching plaids, designers must consider a number of other technical aspects of cutting that depend on the design features of the fabric.

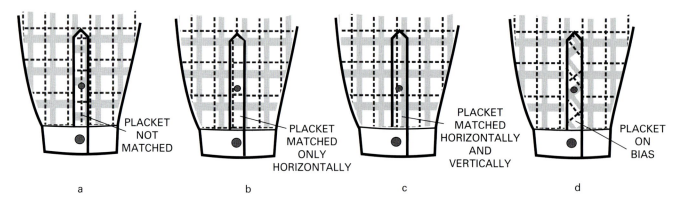

Figure 7.21 **Matching plaid placket.**

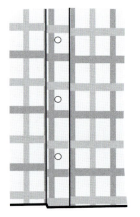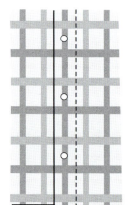

XYZ Product Development, Inc.
CONSTRUCTION PAGE
Cutting information: no nap, cut 2 way lengthwise
Match Horizontal: Across front, side seams
Match Vertical: NA
Match, other: Dominant stripe at CF

Figure 7.22 **Matching plaids at center front.**

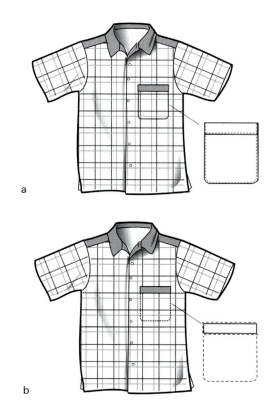

Figure 7.23 **Pocket construction comparison.**

Cost Solution for a Patch Pocket

It is important to understand the construction methods behind the garments to achieve the desired look and cost. The expense and skill needed for plaid matching should be well coordinated with the garment details and construction and the choice of fabric (see Figure 7.23). Designers need to be savvy by using alternative ways to achieve the design they want within the budget. Figure 7.23a has a patch pocket with contrast band. The patch pocket needs to be matched both horizontally and vertically. On the other hand, the shirt in Figure 7.23b has a welt opening and a stitch-through detail that requires no matching. Whether this particular trade-off results in cost savings would be determined by the factory costing it, but the final effect of the pocket is the same, using two different methods.

Directional Fabric

Fabrics may be directional because of a print, nap or pile, surface texture, border element, or uneven stripe or plaid.

Diagonal Weave

Fabrics with an obvious diagonal texture, such as twill, generally need special consideration. A pattern or texture at a 45-degree angle is easier to plan; one with a 70-degree angle (in twill fabric, it's called a *steep twill*), or a 20-degree angle (a *reclining twill*) is more difficult. The diagonal weave also affects the perceived color shade; thus, the garment would need to be cut in a one-way direction. The color-shade effect may be very subtle and difficult to judge on a small swatch, so it is better to err on the side of caution or have a mock-up made in the actual fabric. Twill fabrics that need directional consideration include brocade, gabardine, denim, and herringbone tweed.

Fabrics with Surface Sheen

Satin is an example of a fabric that reflects light and can cause shading when viewed from different angles. Other examples are taffeta, chintz, and polished cotton, and extra consideration should be given when laying out these fabrics. If it is entirely uncertain whether cutting one way will be necessary, the factory can cost it both ways and can send a sample of each for consideration.

Directional Prints

Most prints are designed to allow the pattern pieces to be laid out lengthwise either way (head up or head down) so that direction doesn't matter. However, prints sometimes have a one-way design with an up direction built in, such as a print of Paris landmarks with the top of the Eiffel tower always in the same direction. This requires extra fabric and needs to be noted at the first proto stage to allow for accurate costing. Figure 7.24 shows a floral print arranged as a one-way and as a two-way design. The one way has all the flowers facing up. Extra care must be given to the **fabric layout** (plan for cutting) and the cutting because the garment appearance would suffer if the direction were not considered, or if one panel were accidentally cut incorrectly. This print will also require more fabric in the layout. It is important to establish what is considered up because it is not necessarily clear, so in this example the instructions include the directions "flower stems downward."

The two-way version is quite similar, this time arranged to be able to lay out the pattern pieces either way. Unless there is some specific design advantage, it is preferable to choose fabrics with a two-way design. The cutting instructions for the one-way version appear below the sketches. The two-way version is nondirectional and does not require specific cutting instructions.

Border print fabrics have a different design right-to-left on the roll (see Figure 7.25). These styles need extra consideration and require additional yardage because they are laid out not with the first concern to conserve yardage, but rather to integrate the design into the garment in a pleasing, harmonious way. Border prints must be designed with a lot of thought towards the grain of the fabric, the layout, and the yield. Not every fabric will drape correctly when cut on the crossgrain; for example, if the warp yarns are substantially different from the weft yarns in terms of weight. Border prints add

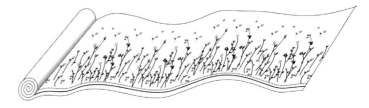

Figure 7.25 **Border print fabric.**

exclusivity and value to a garment; however, they are not always appropriate to every fabric or price point.

Border prints used on a skirt have certain cutting considerations, depending on the silhouette. Figure 7.26 provides examples of three different scenarios.

- Figure 7.26a has a "gentle" design in which there is not a sharp contrast from top to bottom.
- Figure 7.26b shows a way to utilize the straight lines formed at the selvedge edge by giving the garment a zigzag hem and cutting the panels on the bias.
- Figure 7.26c has a woven border design, typical of a hand-woven style of fabric. In this case the border design at the hem is kept level by the choice of a dirndl silhouette, a cylindrical-shape skirt with the top fullness gathered (or pleated) onto a waistband.

Styles with Flare

On a skirt with a lot of flare, the pattern will appear to hang lower at the side seam. By studying the layout in Figure 7.27, you can see why the finished seam creates a miter or a *chevron effect* where the stripes meet up at the seams. This can be incorporated into a pleasing garment, but could also have an unexpected or unwanted effect. On a garment with just a little flare, the pattern could appear to drop down oddly at the side seams. In this case, the cutting instructions should be indicated with a sketch, as in Figure 7.27.

Border prints can sometimes be used for interesting and elaborate effects. Figure 7.28 shows a garment designed to have the border details on the body area using the floral stripe section. (Another type of border fabric is **Schiffli lace**, a kind of eyelet with a finished scalloped border.)

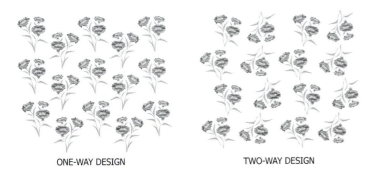

ONE-WAY DESIGN   TWO-WAY DESIGN

XYZ Product Development, Inc.
CONSTRUCTION PAGE
Cutting information: print is 1-way, lengthwise (flower stems downward)

Figure 7.24 **Floral print one way and two way.**

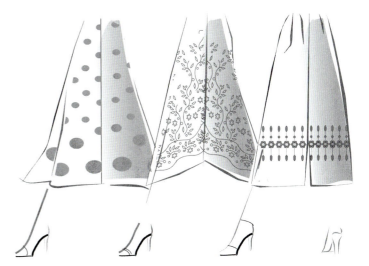

Figure 7.26 **Examples of border designs.**

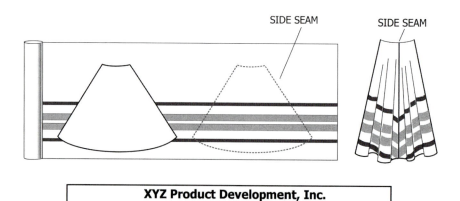

Figure 7.27 **Drop-down effect of a striped border.**

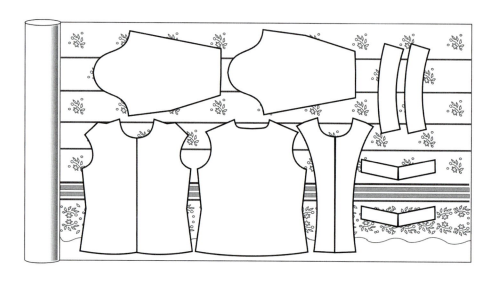

Figure 7.28 **Layout example for border print.**

Fabrics with Large Motifs

Fabrics with larger motifs need to be planned so that the motifs will match after construction. In addition, unless a deliberately asymmetrical look is desired, the motifs should be centered on the body. A simple garment will be most successful.

Figure 7.29 shows a layout for a sleeveless top. The fabric would need to be calculated for the print to accommodate the largest size, so there would be a certain amount of additional fallout for each smaller size. In addition, the motif has to be carefully centered and should not be placed so as to emphasize the stomach. If the back panel is to match as well, there are additional elements to consider, such as matching at the side seams. However, there is more flexibility to the layout if the back panel remains solid. With a simple design and all the details carefully worked out, and with the fabric printed to accommodate it, such a style would be workable.

Engineered Prints

Engineered prints are specially designed prints, a step beyond border prints, in which the pattern is intended to end up in a particular place on the garment, such as collar, cuff, or yoke. The Italian company Pucci is probably the most famous user of this technique. Figure 7.30 shows such a style.

In Figure 7.30a, the pattern is designed to be the shaped collar, a border on the sleeves, and a different, wider border at the bottom. Figure 7.30b shows a border print using different directions, both crosswise and lengthwise. Such a design would need to be carefully planned with the factory because of the way in which it would need to be laid out, but it adds considerable interest and exclusivity. Figure 7.30c shows a third arrangement. Note that the surplice edge of the bodice is on the straight. Because of that, the bodice itself is on the bias.

Figure 7.29 **Layout with large motif.**

a   b   c

Figure 7.30 **Cut for engineered prints.**

Nap or Pile

Fabrics such as corduroy, fleece, velvet, or velveteen, or knits such as velour, that have a raised surface or brushing, have a nap or pile. For these fabrics, the pattern pieces must be laid out in the same direction. The fabric will "read" differently between nap up and nap down; therefore, the two methods cannot be mixed within one garment. Otherwise, the panels will have different shades. All panels in the same garment absolutely must have the same direction (unless there is a design reason why not), but there are three additional choices that affect the yield.

Nap Up for All Units

All the pattern pieces are laid head up on the layout, the same way as for a one-way print. Pile fabrics laid out this way will have the richest color, but over time there is more wear on the surface. It would be a good choice for a high-end velvet jacket.

Nap Down for All Units

All the pattern pieces are laid head down on the layout. The garments will wear better, but will not have such a rich, deep color. This is a good choice for corduroy bottoms, children's wear, and some lighter colors in which a deeper shade has no advantage (see Figure 7.31).

Nap Either Way for All Units

Having some units all up and all down is called one-way for garment/two-way for bulk (*bulk* meaning bulk production, as opposed to sample production). This method has the best yield (least fabric usage), but garments will not be identical to each other. This method works well for fabrics where the difference between nap up and nap down is not dramatic. Otherwise, there will be garments hanging next to each other in the store in the same color, but with different shades. Additional consideration must be given if garments are to be sold as coordinates, such as a

PANEL ACCIDENTLY
REVERSED

XYZ Product Development, Inc.
CONSTRUCTION PAGE

Cutting information: one way, nap down for all units--all visible pieces

Figure 7.31 Cutting instructions for nap and coordinates.

skirt or pant with a jacket; naturally they must be cut so that they will match each other in shade if they are intended to be worn together.

Figure 7.31b is an example of what happens if a small part is sewn with the nap running opposite of all the other pieces. Through an unfortunate series of events at the factory, the jacket has one panel reversed (nap up in a garment with all other panels nap down). Because the inset belt piece is a rectangle with no obvious up or down in the shape itself, it was accidentally reversed during the sewing process. It happens to be at the right front, and is very noticeable, resulting in a lower-quality garment. This is the fault

of the factory, and it may appear on one incorrect garment, or a few, or the entire production run, but it is something that an experienced factory will understand how to control and avoid.

Stripes

Stripe direction is usually specified vertically or horizontally. As with plaids, stripe pattern matching is an important quality indicator. Vertical stripes are the easiest to specify, and a simple shirt or other garment may not need any special consideration. However, with the addition of a patch pocket, choices need to be made concerning matching. Horizontal stripes have more potential matching points than do vertical because of the side seams and the front, if it has a front closure.

A striped fabric can also require a one-way layout. Figure 7.32a, a men's golf shirt, shows an ombre-striped shirt with the maximum points of matching body and sleeves laid out the same direction, sleeves matching body across the chest, sleeves matching each other, and sides seams matching. Figure 7.32a also shows that the construction of the front helps the matching—the placket is not a separate piece, so it's much easier to have it match from right to left. This is a common construction for a men's rugby or polo shirt.

Figure 7.32b shows the same shirt cut with no matching instructions and no consideration to one-way design. This saves money in production, but because neither the right and left sleeves nor the side seams match, it has a rather haphazard look. In addition, the placket is a separate piece, which makes it more difficult to match the seams across the front placket area. This would not be considered high-quality construction.

Cost issues are considered in all phases of the commercialization process. The thoughtful selection of fabrics and the development of a design that works well with the specific fabric, combined with clear and concise cutting instructions, can minimize a great many problems and ensure higher quality.

SIDE SEAM

SIDE SEAM

XYZ Product Development, Inc.
CONSTRUCTION PAGE

| Cutting information: 1 way, lengthwise |
| Match Horizontal: NA |
| Match Vertical: Side seams |
| Match, other: Sleeves match each other |

a

b

Figure 7.32 Striped men's golf shirt.

Summary

Fabric is one of the most important apparel quality indicators. To use fabric appropriately in their chosen designs, designers should carefully consider the unique characteristics of fabrics, design details, cut, and the end use of apparel products. Knits and wovens have different characteristics for each and they affect how each chosen fabric should be laid out and cut. Based on designs of fabric, styles of final garments, and fabric characteristics such as nap or not, technical designers should specify instructions catered to each on how to cut to develop the most cost-effective, high-quality apparel products.

Designers and professionals working in the apparel production process should clearly understand such listed factors of fabrics, design details, cut, and the end use of apparel products and how they interact together to make a completed final product that is functionally sound and aesthetically pleasing, to ultimately meet the highest standard of quality.

Study Questions

1. In your wardrobe, find examples of your personal apparel that have directional fabric. List what they are and why they can be categorized as directional fabric. What cutting instructions can be used for the apparel products? Why do you think the instructions are important for products?

2. Observe the garments you are wearing now. Which are knit and which are woven?

3. Try to find any garments in your wardrobe that are made with plaid. Is each garment even or uneven plaid? Describe the plaid of one garment and draw a diagram of it. Write the cutting instructions that would be sent to the factory. Check each garment part and see if there are any unmatching plaids on the garment. Why do you think the garment has unmatching or matching plaids? Consider various factors related to apparel production before answering.

4. Refer to the *Technical Sourcebook for Apparel Designers* STUDIO. Find a dress style, which is easier to match plaid. Compare the design line of Dress #11 Cheongsam and Dress 14 Sundress and discuss which one would be easier to match plaid.

5. Refer to Appendix C in the STUDIO. Identify which styles of skirts, pants, shirts and tops would not be a good candidate for light-weight knit jersey (T-shirt weight).

Check Your Understanding

1. What are the differences and similarities between woven and knit fabric? Identify the differences and similarities in your writing.

2. What are the differences between lengthwise and crosswise grain? Why do you think it is important to know the differences?

3. What is bias? How is it different from lengthwise and crosswise grain?

4. Identify the main cut instructions for even and uneven plaids.

5. Explain quality issues related to cut in woven fabrics.

6. What are the cutting instructions for styles with flares for skirts?

References

Brown, P., and J. Rice. 2001. *Ready to Wear Apparel Analysis* (3rd ed.). Upper Saddle River, New Jersey: Prentice Hall

Humphries, M. 2009. *Fabric Glossary* (4th ed.). Upper Saddle River, NJ: Pearson-Prentice Hall.

Kadolph, S. J. 2007. *Textiles* (10th ed.). Upper Saddle River, NJ: Pearson-Prentice Hall.

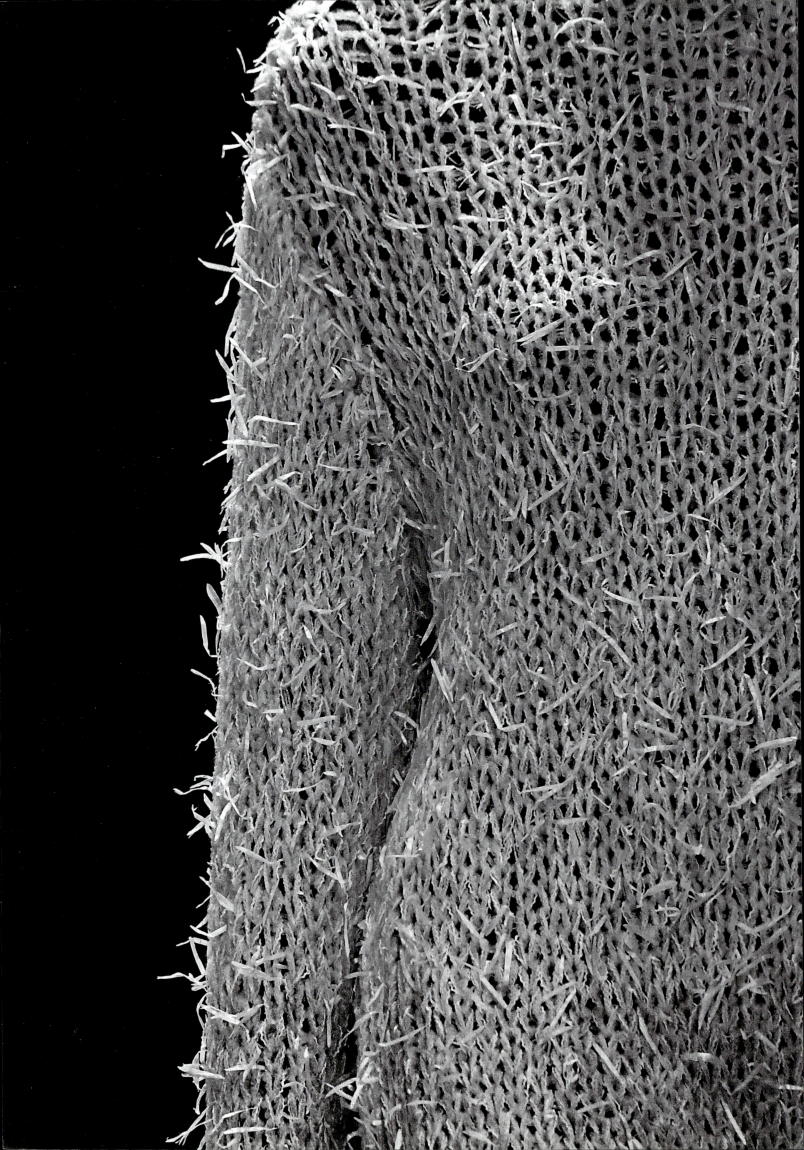

Sweater Design and Manufacturing

Chapter Objectives

After studying this chapter, you will be able to:

- Recognize the differences between knit apparel and sweater apparel
- Evaluate the components that go into a sweater
- Identify the principal stitches used in commercial sweater making
- Differentiate among the main types of sweater construction
- Utilize the terminology of stitches and shaping techniques
- Create and sketch a sweater design
- Build a specialized tech pack for a sweater garment

Key Terms

argyle
binding off
cable stitches
carded
castoff
combed
course
covering power
cut-and-sew apparel
double-face fabric
double jacquard
filament yarns
float thread
full-fashioning
gauge

hand pin knitting
hand-loom machines
intarsia
knitdowns
ladder-back jacquard
latch-hook needle
linking
links-links
live loops
mark
miss stitch
monofilament
plating
pointelle
punch-cards

purl stitch
rib knit structure
single jacquard
staple fibers
stocking frame
technical back
technical face
tuck stitch
wale
weft knitting
woolen yarns
worsted yarns
yarn count

Designing sweaters is somewhat different than designing **cut-and-sew apparel** products, such as shirts and pants. The manufacturing process itself is fundamentally different; sweater panels are shaped through a specialized technique known as **full-fashioning**, which is a method of widening or narrowing each panel as the knitting process progresses. In that sense, the fabric is created at the same time as the garment, something unique to sweaters. A wide spectrum of weights and constructions is used, and sweaters can range from very warm winter garments to cool and lacy summer garments, depending on the yarns and stitches used.

One reason for the enduring popularity of sweater-knit items is that they tend to have a comfortable fit because of the inherent stretch characteristics of the knit construction. They are usually offered in the small, medium, and large sizes, rather than in number sizes, which is less risky for a buyer because fewer units (fewer SKUs) need to be purchased for a single style.

Sweaters are generally designed as tops or coats (garments that cover the upper body), although skirts and dresses are also sweater-knit. Other popular sweater-knit apparel items are accessories such as hats, scarves, mittens, and gloves. The knitting industry is split into two broad segments, one that makes knit *fabrics*, and one that makes *apparel* items, like sweaters. Each of these industries uses specialized machinery (Johnson, Cohen, and Sarkar, 2015).

History and Evolution

The type of knitting most similar to hand knitting of today is known to scholars as **hand pin knitting** to distinguish it from other ancient techniques: knotting, twisting, circular peg frames, and crossed-loop fabrics. With yarn and pins (what we would call *knitting needles*), the craft now called *hand knitting* creates garments with intricate shaping (such as gloves) and equally intricate patterns. Because knitting was easier to learn and did not require expensive equipment like a loom, the craft of knitting developed into an important industry for artisans throughout the medieval period.

Sweaters today mix modern elements with techniques developed over centuries of artistry. The child's sweater example in Figure 8.1 has a traditional feel to the pattern, but includes more whimsical elements and closes with a zipper. The front closure has ribbon trim sewn on either side but also another special touch—knitted lace. The rib start at the bottom introduces the five colors in the colorway with stripes, a charming contrast to the overall pattern.

Invention of the Stocking Frame

The foundation for modern knitting machinery was the invention of the **stocking frame** in 1589 by Reverend William Lee. His device is described nowadays as a flatbed weft knitting machine, in which the operator would add rows in a back-and-forth motion. Such a device enabled the operator to knit courses of loops at ten times the speed of hand-held pins. Hand pins (including the knitting needles of today) are straight and pointed, so skill and dexterity is required to keep the loops in place; by contrast, the stocking frame employs hooked loop holders.

Figure 8.1 Contemporary mix of traditional and modern. Ingrid Schneider.

One major advance in machine knitting technology was the invention of the **latch-hook needle** in 1847. This holds the yarns in place while the loops are being formed and then they release when the needles align. Figure 8.2 shows the mechanism of the hinged latch. On the right is an actual needle from a knitting machine. This type of needle is still used today (Spencer, 1989).

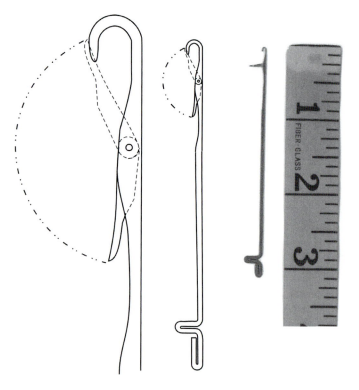

Figure 8.2 Latch-hook needle.

Weft Knitting Fundamentals

The method of construction for fully fashioned sweaters is called **weft knitting** and is generally done on a flatbed machine; fabric is formed by the progressive formation of horizontal rows of loops. The process proceeds in a back-and-forth motion, from bottom to top.

Anyone who has knit even the simplest object (a scarf, pot holder, or even just a swatch) has a basic idea of some of the fundamentals and the most common knitting terms. Students familiar with hand knitting have a distinct head start in understanding the basic structures of knitting over those who do not.

Stitches

The basic unit of knitting is the stitch, which appears as a loop. Both knit fabric and sweater-knit garments share the same structure, which may be described as the interlooping of yarns to create fabric. Of course, the stitches used in fabric are much smaller, with many more per inch, but under a magnifying glass the same loop structure would be seen in a jersey fabric as in a jersey-knit sweater. In sweater knitting, the four basic stitches are knit, purl, miss, and tuck. These stitches, used singly or in combination, form the basis of all sweaters.

Jersey Stitch (Knit Face and Purl Reverse)

The jersey stitch is one of the most common in both hand knitting (where it is known as *stockinette stitch*) and machine knitting, and it is widely used for single jersey fabrics, fully fashioned knitwear, and socks. Jersey has a distinctly different appearance on the face and reverse. Sometimes called *plain knitting*, the jersey side is referred to as the **technical face** in commercial terminology, which means this side is usually the outside (though it need not be). This *knit side* is smoother, and the stitches form a sort of V (see Figure 8.3a).

Figure 8.3b, reverse jersey, is called the **technical back**. In hand-knitting terminology the reverse jersey would be the *purl side*, with its characteristic bumps. It is important to remember that jersey and reverse jersey are not two different stitches; rather they are the front and back of the same loop. Jersey construction has the highest machine productivity and is the least expensive to produce.

Courses and Wales

The technical term for a row is a **course**, and the shaded row in Figure 8.4a is one course. Knitting progresses from bottom to top as courses are added. **Wale** refers to a vertical line of stitches (Figure 8.4b), in which each successive vertical row supports the stitch below and is supported by the row above, one needle per wale. *Wale* (the vertical element) is also a term used to describe corduroy (as in *wide wale* or *pinwale*).

One way to remember the difference between courses and wales is to remember that *course* (the horizontal element) is a term also used in bricklaying. As a brick wall starts at the bottom and builds upwards, with successive courses added on from right to left and left to right, so too a sweater begins at the bottom and has successive courses added from right to left and left to right.

Figure 8.5 shows a swatch of hand-knit sweater-weight jersey. In Figure 8.5a the dark row is one course. When a single course is formed in a contrast color of yarn as in this example, it reads like a horizontal zigzag stripe and highlights the characteristic V appearance of the knit-side stitches on the technical face of the goods. The technical back of the same swatch, the reverse jersey, shows how the same contrasting single row appears as two rows (Figure 8.5b). The bumpy or ridged texture of the purl-side stitches is clearly seen in contrast to the technical face.

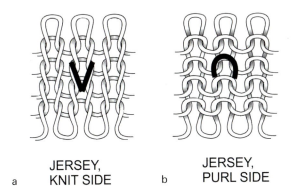

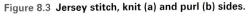

Figure 8.3 Jersey stitch, knit (a) and purl (b) sides.

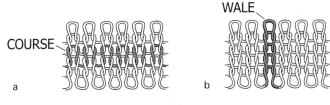

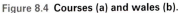

Figure 8.4 Courses (a) and wales (b).

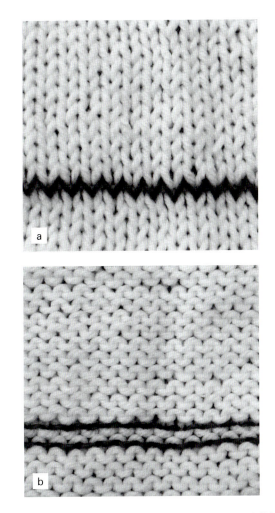

Figure 8.5 Knit swatch, technical face (a) and technical back (b).

One important characteristic of jersey is that the panel tends to curl, with the sides curling toward the back, and the top and bottom toward the front. A long object in jersey stitch will tend to curl into a sort of tube. Unless that is the specific design intention, it is not generally a good choice for a scarf, muffler, or other item intended to lay flat. For a tubular object such as a hat or sweater, that tendency is not a problem. Figure 8.6a shows a scarf in jersey stitch and why it is not the best choice. The actual scarf is 8 inches wide spread open (marked with a tape measure on the wearer's right side), but left alone it curls back up to about 2 inches wide. However, this same tendency can be used for a decorative effect, as seen in Figure 8.6b. There the jersey rolls to the outside, as the neck finish for a lacy sweater. Note that the neck trim stitches are much smaller than the body stitches. This is not uncommon and helps to stabilize the neck and prevent it from stretching out. This sort of specification (stitch gauge) will be noted in the tech pack to guide the sweater maker.

If one of the loops of a sweater were to break or to fall off a needle, it would form a *run* (American term) or *ladder* (British term), which creates holes in a vertical direction along the wale (see Figure 8.7). Great care is taken to prevent this during manufacturing, although on a sweater it is possible to repair.

Knit Stitch

As we touched on previously, knit stitch (or plain stitch) is the basic knitting stitch, and it is also the basis for jersey fabric. A

fabric that is light and sheer, or one that is dense and thick, is still called *jersey*, as long as the jersey construction is used.

Purl Stitch

Purl stitch is the technical back of jersey. A sweater made from alternating rows of knit and purl stitches resembles the technical back of jersey but has the same rather horizontal texture on *both* sides. It is a **double-face fabric** and also lies flat and does not curl at the edges. Another term for this is *garter stitch*.

Purl Knit Fabrics

Also known as **links-links**, this is created by an automated specialty machine with two needle beds that share one set of double-ended latch needles. This enables both knit and purl stitches to be knit on the same wale. This is different than rib construction (in which each wale is all knit or all purl). The fabric is one course of purl and one of knit. The resulting panel is stretchier in length, but has a lower machine productivity, so it is slower and more expensive to produce. This stitch was once commonly used for a type of golf cardigan (Sharp, 2012).

Rib

The **rib knit structure** is created by alternating wales of knit and purl in the same course and requires a double bed machine. One knit and one purl alternating creates a rib called 1×1. Many combinations of rib are possible. Rib is also a double-face fabric because the technical face and back have the same appearance, and have a lengthwise corrugated effect with high width-wise extensibility. The ribs create a certain firmness along the wales, a tendency that is useful for many things, such as a ribbed turtleneck, ribbed cuffs, and so on.

Rib-knit finished goods lie flat and do not curl. This structure can be used for an allover garment, or as trim for collars, cuffs, and bottoms. If used as an allover fabric, it provides a shapely, close-to-the-body fit.

Rib Trims

The knit swatch in Figure 8.8a has a rib start, as might be used for a sleeve cuff. It shows the tendency to draw in and create shape and the distinct vertical effect of the ridges. Figure 8.8b is an example of 2×4 rib. It shows how the goods look different from

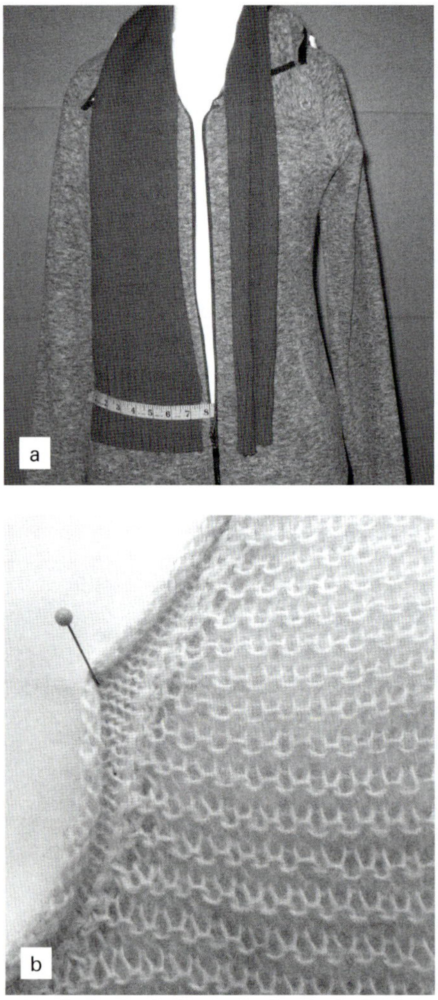

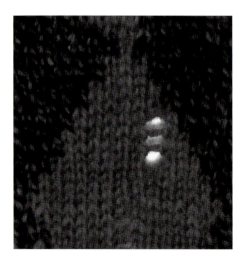

Figure 8.6 **Jersey has a tendency to curl.**

Figure 8.7 **Run formed along the wales.**

face to back, with the knit stitches coming forward and the purl stitches receding.

Miss Stitch

Also called *welt stitch* or *float stitch*, the **miss stitch** is achieved when the machine needles deactivate at patterned intervals and do not move into position to accept a yarn. A **float thread** is formed when a needle stays back. The example in Figure 8.9a shows a miss stitch with two needles deactivated; this is the technical back of the goods. The technique results in a comparatively lighter, narrower, and less stretchy fabric.

Tuck Stitch

A **tuck stitch**, shown in Figure 8.9b, is formed when the latch needle picks up a new stitch without knitting off the previous one. It is possible to hold such stitches for more than one row and then knit them off all at once. Tuck stitches are more successful with a knit stitch on either side, and they can create a highly textured effect, like thermal or waffle knit. The technique increases the weight and width of the fabric compared to plain knitting.

Ottoman Rib

This is created by knitting two or more courses on one bed only, forming a horizontal bump on one side of the fabric. It is often combined with striping (Figure 8.10).

Tuck Rib

One popular variation is known by the term *full cardigan*. For this configuration, both needle beds (for full cardigan) or one needle bed (for half cardigan, a variation) form tuck stitches. The result is a bulky knit construction with a lot of wale-wise stretch useful for heavy knitwear. Full cardigan looks the same on the face and back; half cardigan looks different front to back. The ribs spread and the fabric is wider than conventional rib. Half cardigan is also known as *shaker stitch*. Figure 8.11a is the technical face; Figure 8.11b is the back. Another type of tuck rib is known as *waffle* or *thermal*.

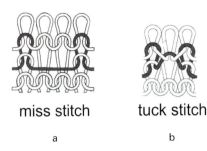

miss stitch   tuck stitch

a   b

Figure 8.9 Miss and tuck stitches.

Figure 8.10 Ottoman rib.

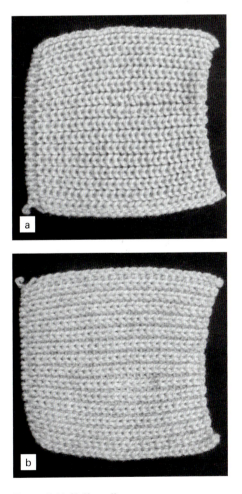

Figure 8.11 Half cardigan.

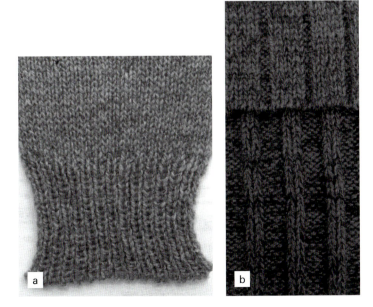

Figure 8.8 Rib trim variations.

Building Sweaters Commercially

Full Fashioning and Panel Knitting

The hallmark of classic sweater making is a weft-knit garment of knitted-to-shape panels with already-finished edges. Shaping is done on a flatbed knitting machine by a technique called **full fashioning**. The machines in a full-fashion **panel knitting** factory have additional shaping guided by instructions from a knit pattern on a punch card or computer file. The panel is shaped by increasing or decreasing the number of needles in action. When narrowing occurs, a stitch is transferred to an adjacent needle, which creates a distinctive stitch called a **mark**. Figure 8.12 shows "marks at two rows in" (fashioning marks at two wales or stitches in from the seam), a popular designation for armhole or sleeve shaping.

The swatch in Figure 8.13 is another example of full fashioning. Notice how the swatch expands in width near the center as stitches are added and then narrows again near the top. The top loops are unsecured where the piece was taken off the needles (also called ***live loops***). If one of these were pulled it would create a run vertically down the wale, so the top edge of a piece is finished by **binding off**. The finished shape and size is incorporated while making the panel itself, something impossible to achieve on a commercial scale with woven fabric. (The equivalent for a woven garment might be for each pattern piece to have its own shaped loom, not something that is even commercially possible.)

Linking

After the panels are completed and taken off the machines, the seams are joined by the technique of **linking**. The swatch in Figure 8.14 shows an example of linking. Notice how the join is a chain-type stitch (shown here in a contrast color), which provides the seam with the ability to flex without breaking. It also creates very little seam allowance or bulk, which helps keep a smooth, flat appearance at the seams. Self yarn is often used for the linking operation rather than sewing thread.

The process of linking uses special machines (see Figure 8.15). The job of linking in a sweater factory is one that requires great skill and care. Live loops (meaning not secured), temporarily held with scrap yarn from one side of the garment, are carefully attached to the machine, and loops from the piece being linked are threaded on. The linking device joins the two; another term for this is *point-to-point linking*. This is seldom performed in the United States due to the cost.

Combination of Fully Fashioned and Cut-and-Sew

A variety of shortcuts can be used to save labor. One shortcut is to knit a sweater sleeve blank in rectangular form, with a rib bottom. After a stack of these are made, the sleeves are cut into the desired shape with a knife and later joined together with an overlock machine. A four-thread overlock (or serger) machine is faster to operate and saves the expense of linking. This type of cutting results in fabric waste, so it is employed either for sweaters made of inexpensive yarns or for high-end sweaters that are very fine gauge. This can potentially save quite a lot in labor costs.

At the other extreme arc garments made from heavy-gauge sweater-like piece goods (roll goods) but using the cut-and-sew method of construction, joined with overlock or flatlock machines. Part of a designer's job is to approach a sweater with the ingenuity needed to keep the look, but to make sure the cost will fall within the parameters set out by the merchandiser and the line plan. Sweaters can be a combination of techniques depending on the overall design. Different factories have different specialties, machines, and expertise, and choosing the right factory is an important consideration.

Figure 8.12 **Full-fashion marks.**

Figure 8.13 **Shaping by full fashioning.**

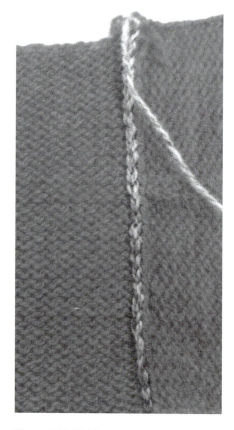

Figure 8.14 **Linking at seams.**

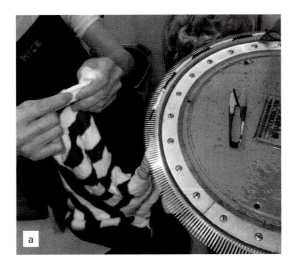

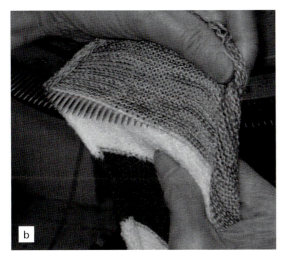

Figure 8.15 **Linking in the factory.**

Figure 8.16 **Hand loom machines.**

Figure 8.17 **Hand loom operations.**

Hand Knitting

Some commercial sweaters are hand knitted by individual knitters using knitting needles. The resulting sweaters are generally very expensive—perhaps several hundred dollars, and sometimes far more. The fashion for hand-knitted sweaters comes and goes but remains a small niche market due to the expense and the difficulty of training and managing hand knitters able to maintain a consistent output of tension and quality. However, there are still certain techniques that can only be achieved through hand knitting.

Hand-Loom Punch Card Machines

Figures 8.16 and 8.17 show some young men working in a sweater factory in Vietnam on machines called **hand-loom machines**. The knit panel in progress (white) can be seen hanging below the bed of the machine. It is weighted at the bottom to help the stitches form smoothly. The decision of whether to use hand-loom machines like these or electronic ones depends on the design of the sweater and the quantity of the order. These machines are less expensive to purchase than electronic ones, but slower and more labor intensive. The yarns being knitted are put up on large white cones, seen in the foreground of Figure 8.17.

Punch-cards (Figure 8.18) guide single-bed hand-loom machines in the same way a computer file would guide an electronic machine, adding colors or patterns and shaping the dimensions of each panel.

Automatic Machines

The most modern knitting machines are electronic and have instructions programmed into a computer. The two major brands of such machines are Stoll from Germany and Shima Seiki from Japan. Electronic machines create texture stitches and color patterns, and the work can be done without the labor costs of a hand-loom machine. However, the initial setup is more complicated, and the factory may require that the expense be paid by the customer. If the design reaches a certain volume (such as 1,000 units) the set-up cost may be waived. In the mass production process, the machines can run with little attention, and one worker can oversee many machines.

There are many advantages to electronic machines. They allow for fully fashioned buttonholes, which are stronger and cleaner than a zig-zag type. Such machines can combine different gauges into one garment, produce several sweaters at a time, and even create

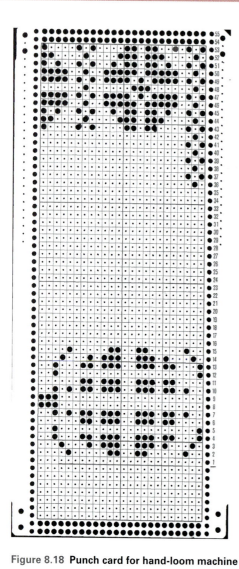

Figure 8.18 Punch card for hand-loom machine

Figure 8.19 Weft knit automatic flat bed with double bed.
Ingrid Schneider.

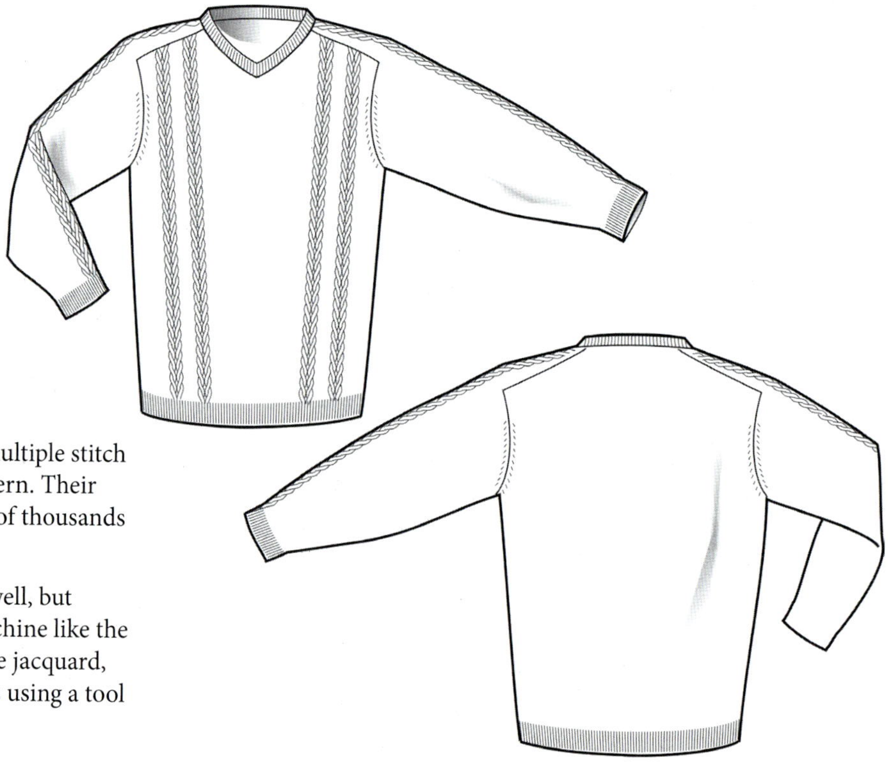

Figure 8.20 Fully fashioned design with engineered cables.

integral, or seamless, garments. They can produce multiple stitch techniques on one garment, mixing texture and pattern. Their main drawback is the price, which can be hundreds of thousands of dollars for each machine.

Hand-loom machines are precision instruments as well, but powered by the operator by hand. A double-bed machine like the one pictured in Figure 8.19 is required for rib, double jacquard, and other stitches. In this photograph the operator is using a tool to transfer stitches.

Example of a Full-Fashioned Sweater

Figure 8.20 is a design appropriate for a men's full-fashioned sweater. It has a handsome *engineered* design that features cables placed individually or in multiples, and other areas without cables (as on the back panel). Panel knitting allows for this sort of special design, with its roots in the design flexibility of hand knitting. Note the full-fashioning marks at the armhole. Tech sketches of sweaters must include those marks in order to indicate where any visible full-fashioning should appear. The side seams, for example, have shaping at the edges but do not usually have marks. All such things are noted in the tech pack. The rib start on the bottom and cuffs is already knit in one (no seam joining) with the panel. The only thing left to finish is the construction and attachment of the 1×1 rib at the V-neck.

Figure 8.21 shows a sweater style in process, with two units being made simultaneously. Because the panels are knitted in the final shape, there is no wasted yarn as there would be in a cut-and-sew operation. The pieces come off the machine with edges finished and ready to be joined together. After the panels are knitted, they are assembled on the linking machine.

Cut-and-Sew Method

The second example is made in a cut-and-sew method from flat (or tubular cut open to lay flat) fabric. This method has certain

Each panel
begins at the bottom
and progresses upward,
in a back-and-forth
motion

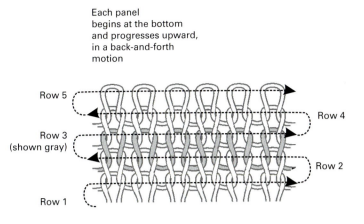

Figure 8.21 Sequence of panel knitting.

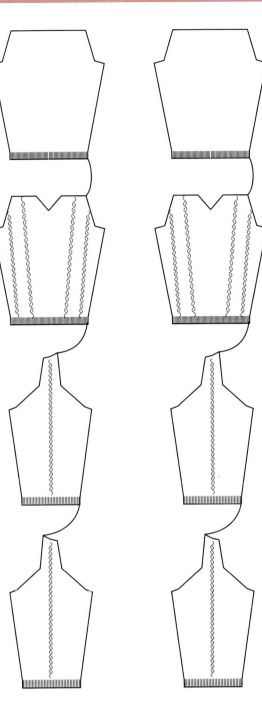

design limitations. The pattern will appear as a regular allover design as in Figure 8.22. This type of sweater is made from roll goods, already made-up fabric delivered to the factory on rolls. The knit fabrics used for this need to be firmer so they can be rolled out for cutting and have the seams joined with overlock machines. This is in marked contrast to fully fashioned sweaters, for which the sweater factory would receive just the yarn itself (on cones, as seen in the factory photo in Figure 8.17).

There are two main types of cut-and-sew sweaters. One is made in a sweater factory but employs ways to reduce labor. In this type, the body panels are knitted to the correct width and have already-finished side seams and a rib start; then the neck and armhole shapes are stacked in layers and cut out. Similarly, after the sleeve is knit to the correct width, the armhole shape is cut out with the knife, and the sweater parts are then joined on the overlock machine (serger). This saves quite a bit of labor but does entail some yarn waste where the pieces are cut.

The second type of cut-and-sew method has a lot in common with woven-garment construction in that the fabric is laid out in plies (layers). Figure 8.23 has a diagram of how that is done in a factory, with the fabric rolled into a stack called a *lay-up* and the plan for all the pieces (the marker) laid on top. The dark area shows what will be discarded after the lay-up is cut out and disassembled for the next steps in production. It also shows how

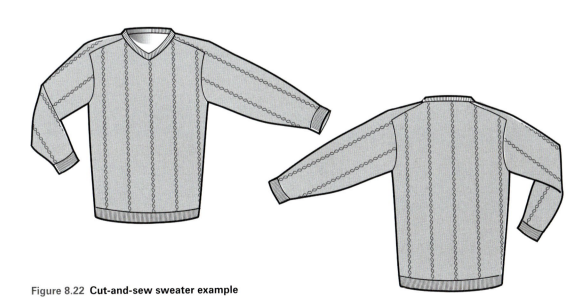

Figure 8.22 Cut-and-sew sweater example

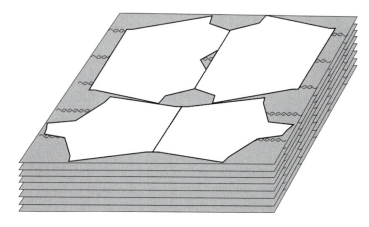

Figure 8.23 Lay-up for cut-and-sew sweater.

Figure 8.24 Finishing for cut-and-sew sweater.

the fabric has a cable-effect pattern knit into it, which will appear as an evenly spaced vertical emphasis. Using this cable-pattern fabric and this lay-up, there is no way to have the cables appear on some areas of the design and not others, as in the fully fashioned example. The garment seams, cuffs, bottom band, and neck trim will all be joined with a serger. All of this has more in common with the way a sweatshirt (an example of a cut-and-sew garment) is made than a traditional sweater.

There are other styles of cut-and-sew sweaters popular in the activewear market. These items are cut from roll goods that are stable enough to roll out and cut easily, and they often have a fleeced back for additional warmth. The garment in Figure 8.24 has the details of a sweater, but the construction of a cut-and-sew garment. The seams were joined with a serger. A single-needle lockstitch (regular sewing machine) is used to set the zipper and for the final topstitching.

The garment in Figure 8.25 shows the seam joining done with flatlock machines; then the garment is hemmed with a coverstitch machine. These are some examples of hybrid techniques between a traditional full-fashioned sweater and a cut-and-sew garment made from fleece (such as polar fleece). Note that full-fashion sweaters are seldom hemmed, so that is usually an easy way to distinguish certain cut-and-sew sweaters from a panel-knit one.

Whole-Garment (Integral) Knitting

Whole-garment knitting machines are an innovation that makes it possible to produce complete sweaters all within one knitting process, bypassing the cutting table and the linking machines altogether. A whole-garment knitting machine knits three seamless tubes—one as the body and the other two as the sleeves—on the same needle bed simultaneously and then finally knits the three tubes together to form a sweater. These sweaters are full fashioned and have no seaming at all, offering a new level of fit and comfort. The clothing comes off the machine as a finished product, including the trims. A small sweater takes about 20 minutes. Intricate effects such as intarsia (see page 149) can also be incorporated, as well as complex details such as pockets.

The complete-garment system's advantages lie in the following:

- A further reduction in materials beyond even fully fashioned production by eliminating seam allowances.
- Faster time to market by eliminating the need for sewing any components. These factors increase cost-effectiveness

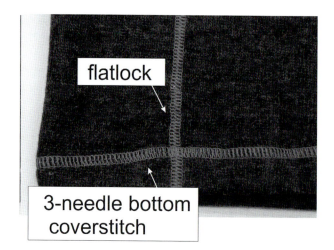

Figure 8.25 Seam and hem for cut-and-sew sweater.

(especially important when using high-performance materials for composites).

One might also argue that cutting down on wasted by-products makes complete-garment knitting better for the environment. The leading manufacturers of complete-garment knitting machines are Shima Seiki and Stoll. For examples, visit the website noted at the end of the chapter.

The complete-garment technique is widely used in the garment industry (from sportswear to sweaters) and for technical textiles (such as car seat covers, which also incorporate additional structural elements such as metal and plastic fasteners). The machines can produce a variety of topologies that were more difficult or impossible to create with knitting machines before, including connected tubes, circles, open cuboids, and even spheres (for helmet shells and other pre-forms).

Complete-garment knitting requires two needle beds for three-dimensional structures (such as clothing). As is the case with all fully fashioned knitting, machines require individual single needle selection (through electronic control) and presser feet (to hold down formed loops). Aspects of complete-garment knitting, such as changing the fabric width or diameter and connecting two sides of the structure together, are also possible with a single needle bed for two-dimensional or *flat* structures and are achieved by:

1. Changing knit structure (e.g., rib to jersey)
2. Varying the structural elements (stitch length, weft insertion, knit, tuck, float)
3. Shaping through loop transfer
4. Wale fashioning by *needle parking*

Yarns

Yarns are the materials formed into loops during knitting. Yarns are made up of fibers, either staple or filament, or any combination of the two. The choice of yarn is fundamental to any sweater design. Sweater yarns need to be relatively smooth and strong, with good recovery properties. The main factors that affect yarns and sweater design are:

- Yarn appearance (whether smooth or rough)
- Yarn structure (staple or filament)
- Length of fibers (staple or filament, and whether combed or carded)
- Fiber content (natural fibers, synthetic, or a blend)
- Twist/tension (direction and degree of twist)
- Number of strands in the yarns (single, plied, or core)
- Count (yarn size, thickness, or diameter)
- Number of ends (how many yarns in each stitch)

Altering the combination of components can change the final product a great deal, and understanding the effect of various elements is an important part of design problem solving.

Spun yarn is formed by the twisting, spinning, or otherwise bonding of fibers. Historically it was done by hand using a spinning wheel. Yarn spinning was one of the very first processes to be industrialized.

Yarn Structure

Yarns are formed from staple fibers or filament fibers. Spun yarns are created from **staple fibers** (relatively short lengths twisted together) and may be a mix of natural and synthetic. They are generally softer and fuzzier, and they are dull rather than shiny in appearance. Cotton yarn fibers are **carded** to disentangle them, remove small bits of debris, and align the fibers. For finer, more expensive yarns, the process goes further and the fibers are **combed**, which removes many shorter fibers and results in yarns of finer denier, smoother feel, and more uniform diameter.

Wool yarn is versatile, popular, and has a long history of use in high-quality garments. Wool and wool-blend yarns are categorized as either woolen or worsted. **Woolen yarns** are carded, but not combed, and the fibers are shorter and more hairy. Woolen yarns are carded and processed to a certain point, and **worsted yarns** are processed even further (see Figure 8.26). There are many cases, however, where woolen is preferred over worsted, and woolen sweater yarns provide more softness, bulk, and a higher warmth-to-weight ratio.

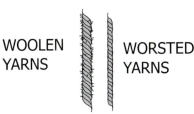

Figure 8.26 **Woolen and worsted yarns.**

Filament yarns are formed from multiple long, continuous lengths twisted together. Generally they have a fine, smooth appearance. The yarns are uniform in diameter and stronger than spun yarns of the same size. The final fabric may have problems with slippage or stability because the smooth surface of the yarns provides less friction to keep the stitches in place.

All synthetic yarns begin as *filament fibers* (very long, continuous fibers), extruded from a chemical base, and may later be cut into staple lengths and twisted. Most filament yarns are multifilament. Silk is the only natural-fiber filament yarn, but synthetic filament yarns are often used to produce silk-like effects.

An example of a **monofilament** yarn would be a length of fishing line. It is interesting to imagine a sweater made of fishing line, and such a garment would not be completely comfortable. Thicker monofilaments are typically used for industrial purposes (such as rope) rather than fabric production or garments.

Yarn Fiber Content

The fibers chosen for yarns vary greatly and impart different qualities. Understanding the trade-offs involved will help a designer make the right choices for cost, quality, and styling decisions. Yarns are selected for different end uses based on the characteristics of the yarn fibers, such as warmth (wool), breathability (cotton or bamboo), durability (nylon blend added to sock yarn, for example), softness (cashmere, alpaca), loft and lighter weight (acrylic), or to reduce cost (ramie). Pilling properties depend on the fiber content as well as on staple length and twist.

Spun yarns may contain a single type of fiber or may be a blend of various types. Combining synthetic fibers (which can have high strength, luster, and fire-retardant qualities) with natural fibers (which have good water absorbency and a comfortable feeling next to the skin) is very common. Yarns such as wool have a natural elasticity that help a sweater retain its shape over time. Cotton and linen yarns have less elasticity and can sag and lose shape.

The washability of the garment has a great deal to do with its marketability. Wool fibers often need special care to prevent shrinking; most of us have experienced having a wool sweater accidently thrown into the dryer, and later emerging 50 percent of its original size. Sweaters for children are more often made with acrylic yarn, which is lightweight and washable.

The most widely used blends are cotton–polyester and wool–acrylic fiber blends. Blends of different natural fibers are common, too, especially with more expensive fibers such as alpaca, angora, and cashmere. A small amount of expensive cashmere can often enhance a yarn while not adding too much to the cost.

Spandex is a generic fiber (Lycra˙ is one brand name used by the DuPont company) often added to yarns to increase their shape retention, especially for cotton, ramie, and rayon blends. It can be combined with any fiber. There are various methods of combining the spandex; the easiest is through a technique called plating (knitting the covered spandex yarn together with a standard yarn). The standard yarn is knit to the outside, and because it is larger, it fully conceals the spandex yarn on the back side. The spandex yarn is fed into the machine with a tensioning device so it is stretched fully. The addition of spandex works especially well with fine gauges (12gg to 14gg) and helps to achieve a smooth, slim-fitting sweater able to retain its shape. The plating technique, using two yarns at once, is employed not just with spandex but for other effects as well.

Certain yarn fiber combinations are chosen for another reason: to reduce the duty rates for importing the product. For example, for goods entering the United States, items with a wool content of less than 23 percent will be classified as *manmade fiber* with a duty rate of 32 percent. If the sweater has 23 percent or more of wool fiber, it falls into the 17 percent duty rate, and if made with a yarn that is more than 50 percent wool, it falls into the wool duty rate of 16 percent. All these things must be carefully weighed and balanced, because the improved duty rate for a higher wool percentage may create a yarn that is itchier, too expensive, or not washable.

Most larger companies have an import specialist who tracks duty rates and the changing regulations applicable to the destination country. That person helps the design department achieve the projected target costs by advising on the best duty rates as well as what to avoid in the materials cost. Different duty rates can apply to style details also, such as a pullover style or a cardigan.

Twist (Direction and Degree of Twist)

Sweater yarns are twisted to add various qualities to the hand, appearance, durability, and texture. Yarns are made by twisting parallel fibers and can be designated as *soft-twist* or *hard-twist*, depending on their twists per inch (TPI). Knitting yarns are usually soft-twist (2 to 12 TPI). The twist direction is known as S-twist or Z-twist. Z-twist yarns have spirals that run upward to the right, like the diagonal part of the letter Z; and S-twist yarns are the opposite (see Figure 8.27). The twist direction is more an element of the final appearance rather than quality or durability.

Number of Strands (Single or Plied)

One yarn is called a *single*, and two or more yarns together are called **plied** (as in 2-ply). Plied yarns increase strength and uniformity, but add cost (see Figure 8.28). A third configuration, *core spun yarns*, has additional yarns wrapped around a central core. An example is a spandex core with cover yarns wrapped around it, used to provide stretch.

Yarn is plied for many reasons: to add strength, texture, color, and elasticity, and to combine the positive qualities of various fibers. A sweater made up of singles has a strong tendency to torque (twist). This problem is commonly found in inexpensive garments. As a remedy, two S-twist singles can be plied in such a way as to form a Z-twist to provide stability and strength and to help eliminate torque (see Figure 8.29).

Z S

Z-TWIST AND S-TWIST

Figure 8.27 **Z-twist and S-twist.**

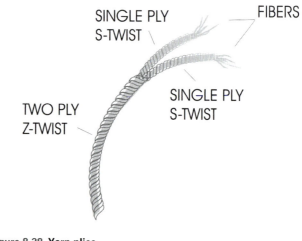

SINGLE PLY S-TWIST

FIBERS

TWO PLY Z-TWIST

SINGLE PLY S-TWIST

Figure 8.28 **Yarn plies.**

TORQUE AT SIDE SEAM

Figure 8.29 **Torqueing.**

Count (Size, Thickness, or Diameter)

Yarn thickness is known as count. **Yarn count** is designated by weight, and many measurement systems for different fibers have evolved through the decades. There are two main methods. The first is called the *direct system* (Decitex system), meaning the larger the yarn, the higher the number, and is used to measure filament yarns. The *indirect system/yarn count system* is a system for spun yarns, and as the number designations increase, the yarns get smaller and thinner—so the higher the number, the finer the yarn. The *Tex system* (a direct system) has evolved in an attempt to create a more universal method of specification, and states the weight of 1,000 meters of a given yarn.

Yarn count has a direct effect on the final product and on the **covering power**. Cover refers to the amount of yarn needed to fill a given space, such as one square inch. A yarn with lower covering power will have a more open effect. It is influenced by yarn shape, configuration, and yarn weight. Metric count (Nm) is a basic unit for sweater knitting. It represents the relationship between unit length and weight of yarn, which indicates how many thousands of meters of yarn weigh one kilogram. For example, a 1/14 yarn means that 14,000 meters of yarn weighs 1 kilogram. Yarn twist and fiber also influence the thickness of yarn and its Nm.

- Typical 7gg yarns are sized around Nm 6
- 5gg yarns are sized around Nm 3, Nm 4
- 3gg yarns are sized around Nm 2
- Two-ply yarn is 2/28 yarn whereas a one-ply yarn is 1/14, which is about the same size as a 2/28 yarn

Novelty yarns are used to add interest and texture to a design. There are many variations, from combinations of thick and thin yarns plied together, to ribbon yarn (arguably not a yarn at all but rather a woven tape), to metallic elements (see Figure 8.30).

Pilling

Most people are familiar with the common quality problem of pilling—tiny balls of short or broken fibers. When the ends of a

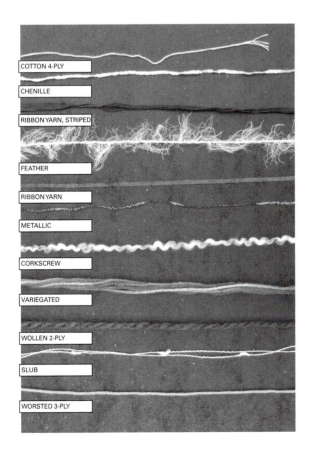

Figure 8.30 Novelty yarns.

fiber break from the surface and tangle with other broken ends nearby, a pill is formed. Pills are created by different factors. Some of the most common are as follows:

- Areas of higher abrasion tend to form pills faster, such as the sleeve opening and the side seam area below the waist. Activewear sweaters sometimes have reinforcement patches sewn in high-wear areas.
- Spun yarns pill more easily than filament yarns, because they have more fiber ends already exposed. The correct balance of spun fibers to filament fibers helps to reduce pilling. In addition, the longer the staple fibers are, the more secure they are within the yarn.
- Blended yarns often have pilling problems that single fibers may not; one example is 100 percent cotton yarns, which often have less pilling than blends of polyester and cotton.
- Certain fibers are more likely to pill than others, and stronger fibers hold the pills to the surface, whereas on yarns formed by weaker fibers, the pills tend to break away and drop off, escaping notice. Pilling on wool yarns is common, because the fibers are strong and the pills remain connected. In addition, wool fibers have a relatively rough, scaly surface that creates the tendency to snag and tangle, forming pills.
- Yarn twist has an effect as well, because soft-twist yarns pill more easily than hard-twist yarns. By increasing the yarn twist somewhat, the fiber ends remain more stable and less likely to protrude and form pills. Because sweater yarns generally have less twist than many fabric yarns, sweater pilling overall is a more common problem than, for example, pilling in a woven shirt.
- Softeners used by the spinner increase the tendency to pill.

Pilling is an issue that can cause a garment to be returned to the store for a refund. By choosing yarns with an eye toward reducing the tendency of the finished sweater to pill, the designer can avoid perceived quality problems and enhance repeat business.

Knitting with Multiple Ends

Multiple ends (strands) of the same yarn can be used to create a thicker yarn. In this way a sweater manufacturer can achieve many looks with one size of yarn, which helps them keep their yarn stock manageable. In the example shown in Figure 8.31, the same fine yarn is used with various gauges to achieve a wide variety of effects, from fine goods to bulky. In the first example there are two strands knit together as one; in the middle example, six strands are knit together as one, and so on. Note that the yarns used in this example of multiple ends are 2-ply (2/30s).

Gauge

In hand knitting, **gauge** refers to stitches per inch (so it could be almost any number), but in commercial parlance there are only a certain number of gauges available, based on the machinery design (see Figure 8.32). On a weft knitting machine, gauge (also referred to as **cut**) refers to the number of needles a particular machine has per inch. Common machine sizes are 3 gauge (written as 3gg), 6 gauge (6gg), 12 gauge (12gg), and 20 gauge (20gg). Three gauge would create a large stitch suitable for a winter sweater. Twenty gauge would be suitable for a very fine, lightweight sweater or twinset.

2/30's yarn used for all

| 2 ends on a 6gg machine | 6 ends on a 6gg machine | 10 ends on a 3gg machine |

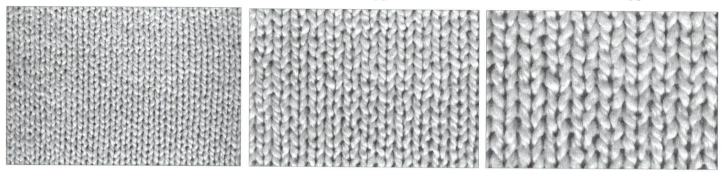

Figure 8.31 Multiple ends.

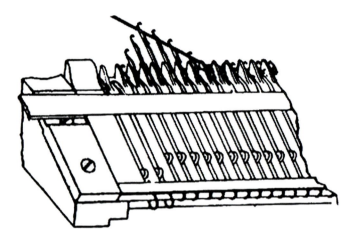

Figure 8.32 Machine needles.

Figure 8.33 Texture stitches.

Tension

The **tension** control can have a big effect on a swatch by making the stitches larger or smaller. A looser tension creates a relatively larger swatch in which the fabric is more elastic. Tighter tension creates a firmer hand and is often desired for areas needing more stability. A tighter tension overall uses more yarn and results in a heavier sweater. Because sweaters are costed by weight, the result will be a more expensive sweater, so the tension is an important costing element.

Texture Stitches

In terms of design and pattern stitches, a smooth yarn enhances the stitch quality of complicated patterns, whereas such a pattern may be obscured by a very textured yarn. For example, an intricate cable pattern in a boucle yarn may not show up enough to warrant the extra labor costs. A novelty yarn with variegated colors often works up best in a simple jersey or rib. Texture can be used in both lighter and heavier yarns, as long as a balance is achieved between the gauge and finished appearance.

Texture can be used in an allover way or as part of a placed design. In the body area of Figure 8.33, stitches create alternating vertical rows. The sleeves begin with a 1 × 1 rib start and are otherwise

plain (jersey). The mock-neck collar treatment is 1 × 1 rib as well. Rib trims reduce the dimensions and hug the body, helping the piece keep its shape.

Pointelle

To achieve a lighter, more feminine appearance, lace or pointelle stitches are often used. **Pointelle** is a type of stitch transfer lace. In this type of pattern, a single jersey stitch is transferred to the needle to the left or right. Repeated in an overall pattern, this creates an openwork effect. Figure 8.34 shows a lace pattern on the left and the charting for that pattern on the right. The piece in Figure 8.35 shows pointelle used in various ways: as an allover pattern on the bottom, as a border used to join the two sections visually, and as a larger pattern of diagonal pointelle on a jersey background.

Another type of lace pattern is achieved through *crochet*, a technique using a single hooked needle (called a *crochet hook*) to produce intertwined loops in a variety of patterns. Crochet can only be produced by hand, not by machine. Crochet is also used for finishing edges and creating plackets, because certain crochet stitches are innately stable. The example in Figure 8.36 has a lace pattern body and a stabilizing button-front placket.

Figure 8.34 **Lace stitches.**

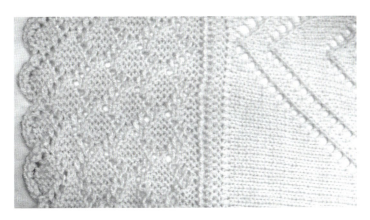

Figure 8.35 **Pointelle stitches.**

Figure 8.36 **Crocheted lace top with placket.**

Figure 8.37 **Cable stitches.**

Cable

Produced on a double-bed machine, cable stitching creates a three-dimensional fabric that seems to have a sort of braided effect sitting on top. There is a twisted effect created by physically switching sets of stitches on the needles. The **cable stitches** (and band intervals) are in a jersey formation and are bordered by loops of reverse jersey (see Figure 8.37). Many intricate cables have been developed over the centuries in hand knitting, the most famous being fisherman's sweaters from the Aran Islands of Ireland. Not all are translatable to machine knitting, but honeycomb and other machine variations follow the cable construction.

The garment in Figure 8.38 is an example of how cables are used to enhance the design lines and combine with other textures. The yarn is lightly tweeded, but not enough to obscure the cables. The collar, a 2 × 2 rib, has a complementary texture and plenty of stretch to lay around the shoulders. The combination of these elements provides a shapely and pleasing design.

Figure 8.38 **Cable design.**

Color Techniques

Sweater knits have many specialized ways of using pattern and color. Because of the nature of a stitch, patterns are often geometric. Since the color not in use is often carried along the back of the fabric, pattern and yarn weight must be carefully balanced to avoid adding too much extra weight.

Striping

The simplest method of adding color is a stripe, in which a color change is made at the beginning of a row. There are usually two rows of a color (or sets of an even number—4, 6, 8, and so on) because the carriage can pass over and then back to the side where the color changes are made. Eight to twelve colors is a common maximum; it is a good idea to check with the factory regarding their requirements or limitations.

The example in Figure 8.39 has stripes paired with other pattern techniques. Stripes are a simple way to combine colors. A graph is usually provided to guide the factory and confirm the color placements. Figure 8.39b in an example of the information the factory needs concerning the placement and color arrangement for a popular stripe known as ombré in which there is a gradual transition from one color to another. The one additional thing they need is the distance where the first stripe (B) begins, measured from HPS. That appears on an additional sketch.

Another type of stripe is called a feed stripe, which looks like a mélange of two different colors. This is an effect achieved by running two or more different colors through the same feeder. Stripes can be added to any stitch (jersey, tuck, and so on). Because of the back-and-forth action of a knitting machine, horizontal stripes are a natural variation. Vertical stripes, however, require additional stopping and starting, piecing, or other more labor-intensive methods (see intarsia, Figure 8.50 on page 149).

Figure 8.40 shows how the exact angle of the seam is important for matching. In this case the angle is about 45 degrees, the point at which stripes match up easily.

Plating

Plating refers to using yarns of two different colors knit together using a special feeder in such a way as to make one side of the goods a different color than the other; in a rib construction, the knit wale will be one color and the purl loops a second color. Depending on the two colors used, a great many subtle dimensional effects can be achieved, especially on things such as a cable. Plating yarns in larger gauges results in a very heavy sweater. Plating is also used to introduce spandex yarns for shape retention (Black, 2002).

Single Jacquard (Fair Isle)

Single jacquard is a method of adding color and pattern in which there are no more than two colors in a single row. It is called *single* because it's made on a single-bed machine. For the color not used, the color is carried along the back as a *float*. Figure 8.41 shows the technical face. This stitch is good for geometric designs and small patterns, in which there is not too much of any one color in any one row, as it is limited

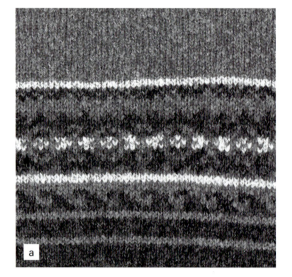

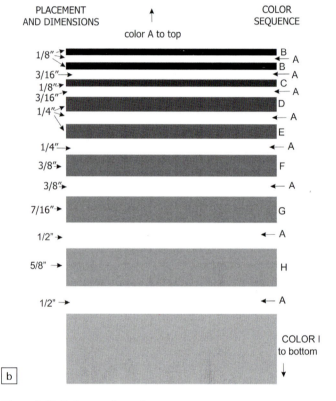

Figure 8.39 **Stripes and graph.**

Figure 8.40 **Matching stripes at the raglan.**

to how many stitches long the floating threads can be (usually no more than six stitches or 1 inch, whichever is less). If the stitches become too long, they are prone to catching and pulling. The floats also add warmth.

The back view of the Fair Isle design shows how the color not being used is carried along the back, so it looks a little like a blurry negative image (the light areas in Figure 8.41 are the dark areas in Figure 8.42). The floats on the back tend to limit the stretch in this area. The resulting goods tend to have a firm rather than drapeable hand, which makes it especially good for heavier outerwear styles (Walker, 1972).

Figure 8.43 has two versions of the same pattern. Figure 8.43a is two-color, and Figure 8.43b is five-color, but neither has more than two colors in any one row. The technical back can be used as the face, as in the design in Figure 8.44. This example has fur lining, braided ties, and a pom-pom. The main decoration on the outside are the floats carried across the technical back, here used as the right side.

There are many effects that can be achieved within the creative limitation of only two stitch colors per row. The design in Figure 8.45 features the traditional curved circular knit yoke from Scandinavian design. The yoke is knit "in the round" with no

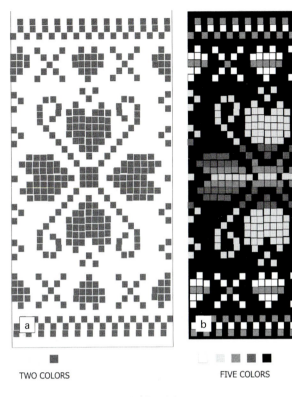

TWO COLORS   FIVE COLORS

Figure 8.43 **Colorations for Fair Isle**.

Figure 8.41 **Technical face of single jacquard.**

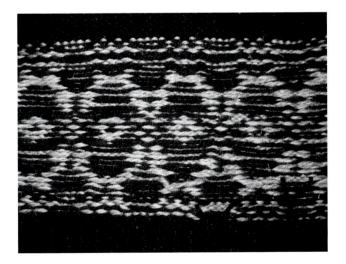

Figure 8.42 **Technical back of single jacquard.**

Figure 8.44 **Technical back used as right side.**

seaming at the armholes. The stitches are decreased as the sweater narrows toward the neckline. This is a fairly expensive technique. This version uses simple neutral colors and a tweed yarn as a base to achieve an effect that is graphic, yet simple. The silhouette is longer than the traditional sweater and updated with three-quarter sleeves.

Fair Isle patterns have a traditional feeling, and as such come and go in popularity. As with all classics it is often revived and re-imagined by designers. Many common traditional hand-knit motifs can be adapted into new shapes, such as the patterned

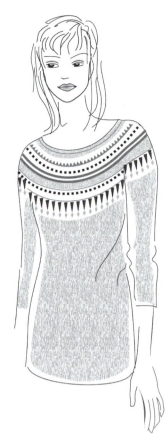

Figure 8.45 **Fair Isle updated.**

Figure 8.46 **Fair Isle motifs in fashion.**

stripes and geometrics combined with an oversized ribbed collar in Figure 8.46a. Snowflakes and reindeer are used to decorate a sweater coat and are merchandised with a shoulder bag (see Figure 8.46b).

Double Jacquard

Double jacquard is a way to achieve more complex patterns and does not have the two-color-per-row restriction. The example in Figure 8.47 has four colors per row. This requires a machine with two beds, but there are no floats on the back. In fact, the technical back sometimes has interesting tweed-like effects that make a nice finish for the interior. Because of the double construction, the overall fabric is fairly heavy.

Figure 8.47a shows the face with various free-form designs and up to four colors per row. Figure 8.47b shows the reverse side with the colors all neatly carried across with no floats. It has a 1×1 rib start and a tubular placket with buttons. The fabric is quite firm with minimal extensibility, appropriate for a sweater-coat. The technical diagram in Figure 8.48 shows one possible jacquard configuration using three colors (Goiello, 1982).

Ladder-Back Jacquard

There is a third style that is a hybrid of single and double, called **ladder-back jacquard**. It has short floats and creates a fabric that is lighter in weight than double jacquard. Figure 8.49a shows the finished pattern; note that it has three colors per row, and is therefore different than single jacquard. Figure 8.49b is the technical (and actual) back and has shorter floats than single jacquard, not as likely to catch.

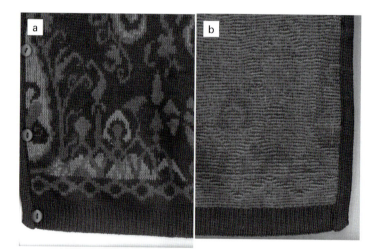

Figure 8.47 **Double jacquard.**

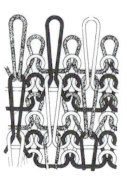

Figure 8.48 **Double jacquard stitch configuration.**

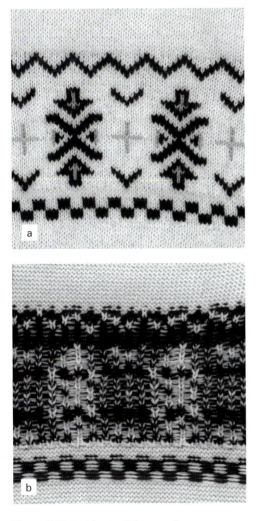

Figure 8.49 **Ladder-back jacquard.**

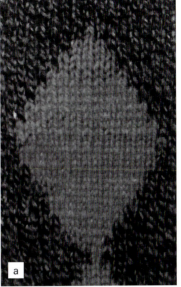

Figure 8.50 **Intarsia technique.**

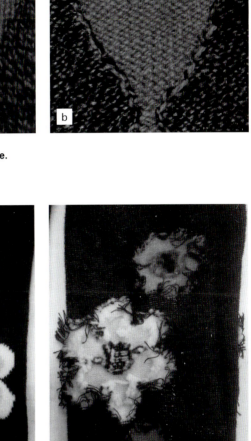

Figure 8.51 **Intarsia, outside (a) and inside (b).**

Intarsia

Intarsia is a technique in which large, non-geometric patterns may be formed. The color change is performed by twisting one yarn over another, and the technique enables designs of many colors and shapes, with few restrictions as to design or colors per row, although the more color changes, the more labor intensive the garment. It is commonly done in jersey, and because a crossover of yarns is made at the point of the color change, there are no yarns carried behind. The separate colors are often wound onto bobbins to help keep the yarns from getting tangled.

Figure 8.50a shows the technical face of a very simple diamond motif, and Figure 8.50b shows the technical back. The crossover stitch appears as a sort of outline at the point where the colors are twisted together. It can also be done on electronic machines if the purchase order is large enough to warrant the setup. The United States has a large seasonal market in novelty sweaters that are often made with intarsia machines, featuring motifs of holiday wrapped gifts, fir trees, ornaments, Santa, and so on.

Intarsia can achieve colorful, even painterly, effects, but it is slow. Done on a hand-loom machine, it takes care to successfully switch colors each row and tie off the yarn at the beginning and end of each motif. It can also be done on a computerized machine, if the quantities per style and color are high enough.

A seemingly simple effect, vertical stripes also require the intarsia technique. Depending on the design, a panel of horizontally knit stripes can sometimes be turned 90 degrees to provide a vertical effect. Careful comparisons would be made by the factory to determine the most cost-effective method of construction. The item in Figure 8.51 is a pair of children's socks with a colorful design of intarsia flowers. In this method the color change is cut rather than twisted, a way to reduce cost for the item when the reverse side does not commonly show.

Argyle

Argyle is a multicolored diamond pattern with thin diagonal lines overlaid. It was first developed to approximate the tartan plaid of the Scottish clan Argyle. It is a traditional pattern that often gains wide popularity for a few seasons. Argyle is a form of intarsia with certain specialized techniques and machinery. In one method, the various colors of yarn feed from bottom to top rather than from side to side like other intarsia. The thin diagonal lines are called the *raker* and can be added in a later step, using another stitch.

When the pattern is set up to a certain dimension, it does not grade, so the sizes being offered must be taken into account. For example, in Figure 8.52 there are three motifs across the chest. There will also be three light blue motifs, in the same dimensions, across the chest for all the other sizes.

The Development Process for Sweaters

As in most garment design, the apparel company begins by determining the desires of the intended customer in terms of price, fit, and styling. In addition, sweaters have a seasonal element and sell better in cooler seasons and climates. However, the use of air conditioning has extended the usefulness of sweaters to near year-round for most parts of the country. Sweater knits can be classic, warm and cozy, sheer and sexy, form-fitting or oversized, depending on the yarn, stitch, and gauge.

Figure 8.52 Argyle example.

Planning

A company that sells sweaters will have a history of what sells and to whom, of what is trending up in sales and what is trending down. All of these crucial pieces of the merchandise puzzle are analyzed and items slated for development go onto the line plan. As always, it will be a mix of carry-over styles and new styles. As with any other part of the line, the merchandisers or product line managers meet with the designers to share their perspectives on the upcoming season so the designers can start the process of developing prototypes. Sweater knits are a very popular accessory category and sometimes even a separate division of the company.

Inspiration

The tools for inspiration are trend books, vintage swatches or garments, stitch books, and knit-downs. The designer will already have their own research along with books of scrap and magazine pulls. In addition, the designer will keep current on general trends through fashion magazines and on market competition by attending wholesale trade shows.

Yarn suppliers also have a great deal of trend information, and attending the yarn trade shows is an inspiring event in itself. The most famous is Pitti Filati, held in Florence, Italy, each January (for spring/summer) and July (for fall/winter). Yarn shows are also held in New York. At all of these shows, yarn suppliers provide samples and swatches to inspire designers to purchase their yarns. Color trends, fashion shows, and other directional information are offered as well.

Back at the apparel company, after the line plan is in place, the design process and prototyping can begin. Commercial designing combines design skill with the understanding of the specific machinery that will be used to produce the items. All the many elements of yarn, machine gauge, and stitch structure must be in harmony before the development can proceed. The more these things are understood by the designer, the fewer prototypes are required, and the more quickly an approved sample can be developed.

The cost of producing the garment is influenced by many elements, from the cost of the yarns, to the complexity of the design, to the weight of the final sweater, to the duty rates imposed on the style. All these things affect the profit margins. Because each style has to perform and contribute to the bottom line, even the costs of buttons or other trims are carefully tracked.

Knitdowns

Because a limited amount of information can be gleaned from a hank of yarn alone, factories and yarn companies depend on swatches, called **knitdowns**, to assist the designer in their decision making. These are around 6 to 7 inches square, and they indicate the gauge, tension, and weight. A number of issues can be resolved with a careful evaluation of a knitdown. For example, if it is too lightweight, an end can be added before sample making proceeds. If the goods seem to be saggy, the stitch tension can be increased or the fabric combined with spandex. A knitdown includes the reference number, yarn size, content, gauge, and ends (Figure 8.53).

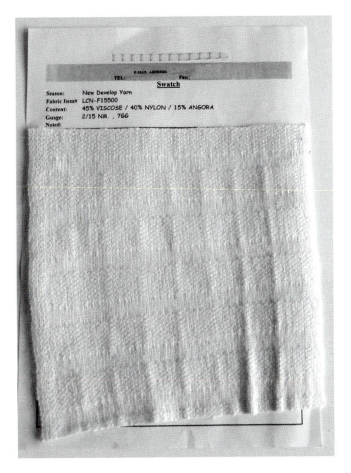

Figure 8.53 **Knitdown.**

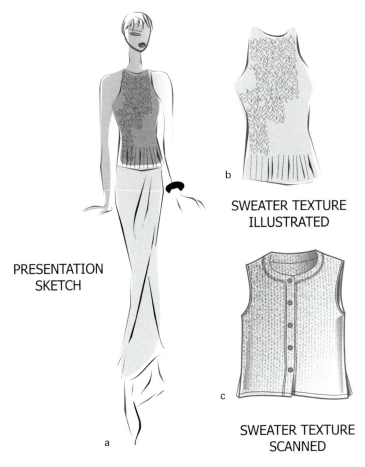

PRESENTATION
SKETCH

SWEATER TEXTURE
ILLUSTRATED

SWEATER TEXTURE
SCANNED

a

b

c

Figure 8.54 **Sweater sketches.**

Presentation

As we saw in Chapter 4, there are various sketch styles used at different stages of development. Presentation sketches (fashion illustrations) are useful for initial concept boards, and often key styles are drawn on figures. Figure 8.54a has the sweater stitch texture in illustration style. The float in Figure 8.54c has the sweater *fill* as a scan of the actual stitch. For example, the knitdown in Figure 8.53 can be scanned and used in the actual presentation sketches. In that way, the viewer can see the real yarn and real texture of the intended design.

Setting Up the Tech Pack for a Sweater

Sweater tech packs have some important differences from cut-and-sew garments. Sweater styles often have fewer findings, linings, and interlinings, and the knit pattern and yarn structure determines weight and drape. There are also important drawing conventions that guide the factory in setting up the panels.

Sketching Styles

Figure 8.55 is a technical sketch for a men's basic crewneck sweater. The notation at the underarm area designates the marks and shows that this is a full-fashioned style. Other areas may be shaped without marks, such as the side seams and shoulders. A

full set of instructions appears in the tech pack. Another thing we see is that the sweater panels (front, back, and sleeves) have a rib start. That means the knitting starts off with a certain amount of rib before transitioning to jersey (or another pattern). Because the rib is not seamed on for a sweater, the drawing should not have a horizontal line above the rib. Sweaters have various ways to start off at the bottom of the body or sleeves, called, logically enough, the *start*. Figure 8.55 shows various start methods as well as how to draw them for the tech pack.

The neck trim is also rib, which is linked to the body. It may be double layer in a fine-gauge knit or single thickness in a heavier gauge. It is important to specify all such details. It is common to allow for a **castoff**, which is a horizontal area that is finished clean at the underarm and improves the shape and the fit of the armhole (Newton, 1992). Figure 8.56 is an example of the construction directions for a sweater like the one in Figure 8.55. It spells out all the details of the sweater, including the stitches, start instructions, marks, castoff, and so on.

Examples of Pattern Layouts and Placements

Patterns are often strictly measured by repeat. For example, for a single jacquard, the repeat on a punch card machine can be 2, 3, 4, 6, 8, 12, and 24. For an argyle, the same principle holds true, so using existing garments for measurements can be very helpful. Providing the yarn size is comparable; the layout can be planned

NO SEAM HERE

	3″
1 X 1 RIB START	
	5″
2 X 2 RIB START	
	1″
TUBULAR START	
SELF START	
	1/4″
SELF START WITH CONTRAST ROW	

Figure 8.55 **Technical sweater sketches.**

LOCATION	CONSTRUCTION	LINKING / JOIN METHOD	FULL FASHIONING
Body and sleeve	Jersey 12gg		
Sleeve, armhole edge	3/4" castoff, front and back		w/ marks 2 rows in
Armhole	3/4" castoff, front and back	Link	w/ marks 2 rows in
Shoulder	with 1/4" elastic tape	Link	without marks
Side and seeve seams		Link	without marks
TRIM			
Neck	1 x 1 rib, single layer	Link	without marks
Sleeve/cuff	1 x 1 rib start (see spec for height) 2 rows spandex thread at edge		
Bottom	1 x 1 rib start (see spec for height) 2 rows spandex thread at edge		

Figure 8.56 **Sweater construction page.**

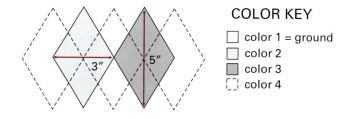

COLOR KEY

- ☐ color 1 = ground
- ☐ color 2
- ☐ color 3
- ☐ color 4

Figure 8.57 **Argyle pattern layout.**

precisely. Notice that one of the diamonds in the pattern is set at center front, so there must be an odd number planned. In the argyle placement sketch in Figure 8.57, the central motif is color 2. So color 2 will always appear as the central motif color.

The pattern layout provides information on the scale of the pattern, as well as the color placements. After the colors are chosen, that information appears on the tech pack on the colorway summary page. An example is shown in Figure 8.58, which shows the sweater offered in four colors. The labels are gray for all, and the shoulder tape is "DTM Color 1" (dyed to match color 1, the main body color). The argyle motif for this design (Figure 8.59) is placed at the chest area, rather than all over, so the grading is calculated from HPS (high point shoulder).

The spec page shown in Figure 8.60 contains the POMs (points of measure) and size specifications for size L, the sample size.

These are based on other sweaters of a similar gauge that fit the standard fit model correctly. At the bottom are three sweater-specific measurements: weight per dozen, courses per inch, and wales per inch. Counting the courses and wales per inch helps to ensure that the knitting tension is correct. Like cut-and-sew knit garments (such as polo shirts, T-shirts, and so on), sweater girth measurements are *half measure*. Those points of measure are noted in Figure 8.60 in boldface, for easy reference (an example is T-F chest).

The grade page has all the grade rules for this style. Like most sweaters it is based on a small/medium/large size scale (known as alpha sizing). Sweaters have an easy fit, like many knits, and alpha sizing will accommodate most customers. As we studied in Chapter 3, the tech pack will also call out labels, packaging, and hangtags, because all these components affect the price.

COLORWAY SUMMARY						
color 1	color code	color 2	color 3	color 4	shoulder tape, DTM color 1	Label
Cadet	4473	Navy	White	Black	Cadet	grey
White	2677	Navy	Fire	Black	White	grey
Navy	0672	Cadet	White	Black	Navy	grey
Black	6037	Fire	Cadet	White	Black	grey

Figure 8.58 Colorway summary page for argyle sweater.

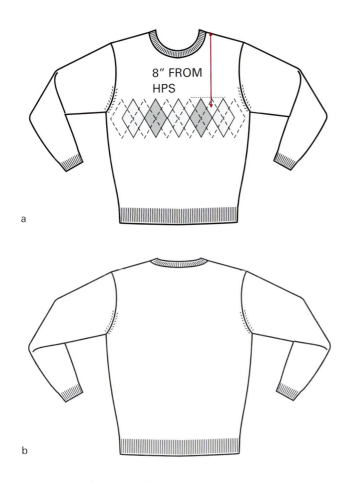

a

b

Figure 8.59 Argyle pattern placement.

PROTO# SM-12-157
STYLE# 0
SEASON: Fall 20XX
DEPT Mens
FIT TYPE Natural/Sweater
BRAND: XYZ Mens
STATUS: Prototype-1

SIZE RANGE: Mens, S-XXL
SAMPLE SIZE: M
DESIGNER: Glinda
DATE FIRST SENT: 1/5/20XX
DATE REVISED: 0
FABRICATION: 12gg

POINTS of MEASURE, M's SWEATER

(GIRTH MEASUREMENTS ARE HALF MEASURE–POMs in **Boldface**)

meas code	BODY SPECS	Spec	+ Spec	- Spec
T-A	Shoulder Point to Point	18 1/4	1/2	1/2
T-B	Shoulder Drop, HPS to seam	1 1/4	1/4	1/4
T-C	Front Mid Armhole	17 1/4	1/2	1/2
T-D	Back Mid Armhole	18	1/2	1/2
T-E	Armhole Drop from HPS	12	1/4	1/4
T-F	**Chest** @ 1" fm seam	22	1	1
T-G	**Waits**	n/a	1	1
T-G2	Waist position fm HPS	n/a	1/2	1/2
T-H	**Bottom** Opening	19 1/4	1	1
T-I	Front Length fm HPS	28	1/2	1/2
T-J	Back Length fm HPS	28	1/2	1/2
T-K	Center Back Sleeve Length (LS)	34 1/2	3/8	3/8
T-L	**Bicep** @ 1" fm Seam	8 1/2	1/4	1/4
T-Q	**Elbow**	6 3/4	1/4	1/4
T-M	**Sleeve Opening**, bottom (LS)	3 3/4	1/4	1/4
T-N	Front Neck Drop, to seam	4 1/2	1/4	1/4
T-O	Back Neck Drop, to seam	1	1/4	1/4
	Collar at Top, closed (1/2 measure)	n/a	1/2	1/2
T-P	Neck Width, seam to seam	8	1/4	1/4
	Cap Height	n/a	1/4	1/4
	STYLE SPECS			
	Collar trim height at CB	1	1/8	1/8
	Cuff height	2	1/4	1/4
	Rib height at bottom	2 1/2		
H-2	Weight per Dozen			
H-3	Courses (per inch)			
H-4	Wales (per inch)			

Figure 8.60 Sweater specification page.

Summary

The sweater has been an important product category in apparel markets. This chapter reviews special knowledge in designing and manufacturing sweater apparel products, such as unique differentiation between sweater-knit and cut-and-sew products, various terminology related to sweater construction and product development, and finally the essential skills and knowledge foundation for building sweater technical packages, including the information on product process and examples of pattern layouts and placements.

Useful Websites

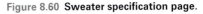

- http://www.shimaseiki.com/wholegarment/

Study Questions

1. For jersey stitch, what is the hand-knitting term for the technical face? For the technical back?

2. Name two advances in knitting technology that have occurred since the 1500s.

3. What sweater knit construction has the greatest width-wise extensibility?

4. What causes a run (ladder)?

5. How are full-fashioning marks created?

6. What is the difference between two ply and two ends?

7. State three reasons for the popularity of sweaters in the marketplace.

8. Why do weft knits usually have stripes in the width direction?

9. Describe some of the different sweater techniques that can be used to produce a four-color sweater.

10. Which of the following are primarily color techniques?

   a. argyle

   b. cable

   c. intarsia

   d. jacquard

   e. jersey

   f. links-links

   g. plating

   h. pointelle

   i. purl

   j. striping

   k. worsted

11. Refer to Appendix C in the *Technical Sourcebook for Apparel Designers* STUDIO. Select Sweater #6: Argyle and remove the argyle detail and replace it with #7: Fair Isle detail.

Check Your Understanding

1. Practice knitting by making an approximately 4-inch swatch in jersey (also called stockinette stitch in hand knitting). Make a second swatch in all purl. Compare the two and make a list of the qualities of each. Bring a jersey sweater to class and identify the knit side and purl side.

2. To create a Fair Isle sweater design:

   a. Starting with a seasonal color palette, choose 7 to 10 colors.

   b. Create a Fair Isle design on graph paper, using a repeat (the distance between repeated elements) of 2, 3, 4, 6, or 12 to

combine small patterns. Remember to use no more than two colors for any one row.

   c. After the design is completed, use it in an original sweater design.

   d. Draw a colored presentation sketch on a fashion figure or float.

   e. Make technical sketches and a tech pack for the style.

3. What are the reasons that yarns are plied? What are the advantages? What are the disadvantages? Bring to class an example of a sweater with plied yarns.

4. Research the internet and find some knit items produced between 1400 and 1700. Bring the images to class and share your observations.

5. Refer to Figure 8.3. Which is the technical face and which is the technical back?

6. Open your closet and find a sweater with linked seams. Take a picture of the seaming detail and bring the hard copy to class.

References

Black, S. 2002. *Knitwear in Fashion*. New York: Thames and Hudson.

Goiello, D. 1982. *Understanding Fabrics: From Fiber to Finished Cloth*. New York: Fairchild.

Johnson, I., Cohen, A., and Sarkar, A. 2015. *J.J. Pizzuto's Fabric Science* (11th ed.). New York: Fairchild Books.

Newton, D. 1992. *Designing Knitwear*. Newtown, CT: Taunton Press.

Sharp, H. 2012. *Machine Knitting Technology*. Self-published in Seattle, WA.

Spencer, D. J. 1989. *Knitting Technology: A Comprehensive Handbook and Practical Guide to Modern Day Principles*. Oxford and New York: Pergamon.

Walker, B. 1972. *Charted Knitting Designs*. New York: Charles Scribner's Sons.

Stitches and Seams

Chapter Objectives

After studying this chapter, you will be able to:

- Identify different stitches from 100 to 600 classifications
- Identify four different seam types in different categorizations
- Identify different sewing machines for different end uses of garments and practices
- Explain the different stitches and seams based on end use of garments
- Evaluate the importance of stitches per inch (SPI) as a quality indicator
- Discuss apparel quality issues related to stitches and seam types

---

Key Terms

bartack	inset corner	seam
booked seam	interlock stitch	seam allowance
bound seam	intersecting seams	seam grin
busted seams	lapped seam	seamline
chain off	lockstitch	serger
chainstitch	looper	stitches per inch
clean finished seam	looper thread	superimposed seam
coverstitch	mitered seam	tuck seam
enclosed seam	overedge	U.S. federal standard
facings	overedger	Underpressing
flat seaming	pinked seam	welding
folder	piping	zigzag stitch
French seam	plain seam	
graded	safety stitch	

This chapter introduces one of the most important factors of garment manufacturing: stitches and **seams**. Different sewing machines used in the industry and different stitch and seam types are explored with in-depth analysis of their end use for apparel products. **Stitches per inch** (SPI) as a quality indicator is also investigated, along with how to count SPI and select appropriate SPI for an apparel product, considering its end use and fabric type. In addition, various seams and seam uses based on stitch types and construction are explored.

Stitches

Stitches are used to hold a garment together; therefore, stitch quality is a critical component of overall apparel quality. To achieve the desired aesthetic and functional performance and quality of apparel products, manufacturers can control the physical features of stitches such as stitch type; stitch length and width; needle type, size, and condition; thread type and size; tension and other sewing machine adjustments; and operator accuracy. Manipulating these physical features of the stitches results in various levels of performance and affects the cost of apparel products. Designers should pay careful attention to select the most appropriate stitch types and stitch length and work with manufacturers to select the corresponding needle size as well as thread type and size for the factory to achieve the desired level of quality. These variables are specified on the tech pack because they affect the price and the look of the garment.

Types of Machines

Unlike home sewing machines, which can perform many stitch types, industrial sewing machines are usually engineered to perform only one stitch type per machine, although they can perform at top speed for 8 or 10 hours per day. Industrial sewing machines are categorized based on their stitch types, such as lockstitch machines and chainstitch machines.

Lockstitch Machines

Lockstitch machines (see Figure 9.1) are the most frequently used for ready-to-wear apparel production. **Lockstitches** are formed by interlocking thread as a top thread and using a bobbin thread as an underthread. One disadvantage of this kind of machine is that the machine operator must stop and refill the bobbin when it runs out. This is most similar to a home sewing machine.

Chainstitch Machines

Chainstitch machines use underthreads called *looper threads* that are fed from large cones of thread. It does not use a bobbin thread as an underthread. A **looper** is a "stitch-forming device

on chainstitch, overedge, and coverstitch sewing machines to form a stitch" (www.amefird.com), and a **looper thread** is "the bottom thread that covers the edge of an overedge seam, used on chainstitch and coverstitch machines" (www.amefird.com). These machines are very fast and more cost effective to operate than the lockstitch machine. For a designer and merchandiser, when placing an order it is important to be aware of what kinds of machines are available at a factory, because there are certain seam types that can be made only by certain types of machines. Figures 9.2 and 9.3 show a computerized chainstitch machine and a regular chainstitch machine, respectively.

Recently, there have been technological advancements in sewing machine manufacturing. Computer systems have been incorporated into sewing machines to allow production managers, designers, and even their customers to track the progress of apparel production through networks and hand-held devices such as smartphones and tablets 24 hours a day (Ramstad, 2013). It is an advancement that can be easily incorporated into a product lifecycle management system. Through product lifecycle management, professionals working in a product development process in-house or remotely can check and keep track of the production progress easily. Figure 9.4 shows a worker at Sunstar Machinery Co. in suburban Seoul, South Korea, using one of the new high-tech sewing machines.

Stitch Types

Different stitch types and seam types are categorized according to the widely accepted U.S. federal standard. This section covers the standard categories of stitches, defined by the method of

Figure 9.2 Computerized chainstitch machine.

Figure 9.3 Single-needle chainstitch machine.

Figure 9.1 Single-needle lockstitch machine.

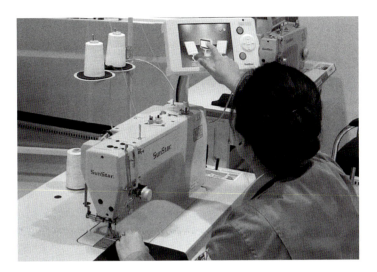

Figure 9.4 **High-tech sewing machine with Internet access.**

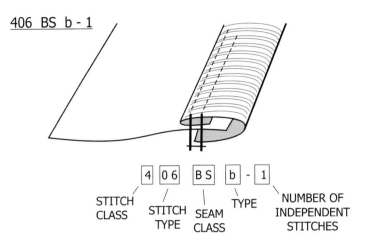

Figure 9.5 **Example of an ASTM standard.**

making the stitch. This standardization enables manufacturers, contractors, and retailers to communicate more accurately and effectively about design details and specifications.

The U.S. government has established six classes of stitches. **U.S. federal standard** was originally set as a foundation for increasing uniformity in sewn products, such as military uniforms, for the contractors who produced them, and was later adopted for the apparel industry for its usefulness (Brown and Rice, 2001). There are different stitch types in each class, although each type is similar. Their numbers vary in the class by the exact arrangement of the threads. The following designations will be seen in the descriptions throughout the chapter. Figure 9.5 gives an example of a system previously known as U.S. federal standard, which is now called ASTM (American Society for Testing and Materials). It is a bound seam (BS) of type (b) sewn with the 406 class machine, a type of 2-needle bottom coverstitch. Two lines of topstitching are set ¹/₄ inch away from each other. More information regarding this seam type is found later in this chapter.

Characteristics of Each Stitch Class

Table 9.1 presents a general overview of the characteristics of each stitch class. The classes are described in more detail in the following sections.

100 Class Stitches

The single-thread chainstitches with no underthreads are called *100 class stitches*. They are frequently used for basting, button sewing, buttonholes, and spot tacking. Economy and stretchability are two advantages of 100 class stitches; however, there are also disadvantages, such as lack of durability. It is very important to note that the stitches are not durable enough for ready-to-wear garments. A 2-thread 401 chainstitch is more common for seaming apparel because the 100 class stitches are not secure or tight when used for seaming and are prone to quality problems. This is discussed as part of the seam information later in the chapter.

There are three main kinds of stitches included in 100 class: 101 single-thread chainstitch, 103 blindstitch, and 104 saddlestitch. They are specified as follows.

- 101 single-thread chainstitch is used for basting, button sewing, buttonholes, and spot tacking. Figure 9.6 shows the top and bottom views of the stitch. They are also good for temporary basting and may be seen in other industrial non-garment items, such as to close the tops of flour sacks.

- 103 blindstitch (see Figure 9.7) is formed with single-needle thread that interloops with itself on the top surface of the material. The thread passes through the top ply and

Table 9.1   Stitch Classes and Their Characteristics

Stitch Class Number	Name	Characteristics	Note
100	Simple chainstitch	Single thread	Stitch formed by chaining, with no underthread
200	Hand stitches and their machine simulations	Rarely seen in ready-to-wear; not used for general seaming for lack of durability; used for decorative purposes in ready-to-wear	Single thread and hand needle
300	Lockstitches	Most common stitch type, frequently used in ready-to-wear	Stitches formed with a needle thread interlocking with a bobbin thread
400	Multithread chainstitch and coverstitch	Frequently used in wovens such as jeans, casual pants; frequently used for seaming in knits	Formed by a needle thread above interlooping with a looper thread below
500	Overedge stitch (non-safety stitches) and safety stitches	Most common edge finished used in the industry	Stitches formed over the edge of the fabric, encasing it with thread
600	Coverstitch or flatlock	Most common stitch type used for knits and cut-and-sew jersey	Stitches interloop on both right and wrong side, used for flat seams where the fabric butts together or overlaps slightly

horizontally through portions of the bottom ply without penetrating the full depth. It is widely used for hemming.

- 104 saddlestitch (see Figure 9.8) is used for decorative stitches.

200 Class Stitches

This class of stitches includes some hand stitches and some specialized machines that simulate hand stitches. Machine imitations of hand stitches are similar in durability, uniformity, and cost to other types of machine stitches, but are often not cost effective. This stitch class is mostly decorative rather than durable, and is not generally used to join seams, so it is important to note that it is seldom used in ready-to-wear apparel products. The stitches are good at creating various styles and add softness and a flexible touch.

The four main stitches included in the 200 class (see Figures 9.9 through 9.12) are the 202 backstitch, 204 herringbone stitch, 205 running stitch, and 205 slipstitch (or saddlestitch).

300 Class Stitches (Lockstitches)

Figures 9.13 and 9.14 show *301 lockstitch*, which is the plain or straight stitch. It is the most frequently used stitch in ready-to-wear apparel production. The threads interlock between fabric

plies. The stitches look the same on the top and the bottom, so they are easily reversible. The stitches are tight and secure, so the lockstitch is the most common type of stitch used for ready-to-wear garments, especially wovens. There are disadvantages to this stitch category; because they don't stretch very far, they rupture easily if used on knits and fabrics where stretchability is required. But even on knits, lockstitch is used for many components, such as setting zippers where stability rather than stretch is required. The machine needs to have the proper tension, balanced between top thread and bobbin thread (see Figure 9.14). Otherwise, it will not have nearly the strength of a properly balanced stitch.

There are two different kinds of lockstitch: regular 301 lockstitch and 301 twin-needle lockstitch. Twin-needle lockstitch is the same as single-needle 301, but it has two rows of stitches, which typically have a $1/4$-inch space in between. The twin-needle lockstitch machines are available to set the space from $3/16$ inch up to 1 inch. The advantage of a twin needle is a neat double row of stitches, perfectly parallel. Attaching elastic tape to the body of shorts—usually with the help of a metering device—would be a good example of when to use a twin-needle machine, and will result in a quality finish. The 304 **zigzag stitch** (see Figure 9.15), a variation of the 301, is stretchable and is frequently used for intimate apparel, infant wear, and sportswear, and for button sew,

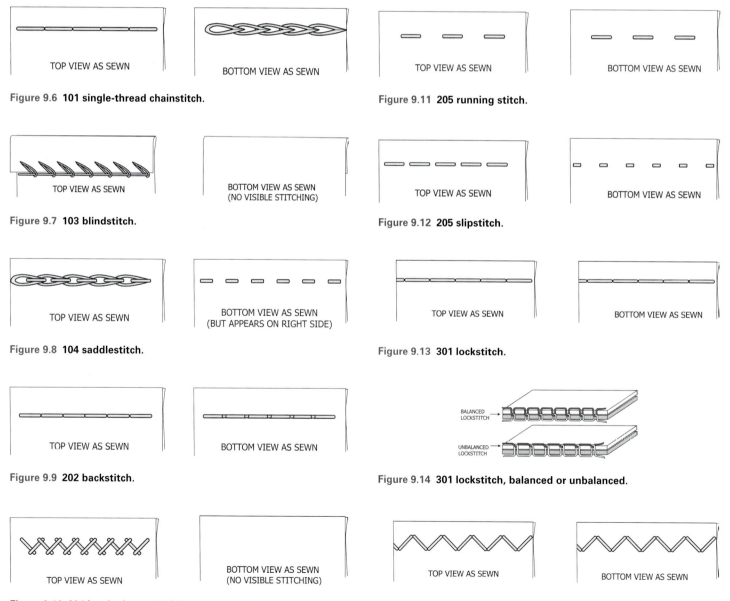

Figure 9.6 **101 single-thread chainstitch.**

Figure 9.7 **103 blindstitch.**

Figure 9.8 **104 saddlestitch.**

Figure 9.9 **202 backstitch.**

Figure 9.10 **204 herringbone stitch (also called catchstitch).**

Figure 9.11 **205 running stitch.**

Figure 9.12 **205 slipstitch.**

Figure 9.13 **301 lockstitch.**

Figure 9.14 **301 lockstitch, balanced or unbalanced.**

Figure 9.15 **304 zigzag lockstitch.**

buttonhole, and bartacking operations. Needle thread and bobbin thread meet in the center of the seam to form a symmetrical zigzag pattern stitch. There are also variations of the zigzag lockstitch. One example is a multi-stitch zigzag, ISO-321 (see Figure 11.31 on page 212).

Bartacks (see Figure 9.16) are repeated zigzag stitches, usually used at the beginning and ending of the seam to secure the seam from unraveling. Bartacks are used to reinforce stress points where needed, such as at the front fly of pants and pockets. They are also used for attaching belt loops. Although there are special machines to sew buttons and buttonholes, buttonholes and button sewing are also created by 304 zigzag stitches.

400 Class Stitches

The 400 class stitches are multithread stitches or double-locked chain stitches. There are advantages related to this class of stitches. The stitches are very stretchable because they have chains. There are also some disadvantages related to the 400 class stitches. The seams tend to be loose when pulled, compared to 300 class stitches for its chains, so there are tendencies toward **seam grin**, which means threads show on the exterior side when the **seamlines** are stretched, looking similar to the teeth in a smile or grin (Brown and Rice, 2001). Seam grin is an indicator of low quality, which affects the durability of garments. To construct chains, the stitch requires considerable thread, and it will cause bulky seams that may feel uncomfortable to the wearer.

Three types of stitches in the class are most frequently used: 401 chainstitch, 406 2-needle bottom coverstitch, and 407 3-needle bottom coverstitch. The 401 2-thread chainstitch is one of the most frequently used stitch types. The others—406 and 407—are variations of bottom coverstitches, and are used to cover seams and attach elastic bands, form belt loops, attach bindings, and create hems.

Unlike the 100 stitch class, the *401 chainstitch* (see Figure 9.17) has both a needle thread and a looper thread below, which

greatly increases the durability and decreases the likelihood of unraveling. Based on total needles and needle thread used, there are two different kinds of chainstitch: 401 chainstitch and 401 2-needle chainstitch (Figure 9.18).

The 401 2-needle chainstitch is formed by two needle threads passing through the material and interlooped by two bottom looper threads, forming two separate rows of stitch set on the underside of the seam. It is one of the more popular stitches used for many main seams on woven apparel. Seams for jeans are a good example of the use of the 2-needle chainstitch.

The 406 2-needle bottom coverstitch (see Figure 9.19) is formed by two needle threads passing through the material and interlooping with a bottom looper thread with the stitch set on the underside of the seam. The bottom looper threads are interlooped between needle threads, providing seam coverage on the bottom side. Although this stitch is never used for seams, this is widely used for belt loops and hemming the bottom of knit shirts. Most knit shirts have this stitch used at the sleeve and bottom hems. It is also used on lingerie and as decorative topstitching on knit garments.

The 407 3-needle bottom coverstitch (see Figure 9.20) is different from 406 in that it is formed by three needle threads passing through the material and interlacing with one bottom looper thread with the stitch set on the underside of the seam. The bottom looper thread is interlooped among needle threads, providing seam coverage on the bottom side only.

The most important advantages of these two bottom coverstitches (406 and 407) are that they conceal raw edges by covering them with loops. They are never used for seam joining, but widely used for seam topstitching and for hems.

500 Class Stitches

The nickname **overedge** for 500 class stitches is probably the best descriptive term for this class. The stitch is formed by a triangle of thread around the raw edge of the seam. Most manufacturers use spun or texturized threads on overedge operations. The three categories of stitches in the 500 stitch class are described in Table 9.2. Interestingly, odd number designations (such as 505) are used for hemming and serging, but even numbers (such as 514) are used only for seaming.

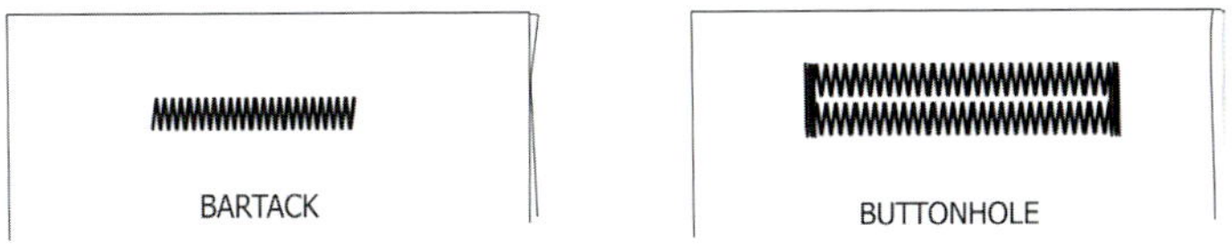

Figure 9.16 **Bartack and buttonhole.**

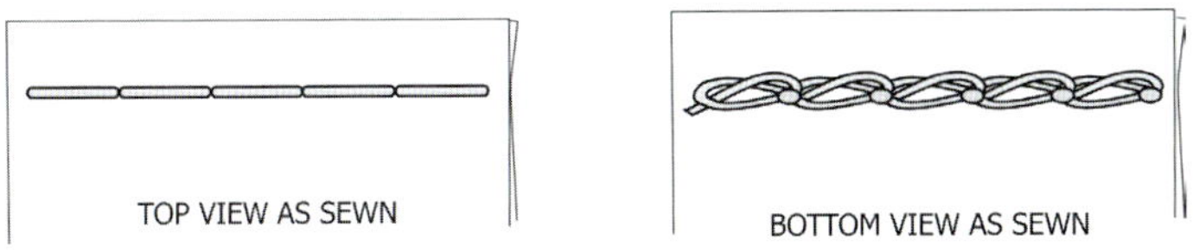

Figure 9.17 **401 single chainstitch.**

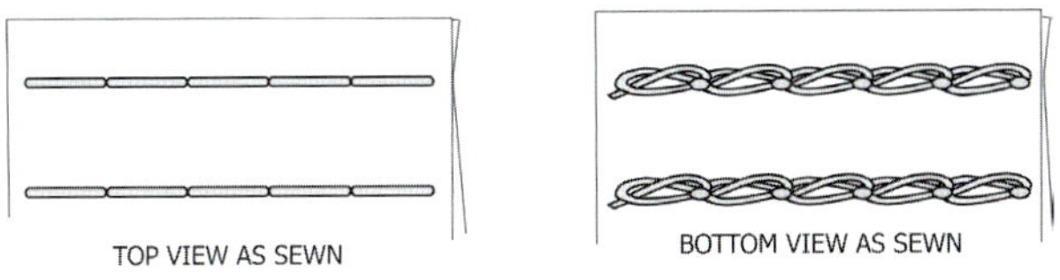

Figure 9.18 **401 2-needle chainstitch. Note that the stitch characteristics in the illustrations are slightly exaggerated to help in identifying the stitch and types.**

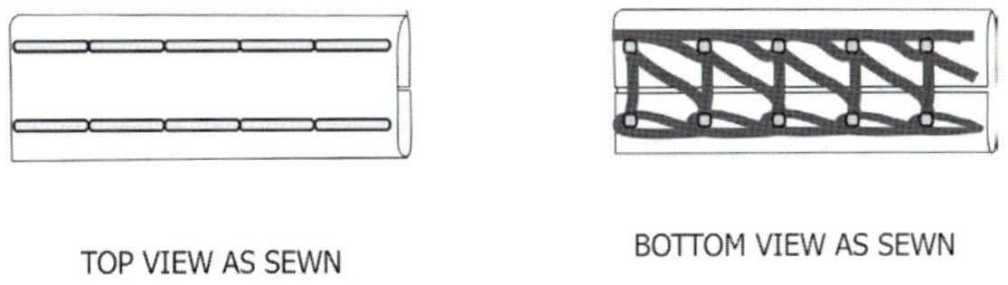

Figure 9.19 **406 2-needle bottom coverstitch.**

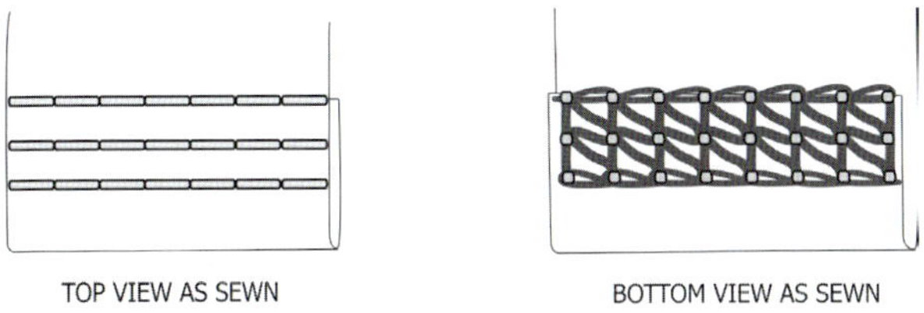

Figure 9.20 **407 3-needle bottom coverstitch.**

Table 9.2 500 Class Stitches

Name of Stitch	Numbers and Uses
Single-needle overedge stitch	501, 502, 503, 504, 505.
	Odd-numbered stitches are for serging (hemming), even-numbered stitches are for seaming.
	504 is the most common stitch used for seaming
2-needle overedge stitch	512 and 514 are for seaming.
	514 is preferred because it chains off better.
Safety stitch	515, 516, 519.
	They provide cost effective construction.

Source: www.amefird.com.

Loops are formed over the edge of fabric, encasing the edge in thread interloopings to prevent raveling. Overedge stitches, a kind of advanced form of chainstitch, sew a seam and simultaneously finish its raw edges to prevent raveling. Overedge stitches are made on small sewing machines called **overedgers** or **sergers**. Sergers stitch only at the edge of a fabric. Unlike other conventional sewing machines used to make other classes of stitches (that can sew anywhere on the fabric), sergers cannot stitch within the body of a garment. Sergers have a detachable knife attachment that evenly trims the edge of the fabric just before the stitches are made, finishing raw edges and preventing them from raveling. A serger can't stitch wide seams. It is set for a certain seam allowance, which is usually around $3/8$ inch or less. It can stitch straight or gently curved seams, but has difficulty stitching around intricate curves or shaped angles because the knife attachment can cut off the curved shape. The 500 class stitches are stretchable and prevent the raveling of the edge of garments by concealing the edges completely.

Sergers use a small amount of seam allowances ($3/8$ inch compared to $5/8$ inch), so they require less fabric. Sergers also reduce the total labor by half because they can finish edging and seaming in one operation. Thus, they are a cost effective way of creating garments. However, they also have some disadvantages. The stitches are loose, so they tend to create seam grin. The seam is not able to be busted, or pressed open, so it can cause a bulky seam and is, therefore, not good for thick fabric.

The best overedge stitches for wovens are the **safety stitches** (515, 516, and 519). The 516 safety stitch is the most frequently used stitch within this category. It creates 401 chainstitch plus 500 serged edges in one operation, so it can result in a sturdy seam with completely serged seam edges. The difference between single purl and double purl is only seen at the cut (raw) edge of the **seam allowances**. One has two purls and the other has one purl. A 503 2-thread overedge (see Figure 9.21) is used for serging. The stitch is formed by one needle thread and one looper thread, which creates a purl on the edge of the seam.

A 504 3-thread overedge (see Figure 9.22) is used for overedge seaming and serging. The stitch is formed by one needle thread and two looper threads, which creates a purl on the edge of the seam. A 505 3-thread overedge (see Figure 9.23) is for edge finishing rather than seam joining. The stitch is formed by one needle thread and two looper threads, which creates a double purl on the edge of the seam.

A 512 4-thread overedge, or mock safety stitch (see Figure 9.24), is formed with two needle threads and two looper threads with the looper threads creating a purl on the edge of the seam. The 512 right needle only enters the upper looper loop. This stitch type will not **chain off** as well as the 514 stitch. This means that the operator continues to sew after finishing the seam, creating a chain of thread.

A 514 4-thread overedge (see Figure 9.25) is formed with two needle threads and two looper threads with the looper threads forming a purl on the edge of the seam. Both needles enter the upper looper loop. This stitch is preferable to the 512 stitch because it chains off better. A 516 5-thread safety stitch (see Figure 9.26) is a combination stitch consisting of a single-needle

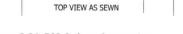
SINGLE "PURL" ON EDGE

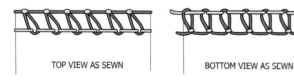
TOP VIEW AS SEWN   BOTTOM VIEW AS SEWN

Figure 9.21 **503 2-thread overedge.**

TOP VIEW AS SEWN   BOTTOM VIEW AS SEWN

Figure 9.22 **504 3-thread overedge.**

DOUBLE "PURL" ON EDGE
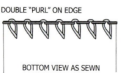
TOP VIEW AS SEWN   BOTTOM VIEW AS SEWN

Figure 9.23 **505 3-thread overedge.**

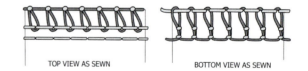
TOP VIEW AS SEWN   BOTTOM VIEW AS SEWN

Figure 9.24 **512 4-thread overedge, mock safety stitch.**

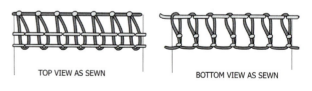
TOP VIEW AS SEWN   BOTTOM VIEW AS SEWN

Figure 9.25 **514 4-thread overedge.**

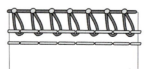
TOP VIEW AS SEWN   BOTTOM VIEW AS SEWN

Figure 9.26 **516 5-thread safety stitch.**

chainstitch (401) and a 3-thread overedge stitch (504) that are formed simultaneously.

600 Class Stitches

Stitches in the 600 class, called **coverstitches** or **interlock stitches**, create excellent coverage of the bottom as well as the top side of the seam or flat-seam stitches. This coverage provides very flat seams. These stitches are used for seaming knit underwear, athletic wear, and intimate wear. They are used to sew flat seams (FS) in which the fabrics abut or lap slightly. The advantages in using 600 class stitches are that they are very strong and stretchable, and therefore widely used for lighter-weight knits. They create coverstitches, so using this class requires little or no seam allowances. However, these stitches also have some disadvantages. They require a large amount of thread, and when used for children's wear or underwear, a special soft thread must be used to prevent irritation. These coverstitches are seldom used for wovens because the stretch qualities have no advantage for wovens.

Usually spun polyester or texturized polyester/nylon threads are used on the machines. The different needle configurations and looper threads used for various 600 class stitches are shown in Table 9.3. One popular fashion detail is using contrasting color threads for loopers in sewing knit apparel products to produce unique design features.

SPI: A Quality Indicator

The number of SPI (stitches per inch) is an important quality indicator for sewn apparel products.

Determining Appropriate SPI

Determining appropriate SPI is important for seam quality, strength, stitch appearance, cost, and seam elasticity on stretch fabrics. More stitches per inch require more thread consumption to complete the seam. Higher SPI will lead to stronger, more elastic seams. Greater SPI means more stitches used in a seam, which also requires longer production time to complete the seam. Longer production time (that is, longer sewing cycles) means higher labor costs as well as lower production levels. For example, a sewing machine operating 5,000 stitches per minute (SPM) at 8 SPI will sew 17.4 yards of seam per minute; however, a machine sewing 5,000 SPM at 14 SPI will sew 9.9 yards of seam per minute.

Sometimes a seam can have too many stitches per inch. A very lightweight or sheer fabric can be weakened by too many stitches,

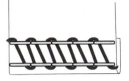

TOP VIEW AS SEWN   BOTTOM VIEW AS SEWN

Figure 9.27 602 2-needle 4-thread coverstitch.

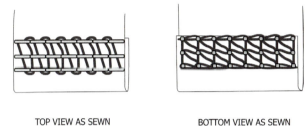

TOP VIEW AS SEWN   BOTTOM VIEW AS SEWN

Figure 9.28 605 3-needle 5-thread top-and-bottom coverstitch.

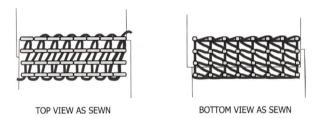

TOP VIEW AS SEWN   BOTTOM VIEW AS SEWN

Figure 9.29 607 4-needle 6-thread flatlock, or flatseamer.

as can leather seams. SPI should be recommended and taken into consideration to provide appropriate seam strength at the price level for each sewn product. Many companies require designers to indicate specific SPI information for each product in the tech pack.

How to Count SPI

SPI is calculated by counting the number of stitches made in one inch of seam or topstitching, starting at needle penetration and ending at 1 inch away. You can place a ruler next to the seam and perform this task. For example, Figure 9.30 shows that approximately nine SPI are sewn in this seam. A stitch counter is used in this figure to make this measurement easier (www.amefird.com/spi.htm). The SPI is important information that always needs to be included in the tech pack and reviewed with

Table 9.3   Various Stitches in 600 Class

ISO number	Needle number	Description	Number of loopers and top threads
602 (Figure 9.27)	2-needle 4 Thread coverstitch	Stitch is formed with two needle threads, a top cover thread, and a bottom looper thread	One looper and one top spreader thread
605 (Figure 9.28)	3-needle 5 Thread coverstitch	Stitch is formed with three needle threads, a top cover thread, and a bottom looper thread	One looper and one top spreader thread
606	4-needle 5 Thread coverstitch	Stitch is formed with four needle threads, a top cover thread, and four bottom looper threads	Four loopers and one top spreader thread
607 (Figure 9.29)	4-needle 6 thread coverstitch	Stitch is formed with four needle threads, a top cover thread, and a bottom looper thread; preferable to 606 stitch because the machine is easier to maintain	One looper and one top spreader thread

Figure 9.30 SPI counter.

a ruler on each sample. Using the correct number of stitches per inch can greatly enhance the strength, appearance, and performance of the seam for a given fabric type and application.

On a typical woven shirt style, the SPI is 10 to 12. That is expressed as 11 SPI +/– 1 stitch, or 11 stitches per inch, plus or minus 1 stitch. That is the same as 10 to 12 stitches per inch because 10, 11, or 12 stitches are acceptable. The difference in expressing it that way is that it includes a tolerance of one stitch. Considering apparel products are not hard science items and human errors are involved in apparel production, it is not only important to give a bit of leeway, but also to meet the standard. Thus, the concept of tolerance is accepted for apparel production standards.

Medium-weight and densely woven fabrics, such as bottom weights, use longer stitches, 8 to 10 SPI. Leather needs long stitches to avoid too many perforations that will weaken the seam. An appropriate SPI is 6 to 8, depending on the weight of the leather, especially for topstitching. Very lightweight fabric requires a higher SPI, such as 12 to 15, often seen on men's shirtings. (Note: A shirt is a garment, and shirting is a fabric, so shirtings are men's shirt-weight fabrics.) Other factors that influence the choice of SPI are the number of plies being sewn, weight of the fabric and thread, and amount of stretch. Both too few or too

many stitches per inch can sometimes result in seam failure and appropriate SPI is a quality indicator.

All types of sewing machines are equipped with regulators that select the number of stitches per inch. Tables 9.4 and 9.5 include lists of garments for wovens and knits and the typical number of stitches per inch recommended by American & Efird (http://www.amefird.com/spi.htm).

Seam Types

A **seam** is the stitched joint between two or more pieces of fabric, or the line of stitching that joins the edges in a single piece of fabric (a dart, for example). In the construction of garments, the cut panels are joined into seams. The cut edge is also known as the raw edge. The **seamline** is the place marked on the pattern to designate where the seams will be joined. The distance from the seamline and the edge of the pattern is the **seam allowance**. The seam allowance varies based on locations and end uses of garments. Higher-quality garments often have wider seam allowances to provide fabric for alterations, and that is considered a quality indicator. Figure 9.31 shows these terms as they would be represented on a pattern. On a properly joined seam, the stitches will not be seen from the right side.

Basic Seam Types

Seams are sewn with different machines for different results, and the same garment can often have a number of different seam types. Different stitches can be used to construct a certain seam type, but *a seam type remains the same regardless of the stitch used to sew it.* Appropriate seam types are an important factor in determining the quality of apparel products. Good seam choices depend on the location of the seam, structure and weight of the fabric, whether the fabric is knit or woven, design details, fit and look of the garment, end use of the garment, and, most importantly, cost limitations.

There are four seam classes (previously known as a *federal standard of seam classes*) in the industry: superimposed seams (SS), lapped seams (LS), flat seams (FS), and bound seams (BS). Within each major seam class, there are several seam types.

Table 9.4 Typical Stitch Lengths Recommended for Wovens

Woven Garments	SPI	Comments
Blindstitch operations on slacks, dresses, skirts, etc.	3–5	A long stitch length is desirable to minimize the dimple or appearance of the needle penetration on the outside of the garment.
Buttonhole (1/2-inch purl or whipstitch)	85–90	Generally sewn vertically; approximately 85 to 90 stitches with a lockstitch buttonhole machine.
Button sew (four-hole button)	16	Button-sew machines are cycle machines with a predetermined number of stitches per cycle.
Casual shirts, blouses, tops	10–14	Lighter weights use more stitches per inch.
Children's wear	8–10	Although there are various size ranges and age groupings, it is a general guideline.
Denim jeans, jackets, skirts	7–8	Fewer stitches per inch generally will give more contrast stitch appearance.
Dress shirt or blouse	14–20	Using more SPI allows the use of smaller diameter threads that will minimize seam puckering.
Dresses, skirts	10–12	This range works for many fabrics.
Twill pants or shorts	8–10	More stitches per inch will help minimize seam grinning.
Trousers, dress pants, slacks	10–12	On some operations, such as serge panels, it may be desirable to use a longer stitch length.

Table 9.5 Typical Stitch Lengths Recommended for Knits

Knit Garments	SPI	Knit Garments	SPI
Dresses, shirts	10–12	Jersey T-shirts, tops, polos	10–12
Fleece	10–12	Sweaters (medium to heavy)	8–10
Hosiery, socks	35–50	Stretch knits (Lycra, spandex, etc.)	14–18
Infants' wear	10–12	Swimwear	12–16
Intimates	12–16	Underwear	12–14

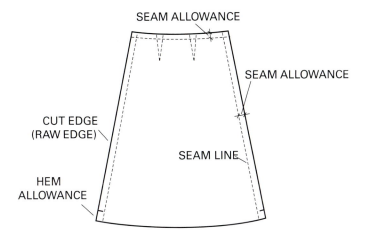

Figure 9.31 Seams and seam allowance.

Superimposed Seams (SS)

Superimposed seams (SS) are created by stacking fabric plies and then sewing them together near the edges. Superimposed seams are those in which one piece of fabric is laying on top of the other, usually right sides together, the raw edges lined up together (see Figure 9.32). This is an example of a straight seam, the easiest to sew and one of the most common seams.

Figure 9.32 illustrates different views of SSa, general seaming. This same general drawing format will be used for all the seam types in this chapter. Note that there is a key included to tell the viewer what is the right side and wrong side of the fabric. Such visual definitions are very important for technical drawings, as we studied in Chapter 4 (see Figure 4.51). Figure 9.32a is a special type of simple drawing, a sort of shorthand, called a schematic. The long horizontal lines represent the plies of fabric, and the short vertical line represents the "point of join," where the needle goes through. Figure 9.32b is a more three-dimensional version of the same, showing how the layers are arranged and stitched. Again, the short vertical line is the point of join, where all the layers are stitched through. Figure 9.32c is a sketch showing the seam "in the making." Here, as in most cases, the panels are sewn right sides (or face sides) together, and we can see that when a lockstitch is used, the stitch configuration for both top and bottom appear the same. Figure 9.32d shows the seam as it would be pressed open, or busted (also called *butterflied*). The point of join, where the needle goes through, is shown highlighted in red. The photograph in Figure 9.32e is an inside view of a **busted seam**; this example has overlock finished edges.

The glossary of stitches in Appendix A lists many variations on this terminology. The most common ways to form superimposed seams are 301 and various 500 class stitches. Examples of popular seams included in the superimposed seam category are:

- Plain seams (curved, inset corner, intersecting seams, mitered seams)
- Enclosed seams
- French seams
- Mock French seams
- False felled seams
- Serge-joined seams
- Decorative seams, such as piping
- Reinforcing seams (taped, strapped, and stayed)

Plain Seams

The **plain seam** (SSa) is used for general seaming and is one of the most common of the SS seams. Figure 9.32 illustrates different views of SSa, general seaming; the inside of a dress is shown in Figure 9.32e as a typical example. Stitches in the 300 class, such as 301 (Figure 9.32a), 321 (Figure 9.33a), and 304, as well as 401 and 516, are frequently used to construct this seam type.

Plain seams are the most common seam type. They are inconspicuous, especially when seam busted, and can be altered easily compared to other seam types. Because it has only a single

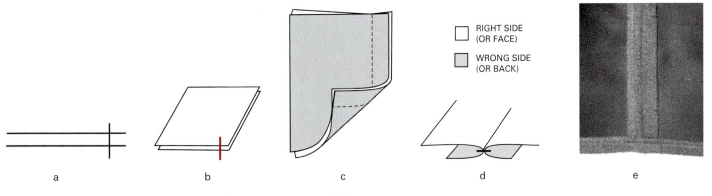

Figure 9.32 Seam type: plain seam, SSa; machine type: 301 lockstitch.

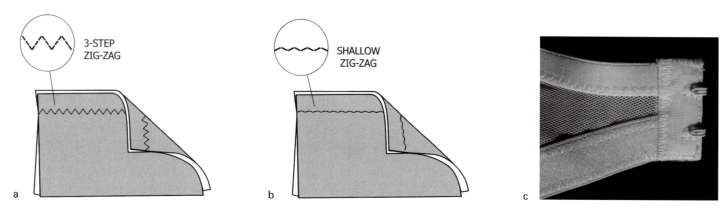

Figure 9.33 Seam type: plain seam, SSa; machine types: 321 (a) and 304 (b) zigzag lockstitch.

row of stitching, it is not designed for strength; however, this type of seam works well for high-quality tailored garments, made from fabrics that press well, that may need to be altered, and that don't take a lot of stress in the way that workwear or active sport clothing may.

Another version of SSa is sewn with a zigzag machine, which is used for fabrics with stretch. It is also used for lace, as a lingerie seam, and other places where the seam needs to have some stretch. Figure 9.33a shows a particular style of zigzag with three steps each way, which provides maximum stretch. Figure 9.33b has a shallow zigzag, a one-stitch zigzag suitable for a seam that is to be busted but still requires some stretch. The photo in Figure 9.33c shows how widely used zigzag is in the lingerie industry; in that small area of bra closure, zigzag is used as joining, as topstitching, and as reinforcement.

Straight seams are the easiest to sew, but other seams have other uses. Three other common seam shapes are curved seams, inset corner, and intersecting seams. Each of these has its own considerations and is best sewn with certain machines.

A **curved seam** (see Figure 9.34) is a plain seam, but with a curved shape. Before sewing, the shape of the panel on the right is concave and the shape of the panel on the left is convex (see Figure 9.34a, face side). The wrong side view shows that the

concave side needs to be clipped after sewing to lay flat or, in this case, to be seam busted. This type of curved shape would be found on a princess seam (see Figure 9.34c). In general, the greater the curve, the more clipping is required to press the seam open. If topstitching is added, it should be on the concave side, especially if it is farther away from the seam than edge stitch (about $1/16$ inch). Figure 9.34d also has a slight curve to the waist seams, but would not require the same amount of clipping because the curve is gradual.

More than one method can be used to create a style with an "S" curve seam (see Figure 9.35a). This curved seam example is sewn with two different stitch types: 301 lockstitch (see Figure 9.35a) and 516 5-thread safety stitch (see Figure 9.35c). It is important to note that this illustrates the rule that *the seam type remains the same regardless of the stitch method used to sew it.*

Both of the examples in Figure 9.35 are superimposed seams, SSa. Wrong side method A (Figure 9.35b) is sewn and pressed in an elaborate and labor-intensive way that requires clipping, seam busting, careful steaming, and very exacting topstitching. Wrong side method B (Figure 9.35d) is sewn with an overlock machine and no topstitching; this would work with a jersey fabric. Unless the price allowed for considerable skilled pressing, a knit construction would make a better choice for this style of seam.

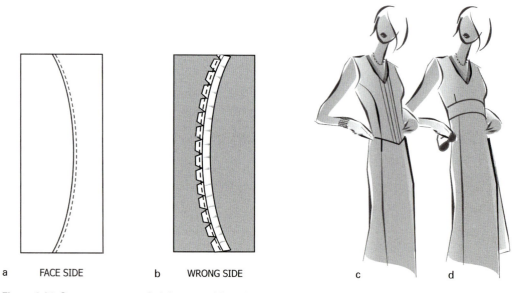

| a | FACE SIDE | b | WRONG SIDE | c | d |

Figure 9.34 Seam type: curved plain seam, SSa, with topstitching; machine type: 301 lockstitch.

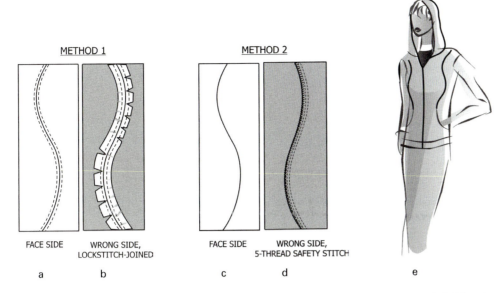

METHOD 1

METHOD 2

FACE SIDE

WRONG SIDE,
LOCKSTITCH-JOINED

FACE SIDE

WRONG SIDE,
5-THREAD SAFETY STITCH

a   b   c   d   e

Figure 9.35 **Seam type: plain seam, SSa, with topstitching; machine type: 301 lockstitch (a) and (b). Seam type: SSa; machine type: 516 5-thread safety stitch (c) and (d).**

Neither is right or wrong; the designer will need to specify the one that is appropriate for the final price of the design and best suits the chosen fabric.

A seam that incorporates an **inset corner** involves greater sewing skill. Figure 9.36 shows an example that is sewn with a 301 lockstitch. The inset corner in Figure 9.36a is a dart that transitions into a stylized princess seam. Figure 9.36d shows the shaped waist seam as an inset corner at center front. Because a clip is required at the very corner point, it is a weak spot and not suitable for a coarse-weave fabric or one prone to ravel. Figure 9.36b shows the direction in which it should be pressed, and topstitching can provide for additional reinforcement. Overlock machines do not work well for joining at sharp points, so the method shown on the wrong side (see Figure 9.36b) would not be suitable for overlock join. If the seam was joined by topstitch only, it would be a lapped seam. In that case, Figure 9.36b would show only one row of stitches.

Inset corners (see Figure 9.37) can sometimes be avoided when necessary by using a seam rather than a corner. Figure 9.37a shows the zipper placket for a child's pullover sewn to the front with two inset corners. Figure 9.37b has a similar appearance, but with the placket ending in a yoke seam, a much easier sewing technique that reduces the construction costs. Part of a designer's job is to understand how design features affect costs, and strategize the use of current trends and balance them with function and price to produce a successful garment.

Intersecting seams form at the point where two or more seams meet and cross each other; the seams must meet exactly on a quality garment. Figure 9.38 shows an example of a garment sewn with a 301 lockstitch. When seams cross over, it is especially important that the seams are pressed open to reduce the bulk. The first seam should be busted and pressed before the second seam is joined. This is also known as **underpressing**, the type of pressing that cannot be done at the end, but must be done in sequence with

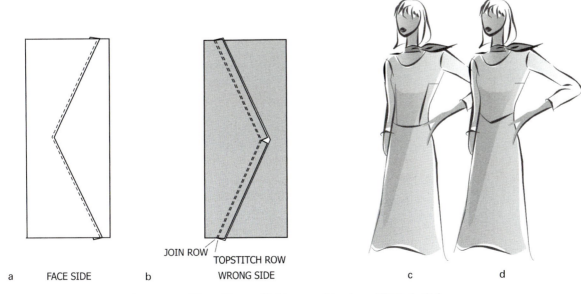

a   FACE SIDE   b

JOIN ROW
TOPSTITCH ROW
WRONG SIDE

c   d

Figure 9.36 **Inset corner. Seam type: SSa, with topstitching; machine type: 301 lockstitch.**

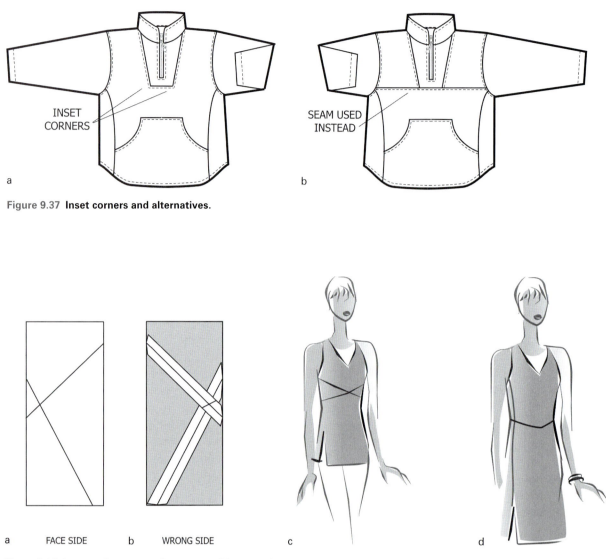

Figure 9.37 **Inset corners and alternatives.**

Figure 9.38 **Intersecting seams. Seam type: SSa; machine type: 301 lockstitch.**

sewing. In Figure 9.38c the crossover seam detail at center front is decorative. Figure 9.38d shows that the side seams would be joined first (skirt and bodice) and then carefully matched when sewing the waist seam. Figure 9.38d also shows an inset corner at the center front waist.

Mitered seams are another type of plain seam that occurs when seaming two pieces diagonally at the same angle, creating a chevron effect. In this case, if the fabric is plaid or striped, patterns should be well matched where mitered. When a braid or edging is applied, the area at a corner is often mitered, rather like the corner of a picture frame (see Figure 9.39). In this case, the miter angle is 45 degrees. Mitering requires more skill than straight seaming because the area is on the bias and prone to stretching. Thus, extra labor is required, and more cost is involved. Sometimes, however, it adds an important focal point and should be considered a design element. Thus, it is a designer's call to decide whether it is appropriate to incorporate the additional cost involved.

The trim in Figure 9.39a has an example of each way: the top example is a mitered corner and the bottom example is a straight seam. Because the trim fabric pattern in Figure 9.39a is more of an all-over pattern, both examples are similar, and the trim does not gain much from the mitering detail. Figure 9.39b, upper

example, is also mitered and shows what may happen if the miter were not sewn precisely; here, the stripes do not match well. If the factory assigned to this style does not have a high level of skilled sewing operators, the lower example is acceptable and would be less problematic to manufacture.

The example in Figure 9.39c shows a crisp stripe, which takes especially well to the mitering detail. The straight seamed version may also be acceptable depending on the application. Figure 9.39d shows both methods of side seam detail. The miter is toward the front, the straight seam toward the back. It is a designer's call to decide which looks better for the specific fabric used. The photo detail, Figure 9.39e, shows a mitered trim used as a facing, to finish off the front edges of a surplice shirt. Figure 9.40 shows additional mitered seams. The neck trim is mitered, and because both angles are 30 degrees, the stripe matches at the mitered corner.

The dolman sleeve has a seam down the center that sets up the opportunity to create a mitered effect with a textured fabric, or in this case, with stripes. Mitered seams can create a distinctive design effect with no more than just a straight seam, provided the stripes are matched up properly.

Leather (or leather substitutes or multicomponent fabrics) is sewn in much the same way as other materials, but because of the thickness, the seams are usually busted. Because leather cannot

Figure 9.39 Mitered seams as border detail. Seam type: SSa; machine type: 301 lockstitch.

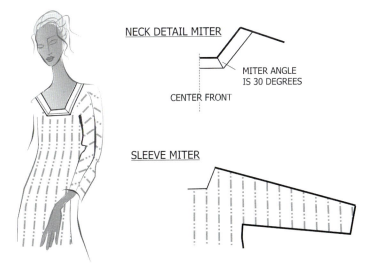

Figure 9.40 Mitered seams in other applications. Seam type: SSa; machine type: 301 lockstitch.

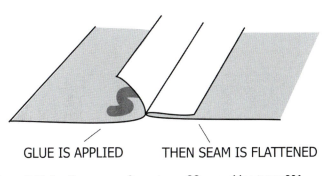

Figure 9.41 Leather seams. Seam type: SSa; machine type: 301 lockstitch.

be pressed open like textile fabric, the seam allowances are glued open (see Figure 9.41) and then pounded flat with a special mallet.

Enclosed Seams

The second seam type found in the superimposed seam category is the **enclosed seam**, or SSe (see Figure 9.42). This seam is the second most common seam type after the plain seam, and requires two separate stitchings: a join and a topstitching. Usually 301 are used.

To create this seam type, the fabric plies are sewn face sides together near the edge (as for SSa) and then opened out and turned back to encase the seam allowances. This type of seam is called an enclosed seam because the seam allowances end up sandwiched between the two layers. These seams occur only at edges: neckline, collars, cuffs, waistlines, waistbands, and facings. One unique feature about this seam type is that there are no visible stitches along the edge, and the stitches and seam allowances are hidden inside the garment because they are sandwiched between the plies of fabric.

As aforementioned, the 301 lockstitch is most often used to construct enclosed seams. Figure 9.42 shows the 301 lockstitch. Figure 9.42a through c shows the rows of stitching; the shorter vertical line represents the join stitch (Step 1 stitch in Figure 9.42c) and the longer vertical line represents the topstitching (Step 2 stitch in Figure 9.42c).

A possible disadvantage of this kind of seam is bulk, so it may not be a good choice for thick fabrics. It would not be necessary to overlock the edges before joining unless the fabric is extremely ravelly. The seam allowances are sometimes trimmed in layers, or **graded** (see Figure 9.42c). Figure 9.42d shows an example in which a square corner is turned (90 degrees or less). This area needs skill in trimming to prevent bulk from showing through or distorting the desired shape.

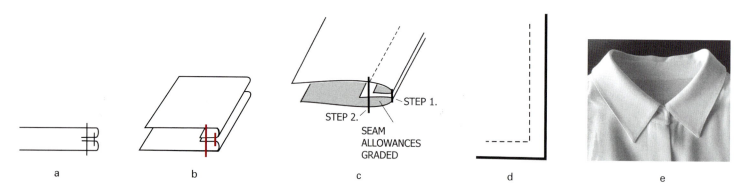

STEP 1.

STEP 2.

SEAM
ALLOWANCES
GRADED

a   b   c   d   e

Figure 9.42 Enclosed seam example. Seam type: enclosed seam, SSe; machine type: 301 lockstitch.

Figure 9.42d is a typical application as a cuff or collar, and shows it finished and turned to the face side. The addition of topstitching (all four views) strengthens the seam further. Figure 9.42e shows a collar and collarband, both of which are examples of enclosed seams. **Facings** are a way of finishing a raw edge of a garment with a separate piece of fabric and are considered enclosed seams. More examples of facings are discussed in Chapter 10.

French Seams (SSae)

The **French seam** (SSae) has the nickname *seam within a seam*. This kind of seam is good for thin, lightweight, or sheer fabrics that may fray, and for lingerie or underwear. A 301 is mainly used to create this kind of seam type as it creates clean, sturdy, and flat seams. Also, to have overedge, for example, showing through a sheer seam would be very unsightly. This is a good seam for straight seamlines but is more challenging for curved seams. Because it requires multiple sewing steps, it is labor intensive and, therefore, costly to make. In addition, it will add more bulk to the seams. Thus, thick fabric is not a good match with this seam type. However, a French seam will create clean, neat seam edge finishes. If a garment requires a similar finish for curved areas (such as an armhole), a bias seam binding is often a good match.

This construction results in a narrow seam encased within a wider seam, and it prevents fabrics from fraying. Figure 9.43 shows a seam constructed with 301 lockstitch. Figure 9.43a is the common schematic used for this style of seam. It has two steps of sewing seen in the top and bottom of Figure of 9.43a. There is nothing incorrect about the schematic (top of Figure 9.43a), but the next step (bottom of Figure 9.43a) has also been added. Figure 9.43b shows that the fabric is flipped back around so that it is once again

face side out. No stitching shows from the face side on this style of seam. The photo in Figure 9.43d shows a garment finished very skillfully; not only are the side seams (which are straight) finished with French seams, but also the curved seams of the armscye. This seam finish is sometimes used in countries that have sewing operators with higher skills and few overlock machines available.

Mock French Seams

French and mock French (or false French) seams have a similar appearance, but for the latter, the seam allowances of a plain seam are folded toward each other and stitched together (see Figure 9.44). Similar to the French seam, the mock French seam is used on transparent fabrics that ravel easily, and is used on straight seams. The mock French seam can be distinguished from the true French seam because the mock French seam features two rows of stitching visible inside the garment rather than one. It can be altered somewhat more easily than a true French seam. Figure 9.44 shows an example that is sewn with 301 lockstitch.

False Flat Felled Seams SSw(b)

Although the flat felled seam is a lapped seam, the false flat felled seam, SSw(b), is a superimposed seam (see Figure 9.45a and b). It is frequently seen in casual woven jackets and pants. The 301 and 401 stitches are usually used to create this seam type due to their smooth seam features.

The example shown is constructed with a 301 lockstitch. Figure 9.45a shows what is required to make a false flat felled seam with at least two separate stitchings. Note that there is a different amount of seam allowance for the layers and extra width has been

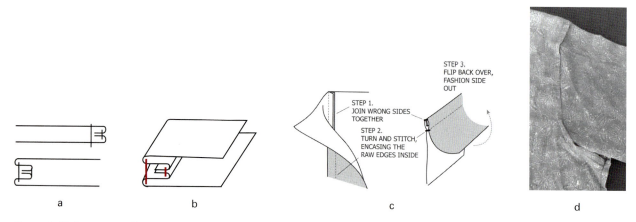

STEP 3.
FLIP BACK OVER,
FASHION SIDE
OUT

STEP 1.
JOIN WRONG SIDES
TOGETHER

STEP 2.
TURN AND STITCH,
ENCASING THE
RAW EDGES INSIDE

a   b   c   d

Figure 9.43 Seam type: French seam, SSae; machine type: 301 lockstitch.

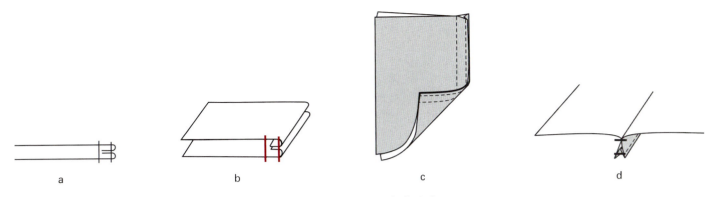

Figure 9.44 Seam type: mock French seam (unclassified); machine type: 301 lockstitch.

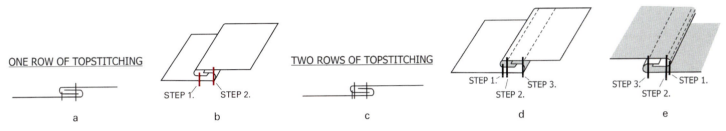

Figure 9.45 Seam type: false flat felled seam, SSw(b); machine type: 301 lockstitch.

added to enclose the raw edge. The machine type here is a single-needle lockstitch, and it could be sewn in a minimally equipped factory, which may not have the more complicated machinery for a flat fell application. Figure 9.45a and b shows alternate versions with only one row of topstitching. A false flat felled seam is created with just a single-needle lockstitch machine. It is a high-quality finish for men's shirts and provides a finished interior with no serging. It is used in place of a flat felled seam because the flat felled application cannot be employed to finish a narrow cylinder such as a shirt sleeve.

To imitate a flat felled seam style with two rows of topstitching requires three separate passes (see Figure 9.45c). The seam is joined at Figure 9.45d, Step 1. The seam is turned and edgestitched at Figure 9.45d, Steps 2 and 3. The underside is clean finished. Note that the appearance of the fashion side is different from the wrong side, which has one additional stitch line showing (see Figure 9.45e). This style of seam is common on men's shirts.

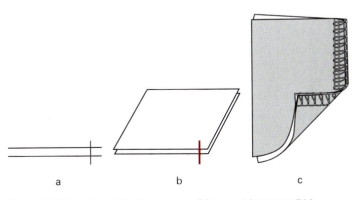

Figure 9.46 Overlock join. Seam type: SSa; machine type: 514.

Serge-Joined Seams

The serge-joined seam is sewn with a 500 class stitch. It is one of the most common types used for budget-priced, ready-to-wear garments. The safety stitch looks similar to a combination of an overlock stitch and one extra row of chainstitch. A single operation using the safety stitch results in finishing at the edges as well as seaming. It is very fast to create, cost effective, and finishes the seam allowances and the stitches simultaneously. It is called an *overedge, merrow, overlock,* or *serged seam.*

This type of seam is common for knits. This is an especially useful seam finish because it is a join and seam finish in one. The overedge refers to stitch formations in which a triangle of thread is formed around the cut edge of the fabric (see Figure 9.46c). This style of seam is functional for even the stretchiest fabrics.

Decorative Seams

Many decorative seams are used for ready-to-wear. They require various skill levels and entail various costs so they deserve careful study to determine which will provide the most benefit for a reasonable price. Variations on the **piping** (SSk or SSaw) technique are used as a decorative insert to accentuate seams and design lines and can be used as flat or corded piping. It is used for many categories, from high-fashion garments (for example, black satin piping with black wool crepe), to children's wear (such as floral piping), to active sports (for example, white piping on red knit). Piping made from woven fabrics can be constructed straight of grain or as a bias insert. Stretch piping can be constructed with knit fabrics. Figure 9.47e shows an example of an athletic pant that is constructed with knit piping.

Figure 9.47a shows a schematic with flat piping and Figure 9.47b shows corded piping. Figure 9.47c shows bias, corded, contrast fabric. Figure 9.47d shows piping used as an insert on an active

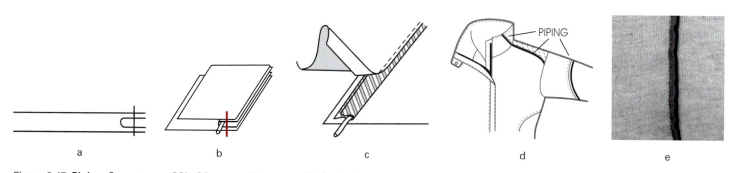

Figure 9.47 Piping. Seam types: SSk, SSaw; machine type: 301 lockstitch.

outerwear piece. It has topstitching added, which is a variation classified as SSaw.

Reinforcing Seams

Seams often need reinforcing for strength and also to maintain shape and prevent stretching. Three common examples of reinforced seams are taped seams, strapped seams, and stayed seams. The 301 and 500 stitches are frequently used to create the seams.

- Taped seams (SSab) are often created at shoulder seams, necklines, and women's waistline to prevent them from stretching out. These seams are frequently seen in knit T-shirts. Taped seams are constructed when a supportive tape such as twill tape, stretch tape, or fabric is sewn *into* the structural seam. A 301, 401, or sometimes 500 stitch are used to create this type of seam. Taped seams are also used to prevent the inside of kick pleats from stretching, to stabilize gathered seams, and for many other applications. Figure 9.48c shows tape used in a 301 lockstitched seam and Figure 9.48d shows it in an overlock joined seam, as would be used for the shoulder and neck seam to prevent stretching. It is not visible from the face side of the garment. Figure 9.48e is a knit shirt with taping at the shoulder seam. In this case it is white, but clear tape can be specified as well. Twill, grosgrain, and transparent stretch tapes are frequently used in this application.

- Strapped seam (SSag) is a strip, usually bias, used to cover a raw seam, and it is sewn through all layers. Figure 9.49c shows topstitching on the interior as well as the exterior. This strip could also be used for an unlined jacket, for example, in a contrast fabric. This wider piece of fabric covers the raw edges of a busted seam. This technique could be used inside (see Figure 9.49d) as a decorative tailored finish for an unlined jacket, or outside a garment as a trim. Strapped seams can also be made using a non-bias or ribbon if used on straight seams. SSf is a variation for which the strap needs no seam allowance,

such as twill tape, and is not illustrated. The easiest place to find a real-life example of a strap seam is to look at the seam finish in the crown of a baseball cap.

- Stayed seams are similar to strap seams, but the join stitching is not seen from the face side and it is sewn to the seam allowance only (see Figure 9.50c). A 301 is used to create this seam type. A section of twill tape, bias binding, or self-fabric is placed over the opened seam inside and attached to each seam allowance ply, without stitching through to the outside layer. The stay is usually the same width or slightly narrower than the busted seam. Figure 9.50a and 9.50b show that the stitching is through the seam allowance only. A common area of this type of reinforcement is at the bottom of a men's fly, inside. The variation SSf signifies a tape that needs no seam allowance (not illustrated).

Lapped Seams (LS)

A **lapped seam** is constructed by joining all thicknesses from the face side. Seam allowances of two or more fabric plies are sewn together, with the fabrics extending in opposite directions. Frequently, the 301 and 401 stitches are used to create this seam type. Seams included in this class are:

- Lap seams
- Patch pocket setting
- Felled seams
- Decorative lapped seams
- Folder applications

Lap Seaming (LSa)

The lapped seam category contains 102 variations, making it the largest seam class. Figure 9.51a is a schematic of a simple lapped seam sewn with 301 lockstitch. This type of seam is made by overlapping two or more layers of fabric and sewing through all layers near the edge (see Figure 9.51b). This is done in situations

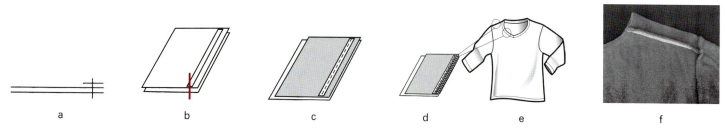

Figure 9.48 Seam type: taped seam, SSab; machine types: 301 lockstitch and 504 overlock.

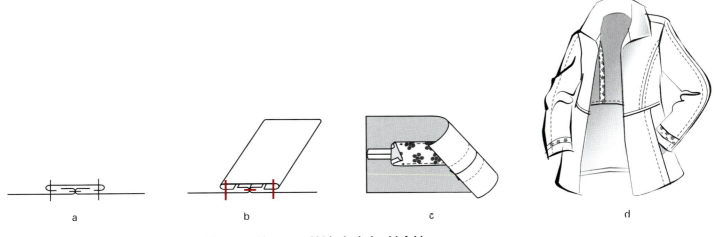

Figure 9.49 Strapped seam. Seam type: SSag; machine type: 301 lockstitch with folder.

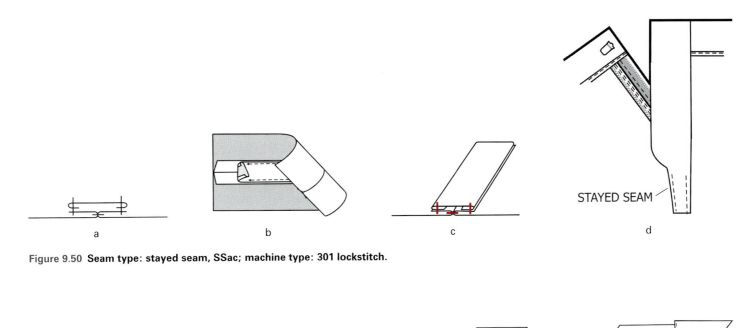

Figure 9.50 Seam type: stayed seam, SSac; machine type: 301 lockstitch.

STAYED SEAM

Figure 9.51 Seam type: Lap seaming, LSa; machine type: 301 lockstitch.

where there is no danger of the edges raveling, and in this method, the plies are overlaid face-to-back. The advantage to this is that the finished seam is flatter than it would otherwise be and that it is easier to sew unusual shapes such as curves and novelty designs. It also uses less seam allowance.

Figure 9.51d could be used for a detail on a leather jacket, for example. Such a shape would obviously be difficult to accomplish as a superimposed seam. The lapped seam is also frequently used for waistband attachment to the body of pants. It is not applicable in many cases, and one disadvantage is that during the sewing process, it can be difficult to judge the overlap from the top. Another is that only one stitching is used, so it is not good for high-stress areas.

Lap seaming is also used for seaming lace panels for an invisible join and for joining lace borders to another fabric. Figure 9.52 shows a common method for attaching lingerie borders in which the preshaped lace is attached with a fine zigzag; then the fabric in back is carefully cut away, leaving the lace as an edging or insertion (see Figures 9.52a and 9.52b). It is also the seam type used for appliqué, such as when applying lace to a lightweight lingerie tricot that will not ravel.

Lapped seams are also used for making a flattened finish on fabrics that won't ravel, such as felt or melton; to join interlining inside, such as for a waistband; and to eliminate bulk, such as for darts on interlining as in tailored jackets. (Even though the

FACE SIDE

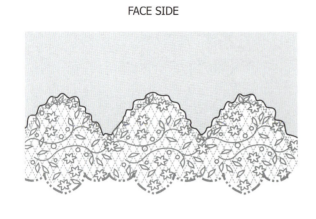

a

WRONG SIDE

b

Figure 9.52 Lace edging. Seam type: lap seaming, LSa; machine type: 304 zigzag lockstitch.

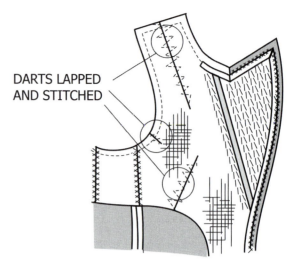

DARTS LAPPED AND STITCHED

Figure 9.53 Tailored jacket, inside view. Seam type: lap seaming, LSa; machine type: 301 lockstitch.

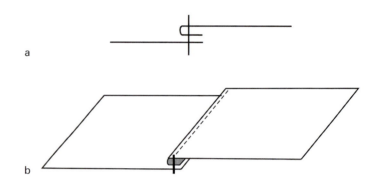

a

b

Figure 9.54 Seam type: lap seaming, LSb; machine type: 301 lockstitch.

stitching in Figure 9.53 has a zigzag appearance, it is actually sewn in a back-and-forth way on a straight stitch machine.)

Figure 9.54 shows another example of lap seaming. The seam is sewn with 301 lockstitch. This is a lapped seam joining all thicknesses from the face, along the folded edge of the top ply, similar to appliqué. This is done where stitching on the face will speed sewing. Because all layers are joined with one stitching, it is not as strong as a superimposed seam that has been top-stitched, although it looks like one. Thus, it should not be used for high-stress areas, such as side seams or at the front rise, below the zipper fly of a pant.

Patch Pocket Setting (LSd)

Figure 9.55 shows a patch pocket sewn with 301 lockstitch. Patch pockets are set in a lap seam application from the top side. The photograph in Figure 9.55c shows a patch pocket stitched to a jacket. This style is interesting because it includes piping in the seam. A very common item, a belt loop, is shown in Figure 9.55e. It is also stitched from the top "through all layers."

Felled Seams

True flat felled seams are seam join and seam finish in one. The difference between true flat felled and false flat felled is based mainly on its operation process. False flat felled seams have three different steps required, but true flat felled seams require only one step.

In this operation, the raw edges pass through a folder and interlock, as they are stitched through all layers. The most common method is with a 2-needle chainstitch machine. The

resulting seam has all raw edges enclosed and two rows of stitching on both the faced and the wrong side. It is strong, durable, and works well on seams that are straight or have, at most, a slight curve. This is commonly used for jeans, workwear, and other similar outerwear, and children's clothing. It creates a stiff seam on heavier fabrics.

Figure 9.56c shows an example where the stitch formation is a chain, visible from the underside, and the thread weight must be carefully matched to the weight of the fabric to avoid seam failure. Figures 9.56d and 9.56e show an actual jeanswear flat felled seam, inside and out. In Figure 9.56e it is possible to see the underside chain formation of the stitches. Figure 9.56f shows the right side and Figure 9.56g shows the underside of the actual denim flat felled seam.

Decorative Lapped Seams

Figure 9.57 shows decorative lapped seams. The seam is sewn with 401 chainstitch or 301 lockstitch. Slot seams are a style of lapped seam that has the two edges stitched to a narrow strip of fabric underneath, which is often of a contrast color (see Figure 9.57c). It could be used for the side seam on tuxedo pants or other straight seams. A seam with one side lapped is called a **tuck seam**. It differs from a standard lapped seam in that the stitching is farther from the edge, creating a tuck effect and adding accent to a seam line (Figure 9.58).

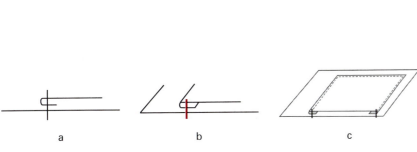
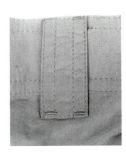

Figure 9.55 Patch pocket setting. Seam type: LSd; machine type: 301 lockstitch.

FLAT FELL

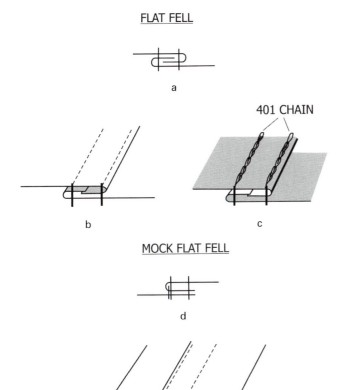

401 CHAIN

MOCK FLAT FELL

OVERLOCK

Figure 9.56 Seam type: flat felled seam, LSc-2; machine type: 401 2-needle chain (a–c). Seam type: mock flat felled seam, LSg; machine type: 301 lockstitch plus 504 3-thread overlock (d) and (e). Right side of the actual denim flat felled (f); underside of the actual denim flat felled seam (g). Note: (g) set with 401 2N chain stitch.

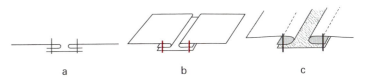

Figure 9.57 Seam type: slot seams, unclassified; machine type: 401 2-needle chain or 301 lockstitch.

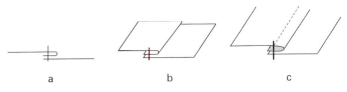

Figure 9.58 Seam type: tucked seam, LSd-1; machine type: 401 2-thread chain or 301 lockstitch.

Flat Seaming (FS)

The seam formed by the **flat seaming** method joins fabrics along the edges, butting them together or overlapping them slightly (see Figure 9.59). Certain specialized machines are used for this; the most common is the 600 series machine. Other methods use 500 series coverstitch, or occasionally 304 zigzag or 406 chainstitch machines. Of course, a single-needle lockstitch machine cannot be used for this type of seaming. The detail photo in Figure 9.59 shows a very common area for flatlock-joining, the seams of a mid-weight fleece garment. The thread color specified is in tonal contrast to the heather fabric, which highlights the body seams in a way often used in active and outdoor wear.

Because of the low-profile seam and stretch capability, it is very comfortable to wear, and it is often paired with high-stretch fabrics such as knits. The 600 stitches are most frequently used in knits. Because there is no seam allowance, it saves on fabric usage, but uses a lot of thread. It is popular for activewear, underwear styles, and children's wear. The style in Figure 9.59c uses flatlock seaming for the sleeve detail, raglan seam, empire seam, and side seams. Thread type is important for flat seaming, and a special type of soft thread called fluff thread, or texturized polyester, is usually specified to prevent chafing.

Sleeve and bottom openings use a similar-looking stitch called a 3-needle top-and-bottom coverstitch to finish the edges. Flatlock and coverstitch are often used on the same garment and are both 600 series machines. Top-and-bottom coverstitch was discussed

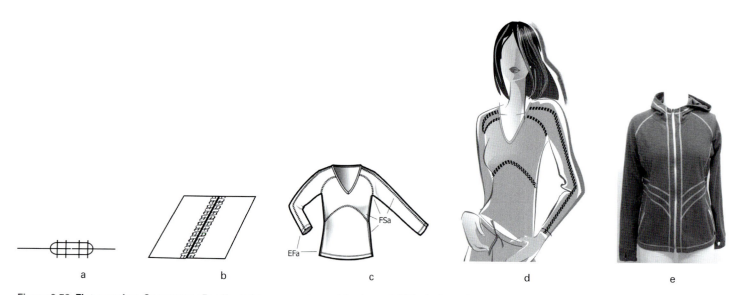

Figure 9.59 Flat seaming. Seam type: Fsa (for joining seams); machine type: 607 flatlock; and seam type: Efa (for hemming); machine type: 605 3-needle 5-thread coverstitch.

previously in this chapter. Special thread with great stretch capabilities is more compatible with flatlock. A flatlock finish works best on fabrics with little tendency to ravel and is not used for joining woven fabrics. Figure 9.59 shows an example that is sewn with a 4-needle, 6-thread, 607 coverstitch, also called a flatlock or flatseamer.

Bound Seams (BS)

Seam binding provides a high-quality finish and can be used when the inside appearance is important. It also provides a good alternative to overlock where that would be too visible. **Bound seams** can be used for decorative applications as well, in a contrast color or fabric. Bound seam application is often found in waistband finishing, on the inside. The bound seam is also used as a seam finish. Usually the 301 stitch is used to create this seam type.

Figure 9.60 shows an example of binding used as a quality interior edge finish. It works best when the binding fabric is lighter weight than the shell fabric (or if both are lightweight). It is a good finish to use for sheer woven fabrics. For this method, two steps are needed: The seam is joined and then a **folder**, a special device to keep the binding precisely folded and set while sewing, is used to attach the binding to both plies of seam allowance. This type of finish also works well for leather bags and other more industrial

uses. Figure 9.60d shows the corner of a grocery bag made from recycled materials; all four corner edges are finished with binding. This fabric does not ravel, so the binding needs no seam allowance.

Figure 9.61 shows a method that uses binding in a busted seam application. This is considered a specialty and high-quality finish. This type of edge is used on better fabrics that take a press well, and it creates a fine finished look when the seams are pressed open. Another name for it is *Hong Kong finish*. Because the binding is applied before the seam is sewn, this is classified as an SS, superimposed seam. The sequence of operations is:

1. Apply bias to raw edges.
2. Join panels at the seam line (superimposed seam).
3. Press the seam open.

It can be sewn as double fold bias (see Figure 9.61a) or with one fewer layer (see Figure 9.61b). Although one edge is left raw, it is not seen, and because the binding is bias, it has little tendency to ravel. Figure 9.61c shows the inside of a plaid jacket finished with bound seams and a bound hem edge at the bottom. Because the jacket is unlined, the binding creates a high quality finish inside. The binding fabric is a lighter weight than the plaid fabric, which works well for this application and avoids extra bulk.

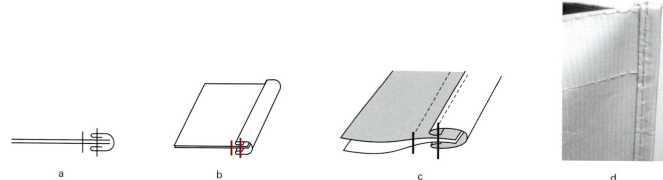

Figure 9.60 Binding as a seam finish. Seam type: BSe; machine type: 301 lockstitch.

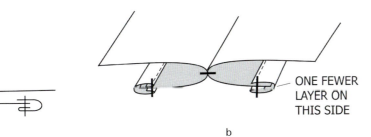

ONE FEWER
LAYER ON
THIS SIDE

a　　　　　　　　　　　b　　　　　　　　　　　c

Figure 9.61 Busted seam with binding edge finish. Seam type: SSbh-3; machine type: 301 lockstitch.

Other Frequently Used Edge Finishes for Seams

Frequently used seam finishes, primarily used for woven fabric, include:

- Overedge
- Clean finished
- Booked
- Pinked seams

These finishes are made *before* joining the seams.

3-Thread Overlock Edges (EFd)

The 3-thread overlock finish is classified EF (edge finish); it is applied before a seam is sewn and then busted. Overedge machines are used for join and edge finish in one (see Figure 9.46). Figure 9.62 utilizes a simpler type of overlock stitch to finish the raw edges for busted seams, either 503 (2-thread overedge), 504 (common 3-thread overedge), or 505 (3-thread overedge). Within the class of 500 stitches, odd-numbered stitches are for serging and even-numbered stitches are used for seaming. The 503 version here is called a 2-thread overlock. It is for edge finish only, such as in this example on a busted seam. The 3-thread overlock is not generally strong enough to be used to join two layers into a superimposed seam.

Clean Finished and Booked Seams

The method for clean finished and booked seams is similar although a different machine is used. The seam type for both is superimposed seam, specifically plain seam. For the **clean finished seams** (see Figure 9.63), the raw edge is turned and stitched with a lockstitch. It works well with less fabrics that will not fray, in lighter fabrics that do not add bulk, and it is better as a finish for straight seaming. Because it uses the same machine type as the seam join (301 lockstitch), it could be a good finish for a factory with limited machine types.

Booked seams (see Figure 9.63c) also have the raw edges turned under and stitched, but use a blindstitch machine (103 blindstitch). This operation is performed prior to the seam join and creates a durable hard-wearing finish often seen on men's unlined summer suits. Neither of these finish types would be used for bulky fabrics or in cases where a hard press would cause seam shine or show through.

Pinked Seam

A **pinked seam** (see Figure 9.64) is an edge finish made with a zigzag cut and is common in lightweight fabrics because it does not add bulk. It appears to have been cut with a pair of pinking shears, but it is actually done with a shaped blade. This kind of seam edge finish is good for fabrics that do not fray. Over time,

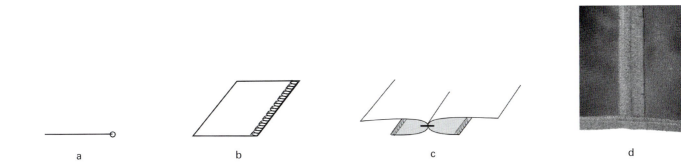

a　　　　　　　　　　　b　　　　　　　　　　　c　　　　　　　　　　　d

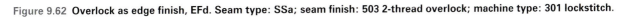

Figure 9.62 Overlock as edge finish, EFd. Seam type: SSa; seam finish: 503 2-thread overlock; machine type: 301 lockstitch.

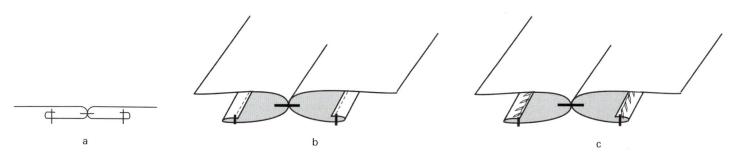

Figure 9.63 Clean finish and booked seam finishes, schematic (a). Seam type: SSa; machine type: 301 lockstitch; seam finish: EFa, hem; machine type: 301 lockstitch (b). Seam type: SSa; machine type: 301 lockstitch; seam finish EFa, hem; machine type: 103 single-thread blindstitch (c).

the fabric will still tend to ravel, but more slowly than without pinking. This type of finish would not be appropriate for very bulky or loosely woven fabrics. After the introduction of overedge machines, this method is seen mainly in vintage clothing and has faded from common use. The garment in Figure 9.64b is the inside view of a vintage wool gabardine skirt. It can also be found in vintage lingerie and other sheer garments.

Selecting Appropriate Seams and Edge Finishes for a Garment

Figure 9.65 shows many seam types used to construct one garment. Each one has been carefully thought through by the designer to provide this garment with the best customer appeal and the best quality for the price point at which it is being offered. Because the fabric is lightweight and sheer, the seam finishes actually show through on the fashion side. For that reason, French seams and bound seams have been chosen rather than overlock, which would show through in an unsightly way and would not be appropriate. This style illustrates how the technical design aspects of this style (and any style) go hand in hand with the design itself.

The Order of Seaming

A particular order is applied when seaming apparel products. The order varies according to the type of garment, but the objective is always to work efficiently while maintaining quality standards.

Armholes

Some styles fit better if the seams are joined round-on-round. A good example is the tailored sleeve (see Figure 9.66a). The sleeve is seamed first at the underarm into a kind of cylinder shape. The side seams and shoulder seams are joined and the two shapes are then sewn together at the armhole, round-on-round. By contrast, the shirt style in Figure 9.66b has the armhole sewn first; then the side seam and underarm seam are sewn as one operation. From the sewing operator's standpoint, it is faster to sew seams while the garment is flat, as in the shirt armhole (see Figure 9.66b). Sewing the tailored garment armhole last (see Figure 9.66a) requires more skill, but the underarm seams are more comfortable and less bulky.

Rises

Figure 9.67 shows two different ways of sewing a rise. For tailored trousers and lined pants, usually the front and back rise are joined all in one (see Figure 9.67a), which allows the crotch seam allowances to stand straight upright and the right and left legs to lie very flat at the crotch point. This is the only practical method if the inseams are busted and pressed, as they would be on a

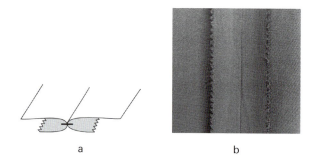

Figure 9.64 Seam type: SSa with pinked seam edges; machine type: 301 lockstitch.

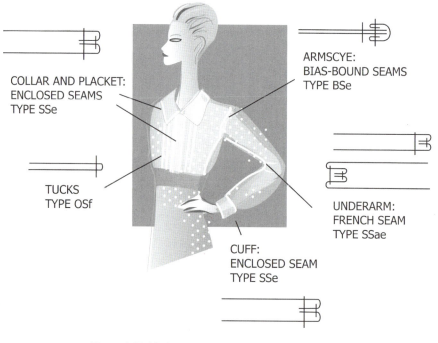

COLLAR AND PLACKET: ENCLOSED SEAMS TYPE SSe

ARMSCYE: BIAS-BOUND SEAMS TYPE BSe

TUCKS TYPE OSf

UNDERARM: FRENCH SEAM TYPE SSae

CUFF: ENCLOSED SEAM TYPE SSe

Figure 9.65 Various seams for a sheer shirt.

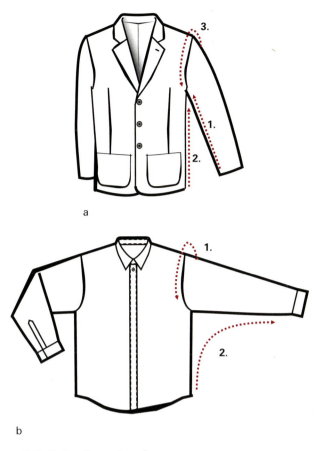

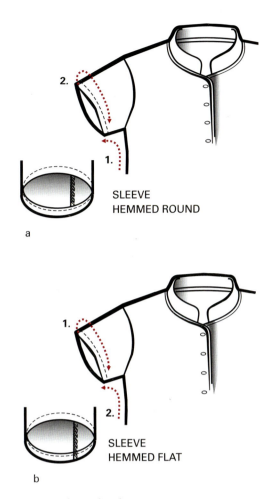

Figure 9.66 **Order of seaming, sleeves.**

SLEEVE
HEMMED ROUND

a

SLEEVE
HEMMED FLAT

b

Figure 9.68 **Order of seaming, hems.**

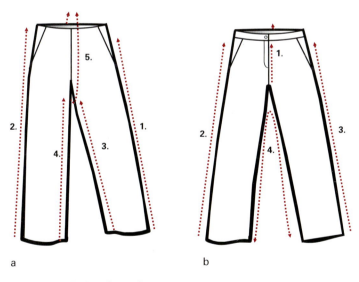

Figure 9.67 **Order of seaming, pants.**

high-quality pair of pants. Figure 9.67b shows the inseams sewn together last, an all-in-one operation. Inexpensive casual pants and jeans are sewn this way, and the crotch point is bulkier than if the rise is sewn last.

Hems

Cuffs and hems hemmed round-on-round (after the underarm seam is closed) are the standard. A cuff that is hemmed flat and then has the underarm/sleeve seam closed would have to have the

seam allowance extend to the edge. This is commonly used for children's apparel and in places where the aperture is too small to hem on a machine. For adult apparel, however, it is generally considered a substandard sewing method. The seam may be uncomfortable, and it may show on the bottom edge (see Figure 9.68b). It is seen more often on inexpensive tops and bottoms. Designers need to take into consideration the way their design details dictate various methods and sequences of construction to ensure the quality of the final products at a given price range.

Innovative Seam Finish Methods: Laser Cut/Welding/Fusing

There have been many innovative technological approaches applied in apparel product development, including new methods of seam. **Seam sealing** is one example and is widely used for technical outerwear. The step of sewing seams in waterproof fabrics creates needle holes that compromise the integrity of the waterproof function, so the application of a special seam seal tape over the previously sewn seam restores the waterproofing. This procedure adds a great deal to the labor costs but is a hallmark of modern technical outerwear.

Another approach is a technique known as **welding** (or fusing). For this method heat and pressure are applied to the seams to weld them, rather than sew them. There are no stitches or thread used, and the result is a watertight seal. The operator carefully monitors heat, pressure, and dwell time to assure the quality of bonding. Figure 9.69 shows a reinforcing piece (the black fabric) being welded to the hand pocket area, over the zipper.

Figure 9.69 **Welding.**

Figure 9.70 **Laser cutting.**

A technique known as *laser cutting* is also used to create a clean edge that does not require a hem. This technique cuts down on thickness, and the heat of the laser seals the edge. Figure 9.70 shows a laser cutting machine at work, cutting circle shapes for reinforcing. The edges of the piece in Figure 9.69 have also been laser cut and require no seaming.

Summary

This chapter reviewed the various stitches and seams in each class and the appropriate use of stitches and seams for various garments depending on these end uses. Stitches and seams have their own characteristics, and other design details should be taken into consideration for ideal selection of stitches and seams. SPI and its appropriate use for various ready-to-wear products is also an important factor determining apparel quality. Order of seaming for each standard product categories was also surveyed. Lastly, some innovative seaming methods were explored. Designers pay careful attention to each design detail of apparel products that affect apparel quality. Understanding the various stitch types and seam types available and selecting appropriate seam types are central factors that determine apparel quality. Chapter 10 provides more information on seam edge finishes.

Study Questions

1. Use any example of a T-shirt in your wardrobe.
   a. List fabric content.
   b. List stitches and seams and the reasons for selecting the stitches and the seams used for each part of the garment (shoulder seam, armhole, side seam, bottom hem, cuff, neckband).
   c. Suggest any alternative stitches and seams that can be used and the reason you selected them for each part of the garment (shoulder seam, side seam, bottom hem, cuff, neckband).
   d. List the possible order of seaming this garment.

2. Select two similar tops that represent two different price ranges, high and low, in your wardrobe.
   a. Note the price range for each.
   b. Think through the various factors that caused the difference in set price ranges for two products.
   c. Are there any construction-related issues? Analyze the differences in stitch types, seam types, construction, and design details. What are the factors causing high cost for production?
   d. If you are a designer who wants to make a knock-off of the high-price-range product for mass market, what suggestions would you have for an alternative way to construct your low-cost product line?

3. Use any pair of jeans in your wardrobe.
   a. List fabric content.
   b. List stitches, seams, and the reasons for the stitches and seams used for each part of the garment (outseam, inseam, bottom hem, waistband, dart, belt-loop construction, belt-loop attachment, pocket, pocket bag).
   c. Suggest any alternative stitches and seams that can be used and the reason you selected them for each part of the garment (outseam, inseam, bottom hem, waistband, dart, belt-loop construction, belt-loop attachment, pocket, pocket bag).
   d. List the possible order of seaming this garment.

4. Design a women's shirt for your target market.
   a. List your target market and price range.
   b. Draw a ¹⁄₈-scale flat for front and back, respectively.
   c. Specify the fabric you want to use.
   d. Put specs in your drawing using callouts and arrows.
   e. Specify stitches and seams and the reason why you choose the stitches and the seams for the shirt for each part of the garment (neckline, collar, armhole, shoulder, bottom hem, cuffs).
   f. What are the reinforcement seams you want to use for your shirt?

5. What are the various factors designers should take into consideration when selecting stitch types and seam types for apparel products?

6. What are the possible stitch types used for constructing enclosed seams?

7. Revise the sketch in Figure 9.60c to specify a binding with no seam allowance.

8. What seam types are appropriate for knits?

9. Look on the tech pack in Chapter 3 and list the seam types for a men's jean. In Appendix B, locate the tech pack for a Men's Woven Shirt and list the seam types.

10. Refer to Appendix A: Standards for Seams and Stitches. Find the one seam type for setting a patch pocket.

11. Refer to Appendix A: Standards for Seams and Stitches. Find a seam drawing for each:

    a) a jean pant 2 piece waistband b) a pajama waistband.

12. Refer to Appendix C: 101 Pockets, page 351. Select an example from Pockets with Piecing and Seaming. Provide a full list of the seams and stitches for making the pocket.

Check Your Understanding

1. List the differences between 300 and 400 stitches and how the differences determine the application based on end uses of apparel products.

2. List differences (advantages and disadvantages for each) between 500 safety and non-safety stitches and describe how they are applied to apparel products.

3. List various sewing machines and explain how they are used in sewing for different end uses of apparel products.

4. Define SPI and explain why it is important for quality of apparel products.

5. List appropriate SPI for five selected product categories each in wovens and knits.

6. List and describe the four basic seam types.

7. List various seam types in lapped seam.

8. List various seam types in superimposed seam.

9. List three types of reinforcement seams and elaborate on the differences among them.

10. List the order of seaming for shirts and pants.

References

American and Efird. (n.d.) Thread education. Available at http://www.amefird.com/technical-tools/thread-education.

Brown, P., and J. Rice. 2001. *Ready to Wear Apparel Analysis* (3rd ed.). Upper Saddle River, New Jersey: Prentice Hall.

Ramstad, E. (February 5, 2013). "Sewing Machines Go High-Tech." U.S. edition of *The Wall Street Journal,* p. B5.

Edge Treatments

Chapter Objectives

After studying this chapter, you will be able to:

- Analyze various kinds of edge treatments for each garment's end use
- Discuss the importance of appropriate edge finishes for each area of seams
- Identify the appropriate edge finishes based on fabrics and design features
- Understand how to construct the various edge finishes

Key Terms

band
belting
binding
contour waist style
cuffs

edge finishes
heading
hemline
padded hem
placket

stitch-in-the-ditch
turned-back hem
understitching

Edge finishes make up a class of stitches designated as EF, which, technically speaking, refers to the methods for finishing the edge of a single ply, including finishing the raw edges before seaming, as we studied in Chapter 9. This chapter focuses on edge treatments as applied to garment edges. Edge treatments in this context include various garment edge finishes, hems, facings, cuffs, and plackets.

Common types of edge finishes with the EF designation include:

- Hems
- Straps and belting
- Tunneled elastic
- Binding
- Facings
- Plackets
- Cuffs and bands

Hems

A common way to finish the edge of a garment is to turn back the raw edge to the inside and secure it with what is known as a **turned-back hem**. Many of the seam finishes we studied in Chapter 9 are used as hem finishes as well, including booked hem, bound hem (Hong Kong finish), bias-edge hem, and pinked hem. Leather items use glued hems in much the same way leather seams are finished. There are a great many possibilities for hems, depending on the weight of a fabric and style of garment.

Other types of hems are faced hems, band hems, and bound hems. Different techniques are often used for stretch knits than for woven fabrics, with certain techniques suitable for either. The **hemline** is the bottom edge, or foldline if there is one, of a dress or skirt, which will be the finished length (see Figure 5.2). All of these techniques are applicable to sleeve openings and other areas as well.

Hems can also be used to add weight and improve the drape of the bottom edge. Sometimes a deep hem can be added to a lightweight knit fabric or a double-fold hem to a sheer fabric to give a better hang to the garment. Fine, sheer garments sometimes have *hand-rolled hems*, as do lightweight scarves. This is a very narrow, twice-turned hem that is stitched by hand. There are also *machine-rolled hems* that are made with the use of a folder. Sometimes actual weights may be sewn on, or a chain is added to the hemline to improve the drape and help the hem fall evenly.

Blindstitched Hem (EFC)

Figure 10.1 shows a common way of securing a turned-back hem, with a finish called *blindstitching*. This approximates the look of

a hem blindstitched by hand in the most invisible way possible. The machine that produces this hem has a curved needle, and the stitches are made with single-needle thread, which forms a chainstitch. A penetration adjuster determines how far the thread will go through the face side layer. Properly set up, the needle will pass through only a portion of the face side ply, without going all the way through. It works well for both wovens and knits and is the most invisible hem. It is not the most durable hem, and it is used for finer fabrics, tailored garments, and items not intended for hard use or constant machine washing.

Figures 10.1a and 10.1b show the short vertical line that represents the needle and where it is penetrating. These sketches indicate that the thread does not penetrate through the face ply and just passes through the inside edge. The use of seam tape (see Figure 10.1d) is common to help bridge the thickness of the fabric and protect the raw edge from raveling, while maintaining just one layer of turnback. This type of finish is used for high-quality fabrics and is better with "dry-clean only" care since, as mentioned earlier, it is less durable than other methods. Because it is a chainstitch, if the chain formation is broken and the loose thread is pulled, the stitching could come out completely.

On a garment with an improperly sewn blindstitch, the thread may show through on the right side as a row of small dimples, or even tiny stitches. This indicates that the machine was not set up properly, or that the fabric is too lightweight to make a blindstitched hem a good choice for the style. The thicker the fabric, the more likely the blindstitch will be invisible.

Figure 10.1e shows a hem using seam tape, first sewn to the raw edge. The fabric is a wool gabardine. Figure 10.2 shows a similar style that has the raw edge first turned back and secured with the blind hemmer; then the hem turn-back is blind hemmed as well. This style of hem is useful when a very clean appearance is desired, such as on the inside of an unlined jacket. (This is similar to the booked hem in Chapter 9, Figure 9.63c.)

Clean Finished Hem

Figure 10.3 shows a clean finished hem. As seen in Figure 10.3a, this configuration is type EFb, no matter how much turn-back is specified. Figures 10.3a top and 10.3b both have a small amount of turn-back. Figures 10.3a bottom, 10.3c, and 10.3d have a deeper hem turn-back, but the sewing method and classification are the same. This finish is very common for woven fabrics but not usually a good choice for jersey knits because it would add bulk and is not extensible (stretchy); it would tend to snap under pressure. In most knits, it would also create unsightly ripples while sewing.

A common example of this hem construction is on the bottom opening of a pair of jeans; in fact, it would be hard to find a pair

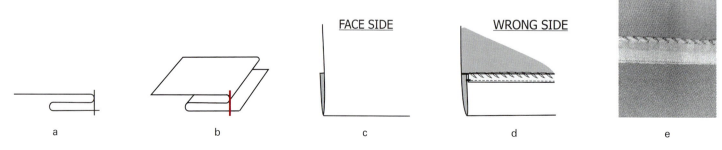

FACE SIDE   WRONG SIDE

a   b   c   d   e

Figure 10.1 Blindstitched hem. Stitch type: EFc; machine type: 103 single-thread blind hemmer.

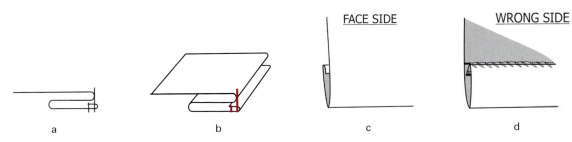

Figure 10.2 **Variation of blind hem. Stitch type: EFc; machine type: 103 single-thread blind hemmer.**

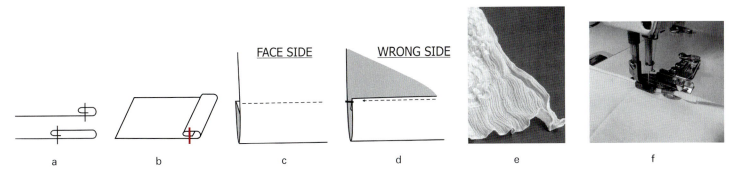

Figure 10.3 **(a–f) Clean-finished hem. Stitch type: EFb; machine type: 301 single-needle lockstitch.**

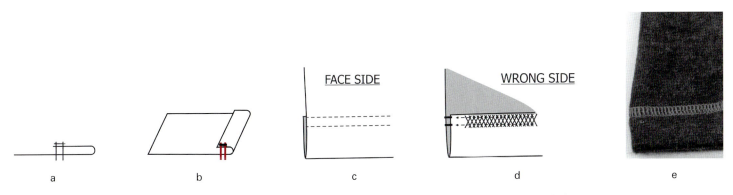

Figure 10.4 **Top-and-bottom coverstitch hem. Stitch type: EFa Inv; machine type: 605 3-needle bottom coverstitch.**

that do not use this hemming method. Another useful application is shown in Figure 10.3e. That is a silk scarf with an extremely narrow hem, around $^1/_{16}$ inch on the edges and bottom. Because the fabric has stretch and the finished hem pulls widthwise, it creates a decorative feminine appearance, a kind of ruffled finish known as *lettuce edge*.

Coverstitch Hem

Coverstitch is a special type of sewing machine that creates the most common knit hem finish (see Figure 10.4). The point of join is through only two layers, so it is less bulky than a clean-finished method. From the face side, the finish appears as 2-needle, and the wrong side shows the looper threads, which also act to finish the raw edge. This type of finish has a lot of extensibility, and when properly applied, will not distort the surface while sewing. Machines with a differential feed system allow knit seams to lay flat after seaming by allowing the knit layers to pass through the machine at different rates. Machine classifications 600 and 406 are frequently used in this application. Figures 10.4c and 10.4d show

2-needle bottom coverstitch. Most T-shirts and knit shirts will likely have this finish used to hem the sleeves and bottom. Figure 10.4e has another type of coverstitch called 3-needle top-and-bottom coverstitch.

Serge and Hem (EFe)

An inexpensive type of hem, *serge and hem*, is used on woven fabrics for items such as placemats, sheer curtains, and places where the finish won't be seen (Figure 10.5).

Faced Hem (LSct-2)

The use of another fabric, usually a strip of single-fold bias to face the edge (see Figure 10.6), is useful in situations where the garment shape is curved (see Figure 10.6c). It is also useful if the fabric is heavy; in that case, the facing will reduce bulk. A type of knit tape can also be used. Bias is also used on the outside (see Figure 10.6d) to provide a decorative effect with either matching or contrasting fabric. Figure 10.6c shows another method of

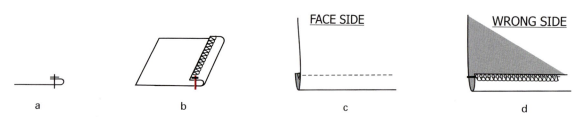

Figure 10.5 **Serge and hem.** Stitch type: EFe, serge and hem (two operations); machine type: first, overlock, 503, 504, or 505; second, 301 single-needle lockstitch.

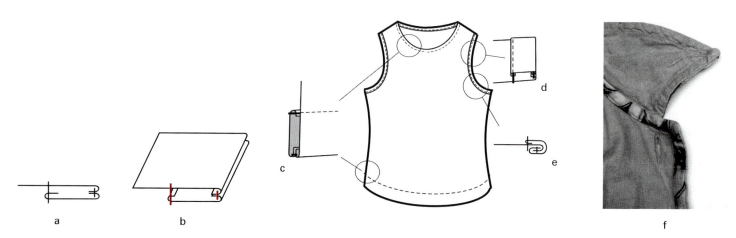

Figure 10.6 **Faced hem.** Seam type: LSct-2; machine type: 301 lockstitch.

using bias to bind the armhole edge, BSg. The photo example in Figure 10.6f shows a decorative printed bias strip used for both embellishment and to finish the center front edge (notice the buttonhole) of a summer-weight linen jacket.

Shaped Hems

It is possible to achieve a great variety of shapes with the use of a facing, and the shaped facing technique can be used for many applications (see Figure 11.12 in the next chapter). Figure 10.7 shows a scallop shape that requires a tightly woven fabric because it needs close clipping in order to turn smoothly. The deeper the scallop, the more challenging the sewing will be. This same scallop shaping could also be used for the front placket shape of a blouse. This particular one would be considered very labor-intensive because of the sewing involved, and it would be seen in a high-quality garment. The steps, most of which require more than average skill and handling, are:

1. Apply seam tape to facing
2. Join facing to shell
3. Trim, clip, and turn
4. Press
5. Edge-stitch scallop shape
6. Blind hem top of facing to shell

Figure 10.7c shows another method, a far less labor-intensive way to achieve a scallop shape. In this example, a type of zigzag embroidery is used to finish the edge. If a factory had this machine, they could achieve a similar effect, and when the designer understands the finishing techniques and the machinery

involved, this makes it possible to have the design cost in at the desired price point. Neither of these methods is right or wrong, but the cost expectations for each style in the line, laid out before designing even begins, must always be met.

When considering whether to use a facing or other edge finish, keep in mind that the heavier the fabric, the more difficult it will be to use a self-fabric facing because of the layers involved. Often a lighter-weight fabric can be used as a facing to reduce bulk, as long as it is compatible with the shell fabric in terms of care. The seam can be layered by trimming each layer to a different width, or graded (see Figure 10.8c). Factories can simulate this effect by sewing with varying seam allowances, but either method requires a bit of additional time and handling.

A facing often requires careful handling and pressing. **Understitching** can be added to help the seams to roll to the inside and prevent the facing layer from slipping out and showing. It also flattens the seam allowance to reduce the bulkiness of the seam. Figure 10.8 shows understitching. Figure 10.8a is a schematic view and shows how the second stitch line goes through only three layers, not four, as topstitching would. Figure 10.8b shows how the layers are positioned while sewing and that the understitching penetrates through three layers only. Figure 10.8d shows how the understitching is visible from the inside, but not from the outside. This method of stitching cannot go around a corner and stops short a couple of inches back from center front. The photograph in Figure 10.8e shows the hood of a fleece garment. The hood facing (the black strip) is made from a flat wide spandex tape, finished all along both edges. The stretch makes it able to shape itself around the hood edge, and the finished edge is secured by 3-needle top-and-bottom coverstitch and does not require a hem. That keeps the hood edge flat on an otherwise bulky fabric.

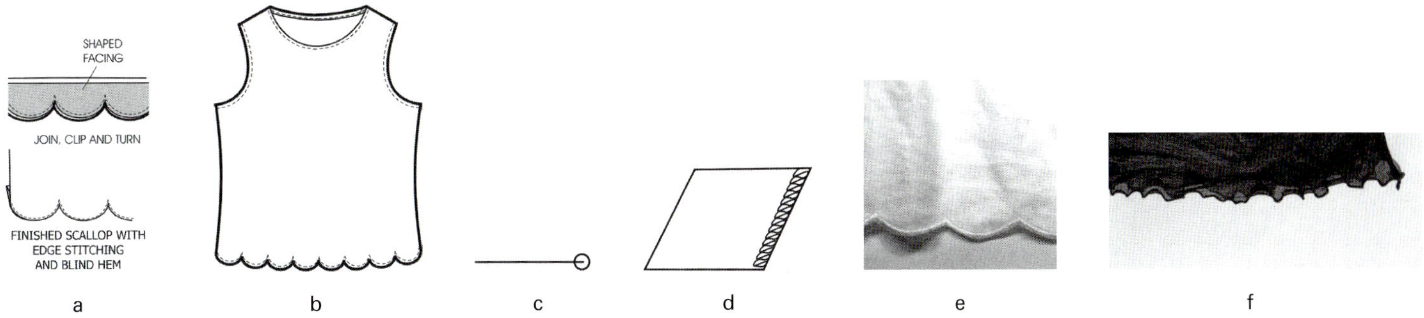

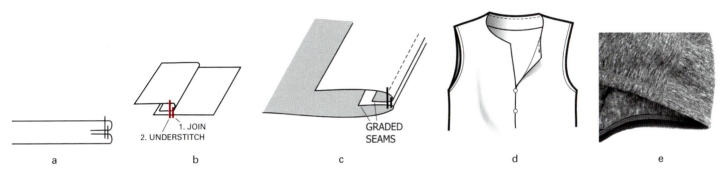

Figure 10.7 Shaped facing (a) and (b); ornamental edge finishing (c–e). Seam type: EFd; machine type: 304 zigzag.

Figure 10.8 Shaped facing with understitched seam. Seam type: understitched seam, unclassified; machine type: 301 lockstitch.

Band Hem

Bands are pieces of fabric that are sewn to the straight raw edges of garments to extend and finish the edge (see Figure 10.9). They can be made of shaped bias or straight-grain fabric and are used at the hem or waist edge of a skirt, pant, or sleeve. They can be self-fabric or contrast, depending on the application. The band hem on a sleeve differs from a cuff in that it has no closure. A **band** finish creates an enclosed seam and is the same construction as is used for many collars and for waistbands. It is often decorative. More sleeve finish examples are shown in Figure 10.34 on page 196.

Decorative Hems

Other hems are used for formal wear or novelty effects. We saw a lettuce edge in Figure 10.3e; a stretch knit fabric can also be pulled while adding a narrow merrowed edge finish to create a similar effect. Sometimes hems have wire of metal or plastic incorporated into the edge. Horsehair, which is a stiff woven bias braid, can be added to introduce flare and create a bouffant silhouette which stands out stiffly. Another type of hem is called a **padded hem**, which has an additional piece of thick, soft bias inserted between the hem and garment to prevent a sharp crease or eliminate a ridge on a heavy fabric.

Straps and Belting

Some very useful techniques are applied to edging straps and belting.

Straps

A narrow round strap is called a spaghetti strap. When it is made, the seam allowances fill the inside of the tube (see Figure 10.10c) and create the shape of a thin cylinder, like a piece of spaghetti. It is used for narrow straps, drawstrings, and other trim, such as a waist insert detail (see Figure 10.10d). The join stitching of this type of strap is on the inside and is not visible.

Other edge finish techniques include straps and belting. Figure 10.11c shows a jacket with a self belt, made from the same fabric as the garment. The fabric may be applied around a kind of stiff interfacing called **belting**, if more body is desired than just the fabric alone. An accessory such as a belt can add considerable value to the garment without adding a lot to the cost.

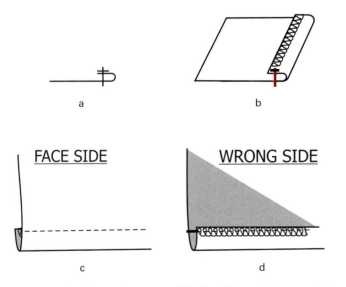

Figure 10.9 Band hem. Seam type: BSg band (bound) hem; machine type shown: 301 lockstitch.

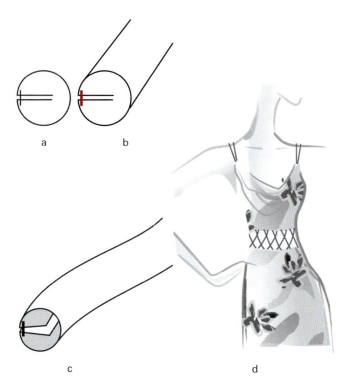

a   b

c   d

Figure 10.10 Spaghetti strap. Seam type: EFu, spaghetti; machine type: 301 lockstitch with folder.

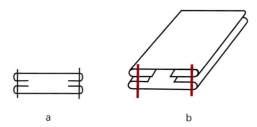

a   b

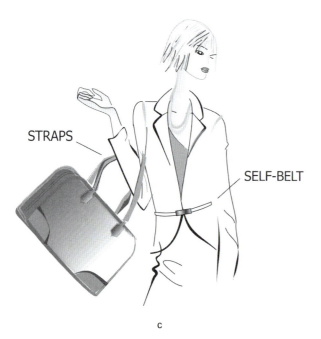

STRAPS

SELF-BELT

c

Figure 10.11 Straps and belting. Seam type: EFn; machine type: 301 lockstitch with folder.

The handbag in the sketch also uses belting to form the straps. A great many types of belt shapes, with piping or without, can be set up to be made with special forms called *folders*, which pull fabric strips off a spool, automatically fold under the seam allowances, and stitch—an all-in-one operation.

Belting

Belt loops and elastic belting are edge treatments sometimes seen at the waist of a skirt or pant.

Belt Loops

Figure 10.12 shows another use of the versatile 2-needle bottom coverstitch, in this case for making belt loops. Figures 10.12a and 10.12b show that the fabric edges butt together, eliminating the bulk of seam allowances. The "cover" (threads over the raw edge) keeps it from fraying. Belt loops of this type are made in a long piece and then cut to length before being sewn to the garment. Traditional jeans and casual pants use this type of belt loop.

Figure 10.12d shows a common construction of belt loops in which the bottom of the belt loop folds up to be caught in the waistband seam. The top is folded over and bartacked or stitch-tacked into place. Traditional trousers have this method of belt loops. Figure 10.12e shows a belt loop in place on a casual pant.

Elastic Belting

Figures 10.13a and 10.13b indicate the construction method for finishing the top edge of a garment with an elasticized edge. The single bar in the middle of Figures 10.13a and 10.13b represents the elastic. This method involves sewing the elastic into the casing and finishing the inside waistband bottom edge with a clean finish, all-in-one step, with the use of a folder designed to perform that operation.

The drawstring for this pair of shorts (Figure 10.13c) is made with another folder setup (see Figures 10.13d and 10.13e) and has only one stitch at the edge. This same construction can be used to make belts, straps, drawstrings, and other accessories. Generally, the drawstring or belting would be cut into very long pieces, passed through the folder and sewn, then cut to length depending on the waist size needed. In the case of these shorts, the drawstring is threaded through the casing formed by the elastic, after the garment is assembled. The entry and exit points would be two buttonholes or grommets near the center front.

Binding

As we saw in Chapter 9, **binding** is an edge finish to one or more plies of fabric in which a separate piece of fabric is used to encase the raw edges. It is also a very popular method to finish garment edges, especially the neck edge of knit garments. The bindings for neck edge treatments need to be at least slightly stretchy, unless they are being applied to a straight edge. If a woven fabric is used for the binding, it is most often cut on the bias, which is better able to accommodate curved shapes.

Figures 10.14a and 10.14b illustrate the use of double-fold bias binding. The binding is either prepared in advance with the folds pressed in place (such as what is available pre-packaged in a fabric store) or just pre-cut in a long strip and set into place with a folder. The binding in the photograph in Figure 10.14c is set that

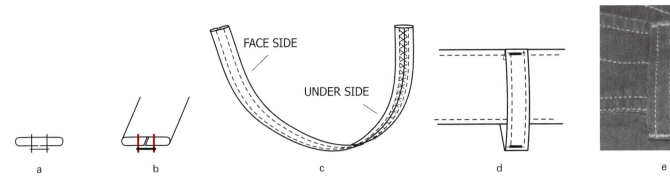

Figure 10.12 Belt loops. Seam type: EFa Inv, coverstitch; machine type: 406 2-needle bottom coverstitch.

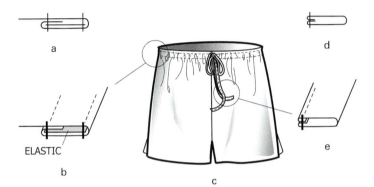

Figure 10.13 Various elastic belt applications. Schematic (a) and diagram (b) show the construction of the elasticized edge for a pair of shorts (c); seam type: EFr, tunneled elastic. Schematic (d) and diagram (e) show the construction of the drawstring; seam type: EFp, belting. Machine type for both: 301 single-needle lockstitch with folder.

top of the previous join seam (the crevice between the garment and binding). This method is also called *crackstitch*. Figures 10.15c and 10.15d show the use of binding with one finished edge. For woven fabrics, it works best on long, fairly straight seams because of the limitations of the bias, and is also often used in certain areas such as the waistband edge inside and the fly-facing edge of pants.

Figures 10.16a and 10.16b show the use of a binding material with finished edges, such as ribbon or tape, which needs no seam allowance turned under. In this case, the finished piece is only three layers, so this is a way to reduce bulk. It could also be made with elasticized binding, which would be useable for curved shapes or on knits because it will stretch. Figure 10.16c shows just such an application for the strap of a stretch camisole. Figures 10.16d and 10.16e show a binding fabric without finished edges. It requires five layers of fabric so it is used in situations in which the fabrics are light enough to avoid extra bulk.

Bias has many uses both as an edge treatment and as decoration. Figure 10.17 shows an example of an infant's bib, which uses bias in two different ways. The two types of bias have the same finished width and visual appearance, but the techniques for applying them are not the same, and they would require the factory to set up its equipment differently to apply each type.

The first method (see Figures 10.17a and 10.17b) has the stripes appliquéd flat onto the bib with the use of a folder and a 2-needle machine. The edges (Figure 10.17c) are also finished with bias binding attached with a different folder setup that covers the raw edge, while folding under a seam allowance on the top and bottom, so that everything is done with one stitching (see Figures

way, and a chainstitch machine has been used; the chain loops are visible on the inside edge. Other solutions to reducing bulk are knit or elastic bindings and fold-over braids. The bindings in Figures 10.14d and 10.14e are sewn with a 406 2-needle coverstitch. Figure 10.14f shows a matching ribbed fabric used for the binding, a good choice for a comfortable flexible edge finish. This is a common method for knits and reduces the seam allowance bulk by one layer (compare Figures 10.14a and 10.14d). Figure 10.14g shows a picture of bias folder.

The **stitch-in-the-ditch** (see Figures 10.15a and 10.15b) is used for a more invisible application where the stitch line is sewn on

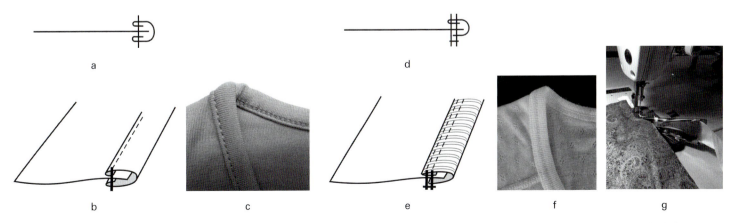

Figure 10.14 Binding as edge treatment. Schematic (a), diagram (b), and actual garment (c); seam type: BSc; machine type: 301 lockstitch or 401 chainstitch. Schematic (d), diagram (e), actual garment (f); seam type: BSc; machine type: 406, 2-needle bottom coverstitch; (g) bias folder.

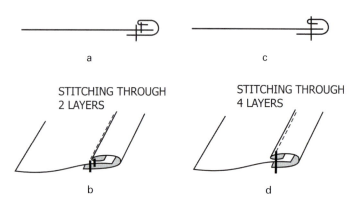

STITCHING THROUGH 2 LAYERS

STITCHING THROUGH 4 LAYERS

b d

Figure 10.15 (a–d) Edge binding. Schematic (a) and diagram (b) show stitch-in-the-ditch; seam type: BSf. Schematic (c) and diagram (d) show binding; seam type: BSb. Machine type for both: 301 lockstitch or 401 chainstitch.

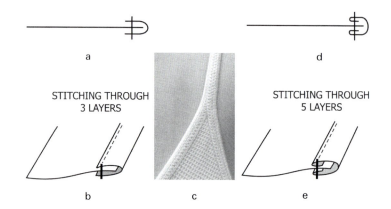

STITCHING THROUGH 3 LAYERS

STITCHING THROUGH 5 LAYERS

b c e

Figure 10.16 Edge binding variations. Schematic (a), diagram (b), and actual garment (c); seam type: BSa. Schematic (d) and diagram (e); seam type: BSc. Machine type for both: 301 lockstitch or 401 chainstitch.

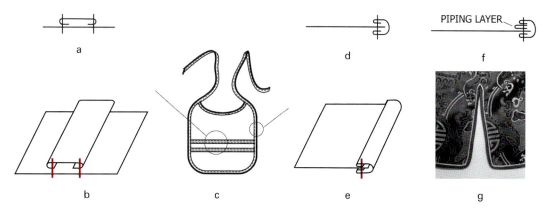

PIPING LAYER

a b c d e f g

Figure 10.17 Flat bias. Seam type: SSat; machine type: 301 2-needle lockstitch with folder (a and b) and bias binding. Seam type: BSc, bias binding for edges and ties. Machine type for both: 301 lockstitch (c and d).

10.17d and 10.17e). Figures 10.16f and 10.16g show a decorative and high-quality finish, which combines a contrast piping with a binding edge.

Elastic binding is a useful finish for many fabrics, especially knits, and is widely used in lingerie (see also Figure 10.16). Figure 10.18 shows binding used to finish the edge of a stretchy knit fabric. Because the binding edges are already finished, they need no turn-under, and the result is a very thin, stretchy finish. The zigzag lockstitch (see Figure 10.18d) has the advantage of stretch and is useful for setting elastic binding onto knits for intimate apparel.

Heat-Cut Edges

Some fibers with a low melting point, such as nylon, may have the edges cut with a hot knife, essentially melting the edge to prevent raveling. This is used in a limited way for garments, but is also used to make kites, flags, and fabric signage. Garment labels often have a heat-cut finish as well.

Figure 10.19 shows lapped seams that are used for joining. This is a cost-effective method for sewing irregular curves and shapes, and after being secured by the heat cutting, some pieces, such as the bottom fringes, need no additional finish at all. Figure

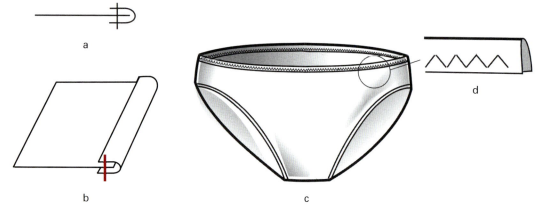

a b c d

Figure 10.18 Elastic binding. Seam type: BSa; machine type (d): 304 zigzag lockstitch.

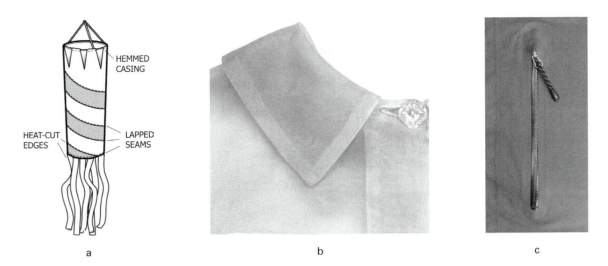

Figure 10.19 **Heat-cut edges with lapped seams.**

10.19b shows a little girls' vintage dress in a sheer nylon fabric. The enclosed seam allowance has been heat cut. That makes a neat finish for this sheer fabric, and the fact that it is heat cut and within an enclosed seam has kept it intact for decades. Figure 10.19c is another example of a precision laser-cut edge. It is fused after cutting and requires no stitching.

Facings

A facing is a piece of fabric, usually seamed on, to finish the raw edges of a garment. We studied one style of facing in Figure 10.7. Facings can be made from self-fabric or a different one, and facings can be constructed to sit on the outside of a garment or, more typically, on the inside. They are cut to conform to the shape to which they will be applied.

Figures 10.20, 10.21, and 10.22 show facings in three different configurations that dictate different finishes, and they illustrate the way in which the technical details affect the design details. Figure 10.20 shows views of both wrong side out and face side out. Figure 10.20a, inside view, shows bias facings for the armholes and a shaped facing for the neck. Bias facings are usually sewn through all layers to keep them in place. Because the armholes have topstitching, the designer chose to carry that detail around the neck as well (see Figure 10.20b).

Figure 10.21a, inside view, has shaped facings at both the neck and armholes. The armhole facings are wider and need to be tacked in place, so decorative topstitching is used to tie the armhole and neckline together visually. Figure 10.21c shows a rather different style of garment, a men's zip-front pullover with a collar. The facing is similar, though, and is widely used in many garment styles.

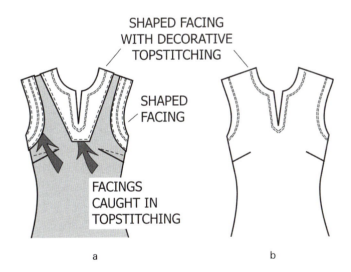

a   b

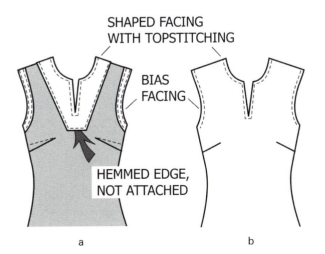

a   b

Figure 10.20 **Shaped and bias facings with topstitching.**

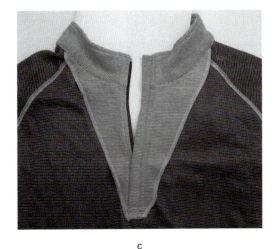

c

Figure 10.21 **Shaped bias facing with topstitching.**

Figure 10.22 presents the opportunity of offering a clean and un-topstitched edge finish with the use of understitching. Understitching helps the facing to roll to the inside and remain invisible. It shows on the inside (Figure 10.22a), but not on the outside (Figure 10.22b). This version has an all-in-one facing, which is used to reduce bulk or when separate facings would overlap. This style of facing is also more secure in the sense that the armhole facings cannot flop around and will not need tacking. Figure 10.22c shows this style employed on a boatneck-style sheath. The bottom edge of the facing could be finished in various ways appropriate to the style, as long as it won't show through to the right side.

Facings are also used at the waist of skirts and pants. Figure 10.23a has a bias facing at the waist, which works well with the **contour waist style** (a style with no waistband) curved to fit the contour of the body. It is stitched through at the bottom to keep it in place, and that stitch will show on the outside. A piece of woven tape will often be sewn into the seam to stabilize it and help prevent the waist from becoming stretched out. Figure 10.23b has a self-fabric facing, hemmed at the bottom edge. It is tacked invisibly to the darts and side seam allowances to keep it in place.

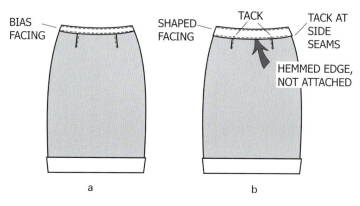

Figure 10.23 Waist facings.

Plackets

A **placket** is a finished opening, such as that found at the cuff of a sleeve or at the center front of a shirt. A side slit is also technically a finished opening, but is not considered a placket because it has no closure. Plackets are used for sleeves as well as at the front or back neckline instead of a zipper, and are planned in such a way as to accommodate buttons, snaps, or other fasteners.

Center Front Placket

Figure 10.24a shows a detail of a typical front placket seamed onto a woven shirt. Figure 10.24b shows a folded placket, a simple style that works well with a plaid or patterned fabric because it eliminates a matching point. Other plackets may be simply folded or pleated. The top placket (see Figure 10.24a, right side) is sometimes slightly wider than the underplacket to help ensure that the underplacket (see Figure 10.24a, right side) will be fully covered when the shirt is buttoned. The examples are men's shirts, buttoned left over right.

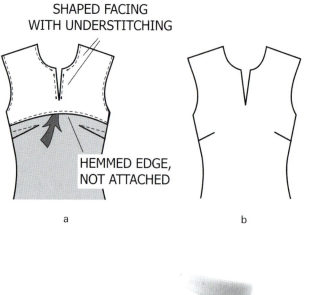

Figure 10.22 All-in-one facing.

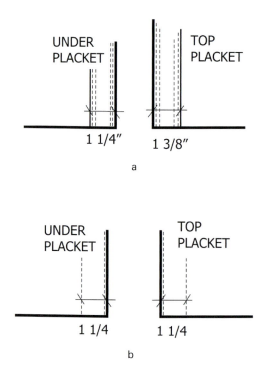

Figure 10.24 Front plackets for woven shirts.

Sleeve Placket

Sleeve cuffs often have plackets to allow them to open and accommodate the hand; plackets should be designed with enough length to allow sufficient expansion. Cuffs often have two buttons to allow the wearer to choose the position that is more comfortable. Many wearers prefer to be able to just slip a hand through the cuff without unbuttoning it.

Classic Tailored Sleeve Placket

The classic sleeve placket (see Figure 10.25a), or tailored placket, has two pleats, binding on the underplacket, and a separate outer placket. The two buttons on the cuff, which allow the wearer to make the cuff a better fit, also adjust the sleeve length slightly. Figure 10.25a shows the sleeve as if it were split open, allowing both top and underplacket to be shown. The placket for a classic tailored sleeve (see Figure 10.25) is long enough to allow the cuffs to be rolled back, and includes a placket button to prevent the placket from gapping open.

Continuous Lap Placket

The sleeve placket in Figure 10.26 is simpler and more suitable for somewhat heavier fabrics. This is called a *continuous lap placket*. Figure 10.26a shows the view from the outside, as it would appear on the finished garment. The girth of the cuff and the cuff height will appear on the sample measurements sheet and so are not noted on this sketch. The center detail (see Figure 10.26b) shows the construction method and how this type of placket is clipped very closely at the top (the sketch is shown opened out). For that reason, a fabric prone to ravel would not be a good choice for this style of placket.

Faced Placket

A faced placket is a simple style that may be used to save money when the pricing targets are tight, for example, on a child's garment. The facing fabric can be lighter weight than the shell fabric to help cut down on bulk. Because it is made with a slash and is clipped very closely at the top, it should be reinforced at the top, or it may fray. On the other hand, if the point is not cut deeply enough, a pucker will form.

Figure 10.27 has the placket edge reinforced with an edgestitch. That also helps to keep the facing to the inside. This style of placket has no overlap, so a cuff extension provides an underlay. Because this underlay is short, the placket edges will cross over when the cuff is buttoned.

In-Seam Placket

An in-seam placket is formed by finishing the raw edges of a seam at the placket opening. Because of a clipped area at the top of the opening, it requires a stitch-tack or bartack for reinforcement. This type of simplified placket may be seen on a denim jacket or other heavier fabrics (see Figure 10.28).

Other Types of Plackets

Other types of plackets are useful for lightweight fabrics. Figures 10.29a and 10.29b are other types of in-seam plackets. Figure 10.29a shows another example of a placket set into a seam, in this case, the underarm seam. This is not the ideal place for a button because it can catch or be uncomfortable when the arm is resting on a table. The advantage is price and simple sewing. Figure 10.29b shows another simplified style that works best on lighter weight fabrics. It is important to observe that even a simple cuff has many measurements that need to be specified in order to have a correct sample returned.

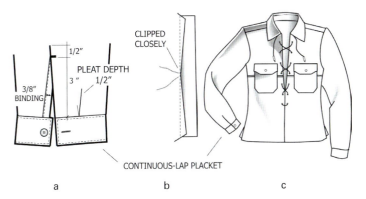

Figure 10.26 Continuous lap placket.

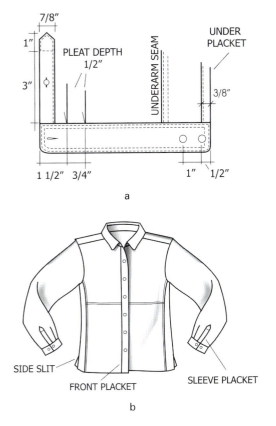

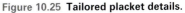

Figure 10.25 Tailored placket details.

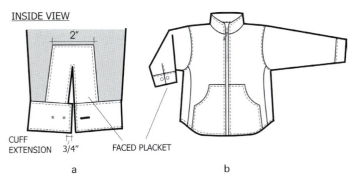

Figure 10.27 Faced placket.

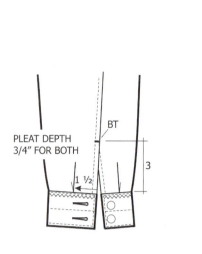

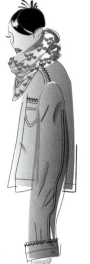

PLEAT DEPTH
3/4" FOR BOTH

BT

3

1 ½

Figure 10.28 **In-seam placket.**

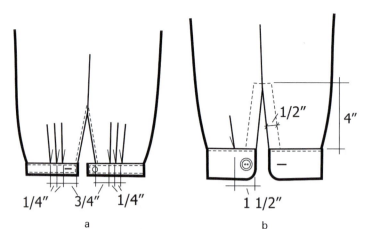

1/4"   3/4"   1/4"

1/2"   4"

1 1/2"

a   b

Figure 10.29 **Other in-seam plackets.**

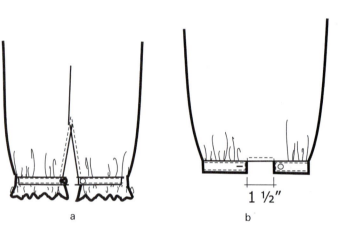

a   b

1 ½"

Figure 10.30 **Placket variations.**

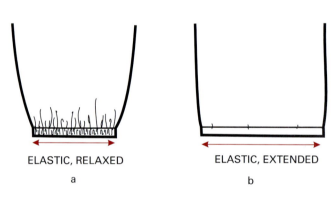

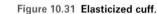

ELASTIC, RELAXED   ELASTIC, EXTENDED

a   b

Figure 10.31 **Elasticized cuff.**

Figure 10.30a shows the sleeve fullness gathered into a ruffle, again a technique for lighter weight fabrics. It is a kind of in-seam placket. The placket edges are clean finished inside. Figure 10.30b is one of the simplest styles of placket, is very economical, and is often seen on children's wear. It is also a good choice for bulky and loosely woven fabrics. When the placket is closed, a pleat is formed.

Cuffs

Among the types of **cuffs** are elasticized cuffs, premade knit cuffs, decorative cuffs, band cuffs, and outerwear cuffs.

Elasticized Cuffs

Some sleeve closures do not need a placket if they can allow for stretch. Figure 10.31a shows an elasticized cuff, such as may be seen on a child's blouse or on a lightweight windbreaker. The tech pack specifications for such a cuff must include the measurements "sleeve opening, relaxed" and "sleeve opening, extended." The relaxed measurement will accommodate the wrist and allow the sleeve to sit comfortably; the extended measurement tells the

patternmaker how wide to shape the pattern and determines how much blouse, or fullness, will be created. The actual sleeve opening measurements (for example, 8 inches for relaxed, 11 inches for extended) will appear on the spec page and not the drawing. This is an important point of measure that is not the same for all sizes, and will be graded larger or smaller, depending on the specific garment size.

Premade Knit Cuffs

Figure 10.32a is a sleeve with a premade knit cuff, often used for active sports apparel. The cuff is ordered through the knitting mill that produces it and comes in a cylinder shape with no seam, twice as long at the finished size. It is doubled over before attaching and is then joined to the sleeve at the bottom, round-on-round. Figure 10.32b is another style of knit cuff which is a heavier yarn and therefore is a single layer. It comes as flat goods and is later seamed at the underarm.

Gathers with Heading

Figure 10.32c has a cuff with an elastic casing set a specified distance from the edge. That section is called a **heading**. Gathers form above and below the elastic, creating a ruffle. This same

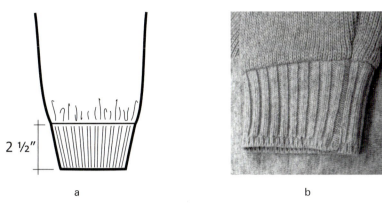

Figure 10.32 Premade knit cuff (a and b) and cuff with elastic encased in a heading (c).

sewing technique is used elsewhere as well, for example, at the waistband of a pant or skirt. In that case, the casing is positioned at the waist of the garment and the heading is at the very top of the garment.

Decorative Cuffs

The wrist is an important focal point, and a decorative cuff can have a flattering effect. Cuffs can be shaped, embroidered, or topstitched, or have ruffles, shirring, or tucks added. Some processes, such as certain embroideries, are sent out from the factory after cutting and returned after the embroidery is completed. This adds to the time to produce these goods, and the production department must include this time in its plan. Figures 10.33a and 10.33b show a sheer blouse with a long pleated cuff detail inserted into a narrow band. There are slight gathers above the band, so the precise amount of gathers is noted. This is another example of a component that is sent from the factory to the pleaters after the garment is cut and then returned for final assembly. Figure 10.33c shows a collar treatment done in the same way. For situations like this, extra time should be allowed to complete the production.

Band Cuffs

Not all cuffs require a placket. Figure 10.34a shows a band cuff that may be seen on a men's robe or smoking jacket. Because

the cuff is wide and decorative, there is no need for a closure. The details are a focal point, and all the proportions are noted, including the dimensions of the quilt pattern (Figure 10.34b). This is an example of how creating a drawing to scale helps the designer decide what proportions will be best. It also shows the precise dimensions of the diamond quilt and exactly how many repeats of the diamond appear to give the most pleasing effect. Figure 10.34c is another decorative cuff. This one has embroidery and beadwork around the cuff.

Outerwear Cuffs

Figure 10.35a shows a cuff that may be used for a specialized outerwear garment, for example, on a jacket designed for snow sports or mountaineering. This type of garment has many considerations concerning cuff closures, which dictate the details. This style of cuff would not have an open placket; instead, a gusset is often used to add fullness to the opening, especially if it is intended to fit over a glove. A secure cuff will provide a tight seal and will prevent drafts and heat loss. A typical closure will adjust by way of a hook-and-loop tab.

Figure 10.35c is an actual example from a travel raincoat. This garment has the lower edge of the cuff extend longer on one side to protect the top of the hand from rain. Cuffs are functional as well as aesthetical features for a design. Selecting an ideal cuff that enhances the whole quality of the garment is an important element for the overall design and function.

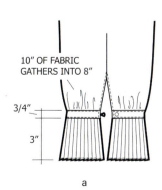

Figure 10.33 Decorative cuffs.

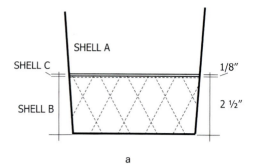

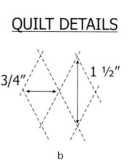

QUILT DETAILS

a

b

c

Figure 10.34 Band cuff with quilting.

CUFF DETAILS

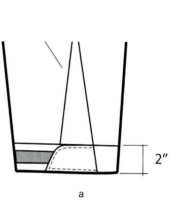

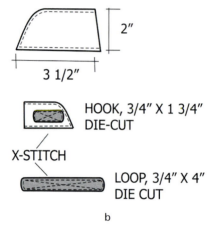

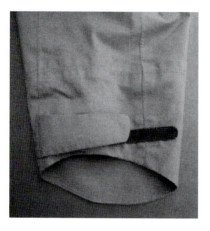

a

b

c

Figure 10.35 Technical design for outerwear cuff.

Summary

In this chapter, we surveyed various edge treatments including various hems, facings, plackets, and cuffs. To create an ideal apparel product with appropriate edge treatments, the class of stitches designated EF, using the various methods for finishing the edge, should be selected. More information related to EF class is found in Appendix A.

Study Questions

1. What are the most frequently used hem treatments for woven shirts? Why are these hems appropriate? Which hem treatments are frequently used for women's formal wear?

2. What are the most frequently used hem treatments for knits? Why are these hems appropriate? Among these, which are most frequently used for children's wear?

3. Design a sleeve placket for a women's shirt for a woven garment. Design one for a knit garment.

4. Design a sleeve placket for a children's shirt for a woven garment. Design one for a children's shirt for a knit garment.

5. Observe three different pairs of underpants. Identify the method for setting the waistbands. Identify the finishing method for the leg opening. Are there different finishes for men's underwear compared to women's? How many examples of different finishes can you find?

6. Open your closet and try to find the following three hem types: clean finished hem, bias or seam taped hem, and faced hem. Take a picture of each hem, print them, and bring them into class.

Check Your Understanding

1. List the various hem treatments and their uses. Give examples of each.

2. List the various facings and the advantages and disadvantages of each.

3. List the various plackets and the advantages and disadvantages for each.

4. Find two different plackets on garments in your wardrobe. Make a schematic sketch and a technical sketch for each.

5. Choose any sleeve placket example from this chapter and adapt it for use elsewhere, such as for a neck opening, leg opening, or waist opening. Adapt the proportions as needed and make a technical sketch. Be sure to include all the measurements.

6. In Figure 10.1e on page 184, the top edge of the seam tape is blind hemmed. What is the seam type along the bottom edge?

7. There are two schematics shown in Figure 10.9a on page 187. Which schematic applies to Figure 10.9b, the band hem on the sleeve? Which applies to the waistband in Figure 10.9c, and which applies to the band hem?

Construction-Related Design Details

Chapter Objectives

After studying this chapter, you will be able to:

- Explore various pocket options used in ready-to-wear apparel
- Understand various technical aspects of designing a pocket and its details
- Select appropriate details for various sewn products, ideal for their end use
- Demonstrate functions and aesthetics of stitches used for reinforcement and design details

---

Key Terms

cargo pocket	patch pocket	welt pocket
flap	reece welt	
on-seam pockets	topstitching	

This chapter provides information on various pockets and their details. This chapter also examines reinforcement stitches used both as design details and for functional purposes.

Pockets

Various pockets are used in apparel production. Each style gives a specific look to the garment on which it appears. Some are durable and functional; some are meant as a fashion statement and are the focal point of the garment. As we saw in Figure 5.41, the four main types of pockets are welt pockets (Figures 11.1a through 11.1e), patch pockets (Figure 11.1f), on-seam pockets (Figures 11.1g and 11.1h), and seam-to-seam pockets (Figure 11.1i). These definitions refer to the construction method used to apply them, and they can appear in many places and different configurations on a garment. Pockets can also be combinations of these types.

In addition, one garment can have various types of pockets. Figure 11.2 shows an example of an outerwear garment representing each type. Pocket 1 is seam-to-seam; pocket 2 is a patch pocket; pocket 3 is a double welt; and pocket 4 is an on-seam pocket. A standard of quality for a prototype is that pairs of pockets—for example, on a jacket—are identical and level with each other. In this section, we will examine which pocket is best suited for particular styles and price points.

A pocket is like a little sculpture. Besides being functional, it is an important decorative focus of the garment. All pockets need specifications for dimensions, construction, stitching, and placement. When careful thought is given to the finished appearance and dimensions as well as to the specifications needed to achieve that appearance, the result is a balance of look and price.

Technical Aspects of Designing a Patch Pocket

A simple **patch pocket** consists of one ply of fabric. It usually matches the main garment and has the opening edge finished first. It has the seam allowances turned back and is appliquéd onto the outside of a garment (sewn through all layers). This type of pocket can be durable and is widely used for workwear, children's wear, jeans, shirts, bathrobes, and tailored jackets. It has a casual feeling, but can also be used for dressy garments. Patch pockets are generally slightly longer than they are wide (see Figure 11.3).

As with most garment details, even a basic pocket has important information that needs to be provided on a tech pack in order to be constructed correctly on the actual garment. Figure 11.4a

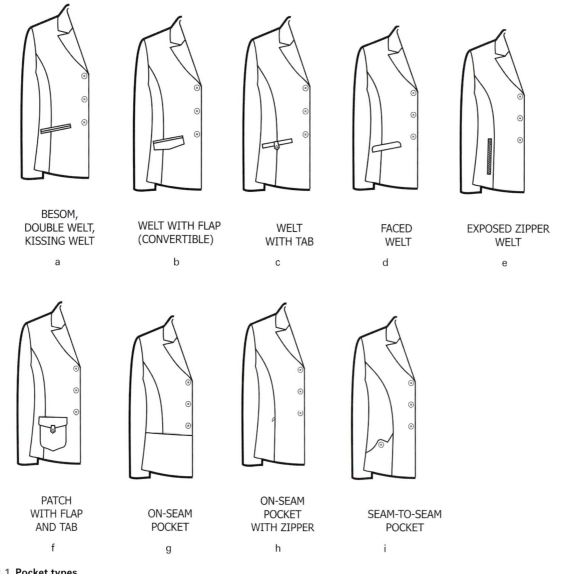

BESOM,
DOUBLE WELT,
KISSING WELT

a

WELT WITH FLAP
(CONVERTIBLE)

b

WELT
WITH TAB

c

FACED
WELT

d

EXPOSED ZIPPER
WELT

e

PATCH
WITH FLAP
AND TAB

f

ON-SEAM
POCKET

g

ON-SEAM
POCKET
WITH ZIPPER

h

SEAM-TO-SEAM
POCKET

i

Figure 11.1 Pocket types.

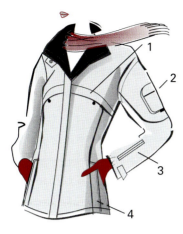

Figure 11.2 **Application of various pockets.**

shows the finished appearance of a simple patch pocket such as would be found on a men's woven shirt. Figure 11.4 shows the same pocket with the details called out: the stitching, dimensions, and construction details. When making the pattern, is the hem width a stitching detail or a construction detail? There is a certain amount of overlap in the definitions, but the prime directive is to make the details clear and understandable. It is good to apply the "three-second rule," meaning, does the viewer understand what is going on in the sketch within three seconds? Of course, that is just an example, and complicated drawings will take longer to understand. But because the goal is communication, it is a good idea to show your drawings to another person who can tell you whether all the information is clear.

The simplest shirt pocket would be set onto the garment with an edgestitch and a plain hem at the opening edge. As seen in Figure 11.4, alternatives would be to overedge the raw edges (in case of a loosely woven fabric that will be machine washed or a pocket that will be near a zipper; see Figure 11.4c) and have a clean-finished hem with the vertical edges enclosed (see Figure 11.4c). These important elements are all indicated in the detail sketch because they will affect the cost.

Corner Curves

The corner curve is another important pocket dimension to specify. Curve shapes have their own vocabulary. Figure 11.5a shows a pocket with a very slight curve, based on a military-style pocket. It would be suitable for either men's or women's wear. Figure 11.5b is somewhat softer in shape and would be suitable for the hand pocket of a women's tailored garment. The difference between the two can be defined precisely by adding the corner curve dimension, as demonstrated. Figure 11.5c has very rounded corners, such as would be used on a child's garment. A pocket with corners that rounded could also be used on a women's garment (most likely a juniors' style), but would probably not be very successful on a men's garment. It is interesting to note that the corner curve on Figure 11.5c is actually less than that on Figure 11.5b, even though the appearance is much rounder. It is another example of how overall proportions affect the final shape, and how drawing to scale can help predict the finished pocket design.

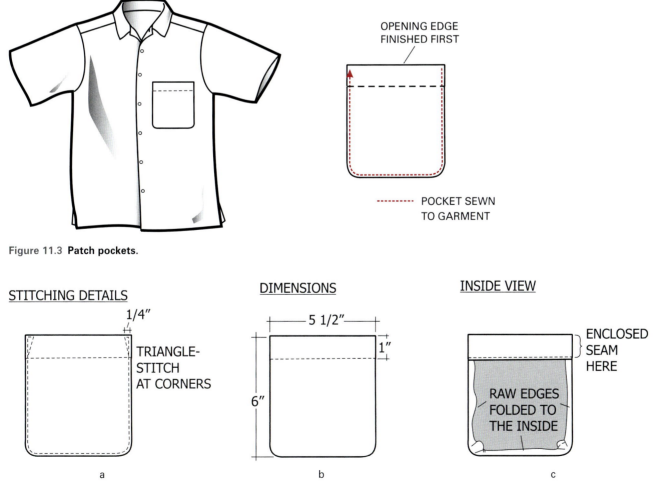

Figure 11.3 **Patch pockets.**

Figure 11.4 **Patch pocket construction.**

CORNER CURVE

5 1/2″

6″   1″

1/4″

a

CORNER CURVE

5 1/2″

6″

3/4″

b

CORNER CURVE

3 1/2″

3″

1/2″

c

Figure 11.5 Corner curved patch pockets.

POCKET DIMENSIONS

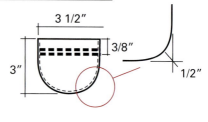

3 1/2″

3/8″

3″

1/2″

Figure 11.6 Patch pocket with details.

A patch pocket with decorative details is a good way to bring other elements together. Figure 11.6 shows the pocket from Figure 11.5c with a trim detail added at the opening edge (in this case the top) and set onto a little girls' shirt. The tech pack would have to make clear what the detail actually is (whether an applied trim or decorative topstitching), but it shows how pockets are used to unify the details of a garment. In this example, the pocket is actually wider than it is tall, a proportion popular for smaller children's garments.

Patch Pocket with Pleat

The addition of a pleat adds a visual focus and increases the storage capacity of a pocket. The pleat depth has its own detail sketch (see Figure 11.7a). This sketch also includes the detail information for reinforcement stitches, such as bartacks set at the stress points (Figure 11.7b). Figure 11.7c shows the finished placement. To save costs, it would be possible to construct a pocket that only appeared to have a pleat. That is not the case here, because Figure 11.7a includes the pleat depth; therefore, a functioning pleat is intended.

This sketch also includes important information on pocket placement. The position can easily look wrong, or the pocket can be ill-positioned for the intended use, so it is important to determine the placement that looks right and is also comfortable and functional to the wearer (see Figure 11.7c). This pocket is intended for a cell phone or other small object, so the position must be double checked for ease of use on an actual wearer (such as a fit model) when the prototype garment is available.

Patch Pocket with Flap

A **flap** is a separate construction, set near the opening edge, to help secure the contents of the pocket. Because it is so visible, the precise dimensions have considerable impact. Figure 11.8 has many shaping instructions, all of which will be included in the tech pack.

How much written information should be called out in the tech pack? A good rule of thumb is, if having the detail wrong would be a problem for the finished design (as it would be here), then it should be included. Because the pockets on this garment are really driving the style, it's better to leave nothing to chance. If the first proto is being developed by a factory experienced in this type of garment and detail, fewer specifications need to be included. If the factory is new or untested, the more details, the better. Avoid contradictory information, having the same information in two places or in an obscure place, or the same sort of information in different places on different tech packs. The more standardized the presentation of information, the fewer errors will result, and the better chance a style will make it into the final line. For most pocket elements, a detail sketch is the best way to communicate and "dimensions, construction, stitching, and placement" make up a good checklist.

The notation *BT* at each end of the flap stands for bartack, a common reinforcing detail. Topstitching details are also crucial elements to the finished appearance. (Some additional topstitching details appear on the construction page of the tech pack.) If there is a pair of pockets, the factory must make them symmetrical in size, shape, and placement.

POCKET WITH PLEAT

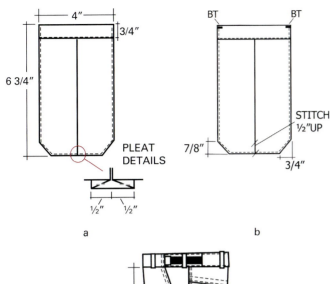

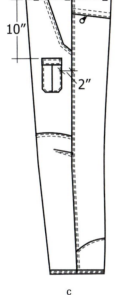

FLAP UP

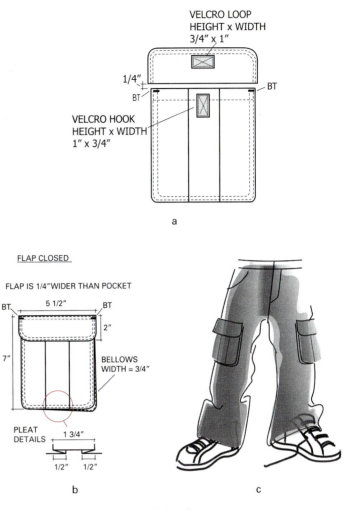

Figure 11.9 **Cargo pocket with Velcro flap.**

c

Figure 11.7 **Patch pocket with pleat detail.**

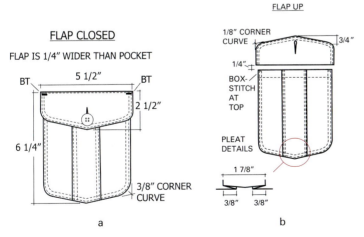

a   b

Figure 11.8 **Patch pocket with flap.**

Cargo Pocket with Velcro Flap

A **cargo pocket** (see Figure 11.9) has its roots in the functionality of military uniforms, and has a seamed panel or pleats to add capacity. The construction often includes a side piece to add dimension to the pocket, so more can be carried in it. Another name for this side piece is a *bellows*.

The hook-and-loop (also called by the brand name of the original producer, Velcro) is positioned horizontally on the flap and vertically on the pocket, which gives it more opportunity to "catch" when the pocket is full (see Figure 11.9). It is important to determine which side is more comfortable as the "hook" side, because it is more scratchy and can be uncomfortable if it is on the wrong side. Figure 11.9a shows the hook on the outside of the patch, where the hand will not touch it on the way in and out of the pocket.

Not all weights of fabric can be used for a pocket bellows, although there are ways to reduce the layers if the area is too thick. The top corners of a patch need to be secured so that the cargo pocket detail is stabilized, under the flap, and in a lighter-weight fabric. Figure 11.10a shows that the top edges are tacked through all layers. How many layers would that be? Figure 11.10b shows the layers involved at the bartack point, and why the fabric weight has to be able to accommodate the layers. There are thirteen layers where the bartacks are set. The garment itself is one layer, the pocket seam allowances are four layers, and the bellows has a total of eight. For that reason, a heavier canvas would not always be suitable for this type of bellows (or at best would require special machines and heavy needles), but another method could be adapted, such as one in which the bellows is not a separate piece, but pleated instead. In that case, the bottom corner would be folded and would have to be square rather than round. The factory is clipped if necessary, turned to the wrong

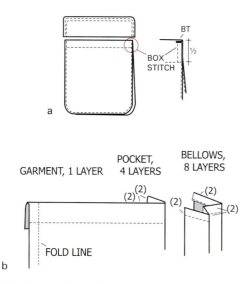

Figure 11.10 **Construction of a cargo pocket.**

side, and can make a mock-up sample if there is a question about the weight of the fabric.

Figure 11.11 shows variations of the cargo pocket, some with and some without a bellows. Figure 11.11a shows an asymmetrical flap and diagonal cargo pleat. Figure 11.11b shows a center pleat reinforced with bartacks, and dart corners with grommet detail. It also has the flap set onto a strip of reinforcement (sewn prior to pocket placement to the inside of the garment). Figure 11.11c shows a flap closed with a snap. It could be used on a more tailored garment because the overall profile is flatter and the topstitching style is more decorative. A pocket can also be made with a partial bellows that has the pocket set into seams on two sides and has a bellows on the free side (see Figure 11.11d). A great deal of creativity goes into choosing the right construction method for all the details.

Patch Pocket with Shaped Facing

A *facing* is a piece of fabric used to finish a raw edge; in this case, the opening edge of the pocket. It adds strength, but also introduces a lot of shaping possibilities. After the facing is sewn to the right side, it is clipped if necessary, turned to the wrong side, and topstitched to create an enclosed seam. A shaped facing can add a lot of style emphasis to a detail such as a pocket. Figure 11.12 shows how the stitch-through at the bottom of the facing (2 inches down from the top edge) becomes part of the pocket design.

Shaped Patch Pocket

The use of a facing enables the patch pocket to take on nearly any shape (see Figure 11.13). Several steps are involved in this particular design, as well as considerable labor. If the appeal of the finished garment is a good match to the intended retail price, it is a good choice. If not, the details will have to be reworked. A factory with skilled operators may suggest alternative ways of construction, such as a simple appliqué. In this method, after the top point is faced, the rest of the shape could be pressed over a template and then sewn directly to the garment, as one layer rather than two. Each factory is set up differently, and will suggest the best construction methods for their factory. If neither the design nor the quality is affected, it's often best to follow their lead.

Technical Aspects of Designing Welt Pockets

A patch pocket sits on the outside of the garment, but a **welt pocket** (other names are *bound* or *slashed pocket*) is a kind of finished hole or opening into the interior. Welt pockets have many variations and are often considered more difficult to construct than patch pockets. Some can be made less expensively with an automatic machine; some are examples of the finest tailoring. Each is appropriate for particular garments.

The most common way to make a welt is with a machine such as a Reece machine. This is often called a **reece welt** (whether it is actually made with a Reece brand machine or not). The Reece machines have standard widths and features, so if the design calls for something else, the welts will need to be made a different way, often at a much greater cost. For example, if the machine's narrowest setting is $3/8$ inch, and the desired finished welt is narrower than that, it would have to be made by hand rather than by the Reece machine. In that case, the decision would need to be made whether this special narrow welt was important enough to the design to justify the additional cost.

A Reece machine has multiple steps and sews at high speed. After the welt piece is placed onto the face side of the garment piece (see Figure 11.14d, a back yoke panel), the first step is to sew two parallel stitches with an automatic stitch-tack on each end. The distance apart is the width of the finished welt (see Figure 11.14a). In the second step, a knife cuts the center and deep into the corners through all layers (see Figure 11.14b).

Fabrics that are too loosely woven to be clipped closely into the corners would not be suitable for this style of welt. To complete, the welt is turned to the inside; the fabric is folded to create the

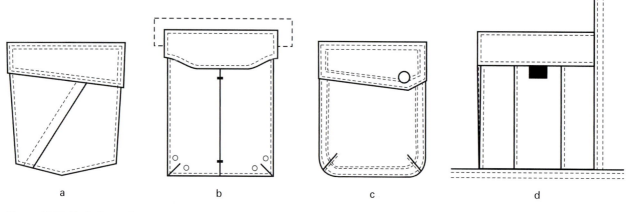

Figure 11.11 **Variations of cargo pockets.**

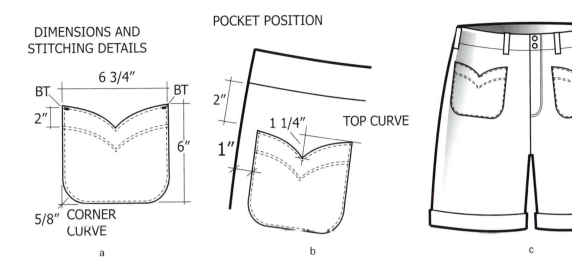

DIMENSIONS AND
STITCHING DETAILS

6 3/4"

BT   BT

2"

POCKET POSITION

2"

1 1/4"

TOP CURVE

1"

5/8" CORNER
CURVE

6"

a   b   c

Figure 11.12 **Patch pocket with shaped facing.**

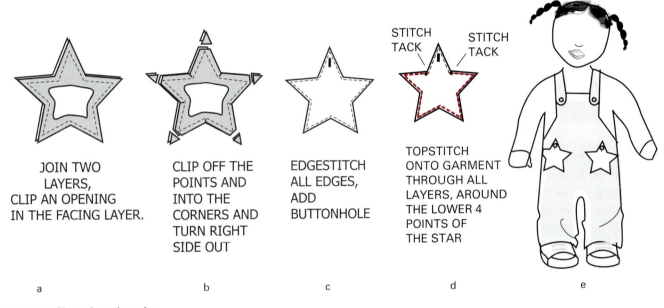

JOIN TWO
LAYERS,
CLIP AN OPENING
IN THE FACING LAYER.

CLIP OFF THE
POINTS AND
INTO THE
CORNERS AND
TURN RIGHT
SIDE OUT

EDGESTITCH
ALL EDGES,
ADD
BUTTONHOLE

STITCH
TACK

STITCH
TACK

TOPSTITCH
ONTO GARMENT
THROUGH ALL
LAYERS, AROUND
THE LOWER 4
POINTS OF
THE STAR

a   b   c   d   e

Figure 11.13 **Shaped patch pocket.**

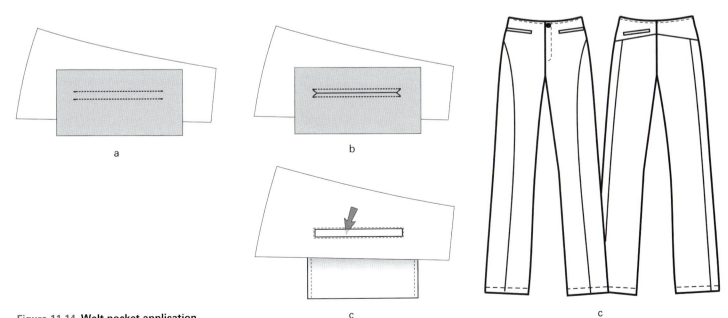

a   b   c

c   c

Figure 11.14 **Welt pocket application.**

welt; the triangle ends are carefully stitched to prevent raveling; the edge stitch around the perimeter is added; and the pocket bags are attached and finished. Figure 11.14c shows the finished welt appearance, and also shows the pocket bag attached.

The handling of this operation is simplified by the fact that the welt is set completely inside the back yoke, a relatively small piece. Figure 11.14d also shows welts on the front view. Because the front panels are a lot longer than the back yoke, and because the right and left must match, it would entail more handling to make.

Figure 11.15 shows the versatility of welt pockets for use in various product types. Figure 11.15a shows a pant pocket with a double welt (also known as *double-besom* or *kissing welt*). It is also a reece-style welt made on an automatic machine. This example includes a button and buttonhole detail below the welt. This serves two purposes: one to secure the contents of the pocket, and the other to support the pocket and prevent it from stretching and gapping open over time. Note that it also has a bartack on either end for reinforcement. A pocket such as this one is often the place where customers will keep their wallets, so it is important to keep the function in mind when designing the size of the welt and the depth of the pocket bags inside. Figure 11.15b shows a skirt on which the welt pockets are pressed flat, rather than edge stitched. The triangle ends are stitched inside, rather than bartacked through all layers. These methods are more in keeping with a tailored type of garment, and require more labor.

The fact that the welts for this style are set over seams means that the entire front must be assembled first, and pressed and topstitched, before the welts are set. That makes the handling a little more difficult because the entire front has to be moved around the factory floor before it is placed on the Reece machine. It is imperative that the right and left sides match in height and angle, and because of that, the operator must watch closely to make sure that nothing is misaligned. The pressing and extra handling must be considered against the projected cost of the skirt.

Functional pockets and details are an important quality indicator. Pockets in a position such as this (small and placed high) may be considered nonfunctional, and they are sometimes sewn closed, with no pocket bags attached. That treatment is usually found in lower-priced garments.

Welt with Flap

Welts are often used in combination with flaps, and Figure 11.16 shows some of the variations used on different products. Figure 11.16a has the flap edge stitched, and the welt is pressed but not stitched. This is a type that may be found on a men's tailored suit. Figure 11.16b is an upward facing welt, shaped with a seam at the upper edge of the welt and with the pocket opening edge at the top; it could be used as a hand pocket or breast pocket. Note that the join seam is on the bottom edge, and that the sides are stitched through in a subsequent operation. Figure 11.16c shows a style that may be seen on a trench coat, and Figure 11.16d shows a convertible welt that could be worn with the flap either out or tucked inside and not seen. It requires a lighter-weight fabric; otherwise, when the flap is tucked in, it will create a bulge.

Welt Pocket with Zipper

A welt pocket with a zipper can have the zipper either exposed or covered. Figure 11.17 shows an exposed zipper and has no actual "welt" piece. It is included because it is also set with a reece-type machine. Figure 11.17 shows two pockets combined: a patch pocket with a flap, and an exposed zipper pocket. In terms of the order of construction, note that the exposed zipper detail is put into place first and then the patch pocket and the flap are carefully lined up and set on afterward. The pocket bag of the zipper pocket goes to the interior of the garment and is visible on the inside. Even though the zipper is not technically "exposed" (because it's covered by the flap) in the final garment, it is still "exposed zipper construction." This type of pocket may be seen on a special-use garment such as a travel shirt where the zipper pocket is useful to secure valuables, and the patch pocket serves as ordinary storage.

Another style of welt pocket with zipper is used for active outerwear such as skiing or snowboarding apparel, and has the zipper covered for protection from moisture. Because this type of garment is used in cold weather, and a person would be wearing gloves during use, it needs a larger zipper pull for its easy operation. Because it is not always immediately obvious, this style needs to have the *opening edge* called out in the tech pack. Having the opening edge toward the side seam works for hand pockets in most situations. Having the opening edge toward center front would be preferable for certain other types of outerwear, such as for snowboarding, for which water repellency is an issue, because that will prevent water from dripping into the pocket.

In the welt examples of the skirt in Figure 11.15b, the opening edge is clearly the top. Figure 11.17 (double welt or exposed zipper) shows that the opening does not need to be called out because it is always in the center. But for the welt in Figure 11.18, the opening edge could be toward center front or toward the side seam and, therefore, needs to be specified. If the zipper pull is included in the sketch, it can serve as the indicator of the opening edge. Figures 11.18a and 11.18b show top opening edge, and Figures 11.18c and 11.18d show bottom opening edge.

The second detail that needs specifying is the direction in which the zipper closes, whether up or down. The sketch in Figure 11.18e matches Figure 11.18c, but we have three other possible choices (see Figures 11.18a, 11.18b, and 11.18d).

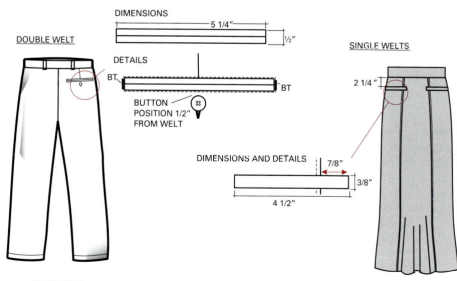

Figure 11.15 Welt pocket details: double welt (a) and single welt (b).

In Figure 11.18a, the pull closes down, but sits at an awkward angle because of the size of the pull. In Figure 11.18b the pull folds down and hides, so it is less suitable for an outerwear style because ski gloves make it hard to catch the pull. This design may be better for another style, such as running wear, in which the wearer is less likely to be wearing gloves. Figure 11.18d closes up and the pull hangs freely, but may be considered too obtrusive. These are all issues that the designer needs to consider and specify.

Curved Welts

The classic Western shirt has a distinctive style of narrow curved welts that are a quality indicator for this type of garment (see Figure 11.19). Another name for this style of pocket is a *smile pocket*. The first step in construction for the welt shown in Figure 11.19 is the welt itself, which is then finished at both ends with a stitched triangle appliqué. Another end finish seen on vintage shirts is a hand-embroidered triangle. Western-style shirts such as this are part of a unique American tradition with its own vernacular, such as contrast piping, bias-cut yokes, pearl snaps, ornate cuffs, embroidery, braiding, border prints, and contrast details.

Figure 11.20 shows that this shape of welt is curved at the top, and would need to be sewn with a facing. It is sewn as an upward facing welt. The curve is set at the bottom; the side edges are sewn down last. This style of curved welt requires a great deal of skill, which only a specialized factory could manage. But for the factory that can do it well, it gives the finished garment a distinctive high-quality detail.

Technical Aspects of Designing On-Seam Pockets

On-seam pockets are set into a seam and used in cases where the seamline is intended to be the focus, rather than the pocket itself. Figure 11.21a shows an on-seam style that also features double welts. Figure 11.21b shows a well-known example of an on-seam pocket, one that can be found on a pair of men's or women's trousers.

Figure 11.22 shows another example of an on-seam pocket. A zipper has been added because it is an active outerwear piece. A zipper takes up room at each end of

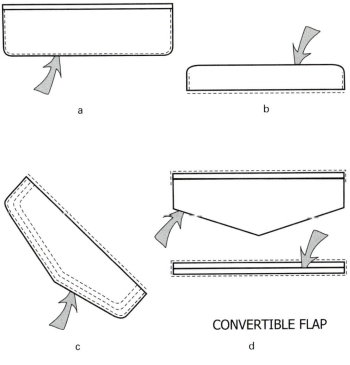

Figure 11.16 **Various shapes of flaps.**

CONVERTIBLE FLAP

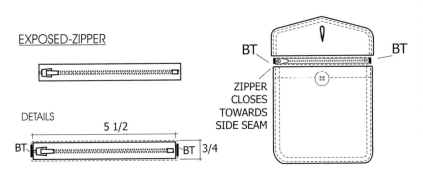

EXPOSED-ZIPPER

DETAILS

5 1/2

BT   BT   3/4

BT   BT

ZIPPER
CLOSES
TOWARDS
SIDE SEAM

Figure 11.17 **Welt with exposed zipper.**

ARROW INDICATES OPENING EDGE

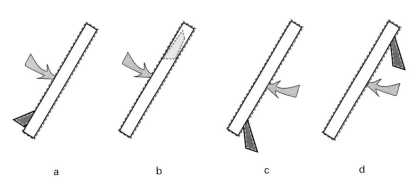

a   b   c   d

Figure 11.18 **Welt with zipper and zipper pull.**

e

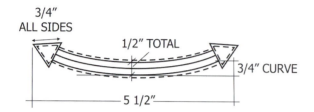

3/4"
ALL SIDES

1/2" TOTAL

3/4" CURVE

5 1/2"

Figure 11.19 Curved welt application.

CURVED WELT

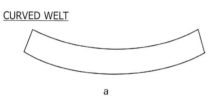

a

DETAILS

1 1/4"

7/8

5 1/2

b

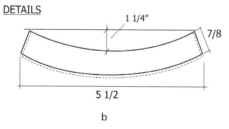

Figure 11.20 Curved welt variation.

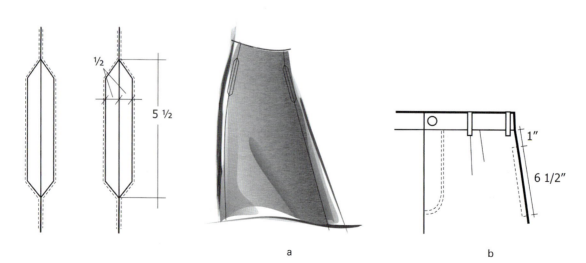

1/2

5 1/2

1"

6 1/2"

a

b

Figure 11.21 On-seam pockets.

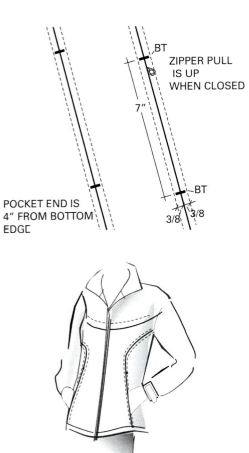

BT
ZIPPER PULL
IS UP
WHEN CLOSED

7″

POCKET END IS
4″ FROM BOTTOM
EDGE

BT

3/8   3/8

Figure 11.22 On-seam pocket details.

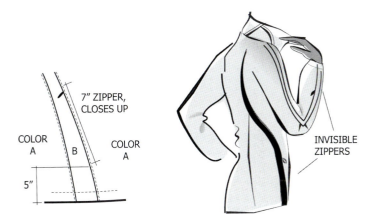

1 3/4″

6 ½″

1/8″
PIPING
AT EDGE

WELT POSITION
BOTTOM EDGE
OF WELT
IS 9″ ABOVE
BOTTOM OF
GARMENT

1″
BOX TACK

Figure 11.23 On-seam pocket with flap.

7″ ZIPPER,
CLOSES UP

COLOR
A   B   COLOR
A

5″

INVISIBLE
ZIPPERS

Figure 11.24 On-seam pocket variation.

the pocket, and the opening also needs to accommodate gloves, so extra length is added. It also includes information that the zipper closes in the up position. The advantage to having the pocket bag close in the up position is that it is easier to open. A possible disadvantage would be if the pulls were too visually dominant in that position, such as if the pulls were too near the bustline. For this jacket, the pull is matching and smaller, so the decision was made to have the pockets close at the top of the opening.

The pocket position is noted also; hand pockets should not be too close to the bottom edge, or there won't be enough depth to the pocket bag to prevent items from falling out (see Figure 11.22). Having the zipper close up also helps keep the contents more secure. Figure 11.23 shows an on-seam pocket with a flap. Setting the pocket into the seam adds a great deal of support for the pocket, and prevents it from stretching and sagging. This example has decorative piping added to the outside edge of the welt.

Invisible zippers were originally used for dress and pant closures, but are increasingly used for pockets as well. Figure 11.24 has two such pockets—one in the sleeve, and one for each of the hand pockets. This shows how this type of zipper is useful when the contrast panel (color B) is the dominant design feature, and the pocket blends in discretely.

Technical Aspects of Designing Seam-to-Seam Pockets

The seam-to-seam style of pocket begins in one seam and ends in another, which makes it strong and durable. A common example can be found on a pair of jeans (see Figure 11.25a). This also shows how a bartack can be positioned for additional strength through all seam allowances.

This style of pocket can come in numerous shapes because of the facing. In the finished pocket, the facing piece is behind the opening edge, and generally the pocket bags are separate and sewn to the inside edge of the facing. Figure 11.25b shows a classic jean-style pocket. The edge is sometimes faced with bias binding and sometimes faced with the pocket bag itself. The image in Figure 11.25b is often called an L-pocket because of its shape. Figure 11.25c shows the pocket bag stitched through the shell. Figure 11.25d, also known as a "quarter-top" pocket, is used for both men's and women's trousers.

Figure 11.26 shows this style of pocket with the pocket bags as a separate fabric, called pocketing. Pocketing is chosen for strength, light weight, and compatibility of care with the garment fabric. Pockets are constructed so that the pocketing fabric will not show. Note that the terms *palm side* and *knuckle side* are specified. The pocket bag edges are caught into the seams as well for support.

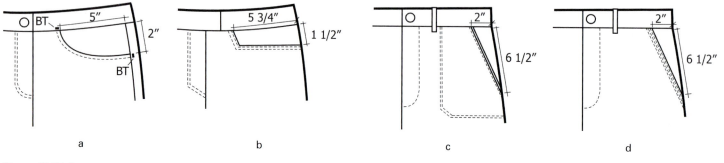

a   b   c   d

Figure 11.25 **Seam-to-seam pockets.**

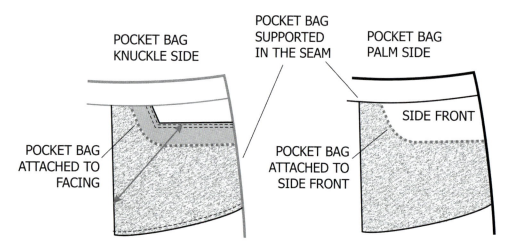

POCKET BAG
KNUCKLE SIDE

POCKET BAG
SUPPORTED
IN THE SEAM

POCKET BAG
PALM SIDE

SIDE FRONT

POCKET BAG
ATTACHED TO
FACING

POCKET BAG
ATTACHED TO
SIDE FRONT

Figure 11.26 **X-ray view of seam-to-seam pocket.**

Reinforcement

Stitch detail is used as a reinforcement in specific areas of apparel products where needed to withstand stress. Reinforcing stitches can also serve as decoration.

Stitch Reinforcement

Many areas of quality garment construction require reinforcement to add strength to seams. At opposite ends of the spectrum, traditional higher-end garments have more invisible reinforcements, and heavy workwear garments have multiple visible bartacks and even metal rivets. Understanding reinforcements helps designers to make choices appropriate to the type of fabric and garment, and add value and durability.

Back Tack

The beginning and end of a quality lockstitch seam should have a *back tack*, which is a short double stitching to secure the ends (see Figure 11.27a). Many industrial machines have a device that allows the operator to back tack automatically. This specification is an industry standard and need not be individually specified for each seam. Some machine types, such as coverstitch, do not have a method for back tacking. They should have an area of overlap for security (see Figure 11.27b).

Bartacks

The most common form of reinforcement for durable fabrics is the bartack. A bartack machine is a type of 304 zigzag lockstitch

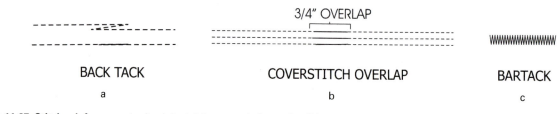

3/4" OVERLAP

BACK TACK   COVERSTITCH OVERLAP   BARTACK

a   b   c

Figure 11.27 **Stitch reinforcements: back tack (a), coverstitch overlap (b), and bartack (c).**

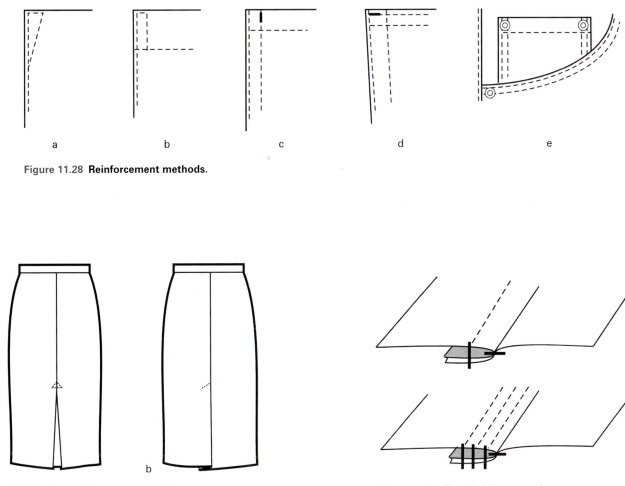

a   b   c   d   e

Figure 11.28 **Reinforcement methods**.

a   b

Figure 11.29 **Stitch reinforcement for kick pleats.**

Figure 11.30 **Topstitching example.**

and shares the same machine number. The stitches for a bartack are very close together (see Figure 11.27c). It is very strong, and in fact, it can be stronger than the fabric, a situation that would cause damage. For example, a bartack on leather would quickly create a hole, and a bartack on very lightweight fabric could damage the fibers. The weight of the fabric will dictate the best style of reinforcement.

Stitch Tacks

A method for securing lighter fabrics that need reinforcement but for which a bartack would not be suitable is called a *stitch tack*. Stitch tacks can have a triangle shape (see Figure 11.28a), or box reinforcement (see Figure 11.28b), or just be multiple stitching "in place," similar to a back tack.

The images in Figures 11.28a and 11.28b would work well on lighter-weight shirting fabrics to keep the top edge of the pocket securely stitched, and they also have a decorative effect. Figures 11.28c and 11.28d show two methods of using bartacks on patch pockets on heavier-weight shirting fabrics, or on bottom weights. Figure 11.28d would be considered the stronger of the two because the horizontal placement is capable of supporting more downward pressure. Figure 11.28e shows how metal rivets are

used to secure pockets. They are an example of the way in which reinforcements can also be decorative; rivets come in an array of metals and finishes, and are often chosen to match metal buttons, zippers, and other trims. A row of rivets is sometimes used in a purely decorative way.

Another type of stitch reinforcement is used to support the top of a pleat detail (see Figure 11.10). Figure 11.29 shows two examples of reinforcement at the top of a kick pleat, used to provide ease at the bottom of a narrow skirt. The reinforcement stitching keeps the pleat from sagging over time.

Topstitching

Topstitching is a line of stitching on the visible side of the garment, parallel to a seam. It is generally stitched through all layers, adding seam strength as well as a decorative effect. On inexpensive garments, topstitching a seam also acts as a substitute for pressing because it also flattens the seam. All lapped seams (by definition) have visible topstitching on the exterior side of garments. Superimposed seams often get topstitching as a second step. Various stitches are used to give design detail on the exterior side of a garment. Thread color contrasting to the fabric color gives a conspicuous design detail, and a heavier weight of thread

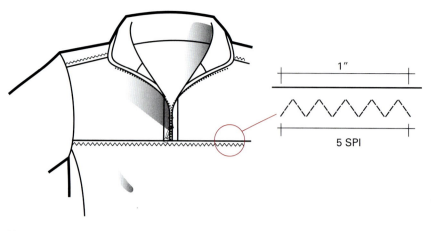

Figure 11.31 **Zigzag topstitching.**

is often used. Stitch width and length can be varied to create a unique look.

Because topstitching is visible, it is an important quality element and must be applied parallel to the seam and without visible thread breaks and joins. The $^1/_4$-inch topstitching (see Figure 11.30a) is a common type. The triple-needle (see Figure 11.30b) is characteristic of heavier fabrics and workwear. If multiple topstitching is required, a multineedle machine works best because the three rows will always appear perfectly parallel, an effect difficult to match while trying to sew three parallel rows individually. Designers should check to make sure the factory has the appropriate multineedle machinery, and that it will not be substituting a method that will not produce the desired quality of stitching. The factory can always be requested to send a mock-up to confirm what type of machinery is available.

A zigzag lockstitch can also be used as topstitching. It provides elasticity and is also used as a design detail. There are different variations of the zigzag lockstitch. One variation is a multistitch zigzag, ISO-321. These machines provide even greater elasticity and, in addition, can be used for a decorative topstitching. Figure 11.31 shows a three-step zigzag, in which the machine travels three steps before changing direction. Makers of zigzag machines consider a stitch as one V; that is, one over and one back. Figure 11.31b illustrates stitches per inch for the multistitch zigzag. For a straight-stitch machine, it would be considered 15 stitches, but it is considered 5 for this type of stitch.

Summary

Various pockets and their design details can be chosen for various apparel products and for their own end uses. Reinforcement stitches are used for creating design details as well as for serving the reinforcement function.

Study Questions

1. What are the necessary considerations for creating tech packs for welt pockets? What callouts are used to specify in tech pack?

2. What are the four pocket specification details?

3. Find a man's patch pocket on an inexpensive shirt and an expensive shirt. Do they differ? Find four different men's patch pockets and specify them all.

4. What are the necessary considerations when designing on-seam pockets? What callouts are used to specify in-seam pockets in the tech pack?

5. Choose a pair of men's size medium (size 32 or 34) jeans and a pair of women's size medium (size 8) jeans. Create a set of cargo pockets for the men's and women's garments drawn to scale. Use paper to create a pocket in actual size. Create a spec and detailed sketches for the pockets, including dimensions, construction, stitching, and placement. Compare the two created pockets and specify any gender-based differences.

6. What is a bartack? Why is it frequently used for sewn apparel products?

7. Select a pair of jeans and list the various reinforcements as well as topstitch details used in the pant. Specify the area (location) on the garment with stitch numbers.

8. Design a woman's casual shirt with two sets of pockets. Create technical specs for the shirt and pockets.

9. Design a man's woven shirt with two sets of pockets. Create a spec sheet for the shirt and pockets.

10. Design four pairs of pants for men and women. Note that each should use one of the following pocket categories: welt, patch, on-seam, and seam-to-seam.

11. Draw a patch pocket to scale. Cut it out of fabric and pin it to a pant or jacket. Is it a good size for a cell phone or an iPod? Does it need any modifications?

12. Visit the *Technical Sourcebook for Apparel Designers* STUDIO. Refer to Appendix C: Pockets With Tabs and Flaps. Select three pockets and complete the specifications for each, including dimensions and details.

Check Your Understanding

1. List the four basic categories of pockets available for apparel.

2. List at least two important technical aspects of designing patch pockets.

3. List at least two important technical aspects of designing in-seam pockets.

4. Look at Figures 11.1a through 11.1e. Which welt would be most unusual for a tailored jacket, and why?

12

Shape and Support

Chapter Objectives

After studying this chapter, you will be able to:

- Utilize various underlying fabrics to achieve shape and support
- Demonstrate other supportive materials used for each design detail and end use of garments

---

Key Terms

braid	hand sample	soutache
braid binding	interfacing	swing tack
bra strap keeper	interlining	twill tape
collar stays	lining	underlining
down	plumules	wet process
hair canvas	shelf bra	wicking

A garment is separated into two types of components: fabric and findings. *Findings* are all the elements on a garment that are not fabric. Findings include internal as well as external elements. *Trims* is a similar term, but generally means the visible elements, such as buttons, zipper pulls, cords, and appliqués.

This chapter studies findings and trims as related to the shape and support of apparel products. *Underlying fabrics* that can change the appearance, function, and quality of the garment, as well as insulations for outerwear and quilting, are also examined. Underlying fabric requires extra labor and materials, and thus adds extra costs. Although it would be possible to save money by avoiding the most expensive of the underlying fabrics, it would not be advisable to forego these fabrics entirely because they add so much to the appearance as well as longevity of the garment.

Underlying Fabrics

The most important aspect when choosing underlying fabrics is to determine their compatibility with the shell fabric in terms of weight, care, and shrinkage related to dimensional stability. There are four different categories for underlying fabrics:

- Interfacing
- Underlining
- Lining
- Interlining

Interfacing

Interfacing refers to supportive fabric placed between the layers of shell and facing that adds weight and body to a garment. It is used on edge parts such as collars, cuffs, flaps, and waistbands, and provides shape and support. It is useful to stabilize detail areas that may stretch and greatly assists in the sewing process. It is designed to be invisible, and lies between the shell and the inner layer, such as inside a hem, facing, or lining.

Interfacings can be lightweight or heavy, crisp or supple, depending on the application and the desired look. Interfacings should be a similar weight to the shell fabric or lighter. If the interfacing is too stiff, it will look incorrect on the finished garment.

Where Interfacing Is Used

Figure 12.1 shows by shading where interfacing would commonly be added for different garment types. Figure 12.1a shows areas of interfacing for a tailored jacket, including the welts, flaps, and hems, as well as the collar and chest piece. Tailored garments have a number of special types of interfacing and special techniques for applying them. More details are given in the section "Tailored Garments" later in this chapter.

Figure 12.1b shows the usual interfacing areas for a hat constructed of a woven fabric. Because a hat is meant to be a more rigid object than a shirt, it has heavier interfacing. If the hat itself is made of a heavier fabric, such as canvas, it may not need interfacing in all areas.

Figure 12.1c has interfacing in the waistband and fly facing. The main function for the fly area is to prevent stretching, and for the waistband, to prevent rolling. Standard-width belt loops (see Figure 12.1c) don't require it, but for wider belt loops on a lightweight fabric, interfacing may be advisable. The bottom leg opening has a twice-turned, clean-finished hem and no interfacing because no stiffness is needed there.

Figure 12.1d shows the interfacing in the edge pieces. Interfacing is especially important for lighter-weight fabrics. Certain areas are traditionally meant to have a crisp appearance, such as men's shirt collars; however, a women's blouse or dress would generally have a softer appearance, and thus a lighter interfacing. The interfacing would usually be set to the outer layer; for example for a shirt collar (see Figure 12.1d), the topcollar would have interfacing, but not the undercollar. That helps to prevent the seam allowances from showing through the topcollar.

If requested, the factory will send a **hand sample**, a swatch with the interfacing applied to the shell fabric, for approval. The interfacing supplier will also provide testing information for a given quality of interfacing. This is an important step to confirm that the desired effect will be achieved and determine whether the interfacing will stay in place through many washings or dry cleanings.

Types of Interfacing

The main types of interfacing structures are woven, knit, and nonwoven. Each of them has a fusible and nonfusible (sewn-in) version. The fusing process is a method of fixing the interfacing

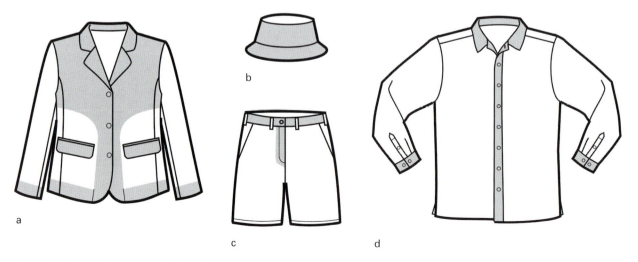

Figure 12.1 **Areas of garments for interfacing.**

to the wrong side of the shell fabric by means of a special adhesive set with heat and pressure.

Sewn-In

Sewn-in *woven interfacings* are often used in the highest-quality garments because they are strong yet flexible and stable. They require more skill to cut and sew because the grain must match that of the shell fabric, and the interfacing must be carefully sewn all around the edges (also called *perimeter stitching*). In the case of tailored garments they may even be hand stitched into place.

Sewn-in *knit interfacings* add lightweight support and stability to knit fabrics and are less expensive than woven interlinings. They also help the fashion fabric retain greater stretch than would a fusible style. Sewn-in *nonwovens* are used where a very stiff hand is required or considerable stabilizing is needed, such as on a hat brim. Some garments use self-fabric interfacings, made from the same fabric as the shell. This may be done if the cost will allow and if compatibility problems are expected. For example, if the finished garment is to be **wet processed**—that is, a special finishing process such as softening, pre-shrinking, or special dyes or rinses—self-fabric interfacings will ensure that all plies will have the same dimensional stability characteristics.

Fusible

Fusible *woven interfacings* are often used in high-quality applications and are the most stable of the three interfacing structures. The grain of the interfacing must be matched to that of the woven shell before fusing, or there may be twisting. They would not normally be used for knits except in certain areas that need greater stability, such as buttonhole areas. Fusing machines are used in apparel manufacturing facilities to speed the production process and to provide consistency.

Fusible *knit interfacings* are useful for knit applications because they often have a better affinity for the shell fabric and add soft body while mimicking the drape of the shell fabric. Fusible knit interfacings have stretchability to make them compatible with the stretchable shell fabric and knits. They are often less expensive than woven interfacings, but more expensive than nonwovens.

Fusible *nonwoven interfacings* (also called *fiber web*) are the most common type. These are formed by fibers, usually polyester, that are fused together into a sheet of fabric. (In other methods, the fibers are entangled, glued, or fused by some combination of these methods.) Because the nonwoven material has no grain, it can often be economically laid out. Some interfacing styles are less stable in one direction or other, which is another reason for having the factory provide a hand sample. Nonwoven fusible interfacings do not have the durability of other types of interfacing, and can break down over multiple washings.

The fusing qualities of each style must be pretested by the factory to ensure that the proper heat and pressure are used to create a complete bond. In addition, the samples should be wash-tested to ensure that the interfacing and fashion fabrics have the same shrink characteristics; otherwise, the garment can separate from the interfacing and create bubbles or blisters and skewing.

Underlining

Underlining (also called *backing*) is used to stabilize fabrics that are loosely woven or sheer, and to conceal construction details such as seam allowances in lightweight woven fabrics. Underlining is usually a tightly woven fabric, cut into the shapes of the main garment pieces and attached to the back of these pieces before the garment is sewn together.

Figure 12.2a shows a panel with perimeter stitching, before assembly. Figure 12.2b shows underlined panels after they are seamed. Figure 12.2c shows the panels joined and pressed open, and a dart sewn through all layers.

Underlining adds more support than lining because each piece is supported individually. Garments can also be partially underlined in areas that need the most support, or areas that may be unsuitably sheer. An example is the lace bodice of a wedding gown. Sometimes places such as the knees on a men's suit or a leather pant, or the back panel of a skirt, are underlined to prevent them from stretching out.

Of course, one of the most important decisions in choosing an underlining fabric is selecting one that has the same care characteristics as the shell fabric. If one of the layers shrank more than the other during dry cleaning, for example, that would be unacceptable.

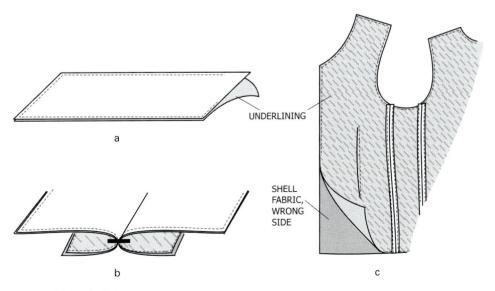

a

b

UNDERLINING

SHELL FABRIC, WRONG SIDE

c

Figure 12.2 Underlining.

Lining

A **lining** is a fabric, usually lighter weight than the shell fabric, used for all or part of the inside of the garment that finishes the interior and covers the seam allowances. It can also be used for pocket bags in place of pocketing. Lining can have a decorative function as well, such as when a lining is in a high-contrast color or printed. It can help the garment to slip on and off and can provide absorbency. The lining should be a bit bigger and roomier than the shell fabric to allow for the possible stretching of the shell fabric. For that reason, lining patterns are usually cut $^1/_8$-inch wider than the shell patterns.

The fabric for jacket linings is generally woven and helps to prevent stretching; however, for comfort and appearance reasons, the lining cannot be smaller than the shell or the shell may appear distorted, so it often has features such as pleats that add range of motion, especially across the back at the shoulder area. In most styles, the lining does not extend to the edge but has a facing that connects it to the outside shell. In developing the tech pack for a lined jacket style, the lining will have its own technical sketch to note all the components and construction elements, including darts, pockets, and pocket positions, and hem and facing details, which may have an impact on price.

Figure 12.3 shows a detail called an *armhole shield*, which is used to prevent perspiration stains and excess wear at the armhole, the point of greatest wear in a lining. Armhole shields (also called *dress shields* for women's wear) are a sign of higher-quality garments.

A lining is considered a quality indicator, although a well-finished interior with a partial lining or no lining can be of equally high quality. Figure 12.4 shows examples of quality partial linings. Figure 12.4a shows a common method for a men's summer suit. The center back seams would require a seam finish, such as the booked finish seen in Figure 9.63c. Figure 12.4b illustrates the use of a decorative bias binding, such as a Hong Kong finish, seen in Figure 9.61 with a partial lining.

A simple lining that is constructed in the same shape and attached to the main garment at the top is called a *drop-in lining* (Figure 12.5a). This is the usual construction method for lined pants and skirts. To provide stability with some give, a thread tether known

as a **swing tack** (also called a *French tack*) is used to connect the lining to the bottom edge of the garment, usually at the seam allowances (see Figure 12.5b). Swing tacks are sometimes made of ribbon or tape, if a sturdier connector is needed.

Lining for Activewear

Linings for ski or activewear jackets often have many specialized features that are included in the tech sketch. Technical outerwear garments have linings with many additional functions, such as **wicking** ability (which pulls moisture from one area and distributes it, letting it evaporate more efficiently), and features such as drawcords to retain heat and multiple pockets for storing gear. A special lining fabric such as fleece or pile can also be chosen to provide additional insulation. Figure 12.6 includes a drawstring casing at the waist, cordlock (also called *stopper*) and grommets, and inside pocket details. This example has one patch pocket with a hook and loop closure (right side wearing), one zipper welt pocket, and an oversized mesh pocket (left side wearing). The mesh pocket would be useful for storing a hat or gloves, and has elastic binding at the opening to help the wearer access the contents and to prevent items from falling out.

Figure 12.6 shows that the back facing is shaped in a way to set off the main label, and there is an action pleat at center back, below the facing, to add ease. The center front has a zipper closure with a storm fly (see Figure 12.6), so the zipper is visible only on one edge of the lining. Because the collar is not part of this drawing, the storm fly is not fully drawn at the top. Details of the collar and storm fly at the top would appear elsewhere in a detail sketch. Additional detail sketches can be added where necessary.

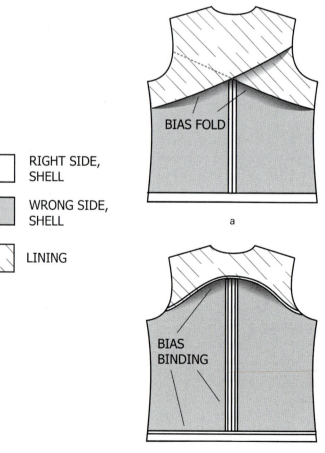

RIGHT SIDE, SHELL

WRONG SIDE, SHELL

LINING

BIAS FOLD

a

BIAS BINDING

b

Figure 12.4 **Lining for a summer jacket.**

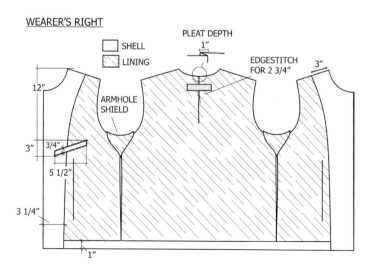

WEARER'S RIGHT

SHELL

LINING

PLEAT DEPTH

1"

EDGESTITCH FOR 2 3/4"

3"

12"

ARMHOLE SHIELD

3"   3/4"

5 1/2"

3 1/4"

1"

Figure 12.3 **Lining.**

DROP-IN LINING

a

PANT HEM DETAIL

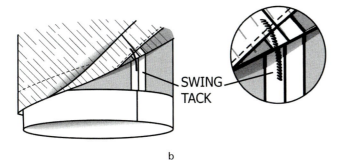

SWING TACK

b

Figure 12.5 Swing tack for lining.

Zip-Out and Button-Out Linings

Linings that can be removed are sometimes added to coats to extend their usefulness into colder seasons. Figure 12.7a shows a quilted button-out liner added. The liner is front and back only (like a vest), made of quilted fabric, and finished with binding at the edges. Figure 12.7b shows a ski coat liner in a two-in-one style of coat. The quilted down liner can be zipped in or out, depending on the weather. In this case, the liner is also designed to be used as a jacket on its own.

Interlining

Interlining is used for additional warmth as an insulated layer placed between lining and shell fabric, and also for quilted effects.

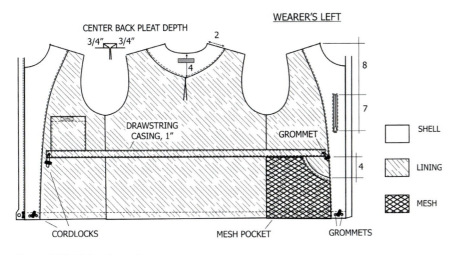

CENTER BACK PLEAT DEPTH
3/4"   3/4"

WEARER'S LEFT

2

4

8

7

DRAWSTRING CASING, 1"

GROMMET

4

CORDLOCKS   MESH POCKET   GROMMETS

□ SHELL

▨ LINING

▩ MESH

Figure 12.6 Lining for activewear.

Interlining for Tailored Styles

In a tailored jacket, a shorter style would not usually be interlined because of the added bulk. Long coats and overcoats are often interlined, sometimes with the interlining cut shorter at the bottom to avoid stiffness. Flannel is a common woven interlining material.

An example of insulation used for a decorative effect is a man's traditional bathrobe with a satin shawl collar and cuffs (a style probably more common in movies than in current fashion). The collar and cuffs may have a diamond-quilt pattern, and the collar and cuffs would be constructed with a layer of cotton batting underneath to emphasize and raise the quilt pattern (see Figure 10.34).

Interlining for Insulation

Casual outerwear or active sport styles use a nonwoven type of interlining known as *insulation* (other terms are *batting*, *polyfill*, and *needlepunch*), which comes in two distinct forms: roll goods and blown-in (such as down). Insulations are used to provide warmth for winter coats, skiwear, and other types of rugged outerwear. There are many types on the market that provide great warmth with very little weight. Insulation is available in a wide variety of different weights and thicknesses. Polyester is the main fiber used for insulation. The insulation can either be sewn to the shell as an interlining, or sewn to the lining.

Figures 12.8a and 12.8b show two casual outerwear jackets that mix quilting and flat panels. The quilt in the quilted sections is called pre-quilt because the shell fabric and insulation are quilted before the goods are cut out. This style mixes quilted panels with underlined panels. In Figure 12.8c the body panels are pre-quilt, but the placket, flaps, and hood are not. To avoid *shading* issues,

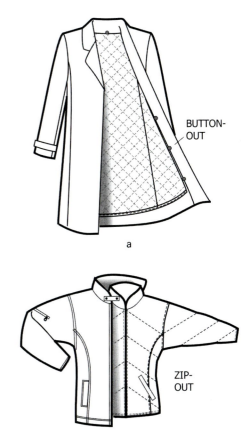

BUTTON-OUT

a

ZIP-OUT

b

Figure 12.7 Zip-out and button-out linings.

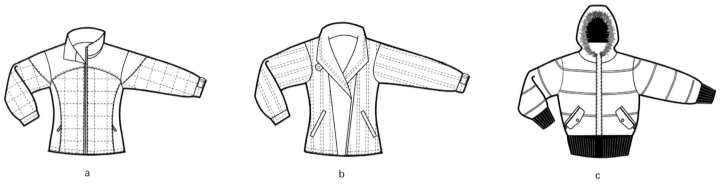

Figure 12.8 Interlining for warmth.

the factory must take care that the quilt and non-quilt sections are from the same dye lot.

Down Insulation

Down is the soft undercoating of waterfowl, most commonly ducks and geese. The advantages of down insulation are superior warmth retention, light weight, and great compaction. A garment or sleeping bag made of down can be pressed into a small container such as a stuff sack, and it will quickly regain its loft when pulled out. The element of down used for the finest fill is called the **plumules**, and the loftiest plumules are from geese; duck down is considered to be of lesser quality. A plumule is entirely different from a feather and has no quill.

The fill used for garments is often a mixture of down and feathers. The mixture of down and feathers is heavier and more compact, has less warmth retention than down alone, and is substantially cheaper. Disadvantages of down are the comparatively higher cost and the fact that it loses its insulation value when wet. Because of its unique qualities, it is considered a premium insulation.

Special consideration needs to be taken in selecting the fabric to be down filled. These garments require a downproof fabric; otherwise, the down will escape through the fabric over time. The best fabrics are downproof by construction, meaning that they are too tightly woven for the down to work its way to the outside. A coating can be applied to the wrong side of the fabric to make it downproof, but that has several disadvantages: it can cause the

fabric to be stiffer, it will retain moisture from the wearer's body, and it can break down over time and let the down escape.

The garment fabric should also be lightweight and strong; lightweight because otherwise the down will be compacted and unable to loft, and strong because if the garment is torn, the down in that chamber will literally fall out. Even the joining thread should be thin and strong, and the sewing needle size should be small enough to prevent needle holes through which the down can escape.

Down Processing

Down is cleaned, sorted, and shipped in bales. The bales are released into a bin, and from there, the down is blown in precise quantities into pre-made parts of a garment. Figure 12.9a shows the sleeve joined to a backing, also downproof. A metered blower blows the correct amount of down into the sleeve, forming a sort of pillow. The designer will have already decided on the look desired for the design (meaning, how puffy it should be), and the factory will translate the down required based on the square inches of each panel.

Figure 12.9b shows the fill opening sewn closed. The quilt lines are then added according to the design. It is important that the sewing operator endeavors to keep the down evenly distributed while sewing to avoid flat spots, because after the quilt lines are completed, the down is locked into one chamber and cannot be redistributed.

Technical Aspects of Designing for Down Garments

Down must have quilt lines to contain it because otherwise, in addition to being rather shapeless, the down will tend to drift to the bottom of the garment. For that reason the most effective quilt lines are horizontal, box, or diamond. Wide vertical lines would be problematic; over time, the bottom of the coat would fill up with all the down.

Because of the filling process, it is better to design a down garment in such a way that it can be filled in fewer pieces, ideally just the fronts, back, and sleeves. For example, rather than having a separate front and back yoke, the quilts lines can be used as an emphasis (see Figure 12.9c). For the same reason, there is no seam at the waist. Collars can be filled with down but are just as often filled with polyester insulation, which is easier to handle for such a small piece.

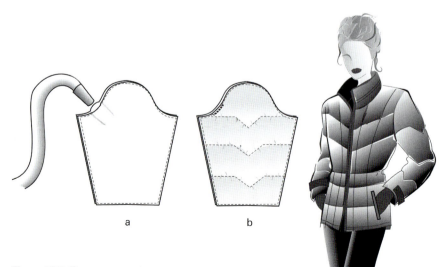

Figure 12.9 Down garments.

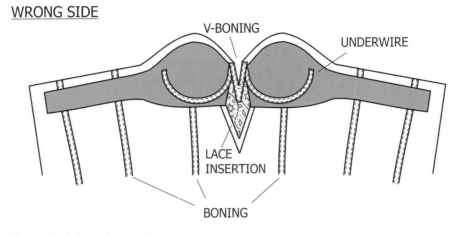

WRONG SIDE

V-BONING
UNDERWIRE
LACE INSERTION
BONING

Figure 12.10 **Bust shape and support.**

Other Supporting Devices

Other supporting devices provide padding, stiffening, or shaping to enhance the current silhouette. General supportive items include boning, crinolines, horsehair braid, collar stays, and bra strap keepers. Two useful devices common in tailored items are shoulder pads and sleeve heads.

Bust Shape and Support

Boning is a strip of stiff plastic covered with a casing, attached to seam allowances (see Figure 12.10a). Boning and underwires are used for women's strapless garment for bust shaping and support. Strapless garments function best when constructed from firmly woven fabric. Boning adds to the support of the garment, and is especially important when the bodice is draped or beaded. Specially formed padding is sometimes added to the bustline in the form of bra cups. This type of garment is often worn for formal occasions, and can become uncomfortable after a few hours.

On the other end of the spectrum is a style called a **shelf bra**, a stretchy second layer of fabric inside a top or dress with thin straps. This provides very light but very comfortable support (Figure 12.10b). Sports bras often have a pad that can be inserted for a smooth shape, or removed if not needed (Figure 12.10c).

Hoops and Crinolines

When fashion calls for considerable volume in a skirt shape, hoops and crinolines come back into use. Hoops are large rings sewn to the lower portion of an underskirt to support a full skirt. *Crinolines* are rows of netting that create a kind of stiff petticoat to shape women's skirts.

Horsehair Braid

A type of braid used for stiffening hems as well as other effects, a *horsehair braid* is woven in a bias and can be used to create volume and flare and stabilize the edges of lightweight fabrics. If it is used for the hem of a long skirt, it can be stretched slightly during application and will naturally pull to the inside to create a graceful and invisible hem. Some varieties have a heavy thread along one edge to help draw it up for shaping.

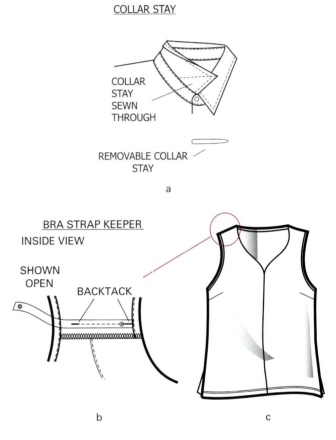

COLLAR STAY

COLLAR STAY SEWN THROUGH

REMOVABLE COLLAR STAY

a

BRA STRAP KEEPER
INSIDE VIEW

SHOWN OPEN

BACKTACK

b   c

Figure 12.11 **Collar stay and bra strap keeper.**

Collar Stays

The plastic sticks inserted inside men's shirt collars are called **collar stays**. They shape the edge of the shirt collar points to look sharp and keep from curling (see Figure 12.11).

Bra Strap Keeper

The loops that hold bra and camisole straps in place are called **bra strap keepers**. They also keep a light or slippery garment aligned to the bra strap to prevent it from sliding off the shoulder. It is functional and aesthetic to support the silhouette of the garments.

This is useful for wide necklines such as the boatneck. Figure 12.11 shows a style of bra strap keeper that has a small snap attached, and opens and closes for easier positioning.

Other Supportive Devices: A Case Study of Tailored Garments

The tailored jacket has many specialized shaping elements. One of the most important is the interfacing, which, in a classic tailored jacket construction, is made of a special springy fabric called **hair canvas**. The fabric is so springy, in fact, that the darts and seams are lapped; if regular superimposed seams were to be used, they could not be properly pressed open. The following is a list of the main components used in shaping high-quality tailored garments. Figure 12.12 shows how some of these main components are applied.

- *Haircloth*: A wiry resilient woven interfacing traditionally made from cotton and horsehair. It is used in tailored garments to reinforce the chest and shoulder areas, more often in men's tailoring.

- *Hair canvas* (also called *hymo* or *foundation canvas*): A strong resilient fabric made from wool and goat hair (see Figure 12.12a). The hair canvas is attached to the fabric with great skill, and with many interior hand stitches (see Figure 12.12a).

- *Covercloth*: A fabric with a slightly napped surface, sewn over haircloth to prevent the sharp ends of the horsehair from protruding. It also adds extra padding to round out the shape.

- *Wigan*: A loosely woven, durable interfacing, stiffened bias strip used for hems. Figure12.12b illustrates the use of wigan in sleeve construction, and how it supports the sleeve hem without showing stitches through to the outside. Wigan is used in the bottom hem as well. It is interesting to note that the tailored jacket sleeve vent used to have functioning buttonholes to enable the jacket sleeve to be folded back, but that feature is extremely rare now.

- *Silesia*: A cotton twill used for pocketing, fly facing and reinforcement, and waistband facing. Also substituted for wigan to reinforce sleeve hems.

- *Undercollar fabric*: A special fabric called Melton cloth, often used in men's tailored styles, which provides reinforcement and extra wear. It is a solid color and may match, harmonize with, or contrast with the main fabric. Women's styles use self-fabric (the same fabric as the body).

- *Tape*: Straight grain or twill woven tape is used for "staying" the crease line, lapel, and front edges.

- *Shoulder pads*: Components constructed of layers of muslin, often with cotton wadding (a nonwoven cotton batting or padding fabric) inside, used to shape and build up the shoulders (Figure 12.13c). Shoulder pads are formed from triangular pieces of fabric with padding in between. They are used to shape the shoulders of the jacket, building them up as dictated by the current silhouette. The pattern must be designed to accommodate the shoulder pads.

- *Sleeve heads*: Strips of fabric placed inside the top of the sleeve to create a smooth line and support the roll at the sleeve cap (Figure 12.13d). They also improve the hang of the sleeve and help it to maintain its shape. Strips of cotton wadding or lamb's wool fleece are used to support the roll of the sleeve cap and maintain the hang of the sleeve.

The roll line of both the shell fabric and the canvas is on the bias (see Figure 12.12a), so the addition of the taping prevents it from lengthening and becoming stretched out of shape. Figure 12.12a shows that pad stitching is one of the most important elements of traditional tailoring; it goes through the interfacing and barely catches the shell fabric, ensuring that the lapel and roll line remain perfectly rolled. The roll line is never pressed flat.

Figure 12.12 shows a jacket with the level of construction that would sell for a few hundred dollars or more, and is, therefore, limited to the upper end of the market. Less expensive tailored items use a combination of fusible interfacings and other less labor-intensive methods to achieve an attractive finished product (Figure 12.13). These garments will probably not wear as well or keep their shape as long as ones that have the more expensive construction features.

Fusible Interfacing for Tailored Garments

Figure 12.13 provides information about how the fusible interfacing is attached to a tailored garment. Ideally, the interfacing provides stability and support to the garment to shape the silhouette and style.

Narrow Fabrics

Ribbon, grosgrain, and other woven trims with a selvedge on each edge are sometimes called narrow fabrics (see Figure 12.14). Trims such as these add to the appeal of a garment and are common on many types of garments, including children's wear, lingerie, and casual wear. Ribbon may be satin, satin with picot edging, velvet, with a novelty-woven design, ruffled, or pleated.

Twill Tape

Twill tape is another type of firmly woven ribbon, usually in a natural (unbleached muslin) color, and is used less for decorative reasons and more often to stabilize seams and edges. It is used as a

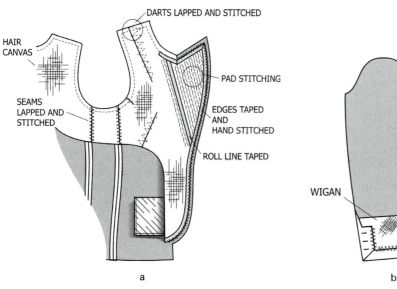

DARTS LAPPED AND STITCHED

HAIR CANVAS

PAD STITCHING

SEAMS LAPPED AND STITCHED

EDGES TAPED AND HAND STITCHED

ROLL LINE TAPED

WIGAN

a

b

Figure 12.12 Supporting devices for tailored garment.

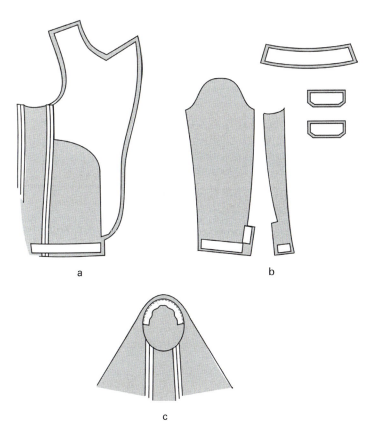

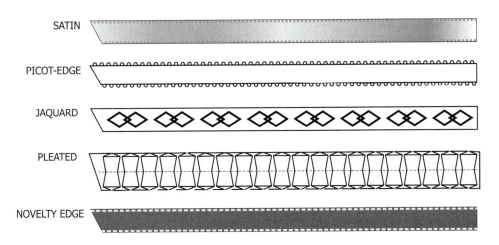

a

b

c

Figure 12.13 **Fusible interfacing for a tailored garment.**

waist stay, or for other stayed seams; to prevent stretching, as on the shoulder seam of a sweater; as reinforcement for a vent; and at the foldline of facings where stretching may be an issue. It is sometimes used as an inexpensive drawcord, or as an inside tie for a wrap garment such as a bathrobe.

Twill tape (see Figure 12.15) is also used to finish the inside neck edge. It can also be used in place of a facing to finish the edge of the zipper tape at center front. In other applications, bias tape would also work. Grosgrain ribbon (see Figure 12.15) is used as waist facing, belting, waist casing, center front facing on a cardigan sweater to support the buttons and buttonholes, and to stay a zipper or placket on knit garments. It is available in stripes and patterns and as decorative trim (see Figure 12.16).

Ribbon and Lace

Ribbon seam tape is a narrow lightweight ribbon used to finish hems and as a preparation for a blindhem (see Figure 12.17). The seam tape is applied to the turn-back in one operation to cover the raw edge and stabilize it. The hem is then blindstitched in a second operation. Because the seam tape is finished along the selvedges at both edges, it needs no turn-back and it creates a flatter hem, even on bulky fabrics.

Lace seam tape may be stretch or nonstretch, and is used in the same way as ribbon seam tape to finish seams. The stretch version works well for knit hems where some give is required. It can also be used decoratively as an edging or insert.

SATIN

PICOT-EDGE

JAQUARD

PLEATED

NOVELTY EDGE

Figure 12.14 **Decorative ribbons and trims.**

TWILL TAPE

GROSGRAIN

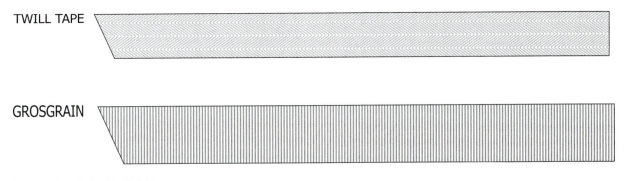

Figure 12.15 **Trims for finishing.**

INSIDE FINISHES

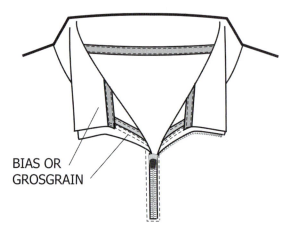

Figure 12.16 **Tape finishes for neckline and zipper edge**.

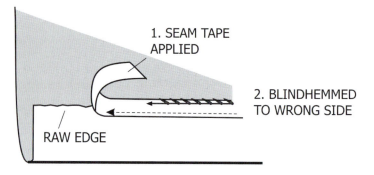

Figure 12.17 **Seam tape for blind hems**.

Braid

Braid is a type of trim formed without the strict structure of woven trims and is used where a more flexible and curved application is needed. Some types are woven on the bias (in the same way as horsehair to finish the edge of the zipper tape at center front). In other applications, bias tape would also work.

Rickrack and soutache are two examples of braid trim used for decorative effects (see Figure 12.18). Rickrack is associated with children's wear and with the 1950s era; it has a simple, homey, naïve charm. Figure 12.19a shows an example of how it is applied to a garment. **Braid binding** is a kind of woven bias used for facings and edgings (see Figure 12.18). A variation on braid binding is scored in the middle so that it folds cleanly. It is generally applied with a folder.

Soutache and similar narrow flexible braids (see Figure 12.18) have a long, colorful history, and have been used for military uniforms and elaborate decorations. It is also used for button loops on garments where a self-fabric loop would be too heavy. Figure 12.19 shows an example of how it is applied to a garment. There are other elaborate styles of braid used for upholstery and home furnishings; simpler, more delicate ones are used for garments. Another term for the finished effect of numerous braid trimmings is *passementerie*.

Elastic

Elastic has been incorporated into many products since its introduction as an apparel component. It is made from rubber or

synthetic rubber, which is extruded and then covered with fabric in a braided or woven configuration, or used as a flat band. Most elastic applications are lap seam construction.

Elastic Thread

Elastic thread is made with a rubber core, wound with cotton or synthetic or metallic yarn. It is indispensable for making elasticized shirring used for waist and cuffs, fitting, and other panels such as collars as a textural effect. It enables a woven garment to fit a wider range of sizes than it would otherwise. The elasticated stitching can be made in multiple rows, depending on the machine setup. The elastic thread is wound onto the bobbin and plain thread is used on top.

Elastic Cord

Elastic cord is either round or flat and narrow, covered with yarn, and sewn directly onto the garment. It is used for creating a ruffled effect or shaping at the waist. It is commonly found on children's clothing and is also used to produce machine smocking. Another type of elastic cord, used in conjunction with a cordlock for drawing a hood closed, or the bottom of an outerwear garment to avoid heat loss, is shown in Figure 13.30.

Braided Elastic

A lightweight style used for waistbands and unfitted garments, braided elastic is usually sewn down through the shell fabric because it curls. It is available in hard and soft stretch. Similar to other braided trim, it gets narrower when stretched, and returns to full width when released.

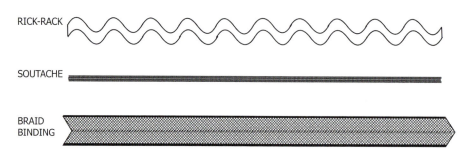

Figure 12.18 **Braid trims**.

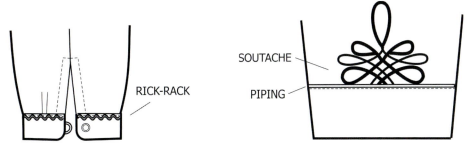

Figure 12.19 **Applications of rick-rack and soutache.**

Woven Elastic

Woven elastic is used in waistbands and for heavier fabrics. It is available in nonroll styles for areas that need a more rigid appearance. It retains its full width when stretched.

Decorative Elastic

Some elastic is available with stripes, and another style is printed in a custom pattern (see Figure 12.20). These tend to have higher minimum order quantities than plain styles, but they enable a simpler construction method to be used.

Elastic Edging

Decorative elastic is commonly used for underwear and in places where a thin stretchy finish is needed. Figure 12.21 shows flat elastic used for the leg opening and finished with a 2-needle bottom coverstitch. This enables the seam to be only two layers: one shell, one elastic.

Elastic Binding

Elastic binding is used to finish the waist in Figure 12.21. Underwear is the garment category in which it is usually seen. Elastic can be set into a casing, either self-fabric or applied in a different fabric. When used for a waist, as in woven boxers (see Figure 12.22), there is no need for a fly closure, provided that the waist-stretched measurement is sufficient to get over the hips.

Other places for elastic in casing are cuffs, bottom opening, and upper edge of a strapless garment or camisole. It is used to create a ruffled effect, for shaping the waist of a one-piece garment, and on children's wear and sleepwear. A casing can be turned to the inside (see Figure 12.22a), or set onto the outside. Elastic can act as a facing, and in that case, it will be exposed on the inside (see Figure 12.22b).

Flat elastic is often used inside hems for stretch fabrics such as those used for swimwear. In that case, the elastic is first attached along the edge; then the hem is turned and stitched with a 2-needle bottom coverstitch. For areas that will be covered, such

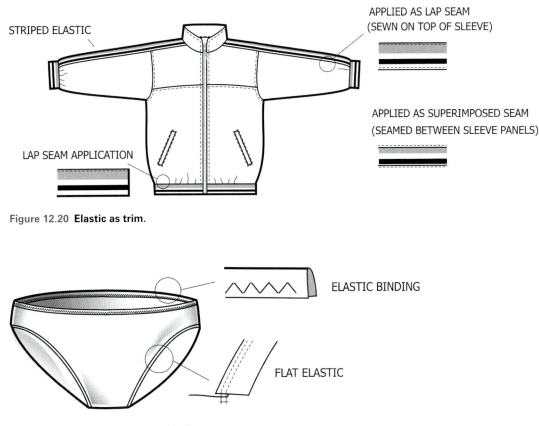

Figure 12.20 **Elastic as trim.**

Figure 12.21 **Elastic edging and binding.**

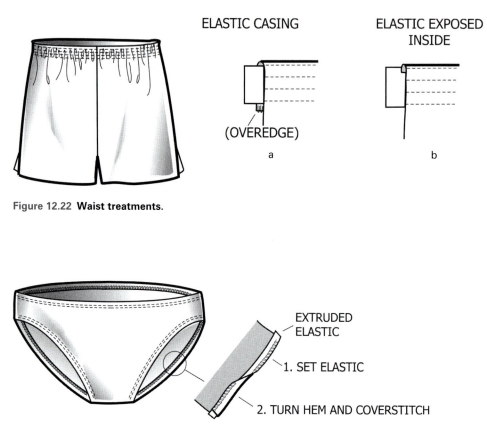

ELASTIC CASING

ELASTIC EXPOSED INSIDE

(OVEREDGE)

a

b

Figure 12.22 **Waist treatments.**

EXTRUDED ELASTIC

1. SET ELASTIC

2. TURN HEM AND COVERSTITCH

Figure 12.23 **Extruded elastic inside a hem.**

as inside a hem, a style of elastic is often used that is extruded (see Figure 12.23). It looks and feels rubbery because it is uncovered by any yarns. It is an inexpensive style that can be used to stabilize the shoulder seams of knit shirts and sweaters, and other areas of knit garments.

Summary

Various findings and trims related to shape and support of apparel products are critical factors when creating ideal appearance, function, and quality of the garment. Selecting desirable underlying fabrics for various functions is important for creating ideal quality apparel products. Understanding various options of shape and support devices helps designers to create products appropriate for their end use and for their target consumers.

Study Questions

1. What are the differences between linings and interfacings?
2. Select one shirt and one tailored jacket in your wardrobe. What are the shape- and support-related materials used for the products? Identify each material and locations of its use and explain why they were used.
3. What are the technical aspects of down garments?
4. Visit Appendix C in the *Technical Sourcebook for Apparel Designers* STUDIO. Select any collars that are constructed without interfacing.

Check Your Understanding

1. Identify various underlying fabrics. State an appropriate use for each.
2. Explain the main reason for using underlying fabrics.
3. Identify the specific considerations for selecting underlying fabrics.
4. Explain the main reasons for using tapes for garments.

13

Fasteners

Chapter Objectives

After studying this chapter, you will be able to:

- Identify different fasteners used in apparel products
- Understand from a technical perspective the application of different kinds of fasteners used in apparel products
- Select fasteners for various sewn products appropriate for their end uses

Key Terms

eyed buttons	gimp	lignes
fasteners	hook and loop	shank buttons
frog	lacing	trims

As described in Chapter 12, *findings* are all the components of a garment except the fabric, including thread, labels, elastic, and trims. **Trims** include external decorative features, which are added on to the basic garment, such as buttons, lace, ribbon, and bows. In this chapter, we will look at one of the most important components for apparel products: fasteners (or closures). **Fasteners** include buttons, zippers, lacing, ties, hook and loop (most commonly known by the brand name Velcro), hooks, and snaps, among the methods used to fasten the openings of apparel products for the wearers' ease in dressing and undressing. This chapter examines the following fasteners:

- Buttons and buttonholes
- D-rings and toggles
- Frogs
- Lacing
- Hook and loop
- Zippers
- Hooks
- Snap fasteners
- Cordlock

Designing the appropriate style and types of fasteners is one of the integral parts of each design and an indicator of the quality of the garment.

Buttons

One of the most common fasteners is the button, which is designed to slip through a buttonhole or other opening, such as a loop. Selecting appropriate types is influenced by the style as well as the end use of apparel products.

Advantages of Using Buttons

Buttons have been used as an apparel closure method for centuries. They are often decorative as well as functional, and come in a wide variety of shapes and materials. In many styling situations, a button is preferred to a zipper; for example, for blouses and most tailored jackets; for garments with lightweight and drapery fabrics; and for blouson silhouettes, where a zipper would be too stiff and heavy, and would distort the structural line of the intended silhouette.

Button Sizes

The button size is an important visual statement, and sometimes large or small buttons are used for novelty. Generally, larger buttons have more holding power than smaller buttons. When it comes to placing them, therefore, larger buttons are spaced farther apart than smaller buttons. Larger buttons are used for jackets and outerwear, and smaller buttons for shirts and blouses.

Buttons are sized by their diameter, designated as **ligne** size. This is a special measuring unit used specifically for sizing buttons. A 40-ligne button is 1 inch, so a ligne equals one fortieth of an inch, or .025 inch (.635 mm). For other size comparisons, a dime is equivalent to 24 ligne, and a quarter to 36 ligne. Typical sizes for a blouse or dress would be 18 ligne to 20 ligne. It would be possible to custom-order *any* size, but there are standard sizes, such as 18 or 20 ligne for a shirt and 30 to 50 ligne for a coat. A common jean-tack button size is 30 ligne. Jacket buttons are commonly 30 to 36 ligne, but larger buttons often are used as a fashion statement. Larger buttons cost more than smaller ones, so the ligne size is an important factor for costing purposes.

Button Styles

Button shape is generally flat and smooth, thus making them easy to manipulate. There are two kinds of button styles: shank buttons and eyed buttons (Figure 13.1). **Eyed buttons** are also called sew-through buttons because they have holes to sew through. They are useful in places where a flat button will be most comfortable, such as on pajamas, back closures, and children's wear. Two-hole and four-hole varieties are most common, but there are some novelty buttons with three holes and other configurations.

Shank buttons are created with a premade attached shank or thread shank. Shanks raise buttons above the garment surface, allowing the button to sit sufficiently higher than the buttonhole to avoid distorting the garment. Shank buttons offer a dressy look because the attachment threads are concealed.

Button Shanks

All buttons have a shank of some type. For eyed buttons, a thread shank is created to provide the space between the button and overlap of the garment (see Figure 13.2a). Buttons with a molded shank (see Figure 13.2b) have an attached loop made of wire,

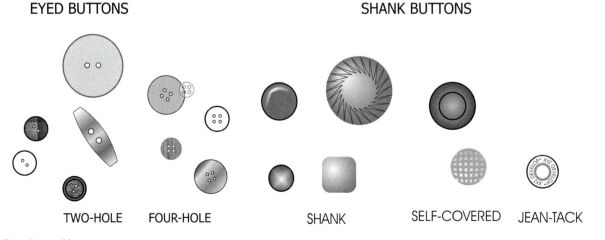

EYED BUTTONS   SHANK BUTTONS

TWO-HOLE   FOUR-HOLE   SHANK   SELF-COVERED   JEAN-TACK

Figure 13.1 Top views of buttons.

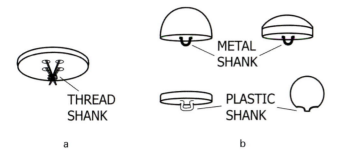

Figure 13.2 **Button shanks.**

metal, or the button material itself. Self-covered buttons (see Figure 13.2c) have fabric in the center that acts as the shank, together with the attaching threads. Figure 13.2d is called a *jean tack* button, and is very durable. For that reason, it is used on jeans and workwear. It is not sewn, but is set by machine through the fabric and into a bottom stud.

The height of the shank needs to be considered when selecting buttons. The shank provides the space needed to accommodate the thickness of the overlay of the garment so that the buttons lie smoothly on the surface. When buttoned, the button should sit on top of the overlap without pulling or distortion, and the shank or thread shank should not show. A shank too short will distort the area around it when buttoned. Shank buttons that are not round will tend to twist on a garment and appear mismatched.

Compositions of Buttons

A wide variety of materials are used to make buttons. At one time all buttons were made from natural materials such as bone, mother of pearl, or porcelain. Most buttons are now made of polyester or nylon because those materials can be easily shaped and dyed. The following are other frequently used button materials.

- *Wood* is used for casual wear. It is not recommended for frequent laundering.
- *Bamboo* is a common material and has some of the warm feeling of wood but with greater washability.
- *Leather* is often used on casual suiting styles. It cannot be laundered or dry cleaned, so the dry cleaner wraps the buttons carefully with a foil cover before the dry cleaning process. A plastic molded leather-look button is often used as a cheaper substitute.
- *Horn* (or *bone*) is an expensive material, good for dressy apparel products. It can be washed or dry cleaned without any special care instruction.
- *Mother of pearl* (or *shell*) is good for dressy wear. Most can be washed or dry cleaned, although some types of shell buttons are fragile and will break if machine washed. Pearl buttons are feminine in appearance, and work well with many colors. Plastic is often used to imitate mother of pearl.
- *Metal* can be cheap or expensive, and can be washed and dry cleaned. However, metal buttons should not be left in the water too long or they can discolor.
- *Rubber* is appropriate for casual apparel and is a traditional material for rugby shirt

buttons. It does not withstand the heat of a dryer, and it can melt, but is good for regular laundering.

- *Plastic* is the most frequently used button material. Care is easy because it can be washed, dried in a dryer, or dry cleaned. However, it can melt with enough heat, and may crack or break during rough laundering.
- *Cord* or braid buttons are often seen paired with frog closures.
- *Fabric buttons* may be fully covered with the garment fabric, or used together with a metal rim.

Button Attachment

The attachment method for most buttons is by sewing machine. A properly sewn button will remain in place for the life of the garment. There are two stitch types used for machine attachment of buttons: a chainstitch (stitch type 101) and a lockstitch (stitch type 304). For durability, the 304 lockstitch machine should be specified; 101 is not recommended.

The four-hole button is sewn with separate stitchings, and can be sewn either parallel (two sewings), in an X (two sewings), or square (four sewings), and is, therefore, safer from failure than a two-hole button. Buttons falling off is a major source of customer dissatisfaction and an important quality issue. For children's wear, it is important to check the strength of the button attachment because buttons can create a choking hazard.

Some buttons are hand sewn, such as the hidden button on a French fly. Hand sewing can add a shank to a two- or four-hole button, as would be desirable for very thick fabric. If a button is hand sewn, it should be done with the thread creating the appropriate length of shank and the shank encircled for strength (see Figure 13.3).

HAND-SEWN BUTTON

PASS THREAD THROUGH ALL FOUR HOLES THREE TIMES, WITH DOUBLE THREAD

THEN WRAP THE THREADS FIVE TO SIX TIMES BEFORE KNOTTING

Figure 13.3 **Hand-sewn buttons.**

Button Placement

Buttons are sewn or attached to the part of the garment called the *underlap*; the part of the garment with the buttonholes is called the *overlap*. Traditionally, positions of buttons at the center front opening are determined by the gender of the wearer. We can express this convention by saying that for the underlap, buttons are on the right (left over right) in men's wear, and buttons are on the left (right over left) in women's.

As a rule for tops, buttons are placed along the center front (see Figures 13.4a and 13.4b) or center back for back opening styles. Buttonholes may be placed vertically and horizontally, and sometimes diagonally. When they are set horizontally, one end point starts from approximately 1/8-inch away from the center front (see Figures 13.4a and 13.4b). An exception to the center front rule is for most pants, for which the *edge of the fly* is center front and the button is set back from there (see Figure 13.4c).

The part of the garment from center front to the edge is called the *buttonhole extension*. To maintain good proportion, the larger the buttons, the wider the buttonhole extension should be, and the greater the distance apart the buttons should be as well. Note that a good width from the edge is generally the width of the button (Figure 13.4a). The top button should be placed about half of the button width below the top edge.

Double-breasted styles have the buttons in pairs, positioned equidistant from center front (see Figure 13.5a). This style of closure sometimes has buttonholes for each button, but more often only the set nearest to the edge has buttonholes. In that case, to support the extra weight of the underlay, a backing button is sewn inside. Figure 13.5b shows the cross-section detail. The backing button is often a bit smaller to make it easier to manipulate, and may be clear plastic. Backing buttons are a good method of support and are used with large-eyed buttons, heavy buttons, buttons sewn to loosely woven fabrics, and often on buttons sewn on leather. They are an indicator of high apparel quality as well.

Buttons are positioned at areas of horizontal stress, such as waist and bustline (see Figure 13.6). If a style is fitted through the bustline, a button should be placed at or slightly below the bustline to prevent gapping. For a jacket or coat with a belt, the buttons are often positioned above and below the belt to give a balanced look (see Figure 13.7).

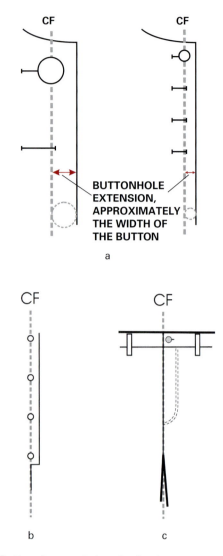

BUTTONHOLE EXTENSION, APPROXIMATELY THE WIDTH OF THE BUTTON

a

b   c

Figure 13.4 Button placement at center front.

Garments with specialty buttons generally have a spare button provided, either attached inside, or if too large or bulky for that, attached to the hangtag inside a plastic bag. A button of each size should be included; otherwise, if one is lost, the owner of the jacket would need to replace all the buttons, an expensive and difficult task, especially if the buttons were dyed to match (DTM).

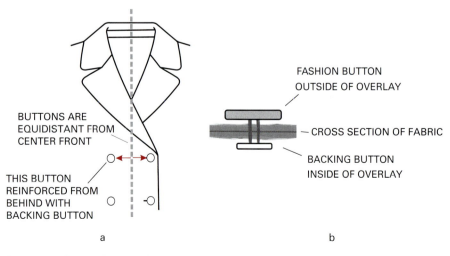

BUTTONS ARE EQUIDISTANT FROM CENTER FRONT

THIS BUTTON REINFORCED FROM BEHIND WITH BACKING BUTTON

FASHION BUTTON OUTSIDE OF OVERLAY

CROSS SECTION OF FABRIC

BACKING BUTTON INSIDE OF OVERLAY

a   b

Figure 13.5 Double-breasted button details.

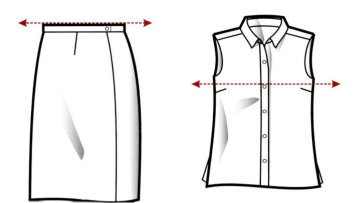

Figure 13.6 **Button placement for skirts and shirts.**

Figure 13.7 **Button placement for a jacket with a belt.**

Purely Decorative Buttons

Buttons are also used in purely decorative ways. Figure 13.8a shows buttons that are used in combination with braid in a decorative way (the actual closure method is a front zipper). Figure 13.8a shows sleeve buttons that are strictly ornamental. This is true on most tailored jackets, as well. Buttons in various sizes are used as a border detail for the skirt in Figure 13.8b.

Buttons have been used as decoration in many cultures. A traditional style from Cockney London is a coat worn by the Pearly Kings and Queens (see Figure 13.9). It is not a commercial product, of course, but rather a hand-embellished garment with mother-of-pearl buttons. The exuberant and fanciful designs are an example of inspiration drawn from traditional sources.

Buttonholes

Buttonholes are the openings through which buttons are inserted and, therefore, need to be compatible with the chosen button. The main types of buttonhole are zigzag, keyhole, slit, bound, and on-seam (see Figures 13.10 and 13.11). Tailored clothing sometimes has hand-worked buttonholes, but their shape is similar to a keyhole buttonhole, and the general guidelines cover them as well. Loop closures serve the same purpose as a buttonhole, and are also included here.

Zigzag and keyhole buttonholes are set with an automatic machine, which first stitches the threads and then cuts an opening through the garment. The zigzag buttonhole (see Figure 13.10a) is the most common and inexpensive style. The zigzag prevents raveling at the edges, and the bartack at either end provides reinforcement. It should always be formed with a 304 lockstitch; otherwise the buttonhole could inadvertently be pulled out entirely. Figure 13.10b shows two examples of a keyhole buttonhole, in which the front edge has a round area that provides extra clearance for the button shank. They are often made with the stitches formed over a cord called **gimp** (as shown in the lower sketch), which adds stability. It is frequently used for jeans, jackets and coats, and other situations where the button shank is larger.

A slit buttonhole (see Figure 13.10c) is used in fabric that doesn't need stitches, or would be unable to support the stitches in a zigzag buttonhole. Leather or imitation leather and thermoplastic fabrics are examples of fabrics that could not support the stitches

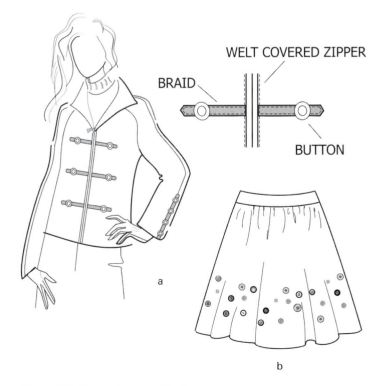

BRAID

WELT COVERED ZIPPER

BUTTON

a

b

Figure 13.8 **Decorative use of buttons.**

Figure 13.9 **Buttons as embellishment.**

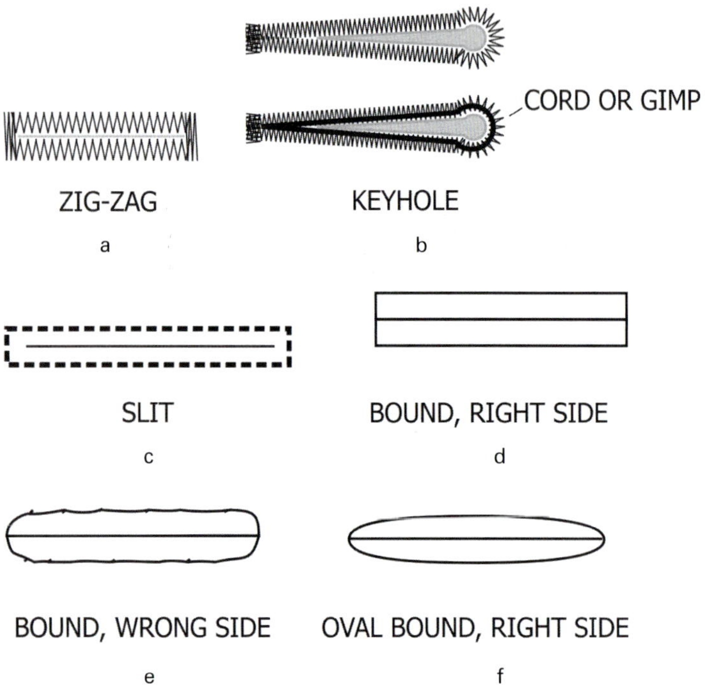

Figure 13.10 Various buttonholes.

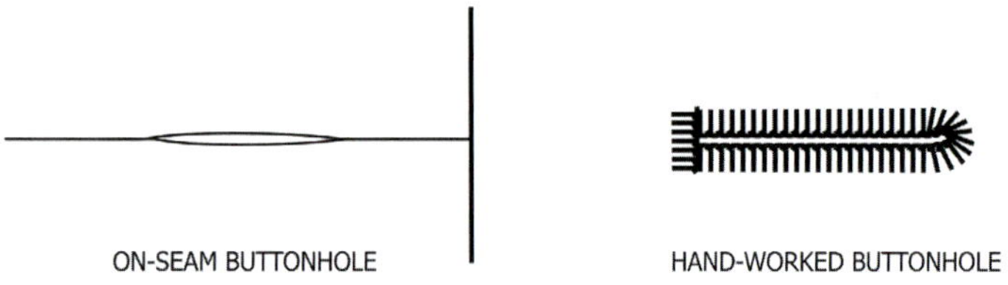

Figure 13.11 On-seam and hand-worked buttonholes.

of a regular buttonhole, and that does not fray at the cut edges. Sometimes the slit edge is simply fused or melted by heat for vinyl and other film fabrics. It is good for low-priced lines, for example, raingear. Bound buttonholes (see Figure 13.10d) are similar to miniature welt pockets. They are generally in self-fabric (the same fabric as the garment shell), but could also be in a contrast color or fabric such as leather for aesthetic appearance. They need to be carefully finished on the wrong side as well, by hand stitching. As with pocket welts, lightweight or loosely woven fabrics would not be good candidates for this style of buttonhole. The oval band buttonhole in Figure 13.10f is very detailed and would require highly skilled sewing.

Bound buttonholes appear almost exclusively on women's apparel and are an indication of high quality. Because they require considerable skill to sew, this type of buttonhole is expensive to make. Bound buttonholes were more common in recent decades, when more garments were made by dressmakers. Bound buttonholes are often found on leather garments and are considered an important quality indicator because they require extra workmanship.

On-seam buttonholes have a sleek, inconspicuous look and are formed by leaving a seam unstitched. They do need to be hand finished on the back, but are simpler than bound buttonholes. Of course, there may not always be a handy seam where a buttonhole is needed, so their use is somewhat rare. The example of a coatdress in Figure 5.8b shows the use of the on-seam buttonhole for a double-breasted style.

Figure 13.11 shows hand-worked buttonholes made with buttonhole twist thread and used in places where the fabric is too fragile to receive a machine buttonhole, or in place of a bound buttonhole to avoid the bulk it would create. They work best in firmly woven fabrics that won't ravel.

Quality problems (Figure 13.12) are usually caused at the end of the buttonhole-machine cycle, when the knife cuts the buttonhole open by cutting a thread that formed the buttonhole, or when the knife is dull and doesn't cut the hole cleanly all the way to the bartack, causing the buttonhole to be too short. The latter problem creates difficulty in buttoning and unbuttoning, a major quality problem if not corrected.

Buttonhole Size

The length of a buttonhole is determined by the shape of the buttons. For flat buttons, it is usually equal to the width of the button plus ⅛ inch. Thicker buttons may need a larger allowance, and that can be determined by slipping the proposed button through a slit cut into a swatch of fabric. The following are three different possibilities for buttonhole length based on button shape.

- Flat buttons: the length of the buttonhole = the width of the button + the height of the button
- Rounded buttons (ball buttons): the length of the buttonhole = the circumference of the button divided by 2
- Unusually shaped buttons: the length of the buttonhole = width of the button + the height of the button + extra length (based on button shape)

Because ease of buttoning is important for consumer satisfaction, this is something that should be checked on each new sample before the fit meeting. Buttonholes too small would be considered a major defect for a garment shipment and would make the garments undeliverable as first quality. Buttonholes too big will not stay buttoned. But generally, the exact buttonhole length would not need to appear in the tech pack because the factory is responsible for making buttonholes compatible with the specified button.

Button and Buttonhole Placement

Buttonhole direction influences the placement. The horizontal buttonhole is not centered at center front (as the button is) because a button seats itself at the end of the horizontal buttonhole, and not at the center. Horizontal buttonholes need to be precisely lined up to prevent gapping or pulling (see Figure 13.13a). Because the button seats itself at the front edge, the horizontal pulling direction, especially for a tight-fitting garment, keeps the button securely in place.

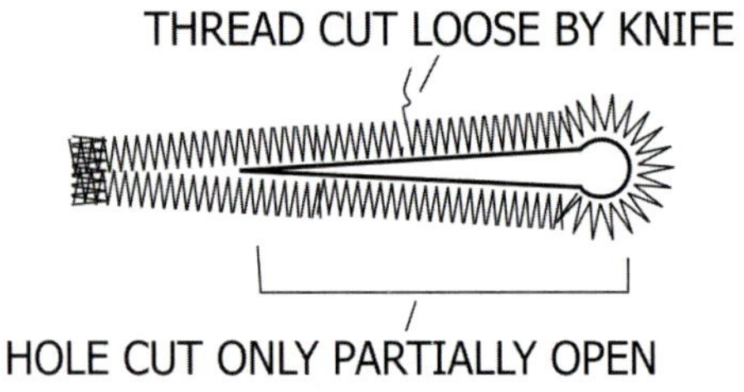

Figure 13.12 Quality problems in a buttonhole.

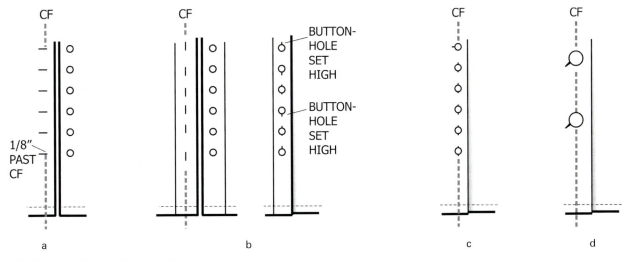

Figure 13.13 **Button and buttonhole direction.**

A set of vertical buttonholes could be a little less precisely equidistant and still allow the placket to lie flat (see Figure 13.13b). For that reason, a less-skilled factory would do a better job with vertical buttonholes. Some potential problems with vertical buttonholes are that they tend to pop open more easily and that they allow the placket to slide up and down too much.

Sometimes the top button is set horizontally, and the rest vertically (see Figure 13.13c). That way the placket can't slip up and down, but it still has the advantage of easier setting. Figure 13.13d shows an angled buttonhole, which may be used as a novelty tailoring detail. It would need to be set with adequate interfacing to avoid stretching. Another use would be in a bias-cut garment, which would allow the buttonhole to be set along the straight-of-grain.

Loops

Loops are narrow strips used for button or hook closures. Figure 13.14a shows a thread loop, such as may be used with a button or hook to secure the top of a zipper. Loops are often made of turned bias (also called *spaghetti*), but a braid or cord loop can also be used. A series of buttons and loops are often used for formal gowns or bridalwear (see Figure 13.14b and 13.14d). The ends of the loops are caught into a seam and generally hidden by a facing (see Figure 13.14c). It is important that the ends are reinforced to avoid them pulling out. It is often not designed to be a durable button closure method, so it is more often used for low-stress areas.

Button Reinforcement

Interfacing should be used in all button and buttonhole areas to help prevent the fabric from stretching out. In areas where the fabric is single ply, a round patch of interfacing or self-fabric should be used behind buttons on the wrong side of the fabric where the stress occurs. Figure 13.15 provides information on where the interfacing is placed. In shirts, interfacing is placed on the interior side where the collar button is set.

Specifying Buttons

Button placement is shown in the tech pack sketch; the specific button information appears on the Bill of Materials page and includes all the details needed for ordering. Figure 13.16 shows a men's shirt style, similar to the style shown in Figure 13.15. The Bee Button Company has furnished XYZ Product Development with button sample books from which to choose and that give the item numbers of each button. The placement information shows the quantities for each area, and the ligne size is indicated with an L, as in 18L. Buttons may have finish options, which in this case is a dull finish, usually better for men's shirt styles. The +1 designation under the quantity column indicates an extra button, one of each size, to be included as a spare.

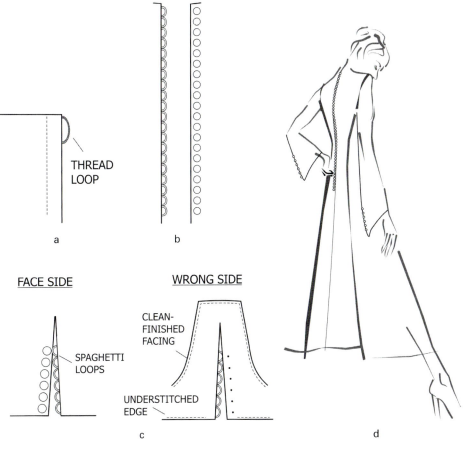

Figure 13.14 **Loops.**

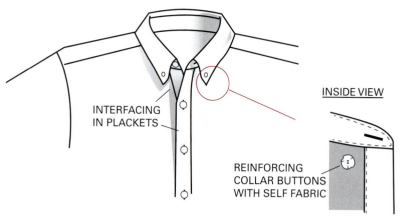

INSIDE VIEW

INTERFACING
IN PLACKETS

REINFORCING
COLLAR BUTTONS
WITH SELF FABRIC

Figure 13.15 **Interfacing for buttons and buttonholes.**

The MOQ column shows the *minimum order quantity* required by the supplier, Bee Button. This can be negotiated to some extent, based on the total buttons that XYZ Product Development buys from Bee Button each year as well as on other factors, but the minimums need to be observed rather carefully to avoid a surcharge. Buttons are governed by MOQ, such as 10 gross, and any buttons unused in an order have to be paid for anyway. For example, if the minimum order is 50 gross, then that is how many buttons must be purchased, whether they are used or not. If the garment order is for 1,200 blouses each requiring six buttons, it would need to be calculated whether or not the minimum order was satisfied.

For that reason, the horn finish has been chosen because it goes with all the colorways offered in this shirt style. If the buttons were DTM, then each colorway would need to satisfy a certain minimum order quantity. For a large company with a high volume of styles produced, that would be no problem, but for a smaller company, it is important to strategize the trims used to make your minimums (use up all the components), such as by using a button in numerous garment styles being made at the same factory.

In the product development stage, the prototypes often get substitute buttons, and that will be marked on the sample card. Often, the button supplier will make special small sample runs for the company's sales samples.

D-Rings and Toggles

D-rings (see Figure 13.17) are sets of rings for adjusting a strap detail. They are used on raincoats to tighten a sleeve, at the waistline to adjust the size, and for other details. A toggle closure

(see Figure 13.17b) has two loops, one of which has a long button attached. This detail is used for garments of heavy fabric, such as fur or faux-fur or outerwear where a buttonhole would be difficult to make.

Frog Closures

A method of closure that is functional but largely decorative is known as a **frog**. The actual closing elements are a button (called a knot button) and a loop. Frogs are usually made of cord or bias-covered cord or wire; the button shank is made from the same cord as the button. This style first appeared on traditional Chinese garments.

Figure 13.18a shows some of the configurations seen in frog closures. The straight version in the center is one of the simplest. Figure 13.18b is a sweater style with a frog closure at the throat. Figure 13.18c shows the principle of the straight frog closure adapted to other methods. In this example, for the closure across the placket, the usual cord is replaced by decorative ribbon and the knot button by a ball button.

Lacing

Lacing is a closure in which cord, braid, or ribbon is threaded through eyelets, grommets, hooks, or buttonholes. It is used decoratively as a placket closure, and because it is always connected at one end, is not used as a full center front opening. It is also used as a shaping device, a fitting device, or dart equivalent (see Figure 6.18). To draw up the closure, the lacing is pulled and tied at the top or bottom.

Hook and Loop

The standard **hook and loop** fastener (also called *Velcro*) consists of two tapes, one a woven hook-tape and the other a woven or knitted loop-tape. This closure method works with simple pressure, and is especially useful for people with arthritis and as closures that need to be manipulated without looking. It is also used for detachable elements such as cuffs, collars, and trims. It is popular for some children's applications because it is simple to manipulate, and also makes a pleasing ripping sound when opening.

Different engagement strengths can be specified, depending on the holding power required. With a stronger holding style of tape,

ITEM / description	CONTENT	PLACE-MENT	SUPPLIER	WIDTH / WEIGHT / SIZE	FINISH	QTY	MOQ
878G button, horn, 4-hole,		CF placket (8), cuff (4)	Bee Button	18L	dull	12+1	12 gross
878G button, horn, 4-hole,		Cuff placket (2), collar(2)	Bee Button	14L	dull	4+1	12 gross

XYZ Product Development, Inc.
Bill Of Materials

Figure 13.16 **Specifying buttons.**

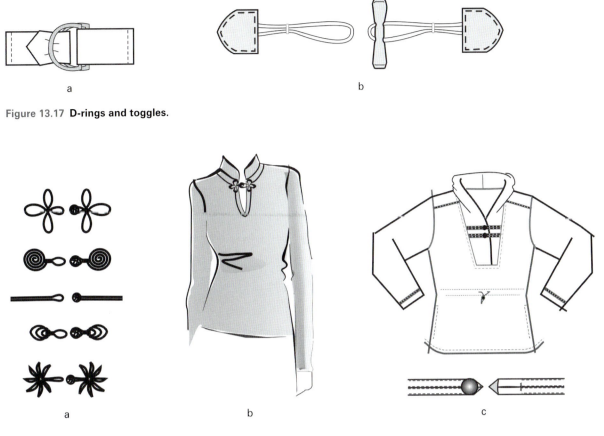

Figure 13.17 **D-rings and toggles.**

Figure 13.18 **Frog closures.**

it is especially important to include an X-stitch through the center (see Figures 13.19a and 13.19b). Otherwise, the stitches around the tape can break with repeated use.

Drawbacks to hook and loop closures are its stiffness (although softer versions are now available) and the tendency for lint to collect in the hooks. For that reason, the two sides should be engaged during laundering. The application should be used with more caution in a place such as a pant fly (see Figure 13.19d), which could eventually get "gummed up" with lint and no longer function. There is also a style in which both hook and loop are mixed together on the same face of the tape. This style is softer feeling and is more lint resistant than regular hook and loop.

Hook and loop fasteners may not be suitable for certain fabrics, such as a garment with loopy or lacy elements, because the loop could catch on the fabric.

Various other considerations should also be addressed when specifying hook and loop. One is that the corners can be very sharp; if so, they should be trimmed off (see Figure 13.19a). For children's wear, dye-cut shapes can be specified, such as round or oval with no corners.

The stitching that sets the hook and loop to the body can be hidden, or sewn through all layers. Figure 13.19b shows the loop side sewn through all layers of the flap, which would make it stronger. For appearance sake, it can be sewn just through the underflap. That detail needs to be made clear (see Figure 13.19c).

Zippers

Zippers first appeared in the late nineteenth century in Chicago at the World's Fair, and were widely adopted after World War I (Burns and Bryant, 2007). They are common and useful, especially for

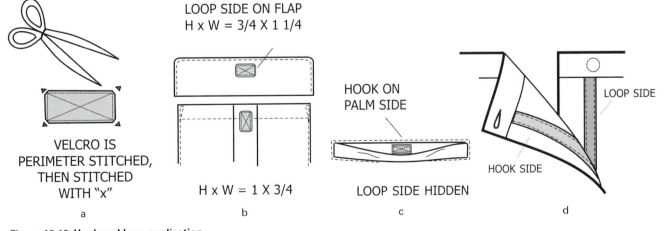

Figure 13.19 **Hook and loop application.**

medium- to heavier-weight fabrics, trouser flies, and outerwear. The use of invisible zippers is increasingly common as well.

Zippers are less well suited to very lightweight fabrics because of their stiffness. On the other hand, on certain slim-fitting garments, especially knits, zippers work better than buttons because they prevent gapping. Figure 13.20a shows that the garment closed with buttons would be prone to gapping. Additional buttons would reduce the gapping, but would not be convenient for opening and closing. Figure 13.20b shows that the zipper provides a clean, consistent closure. For a designer, it is critical to develop an eye when selecting the most ideal design features that affect the style and fit of the garment as a whole.

Common Types of Zippers

Figure 13.21 shows two of the most common types of zippers. The *closed-end zipper* (see Figure 13.21a) is the type most frequently used for openings in skirts and pants, and neckline openings in tops. This type is also used for pockets. The *separating zipper* (see Figure 13.21b) is used for the front opening on tops and outerwear (see Figure 13.21c). These zippers are also used for detachable items such as hoods, sleeves, and pant legs, adding to the functions of the garments for which they are used.

A separating zipper would not be suitable for a back-closing blouse because of the difficulty in getting the insertion pin engaged without looking. Learning to use a separating zipper is a rite of childhood. Engaging the beginning of the zipper is second nature for most adults and, in the United States, separating zippers are overwhelmingly left-hand insert/right-hand pull for men's, women's, and children's wear. Faced with a right-hand insert zipper (such as may be found on a garment from Europe), a person's fingers fumble a bit. For that reason, the left-hand insert information is important when specifying a separating zipper for the front opening. Figure 13.22 shows how a jacket is designed to convert to a vest by having the sleeves zip off.

Specifying Zippers

The Bill of Materials portion of the tech pack has the information for the zippers (see Figure 13.23). Zippers have many elements,

and all of them should be specified in the tech pack, including the zipper type, teeth size and configuration, and the pull appearance and function. Figure 13.23 shows details about a zipper that would be for center front, and the example in the tech pack is for a YKK zipper, a brand noted for high quality.

Parts of a Zipper

Zippers have three main parts: the teeth (also known as elements), the tape, and the slider.

Teeth

Zipper teeth can be coil, metal, or molded plastic. Coil is the lightest weight, and is used for skirts, dresses, pockets, and lightweight fabrics. Invisible zippers are also a coil style of teeth, in which the chain of the zipper is concealed when the zipper is closed.

Metal teeth are strong and are common in work-wear, denim garments, and other bottom weights, and come in different metals and finishes. Brass teeth are used for durability and tarnish resistance. Aluminum zippers are less durable and more prone to discoloration and corrosion.

Molded plastic teeth are versatile for many medium- to heavier-weight applications, and are superior in cold weather applications because they don't freeze and they block cold air more effectively than metal. There are also specialized teeth that are airtight and watertight and are used for underwater dry-suits.

Zipper Tape

Zipper tape comes in special finishes, such as fire retardant; antistatic; indigo, designed to fade with denim; cotton tape for garment-dye; printed designs, such as leopard pattern or other graphics; reflective-striped tape; recycled polyester; jacquard patterns; and woven stripes. There are two zipper tape variations: woven and knitted.

- *Woven* is durable, but can shrink after washing. It is important to have a preshrunk zipper. Usually it is made of cotton or cotton blend. Woven tape is used primarily with scoops (metal) and sometimes with coils.

- *Knitted* is flexible and tends to be lightweight. It is used only with coils. It is made of synthetic fibers so it tends not to shrink after washing as much as woven tapes.

Sliders

Sliders can be locking or nonlocking. The slider on a pair of pants must be a locking type, or it will allow the zipper to work its way open. The slider of a front separating zipper should also be locking. Nonlocking sliders are good for pockets, especially if the zipper is set horizontally. They often employ a swivel-type pull that allows for easier access to the pocket while still providing security. Slider pulls come in a great variety of appearances and functions.

There are zippers for many functions and styles. Figure 13.24a shows a two-way separating zipper that allows the garment to be zipped up from the bottom or down from the top. This enables the user to zip the garment open for more comfort while sitting. The two zipper styles with double heads often appear on technical active

a   b

Figure 13.20 Buttons versus a zipper.

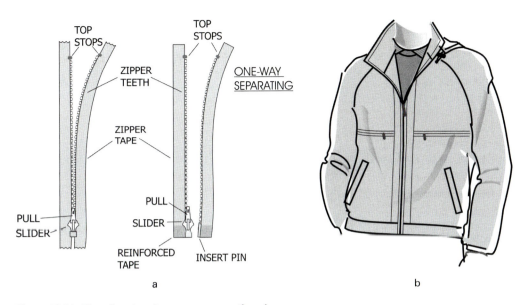

TOP STOPS

TOP STOPS

ZIPPER TEETH

ZIPPER TAPE

ONE-WAY SEPARATING

PULL

SLIDER

PULL
SLIDER

REINFORCED TAPE

INSERT PIN

a

b

Figure 13.21 Closed-end and one-way separating zippers.

outerwear and allow for heat to escape in a controlled way. They are also used for luggage applications. Figure 13.24d shows a type of zipper used for a reversible jacket.

Sewing a Zipper into a Garment

Zippers can be sewn in different ways. The side lap, shown as it would be placed on the left side of a skirt (see Figure 13.25a), is sewn so that the open edge is toward the back. The center lap (see Figure 13.25b) or welt (see Figure 13.25c) is used for a back, front, or sleeve zipper. Invisible zippers (see Figure 13.25d) are useful in many applications in lighter weights of fabric. The exposed style (see Figure 13.25e) is used in leather styles and other applications where the teeth are part of the design. Figures 13.25b, c, and e show methods that are also used for separating zipper applications, such as the front of a jacket.

In general, zippers should be applied on a straight seam; curved areas are much more difficult to apply, and can create a bulgy shape. For example, an invisible zipper set into the side seam of a skirt can cause the right and left side seams to have a different shape. When a zipper malfunctions, the garment becomes largely unusable. That is why the best quality zippers are a good value.

Hooks

There are two different kinds of hooks that are identified by their applications: sew-on hooks and machineset hooks.

Figure 13.22 Zip-off sleeves.

XYZ Product Development, Inc. Bill Of Materials								
ITEM / description	PLACE-MENT	SUPPLIER	PULL	PULL FINISH	TAPE COLOR	COIL FINISH	LENGTH	QTY
CFO-56-DA, LEFT INSERT	CF PLACKET	YKK	DA		580	EL-BLK-2	25"	1

Figure 13.23 Specifying zipper in a tech pack.

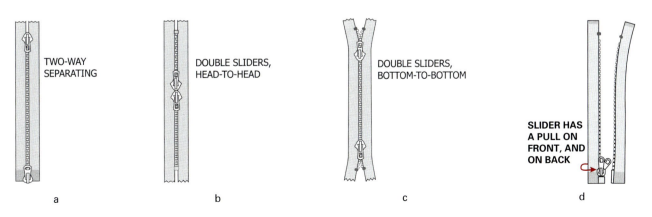

TWO-WAY SEPARATING

DOUBLE SLIDERS, HEAD-TO-HEAD

DOUBLE SLIDERS, BOTTOM-TO-BOTTOM

SLIDER HAS A PULL ON FRONT, AND ON BACK

a

b

c

d

Figure 13.24 Various slider types.

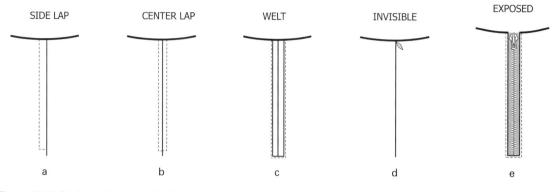

Figure 13.25 Various zipper applications.

Sew-On Hooks

Sew-on hooks usually come in a set with a companion piece called an eye, although the eye can sometimes be made of thread or fabric. The most common, everyday use of a hook and eye is for the back closure of a brassiere. The application is concealed from the outside in most cases, but it can be exposed on casual or work clothing or for design reasons.

Hooks can carry more stress than a snap closure, and the sew-on type of a hook and eye is common for securing the edges above a zipper closure. They must be sewn with care, in such a way that they are not visible from the outside, and they should be sewn through the interlining for extra support.

Figure 13.26a shows how they are positioned toward the edge and the stitches used to secure them. The first eye shown (round) would be used for edges that butt together; the second eye (straight) is used in a place where the edges overlap. Figure 13.26b shows a larger covered loop that may be used for a fur coat. The design advantage of such a hook closure is that the edges can butt together with no overlap. Figure 13.26c shows a larger style with a flat plate for the hook. This style is used for the waistband of a pant or skirt. Figure 13.26d shows a plastic, color-matching hook, and the eye is a loop made of the covered elastic band. This example would be used to close a bathing suit top.

Machine-Set Hooks

Machine-set hooks (sometimes called hook and bar) are set mechanically, can carry a lot of stress, and are commonly used for the waistband of pants. This type of hook works well on heavyweight fabrics. Figure 13.27 shows a common application

for a hook and bar on a fly closure, and includes a hidden button. This type of fly, with a buttonhole on the underlay side, is called a *French fly* and is used on better trousers. Because the button is not meant to show on the right side, it is often hand sewn through the inside layers of the waistband only.

Snap Fasteners

A sewn-on snap consists of a mated interlocking ball and socket, designed to snap open and closed (see Figure 13.28a). The ball part is attached to the overlap of the garment, and the socket is attached to the underlap. Ball direction is not set toward the body because it will not be comfortable to the wearer when pressed. Sewn-on snaps are often used to fasten the topmost corner of a closure such as a front placket. They are also useful for other concealed closures and for removable elements such as dress shields.

Machine-set snaps (see Figure 13.28b) have four components. Snaps are often used in place of buttons for garments such as activewear because their flat profile won't catch on objects, and on outerwear because they are easier to manipulate while wearing gloves. Machine-set snaps tend to be durable and long wearing, but when planning their placement on a garment, care should be taken not to set them too near an uneven thickness (such as half on, half off a seam allowance). They may not set properly, and may pop off.

Snap tape is a pair of woven tapes (such as twill tape) with opposing snaps already set at regular intervals (see Figure 13.29). This eliminates the need to set individual snaps and is used on children's wear and playwear, toddlers or baby's clothing, and other placket applications. Snap tape can shrink when washing, so the twill tape should be preshrunk before applying to garments.

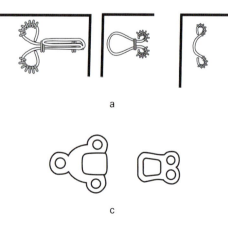

a

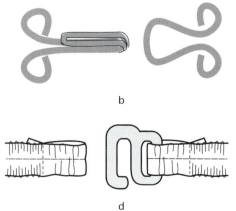

b

c

d

Figure 13.26 Types of hooks.

FRENCH FLY

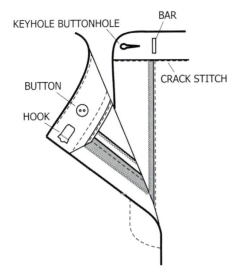

Figure 13.27 **Machine-set hooks on a trouser.**

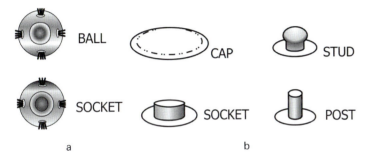

a   b

Figure 13.28 **Snaps.**

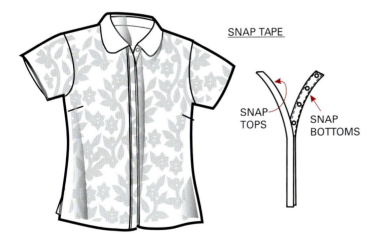

SNAP TAPE

SNAP TOPS

SNAP BOTTOMS

Figure 13.29 **Snap tape.**

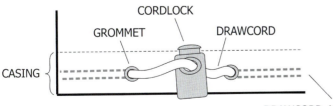

CORDLOCK

GROMMET   DRAWCORD

CASING

DRAWCORD, X-RAY VIEW

Figure 13.30 **Drawcord and cordlock.**

Cordlock

A *cordlock* (see Figure 13.30) is a way of adjusting a drawcord in a casing. It allows the casing to be drawn up and secured until the cordlock is released. This is used for outerwear details, often at the bottom or waist of a garment, and for packs and luggage. The drawcord itself is sometimes made of an elasticated cord called *bungee cord*.

Summary

For the design of a garment to be successful, it is critical that the designer select fasteners appropriate for the end uses of the design, the style, and target market of the garment. In this chapter, we explored various fasteners used on apparel products, and investigated the technical perspective of applying them.

Study Questions

1. Design a children's top and determine two possible fastener types. List why the two you selected are the best choices for your design, and list at least two pros and cons for each type.
2. List some quality issues related to using a button as a fastener.
3. What size, in inches, are a 40-ligne button and 30-ligne button? What ligne size is a 11/2-inch button?
4. If the minimum button order is 50 gross and the garment order is for 1,200 blouses with each blouse requiring six buttons, does that satisfy the minimum order quantity?
5. Design a pant and top for a patient who uses a wheelchair. What are the possible fastener choices in this case? List two possible choices and specify the reasons for your decision.
6. How can you determine the length of buttonholes?
7. What are the points that need to be considered when it comes to button placement?
8. What is the indicator you need to use when you determine the shank height?
9. List the instructions for applying hook and loop.
10. Visit any outerwear/ athletic wear store of your choice. Identify 3 interesting closures used for your selected garments. Take a picture and add suggestions of any alternatives. Discuss which would be cost effective. Bring the hardcopy to class.

Check Your Understanding

1. List different kinds of fasteners used in apparel products, and indicate the types of apparel on which each would be used.
2. What are the different kinds of buttonhole types?
3. How are button and buttonholes placed?

Reference

Burns, L. D., and N. O.Bryant. 2007. *The Business of Fashion*. New York. Fairchild Publications.

14

Labels and Packaging

Chapter Objectives

After studying this chapter, you will be able to:

- Examine the regulations related to care labels for apparel products
- Examine different methods of care for garments
- Identify exemptions and violations related to labeling
- Demonstrate how to label apparel products
- Illustrate various design perspectives of labeling

Key Terms

care label
Federal Trade Commission
(FTC)

ornamentation
registration number (RN)

Textile Fiber Products
Identification Act (TFPIA)

Labeling has become an important feature of fashion design. Designers exhibit their creativity in the designs of their labels and use labels as a way of communicating to consumers the unique characteristics of their brands. Placement of labels, as well as methods of attachment, has also become more and more creative. Instead of being used as a design feature, the main purpose of a label is to inform the consumers about the brand, fiber content, and related care, and labels should clearly communicate this practical information to the customers.

It is required by U.S. law, specifically the **Textiles Fiber Products Identification Act (TFPIA)** and the Care Labeling Rule, that all apparel products should contain permanent labels. The **Federal Trade Commission (FTC)** administers all regulations related to apparel labeling. Most importantly, government regulations about labeling have been updated frequently, so apparel manufacturers and importers need to keep informed and up to date about the information required on labels for their apparel products.

Labels have many different functions. The main label, which carries the brand identity, adds value and suggests to customers that they are getting what they are paying for. Other labels provide information to the consumer about sizing, fabric, and care to help guide their purchase. Some labels comply with legal requirements, such as the **registration number** (**RN**) and country of origin. Others, such as the factory tag, are designed to help the company track production and quality issues.

Basic Rules of Labeling

There are basic rules related to labeling. The garment must be labeled with the following information:

- Brand name
- Garment size
- Country of origin
- RN, Wool Products Label (WPL), or the name and address of the manufacturer or distributor
- Fiber content
- Care information

Also, each factory voluntarily adds its own factory label for its own information. Figure 14.1 shows a typical arrangement of labels.

Brand Name

The brand name label (sometimes called the ID label or identification label) is the main label. Brand name labels are conventionally attached to the main part of the garment at the center back neck for tops (see Figure 14.1) and center back waist for bottoms. Creative labeling for brand name has been used to enhance the uniqueness of design and styles. Examples such as clamp label (labels wrapped around the edge of the garments at the bottom hem or cuffs) and flag label (labels inserted into the seams) are attached to garments. Attachment methods such as sewing, embroidering, graphic designing, and attaching accessories and hardware are other interesting ways of adding flavor to the design.

The brand identity includes more than just the name; it also includes the font, colors, and proportions. The art for the labels is part of a larger brand identity, and the graphics are adopted with great fanfare. The corporate rules for adapting the graphics to labels are usually strict; for example, a navy background with silver letters needs to have the colors navy and silver be an exact match to the corporate graphics standard.

Garment Size

Size is the specific, overall dimension of the garment. Other specialized sizing information is often included, such as the inseam length or whether the garment is petite or tall. The garment size label is attached with the main label or care label where consumers can easily find it. Each company has its own set of sizing, meaning Company A might have a different standard size M (medium) for women than Company B.

Country of Origin

The country of origin (COO) label is important for goods made outside of the United States. If this label was missing, it could lead to a costly error, such as goods shipped to the United States being impounded by U.S. Customs. This label is required to be placed in a visible spot, generally near the main label.

Overall, labels for textiles and apparel worn to cover or protect the body are required to show country of origin. There are exempt accessories, such as shoes, gloves, and hats, and other excluded items that do not cover the whole body or protect the body, such as suspenders, neckties, and shoe laces. Piece goods sold for producing apparel are also required to have this information on their labels.

The Textile Fiber Products Identification Act requires that labels disclose three different pieces of information: fiber content, manufacturer or importer, and country of origin. This information should be permanently affixed to all garments sold in the United States. Goods produced in the United States do not

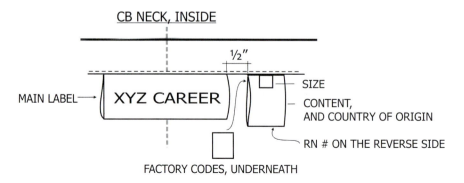

Figure 14.1 Typical label arrangement.

have to display a country of origin label on the exterior, but they often do, sometimes with an American flag tag as a selling feature.

Some consumers might have preconceived notions about the relationship between country of origin and product quality, so it is important to specify the information with the products. Some countries are known for producing high-quality goods; for example, Italy is known for its high quality of leather shoes and silk. In the current trend of global production of apparel products, however, products are processed by teams in different countries. Therefore, it is harder to determine the country of origin of apparel products, and it is important to follow the rules for the decision (https://www.gpo.gov/fdsys/granule/CFR-2003-title19 -vol1/CFR-2003-title19-vol1-sec12-130).

Manufacturers decide the country of origin of their products. This is determined by the "substantial transformation of the product," meaning where the product was produced. According to the trade regulations such as Chapter 98 and Item 807, apparel products should be labeled "Made in [the name of country where the components were assembled]." For example, if the material and fabric were cut and prepared in Country A but shipped to Country B for assembly, the final garment is labeled "Made in Country B."

Many consumers in the United States want to support domestic manufacturers. A "Made in U.S.A." label adds more value to products in the eyes of these consumers. They willingly pay more to support domestic manufacturers and the apparel industry. Manufacturers in the United States are required to attach a "Made in U.S.A." label to their garments. If a garment is not assembled in the United States but is finished in the United States, the garment is labeled "Made in [name of the country], Finished in U.S.A."

If the garment is made in the United States but the materials are from other countries, it is labeled "Made in United States of Imported Fabrics." "Made in U.S.A." is only for products made completely in the United States of materials that were also made in the United States. If a U.S. manufacturer uses imported greige goods that are dyed, printed, and finished in the United States, for instance, they are not eligible for a "Made in U.S.A." label. If processing or manufacturing takes place both in the United States and abroad, the label must clearly specify both: "Assembled in U.S.A. of Imported Components." The main order of components is also subject to regulations. Refer to www.ftc.gov for further information.

RN or WPL Number

The RN of the company doing business is a registered identification number issued by the Federal Trade Commission. Upon request, the number is assigned to a business residing in the United States that is engaged in the manufacture, import, distribution, or sale of textile, wool, or fur products. The RN is not required by law, but such businesses may use the RN in place of a name on the label or tag that is required to be affixed to these products.

In the case of imported products, "Importer of record" can substitute for the manufacturer's name. For several older manufacturers, a WPL (Wool Products Label) number has been used in place of an RN. It is important to many consumers that apparel product labels specify the manufacturers because consumers may have an impression of product quality based on that information.

Given the current globalized manufacturing practices, retailers have different contractors for the same product category. In that case, some manufacturers use their own RN as well as additional numbers specifying contractors who assembled the apparel products. An RN database is available at https://rn.ftc.gov /Account/BasicSearch.

Fiber Content

The main rules for fiber content are explained in "Threading Your Way Through the Labeling Requirements Under the Textile and Wool Acts" (https://www.ftc.gov/tips-advice/business-center /guidance/threading-your-way-through-labeling-requirements -under-textile#fiber).

Generic Names of Fibers

Per the Textiles and Wool Act and Rules, fiber content must be identified on a label. According to the rules, generic fiber names need to be specified, with the percentage by weight of each fiber in descending order of predominance. For all content labels, all fonts should be equal in size and conspicuous:

70% rayon

30% polyester

If the product is made from one fiber, "All" or "100 percent" can be used; for instance, "100 percent cotton" or "All cotton." Any information on specialty fibers cannot be misleading or deceptive. If a sweater has 2 percent cashmere and 98 percent wool, it may not be labeled as "Fine Cashmere Blend" unless all the labels and tags repeat the full fiber content information with percentages by weight.

If a nonfibrous material, such as plastic, glass, wood, paint, or leather is used, the information does not need to be included in the label. This means that the manufacturer does not need to disclose the contents of zippers, buttons, stoppers, sequins, leather patches, painted designs, or any parts that are not made from yarns, fibers, or fabric, but are used for apparel products.

Five Percent Rule

The five percent rule is as follows: if less than 5 percent of a particular fiber or fibers are contained in a garment, the label does not need to disclose the name of the fiber. It should be disclosed as "Other Fiber" or "Other Fibers" instead of their generic names.

Exemptions to the Five Percent Rule

There are exemptions to the five percent rule. Wool or recycled wool must always be specified, even if the percentage by weight is less than 5 percent. Although the fiber content is less than 5 percent of the product, if it has functional significance, it needs to be disclosed. For example, 3 percent of spandex for stretch will make the garment different from other products that do not contain it. So in that case, it needs to be clearly labeled as:

97% Cotton

3% Spandex

If nylon is used for durability, the label could specify it as:

97% Cotton

3% Nylon

In the case of multiple, nonfunctional fibers that are less than 5 percent of the content of each, but greater than 5 percent together, they should be mentioned with their aggregated percentage as:

82% Polyester

10% Cotton

8% Other Fibers

or

90% Polyester

4% Cotton

6% Other Fibers

Exemptions to the Fiber Disclosure Requirement

Trims, small amount of ornamentation, linings (unless used for warmth), and thread do not need to be counted for labeling purposes.

Trimmings

Trims used for clothing and other textiles that are excluded from the labeling requirements include items such as collars, cuffs, braiding, waist or wrist bands, rickrack, tape, belting, binding, labels, leg bands, gussets, gores, welts, findings, and superimposed hosiery garters. Findings include elastic materials and threads added to a garment. If the elastic goes over 20 percent of the surface area, labeling about fiber content needs to specify "exclusive or decoration." Decorative patterns or designs that are a main part of the fabric are also excluded in this case.

Specific items such as collars and cuffs are exempt from fiber content disclosure whether decorated or not decorated. Thus, decorations on collars and cuffs do not count toward the 15 percent of decoration that is exempted. To apply the exemption, the decoration must not exceed 15 percent of the surface area of the item; if the fiber content of the decoration is not disclosed, it should be labeled as "exclusive of decoration."

If the decorative trim or designs exceed 15 percent of the surface area of the product and are made of a fiber different from the base fabric, such as a 100 percent cotton shirt with silk trim piping and embroidery that covers less than 15 percent of the shirt, and there is no other information on the fiber of the decoration, the label must show a "sectional disclosure" as:

All Cotton

Exclusive of decoration

or

100% Cotton

Exclusive of decoration

If the decorative trim is less than 15 percent of content, but information about its content is referenced somewhere, it is necessary to label the fiber of the decoration. For example, to sell the shirt previously described but to market it as a "silk-trimmed T," the manufacturer should disclose the trim content on the label.

To sell a cotton shirt with 20 percent of decorative silk trim piping and embroidery, the label should disclose the content of the body of the shirt as well as the trim. Thus, both shirts would have the same fiber content label:

Body—100% Cotton

Decoration—100% Silk

Ornamentation

Ornamentation is defined as "any fibers or yarns imparting a visibly discernible pattern or design to a yarn or fabric."

Linings and Interlinings

There are two reasons for the use of linings and interlinings: structural use and use for warmth.

Structural Use

If linings, interlinings, fillings, or paddings are added for structural purposes, it is not necessary to disclose their fiber. If you voluntarily disclose the information, however, you need to follow the rules and requirements.

Use for Warmth

If linings, interlinings, fillings, or paddings are used for warmth (including metallic-coated textile linings and linings or fillings that contain any amount of wool), it is required to disclose their fiber as a sectional disclosure:

Shell: 100% Cotton

Linings: 100% Polyester

or

Coverings: 100% Polyester

Fillings: 100% Cotton

If the outer fabric and lining or interlining are made of the same material, the fiber content is required to be disclosed separately:

Shell: 100% Cotton

Lining: 100% Cotton

If the outer part of the garment is a nontextile material, such as rubber, fur, or leather, and the lining, interlining, filling, or padding is the only textile portion of the garment used for warmth, it must be disclosed.

Sectional Disclosure of Fiber Content

If there are different fiber compositions for separate sections of the product, the content of each section of the product should be disclosed separately. If ornamentation or trim creates a uniquely distinctive section of the product, and it is in sufficient quantity not to be exempt from fiber disclosure, its fiber should be disclosed as a separate section:

Red: 100% Cotton

Blue: 100% Polyester

Green: 80% Cotton, 20% Silk

Ornamentation: 100% Silk

or

Body: 100% Polyester

Sleeves: 80% Cotton, 20% Polyester

Note on Elastics

It must be disclosed if the fiber content of a product is partly elastic and partly other fabric.

Note on Superimposed Fibers

Fibers are sometimes added to some part of a product to reinforce the area (e.g., the heel or toe of a sock) or for another purpose. The label may state the content of the base fabric (total number adding up to 100 percent), followed by the word "except" and the name of the superimposed fiber, its weight relative to the base fiber(s), and the location where it was added:

> 55% cotton
>
> 45% Rayon
>
> Except 5% Nylon added to heel and toe

Pile Fabrics

There are two ways to label pile fabrics. You may state the fiber content as a whole. Also, the fiber content of pile and backing can be disclosed separately. In this case, the ratio of the two must be specified as a percentage of the fiber weight of the whole. For instance:

> 100% Nylon Pile
>
> 100% Cotton Back
>
> (Back is 60% fabric and 40% pile)

Fiber Names

Whether they are natural or manmade, fibers must be identified by their generic names. Certain generic names must be used for manmade fibers, even though manufacturers may give them brand names. The generic names are listed here in alphabetical order: Acetate (Triacetate), Acrylic, Anidex, Aramid, Azlon, Elasterell-p, Elastoester, Fluoropolymer, Glass, Lastol, Lastrile, Lyocell, Melamine, Metallic, Modacrylic, Novoloid, Nylon, Nytril, Olefin, PBI, PLA, Polyester, Rayon, Rubber, Saran, Spandex, Sulfar, Vinal, Vinyon.

Many fiber names are listed on the International Organization for Standardization (ISO) Standard 2976: 1999 (E), "Textiles-man-made fibers-generic names." Those ISO names permitted, although not listed in textile rules, are: Alginate, Carbon, Chlorofibre, Cupro, Elastane, Elastodiene, Fluorofibre, Metal Fiber, Modal, Polyamide, Polyethylene, Polyimide, Polypropylene, Vinylal, Viscose. Those names do not appear in the commission's rule. However, they may be used on labels to satisfy the fiber identification requirement. A copy of the standard is available from:

> American National Standards Institute
>
> 25 West 43rd St., 4th Floor
>
> New York, NY 10036

Some names of fibers commonly identified by the commission have different names in the ISO standard. For example, the ISO standard uses the name "viscose" for the predominant form of "rayon," and "elastane" for "spandex." In this case, either name can be used.

If a manmade fiber is a mixture of two or more chemically distinct fibers, combined during or before extrusion, the content disclosure should state:

- Whether it is a biconstituent or multiconstituent fiber
- The generic names of the component fibers, in order of predominance by weight
- The percentage of each component by weight

For instance:

> 100% Biconstituent Fiber
>
> (65% Nylon, 35% Polyester)

Premium Cotton Fibers

The fiber content may be identified by its name as a type of cotton, for example Pima, Egyptian, or Sea Island, as long as the information is correct. For instance:

> 100% Pima Cotton

If only 50 percent Pima cotton is used in a shirt and the manufacturer wants to use the term "Pima" on the label (or elsewhere), the percentage of the premium cotton can be indicated as "100% Cotton (50% Pima)" or "50% Pima Cotton, 50% Upland Cotton," or "50% Pima Cotton, 50% Other Cotton." If a hangtag on the garment has information on Pima cotton, the label should repeat information about the fiber content that includes the use of a trademark that implies the use of Pima cotton.

Wool Fiber Names

Any fiber made from the fleece of the sheep or lamb and the hair of the Angora goats, cashmere goat, camel, alpaca, llama, or vicuña is considered wool. If reclaimed or recycled wool fibers are used, they must be identified as recycled wool.

Specialty Wool Fibers

Fibers listed as wool may also be specified by their specialty fiber names: mohair, cashmere, camel, alpaca, llama, and vicuña. When the names of specialty fibers are used, the percentage of the specialty fiber must be identified on the label. If any recycled specialty fiber is used, it must be identified as recycled:

> 50% Recycled Cashmere
>
> 50% Wool

or

> 55% Camel Hair
>
> 45% Alpaca

or

> 40% Recycled Llama
>
> 35% Recycled Vicuña
>
> 25% Cotton

If specialty fiber names are identified, they must be seen on the required fiber content label and in any other references to the fibers. If the fiber is simply identified as wool, a specialty fiber name cannot be used in other nonrequired information (such as a hangtag) that may appear anywhere on the product. For instance, if a fiber content label simply says "wool," one may not put "Fine Cashmere Garment" on any required label or any other label or tag.

If a product has a small amount of cashmere and the manufacturer would like to emphasize it, cashmere should be listed on the label with the actual percentage, for instance:

> 97% Wool
>
> 3% Cashmere

Other Hair or Fur Fibers

Any animal fibers other than the wool fiber can be disclosed as hair or fur fiber, or mixtures thereof. If more than 5 percent of hair or fur fibers is used, another animal name may be identified. Because of technological developments, the hair of new varieties of cross-bred animals is available. Cashgora hair or paco-vicuña hair can be identified by name:

60% Wool

40% Cashgora hair

Fiber Trademarks on Label

If the generic fiber name appears on the label, a fiber trademark may also be used on a content label. A complete fiber content disclosure must be done on the label or tag if a fiber trademark appears:

75% Cotton

25% Lycra- Spandex

If no trademark information is provided in the fiber content disclosure, but it appears elsewhere on the label, then the generic name of the fiber must appear together with the trademark the first time the trademark is used. For instance:

75% Cotton

25% Spandex

Made in the USA

Lycra- Spandex

Lycra- for Fit

Products Containing Unknown Fibers

If unknown fibers are used for a product, in whole or in part, the undeterminable fiber content should be disclosed (https://www .ftc.gov/tips-advice/business-center/guidance/threading-your -way-through-labeling-requirements-under-textile#unknown). For example:

45% Rayon

30% Acetate

25% Unknown Reclaimed Fibers

Tolerances for Fiber Content Textile Products

Fiber content should be precisely disclosed based on its percentage of content. For most fibers (except wool), the fiber content percentage may be rounded up to the nearest whole number. For instance, 61.2 percent cotton and 38.98 percent wool can be labeled as "61% Cotton 39% Wool." As to the practical reason, the commission allows a 3 percent tolerance rate for other textile products to wool (https://www.ftc.gov/tips-advice /business-center/guidance/threading-your-way-through-labeling -requirements-under-textile#tolerance).

Care Labeling Rule

Apparel products have different care requirements based on product characteristics, such as end use, fabrics and fibers used, and target consumers. Care of products is often an important factor when consumers make the decision of purchase. The care label describes how to clean the garment and what restrictions there may be, if any, on the processing. Because woven labels have a high minimum order quantity (MOQ), some lesser quality options are sometimes chosen, such as printed labels. If a label will touch the skin, a satin label helps prevent discomfort. Sometimes a nonwoven label is used; this is generally the least expensive option.

The FTC's Care Labeling Rule requires manufacturers and importers to attach care instructions to garments. This requirement is based on the updates to the rule effective on September 1, 2000. This information has been changed to harmonize with the terms and definitions used by the American Association of Textile Chemists and Colorists (AATCC). More information on care labels and regulations can be found at www. ftc.gov/os/statutes/textile/carelbl.shtm.

The Care Labeling Rule requires the following: all care labels must remain legible and securely attached through the laundering cycle and for the life of the garment; manufacturers determine the care labeling according to the results of lab testing upon completion of all colorways of the actual production sample. All trims and related hardware attached to the garment must withstand the selected care method.

The FTC developed the guideline to help the consumer understand how to comply with the Care Label Rule. This information is available at www.ftc.gov, or FTC's Consumer Response Center, 600 Pennsylvania Ave. NW, Washington, DC, 20580, or by calling toll-free 1-877-FTC-Help (1-877-382-4357). As previously mentioned, the FTC has specific label rules (www. ftc.gov). Figure 14.2 provides information on care symbols.

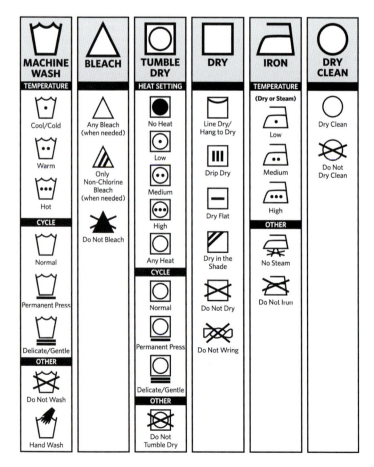

Figure 14.2 **Care symbols.**

Instructions and Warnings

Manufacturers should provide instructions and warnings about the garment, such as the following:

- There must be complete instructions regarding regular care for the garment, or warnings provided if the garment cannot be cleaned without harm.

- The manufacturer should ensure that the care labeling instructions will cause no substantial harm to the product.

- If there are certain procedures that are consistent with the instructions on the label but that would harm the product, then consumers should be warned. For example, if a skirt is labeled for washing, then consumers can assume that it is OK to iron it. If the skirt would be harmed by ironing, the label should specifically say, "Do not iron."

- The labels should remain attached to the garment and legible throughout the useful life of the product.

Reasonable Basis

There must be a reasonable basis for all care instructions, including warnings. This means that the manufacturer should provide evidence of its statement. For example, if the label says, "Dry Clean Only," there should be proof that washing is harmful to the garment. Reliable evidence depends on various factors, such as the following:

- In some instances, experience and industry expertise can serve as a reasonable basis.

- Some trims (e.g., beads) or dyes can be damaged or harmed during dry cleaning or washing, so a recommended way of cleaning should be provided.

- If a garment contains several components, the manufacturer should have reliable evidence showing that the garment as a whole will not be damaged when cleaned as directed.

When to Label Garments

All manufacturers, including domestic and imported, should attach **care labels** before they sell their products.

Where to Label Garments

Care labels may be provided in the following ways:

- Attached labels should be visible or easily found by consumers at the point of sale.

- In the case of labels that cannot be seen easily because of packaging, additional care information must appear on the outside of the package or on a hangtag attached to the product.

- Labels must be attached permanently and securely, and be legible during the useful life of the product.

- If the garment has different parts packaged together as a set and sold as a unit (for example, a pair of gloves), the set needs only one care label if the instructions for all parts are the same. The label should be attached to the major piece. If the set has different care instructions for some of its parts, or if they are designed to be sold separately, then each item must have its own care label.

Labeling Piece Goods

In the case of rolls or bolts of fabric, importers and manufacturers must provide care information clearly and conspicuously. The information should apply to the fabric on the roll or bolt. If other items possibly add to the fabric, such as trim, lining, or buttons, the information is not required to apply to those items.

Exemptions Listed by the FTC

For the following items, there is no need for permanent labels, but temporary labels at the point of sale would be acceptable:

- Totally reversible clothing without pockets.

- Products that may be washed, bleached, dried, ironed, and dry-cleaned by the harshest procedures available, as long as the instruction, "Wash or dry-clean, any normal method" appears on a temporary label.

- Products that have been granted exemptions on the grounds that care labels will harm their appearance or usefulness. The manufacturer must apply for this exemption in writing to the secretary of the FTC. The request must include a labeled sample of the product, and a full statement should be submitted, explaining why the request should be granted.

Several items do not need care instructions:

- Products sold to institutional buyers for commercial use; for example, uniforms sold to employers for employee use in job-related activities but not purchased by the employees.

- Garments custom-made of material provided by the consumer.

- Products that are completely washable and sold at retail for three dollars or less are granted exemptions under Section (2). Anytime the product no longer meets this standard, the exemption is automatically revoked.

Violations

Manufacturers and importers who violate the labeling rules are subject to enforcement actions and penalties of up to $11,000 for each offense. More information on violation can be found on www.ftc.gov/os/statutes/textile/carelbl.shtm.

Extra Labeling: The Factory Label

Figure 14.3 shows that companies often provide a factory tracking label that reflects the factory, agent, purchase order number, style number, season, and other inventory tracking information. This information is not required by law but is extremely helpful for internal reasons, one being the possibility of a quality failure after the goods are shipped to retail.

Application of Labels

Main labels generally come in one of three configurations—endfold, loop (sometimes called center fold), and mitre—and are usually placed at the center back neck area for tops, and center back waist for bottoms (Figure 14.4). If the label material allows (and does not need seam allowance), the label can be a flat style. This would be a label made of faux suede, plastic, or other nonwoven material.

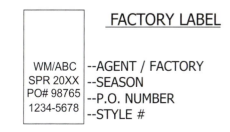

Figure 14.3 Factory label.

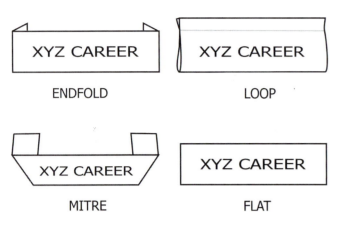

Figure 14.4 **Various main label applications.**

Materials of Labels

The following materials are commonly used for labels:

- *Woven*: Woven labels are made on narrow looms, and jacquard and damask labels are considered the highest quality.

- *Other Materials*: Other materials for a main label include taffeta, satin broad loom, woven grosgrain, and even printed twill tape, faux suede, and plastic. Each material has its own character. One type would be suitable for high-quality tailored garments, others for T-shirts, and still others for children's wear or athletic garments.

- *Heat-Set Merrowed*: Heat-set merrow-edge patches, such as found on ball caps, and heat transfer labels are used on knits, underwear, and other places where a woven label would be uncomfortable.

- *Tear-Away*: Accessories such as a neck scarf sometimes have a tear-away label because a sewn label would get in the way of wearing the product. Some labels may be glued on, but these would be seen only on low-end products.

- *Heat Transfer*: The heat transfer label has become increasingly popular because it is, by its nature, very flat (see Figure 14.5). This label is useful for underwear and other close-fitting sport styles. It is also called tagless labeling.

Setting Main Labels

A quality garment won't have the label show to the outside. Exceptions are casual garments, such as T-shirts. Sweaters often have no other way to set the label, and in that case, the thread is carefully matched to minimize the appearance of the stitching.

Label Position: Endfold

Endfold labels are often sewn around all four sides. Considerable care is taken to avoid having the label-setting stitching showing on the outside. It is generally desirable that the label stitching not show through to the outside. Figure 14.6a shows a label set $1/2$-inch below a bound edge, so this stitching would show to the outside and would need a facing. Figure 14.6b is the preferred method and has the label sewn to the inside of a band collar, through the inner collar only so that the stitching is not showing through the outside.

Endfold labels are sometimes sewn down at the ends only. Figure 14.7 shows a garment with no collar, with the back neck finished with a facing. In that case no stitching will show through to the

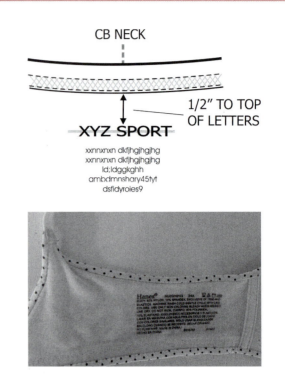

Figure 14.5 **Heat transfer label.**

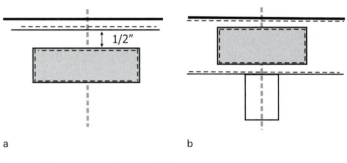

Figure 14.6 **Label position: endfold.**

outside. This figure shows a label set onto a dress with a center back zipper. It works best when a facing construction is specified, as seen in this figure. The balance of the labels are set into the side seam. Another common example of end-stitching is on a sweater or T-shirt (see Figure 14.8). A sweater has no facing or extra layer there, so it will show through, and the end-stitching helps minimize that.

Because the label is probably a different color from the garment, the factory needs to use two different colors of thread—one for the bobbin and another for the needle side. The label is sometimes set with a small amount of ease ($1/8$-inch in this case) so that on a tighter style such as a crewneck, little stretch will be lost to the label (see Figure 14.8a). The advantage to this construction is that the label can also be used as a hanger loop, as on a men's casual shirt. Figure 14.8b shows the second label sewn to the bottom of the main label.

Label Position: Loop

Loop labels are used on pants or other garments that are finished with a band at the top. Their extra thickness is not a problem on

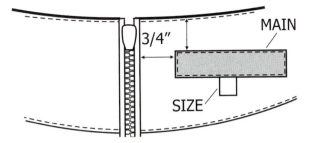

Figure 14.7 **Endfold label on facing.**

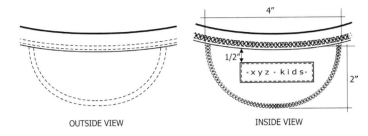

OUTSIDE VIEW   INSIDE VIEW

Figure 14.9 **Half-moon facing.**

CB NECK, INSIDE

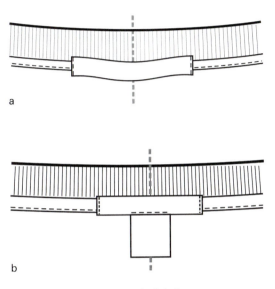

a

b

Figure 14.8 **Endstitching on the label.**

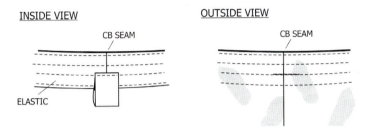

INSIDE VIEW   OUTSIDE VIEW

Figure 14.10 **Label for elastic band on underwear.**

pants or jackets, but could be uncomfortable on a garment such as a lightweight knit shirt. Figure 14.1 shows the size and main labels as good examples of loop labels.

Half-Moon Facing

A popular type of facing on which to set labels is a called a half-moon facing (see Figure 14.9). This is used for knits, and provides a way to avoid having the label stitching show through.

Underwear

Lighter-weight loop labels, such as satin, can be used for lighter-weight garments. Figure 14.10 shows an example of a men's woven boxer short, and the label is sewn through all layers but in a way so that it is all but invisible from the outside.

Exterior Identification

Some types of garments, usually more casual styles, have labels on the outside as well (see Figure 14.11). A common example is Levi's, which have a loop label (also called a flag label) sewn between the back pocket and the garment (see Figure 14.11a). The appliqué method for labels, sewn down on all four sides, is also common (see Figure 14.11b). Embroidery is also used on the exterior (see Figure 14.11c). Embroidery provides considerable freedom in terms of shape, but cannot provide the same amount of fine detail as a woven label can.

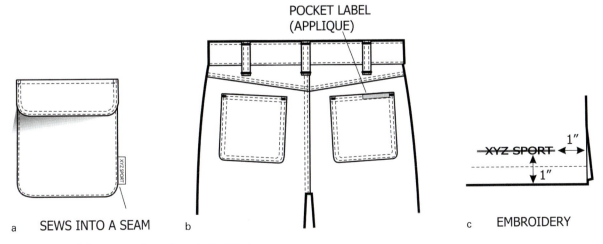

POCKET LABEL (APPLIQUE)

a   SEWS INTO A SEAM   b   c   EMBROIDERY

Figure 14.11 **Other applications for exterior labels.**

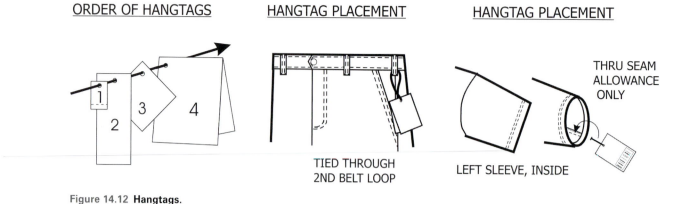

ORDER OF HANGTAGS

HANGTAG PLACEMENT

TIED THROUGH
2ND BELT LOOP

HANGTAG PLACEMENT

THRU SEAM
ALLOWANCE
ONLY

LEFT SLEEVE, INSIDE

Figure 14.12 **Hangtags.**

Hangtags, Folding Instructions, and Packaging

Other elements of the tech pack are the hangtags, folding instructions, and packaging. Only one of these (the hangtags) is seen by the customer, but folding and packaging also appear on the tech pack because they are items that contribute to the cost. Similar to labels, hangtags contain important information. Besides brand messages conveyed by photos and graphics, they also have details such as color code and color name, often as part of the bar code label. Other hangtags include trademarks such as the Woolmark hangtags, Teflon, or other branded components, and the price tag, if that is furnished by the manufacturer.

Figure 14.12 shows how the hangtags are attached per the tech pack. They are usually attached with a safety pin and string, or with a Swiftacher, a machine that attaches a small plastic strip to the garment. There is usually a corporate standard for the attachments and a standard set of descriptions or sketches, but sometimes a new type of garment may be designed that does

not fit any of the previous methods. In that case, the design or technical design department will find the best solution.

Other hangtags, used where appropriate, are reversible. Some garments are shipped on hangers and are packed in special cartons called garment on hanger (GOH) cartons. It is more expensive than the flat pack method, and fewer items can fit into a carton. For some garments, however, such as fine tailored jackets or fabrics prone to wrinkle damage, a flatpack would create creases that are not easily removed, and GOH is specified.

Folding instructions may appear on the tech pack or in another document such as the vendor manual, but it is another point that gets specified along with plastic bags, tissue paper, folding clips, and other items appropriate to the style. Figure 14.13 shows a typical set of sketches reflecting the folding method. In this case, the hangtags are folded in such a way as to have the bar code face up. This will allow the garments to be scanned as part of inventory control. Similar to the hangtags, folding instructions are usually part of an already established set of standards and don't need to be revised except in the case of an unusual new style.

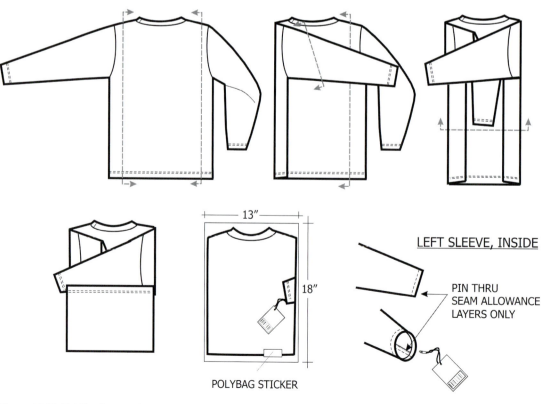

13″

18″

POLYBAG STICKER

LEFT SLEEVE, INSIDE

PIN THRU
SEAM ALLOWANCE
LAYERS ONLY

Figure 14.13 **Folding instructions.**

Summary

In this chapter, we have explored and learned various regulations and requirements related to labels for apparel products. It's important to understand how to appropriately label apparel products. Designers and professionals working in the global apparel production process use labels as a way of communicating information about the products to everyone in the team as well as consumers who purchase the products. That is the reason appropriate labeling including precise information is reinforced by law. Labeling regulations about apparel products are frequently updated to ensure clear communication to all. To create high-quality apparel products, it is essential to have a clear understanding of the laws and regulations in terms of labeling and packaging. There has been a trend to more creative labeling and hangtags, which in themselves create more value and salability for the product.

Study Questions

1. Bring three garments (shirt, pant, and skirt) to class and analyze the label of each, based on the following factors:
   a. List how many labels are used as well as their type.
   b. Analyze content labels and care labels. Are they compatible?
   c. List label attachment method and location.
   d. List any interesting design features of the label.
   e. List the country of origin of each product.
   f. List any missing labels based on U.S. law, the Textiles Fiber Products Identification Act, and the Care Labeling Rule.

2. Design a pair of basic jean pants for women. Create all related labels for the product. Make sure to list the material of the labels, attachment method, and location.

3. Design a basic T-shirt for teen girls. Create all related labels for the product. Make sure to list the material of the labels, attachment method, and location.

4. Visit https://rn.ftc.gov/Account/BasicSearch to get RN data for five different apparel companies in the United States.

Check Your Understanding

1. List general labeling requirements for apparel products.
2. List basic rules related to the country of origin.
3. List ten ways of attaching labels.
4. Visit the Federal Trade Commission website and check the most updated regulations related to Country of Origin label.

References

Federal Trade Commission. Writing care instructions: https://www.ftc.gov/tips-advice/business-center/guidance/clothes-captioning-complying-care-labeling-rule#writing.

Federal Trade Commission. Registered Identification Number Database. https://www.ftc.gov/tips-advice/business-center/selected-industries/registered-identification-number-database.

How to Measure, Size, and Grade

Chapter Objectives

After studying this chapter, you will be able to:

- Understand principles regarding measuring apparel products
- Practice measuring different kinds of apparel products
- Create specs for apparel products
- Demonstrate various size systems for apparel products for their target consumers
- Communicate size- and spec-related fit issues on technical packages in written and oral forms
- Understand the principles related to grade

Key Terms

fit history	hat ring	minimum stretched
grade rules	knock-offs	NAHM board

This chapter covers measuring guidelines for various apparel items, including tops, bottoms, underwear, hats, and socks. It offers tips for how to set up for measuring and what kinds of tools are needed. Special technical tips are also discussed. Given that measuring accurately is a critical factor closely linked to the fit of a garment, designers should understand the importance of measuring and be able to clearly communicate their expectations. The chapter also covers how to keep the fit history and fit comments. Size charts for various target markets in terms of gender and age are explored, with grades for each.

How to Measure

The arrival of a first proto is an exciting event, when a person's design ideas are first seen made into an actual garment. Sometimes the first proto is interpreted by the factory exactly right, will fit the size model perfectly, and will be perfect in every other way, with no revisions needed. That would be an exception, however. More often than not, some details will need refinement or revision or if the factory got something wrong, a return to the correct specification.

The careful measuring of a new prototype is a way not only to check the size, but a chance to review the overall appearance and sewing quality and make sure the details are in good proportion and have been executed correctly. Being able to measure efficiently can result in the difference between spending the New Year's Eve holiday with your family and friends or spending it at the office working on tech packs to meet the due date. Note that keeping the due date is one of the designer's most important job responsibilities.

The first proto will, therefore, be carefully measured, and all the details will be reviewed against what was specified. The item will be fit on a model or dress form, and the tech pack updated to reflect any changes needed. It is an important step in the commercialization process, together with writing comments. Every subsequent sample will also be measured, and the measurements recorded as a kind of **fit history**, which is the review of each sample against the tech pack and the points of measure. This review is also the opportunity to judge whether or not the factory understands the measurements and requirements. A measurement may be off-spec for a number of reasons; perhaps the pattern is incorrect, or the sewing may be incorrect, or the garment is not engineered properly, or the spec is not correct, or the problem is a combination of these and other factors. Evaluating samples is a process of continually comparing what was requested against what was received. Measuring correctly and consistently is essential to understanding how the existing garment fits and analyzing what comments and revisions are needed. In addition to the design department personnel, factories and quality assurance departments must all measure in the same standardized way so that the results will be consistent and they can communicate with each other correctly.

Setting Up for Measuring

The basic principle is that garments are laid flat on a table to measure. The tools for measuring various apparel products are described in the following sections.

Table and Surface

The garment must fit onto the table without hanging over the edge, and the table height should allow the user to reach across comfortably. The surface should be smooth. A surface such as cork or fabric should be avoided because it will impede the garment from relaxing completely.

Tape Measure and Ruler

The primary measuring tool is a tape measure. The tape measure should be fiberglass-coated for stability. When the edges of the tape measure begin to warp or curl, it should be checked against a ruler for accuracy. Short straight distances can be measured with a ruler. These include sleeve openings and detail areas such as pockets and collars.

Other Tools

Basic tools include the following:

- Masking tape, 1/4 inch wide
- Tailor's chalk or chalk pencil
- Straight pins
- Safety pins
- Clear grid ruler (quilt ruler)
- L-square
- SPI stitch counter

Based on specific product categories the following items are also needed:

- For sweaters: stitch counter for checking gauge, scale for weighing
- For socks: NAHM (National Association of Hosiery Manufacturers) boards in the sample sizes. The fitting of socks is not done on a fit model, but rather on a device called a **NAHM board** (see Figure 15.1) developed to ensure consistency in sock fit. They are available in standardized sizes from 3 to 16. Most people know their shoe size, but few know their sock size. (Table 15.1 is a chart of corresponding shoe and sock sizes.)

Figure 15.1 shows an example of a child's sock on the far left. The center figure shows the same sock on the appropriate NAHM board. The figure on the right is an adult size board; the proportions are slightly comical (rather like a cartoon figure run over by a steam roller), but the board is useful in gauging whether a sock will be comfortable on the foot, ankle, and leg dimensions. If the sock sample is hard to slip onto the NAHM board or hard to pull up, it must be re-tried on the next size down. The NAHM board serves the same purpose as a dress form. The hole at the heel (see Figure 15.1) is a guide to where the gore hole should fall.

For hats: the **hat ring** is a spring device used to measure the inside of a hat. It looks somewhat like a pair of scissors, and when set inside a hatband and squeezed, it expands to the inside diameter and the size can be taken from the calibrated numbers. Figure 15.2 shows a hat ring that indicates measurements in hat sizes and centimeters.

It sometimes seems that a garment measures differently every time it's measured. Practice will help establish a set of standard measuring techniques that will give consistent results.

Table 15.1   NAHM Sock Size Chart and Corresponding Shoe Size

| | Shoe Size | | |
Sock Size	Children	Men/Boys	Ladies
3	Baby		
3½	0		
4	0–1		
4½	1½–2		
5	3–4		
5½	4½–5		
6	6–7		
6½	7½–8½		
7	9–10		
7½	10½–11½		
8	12–13	1	
8½	13½–1½	1½–2½	2½–3½
9	2–3	3–4	4–5
9½		4½–5½	5½–6½
10		6–6½	6½–7½
10½		7–8	8–9
11		8½–9	9½–10½
11½		9½–10	10½–11½
12		10½–11	11½–12
12½		11½	12½–13
13		12–12½	
14		13–14	
15		14½–16	
16		16½–18	

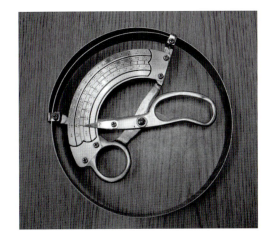

Figure 15.2 **Hat measure tool.**

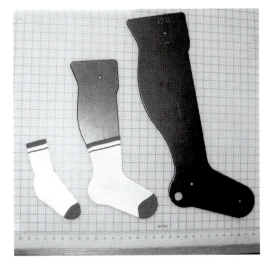

Figure 15.1 **NAHM board.**

Preparation

New prototype garments must be measured before they can be tried on to avoid any stretch or related errors. All garments should be measured before being evaluated so that it is clear whether they are on-spec or off-spec. For knit garments especially, the dimensions are often different before and after wearing; they can stretch out, and the measurements will be inaccurate.

Lay the garment on the surface, beginning with face up. The garment should be patted smooth, without slack, but not stretched or pulled out. All folds and wrinkles should be removed from the underside. For tops, the side seams need to be carefully smoothed to make sure that the high point shoulder (HPS; see Figure 15.3) position is correctly represented and has not shifted forward or back. HPS information was introduced in Chapter 4, but the main guidelines are reviewed here. HPS is the point at which the garment naturally folds when the side seams are lined up. It is helpful to mark the HPS with a safety pin or chalk for reference later, such as when the garment is on a dress form or body, if it is flipped to the back side, or when measuring garments with a hood (in which hood height is measured from HPS; see Figure 15.18a). Figures 15.3a, 15.3b, and 15.3c show that the HPS is at the neck seam. Sometimes a garment has no seam (if it has no collar), and in that case it is measured "to edge."

Closures should be closed, zippers zipped, and buttons buttoned. For horizontal buttonholes the button should be pulled tight into the buttonhole. A garment with no closure, such as a bathrobe, should be overlapped exactly (e.g., how many inches overlapping) as specified in the tech pack. Vents should be smoothed and taped or pinned closed. Slits should lie edge to edge. Many knit garments and all sweaters should be stored folded because hanging on hangers will distort them over time, making the measurements inaccurate.

Steps for Measuring

Work through the following points of measure and follow the order on the spec form.

1. Place the tape at the measurement starting point and press firmly. Walk the tape across the garment to the end point, pressing the tape against the garment at intervals along the way, and press down at the end to determine the measurement. Measure to the nearest ¹/₈ inch.

2. Note the measurement on the sample evaluation sheet in pencil.

3. Proceed through all the points of measure (POM).

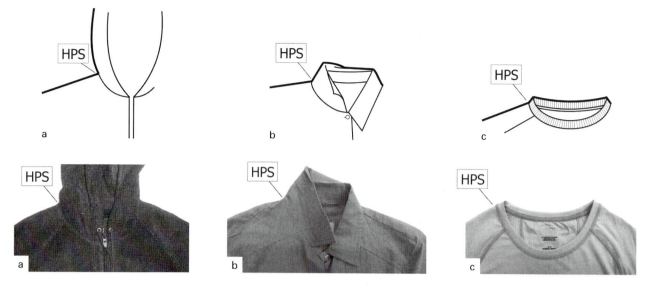

Figure 15.3 **Mark the high point shoulder position.**

4. While measuring, check that all the points of measure are clear and concise and that the factory has understood them. For example, if the point of measure is the front neck drop from HPS, then make sure it is clear whether it should be measured to the seam or to the edge. Add clarification as necessary. Figure 15.4a shows where there could be some confusion about where to measure a neckline. The points of measure in Figure 15.4b are spelled out explicitly.

5. Compare your measurements with the factory's measurements to make sure the factory understands. For example, if the neck width spec is 7 inches and the sample measures 8 inches, it may have been unclear where to begin and end the measurement or it may be that the factory made the pattern a bit wide and should revise it to achieve the spec for the next sample.

6. For a top, only one sleeve is measured (not both). For a pant, only one inseam is measured.

7. For curved seams and edges, the tape may be shifted around a curve, pivoting carefully, or the tape may be stood on edge. Do not stretch or straighten out the curves while measuring. For rises, necks, and armholes, the shape should reflect the shape of the pattern and should curve as much as the pattern would; Figure 15.5 shows the armhole shape curve. It's not uncommon for the factory to make the pattern, so reviewing the sample is also reviewing the pattern. If problems appear that may be pattern-related problems, the factory can be requested to send a pattern tracing with the next sample.

8. Measurements that are squared are designated "drop," such as armhole drop and shoulder drop, and can be measured with an L-square. Figure 15.6a shows an example of how to measure armhole drop with an L-square. This point of measure can also be measured with ruler and tape measure (see Figure 15.6b). The measurement will be the same, and both are accurate. Figure 15.6c shows the advantage of working on a surface marked in grid. When the HPS spot is lined up at the top, armhole drop can be calculated from there.

Neck drop and shoulder drop can be easily measured with a large clear grid ruler known as a *quilting ruler* (Figure 15.7). A smaller version goes by the brand name *C-thru ruler*. When the edge of the quilting ruler has been aligned across from HPS

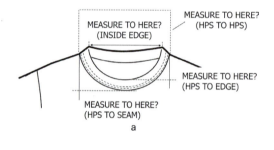

code	**BODY SPECS**	Spec
T-P	Front Neck Drop, **to seam**	4 1/4
T-Q	Back Neck Drop, **to seam**	3/4
T-R	Neck Width, **seam to seam**	7 1/2

b

Figure 15.4 **Clear understanding of points of measure.**

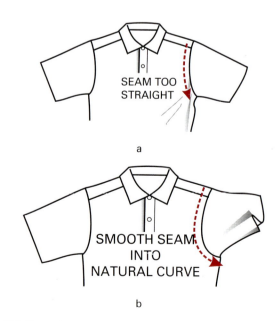

Figure 15.5 **Smooth seams into their natural curves.**

ARMHOLE DROP
MEASURED WITH L-SQUARE

ARMHOLE DROP
MEASURED WITH RULER AND TAPE

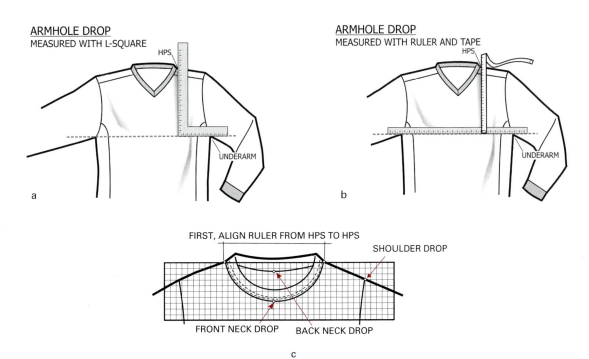

a

b

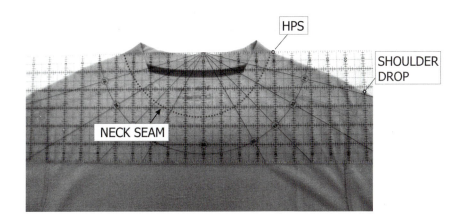

FIRST, ALIGN RULER FROM HPS TO HPS

SHOULDER DROP

FRONT NECK DROP   BACK NECK DROP

c

Figure 15.6 **Measuring armhole drop.**

HPS

SHOULDER DROP

NECK SEAM

Figure 15.7 **Measuring with quilting ruler.**

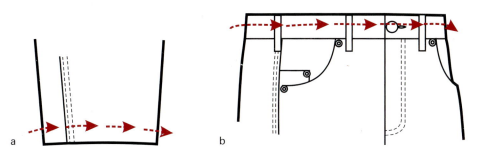

a

b

Figure 15.8 **Roll seam to avoid bulk at edges.**

to HPS, shoulder drop and front neck drop can be measured by sight. (In Figure 15.7 the neck seam position is shown by the dotted line.) This also enables one to measure the back neck drop without having to flip the garment over (see Figure 15.7).

9. For areas with thick seams at the edge, roll the seam toward the front or back so the girth can be measured flat edge to flat edge, without distortion (see Figure 15.8).

10. Stretched measurements require special attention. A relaxed measurement such as on an elastic cuff (see Figure 15.9a) is measured side to side, the same as non-elasticated. The extended measurement of the same cuff (as on an elasticated woven) is fully extended until the fabric stops (see Figure 15.9b). A **minimum stretched** measurement is a particular type of extended measurement used for knits. It often is

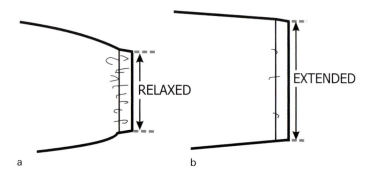

Figure 15.9 Relaxed and extended measurement.

used for neck openings, such as on the neck of a T-shirt. It is measured fully stretched without pulling the seams open and is used to make sure that the neck can extend enough to comfortably get over the head. Minimum stretched measurement is an important standard for children's wear also.

11. Girth means the same as circumference, all the way around the garment. At XYZ Product Development, as with many other companies, the girth measurement for woven garments will be *total circumference*, or whole measure, and in that case, the measurement across must be doubled for total measurement. Figure 15.10 provides information on some of

the girth measurements. A half-measure ruler (on which the measurements are already doubled) can be used, or the total circumference is calculated with a calculator or mentally, before recording in the comments page.

Traditionally, measurement for knits and sweaters is the side-to-side measurement, or *half-measure*. This applies to all categories—men's, women's and children's—and most companies follow this procedure (see Figure 15.11). Points of measure are one of the most important methods of communicating details, especially pattern details. Every company has a skeleton or two in its closet concerning a garment that had a mismatch between the points of measure and the fit. One of the most distressing ones involves the rise on a pant, whether it's measured "to seam" or "to top."

Figure 15.12 shows where the front rise was intended to be measured to seam (7 inches). The front rise does not include waistband height; the waistband is added on top of that for a total of $9^{1}/_{2}$ inches. Somehow the factory misunderstood and made the front rise of the pant 7 inches total, to the top of the waistband. Even supposing that is an acceptable front rise length for certain low-rise garment styles, the waist would be far too small at that point. The zipper would be too long, among other problems, and it would be hard to imagine how to salvage this production run. Luckily such problems can be avoided by careful definitions of the points of measure from the first proto stage and by not changing the point of measure definitions late in the approval process.

EXAMPLE FOR WOVEN SHIRT:
1. EDGE TO EDGE CHEST MEASUREMENT IS 25".
2. THAT IS DOUBLED, AND CHEST SPEC IS 50"

WHOLE MEASURE--
MEASURE ACROSS,
THEN DOUBLE

HALF MEASURE--
MEASURE ACROSS

Figure 15.10 Whole measure and half measure.

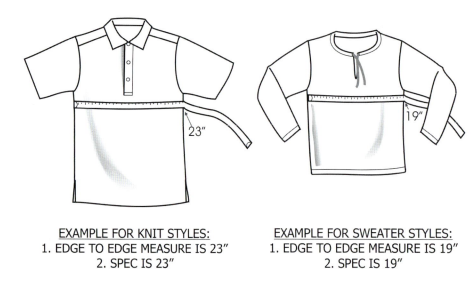

EXAMPLE FOR KNIT STYLES:
1. EDGE TO EDGE MEASURE IS 23"
2. SPEC IS 23"

EXAMPLE FOR SWEATER STYLES:
1. EDGE TO EDGE MEASURE IS 19"
2. SPEC IS 19"

Figure 15.11 Half measure: knits and sweaters.

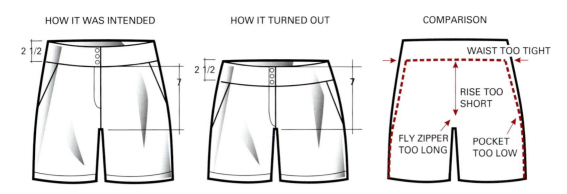

Figure 15.12 **Clearly defined points of measure help avoid problems.**

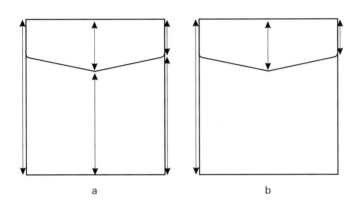

Figure 15.13 **Specify specs logically.**

Just as important as ensuring clear points of measure is avoiding too many points of measure. Many points of measure are standard, but detail measurements must be added, depending on individual style. Generally, out of all measurements possible, enough should be chosen to get the job done without the possibility of contradictions. Figure 15.13 shows a pocket and flap. Figure 15.13a shows every vertical measurement possible and Figure 15.13b shows three that define all of them and are the only three that are necessary. Over-specifying (see Figure 15.13a) can cause unnecessary work and confusion, and can be just as problematic as under-specifying.

Measurement Guide for XYZ Product Development, Inc.

The following is an example of a standard measurement guide for tops and bottoms of different types. The measuring information is based on our fictitious company, XYZ Product Development, Inc. Each company has its own set rules, and XYZ Product Development's set is typical of the industry.

Companies develop a manual of standards, which is sent to the factories and followed by everyone who measures garments to ensure that the factory and the design and technical staff are all following the same methods and terminology. Although it may seem long, this set of measurements is actually quite simple and concentrates on points of measure that get graded (points of measure that change to create different sizes). Generally, the measurement process begins at the top of the garment and works toward the bottom. The basic points of measure are laid out accordingly.

Unless a measurement is specifically a back detail, the girth measurements are taken from the front. Many back measurements can be measured from the front, such as back length from HPS (it is easy to lift up the hem while measuring front length, and check the back length). Figure 15.7 shows the back neck drop measured by the method explained. The garment will then not have to be repositioned so often.

Measurement Guide for Tops for XYZ Product Development, Inc.

As previously noted, measurements marked girth measurements are measured differently between wovens (full-measure) and knits and sweaters (half-measure). The other points of measure are all the same. It is not unusual for a company manual to have gaps in the sequence of codes, where new points of measure are added and obsolete ones deleted.

Points of Measure for Basic Tops

The first set, T-A through T-O, are the basic garment measurements for tops (see Figure 15.14).

- *T-A. Shoulder Point to Point* (see Figures 15.14a and 15.14c): Measure straight across the shoulders from shoulder point to shoulder point where the shoulder fold meets the top of the armhole.
- *T-B. Shoulder Drop* (see Figure 15.14d): Measure the height distance from HPS shoulder to shoulder point, squared across.
- *T-C. Front (across)* (see Figure 15.14c): Locate measuring position from HPS, at front (such as across front at 8 inches from HPS). Measure straight across front, seam to seam, or edge to edge as noted.
- *T-D. Back (across)* (see Figure 15.14d): Locate measuring position from HPS, at back, (such as across back at 8 inches from HPS). Measure straight across back of shirt, seam to seam or edge to edge as noted.
- *T-G. Armhole Drop, Set-In, Raglan, or Saddle* (see Figures 15.14a and 15.14d): Measure from HPS to underarm point, squared across.
- *T-H. Chest Girth Measurement* (see Figures 15.14a and 15.14c): Measure straight across chest from side to side, 1 inch below armholes.
- *T-I. Waist Position* (see Figure 15.14c): Measure from HPS to waist position (as noted on spec).

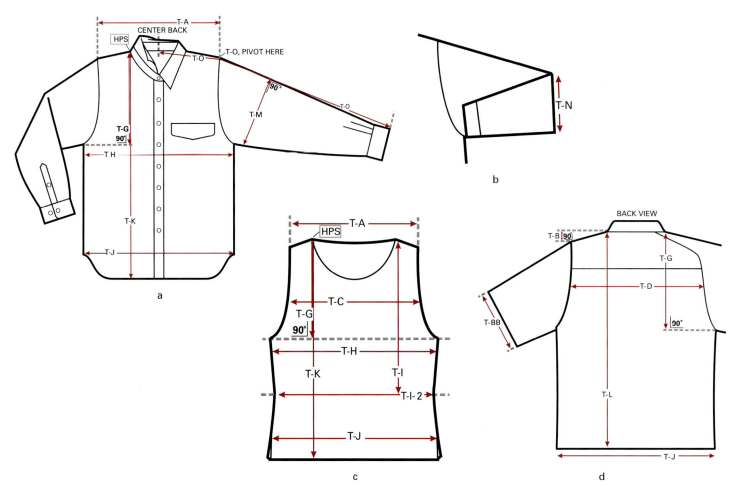

Figure 15.14 Basic garment measurements for tops.

- *T-I-2. Waist Girth Measurement* (see Figure 15.14c): Measure across waist from edge to edge at designated waist position.
- *T-J. Bottom Opening Girth Measurement* (see Figures 15.14a, 15.14c, and 15.14d): Measure straight across bottom from edge to edge. For garments with shirttails or side slits, measure at top of shirttail curve or slit, straight across from edge to edge.
- *T-K. Front Length* (see Figure 15.14a): Measure at front HPS to bottom edge of hem, parallel to center front (CF).
- *T-L. Back Length* (see Figure 15.14d): Measure at back from HPS to bottom edge of hem, parallel to center back.
- *T-M. Bicep Girth Measurement* (see Figure 15.14a): Measure from 1 inch below armhole, squared across (at a 90 degree angle to the folded edge).
- *T-N. Elbow Girth Measurement* (see Figure 15.14b): Align end of sleeve with underarm seam, then measure across at fold.
- *T-O. Center Back Sleeve Length, 3 Point* (see Figure 15.14a): Measure from center of neck seam straight to shoulder point, pivot, and then measure straight to bottom of sleeve.

Points of Measure for Neck and Collar

T-P through T-W are neck and collar variations (see Figure 15.15).

- *T-P. Front Neck Drop* (see Figures 15.15a and 15.15c): Place a ruler across neck width from HPS to HPS. From that center point, measure down to neck seam or neck edge, as specified.
- *T-Q. Back Neck Drop* (see Figure 15.15b): Place a ruler across neck width from HPS to HPS. From that center point measure

down to neck seam or neck edge, as specified. This can also be measured from front (see Figure 15.7).

- *T-R. Neck Width* (see Figures 15.15b and 15.15c): Measure straight from HPS at left to HPS at right.
- *T-S. Collar Spread* (see Figure 15.15e): With all buttons closed and collars lying relaxed, measure across from collar tip to collar tip.
- *T-T. Collarband Length* (see Figure 15.15d): With neckband unbuttoned and flat, measure along center of neckband from outside end of buttonhole to center of button, following contour of band.
- *T-U. Neck Band Height* (see Figure 15.15d): Measure from neck joining seam to collar joining seam at center back.
- *T-V. Center Back Collar Height* (see Figure 15.15d): Measure from neck joining seam to upper edge of collar at center back.
- *T-W. Collar Point* (see Figure 15.15d and 15.16b): With collar flipped up, measure from collar joining seam to outer edge of collar along collar point edge. If the collar point is rounded, measure to collar end before it is rounded.

Points of Measure for Collar Variations and Lapels for Tops

Figure 15.16 illustrates the points of measure for collar variations and garments with lapels. Figure 15.16a shows a collar with a center front zipper, and Figure15.16b shows a tailored collar.

- *T-P-2. Front Neck Drop to Top Button* (see Figure 15.16b): For tailored collar, place a ruler across neck width from HPS to HPS. Measure down to center of top button.

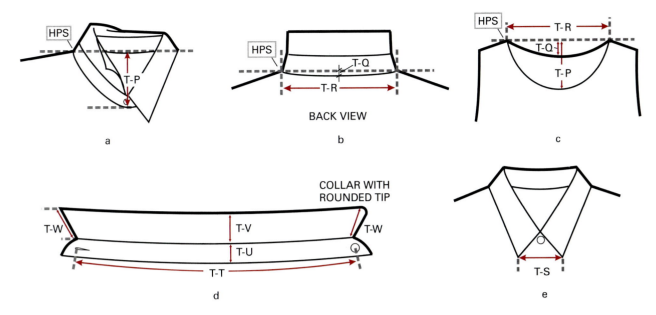

Figure 15.15 Basic measurements for neck and collar variations.

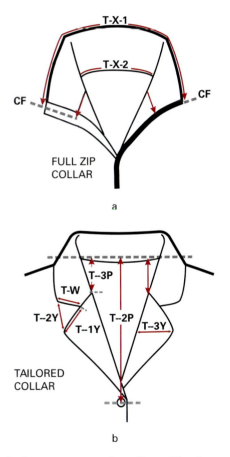

Figure 15.16 Basic measurements for collar and lapel.

- *T-P-3. Gorge Position* (see Figure 15.16b): Measure from HPS to gorge at roll line.
- *T-X-1. Collar Length at Top* (see Figure 15.16a): Measure from one end of collar to other, at outside edge, CF to CF.
- *T-X-2. Collar Length at Neck Seam* (see Figure 15.16a): Measure from one end of the collar to the other, at neck edge, CF to CF.
- *T-Y-1. Lapel Point* (see Figure 15.16b): Measure from lapel point to seam (the seam that joins collar to lapel).

- *T-Y-2. Lapel Point to Collar Point* (see Figure 15.16b): Measure the distance between collar point and end of lapel.
- *T-Y-3. Lapel Width* (see Figure 15.16b): Measure from roll line to lapel point, perpendicular to center front.

Points of Measure for Sleeve Openings and Cuffs for Tops

Figure 15.17 shows each point of measure for the following cuffs.

- *T-Z-1. Sleeve Opening, Relaxed Girth Measurement* (see Figures 15.17a, 15.17b, and 15.17c): Measure sleeve at bottom, edge to edge, with elastic or knit relaxed. For garment with button cuff, measure cuff at bottom, edge to edge with cuff buttoned and flat.
- *T-Z-2. Sleeve Opening, Extended Girth Measurement* (see Figure 15.17d): Measure sleeve at bottom, edge to edge, with elastic stretched.
- *T-Z-3. Sleeve at Cuff Seam* (see Figure 15.17b): Measure sleeve edge to edge at cuff joining seam.
- *T-AA. Cuff Height* (see Figures 15.17a and 15.17b): Measure from cuff joining seam to bottom edge of cuff.
- *T-BB. Sleeve Opening, Short Sleeve Girth Measurement* (see Figure 15.14d): Measure edge to edge of sleeve opening, fold edge to underarm edge

Points of Measure for Pockets and Hoods for Tops

Figure 15.18 illustrates points of measure for hoods (a) and pockets (b) for tops.

- *T-DD-1. Chest Pocket Placement* (see Figure 15.18b): Measure from HPS to top edge.
- *T-DD-2. Chest Pocket Placement* (see Figure 15.18b): Measure from edge of pocket to center front.
- *T-EE. Hood Height* (see Figure 15.18a): Mark HPS position, then align neck seams of hood and lay hood flat. Measure at front of hood from neck seam at HPS to fold at top of hood.
- *T-FF. Hood Width* (see Figure 15.18a): Align neck seams of hood and lay hood flat. Measure across widest part of hood from front edge to fold at center back edge.

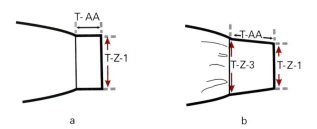

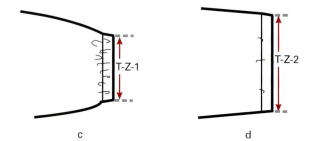

Figure 15.17 Basic measurements for cuffs.

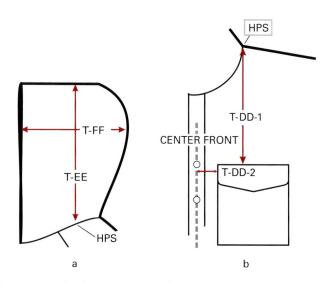

Figure 15.18 Basic measurements for hood and pocket.

Points of Measure for Bottoms for XYZ Product Development, Inc.

Measurements marked *girth* will be *full measure* for wovens and *half measure* for knits and sweaters. Sweater bottoms are rather rare, with the exception of skirts.

Points of Measure for Bottom Body Specs

Figures 15.19 and 15.20 provide illustrations of points of measure for skirt specs. Figure 15.21 illustrates points of measure for pants specs.

- *B-A. Waist, Relaxed Girth Measurement* (see Figures 15.19a and 15.19e): Measure across top of waistband from edge to edge. For contour waist, measure curve of garment at top.
- *B-B. Waist, Stretched Girth Measurement* (see Figure 15.19e): Measure across top of waistband, fully extended, from edge to edge.
- *B-D. Front Waist Drop, Skirt* (see Figure 15.20): With garment front side up, place ruler across waistband from side to side. Measure down from center of this line to top of skirt front.
- *B-E. Back Waist Drop, Skirt* (not shown): With garment front side down, place ruler across waistband from side to side. Measure down from center of this line to the top of skirt back.

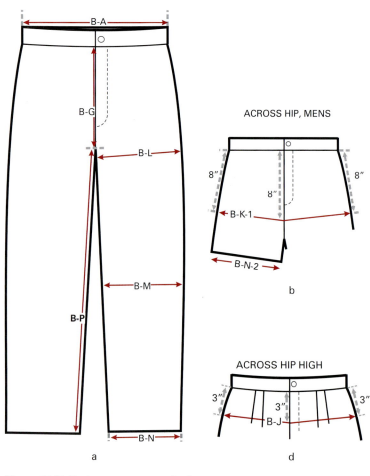

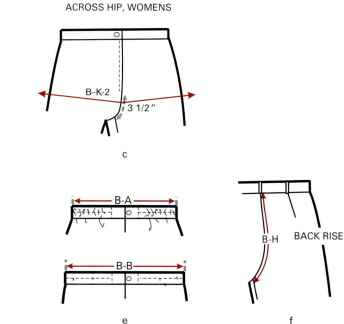

Figure 15.19 Basic measurements for bottoms.

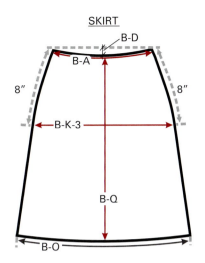

Figure 15.20 **Basic measurements for skirts.**

- *B-G. Front Rise* (see Figure 15.19a): Lay garment flat. Measure from crotch point to waistband seam with rise seam flat. For pant with no waistband, measure to top edge.

- *B-H. Back Rise* (see Figure 15.19f): Measure on curve from waistband seam to crotch point. For pant with gusset, measure to gusset joint. For pant with no waistband, measure to top edge.

- *B-J. Across High Hip Girth Measurement* (see Figure 15.19d): Use three-point measure technique by marking 3 inches below waist seam at center front and 3 inches below waist seam at each side seam. Measure from edge, to CF point, to edge. If front has pleats, measure *without* spreading pleats.

- *B-K-1. Across Hip, Pant Girth Measurement (Men's Method)* (see Figure 15.19b): Use three-point measure technique by marking 8 inches below waist seam at center front and 8 inches below waist seam at each edge of garment. Measure from edge to edge to center front, with all fullness spread.

- *B-K-2. Across Hip at 3¹/₂ Inches up From Crotch Point—Girth Measurement (Women's Method)* (see Figure 15.19c): Using the three-point technique, measure in a slight V along crossgrain from edge to center front to edge, at the point 3¹/₂ inches up from inseam.

- *B-K-3. Across Hip, Skirt Girth Measurement* (see Figure 15.20): At 8 inches down side seams from waist seam, measure from edge to edge, straight across.

- *B-L. Thigh Girth Measurement* (see Figure 15.19a): Measure across leg from edge to edge along crossgrain 1 inch below crotch point.

- *B-M. Knee Girth Measurement* (see Figure 15.19a): Measure across leg from edge to edge 16 inches below crotch for men's garments and 13 inches below crotch for women's garments.

- *B-N. Leg Opening, Long Pants Girth Measurement* (see Figure 15.19a): Measure along bottom opening from edge to edge.

- *B-N-2. Leg Opening, Short Inseams Girth Measurement* (see Figure 15.19b): Measure along bottom opening from edge to edge.

- *B-O. Bottom Opening, Skirt Girth Measurement* (see Figure 15.20): Measure along bottom edge following contour of hem with bottom edges together, with vent or slit in place.

- *B-P. Inseam* (see Figure 15.19a): Measure from crotch point to bottom edge, on inside leg seam.

- *B-Q. Skirt Length* (see Figure 15.20): Measure from waistband seam to hem at center front. For skirt without waistband, measure to top edge.

A few measurement techniques for skirts are different from those for pants. For skirts, the hip measurement method is a straight line, not a three-point measurement (see Figure 15.20). There is also a measurement for front waist drop and back waist drop. (Pants use the rise measurement to regulate how high or low the rise will sit, so they don't need front waist drop.)

Points of Measure for Detail Specs for Bottoms

Figure 15.21 illustrates the method for basic measurements for some pant or skirt design details.

- *B-T. Pocket Opening* (see Figure 15.21b): Measure opening from edge to edge. If bartacked, measure area between bartacks. If riveted, measure area between rivets.

- *B-U. Pleat Depth* (see Figure 15.21a): Measure into pleat to the fold.

- *B-V. Vent or Slit Height* (see Figure 15.21c): Measure from pleat opening to bottom.

Points of Measure for Underwear for XYZ Product Development, Inc.

Figure 15.22 illustrates for basic measurements for underwear. Underwear is measured half measure, and the girth measurements will not need doubling. The following does not note which measurements are girth measurements.

- *U-A. Waist, Relaxed* (see Figure 15.22a): Measure across top of waistband from edge to edge. For contour waist, measure curve of garment at top.

- *U-B. Waist, Stretched* (not shown): Measure across top of waistband, fully extended, from edge to edge.

- *U-L. Thigh* (see Figure 15.22e): Measure across leg from edge to edge 1 inch below rise seam, at right angles to side seam.

- *U-N. Leg Opening* (see Figure 15.22e): Measure along bottom hem from edge to edge.

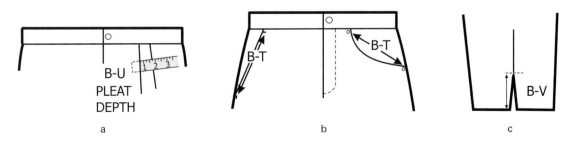

Figure 15.21 **Basic measurements for design details.**

BRIEF

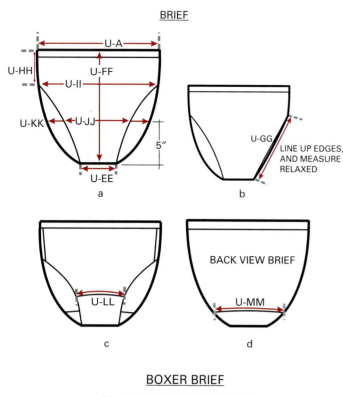

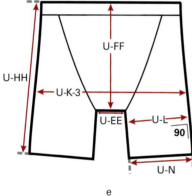

BOXER BRIEF

Figure 15.22 Basic measurements for underwear.

- *U-EE. Brief Crotch Width* (see Figures 15.22a and 15.22e): Measure along the natural crotch fold line from edge to edge.
- *U-FF. Brief Rise* (see Figure 15.22e): Align front to back at waist. Measure from top to bottom of crotch fold line, without stretching.
- *U-GG. Brief Leg Opening* (see Figure 15.22b): Line up edges, then measure straight, without stretching.
- *U-HH. Brief Side Seam* (see Figures 15.22a and 15.22e): Measure from top edge to top of leg opening along side seam.
- *U-II. Brief Width at Top of Leg Opening* (see Figure 15.22a): Measure across at top of leg opening.
- *U-JJ. Brief Width Front, 5 Inches up From Crotch Fold* (see Figure 15.22a): Measure across at lower front, at a point 5 inches up from crotch fold.
- *U-KK. Brief Width Back, 5 Inches up From Crotch Fold* (see Figure 15.22a): Measure across at lower back, at a point 5 inches up from crotch fold.
- *U-LL. Brief Width Front, at Crotch Seam* (see Figure 15.22c): For garments with a crotch seam, measure across front, at seam.
- *U-MM. Brief Width Back, at Crotch Seam* (see Figure 15.22d): For garments with a crotch seam, measure across back, at seam.

Points of Measure for Socks for XYZ Product Development, Inc.

Figure 15.23a illustrates sock terminology and Figures 15.23b and 15.23c show basic measurements for socks.

- *S-A. Leg Length* (see Figure 15.23b): Measure from top of sock to bottom of heel, past last gore hole.
- *S-B. Foot Length* (see Figure 15.23c): Measure from center of toe to heel end of sock, past last gore hole.
- *S-C. Welt at Top* (see Figure 15.23c): Measure across, edge to edge.
- *S-D. Leg Across, 1 Inch From Bottom of Welt* (see Figure 15.23c): Measure across edge to edge 1 inch below the bottom of rib section.

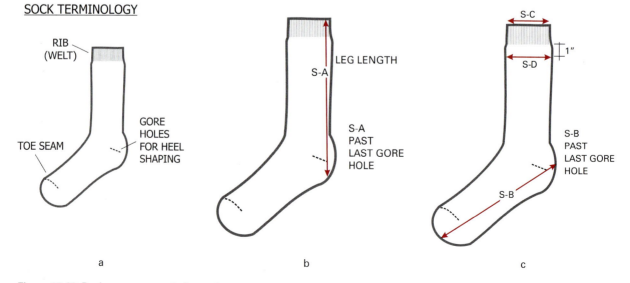

Figure 15.23 Basic measurements for socks.

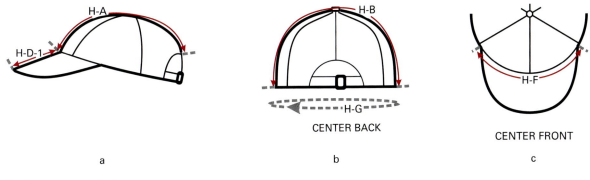

Figure 15.24 **Basic measurements for caps.**

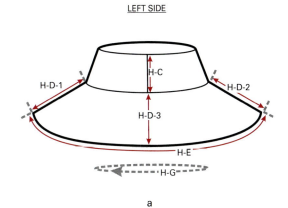

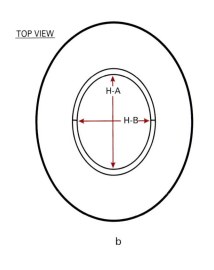

Figure 15.25 **Basic measurements for hats.**

Points of Measure for Hats for XYZ Product Development, Inc.

Figure 15.24 and Figure 15.25 illustrate basic measurements for the two most common styles of headwear, caps and hats.

- *H-A. Crown Length Front to Back* (see Figures 15.24a and 15.25b): Measure front to back, seam to seam.
- *H-B. Crown Width Side to Side* (see Figures 15.24b and 15.25b): Measure side to side, seam to seam, or edge to edge.
- *H-C. Crown Height at Side* (see Figure 15.25a): Measure top to bottom at side.
- *H-D-1. Brim or Bill at Center Front* (see Figure 15.24a): Measure outer edge to seam.
- *H-D-2. Brim Center Back* (see Figure 15.25a): Measure outer edge to seam.
- *H-D-3. Brim at Sides* (see Figure 15.25a): Measure outer edge to seam.
- *H-E. Brim* (see Figure 15.25a): Measure at outer edge of brim CF to CB. Note: This is half measure of total brim circumference.
- *H-F. Bill Width* (see Figure 15.24c): Measure along seam, edge to edge.
- *H-G. Inside Circumference* (see Figures 15.24b and 15.25a): Measure using hat ring.

Working with the Technical Package

When the first proto arrives from the factory, the garment is measured and checked against the specs. The comparison measurements are recorded on the fit history page in the tech pack (see Figure 3.13 in Chapter 3).

Keeping the Fit History

Measuring the garment is the first step for evaluating it. Figure 15.26 shows a simple style of hat, which has few points of measure and simple fitting requirements. All the steps are represented, and the same procedure holds true for any style, whether a hat or the most complicated evening gown.

In the measuring process it is important to answer the question "compared to what?" and to determine whether any points of measure need adjusting. In Table 15.2, column A has the points of measure code and column B has the points of measure descriptions. Columns C and D are the standard tolerances and column E contains the sample specs, the same ones that were sent to the factory along with the original sample request. That is what the sample *should* measure.

Column F will contain the *actual* measurements of the newly arrived first proto sample, measured by the designer or technical designer. Column G is how much the garment is off spec, if at all, for each point of measure. Notes in column H will have the codes for how to proceed and column I will hold the measurements for the next proto sample. The factory often sends its own measurements along with the sample; the value of that information is to see whether the factory is measuring the same way. If there is a large difference between the company measurements and the factory measurements, it means that there is some misunderstanding about how to measure, a problem that should be addressed right away. The code for the notes, or what to do next time, are *OK*, meaning on spec; *RTS*, meaning return to spec; and *Revise*, meaning we are revising the original spec for this point of measure.

Table 15.2 is the same measurement history sheet with the figures filled in. The dates have been added as well, telling us that the sample request went out January 2, and the first proto was

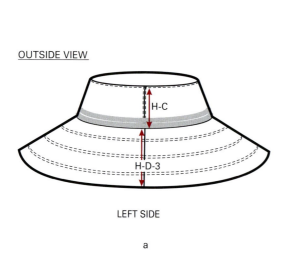

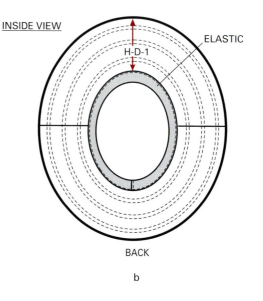

Figure 15.26 Hat example: first proto for measuring.

returned three weeks later on January 22, about average turn-around time. It also shows that the samples were measured that same day, and the comments were finished the next day.

The fit history is quite interesting, and we can see by comparing columns E and F that the factory made the brim the same size all around (3 inches), which is not correct. One of the features of this hat is that it has extra shade coverage in back, so clearly H-D-2 Brim at Center Back will need to be corrected for the next sample and will need to be returned to spec of 4 inches, as noted by RTS, column H, code H-D-2. We will review the brim points of measure and follow them through all of the steps for one prototype. The three brim measurements are H-D-1, Brim at CF; H-D-2, Brim at CB; and H-D-3, Brim at Sides.

In Table 15.4, column G shows how much the factory's sample is off and calculates the difference in the sample spec (what was requested) and the first proto (what was received).

Writing Comments

In addition to the measurement evaluation, other aspects of the sample hat are reviewed, such as the topstitching, details, and colorway. These notations will go into the sample evaluation comments. Writing comments is a balance between saying enough to be clear and not adding unnecessary information.

The following is an example of comments for this hat (see spec in Table 15.5) that are confusing, and a mix between overly wordy and overly abbreviated:

> Please note that we would like to make some modifications to the hat brim. Sending smpl for ref. It is for general brim construction, and not for fabric or for st'ing. The brim s/b made without any binding at edge, just an enclosed seam. Once you have a chance to review it, let me know if you have any questions or if you anticipate any problems making this change. Note that the topstitching at the crown is incorrect, and should be straddle stitch, centered over the seam, i/o 2-needle with both threads toward the back like this one. We have to have the straddle stitch for consistency. Also the bottom of the brim is supposed to be honeycomb shell color, was that avail? Did you use the bamboo color as a sub? Let me know about that. Also the elastic hatband inside is black, and it is supposed to be tan. Is it sub? The brim length in

back is supposed to be 4" in back and this sample is only three, so make sure you rev that for next smpl.

The "brim length in back" information is already in the fit history, and individual points of measure corrections do not need to be recapped here, unless there is some other point to be made.

Table 15.6 is an example of acceptable fit comments, and shows the format for our first proto hat comments. This format for the comments page helps to break the comments into more concise phrases, rather like an outline. In the Area column, the subject and location on the garment are given. The Problem column shows the trouble and the Solution column shows how to correct it. All the same points are addressed as in the poorly written comments example, but in a simpler way in which the conclusions and action points are clearly spelled out. Adding a reference to the place on the tech pack where a person can double-check helps to ensure that the person reading the comments understands.

It is good to have certain stock phrases that can be used all the time for situations that arise frequently. It is better to use short, simple sentences or phrases for giving directions and use capital letters to begin a sentence, periods to end a sentence, and proper spelling, so the nonnative English speaker reading it can understand the directions without ambiguity. It is a good practice to avoid idiomatic phrases (for example, rather than "We have to have," using "We need" is more direct and clear). Abbreviations can be used to simplify commenting as long as all the abbreviations are known and agreed upon. CF for center front, CB for center back, sub for substitution can all be used as long as they are part of the established set of abbreviations, which companies usually list in the vendor manual. If everyone knows s/b stands for should be and i/o stands for instead of, it saves time; if not, it creates confusion.

Many countries have a more formal social structure than that of the United States and a more polite method of expressing themselves. It is common to read comments such as "Please kindly confirm" and to be addressed as "Dear" before your name. The tone is very calm and reasonable, and one should reply the same way. It is best to wait until something serious goes wrong before pulling out the *underlining*, **boldface**, ALL CAPS, and exclamation points! The factory is an important partner in the process and its employees are probably set up to manufacture in a certain way. If a detail can be changed as they suggest, it will speed the garment's process through their factory.

Table 15.2 XYZ Product Development, Fit History

A	B	C	D	E	F	G	H	I
Code	Hat Spec Measurements	Tol (+)	Tol (−)	Spec	1st Proto Meas	Difference	Notes	Spec for 2nd Proto
H–A	Crown length front to back	$\frac{1}{4}$	$\frac{1}{4}$					
H–B	Crown width side to side	$\frac{1}{4}$	$\frac{1}{4}$					
H–C	Crown height at side (at seam)	$\frac{1}{4}$	$\frac{1}{4}$					
H–D–1	Brim or bill at center front	$\frac{1}{4}$	$\frac{1}{4}$					
H–D–2	Brim center back	$\frac{1}{4}$	$\frac{1}{4}$					
H–D–3	Brim at sides	$\frac{1}{4}$	$\frac{1}{4}$					
H–E	Brim circumference (half)	$\frac{1}{4}$	$\frac{1}{4}$					
H–G	Inside circumference, w/hat meas	$\frac{1}{4}$	$\frac{1}{4}$					

Table 15.3 XYZ Development, Fit History Completed

A	B	C	D	E	F	G	H	I
	Fit History	Dates: 1/2/XX	1/22/XX	1/22/XX	1/23/XX	1/23/XX		
Code	Hat Spec Measurements	Tol (+)	Tol (−)	Spec	1st Proto Meas	Difference	Notes	Spec for 2nd Proto
H–A	Crown length front to back	$\frac{1}{4}$	$\frac{1}{4}$	$7\frac{1}{8}$	$6\frac{7}{8}$	$-\frac{1}{4}$	RTS	$7\frac{1}{8}$
H–B	Crown width side to side	$\frac{1}{4}$	$\frac{1}{4}$	$5\frac{1}{2}$	$5\frac{3}{8}$	$-\frac{1}{8}$	RTS	$5\frac{1}{2}$
H–C	Crown height at side (at seam)	$\frac{1}{4}$	$\frac{1}{4}$	$3\frac{1}{2}$	$3\frac{1}{2}$	0	OK	$3\frac{1}{2}$
H–D–1	Brim or bill at center front	$\frac{1}{4}$	$\frac{1}{4}$	$3\frac{1}{8}$	3	$-\frac{1}{8}$	Revise	3
H–D–2	Brim center back	$\frac{1}{4}$	$\frac{1}{4}$	4	3	−1	RTS	4
H–D–3	Brim at sides	$\frac{1}{4}$	$\frac{1}{4}$	$3\frac{1}{8}$	3	$-\frac{1}{8}$	Revise	3
H–E	Brim circumference (half)	$\frac{1}{4}$	$\frac{1}{4}$	21	$21\frac{1}{2}$	$+\frac{1}{2}$	RTS	21
H–G	Inside circumference, w/hat meas	$\frac{1}{4}$	$\frac{1}{4}$	$22\frac{3}{4}$	$22\frac{1}{8}$	$-\frac{5}{8}$	RTS	$22\frac{3}{4}$

Table 15.6 Examples of Acceptable Hat Comments

A	B	C	D	E	F	G	H	I
Code	Hat Spec Measurements	Tol (+)	Tol (−)	Spec	1st Proto Meas	Difference	Notes	Spec for 2nd Proto
H–D–1	Brim or bill at center front	$\frac{1}{4}$	$\frac{1}{4}$	$3\frac{1}{8}$	3	$-\frac{1}{8}$	Revise	3
H–D–2	Brim center back	$\frac{1}{4}$	$\frac{1}{4}$	4	3	−1	RTS	4
H–D–3	Brim at sides	$\frac{1}{4}$	$\frac{1}{4}$	$3\frac{1}{8}$	3	$-\frac{1}{8}$	Revise	3

Table 15.5 Spec Comparisons

A	B	C	D	E	F
Code	Hat Spec Measurements	Tol(+)	Tol(−)	Spec	1st Proto Meas
H–D–1	Brim or bill at center front	$\frac{1}{4}$	$\frac{1}{4}$	$3\frac{1}{8}$	3
H–D–2	Brim center back	$\frac{1}{4}$	$\frac{1}{4}$	4	3
H–D–3	Brim at sides	$\frac{1}{4}$	$\frac{1}{4}$	$3\frac{1}{8}$	3

Table 15.6 Examples of Acceptable Hat Comments

Area	Problem	Solution
Crown at side seams	Sample topstitching is 2N—¼" toward back. That is incorrect.	Return to ¼" straddle stitch, see sketch, page 1.
Bottom brim	Sample is color A. That is incorrect.	Please make bottom brim color B, see colorway information, page 1.
Elastic band	Sample is black.	Should be tan, see colorway summary BOM page. Please advise if the black is a substitution.
Brim construction	Sample has binding at outer edge. That is incorrect.	No binding, make clean finished enclosed seam. Sending sample to you for reference, Fedex AWB# 1234-?5678-?9897. Pls return sample when finished reviewing it. See sketch page 1 for finished appearance.

Table 15.6 shows that a solution to the topstitching problem was offered. The factory sewed the 2-needle topstitch toward the back because that is stronger than a straddlestitch. After evaluating it, the specs can be revised same as sample or returned to the original topstitching method, whichever is in keeping with the function and design of the hat. A hat does not entail a great deal of fitting on a fit model because it has only one main fit point, the inside circumferences, but it should still be tried on a person with the appropriate head size. Garments have many more points of measure than the hat example, but the process of measuring, evaluating, fitting, and commenting has all of the same steps.

Developing Knock-Offs

Companies often use garments from other companies for reference. It is helpful to study a sleeve, pant leg shape, collar, or other details at close range rather than just through a magazine photograph. In that way more precise measurements can be arrived at and adapted as needed. Some companies go further and produce styles called **knock-offs**, which are close facsimiles of the original, generally in cheaper fabrics and trims and offered to the mass market at a much lower cost.

Designs are difficult to patent because it is widely acknowledged that most ideas have been seen in the market in some incarnation or other in the past and not that much is truly new. Thus, in the United States and many other countries, after a design is shown on the runway, it is considered to be public domain. What is new each season is a color, attached to a silhouette, attached to a fabric that has a fresh look that captures the imagination and sense of the moment. That is not easy to patent, nor would it be worthwhile because the design is subject to change the next season. Nonetheless, some elements of a design are occasionally patented, usually a detail or functional element; an example is a pocket that zips off and is also watertight. Such elements have less to do with fashion and more with technology. Copyright is a different protection, one that would apply to visual or graphic elements such as a logo, print, or fabric pattern.

A knock-off that is an exact copy, including the label and logos, is a counterfeit and is clearly illegal. The demand for certain high-end brands is so great that some manufacturers produce them illicitly and sell them outside the usual retail distribution channels, such as through street vendors and other more shady venues. A reputable retailer would not sell this type of item.

If a new style comes onto the market and is in great demand, a version of it may arrive in the design department as an inspiration. It would be unusual to copy it precisely as an exact knock-off. It is much more likely to be adapted into the apparel company's sample size, adjusted for silhouette, measured, and fit on a fit model to make sure it will be attractive and flattering to the customer in question.

Such an adaptation should be treated similar to a first fit sample and measured, reviewed, and adapted into a tech pack format, the same as any new style. Figure 15.27a shows the original style, a silk charmeuse slipdress for evening from a boutique in Los Angeles. Figure 15.27b shows the adaptation, which uses the general ideas, seaming, and strap shape. It is now appropriate for the missy customer for whom it is intended and the tech pack can be sent out to get the style produced as a first proto. Thereafter, all the other development steps will proceed as for any other style.

The steps it has undergone are:

- The bust, waist, and hip measurements are adapted to fit the XYZ Product Development sample size 8, with the fit and details easier for that customer to wear.
- The thigh-high slit is now two shorter side seam slits.
- The plunging neckline is adapted and raised, allowing a bra to be worn while retaining the characteristic U shape.

a   b

Figure 15.27 Style adapted from original designer garment (a) for XYZ's mass market customer (b).

- The straps are slightly less exaggerated.
- The length is slightly shorter.
- The fabric is a synthetic charmeuse rather than silk charmeuse.

The original dress in Figure 15.27a is bright turquoise, which is not in the XYZ palette this season. Colors offered for the dress in Figure 15.27b will be black, white, and lavendrine. In this way the style is made workable for the target customer, and is adapted to reach its sales goals.

Size Charts

There are a great many ways of sorting various types of garments, including categories based on gender, height, body type, and age. Some are high volume, some are specialty, and some are niche. Sizing designations for each category are consistent throughout the apparel industry, but the measurements for each size vary from one producer to another.

Missy Size Chart

A great many shapes and sizes are accommodated in the missy category, an example of a high-volume size range. This customer is average height (around 5 feet, 6 inches) and the range is from size 2 or 4 to size 18 or 20. What do those sizes actually mean? What is a size 8? Although every company has a slightly different answer to that question, Table 15.7 shows typical missy sizes. Since there are no mandatory regulations, a new company just starting out could say "a size 8 is what I say it is." However, if they fail to deliver the fit their customer is looking for, they will not be very successful. For that reason, companies try to follow the lead of others in their field.

As with all size charts, the numbers represent body (not garment) measurements. The vast majority of missy size charts will follow within 1 inch of any of the measurements shown. There has been a gradual shift in the past couple of decades toward more generous sizing. Two identical dress forms from different eras would have the same bust waist and hip measurements, but would be considered different sizes. Twenty years ago, what was a size 8 is now a size 6. It's a kind of size inflation, often called vanity sizing, as if we can't take the awful truth. A paper pattern from the 1950s would designate the size 8 measurements in our chart to be a size 14. Figure 15.28 compares two mannequins from different decades. Figure 15.28a is from the 1960s, Figure 15.28b is from 2010. Their measurements are nearly identical but in its day, the first was known as a size 10; the second is known these days as a size 6. There are other interesting differences as well. The so-called size 10 is more "filled in" right below the waist (through the high hip); the contemporary size 6 has a more gradual high hip shaping, ending in a 1-inch larger hip (38 inches rather than 37 inches) Nonetheless, this overall *proportion* is quite similar: the hip measurement for both is 2 inches or more larger than the bust and 9 inches to 10 inches larger than the waist.

In the past, there was more reliance on one ideal standard proportion. In the last few years more information has been assembled to support different "fit types." A company that has emerged as a leader in this field is Alvanon, Inc. Based on research from ASTM (formerly called American Society for Testing and Materials, now known as ASTM International), they have developed standards and actual mannequins for two distinct fit types: one called "straight" and one called "curvy." These describe the differences between hip and waist, the places with the greatest variation within any randomly chosen group of women (shown in Figure 15.29).

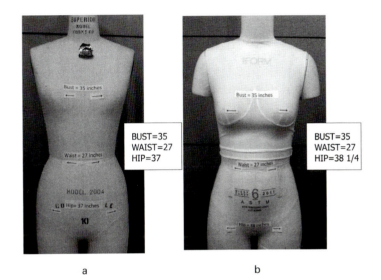

a   b

Figure 15.28 Comparison of dressform shapes: 1960s (a) and 2010s (b).

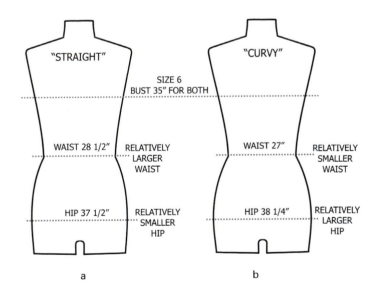

a   b

Figure 15.29 Comparison of dressforms: measurements.

Table 15.7   Missy Size Chart, XYZ Product Development, Inc.

(Alpha)	XS		S		M		L		XL	
(Numeric)	2	4	6	8	10	12	14	16	18	20
Bust	33	34	35	36	37	38½	40	41½	43½	45½
Waist	25	26	27	28	29	30½	32	33½	35½	37½
Hip	35	36	37	38	39	40½	42	43½	45½	47½

Are women's bodies actually changing with the generations, or are we just getting better at defining the differences? Different ethnic populations certainly have different shapes and many jeans manufacturers have begun adding such descriptions. With additional data that reflects things such as how the body changes as we age, apparel companies have the opportunity to further refine the fits their customers are seeking.

Sample Size

All apparel companies choose a certain size in which to develop their product and produce their samples. Theoretically, a size close to the middle of the size range would provide the most accurate costing and grading information. More often though, a smaller size is chosen so that the samples (generally shown flat on hangers) will have more appeal to buyers. For a missy 2–18 offering, size 10 is in the middle, but 8 or 6 is a more common choice for sample size.

There is a lot to be learned from size charts. The one in Table 15.7 combines two typical sizing standards: alpha, which goes by letters, and numeric. Unlike men's sizing, the numbers in the women's numeric chart are arbitrary and do not refer to an actual measurement of anything. Notice that each alpha size encompasses two of the numeric. The advantage to offering a style this way is that the retailer will not have to purchase as many stock-keeping units (SKUs) and the risk of unsold items is theoretically less. There is a possible disadvantage, which is if the garment is slim fitting, there may be too much difference between the sizes to fit everyone; for example, the medium may be too small for a certain customer and the large too big for her. That would definitely be the case for jeans and other bottom-weight pant styles, which would be offered in alpha sizes at the apparel company's peril, because too many customers could not find their size.

For alpha sizes there is sometimes confusion about which size to buy, especially for a mail-order customer. What is a medium, a 10, or a 12, or a size in between? Or a magical garment that shape-shifts according to the wearer? Because a person who reads the company size chart and determines that she is a size 12 (the upper side of the size range) has every right to suppose that it will fit her correctly, the wise company will make sure that a small is the same as an 8, the medium the same as a 12, and so on; in other words, to assign specs according to the upper end of the range. Because the size 6 person, the size 10 person, the size 14 person, and so on, do not really have their size represented in the alpha range, that sizing should be used only for styles where a precise fit does not matter, such as looser or baggier styles, in lighter weight and stretch fabrics.

Another interesting point about size charts is that they are a kind of simplified version of the company grade chart, which we examine at the end of this chapter. There is a 1-inch difference between girth measurements at the smaller end of the scale, from size 2 to size 10 (bust is 33-34-35-36, and so on). Then it accelerates to $1^1/_2$ inches between sizes 12 and 16, and at the upper end, there is a 2-inch difference between sizes, twice as much as at the lower end.

In the alpha size range, there is a 2-inch difference in girth between a 4 and an 8, but between an L and an XL, there are 4 inches. That makes fitting the size 18 person in an XL a bit of a challenge because she may really find herself between sizes. Therefore, it is even more important that styles offered in alpha sizing be chosen carefully, according to fabric and styling, and to be aware that they will not be workable for all styles.

It is also interesting to notice that **grade rules** (difference between sizes) have certain relationships that remain the same for all sizes. If the difference between hip and waist is 10 inches for a size 8 (for example 28 and 38), it remains 10 inches for larger and smaller sizes; the difference between hip and waist for the size 20 is also 10 inches, the same as for the size 4. That represents the average for all the women measured, and the majority of women fall into these proportions. That is how the sizes remain proportionate to each other. Figure 15.30a is a representation of all the Alvanon body proportions from size 00 to size 20. The bust, waist, and hip proportions (the differences between the numbers) are exactly the same for size 00 as they are for size 20.

That leaves a minority who have either more than 10 inches or less than 10 inches between their waist and hip measurements and may have more challenges in finding a good fit. Figure 15.30b shows common variations of body proportions when they are *not* average. Women outside this size chart in other dimensions (for example, smaller than size 2, taller than 5 feet, 8 inches) will also have challenges finding clothes to wear off the rack.

Petite Size Chart

Petite sizes are geared toward women approximately 4 feet 11 inches to 5 feet 3 inches. The principal areas of difference between missy and petite are inseam and sleeve length. Table 15.8 shows that all the girth measurements for petite sizes are slightly smaller across the board (1/2 inch smaller) than for missy. But the proportions between waist and hip and between waist and bust are exactly the same as for missy; the increments between the sizes are also exactly the same. The petites department is an important one for retailers because about half of all women are under 5 feet, 4 inches tall. Petite pant styles have not only a shorter inseam, but a proportionately shorter rise.

Tall Size Chart

Tall sizes are for women over 5 feet, 7 inches and have a T designation after the size. The size chart in Table 15.9 reflects the fact that there are very few size 2 women 5 feet, 7 inches or taller, so that size no longer appears on this chart. Because tall sizes are a smaller market than missy, they are often a sort of add-on to a brand's offering and only a certain percentage of styles will be chosen to produce in tall sizes—the ones that will flatter the taller figure. Pants in tall sizes also have a proportionately longer rise.

Women's or Plus Size Chart

Women's sizes, sometimes called plus sizes, are a growing market in the United States. The alpha sizes have 4-inch increments between sizes and the numeric sizes have 2-inch increments. There is also a size range known as women's petite sizes for large-size, shorter women.

When styling for these size ranges, it is important to define the figure type because large-size women tend to fall into different silhouettes: hourglass, pear, inverted triangle, or rectangle. The size chart in Table 15.10 is the standard one, based on an hourglass figure, and it has the same 10-inch difference between waist and hip as the missy size chart. Companies may revise it as appropriate to them, or more likely, try to accommodate their variety of customers through styling. For example, if there is a call for more garments to fit the rectangular body (one with a nearly

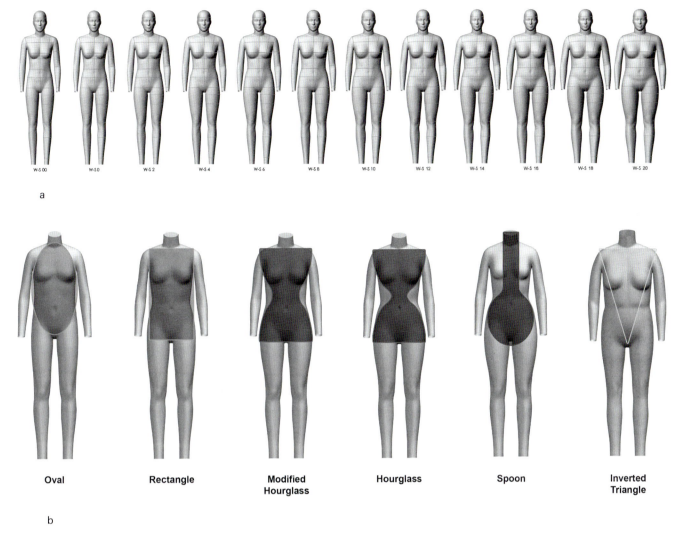

Figure 15.30 **Body proportions: Alvanon size 00 to 20 (a) and fit type variations (b).**
ASTM (a); Alvanon (b).

Table 15.8   Petite Size Chart, XYZ Product Development, Inc.

(Alpha)	XS		S		M		L		XL	
(Numeric)	2P	4P	6P	8P	10P	12P	14P	16P	18P	20P
Bust	32½	33½	34½	35½	36½	38	39½	41	43	45
Waist	24½	25½	26½	27½	28½	30	31½	33	35	37
Hip	34½	35½	36½	37½	38½	40	41¹¹½	43	45	47

Table 15.9   Tall Size Chart, XYZ Product Development, Inc.

(Alpha)	XS	S		M		L		XL	
(Numeric)	4T	6T	8T	10T	12T	14T	16T	18T	20T
Bust	33½	34½	35½	36½	38	39½	41	43	45
Waist	25½	26½	27½	28½	30	31½	33	35	37
Hip	35½	36½	37½	38½	40	41½	43	45	47

Table 15.10   Women's Plus Size Chart, XYZ Product Development, Inc.

(Alpha)	1X		2X		3X		4X	
(Numeric)	14W	16W	18W	20W	22W	24W	26W	28W
Bust	40	42	44	46	48	50	52	54
Waist	32½	34½	36½	38½	40½	42½	44½₂	46½
Hip	42½	44½	46½	48½	50½	52½	54½	56½

equal waist and hip), the solution may be to feature drawstring waists. That way the same style could fit all silhouettes, not only the rectangular and hourglass shape.

Junior Size Chart

The junior figure type encompasses a large age range and a time when the customer's size is changing. The customer is often a couple of inches shorter than her full adult height and is typically still smaller through the bust line; the difference between bust and hip is 31/2 inches, whereas in the missy range it is 2 inches. The waist is slightly smaller compared to the hip than on the missy chart, but only by 1/2 inch. Clothes in this size range are often geared toward a younger customer. Junior sizes are designated by odd numbers and missy sizes by even numbers to help customers distinguish them easily (Table 15.11).

Women's Panty Size Chart

Women's panty sizing is unique among the size charts and does not closely follow the missy chart (Table 15.12). For example, the customer with a 40-40 1/2" hip on Tables 15.6, 15.7, and 15.8 is considered a size 12. That same customer on the panty size chart is a size 7.

Men's Size Chart

Men's sizing has a couple of important size methods. Unlike women's sizing, men's sizes represent the actual measurement of the body, in inches, whether the neck size, chest size, or waist size.

Woven dress shirts are sized by neck circumference, by sleeve length, and sometimes by overall length. The neck is the only place where the shirt fits close to the body, and it can predict what the chest measurement should be. To actually offer sleeve lengths for all the collar sizes, a retailer would be required to offer an impressive array of SKUs—around 26. That would be to accommodate from neck size $14^1/_2$-sleeve length 32 to neck size $18^1/_2$-sleeve length 35, in regular only. If talls are added, the figure jumps to around 41 SKUs, and the range offered from a better men's retailer, which includes body lengths from 32 inches to 36 inches, will be around 87 SKUs—and that is in just one color. So to really offer even a good mid-range of sizes requires a store to maintain a lot of stock, which is one reason why men's dress shirts do not always have a lot of seasonal variety in styling.

Casual and knit tops (polo shirts, sleepwear, and underwear) are cut in alpha sizing. Men vary in height for the same girth more than they vary by categories, so it is more common to offer short, regular, and tall in pants. Men's tailored jackets run by chest measurement and height, such as 42 long, or 44 medium.

Pants are sized by waist size. Hip dimension is not usually noted on a men's size chart, but it is shown in Table 15.13 to compare proportions. It is interesting to note that for men, the chest and hip girth are the same up to size 44; after that the hip grows more slowly. The standard difference between hip and waist for women is 10 inches, and for men, as seen here, it is 6 inches. That is why unisex sizing is seldom successful, especially in bottoms. Because the size numbers are connected to an actual body dimension, it's somewhat harder to introduce the notion of vanity sizing for men: 34 inches is 34 inches. For that reason, men's sizing tends to be fairly consistent from brand to brand and decade to decade.

Table 15.11   Junior Size Chart, XYZ Product Development, Inc.

(Alpha)	XS		S		M		L		XL	
(Numeric)	00	0	1	3	5	7	9	11	13	15
Bust	29½	30½	31½	32½	33½	34½	35½	37	38½	40
Waist	22½	23½	24½	25½	26½	27½	28½	30	31½	33
Hip	33	34	35	36	37	38	39	40½	42	43½

Table 15.12   Women's Panties and Shapers, XYZ Product Development, Inc.

Panty Size	XS / 4	S / 5	M / 6	L / 7	XL / 8	2X / 9	3X / 10	4X / 11
Waist	23-24	25-26	27-28	29-30	31-32	33-34	35-36	37-38
Hip	34-35	36-37	38-39	40-41	42-43	44-45	46-47	48-49

Table 15.13   Men's Size Chart, XYZ Product Development, Inc.

(Alpha)	Small		Medium		Large		X-Large		XX-Large	
Shirts										
Neck (numeric)	14	14½	15	15½	16	16½	17	17½	18	18½
Chest (numeric)	34	36	38	40	42	44	46	48	50	52
Arm (reg)	32½	33	33½	34	34½	35	35½	36	36½	36½
Arm (tall)	34	34½	35	35½	36	36½	37	37½	38	38
Bottoms										
Waist (numeric)	28	30	32	34	36	38	40	42	44	46
Hip	34	36	38	40	42	44	45½	47	48½	50

Children's: Girls' and Boys' Size Charts

It is interesting to note that in children's sizing, height and weight are just as important as the girth measurements. Children often have sudden growth spurts that change the proportions of a garment in unusual ways, unlike the orderly predictable charts for adults. For example, there are times in their development when the pant inseam may grow 2 inches in length, the chest girth 1 inch; at other times the inseam will be only 1 inch longer when the chest grows 1 inch. The difference in girls and boys sizing is slight up to about 60 pounds, after which the difference is greater each year, and the sizes can no longer be combined. The R designates regular sizing (rather than slim or husky).

The girls' size chart goes up to size 16 (Table 15.14); while the boys' size chart goes up to size 20 (Table 15.15), and thereafter it transitions into men's 32 waist pant size. Often the sizes offered at retail will be just the even sizes, 8 through 20.

Size Chart for Hats

Table 15.16 provides information on sizing for hats.

Size Charts for Socks Corresponding to Shoe Size

Refer back to Table 15.1 on page 257, which shows sock sizes that correspond to shoe sizes for children, men and boys, and ladies.

Grading

Grading is the process of proportionately increasing the perfected sample size pattern for the larger sizes and decreasing it for the smaller sizes. Figure 15.31 shows one pattern piece (the right front bodice) with all sizes stacked (also called a nested set). In one way, the sizes don't seem extremely different, but incrementally and multiplied times four (two backs and two fronts) they will encompass all the sizes from 4 to 20.

Purposes of Grading

The grade increments are called the grade rules, and they vary somewhat between brands, but in the same way that the sample size is standard to any one company, the grade rules are also. This ensures that if a customer wears an 18 in this brand, she can count on all styles in 18 fitting the same way. For that reason, the larger sizes should be fit on the corresponding fit model and size 18 or size 20 double-checked as carefully as the size 8 sample size.

The goal is to achieve all the sizes while still maintaining the original style in flattering proportions. If there is a flaw in the sample size pattern, that flaw will be included, or even amplified, in the graded set. For that reason, the grading cannot proceed before the sample size garment fitting is perfected and the darts, notches, drill holes, and grainlines confirmed on the sample size pattern.

Table 15.14 Girls' Size Chart, XYZ Product Development, Inc.

(Numeric)	7R	8R	10R	12R	14R	16R
Height (inches)	51	53	55	57	59	62
Weight (pounds)	59–61	65–67	73–75	83–85	95–97	109–111
Chest/Bust	26	27	28	30	31	33
Waist	22	23	24	25	26	27
Hip	27½	28½	30	32	34	36

Table 15.15 Boys' Size Chart, XYZ Product Development, Inc.

(Numeric)	8R	9R	10R	11R	12R	14R	16R	18R	20R
Height (inches)	50	52	54	56	58	61	64	66	68
Weight (pounds)	59–61	65–68	73–76	80–83	87–90	100–103	115–118	126–129	138–141
Chest	26½	27½	28	28½	29½	31	32	34	35½
Waist	23½	24	24½	25	25½	26½	27½	28½	29½
Hip	26½	27	28	29	30	32	34	35½	37

Table 15.16 Hat Size Chart, XYZ Product Development, Inc.

	Small	Medium	Large	X-Large
Head size*	21½ to 21⅞	22.25 to 22⅝	23 to 23½	23⅞ to 24¼
Hat size	6⅞ to 7	7⅛ to 7¼	7⅜ to 7½	7⅝ to 7¾

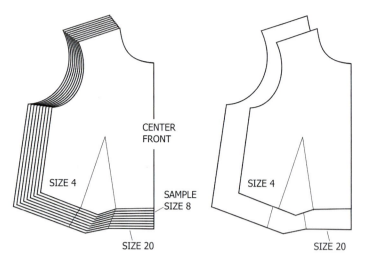

Figure 15.31 Nested set of patterns for bodice grade.

Technical Design Aspects of Grading

In the past, grading was done one piece at a time, by shifting each piece slightly and re-tracing around it onto special tagboard paper. Markers would then be created by tracing around the tagboard pieces onto marker paper. Most factories today have computer programs that allow them to grade a pattern and create markers far more quickly, with fewer steps.

Most companies have a system of grade chart templates; when the sample size is loaded, the rest of the figures populate automatically according to the grade rules. Most of the process is automatic and is straightforward for the main body spec measurements. Some styles may have some contradicting information that will need to be justified. For example, on pants, the hand pocket assembly is usually graded "same for all sizes." (Figure 15.32a, size 8, and Figure 15.32b, size 16, have the same dimensions for the pocket details.) Belt loops are usually graded a given distance from center front, so that the belt loops don't end up too far away from each other, unable to hold the belt down. Figure 15.32b shows the belt loops are too far toward the side seam. So in a garment with cargo pockets ending in belt loops, a decision will have to be made about which grade to follow. Figure 15.32c shows the pocket assembly graded in width, so the belt loops end up where they should. Figure 15.32c would be an excellent candidate to sample and fit in order to see whether the pockets look good, or too big, on the size 16 fit model.

Another example of checking the grade involves a garment known as a skort, a short skirt that has shorts attached inside. Figure 15.33a is how it looks on the outside, and the shorts inside are just $1/2$ inch shorter than the skirt. If the skirt is not graded in length and the shorts receive their standard grade of $1/4$ inch, then by the time the largest size is reached, the shorts will be longer than the skirt, as in Figure 15.33c. That would be disastrous.

Even though most grading situations are straightforward, there are others where careful analysis is essential, and in which getting a larger sample made will help to prove out the grade and avoid problems.

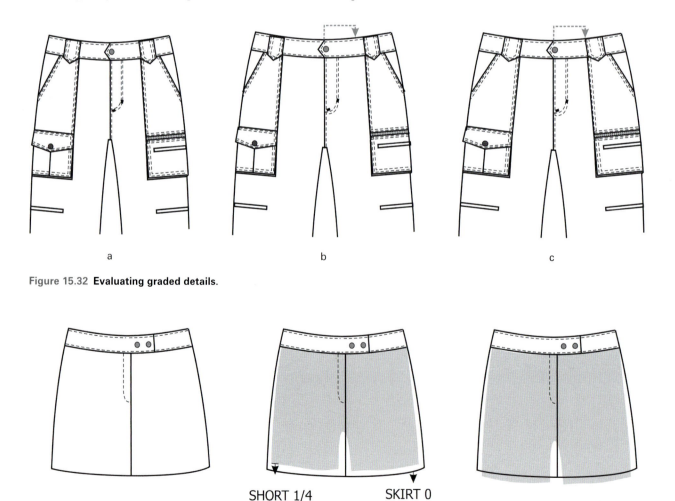

a   b   c

Figure 15.32 Evaluating graded details.

a   SHORT 1/4   b   SKIRT 0   c

Figure 15.33 Making grades compatible.

Summary

Measuring guidelines for various apparel items including tops, bottoms, underwear, hats, and socks are a bit different based on each product's unique characteristics. A thorough understanding of the principles for measuring apparel products can be obtained by ample practice in measuring various items. To clearly communicate size- and spec-related fit issues on technical packages, a designer needs a solid knowledge foundation of size charts for various target markets based on gender and age.

Study Questions

1. Follow these steps to practice measuring shirts:

   a. Bring a shirt from home to measure. Create a spec page for each item followed by the points of measure in the chapter. Measure and record the figures. Add detail specs as needed, making sure to specify dimensions and position.

   b. Draw a proportionally correct front and back sketch by 1:8 scale.

   c. Swap garments with another person. Measure that person's garment and have your partner measure yours, then compare the measurements. Refer to the technical packages in Appendix B to get the information on tolerance. Are there any that differ more than the tolerance?

   d. Review your measuring method with each other. Re-measure until you agree (within tolerance or less).

2. Follow these steps to practice measuring jeans:

   a. Bring a pair of jeans from home to measure. Create a spec page for each item followed by the points of measure in the chapter. Measure and record the figures. Add detail specs as needed, making sure to specify dimensions and position.

   b. Draw a proportionally correct front and back sketch by 1:8 scale.

   c. Swap garments with another person. Measure that garment and have your partner measure yours, then compare the measurements. Refer to the technical packages in Appendix B to get the information on tolerance. Are there any that differ more than the tolerance?

   d. Review your measuring method with each other. Re-measure until you agree (within tolerance or less).

3. Select one hat in your wardrobe. Create a spec page for the item following the specs in this chapter.

4. Select one pair of socks. Create a spec page for the item following the specs in this chapter.

5. Select one item of underwear from your drawer. Create a spec page for the item following the specs in this chapter.

6. What are the differences in the girth measurements between missy and tall?

7. What are the differences in proportion between bust, waist, and hip between missy and tall?

8. How does the girls' size 16 compare to the women's size chart?

9. Select one of your favorite retailers for men's, women's, or children's wear.

   a. Find two competitors for each.

   b. Visit the websites for the company and its two competitors. List the web address (URL) for each.

   c. Specify the reasons why the competitors were selected. Why do you think they are competitors? What is the strength for each? What is the brand positioning for each?

   d. Download their size charts and compare the differences of fit.

10. What is the armhole drop for the garment in Figure 15.6c?

11. What is the shoulder drop in the garment in the photograph in Figure 15.7? What is the front neck drop?

Check Your Understanding

1. List some of the dos and don'ts of measuring in general.

2. Why is measuring important for apparel production?

3. What is grading and why is it used?

4. What are the various size charts available for children's wear?

5. Complete a point of measure chart of your favorite pair of jeans. Refer to Missy Woven Pants in Appendix B, Selected Technical Packages.

16

Fit and Fitting

Chapter Objectives

After studying this chapter, you will be able to:

- Understand fit and fit-related issues for your target consumers
- Communicate fit and fit-related issues in writing and orally
- Develop critical thinking skills to solve fit-related problems
- Understand the relationship between fit and patterns for various body shapes

---

Key Terms

balance	fit ease	sloper
design ease	go-see	
drag lines	set	

The main thrust of this chapter is to understand the importance of fit for developing products for target consumers. Various factors that influence fit and fit-related issues are explored and design features, silhouettes, and body shapes are taken into consideration. The chapter discusses frequent fit-related issues and applies critical thinking to find solutions for various fit problems.

The Importance of Fit

The purpose of clothing is to conceal and reveal. The fit of our favorite garments allows us to conceal what we want to conceal and reveal what we want to reveal. There are many personal elements to a garment fit, and a "perfect fit" for one customer would be completely unworkable for another; some customers want to conceal and others to reveal more, in terms of their shape. Companies that best understand their target customers' desires and expectations are best equipped to provide the fit they want. Consistent fit is an important element for apparel within a given brand and is also essential for building customer loyalty.

Providing the fit that customers expect is influenced by many factors. The following are some important elements that should always be taken into consideration:

- Fashion trends and styles
- Fabrics (textures, weight, hang, and hand)
- Context (social, cultural, political, and other issues)
- Intended function of the garment
- Target consumers (age, gender, body type, lifestyle, demographic, income)

Good fit can vary based on each target market. For example, if skinny pants are the trend, the fit standard for the trendy target consumers may be a skintight fit. However, that same trend adapted for older consumers (even ones with the same girth measurements as their younger counterparts) would be slim, but not extremely tight.

Elements of Fit

There are various elements related to garment evaluation in terms of fit: ease, balance, and set.

Ease

It's often the case that some areas of the body are fit tightly and others more loosely. A key part of the design process is assigning the correct measurements to precisely define the desired silhouette. It is important that the designer understands what they want in terms of the garment fit and that they are clear about how to achieve it by assigning the correct garment measurements.

Ease is used in order to establish various silhouettes and their fit. Ease means the difference between the measurement of the garment and the measurement of the wearer at any given point—at the hip, for example. There are two types of ease: fit (or wearing) ease and design (or style) ease. **Fit ease** is for ordinary movement and **design ease** is added or removed to emphasize a certain silhouette.

Fit Ease and Slopers

As noted, ease is the difference between the garment and the wearer's body. For example, if the hip measurement of our size 8 person is 38 inches and the garment measures 40 inches at that point, the ease is 2 inches. Whether that is the correct amount of ease or not it is determined by the designer and/or technical designer, based on company standards, the proposed fabric, and on the silhouette being developed. In any case, the designer must be able to communicate whether a given amount of ease represents the intent of the design. That communication is done through the numbers on the spec page, which are determined before the first prototype can be requested.

Most apparel companies have a special set of standard patterns, or **slopers**, from which all other styles are developed. Other names are *block patterns*, *basic patterns*, or *foundation patterns*. These patterns provide fit ease only (not design ease) and represent the slimmest version that a woven garment in the sample size would be for that category of garment (such as shirt, dress, or pant). All other shapes are developed from this starting point. A garment made from the sloper pattern alone usually looks rather unfashionable because it represents fit ease only, but its purpose is not as a *style*, but rather as a *shape* to be used as a fit reference.

The sloper is in the sample size and is developed to fit the average shape (average for the company using it). A new one often takes a certain amount of trial and error to perfect. When perfected, it will eliminate pattern inaccuracies that would otherwise be passed on to every pattern using it. The sloper pattern is designed to shape around the curved areas of the body. The side seams of the bodice have an effect similar to a dart, tapering the bodice to the waist. These seams can be straight lines because the body around the rib cage tapers straight down. The side seams of the skirt are curved, however, to better fit the more pillowy shape of the body beneath. The bust, seat, waist, shoulder blades, and elbows are also shaped through seams and darts. The neck shape curve is also important and is related to the garment points of measure we studied in Chapter 15, such as front neck drop, back neck drop, and neck width.

The sloper pattern has many points represented that are important references during the garment fitting process. One is the apex, or bust point (Figure 16.1b). Another key measurement is the waist position because it varies according to a person's height and is important to the smooth drape of the bodice. All of these areas are important to establish according to what will best complement the target customer. When a designer is familiar with the basic specifications and proportions of the sloper, those numbers will be used again and again for reference and for fit checking.

Sloper patterns often have no seam allowances. This is to simplify the dart manipulation and the addition of design ease. Seam allowances are added after the pattern changes are made and before the sample is cut out in preparation to sew up the sloper garment. Figure 16.1a is the assembled garment and Figure 16.1b is the pattern (wearer's right side only) with the darts and reference points noted. In Figure 16.1b, the top part of the sloper is called the waist, another term for bodice.

The back view (Figures 16.2a and 16.2b) follows the same principles as the front in terms of ease and seam and dart shaping. The sleeve sloper includes the elbow line (see Figure 16.2c) and is an important point of measure to ensure that the sleeve will not become too slim to bend comfortably. The armhole position

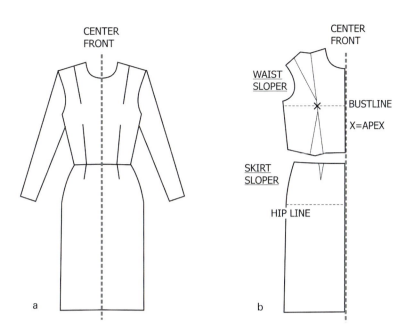
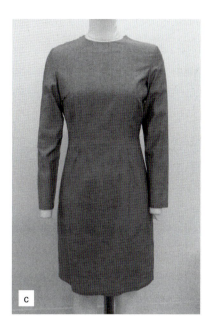

Figure 16.1 Dress sloper garment and pattern pieces, front.

affects the comfort and mobility of the sleeve and the sleeve is perfected to fit into the bodice to hang smoothly and without wrinkles.

The features and usefulness of the slopers are the same for all companies, although different manufacturers will have somewhat different specifications for their slopers according to their target customer and according to what measurements represent their sample size. For example, if a size 8 is considered to be bust 36 inches, waist 28 inches, and hip 38 inches, that represents the average of many bodies, but very few customers will have all three of those precise measurements. Those figures are a composite of many people's measurements, combined to arrive at an average, but ironically, very few individuals are "average."

There may be some variation in the neck shape, for example, or the position of the apex, or the amount of dart depth. In addition, the ideal figure for women changes over time according to the current silhouette, and may be based on American or European averages or other body types, depending on the customer profile. A good sloper helps to bridge the slight variations found among individual customers' measurements.

Companies may develop a number of slopers, depending on what products they run. For example, they may not need a dress sloper because they don't offer dresses, but rather use a separate skirt and blouse sloper. Knits have somewhat different fitting rules and often require less ease, so if a company specializes in a certain type of knit (such as jersey or wool double-knit), they often have a special sloper developed. A jersey dress sewn from the woven sloper pattern in Figure 16.1 would have too much ease and an overly baggy fit on the size 8 customer. Because of the inherent stretch of knit fabrics, it would not need certain details such as the elbow dart. Because every knit has different stretch characteristics, there may or may not be a sloper developed for

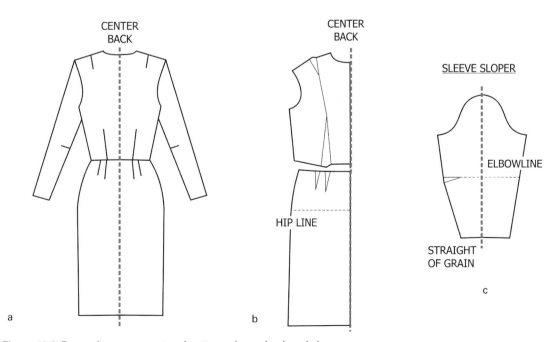

Figure 16.2 Dress sloper garment and pattern pieces, back and sleeve.

each. An alternative is for the apparel company to choose one of its own popular, good-fitting styles to use as an informal sloper garment. Those measurements can serve as starting specifications for other garments of that type.

Sloper garments are also very useful when choosing a fit model. If the sloper garment fits a prospective fit model well, it is an indicator that he or she will predict correct or incorrect fit points for future developments.

Men's Styles

As mentioned earlier in this chapter, the more close fitting a garment, the more important it is to establish the unique contours of the basic sloper. A typical men's dress shirt is fairly loose, but the collar and collarband are fitted; therefore, the exact curve of the collarband is vital to establishing the collar fit and ease. Other fit points, such as how much curve is built into the back yoke, are important, as well as the sleeve cap height.

The cuff is also rather fitted and generally will have a standard spec for all styles. Cuffs often have two buttons to allow the customer to customize the cuff fit. A slightly tighter cuff fit will also allow a person with shorter arms to wear a longer-sleeved shirt because the cuff will stop at the wrist and not fall too long onto the hand. This is one example of strategies that companies use to help accommodate the widest variety of customers.

The company may have a sloper for a men's dress shirt and a different one for a casual shirt, reflecting a slightly different customer expectation. For example, the company may have discovered that its casual shirts experience better sell-through when the front neck drop is lower and the fit is more boxy (with no taper from the chest to the bottom opening). That would be in keeping with a less formal, more comfortable shirt that does not have to fit under a suit, be tucked into pants, or be worn with a tie.

Men's and women's pants often have a sloper (or slopers) established for them, since good-fitting pants are crucial to sales. As at many other companies, the sample size for a pair of men's pants at XYZ Product Development is 34. Not all the men who wear a size 34 measure precisely 34 inches around the waist; in fact, probably very few do. The key pant fit measurements are waist, hip, and rise, and there are an uncountable number of variations in the waist, hip, and rise dimensions of men whose size is 34, the average of which, plus ease, becomes the 34 pant sloper dimensions. For a men's pant sloper, depending on the customer, the actual waistband garment specification may be 35 inches (1 inch of ease included), 35 inches (relaxed measurement) including an elastic insert that adds additional stretch, $35^1/_2$ inches ($1^1/_2$ inches of ease), or even 36 inches (2 inches of ease) if the customer wants the pant to ride lower on the hips. All these variations are taken into account during the establishment of a particular sloper.

Children's Styles

Children's styles are less close fitting and are not quite as influenced by silhouette concerns as other categories, but a sloper is valuable nonetheless to determine that the garments have the correct fit ease and will be consistent over many seasons.

Choice of Ease Slopers

Choice of ease slopers are important tools and are developed for each category as necessary. To arrive at a good fitting, a perfected sloper is well worth the time and effort that companies expend.

It cuts down on development and fitting time and helps to ensure a good-fitting and predictable garment, which is the basis for customer loyalty and repeat business.

There are several considerations when it comes to the choice of ease:

- *Age of the customer*: Junior sizes and younger fashion customers often wear their clothing tighter, requiring less ease.
- *Style and intended use of garment*: A stretch garment in knit or a stretch-woven fabric intended for sports or exercise is often more close fitting, requiring less ease.
- *Fabric weight*: A lighter-weight fabric will drape down in a way that allows for more ease to be built in to allow the garment to fall farther from the body. By contrast, a heavier bottom weight will need less ease to prevent the garment from appearing bulky.
- *Fabric construction*: Generally, knit garments require less ease and sit closer to the body than wovens because the knit structure has "give." Stretch wovens can also have less ease.
- *Tolerance*: The garment specs allow a tolerance to the factory, a given allowance that the garment can be under or over spec. The spec must have an awareness of the tolerance. For example, if only 1 inch of ease is planned (a very slim fit) and the grade rules allow for 1 inch of tolerance, it would be possible for the garment to arrive with zero ease, which would be skin tight. For a woven style with no stretch, that would be unacceptably tight. For that reason, more ease must be included in the spec. Girth tolerances are generally no more than half of the grade for that point of measure. For example, if the grade between sizes for the hip is 2 inches, the tolerance will be +/− 1 inch. Any more than that and the difference between sizes will begin to blur. For certain design areas, such as the collar of a men's dress shirt, the tolerance for things like the collar points may be quite small, such as +/− 1/8 inch. That is because it is considered a key part of the design.

Fit Ease and Fabric

Fabrics have a big effect on how much ease is added and on the details appropriate. Figure 16.3 is an example of the importance of matching specifications and design details with the appropriate fabric weight. More fabric (more ease) is needed for lighter-weight fabrics. Figure 16.3a shows a lightweight summer fabric with a drawstring waist. The specification for hip girth would be one or two inches greater than Figure 16.3b, which shows a heavier cotton canvas style. Heavier bottom-weight fabrics require less ease in the hip girth because heavier fabrics tend to hold themselves away from the body. Heavier fabrics would not look good with a drawstring waist because the gathers would drape "out," not "down," and would tend to add bulk.

Table 16.1 provides the actual comparison measurements for each style in Figure 16.3. The lighter-weight pant has a little longer rise and more fullness in the hip and thigh. It would not be comfortable sitting too close to the body because it would be too revealing. Heavier-weight fabrics tend to "hold you in"; for example, the pant fabric shapes and smooths the body and looks better with less ease. Too much ease will create a bulky look.

Table 16.1 shows one important measurement not needed for the pant in Figure 16.3b: waist stretched. This is a key piece of information for the pattern maker and would be included in the measurements for any drawcord or elastic waist style. This

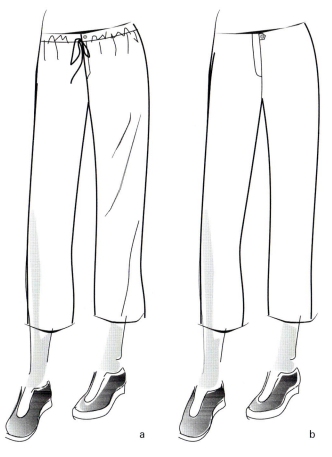

Figure 16.3 Fabric weight and ease.

represents a dart substitute that we studied in Chapter 6 (the canvas style in Figure 16.3b is a flat front style with no front darts and would utilize the back darts from the block pant pattern, which do not need to be called out). This style has a front fly, so the waist stretched measurement does not have to be large enough to fit over the hips. A pull-on pant with no fly closure has to have a large enough waist opening, at least 38 inches for size 8, to fit over the hips. Table 16.2 provides typical ease measurements for some common garment categories.

On the women's ease chart, the bust ease can vary depending on the closure and whether the garment has a button placket, because it must fit without gaping. A dress with a back zipper can fit slightly smaller. The designer must also keep in mind the tolerance, because the production garment may be smaller than spec and still accepted. For that reason, it is wise to build $3^{1}/_{2}$ to 4 inches into a shirt or blouse with a front button closure. Another thing to consider is the sizing chart and whether the style is offered in numeric or alpha sizes. Alpha-sized products require a bit more ease because the tolerances are typically greater.

Jackets and coats can have variation based on layering and what is intended to be worn underneath. People in Chicago may "size up" when purchasing a winter coat because they may plan to wear a sweater or fleece garment under the item. A person in Georgia may not need the extra layer. Outerwear often has a lot of variation in the insulation used; for example, a wool overcoat is typically thinner than a down jacket, possibly by 2 or 3 inches in the chest spec. The waist does not have a great deal of variation for ease. It can't be too small, or it won't be comfortable. It can't be too large, or it won't stay in place. The hip area is greatly affected by the garment style and the fabric weight, as discussed with

Table 16.1   Ease Comparison for Two Different Fabrics

Code	Pant Spec Measurements, Size 8	Tol (+)	Tol (–)	A Spec for Lighter Weight	B Spec for Heavier Weight
B–A	Waist relaxed	$^{3}/_{4}$	$^{1}/_{2}$	31	32
B–B	Waist stretched	$^{3}/_{4}$	$^{1}/_{2}$	35	
B–G	Front rise (to top)	$^{1}/_{4}$	$^{1}/_{4}$	$10^{1}/_{2}$	10
B–H	Back rise (to top)	$^{1}/_{4}$	$^{1}/_{4}$	$15^{1}/_{2}$	15
B–K–2	Hip , $3^{1}/_{2}$" up from inseam	$^{3}/_{4}$	$^{1}/_{2}$	43	39
B–L	Thigh , 1"	$^{1}/_{2}$	$^{1}/_{2}$	27	25

Table 16.2   Fit Ease Guidelines for Woven Garments

Women's Woven Styles, Full Measure Fabric with No Horizontal Stretch

Point of Measure (of Garment)	Garment Type	Fit Ease Required
Bust measurement at 1" below armhole	Blouse/dress	$2^{1}/_{2}$" to 4"
Bust measurement at 1" below armhole	Jacket	3 to 4"
Bust measurement at 1" below armhole	Coat/outerwear	4 to 5"
Waistband	Pant/skirt	1"
Hip at $3^{1}/_{2}$" up from crotch point	Pant/skirt	$^{1}/_{2}$" to 2"

Men's Woven Styles, Full Measure Fabric with No Horizontal Stretch

Chest measurement at 1" below armhole	Shirt	6" to 10"
Chest measurement at 1" below armhole	Jacket	6" to 10"
Chest measurement at 1" below armhole	Coat/outerwear	6" to 10"
Waistband	Pant	1"
Hip at $3^{1}/_{2}$" up from crotch point	Pant	4" to 6"

Figure 16.3 and later by the fit type (Figure 16.6). But if we are only considering fit ease and not design ease, the guidelines in Table 16.2 hold true.

Notice that men's and women's ease are much different. One reason for the wide variation in chest ease for men is that a size L man who has broad shoulders but a slimmer rib cage still needs the L garment, even though it has lots of extra ease in the chest. In general, men wear their clothing with more ease than do women.

Figure 16.4 shows how ease is incorporated into the actual garments. For specified parts of the body and garments, the actual measurements are indicated. The human body needs to have fit ease for movement. The body measurements are from the XYZ Product Development missy size chart size 8 (see Table 15.7 in Chapter 15). For example, Figure 16.4 shows that the body has a bust measurement of 36 inches, but the bust on the sample garment is 39 inches (3 inches ease). The waist on the body is 28 inches, but the actual sample top has a waist of 37 inches (9 inches ease). The skirt waist is 29 inches (1 inch ease), and so on.

Design Ease

At any given moment in the fashion cycle, certain areas of a garment are tighter and others are looser. For that reason it's important for the designer to have a grasp of the precise measurements needed to interpret the silhouette the way it is intended, and specifically where the garment may need more or less ease.

One element of fashion is a kind of planned obsolescence, in which our eye, tired of a silhouette grown stale, looks for something exciting and novel. Young people look for a new shape they can own, one that older people don't like or cannot wear. An example is the low-rise jean, which reveals a slim, flat stomach. A new style like that is first introduced as high fashion, then taken up by those seeking exclusivity—and with the money and interest in searching out the most forward styles. Gradually the silhouette becomes the norm and is often adopted by those less able to wear it well. The older customer adapts it in a modified way, and soon the look loses its charm among trendsetters. Then the cycle starts all over again.

Because of that cycle, there may be a lot of overlap between what is *design ease* and what is *fit ease*, especially in garments without

a lot of ease, such as pants. Figure 16.5 shows two very different styles of pants, from different eras—they are different in every single point of measure. Both have size 8 specs and both fit the same fit model perfectly, as defined by the designer at the time. Each silhouette defines a moment in (fairly) recent fashion, and together they represent the swing of the pendulum. Each style at one time was considered the latest thing, the "rightness" of which was unquestionable. But whereas it's possible that at a given moment neither will be in style, it's also highly unlikely that they would both be in style at the same time. They are just too opposite.

As with most fit evaluations, the shapes can be much more precisely defined in technical design terms with garment measurements rather than with a sketch alone. Compare each point of measure against its counterpart to get a sense of how much variation there can be for what is considered fit ease, depending on the current silhouette (see Figure 16.5).

So is *bottom opening*, for example, a fit spec or a design spec? Clearly a 23-inch bottom opening has nothing to do with fit and was chosen purely for design. But if the 18-inch bottom opening becomes too small, it won't go over the foot, so for this style it is a fit spec. As silhouettes develop over time from one extreme to another, so do ideas of proper ease, and of fit versus design ease.

Design ease is the way a style is defined through measurements that go beyond the fit. The styles in Figure 16.6 have similar basic neckline and many details in common (long sleeves, similar overall length, and inset waistline). But nearly all of the fit specifications for Figure 16.6a could probably be taken from the sloper pattern. The design specs (see "Points of Measure for Neck and Collar" in Chapter 15) include:

- T-P (front neck drop)
- T-Q (back neck drop)
- T-R (neck width)
- B-O (bottom opening)

The back will probably need a vent or pleat incorporated into the design for movement, the style will possibly need a side seam zipper if the fit is close, and perhaps a couple of other things.

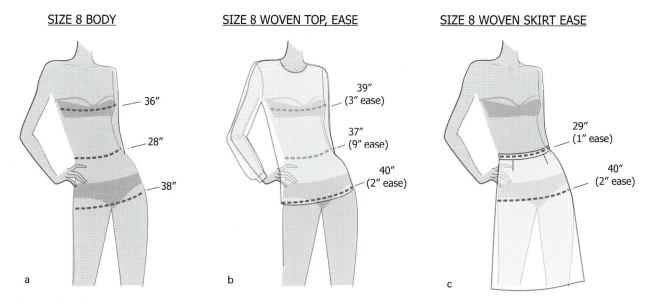

SIZE 8 BODY   SIZE 8 WOVEN TOP, EASE   SIZE 8 WOVEN SKIRT EASE

Figure 16.4 Fit ease for tops and bottoms.

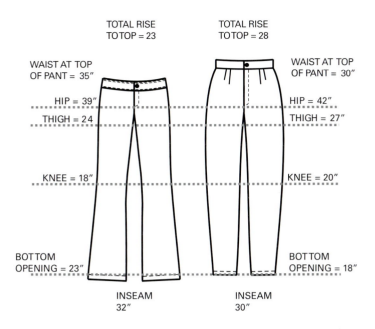

Figure 16.5 Fit ease and design ease comparison of size 8 garments.

Figure 16.6 Design ease example.

Figure 16.6b, in addition to T-P (front neck drop), T-Q (back neck drop), and T-R (neck width), will need the chest (T-H), cuff relaxed and extended (T-Z-1 and T-Z-2), and the cuff height (T-AA). It will need the sleeve length (T-O), since it's likely to be longer than the sloper basic sleeve. The waist insert could probably be the same for both, since it appears to hit at the same spot.

It will also need the bottom ruffle height specified, and key to this style, it will need the gathering ratio of all the spots that gather into a flat seam (above and below the waist and the ruffle seam). This is fairly easy to calculate with a header of the actual fabric or something close in weight, but difficult without it. After all, the goal is to get it right the first time, so having the design tools (a sample of the fabric and trims) is quite important. The area above the waist should have volume, because that accentuates the smallness of the waist, but still appear soft. The area below the waist needs gathers to introduce fullness for the skirt, but not so many as to make the hips look bulky. The ruffle needs to have enough fullness to carry through the gathering theme, but must not require too much or too little fabric and must "look good," a judgment call made by the designer. All these elements are communicated to the factory and pattern maker by the number specifications on the tech pack spec page.

Ease and Silhouettes

Various degrees of ease are used for tops and bottoms, often a mix of fit and design ease.

Ease and Silhouettes for Pants

Figure 16.7 provides pant fits for various silhouettes. The following shapes would be defined through the amount of ease at the hip. (The waist ease would be constant between silhouettes, about 1 inch.)

- Slim: $1/2$–1 inch ease
- Natural: 1–2 inches ease
- Relaxed: 2–4 inches ease
- Oversized: More than 4 inches ease

"Oversized" for bottoms is not a common silhouette, but comes into style occasionally, especially when the fashion emphasis is on a small waist. The greater hip ease of the garment makes the waist appear smaller by comparison. Figure 16.7d shows the waist on the oversized style appears smaller than the waist on the slim style (see Figure 16.7a), although it's not.

Ease and Silhouettes for Tops

The ease for tops has more variation. It is important that the final use of the garment be clearly agreed upon between the merchandiser and designer and that it's what the buyer is looking for. To make sure that the fit of garments is consistent, all new prototypes or repeat styles in new fabrics must be fit. The target customer should be able to buy a certain size in every style. Figure 16.8 shows that if the customer is a size 8, then every 8 should fit her, looser or tighter, depending on the style and the design ease. If her arms are a bit shorter than the standard, then *all* full-length sleeves should be a touch too long. Whether the garment is a slim fit or relaxed fit style, she can still buy the size 8.

The intent of the design in terms of ease must be clearly communicated, and the retail customer must understand and be ready for it. For example, if the garment is intended to have a new, looser fit, and the customer does not want it so loose looking or is not yet ready for that silhouette, she may choose to purchase a smaller size. If the garment is otherwise proportional, that would be a natural choice and a good solution for the people in the middle of the size run. But if all the customers have the same reaction and all buy a smaller size than usual, then the smallest customers will not have a size she considers appropriate. Similarly, the largest sizes may not be considered a good fit and may not

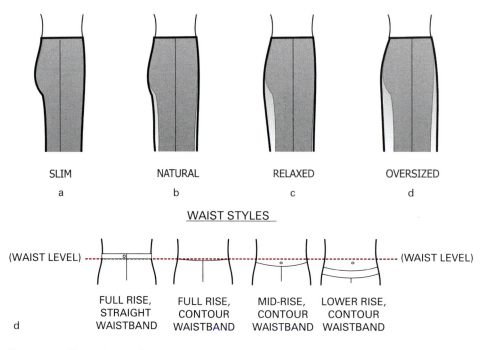

SLIM
a

NATURAL
b

RELAXED
c

OVERSIZED
d

WAIST STYLES

(WAIST LEVEL) - (WAIST LEVEL)

d

FULL RISE,
STRAIGHT
WAISTBAND

FULL RISE,
CONTOUR
WAISTBAND

MID-RISE,
CONTOUR
WAISTBAND

LOWER RISE,
CONTOUR
WAISTBAND

Figure 16.7 **Women's pant fit types.**

sell. This is an example of the importance of understanding the expectation of the target customer in terms of designing ease. Figure 16.8 shows some guidelines, such as what may be seen in a mail-order catalog. It provides various fit descriptions based on fabrication and design silhouettes.

Balance

It is important to check garments for **balance**, which is related to grainline and structural lines. The length grain should run parallel to the length of the body at center front and center back, down the center of the arm from shoulder to elbow and down the center front of each leg. The crosswise grain should run perpendicular to the length of the body at bust and hip. An on-grain garment hangs evenly and appears symmetrical. Structural lines such as darts, pleats, princess seams, and other design lines should be checked to see if they are balanced left to right. Yokes, pockets, and prints or plaids should be symmetrical, and the hemline should be even and parallel to the floor.

Garments can be tried on the mannequin to check for balance and for the general position of details (see Figure 16.9). This is an important step because although the straight lines are easy to check by measurement alone, the curves are not. Armholes on tops and rise shapes on pants are especially important to review in 3D, and only a live fit model can test for comfort and range of motion.

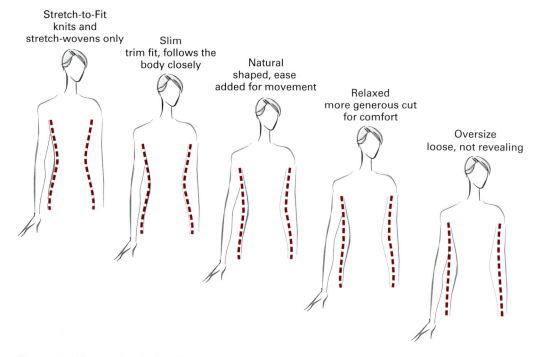

Stretch-to-Fit
knits and
stretch-wovens only

Slim
trim fit, follows the
body closely

Natural
shaped, ease
added for movement

Relaxed
more generous cut
for comfort

Oversize
loose, not revealing

Figure 16.8 **Fit-type descriptions for tops.**

Set

A garment that does not fit well on the body will often produce **drag lines** where there is not quite sufficient fabric or too much fabric to span the distance required. Fabric is pulled in an unattractive way and indicates either not enough, or an excess of, ease. **Set** means a smooth fit of garments without any unwanted drag lines or wrinkles. Generally, drag lines will point to the problem area. For example, drag lines at the underarm indicate that there is too much or too little fabric provided at that point and that the pattern should be revised.

Dress Form

A *dress form*, or mannequin, is an invaluable tool for studying fit issues. It is a good place to review samples prior to fitting on a live model and helps to evaluate potential pattern problems. A mannequin with legs is ideal and is useful for fitting pants, swimwear, and underwear, as well as skirts and dresses. Removable arms (see Figure 16.10a) help when studying sleeve fit and simplify dressing and undressing the dress form. A smooth-fitting cover such as stretch tricot will help the garments slip over the form and avoid inaccuracies due to the fabric sticking to the form. The dress form is a good tool to check for balance because it is symmetrical right to left and does not vary in posture. Unlike a fit model, a mannequin is unchanging and uncomplaining and can be pinned into.

A new mannequin comes with a checklist of measurements provided by the manufacturer, but there are other measurements that may not be included and that are helpful for understanding fit. Figure 16.10 shows a set of measurements that should be recorded and kept near the mannequin for reference. It is also helpful to translate the high point shoulder (HPS) position from a garment to the mannequin and mark it permanently with a pin or thread. Other reference marks can be made at the bust point and underarm level. Nonpermanent reference marks can be made by marking on top of masking tape. For women's styles, the dress form should have a bra available to wear to check for coverage on sleeveless items.

Neck Width and Neck Drop

The human body does not have a "high point shoulder" like a pattern does, and many other garment measurements such as neck drop are useful first in making a pattern. But ultimately all those points of measure correspond to areas of the customer wearing the garment.

Fit Issues and Pattern Corrections

The following sections examine fit issues and common pattern corrections. Sometimes a problem is a combination of specs, sewing, and fabric, so the figures here are not meant to be a comprehensive guide, but rather to serve as a logical starting point. In this section, all patterns and the pattern corrections are shown without seam allowances.

--GRAINLINES HORIZONTAL AND VERTICAL

--DETAILS SYMMETRICAL LEFT-TO-RIGHT FOR SIZE AND FOR PLACEMENT

--BUST DARTS IN CORRECT POSITION

Figure 16.9 Check the sample for balance.

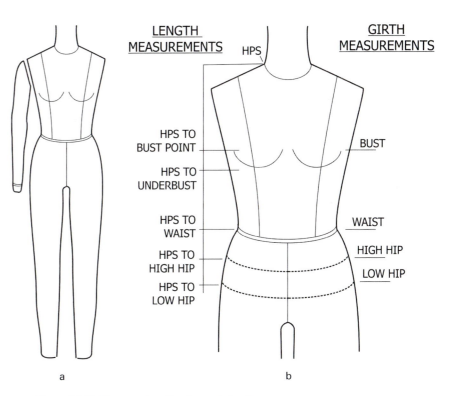

Figure 16.10 Mannequin, other key points of measure.

Drag Lines Across the Chest: Too Tight

Places to check for drag lines on knit tops include the chest, underarm, and across the front. In the following example, drag lines appear from bust point to bust point, indicating that the bust girth is not great enough. In that case the pattern should be extended at the side seam top; Figure 16.11b shows the pattern correction sketch. If the waist girth appears correct, the side seam correction can be blended to nothing at the waist, as shown. To keep the pattern balanced, the back pattern would get the same revision.

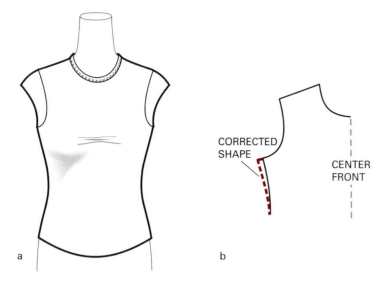

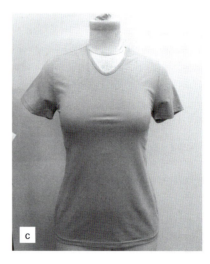

Figure 16.11 Drag lines across bust: too tight at chest.

This style is a knit top, and every knit has different stretch characteristics. If a new style of knit fabric is being introduced, one that has no fit history with the company, it is better to err on the larger size for the first proto because it is easier to pin out extra ease than it is to guess how much extra to add.

The way this change would be noted in the fit history is shown as follows. Because it is a knit style, the specs are half measure. When working with the fit history, it is important to understand what is being compared to what. The spec is shown in Table 16.3, column A. Column B is what the garment actually measured, and column C is the difference. The chest was on spec, but after review on the mannequin, it is clearly too tight. For that reason, the spec is shown revised to $17^1/_2$ inches for the next sample, the second proto (see column E). Waist position and waist girth are correct to spec and also look good on the mannequin, so those and two figures are marked *OK* and carried over to the second proto spec, column E. The bottom opening spec is 18 inches and the sample is $17^1/_2$ inches, past spec. The revision notes we will be using are *OK*, *Revise*, and *RTS* (return to spec).

Drag Lines Radiate at Underarm: Armhole Drop Too High

If the chest spec is correct and drag lines radiate to the underarm, then the underarm is too high. The fit history in Table 16.4 shows that the correct figure for armhole drop from HPS was specified ($8^1/_2$ inches), but that the garment came in incorrectly high ($7^1/_2$ inches). This shows the importance of measuring a sample before fitting. Otherwise, the armhole drop spec may seem incorrect, but there is nothing wrong with the spec, only with the sample. In addition, especially for knits, the garment may stretch out after being worn and be difficult to measure accurately. The solution is to mark it RTS. The front pattern sketch (Figure 16.12b) shows how the problem is corrected when the factory revises the pattern (the way it should have been in the first place).The back pattern would get the same revision.

Drag Lines at Lower Armhole: Pattern Needs More Scoop

Figure 16.13 shows drag lines across the front along the armscye. In this case they indicate that the garment is a bit too large rather than too small, not in any of the girth measurements, but at the lower

Table 16.3   Fit History: Revising Chest

				A	B	C	D	E
					1st Proto			Revised Spec,
Code	Top Spec Measurements	Tol (+)	Tol (−)	Spec	Meas	Difference	Notes	2nd Proto
T–H	Chest , 1″ from armhole	½	½	16	16	0	Revise	17½
T–I	Waist position	½	½	16½	16½	0	OK	15
T–I–2	Waist	½	½	15	15	0	OK	15
T–J	Bottom opening	½	½	18	17½	½	RTS	18

Table 16.4   Fit History: Revising Armhole Drop

				A	B	C	D	E
					1st Proto			Revised Spec,
Code	Top Spec Measurements	Tol (+)	Tol (−)	Spec	Meas	Difference	Notes	2nd Proto
T–H	Chest , 1″ from armhole	½	½	17	17	0	OK	17
T–G	Armhole drop from HPS	½	½	8½	7½	1	RTS	9

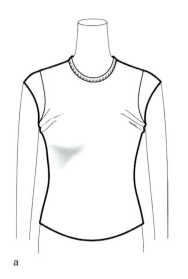

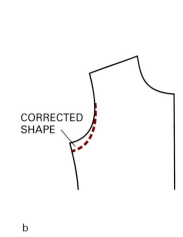

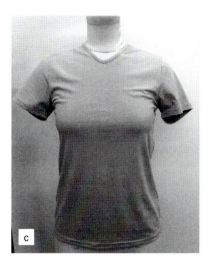

Figure 16.12 Armhole drop too high.

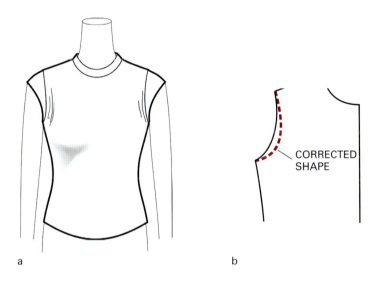

Figure 16.13 Revising across front: more scoop.

armhole. The garment is wider than the body at that point and the excess fabric creates a fold. Across front is the point of measure that helps to control the armhole and is measured across the chest, armscye to armscye, at the specified distance from HPS. The pattern sketch, corrected shape, shows how to remove the excess fabric.

The fit history shows that the across front spec was not followed and the first proto measurements differ from the spec. The note in Table 16.5, column D directs the factory to RTS. Table 16.5 shows a good rule of thumb for first prototypes. Starting with the shoulder point to point measurement (14^1/$_2$ inches), the across front is 2 inches smaller (12^1/$_2$ inches) and the across back is 1 inch smaller (13^1/$_2$ inches).

Drag Lines at Neckline: Neck Drop Too High

Neck drop is an important focal area for design, as well as one that must be comfortable. Figure 16.14a shows what happens when the neck drop is too high. The wrinkles are formed because there is too much fabric below the neck seam. When the pattern is scooped out (see Figure 16.14b), the excess fabric goes away and the area can lie smooth.

The collar also seems to lie a bit wide at the sides and not next to the neck. This could be the design intention or it could be an error. That should be clarified before proceeding, and we can see by the fit history that it does not follow the spec. In this case the decision was

Table 16.5 Fit History: Revising Across Front

			A	B	C	D	E
				1st Proto			Revised Spec,
Code	Top Spec Measurements	Tol (+)	Tol (−)	Spec	Meas	Difference	Notes	2nd Proto
T–A	Shoulder point to point	½	½	14½	14½	0	OK	14½
T–C	Across front at 6" from HPS	½	½	12½	14	1½	RTS	12½
T–D	Across back at 6" from HPS	½	½	13½	13½	0	OK	13½

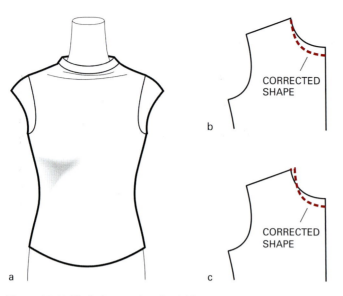
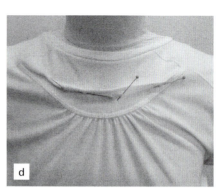

Figure 16.14 Neck drop and neck width.

made to return to spec rather than to revise it to be the same as the sample, and Figure 16.14c shows the pattern correction.

In Table 16.6, the lower pattern correction (T-R) is for neck width. The sample was judged to be standing too far away from the neck and should return to spec. A style such as this, with no closure, must be able to slip over the head. The spec and fit history includes the point of measure *minimum neck stretch*. Because it is a minimum measurement, the negative tolerance is zero, meaning it must be at least 12^1/$_2$ inches. It can stretch to a greater size than 12^1/$_2$, but no less than that. The plus tolerance does not apply because it is acceptable to be over spec.

Bottom Opening Too Wide

The importance of measuring and reviewing samples before trying them on can be seen in the next example (see Table 16.7). The problem is that the bottom opening is too wide, but there is more than one possible solution. Figure 16.15b shows the first solution on the front pattern and the method for reducing the bottom opening. The back pattern would get the same revision to keep the pattern balanced.

Table 16.8 shows a different cause for the problem. Because the garment is far too short, the bottom opening hits at a place at the high hip, where it is smaller. The solution has nothing to do with the bottom opening spec, and after the garment is the correct length the bottom opening will fit fine. Table 16.8 shows how that is communicated to the factory.

In some cases, the girth specs for bust, waist, and hip can be correct, but the transition shaping between them can be wrong. Figure 16.16a shows what can happen when waist position is too low. The side seam at the narrowest part is too low. This causes the fabric above it to crumple, which requires the garment to constantly be pulled down. The corrected waist position (see 16.16b) is higher and adds width at the high hip, allowing a smoother transition to the bottom.

All the girth specs for Figure 16.16 came in as requested, but based on the fitting the waist position will be revised for the next proto. Figure 16.16b shows the correction on the front pattern. The back pattern would get the same revision to keep the pattern balanced. Table 16.9 shows how that is communicated to the factory.

Table 16.6   Fit History: Revising Neck Drop

				A	B	C	D	E
					1st Proto			Revised Spec,
Code	Top Spec Measurements	Tol (+)	Tol (−)	Spec	Meas	Difference	Notes	2nd Proto
T–P	Front neck drop, to seam	½	½	2	2	0	Revise	3½
T–R	Neck width, seam to seam	½	½	6¾	8	1¼	RTS	6¾
	Minimum neck stretch	N/A	0	12½	12	1.2	RTS	12½

Table 16.7   Fit History: Revising Bottom Opening

				A	B	C	D	E
					1st Proto			Revised Spec,
Code	Top Spec Measurements	Tol (+)	Tol (−)	Spec	Meas	Difference	Notes	2nd Proto
T–H	Bottom opening	½	½	19	20	1	RTS	19
T–I	Front length from HPS	½	½	24	24	0	OK	
24								

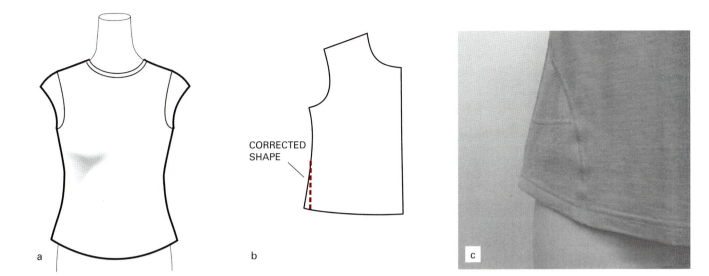

Figure 16.15 **Bottom opening too wide.**

Table 16.8   Fit History: Garment Too Short

				A	B	C	D	E
					1st Proto			Revised Spec,
Code	Top Spec Measurements	Tol (+)	Tol (−)	Spec	Meas	Difference	Notes	2nd Proto
T–H	Bottom opening	½	½	19	19	0	OK	19
T–I	Front length from HPS	½	½	24	22	2	RTS	24

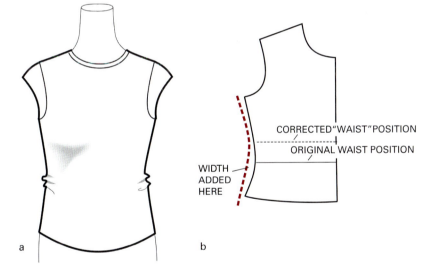

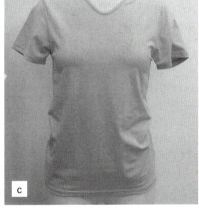

Figure 16.16 **Waist position.**

Table 16.9   Fit History: Waist Position Too Low

				A	B	C	D	E
					1st Proto			Revised Spec,
Code	Top Spec Measurements	Tol (+)	Tol (−)	Spec	Meas	Difference	Notes	2nd Proto
T–H	Chest , 1″ from armhole	½	½	17½	17½	0	OK	17½
T–I	Waist position	½	½	16½	16½	0	Revise	15
T–I–2	Waist girth	½	½	15	15	0	OK	15
T–J	Bottom opening	½	½	18	18	0	ok	18

Sleeve

To fit correctly, sleeves should be as slim as called for in the design without restricting movement. The sleeve of a woven garment should form a smooth cylinder when the arm is relaxed. A knit fabric fits similarly but often with less ease than a woven. If the garment is intended to be worn over or under something, it should be fit in tandem with the companion garment to make sure they are compatible. When writing fit comments the designer can refer to the specific parts of the sleeve pattern.

Figure 16.17 shows a bicep level on the pattern; bicep on the garment is measured 1 inch below the armhole as indicated in the measurement guide in Chapter 15. The reason the garment is measured lower is that the seam is the area of greatest bulk. When measured at 1 inch down, the tape measure clears the armhole seam allowances, which would otherwise distort the measurement.

Figure 16.18 shows that there is a close connection between the cap height and the width at bicep level. The higher the cap, the narrower the bicep, and vice versa. A way to demonstrate that is to draw a sleeve shape like the one in Figure 16.18a onto cardstock. Crisp Pellon works well, too. Cut it out around the edges and then cut along the bicep line and grainline, nearly to the very edge but

leaving a small connection. Then pull open the bicep at the edges (see Figure 16.18b), and you will see the cap height drop (see Figure 16.18c); yet the perimeter, or distance around the outside edge, is unchanged. It is a good representation of the relationship between cap height and bicep.

Figure 16.19a through d shows how cap height affects sleeve mobility. Figure 16.19a and b shows a shirt where a low, wide armhole provides a great deal of "lift" and does not even pull the front of the shirt until the arm is already quite high. Conversely, when the arm is down, it has the extra fabric folding into the armhole area.

A high narrow cap (Figure 16.19c and d), such as is found on a tailored suit coat, can limit mobility. When the arm is lifted, the cap area begins to fold and the front of the garment "grabs" and lifts outward, following the sleeve. The trade-off is that when the sleeve is down, it is perfectly smooth, without wrinkles, bubbles, or drag lines. In fact, the perfectly smooth sleeve is the hallmark of fine tailoring; nonetheless, it would be a hindrance for very active movements. The armhole drop also has a big effect on mobility. One way to help increase the mobility of a high cap garment is to make sure the armhole is as high as it can comfortably be. The armhole drop has a big effect on shirt sleeve mobility in this style as well. As on any garment, if the armhole drop is too low, it can hinder the range of motion.

Shirts

Figure 16.20 shows fit areas for a men's shirt and common details. Shirts have a certain looseness built into the shape that is part of the style. A classic woven shirt should not be overly fitted. If the fabric has give to it, such as either a knit or stretch woven, it can be fit closer to the body by use of vertical darts and seams, if desired, but it must function and be comfortable in the elbows, across the back, and other areas of movement.

A men's shirt is such a traditional garment that the style changes very slowly over time. There are only a few actual style points, such as collar point and collar spread. The other specifications are usually company standards and do not change much from one men's shirt style to another. An exception is for a different fit type, such as slim shirt. In that case, once again, all the shirts of that fit type would have essentially the same specifications.

The collar is sometimes called "the soul of a men's shirt" and must be perfectly symmetrical and smooth. The fit model will

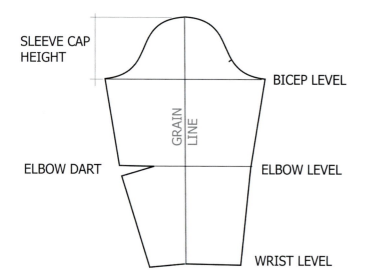

Figure 16.17 **Sleeve pattern terminology.**

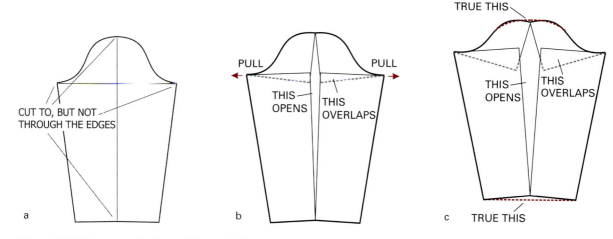

Figure 16.18 **Sleeve cap height and bicep width.**

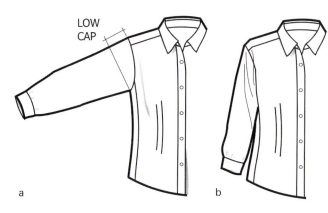

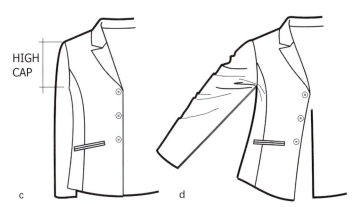

Figure 16.19 Cap height and immobility.

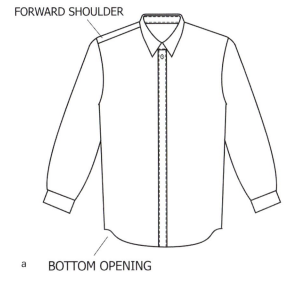

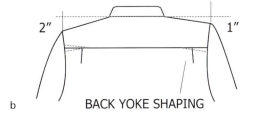

Figure 16.20 Fit points on a men's shirt.

say whether the sample is comfortable, and if it is correct to spec for neck drop and collarband length, it will fit the appropriate customer. The tolerances for men's collarband are small, usually $^1/_4$ inch, so factories must take great care at this point of measure. After all, the collarband is the actual size of the shirt (such as $15^1/_2$ neck), so it must be in correct proportion to the chest.

Certain areas of men's shirts should be reviewed carefully because they can improve the look significantly:

- Shoulder drop: If the shoulder drop—the slope or angle of the shoulder—is too high, the fit of the sleeve will be overly droopy. Usually 2 inches is a good standard for men's shoulder drop spec. Figure 16.20b shows what 1 inch would look like and how it adds too much to the sleeve; after it drops into place on the wearer's shoulder, it will create excess fabric at the underarm. Of course, for a customer with very square or

muscular shoulders, less shoulder drop would be preferable, so each company adapts its specifications to fit its target customer.

- Forward shoulder: The shoulder seam should be positioned around 1 inch forward of the HPS; 2 inches forward also looks good and creates an attractive focal point across the top of the shirt, adding width to the shoulders. You can compare the effect with and without the forward shoulder seam in Figure 16.20a.

- *Back yoke seam*: The back yoke creates a fit opportunity in which fabric can be trimmed out on the pattern, as shown in the back view (see Figure 16.20b). This serves the same purpose as a shoulder dart and gives the back and sleeve a better fit with fewer wrinkles. The left side method in Figure 16.20b works well for most fabrics. The right side method in Figure 16.20b, in which all the shaping is taken from the lower back, is good for plaids. About $^5/_8$ inch should be removed and is blended to around 7 inches in from the edge.

- Bottom opening: The bottom opening is generally around 2 inches smaller (full measure) than the chest so there is not too much fabric to tuck in.

Pants

Pants are challenging to fit for many reasons. Women's pants often fit more closely to the body than men's, and depending on the style, have less ease. Women's pants often have a smaller distance between sizes, so the window between too large and too small is narrow. The precise curve of the rise is of critical importance and cannot be confirmed in measurements alone. A good fit depends on the relationship of hip-waist-thigh and rise.

People are sensitive about how their pants fit, and if they find a company whose fit they like, they are apt to become very loyal. For that reason, consistency is important, and being able to fit the same customer the same way (with variations for different styles) determines the success of the pants business.

Figure 16.21 shows the parts of a pant pattern. When making comments to the factory and noting what revisions are needed, it is important to use the terms consistently. There are various scenarios related to fit issues for pants. Several are described in the next sections, with recommended solutions.

Droop or Drag: Looseness or Tightness

There are a couple of factors that cause V-lines at the front rise: looseness and tightness. Figure 16.22 shows that the effect is caused by looseness at the side seams. The pattern solution is to

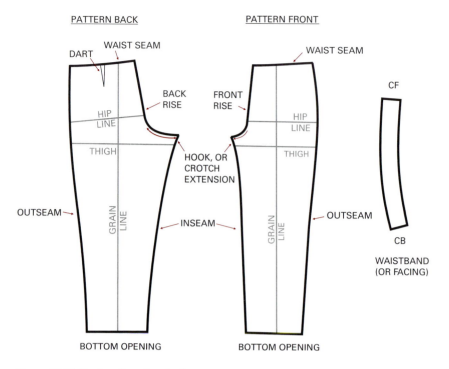

Figure 16.21 Pant pattern terminology.

reduce the girth at the side seams (see Figure 16.22b). The same amount would be taken off the pattern back. Another contributor in this case is a front hook that is too shallow (see Figure 16.22b). Figure 16.23 shows a similar-looking problem, drag, with a different cause. In this case the front rise is too short, either at the top or at the hook (or both).

Greedy Bum: Back Rise Too Short or Too Long

Figure 16.24c and d shows a common pattern problem in which drag lines radiate out from the back crotch. It is sometimes jokingly called "greedy bum" and is caused by the back hook being too short. There are certain advantages for the manufacturer in making the pattern the *incorrect* way because it uses less fabric and makes a tighter production marker. The incorrect shape is actually perfectly appropriate for a person with a small, flat seat shape. For a person with a rounder seat, however, the fabric is

pulled into the crotch point area. This may not necessarily be uncomfortable, but it is certainly unsightly. Figure 16.24a shows corrections that will solve the problem.

This problem cannot be detected by the back rise specification alone. The back rise measurement is 15 inches for both the right way and the wrong way. This is an important example of why a garment should be tried on the dress form or mannequin. The hook shape can sometimes even be correct on the sample size 8, but problems will show up on the larger sizes of a grade if the hook is not graded enough. This problem is an example of why it's important to review all sizes. It is also an example of the importance of a sloper pattern, which can be laid on top of and compared directly to the factory's pattern, and should be sent with all first protos.

Figure 16.24c also shows a related problem, a result of the back rise being too steep at the top. It collapses back and creates

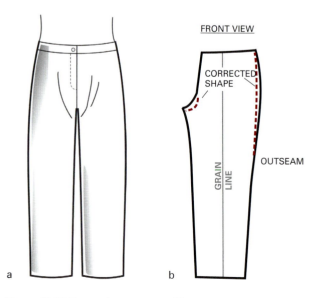

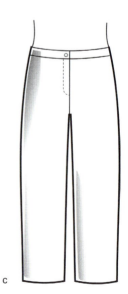

a   b   c   d

Figure 16.22 Droop: looseness at sides.

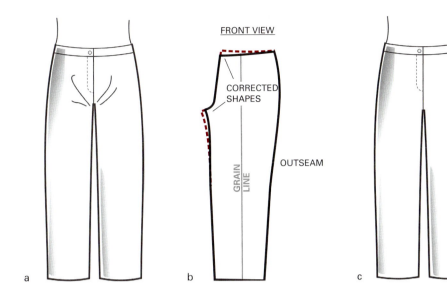

Figure 16.23 **Droop: short front rise.**

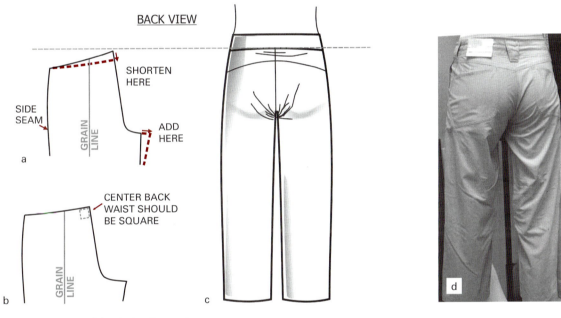

Figure 16.24 **A back hook that is too short.**

horizontal folds at center back, directly under the waistband. Unless there is a design reason not to, the center back seam at waist should be square (see Figure 16.24b).

Too Shallow Back Rise

When the back rise is too shallow, it feels uncomfortable in the back. It is not too tight in the hip, but it constantly feels like it needs to be adjusted in the back, especially when standing after having been seated. There is fabric where there should not be any. Sometimes other things need to be adjusted as well. The photographs in Figure 16.25 show various areas that could be improved:

- The back rise is dipping down. Extra should be added to the center back rise to "true it" (make it lie straight across). Note that there is nothing wrong with the waistband itself, just with the pattern piece below it.

- The elastic waist insert is creating extra gathers (that part is a result of the center back waistband elastication and must be accepted). Adding elastic to a waistband is a popular detail and helps a pant to "sell in" because buyers like it and perceive that it will fit more potential customers. In order for the style to "sell through," however, it has to be functional and flattering in all other areas as well.

- That same extra fabric is also ending up in the center back rise. The pattern should be re-shaped as indicated. (This same effect can also occur for another reason: too much dart shaping.)

- One side effect of re-shaping is that it will reduce the hip measurement. Since the pant is already a bit tight, more will need to be added at the side seam to compensate. The indication that it is tight is that it's very smooth horizontally below the 4 arrow. Above the arrow, there is more room. But it appears to be because the front hand pocket (not shown) is suddenly released above point 4, now free to gape open,

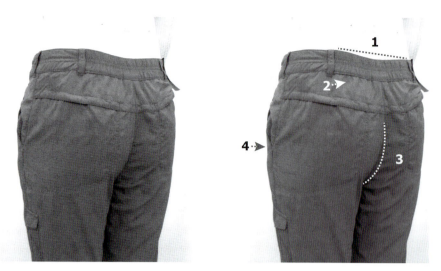

Figure 16.25 **Too shallow back rise.**

it up." (The photo in Figure 16.26c is the same as Figure 16.24d, since that pant had more than one problem, and more than one solution.)

This section would not be complete without a mention of muffin, or muffin top, the phenomenon that occurs when compressed flesh is suddenly released (see Figure 16.27b). The solution is nearly always that the area needs more girth. In this example the waistband is too tight.

Actual Fitting

The true test of the success of the design is in the actual fitting. Whether the design specs need to be adjusted or the factory's interpretation of the specs need to be corrected, problems with the fit are most clearly revealed in a fit session.

which is not a good effect. More ease added to the pattern at the side seam will allow the hand pockets to lie flat. This is a good example of how one or more things may need to be adjusted as the result of a design revision. If the company has a good block pattern to begin with, and the pattern changes are implemented by an experienced pattern maker, many of these effects are reduced, and many fewer samples are needed.

Up the Elevator: Too Small Waist

Figure 16.26 shows a problem called *up the elevator*, which occurs when the waist is too small. That in turn pulls the front and back rise too high. The pant essentially feels too small all over. The most important correction here is the waist dimension. This shows the way that the waist governs how the whole rise will sit. If only one adjustment is made, and that is to the waist, the entire pant will be able to move down into a comfortable spot. If the result is that the whole pant now sits too low, extra fabric can be added back to the rise so the top of the pant can return to the original location. A too small waist spec is a common problem. It would be the same as saying, "The pant fit great until I zipped

Conducting a Fit Session

The fitting process and sample evaluation are affected by the following factors:

- The spec and tolerances sent out (what the manufacturer was asked for). This includes intent of the garment as visualized by the designer.
- The actual measured garment, and where and how much it may vary from spec.
- The fit model, and how he or she varies from the size chart and ideal, sample-sized customer.

The ideal fit session is one in which the fit model represents the correct fit type and measures exactly to the size chart, the sample garment is precisely to spec on every point of measure, and of course, the original specs were flawless and perfectly suited to the fabric weight and garment purpose. This, however, is not generally the case. The fit meeting is the place to compare all the variables and then determine what changes need to be made for the next sample.

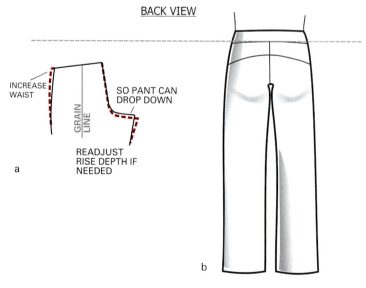

Figure 16.26 **Waist too small.**

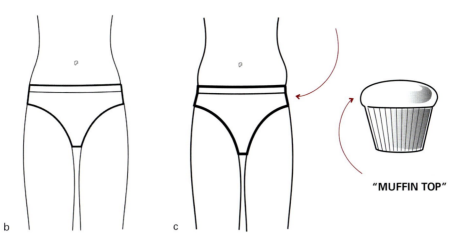

Figure 16.27 **Muffin top.**

Choosing a Fit Model

If the model is from an agency, measurements can be sent to the agency, which will then contact people close to those measurements and send them to the apparel company for confirmation. The model's first trip to get measured is called a *go-see* and is not usually billed; the policies of the agency should be confirmed in advance.

The models can bring their composite card (similar to a postcard with a head shot and at least three body shots) for the records. The composite card often has body measurements on it, such as bust, waist, and hip, but they are notoriously inaccurate, and correct measurements must be taken. For measuring, the prospective model should wear regular undergarments. A measurement chart should also be filled out for each model. Models have many individual variations in posture, musculature, and shape that make certain fit areas hard to predict just from measurements. Figure 16.28 shows key measuring points on the human body.

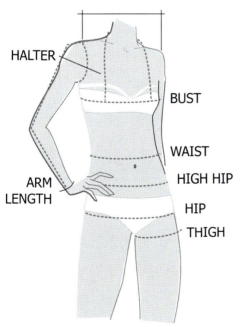

Figure 16.28 **Principal body measurements.**

The standard way to measure a fit model is as follows:

- *Shoulder point to point*: With arms hanging down, measure across the back from shoulder joint to shoulder joint.
- *Bust*: Measure around the fullest part of the bust.
- *Halter*: Measure around the neck, bust point to bust point.
- *Waist*: Measure around the waist.
- *High hip*: Measure around at high hip level, three inches down from the waist.
- *Hip*: Measure around the fullest part of the hip.
- *Thigh*: Measure around the fullest part of the thigh, close to the crotch.
- *Arm length*: Starting at the cervical vertebrae (the prominent bone at the bottom of the neck), measure to the shoulder joint, then along the outside of the arm with elbows lightly bent to just below the prominent bone at the wrist.
- *Inseam*: Ask the model to hold the tape at the crotch level, and measure straight down to the floor without shoes.
- *Height*: Measure from the top of the head to the floor.
- *Weight*: Record the model's weight from the scale. This is useful for future fit sessions because if the weight does not change, the model does not need to be re-measured. If their weight fluctuates more than two pounds, they should be remeasured.

After measuring, have the model try on a block garment, or a basic slim-fitting woven garment from the line that is known to have a good fit, for top and bottom. It is best to keep these garments available to use for all go-sees so you can compare apples and apples. Photos of front, back, and side should be taken for later review.

Prior to Fit: Preparation for Fitting

The samples for review should be measured in advance. This is the only way for the design team to truly know what is being reviewed as well as what they are looking at. A technical designer working on the design is the person who will usually do the advance measuring, but it should be reviewed beforehand by the designer. If time allows, try the garments on the mannequin first to check for balance and general position of details. The measurements should be noted on the fit history page and the out-of-tolerance measurements highlighted.

The Fitting Room

It is helpful to have a full-length mirror in the fitting room so that the fit model can review the garment appearance on herself or himself and comment when needed. After all, the model is representing the customer and customer concerns. There should be a table large enough to seat everyone comfortably, with a clear view of the fit model. A set of tools such as tape measures, chalk, and pins should always be available for meetings. These tools can be kept in a box to be available at all fit meetings.

At the First Proto Fitting

Each company has a different protocol for each type of fitting, but the designer, merchandiser, and other decision makers (and often a technical assistant) will usually attend. It is helpful to assign someone to take front, back, side, and detail (collar fit, for example) photos, if needed. Photos are helpful later to double check a point and compare fit from season to season. For outerwear and sweaters, the correct end use of the garment should be considered. For example, for outerwear, a shirt and a vest should be worn in the fitting to confirm that there is enough ease built in.

It is often complicated to schedule so many people for such a meeting, so it is vital to be prepared. The person running the meeting will read out all the measurements, do the pinning, and work with the garment on the model. The trims and other visual elements will be reviewed and confirmed. Any measurements that need to be changed will be agreed upon.

The job of the model is important, and a good model can be helpful in the fitting process. The fit model can comment on aspects such as how easy the garment is to get on; pocket positions and accessibility; sitting, standing, and reaching; and other questions about utility, appearance, and salability. At other times the model's job is just to be present for long periods while the design team members stare at the garment, discuss obscure fit subjects, and determine the impact of a quarter of an inch here and there.

Because the model is being paid by the hour, if there are issues that can be reviewed off the body, such as how far away two pockets are from each other, or how high a shirt cuff should be, those discussions can take place after the fit part of the meeting. The meeting itself should stay within its allotted time. After the meeting, the fit history is updated, the comments are sent to the factory, and a second proto sample is requested if it is needed.

At the Second Fitting

The second sample will again have been measured in advance and points of measure that were previously confirmed can be skimmed over quickly. Review what worked or did not work and note the out-of-tolerance measurements. Confirm the balance of the details. After the meeting, again update the fit history, send the comments to the factory, and request a preproduction sample (or another fit sample if needed). When the style is bought and put into the production schedule, it will be graded into the size set samples. These are reviewed in the same way, each on an appropriately sized fit model, and, when the style is ready, can be approved to preproduction.

Preproduction Review

Before the meeting, review the fit history and measure the sample. At the meeting, review only what is off-spec. At this point there cannot be any design or measurement changes made. The garment has long since been costed and most changes would negatively affect the margins. If there appears to be a problem, then the agent will need to be consulted to see what can be done. At this point the production department should be brought in to make sure there will be no shipping delays.

Reviewing Details: A Case Study

Let's take an actual example of a long-sleeved T-shirt (see Figure 16.29) and review the details together. Quality-related issues are important points to cover in this review. Figure 16.29 shows a first prototype garment, a long-sleeved cotton interlock T-shirt that is being reviewed on a mannequin. The main problem is that the neckline seems stretched out. The construction method for the neck edge is a self-fabric binding, using a 2-needle bottom coverstitch and a folder.

Some possible solutions are as follows:

- *Pattern Solution 1*: The knit trim pattern may be too long compared to the neck opening. If the neck is stretched while setting the binding, it will not be able to relax back to shape. Checking the pattern will confirm whether this is the problem;

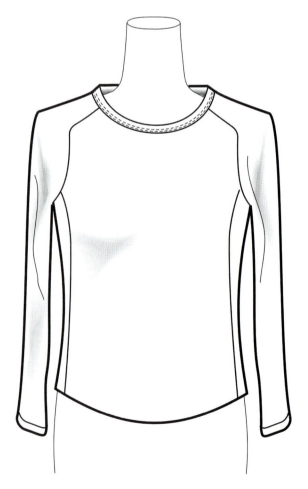

Figure 16.29 **Neckline problem analysis.**

the knit trim pattern should actually be *shorter* than the neck opening so it can be stretched on as it's sewn.

- *Pattern Solution 2*: The shoulder drop may be too steep. If so, it will tend to push up at the neckline (see Figure 16.29). Checking the pattern will confirm if this is the problem or not.

- *Fabrication Solution*: The interlock fabric may be too heavy for self-fabric binding, and neck trim in another fabric would result in less bulk. That would help the neckline to relax back to shape. A neck trim of 1×1 rib instead of self-fabric could be specified.

- *Construction Solution*: The binding folder setup has a setting known as "differential feed," in which the neck edge goes through the folder at a different rate from the binding. It may not be set correctly. The more stretch in the fabric, the more differential is required.

If the source of the problem is not clear, discussing it with a technical person in the company and then taking a photo to send to the factory will help when looking for a solution.

Summary

This chapter covers various aspects of fit and fit issues. *Fit* is a large term that connects many factors. A clear understanding of fit and the variables influencing fit is key to success for providing the products that the customer wants to buy. To creatively solve fit-related issues, critical thinking skills and knowledge of various aspects of apparel products are required.

Study Questions

1. What are the differences between the design ease and fit ease?
   a. Explain the differences in your own words. What is the ease for bust, waist, and hip on a woven shirt? What is the ease for waist and hip on a woven skirt?
   b. In Figure 16.4, why is the skirt waist so much smaller than the shirt waist spec?
   c. Refer to the *Technical Sourcebook for Apparel Designers* STUDIO. Find the Ease Chart and print it out.

2. Grab your favorite pair of pants. Measure all the girth measurement.
   a. Work with your partner to measure the same measurements.
   b. Compare the body measurements to the garment measurement and determine the ease.

3. When would the knee measurement of a pant be considered a design point of measure? Or a fit point of measure? What about a pant bottom opening? Suggest specs for each, based on pants of your own.

4. If your front rise is too short or too long, how can you solve this fit problem?

5. Look at the diagram in Figure 16.21. Which of the exterior lines are seam lines and which are hems? Identify which seam sews to which (inseams, outseams, front and back rises, waistband). Looking at a finished pair of pants as you go will help guide your answers.

6. Work with a partner. Each should bring one dress and one shirt from home. Measure your bodies and the garments and discuss with your partner what the design ease and fit ease is in the two garments.

7. How does the cap height for tops influence the design details and fit?
   a. Visit one of your favorite Internet retailers. Select three apparel products that show three different levels of cap heights (high, medium, and low).
   b. Provide visuals for each and explain the differences of product categories and styles based on each level of cap height.

8. What factors need to be taken into consideration before the fit session?

Check Your Understanding

1. List various factors taken into consideration to achieve a perfect fit.

2. List the various factors related to determining ease.

3. List standard ease for tops and bottoms.

Standards for Seams and Stitches

Standards for Seams (pages 302–307) shows a number of seam configurations and the common places they may be found. Two examples are seam type LSa and LSr (page 305). The illustrations show two alternative methods by which a sewing factory might assemble the waist area of a pair of bib overalls, depending on the finished style.

Standards for Stitches (pages 308–310) has examples of the stitch types produced by various machines to create different seam types. (A downloadable version of Appendix A appears in the *Technical Sourcebook for Apparel Designers* STUDIO.)

Standards for Seams

SEAMS DRAWINGS - INDEX

By Operations	Seam	Pg. #	By Operations	Seam	Pg. #
Attach & Edgestitch (usually 301 stitch)	SSae	5	Joining Bib to Overall	LSar	5
Bag Seaming - 401	SSd	6	Joining Bib to Overall	LSl	5
Bagging Welt Pockets on Trousers (usually 301)	SSc	6	Joining plies	SSv	6
Binding (2 needle - clean finish - 301 or 401)	BSe	2	Lap Seaming	LSa	4
Binding (2 needle - selvedge edge - 301 or 401)	BSd	2	Lap Seaming - top edge turned under	LSb	4
Binding (bottom coverstitch - 406 stitch)	BSb	2	Lining Cuffs for Dress Shirts	SSbc	6
Binding (clean finish - usually 301)	BSc	2	Making Belt Loops (for jeans, chinos)	EFh	2
Binding (coverstitch - 602 or 605)	BSa	2	Making Spaghetti	EFu	3
Binding (Mock clean finish binding - 2 operations)	BSg	2	Making Strap or Belt (1 needle)	EFj	3
Binding (Mock clean finish binding - 2 operations)	BSj	2	Making Strap or Belt (1 needle)	EFp	3
Binding (selvedge edge binding - 301 or 401)	BSa	2	Making Strap or Belt (1 needle)	EFy	3
Bolt-end seaming (501 - single thread overedge)	FSf	5	Making Strap or Belt (1 needle)	EFz	3
Butt seam & tape - generally 301 lockstitch	SSf	6	Making Strap or Belt (2 needle - 2 piece)	EFad	3
Centerplait (Cut-on centerplait - 401/301 stitch)	EFv	2	Making Strap or Belt (2 needle - 2 piece)	EFn	3
Centerplait (Set-on - generally 401 stitch)	LSm	4	Making Straps, Belts (hidden stitch w interlining)	SSaz	6
Cord seam only - generally 301 or 401 stitch	LSq (b)	4	Patch Pocket Setting - 301 stitch	LSd	4
Coverseaming only (straddle stitch - 406 stitch)	SSh (b)	6	Pocket Set (hem & set front pocket - jeans)	SSl	6
Crotch seam (Flatseaming with 607 stitch)	FSa	5	Pocket Set (patch pkt. - 2 operations)	LSs	4
Crotch seam (Flatlock seaming with 606 stitch)	LSa	4	Runstitch & Topstitch - generally 301 stitch	SSe	5
Crotch seam on Jeans - usually 301 stitch	LSas	4	Seam & Cord Seam	LSq	4
Darting (panel not cut - generally 301 stitch)	OSf	5	Seam & Topstitch Seam	LSq	4
Deco Stitching	OSa	5	Seam with Piping	SSk	5
Elastic attaching - 3 or 4 needle 401 stitch	SSt	6	Seam with Piping & Topstitch	SSaw	5
Elastic attaching - 406 or 407 stitch - underwear	LSa	4	Seam with Piping & Topstitch	SSav	5
Facing to front with Zipper	SSj	5	Seaming & Coverseaming	SSh	6
Felling (Mock Felled Seam)	SSw	6	Seaming (1st part of 2 part operation)	SSa	5
Felling or felled seam (2 or 3 needle 401 stitch)	LSc	4	Seaming (General)	SSa	5
Flatlock seaming (with 606 stitch)	FSa	5	Seaming then Taping Seam	SSag	6
Flatseaming (with 607 stitch)	FSa	5	Seaming with Stay Tape	SSab	5
French Seam	SSae	5	Serging - generally with 503, 504 or 505 stitch	EFd	3
General Seaming	SSa	5	Sleeve Set (2 operations)	LSr	4
Hem Seaming (clean finish)	SSp	6	Stripes attaching - 2 needle - either 301 or 401	SSat	6
Hem Seaming (raw edges)	SSn	5	Taping Edge - generally 301	SSaa	5
Hem Serging	EFe	3	Taping only - 2nd part of 2 part operation	SSag (b)	6
Hem with Elastic	EFf	3	Topstitch only - 2nd part of 2 part operation	SSe (b)	5
Hem with Elastic (2 needle)	EFg	3	Waistbanding (1 piece - binding - jeans)	BSc	2
Hem with Elastic (2 needle)	EFq	3	Waistbanding (1 piece)	LSk	4
Hem with Piping	LSn	4	Waistbanding (2 piece banc)	LSg	4
Hemming - 2 Ndl. hemming on knits	EFa Inv.	2	Waistbanding (2 piece w interlining)	LSj	4
Hemming - blindhemming w overedge	EFc	2	Waistbanding (with Elastic - 3 or 4 needle)	SSt	6
Hemming - blindstitch hemming (clean finish)	EFm	2	Waistbanding (with Elastic - 406 / 407 stitch)	LSa	4
Hemming - blindstitch hemming (serged or pinked)	EFl	2	Waistbanding (with "stitch-in-a-ditch" topstitching)	BSf mod	2
Hemming - Tunneled Elastic (2 needle)	EFr	3	Yoking (1 operation - w folder)	LSe	4
Hemming (clean finish)	EFb	2	Yoking (1 operation - wo folder)	LSf	4
Hemming (selvedge edge)	EFa	2	Yoking (2 operations)	SSq	6
Join & Tape Front (flatseamer)	LSz	4	Mock Felled Seam	SSw	6

Courtesy of American & Efird, Inc., www.amefird.com

8/25/2006

AMERICAN EFIRD, INC.

Seam Drawing	751a Number	ISO 4916 Number	Common Application	Requirements
	BSa	3.01.01	Binding Carpets, etc., with selvedge edge binding	1) Specify the Binding finished width.
	BSa	3.01.01	Setting collarettes & Sleeve Binding on Undershirts, etc. Usually sewn with a 602 or 605 coverstitch	1) Specify the needle spacing if 602 or 605 stitch is used; 2) specify the Binding finished width.
	BSb	3.03.01	Setting collarettes on T Shirts; binding legs and fly on knit briefs, etc. Usually sewn with a 406 bottom coverstitch	1) Specify the needle spacing if 406 stitch is used (Ex: 1/8", 3/16"); 2) specify the Binding finished width.
	BSc	3.05.01	For setting sleeve facings to shirts, piping edges of outerwear, etc. Can be sewn with a 301 lockstitch or 401 Chainstitch	1) Specify the width of the binding. Example: 1/2" Binding. 2) Requires a binding folder.
	BSd	3.01.02	Seaming with selvedge edge binding on Outerwear	1) Specify the needle spacing; and 2) Width binding. Example: 3/8" needle spacing and 1/4" Binding. 3) Requires a binding folder.
2 Ndl. Hem	EFa	6.02.01	Hemming Selvedge Edge Shirt Front	1) Specify width of hem.
	EFa Inv.	6.02.07	Hemming Tee Shirts, Polo Shirts, etc. Generally sewn with a 406 stitch.	1) Specify width of hem; and 2) Needle Spacing. (Ex. 1" hem with 1/4" needle spacing).
Clean Finish Hem	EFb	6.03.01	Hemming Shirts, Jeans, Shorts, etc.	1) Specify width of hem. 2) Generally a hemming folder is required or a hemming PF.
Blindhemming	EFc	6.06.01	Hemming bottoms of Tee Shirts, Undershirts, etc. Usually sewn with a 503 Stitch.	1) Specify width Hem. (Ex. 1" hem); 2) Generally a hemming guide is required.

Seam Drawing	751a Number	ISO 4916 Number	Common Application	Requirements
Topstitch hidden in seam line	BSf mod		"Stitch in a Ditch" - Topstitching Waistband with stitch line on top of previous seam line.	1) May require special PF with Guide so stitch is totally hidden
	BSg	3.14.01	Mock Clean Finish Binding	1) Specify width of Binding
Sewn in 2 Operations	BSj	3.05.06	Mock Clean Finish Binding	1) Specify the width of the binding. Example: 1/2" Binding.
Sewn in two operations	BSc	3.05.01	For setting waistbands to jeans, etc. Can be sewn with a 401 chainstitch or 301 lockstitch	1) Specify needle spacing; and 2) Specify the width of the binding. (Example: 1- 3/8" and 1- 5/8" Binding.) 3) Requires a binding folder.
Waistbanding on Jeans	BSe	3.05.05	Seaming and binding on Outerwear	1) Specify the needle spacing; and 2) Width binding. (Example: 3/8" needle spacing and 1/4" Binding.) 3) Requires a binding folder.
Blindstitch Hem	EFl		Hemming Dresses, Slacks, Coats, Bedspreads. Generally sewn with 103 blindstitch	1) Specify Width Hem
Belt Loops	EFh		Making Belt Loops for Jeans and Casual Pants, Shorts, Etc. Usually sewn with 406 stitch.	1) Specify needle Spacing & 2) Width of Belt Loop. (Ex. 1/4" needle spacing and 3/8" width belt loops) 3) Requires belt loop folder.
Blindstitch Hem	EFm		Hemming Dresses, Slacks, Coats, Bedspreads. Generally sewn with 103 blindstitch	1) Specify Width Hem
Centerplaiting	EFv		Cut-on Centerplait. Generally sewn with 2 rows of 401 stitch. (See also LSm - set-on centerplait)	1) Specify needle spacing; and 2) Width centerplait. (Ex. 1" needle spacing & 1 1/2" centerplait. 3) Requires centerplait folder.

AMERICAN EFIRD, INC.

8/25/2006

Seam Drawing	751a Number	ISO 4916 Number	Common Application	Requirements
Serging	EFd	6.01.01	Serging Pants Panels, Flys, Facings, etc.	1) Specify width Bite. (Ex. 3/16")
	EFe		Serging edges of napkins, sheer curtains, etc.	1) Specify width Bite. (Ex. 3/32") 2) A hemming P.F. is required.
Serge & Hem	EFf	7.24.02	Hem and Insert Elastic to Infants Panties, etc.	1) Specify the width of hem
Hem & insert	EFg	7.24.03	Hem and Insert Elastic to Infants Panties, etc.	1) Specify the needle spacing; and 2) Specify the width of hem. (Ex. 1/4" needle spacing and 1/2" width hem.) 3) Requires hemming folder & elastic guide.
	EFq	7.26.05	Hem and Insert Elastic to Infants Panties, etc.	1) Specify the needle spacing; and 2) Specify the width of hem. (Ex. 1/4" needle spacing and 1/2" width hem.) 3) Requires hemming folder & elastic guide.
	EFr	7.26.05	Hem and Insert Elastic to Infants Panties, etc.	1) Specify the needle spacing; and 2) Specify the width of hem. (Ex. 1/4" needle spacing and 1/2" width hem.) 3) Requires hemming folder & elastic guide.
Tunnelled Elastic				

Seam Drawing	751a Number	ISO 4916 Number	Common Application	Requirements
Making Spaghetti	EFu	8.07.01	Making straps. The stitch is hidden and not visible.	1) Specify with of strap.
	EFj	8.05.01	Making straps or belts with clean finish.	1) Specify with of strap.
	EFn	8.19.01	Making straps or belts with clean finish.	1) Specify needle spacing; and 2) Specify with of strap.
	EFp	8.06.01	Making straps or belts with clean finish.	1) Specify with of strap.
	EFad	8.17.01	Making straps or belts with clean finish with interlining.	1) Specify with of strap.
	EFy	8.03.03	Making straps or belts with clean finish.	1) Specify with of strap.
	EFz	8.03.04	Making straps or belts with clean finish.	1) Specify with of strap.

Left section

Seam Drawing	751a Number	ISO 4916 Number	Common Application	Requirements
Lap Seaming	LSa	2.01.01	Attaching knitted cuffs - generally sewn with a coverstitch - 605 or 607	1) A seaming guide or trimmer is used to keep the edges even. 2) Specify Needle Spacing. (Ex. 1/4" ndl spacing)
Lap Seaming	LSb	2.02.01	Not as common as LSq where the piece is attached and then corded or topstitched.	1) Specify the dimension from stitching to edge of top ply. Example: 1/8" header.
Felled Seam	LSc	2.04.06	Seaming Jeans, Shirts, Jackets, etc. Generally with a two or three needle 401 Chainstitch	1) Specify needle spacing & seam width. (Ex: 1/4 needle spacing w 3/8" seam width). 2) A felling folder with correct capacity is required.
Patch Pocket Setting	LSd	5.31.01	For setting patch pockets, flaps, pocket facings, etc.generally with a 301 Lockstitch	1) Specify margin (example: 1/16" or 3/32"). 2) A pressure foot with a yielding section is used to maintain a uniform margin from the stitch to the edge.
Patch Pocket Setting	LSs	2.05.02	For setting large patch pockets on Suit Coats, Overcoats and Jackets	1) 1st Operation - highly skilled operation; 2) Specify margin (example: 1/16" or 3/32").
Yoking	LSe	1.22.01	Seaming yokes to back on Shirts or Blouses in one operation. Not as common as SSq.	1) Specify margin (example: 1/16" or 3/32"); 2) A folder consisting of upper and lower scrolls are required.
Set-On Center Plait	LSm	7.62.01	Attaching Set-On Centerplaits to Shirts and Blouses	1) Specify Needle Spacing (Ex. 1"); 2) Specify width of Centerplait (Ex. 1 1/2") 3) Requires a Folder with Top Strip Folder with
	LSn		Not Common	
Joining & Taping	LSz	2.14.02	Joining & Taping Fronts of Knit Briefs & Thermal Underwear	1) Generally done on a 607 Flatseaming machine with or with the upper spreader thread. 2) Requires an upper Taping Folder with Folder.

Right section

Seam Drawing	751a Number	ISO 4916 Number	Common Application	Requirements
Attaching Elastic	LSa	2.01.01	Setting Elastic to panties or briefs - 406 or 407 stitch; Attaching knitted cuffs - generally sewn with a coverstitch - 605 or 607	1) A seaming guide or trimmer is used to keep the edges even. 2) Specify Needle Spacing. (Ex.- 1/4" ndl spacing)
Seam & Cord Seam	LSq	2.02.03	Sideseam on jeans; Chinos; Jackets, etc.	1) 1st Operation - specify seam width; 2) 2nd Operation - specify number of needles (1, 2, 3) and needle spacing.
Seam & Cord Seam	LSk	7.32.03	Waistbanding on Pajamas; Making Rod Pkt.on Curtains & Shower Curtains, etc.	1) Specify needle spacing and 2) Tape width.3) A folder combining a turn down folder and strip folder is required.
Two piece Waistband	LSg	7.57.01	Attaching a Waistband to Chinos or Work Pants	1) Specify the needle spacing; 2) width of W.B.; 3) A folder consisting of an upper strip folder and lower strip folder is required.
Two piece Waistband	LSj	7.76.01	Attaching a Waistband to Chinos or Work Pants	1) Specify the needle spacing; 2) width of W.B.; 3) A folder consisting of an upper strip folder with guide for interlining; and lower strip folder is required.
	LSf		Seaming yokes to back on Shirts or Blouses in one operation.	1) Specify margin from stitch line to edge (example: 1/16" or 3/32")
	Lsas		Crotch Seaming on Jeans & Chinos	1) Specify needle spacing - (Ex. 1/4")
	LSbj	5.30.01	Facing front pockets on jeans	1) Facing should be serged prior to being set.
Sleeve Set	LSr	2.06.02	Setting Sleeves on Dress Shirts or Blouses	1) 1st Operation - specify the seam width - a folder may be required; 2) 2nd Operation - specify topstitch margin.

AMERICAN EFIRD, INC.

8/25/2006

Seam Drawing	751a Number	ISO 4916 Number	Common Application	Requirements
	LSI	2.28.03	Joining the Bib to Pants of Bib Overall in 1 operation.	1) Needle Spacing and 2) Strip width are required.
	LSar		Joining the Bib to Pants of Bib Overall in 1 operation.	1) Needle Spacing and 2) Strip width are required.
Sewing Darts	OSf	6.05.01	Dart panel on Slacks, Chinos, Blouses, etc.	1) Specify width of Dart and length. (Ex. 3/8" wide and 3" long).
General Seaming	SSa	1.01	Most common seam construction for both wovens & knits.	1) Seam Margin must be specified to maintain fit. 2) A seaming guide or trimmer is used to keep the edges even.
Seaming & Taping	SSab		Joining Shoulders with Stay Tape; Attaching Facing to Jacket Front with Stay Tape	1) Specify width of Stay Tape; 2) Specify Seam Margin
Attaching Tape to Edge	SSaa		Attaching a Zipper tape to Fly Facing; Attaching Stay Tape to Armhole	1) Specify width of tape; and 2) Specify seam margin
Runstitch & Topstitch	SSe	1.06.02	For making collars & Cuffs on Shirts; attaching front pockets, bagging front pockets, setting fly on Chinos, etc.	1) Seam Margin must be specified on both 1st & 2nd operations. 2) A seaming guide is used to keep the edges even. 3) There is a turning process between 1st & 2nd process.
French Seaming	SSae	1.06.03	For edgestitching front facings on Jackets, Dresses.	1) Seam Margin must be specified on both 1st & 2nd operations. 2) A seaming guide is used to keep the edges even. 3) There is a turning process between 1st & 2nd process.

Seam Drawing	751a Number	ISO 4916 Number	Common Application	Requirements
Flatseaming	FSa	4.01.01	Flatseaming Underwear, Fleese, Exercisewear, etc. Generally sewn with a 607 stitch.	
Bolt End Seaming	FSf		Bolt-End Seaming with a 501 Stitch	
Decorative Stitching	OSa	5.01.01	Decorative Stitch Back Pockets on Jeans; Saddle Stitching	1) Specify Design Pattern with dimensions of stitch location
	SSj	1.11	For attaching a Zipper Tape between the Shell and Facing.	1) Seam Margin must be specified to maintain fit; 2) A seaming guide is used to keep the edges even. 3. A zipper Foot may be required.
Seam with Piping	SSk	1.12	For seam apparel, furniture with piping in seam	1) Seam Margin must be specified to maintain fit. 2) A seaming guide is used to keep the edges even. 2) May require a Foot with grooved bottom if cord is used in piping.
Seam, Fold, & Topstitch	SSax	1.18/1.19	For seaming and piping edges of pillow; Pajama Tops, etc.	1) Specify Seam Margin; 2) Topstitch Heading / Margin; and 3) a Folder may be used to make the piping w/ or wo cord
Seam, Fold, & Topstitch	SSaw	2.19.02	For seaming and piping edges of cushions; pillows; attaching yokes to backs on casual shirts, dresses, etc.	1) Specify Seam Margin; and 2) Topstitch Heading / Margin
Hem Seam	SSn	1.20.01	For seaming fabrics that may be susceptable to Seam Slippage	1) A hemming folder or guide is generally used. 2) Hem width should be specified. Example: 3/8" Hem.

Seam Drawing	751a Number	ISO 4916 Number	Common Application	Requirements
Seam, Fold & Cord	SSq	2.42.04	For attaching Yokes to Back or Shoulder Joining on Shirts, Blouses, etc. Similar to LSe but done in 2 steps.	1) A swing out marging guide is required along with a Yielding Presser Foot. 2) The correct PF with the preferred margin guide should be used (example: 1/16 or 3/32 inch).
Butt Seam & Tape	SSf	4.08.02	For Butt seaming & Taping heel seams on Shoes, etc.	1) Seam margin must be specified on 1st Operation. 2) Needle spacing and Tape width specified on 2nd operation.
Seaming & Coverseaming	SSh	4.04.01	For coverseaming knit tops, undergarments to reenforce the seam and give it a decorative appearance	1) Suggest using a 504 for 1st operation and 406 with 1/4" needle spacing for 2nd operation; 2) Seaming guide on Coverseaming machine.
Seaming, then Taping Seam	SSag	4.10.02	For taping the shoulder and neck of Tee Shirts	1) The finished width of the Tape and 2) needle spacing on the taping operation is generally required. 3) A taping folder is required to fold and guide the tape on to the seam.
Setting Stripes Shirts, Shorts, etc.	SSat	5.06.01	For attaching stripes to Shirt Fronts, etc.	1) Specify Tape Finshed Width and 2) Needle Spacing. (Ex.: 3/4" Tape with 1/2" needle spacing)
Mock Felled Seam	SSw	2.04.06	For Side Seaming Shirts, Blouses, Dresses, etc.	Manual method for making a felled seam. 1) Hem ply 1 around ply 2 - Specify Hem width and 2) Topstitch seam - Heading /Topstitch Margin
Mock Felled Seam	SSw (b)		For Side Seaming Shirts, Blouses, Dresses, etc.	Manual method for making a felled seam. 1) Lay ply 1 on top of ply two with edges uneven; 2) Fold and Toptitch - Heading /Topstitch Margin
	SSd	1.07	Not common.	1) Manual method for making a felled seam. 2) Specify Hem width and 3) Heading /Topstitch Margin
	SSv	5.01	Not Common	

Seam Drawing	751a Number	ISO 4916 Number	Common Application	Requirements
	SSp	1.21.01	For seaming fabrics that may be susceptable to Seam Slippage	1) A hemming folder is generally required. 2) Hem width should be specified. Example: 3/8" hem.
Hem Seam	SSs	7.09.01	Hemming and attaching zipper tape.	1) Specify width of tape; and 2) Specify seam margin.
Attaching Elastic	SSt	7.09	For seaming knitted or woven elastic to Boxers, Gym Shorts	1) Specify Width of Elastic; 2) Usually 2, 3, or 4 rows of 401 chainstitch are used to make this seam - Specify Needle Spacing. (Ex.: 1 1/4" Elastic with 4 rows 1/4" needle spacing)
Lining Cuffs	SSbc	1.03.01	Attaching Lining to Cuffs for Shirts & Blouses	1) Specify the Width Hem, if necessary.
	SSb	1.04	Not common	
	SSaz	8.11.01	Making Straps, Belts, etc.	1) Specify finished width. 2) This seam is made on a special "spaghetti" machine.
	SSl	1.08	For setting front pockets on Jeans	1) A hemming folder is used to hem the bottom ply uniformly. 2) Hem width should be specified. 3) If more than one needle, specify needle spacing (ex. 1/4")
	SSc	1.06.01	Not common. SSe is more common.	

Courtesy of American & Efird, Inc., www.amefird.com

Standards for Stitches

Stitch Drawing		ISO 4915 Number	Common Application	Requirements	Stitch Description
Top View As Sewn	Bottom View As Sewn				
Single Thread Chainstitch		101	Basting Stitch for Tailored Clothing; Bag Closing	Specify SPI.	Stitch formed by a needle thread passing through the material and interlooping with itself on the underside of the seam with the assistance of a spreader.
Single Thread Chainstitch or Lockstitch Buttonsew, Buttonhole or Bartack	* 304 Lockstitch is preferred when stitch security is a Must.	101 or 304	Buttonsew, Buttonhole, or Bartack	1) Buttonsew - specify stitches per cycle (Ex. 8, 16, 32) 2) BH - specify length & width (1/2", etc.) 3) Bartack - specify length & width of tack.	Knit Shirts - Buttonhole length generally is 1/2 inch, is placed horizontally, with approximately 85-90 stitches
Single Thread Blindstitch	No stitch visible on the Bottom or Outside of Sewn Product	103	Blindstitch Hemming, Felling, Making Belt Loops	Specify 1) SPI 3 - 5 SPI 2) Non-skip or 2 to 1 skipped stitch	Stitch is formed with one needle thread that is interlooped with itself on the top surface of the material. The thread passes through the top ply and horizontally through portions of the bottom ply without completely penetrating it the full depth.
Lockstitch - Most Common of All Stitches	Bobbin Thread on Bottom	301	Topstitching, Single Needle Stitching, Straight Stitching	Specify SPI.	Stitch formed by a needle thread passing through the material and interlocking with a bobbin thread with the threads meeting in the center of the seam. Stitch looks the same top & bottom.
Zig Zag Lockstitch		304	Intimate Apparel, Athletic wear, Infantwear, Exercisewear	Specify 1) SPI 2) Throw or width Zig-Zag (1/8", 3/16", 1/4")	Stitch is formed with a needle and a bobbin that are set in the center of the seam and form a symmetrical zig-zag pattern. Also, used to identify bartacking and lockstitch buttonsewing and buttonholing.
Chainstitch	Looper Thread on Bottom	401	Single Needle Chainstitch - Mainseams on Wovens	Specify SPI.	Stitch formed by 1-needle thread passing through the material and interlooped with 1-looper thread and pulled up to the underside of the seam.
Zig Zag Chainstitch	Looper Thread on Bottom	404	Zig-Zag Chainstitch for Infantwear and Childrenswear: Binding, Topstitching, etc.	Specify 1) SPI 2) Throw or width Zig-Zag (1/8")	Stitch is formed with a needle and a looper that are set on the underside of the seam and form a symmetrical zig-zag pattern.

Stitch Drawing		ISO 4915 Number	Common Application	Requirements	Stitch Description
Top View As Sewn	Bottom View As Sewn				
2 Needle Bottom Coverstitch	Looper Thread on Bottom	406	Hemming, Attaching, Elastic, Binding, Coverseaming, Making Belt Loops	Specify 1) Needle spacing (1/8", 3/16", 1/4") 2) SPI	Stitch formed by 2-needle threads passing through the material and interlooping with 1-looper thread with the stitch set on the underside of the seam. Looper thread interlooped between needle threads providing seam coverage on the bottom side only.
3 Needle Bottom Coverstitch	Looper Thread on Bottom	407	Attaching Elastic to Men's & Boys Knit Underwear	Specify 1) Needle spacing (1/4") 2) SPI	Stitch formed by 3-needle threads passing through the material and interlooping with 1-looper thread with the stitch set on the underside of the seam. Looper thread is interlooped between needle threads providing seam coverage on the bottom side only.
2 Needle Chainstitch with Cover Thread	Looper Thread on Bottom	408	Attaching Pocket Facings to Jeans & Chino Casual Pants		Stitch formed by 2-needle threads passing through the material and interlooping with 2-looper threads with the stitches set on the underside of the seam. A top spreader thread is interlaced on the top side of the seam between the two needle threads.
2 Thread Overedge	Single "purl" on Edge	503	Serging & Blindhemming	Specify 1) Width Bite (Ex. 1/8", 3/16", 1/4") 2) SPI.	Stitch formed by 1-needle thread and 1-looper thread with purl on edge of seam for serging or blindhemming ONLY.
3 Thread Overedge	Common Overedge Stitch	504	Single Needle Overedge Seaming	Specify 1) Width Bite (Ex. 1/8", 3/16", 1/4") 2) SPI.	Stitch formed with 1-needle thread and 2-looper threads with the looper threads forming a purl on the edge of the seam. For overedge seaming and serging.
3 Thread Overedge	Double "purl" on Edge	505	Serging with Double purl on Edge	Specify 1) Width Bite (Ex. 1/8", 3/16", 1/4") 2) SPI.	Stitch formed with 1-needle thread and 2-looper threads with the looper threads forming a double purl on the edge of the seam for serging ONLY.
Mock Safety Stitch	2 Needle Overedge	512	Seaming Stretch Knits, Wovens	Specify SPI.	Stitch formed with 2-needle threads and 2 looper threads with the looper threads forming a purl on the edge of the seam. 512 – right needle only enters the upper looper loop. Stitch does NOT chain-off as well as 514 Stitch
2 Needle 4 Thread Overedge	2 Needle Overedge	514	Seaming Stretch Knits, Wovens	Specify SPI.	Stitch formed with 2-needle threads and 2 looper threads with the looper threads forming a purl on the edge of the seam. 514 – both needles enter the upper looper loop. Preferred over 512 Stitch because it chains-off better.

Stitch Drawing		ISO 4915 Number	Common Application	Requirements	Stitch Description
Top View As Sewn	Bottom View As Sewn				
4 Thread Safetystitch		515 (401+503)	Safetystitch Seaming Wovens & Knits	Specify 1) Needle spacing & bite - Ex.: 1/8"- 1/8", 3/16"- 3/16'''- 3/16" – 1/4" 2) SPI	Combination stitch consisting of a single-needle chainstitch (401) and a 2-thread Overedge stitch (503) that are formed simultaneously. Uses less thread than a 516 stitch; however, many manufacturers prefer a 516 stitch.
5 Thread Safetystitch		516 (401+504)	Safety Stitch Seaming Wovens & Knits	Specify 3) Needle spacing & bite - Ex.: 1/8"- 1/8", 3/16"- 3/16'''- 3/16" – 1/4" 4) SPI	Combination stitch consisting of a single-needle chainstitch (401) and a 3-thread Overedge stitch (504) that are formed simultaneously.
2 Needle 4 Thread Coverstitch		602	Binding A Shirts, Infants Clothing, etc.	Specify 1) Needle spacing (Ex: 1/8", 3/16", 1/4") 2) SPI	Stitch formed with 2-needle threads, a top cover thread and a bottom looper thread.
3 Needle 5 Thread Coverstitch		605	Lap Seaming, Coverseaming, Binding on Knits	Specify 1) Needle spacing (Ex: 1/4") 2) SPI	Stitch formed with 3-needle threads, a top cover thread and a bottom looper thread.
4 Needle 6 Thread Coverstitch	Flatseamer/Flatlock	607	Flat or Lap Seaming Knit Underwear, Fleece, etc.	Specify SPI	Stitch formed with 4-needle threads, a top cover thread and a bottom looper thread. Preferred over 606 stitch because machines are easier to maintain.

XYZ Product Development, Inc. Selected Technical Packages

Notes on the Tech Packs

This section contains three tech pack examples, exactly as they might be created for product development. They are Women's Tank, Men's Woven Shirt, and Skiwear. The *Technical Sourcebook for Apparel Designers* STUDIO has 6 more tech pack examples included: Women's Skirt, Women's Woven Pant, Men's Tee, Hat, Men's Sweater, Bra.

The first tech pack, Women's Tank, has an example of a blank fit history and comments pages. The others do not repeat those because they represent new styles and there is not yet any history. Following the rules laid out in the book, knit girth specs (such as on the men's tee) are half measure, and woven girth specs are full measure.

Inch designations (such as 2 inches, $^3/_4$ inch, and so on) are used in the sketches but not on the Points of Measure page or Grades page. There, the inch measurements are plain (2, $^3/_4$, and so on) because the inch marks would interfere with the formulas.

Women's Tank

XYZ Product Development, Inc.
FRONT VIEW

PROTO# MWT1770	SIZE RANGE: Missy, 4-18
STYLE#	SAMPLE SIZE: 8
SEASON: Fall 20XX	DESIGNER: Monica Smith
STYLE NAME: Woven Tank	DATE FIRST SENT: 2/2/20XX
FIT TYPE: Natural	DATE REVISED:
BRAND: XYZ, Career	FABRICATION: A7777, Challis
STATUS: Prototype-1	

XYZ Product Development, Inc.

DETAILS VIEW

PROTO# MWT1770	SIZE RANGE: Missy, 4-18
STYLE#	SAMPLE SIZE: 8
SEASON: Fall 20XX	DESIGNER: Monica Smith
STYLE NAME: Woven Tank	DATE FIRST SENT: 2/2/20XX
FIT TYPE: Natural	DATE REVISED:
BRAND: XYZ, Career	FABRICATION: A7777, Challis
STATUS: Prototype-1	

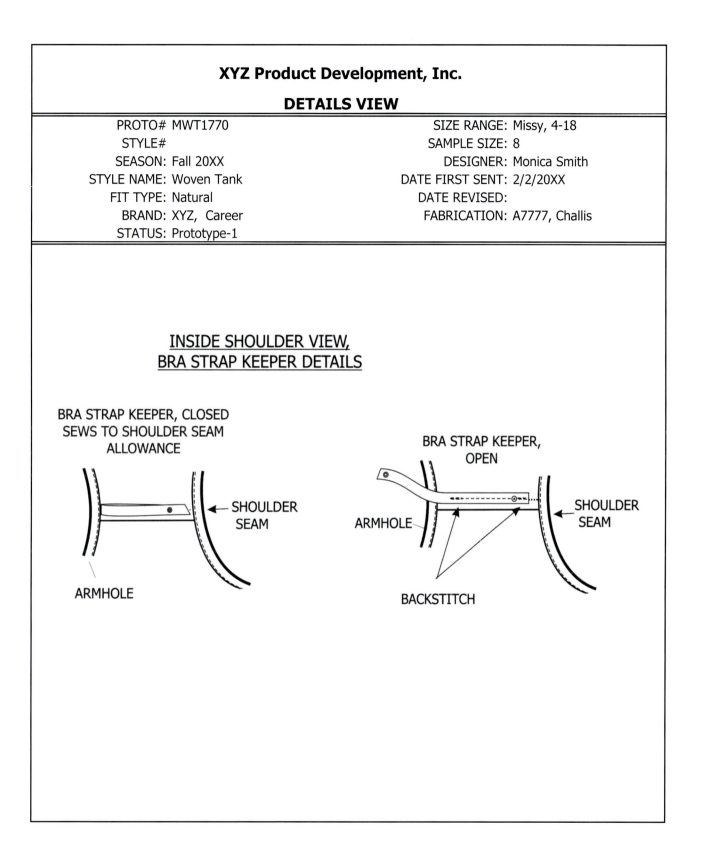

INSIDE SHOULDER VIEW,
BRA STRAP KEEPER DETAILS

BRA STRAP KEEPER, CLOSED
SEWS TO SHOULDER SEAM
ALLOWANCE

SHOULDER SEAM

ARMHOLE

BRA STRAP KEEPER, OPEN

ARMHOLE

SHOULDER SEAM

BACKSTITCH

XYZ Product Development, Inc.

DETAILS VIEW

PROTO# MWT1770

STYLE#

SEASON: Fall 20XX

STYLE NAME: Woven Tank

FIT TYPE: Natural

BRAND: XYZ, Career

STATUS: Prototype-1

SIZE RANGE: Missy, 4-18

SAMPLE SIZE: 8

DESIGNER: Monica Smith

DATE FIRST SENT: 2/2/20XX

DATE REVISED:

FABRICATION: A7777, Challis

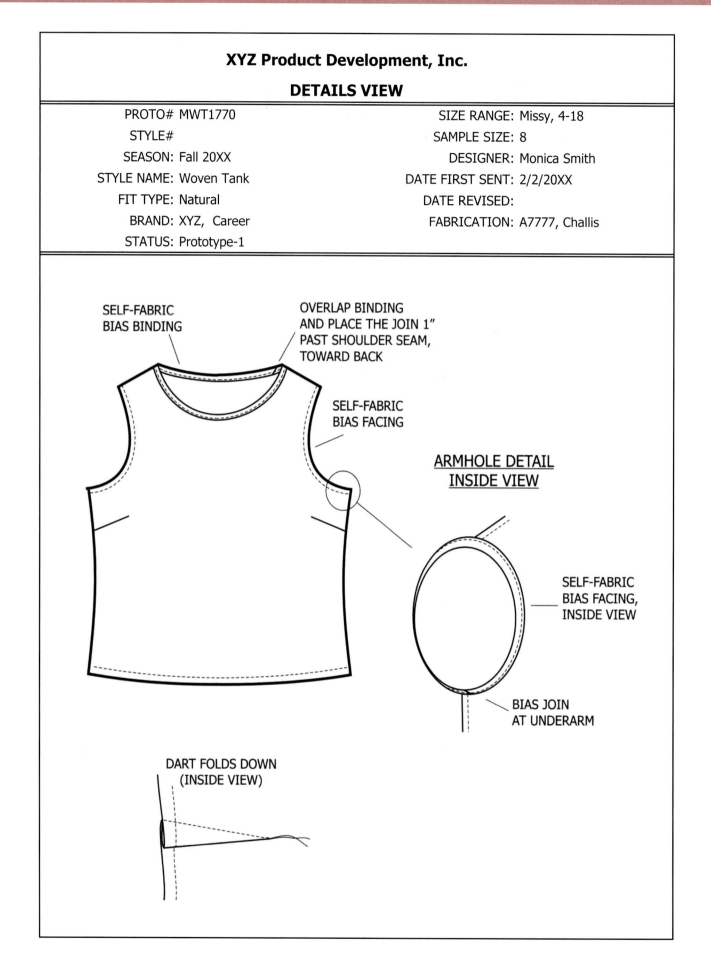

SELF-FABRIC
BIAS BINDING

OVERLAP BINDING
AND PLACE THE JOIN 1"
PAST SHOULDER SEAM,
TOWARD BACK

SELF-FABRIC
BIAS FACING

ARMHOLE DETAIL
INSIDE VIEW

SELF-FABRIC
BIAS FACING,
INSIDE VIEW

BIAS JOIN
AT UNDERARM

DART FOLDS DOWN
(INSIDE VIEW)

XYZ Product Development, Inc.
BACK VIEW

PROTO# MWT1770

STYLE#

SEASON: Fall 20XX

STYLE NAME: Woven Tank

FIT TYPE: Natural

BRAND: XYZ, Career

STATUS: Prototype-1

SIZE RANGE: Missy, 4-18

SAMPLE SIZE: 8

DESIGNER: Monica Smith

DATE FIRST SENT: 2/2/20XX

DATE REVISED:

FABRICATION: A7777, Challis

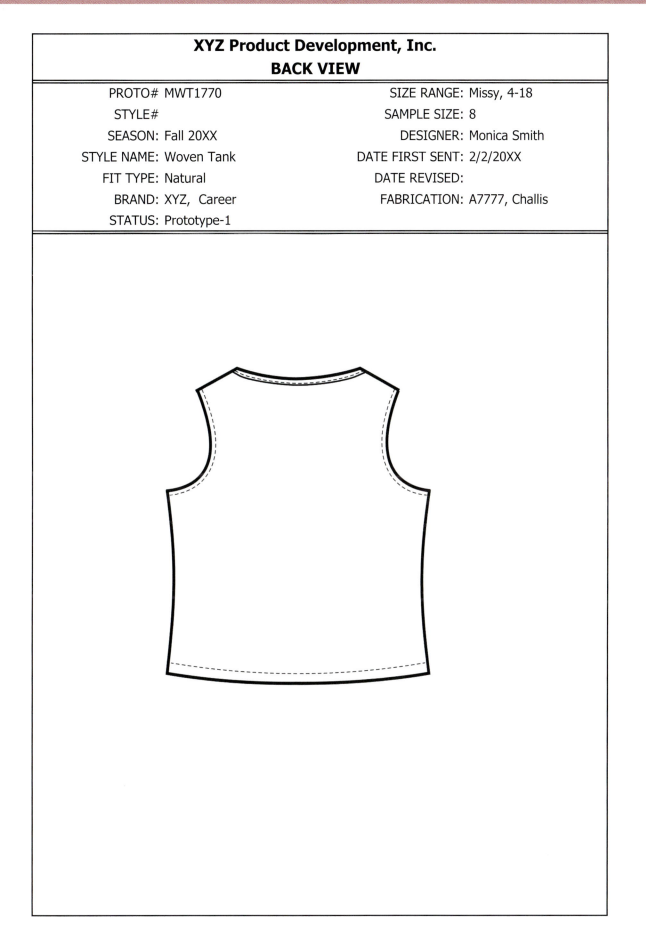

XYZ Product Development, Inc.
POINTS OF MEASURE

PROTO# MWT1770	SIZE RANGE: Missy, 4-18
STYLE# 0	SAMPLE SIZE: 8
SEASON: Fall 20XX	DESIGNER: Monica Smith
STYLE NAME: Woven Tank	DATE FIRST SENT: 2/2/20XX
FIT TYPE: Natural	DATE REVISED: 0
BRAND: XYZ, Career	FABRICATION: A7777, Challis
STATUS: Prototype-1	

POINTS of MEASURE, **WOVEN** (GIRTH MEASUREMENTS ARE WHOLE MEASURE)

code	TOP SPEC measurements	Tol (+)	Tol (-)	size 8
T-A	Shoulder Point to Point	1/4	1/4	15
T-B	Shoulder Drop	1/4	1/4	1
T-C	Across Front at 6" from HPS	1/4	1/4	13
T-D	Across back at 6" from HPS	1/4	1/4	14
T-G	Armhole Drop from HPS	1/4	1/4	8 1/2
T-H	Chest at 1" fm armhole	1/2	1/2	40
T-I-2	Waist	1/2	1/2	38
T-I	Waist position fm HPS	1/2	1/2	15 1/2
T-J	Bottom Opening	1/2	1/2	40
T-K	Front Length fm HPS	1/2	1/2	24
T-L	Back Length fm HPS	1/2	1/2	24
T-O	Center Back Sleeve Length (LS)	--	--	N/A
T-M	Bicep	--	--	N/A
T-Z-1	Sleeve Opening, Bottom	--	--	N/A
T-P	Front Neck Drop, to seam	1/4	1/4	5
T-Q	Back Neck Drop, to seam	1/4	1/4	1
T-R	Neck Width, seam to seam	1/4	1/4	10
	Bust Dart Position from Underarm	1/4	1/4	4
	STYLE SPEC measurements			
	Strap Width	1/8	1/8	2 1/2

SKETCH IS FOR REFERENCE ONLY, NOT FOR DETAIL

XYZ Product Development, Inc.

GRADE

PROTO# MWT1770
STYLE#
SEASON: Fall 20XX
STYLE NAME: Woven Tank
FIT TYPE: Natural
BRAND: XYZ, Career
STATUS: Prototype-1

SIZE RANGE: Missy, 4-18
SAMPLE SIZE: 8
DESIGNER: Monica Smith
DATE FIRST SENT: 2/2/20XX
DATE REVISED:
FABRICATION: A7777, Challis

POINTS of MEASURE, **WOVEN** (GIRTH MEASUREMENTS ARE WHOLE MEASURE)

code	TOP SPEC measurements	Tol (+)	Tol (-)	4	6	8	10	12	14	16	18
T-A	Shoulder Point to Point	1/4	1/4	14 1/2	14 3/4	15	15 1/4	15 5/8	16	16 3/8	16 3/4
T-B	Shoulder Drop	1/4	1/4	1	1	1	1	1	1	1	1
T-C	Across Front at 6" from HPS	1/4	1/4	12 1/2	12 3/4	13	13 1/4	13 5/8	14	14 3/8	14 3/4
T-D	Across back at 6" from HPS	1/4	1/4	13 1/2	13 3/4	14	14 1/4	14 5/8	15	15 3/8	15 3/4
T-G	Armhole Drop from HPS	1/4	1/4	8	8 1/4	8 1/2	8 3/4	9	9 1/4	9 1/2	9 3/4
T-H	Chest at 1" fm armhole	1/2	1/2	38	39	40	41	42 1/2	44	45 1/2	47 1/2
T-I-2	Waist	1/2	1/2	36	37	38	39	40 1/2	42	43 1/2	45 1/2
T-I	Waist position fm HPS	1/2	1/2	15	15 1/4	15 1/2	15 3/4	16	16 1/4	16 1/2	16 3/4
T-J	Bottom Opening	1/2	1/2	38	39	40	41	42 1/2	44	45 1/2	47 1/2
T-K	Front Length fm HPS	1/2	1/2	23 1/2	23 3/4	24	24 1/4	24 1/2	24 3/4	25	25 1/4
T-L	Back Length fm HPS	1/2	1/2	23 1/2	23 3/4	24	24 1/4	24 1/2	24 3/4	25	25 1/4
T-O	Center Back Sleeve Length (LS)	--	--			N/A					
T-M	Bicep	--	--			N/A					
T-Z-1	Sleeve Opening, Bottom	--	--			N/A					
T-P	Front Neck Drop, to seam	1/4	1/4	4 3/4	4 7/8	5	5 1/8	5 1/4	5 3/8	5 1/2	5 5/8
T-Q	Back Neck Drop, to seam	1/4	1/4	1	1	1	1	1	1	1	1
T-R	Neck Width, seam to seam	1/4	1/4	9 1/2	9 3/4	10	10 1/4	10 1/4	10 1/2	10 1/2	10 3/4
	Bust Dart Position from Underarm	1/4	1/4	3 3/4	3 7/8	4	4 1/8	4 1/4	4 3/8	4 1/2	4 5/8

STYLE SPECS

		Tol (+)	Tol (-)	4	6	8	10	12	14	16	18
	Strap Width	1/8	1/8	2 1/2	2 1/2	2 1/2	2 1/2	2 1/2	2 1/2	2 1/2	2 1/2

sample size

XYZ Product Development, Inc.

Bill of Materials

PROTO# MWT1770		SIZE RANGE: Missy, 4-18	
STYLE#		SAMPLE SIZE: 8	
SEASON: Fall 20XX		DESIGNER: Monica Smith	
STYLE NAME: Woven Tank		DATE FIRST SENT: 2/2/20XX	
FIT TYPE: Natural		DATE REVISED:	
BRAND: XYZ, Career		FABRICATION: A7777, Challis	
STATUS: Prototype-1			

item / description	content	placement	supplier	width / weight	finish	quantity
woven plain georgette, 110D tex, 27 x 116	100% viscose	body	Imprimee Thai	135 cm, 200 gm/m²	peach, washable	
interlining	--	--	--	--	--	
bra-keeper, style A22	100% polyester	shoulder--see detail page	Parma Supply	--	--	2
thread-DTM body	100% polyester	join and overlock	A & E	60's x 3 (tex 30)		
woven loop label, #IDC12		CB neck	Standard Label, factory sourced			1
woven loop label, #CCO14		left side seam	Standard Label, factory sourced			1
hang tag-career		right underarm				1
retail ticket						1
poly bag, and bag sticker (Flatpack)		see label page	factory sourced	H X W = 18 X 15	self stick, closes at bottom	1
safety pin--brass -- with string, for hangtags		see label instructions for placement	factory sourced			1
colorway summary						
color #	**main body color**					
477	coral print					
344B	aqua print					

XYZ Product Development, Inc.
CONSTRUCTION PAGE

PROTO#　MWT1770
STYLE#
SEASON:　Fall 20XX
STYLE NAME:　Woven Tank
FIT TYPE:　Natural
BRAND:　XYZ, Career
STATUS:　Prototype-1

SIZE RANGE:　Missy, 4-18
SAMPLE SIZE:　8
DESIGNER:　Monica Smith
DATE FIRST SENT:　2/2/20XX
DATE REVISED:
FABRICATION:　A7777, Challis

Cutting information: no nap, 2 way, lengthwise

Matching: NA

Stitches per inch (SPI) 11 +/- 1

AREA	DESCRIPTION	JOIN STITCH	SEAM FINISH	TOP STITCH	FUSIBLE	CLOSURES
neckline	bias binding finish, 1/4"	S/N-L		E/S		
shoulder seam	Fr/Sm	S/N-L		--		
armhole	bias facing	S/N-L		1/4"		
side seams		5T-safe		--		
bottom hem	clean finish (twice turn)	S/N-L		1/2"		
CLOSURES						

XYZ Product Development, Inc.
Fit History

PROTO# MWT1770
STYLE#
SEASON: Fall 20XX
NAME: Woven Tank
FIT TYPE: Natural
BRAND: XYZ, Career
STATUS: Prototype-1

SIZE RANGE: Missy, 4-18
SAMPLE SIZE: 8
DESIGNER: Monica Smith
DATE FIRST SENT: 2/2/20XX
DATE REVISED:
FABRICATION: A7777, Challis

dates:

code	BODY SPEC measurements	Tol (+)	Tol (-)	SPEC	1st proto meas	Difference	notes	Revised Spec, 2nd proto	2nd proto meas	Difference	notes	New Spec
T-A	Shoulder Point to Point	1/4	1/4	15								
T-B	Shoulder Drop	1/4	1/4	1								
T-C	Across Front at 6" from HPS	1/4	1/4	13								
T-D	Across back at 6" from HPS	1/4	1/4	14								
T-G	Armhole Drop from HPS	1/4	1/4	8 1/2								
T-H	Chest at 1" fm armhole	1/2	1/2	40								
T-I-2	Waist	1/2	1/2	38								
T-I	Waist position fm HPS	1/2	1/2	15 1/2								
T-J	Bottom Opening	1/2	1/2	40								
T-K	Front Length fm HPS	1/2	1/2	24								
T-L	Back Length fm HPS	1/2	1/2	24								
T-O	Center Back Sleeve Length (LS)	3/8	3/8	NA								
T-M	Bicep	--	--	NA								
T-Z-1	Sleeve Opening, Bottom	--	--	NA								
T-P	Front Neck Drop, to seam	1/4	1/4	5								
T-Q	Back Neck Drop, to seam	1/4	1/4	1								
T-R	Neck Width, seam to seam	1/4	1/4	10								
	Bust Dart Position from Underarm	1/4	1/4	4								

STYLE SPECS

		Tol (+)	Tol (-)	SPEC								
	Strap Width	1/4	1/4	2 1/2								

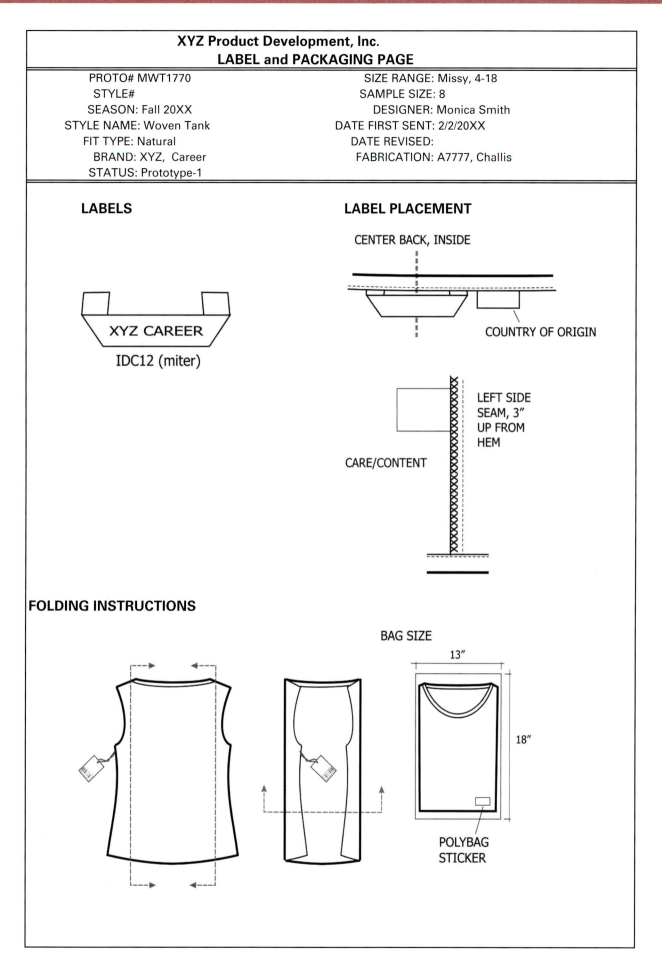

XYZ Product Development, Inc.
LABEL and PACKAGING PAGE

PROTO# MWT1770
STYLE#
SEASON: Fall 20XX
STYLE NAME: Woven Tank
FIT TYPE: Natural
BRAND: XYZ, Career
STATUS: Prototype-1

SIZE RANGE: Missy, 4-18
SAMPLE SIZE: 8
DESIGNER: Monica Smith
DATE FIRST SENT: 2/2/20XX
DATE REVISED:
FABRICATION: A7777, Challis

LABELS

XYZ CAREER

IDC12 (miter)

LABEL PLACEMENT

CENTER BACK, INSIDE

COUNTRY OF ORIGIN

CARE/CONTENT

LEFT SIDE SEAM, 3" UP FROM HEM

FOLDING INSTRUCTIONS

BAG SIZE

13"

18"

POLYBAG STICKER

XYZ Product Development, Inc.

Sample Evaluation Comments

PROTO# MWT1770		SIZE RANGE: Missy, 4-18	
STYLE#		SAMPLE SIZE: 8	
SEASON: Fall 20XX		DESIGNER: Monica Smith	
NAME: Woven Tank		DATE FIRST SENT: 2/2/20XX	
FIT TYPE: Natural		DATE REVISED:	
BRAND: XYZ, Career		FABRICATION: A7777, Challis	
STATUS: Prototype-1			

Date	
SAMPLE TYPE / ID#	preproduction
STATUS	**Approved to production**

Detail review

Date	
SAMPLE TYPE / ID#	size set
STATUS	**Approved to preproduction, use production quality fabic and trims**

Detail review

Date	
SAMPLE TYPE / ID#	sales sample
STATUS	**Approved to size set, send 32-40**

Detail review

Date	
SAMPLE TYPE / ID#	Prototype-1
STATUS	**Approved to Sales Samples, send pattern tracing**

Detail review

DATE	
SAMPLE STATUS	request for 1st prototype

Women's Tank, page 11 of 11

Men's Woven Shirt

XYZ Product Development, Inc.
FRONT VIEW

PROTO# SWT 4343

STYLE#

SEASON: Fall 20XX

NAME: Woven Shirt

FIT TYPE: Standard Shirttail

BRAND: XYZ, SPORT

STATUS: Prototype-1

SIZE RANGE: Mens, S-XXL

SAMPLE SIZE: L

DESIGNER: Rita Wilson

DATE FIRST SENT: 1/11/20XX

DATE REVISED:

FABRICATION: YD2w3,stripe

XYZ Product Development, Inc.
BACK VIEW

PROTO# SWT 4343	SIZE RANGE: Mens, S-XXL
STYLE#	SAMPLE SIZE: L
SEASON: Fall 20XX	DESIGNER: Rita Wilson
NAME: Woven Shirt	DATE FIRST SENT: 1/11/20XX
FIT TYPE: Standard Shirttail	DATE REVISED:
BRAND: XYZ, SPORT	FABRICATION: YD2w3, stripe
STATUS: Prototype-1	

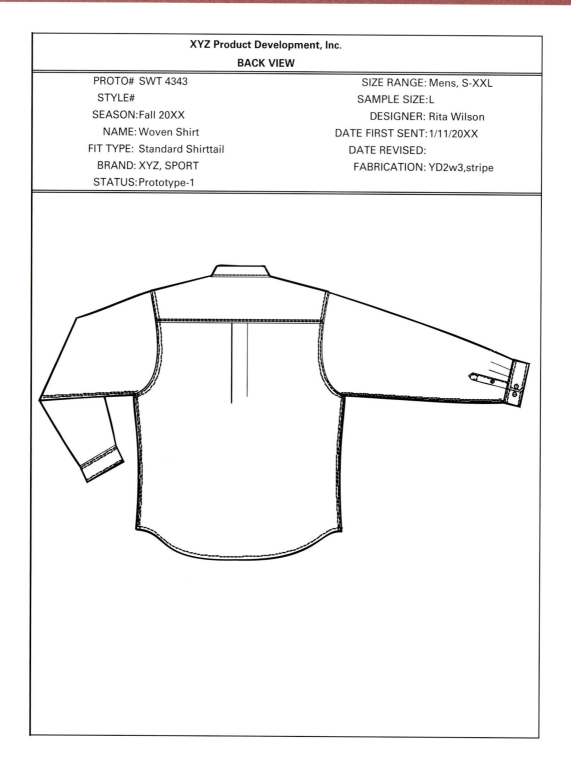

XYZ Product Development, Inc.

DETAILS VIEW

PROTO# SWT 4343
STYLE#
SEASON: Fall 20XX
NAME: Woven Shirt
FIT TYPE: Standard Shirttail
BRAND: XYZ, SPORT
STATUS: Prototype-1

SIZE RANGE: Mens, S-XXL
SAMPLE SIZE: L
DESIGNER: Rita Wilson
DATE FIRST SENT: 1/11/20XX
DATE REVISED:
FABRICATION: YD2w3,stripe

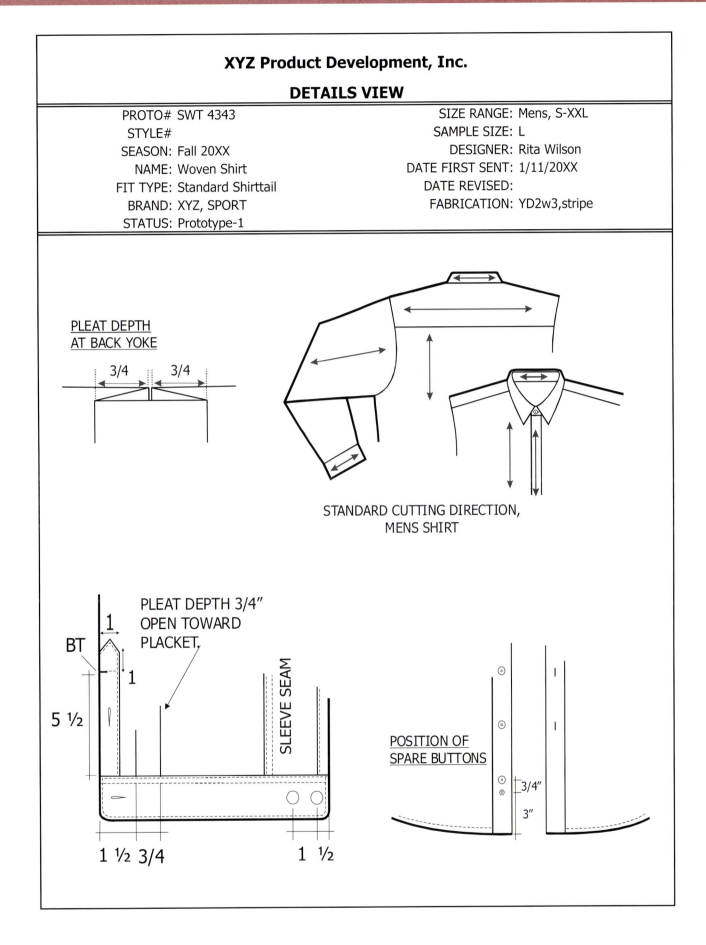

PLEAT DEPTH
AT BACK YOKE

3/4   3/4

STANDARD CUTTING DIRECTION,
MENS SHIRT

PLEAT DEPTH 3/4"
OPEN TOWARD
PLACKET,

BT

1

1

5 ½

SLEEVE SEAM

1 ½ 3/4   1 ½

POSITION OF
SPARE BUTTONS

3/4"

3"

XYZ Product Development, Inc.

DETAILS VIEW

PROTO#	SWT 4343	SIZE RANGE:	Mens, S-XXL
STYLE#		SAMPLE SIZE:	L
SEASON:	Fall 20XX	DESIGNER:	Rita Wilson
NAME:	Woven Shirt	DATE FIRST SENT:	1/11/20XX
FIT TYPE:	Standard Shirttail	DATE REVISED:	
BRAND:	XYZ, SPORT	FABRICATION:	YD2w3,stripe
STATUS:	Prototype-1		

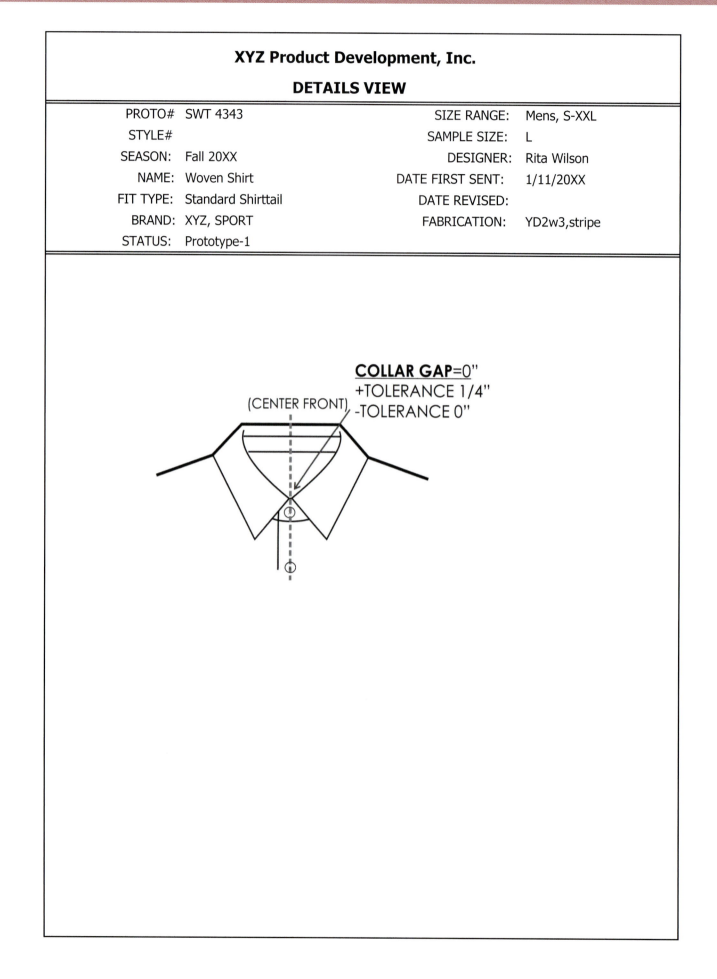

XYZ Product Development, Inc.

POINTS OF MEASURE

PROTO#	SWT 4343	SIZE RANGE: Mens, S-XXL
STYLE#		SAMPLE SIZE: L
SEASON:	Fall 20XX	DESIGNER: Rita Wilson
NAME:	Woven Shirt	DATE FIRST SENT: 1/11/20XX
FIT TYPE:	Standard Shirttail	DATE REVISED:
BRAND:	XYZ, SPORT	FABRICATION: YD2w3,stripe
STATUS:	Prototype-1	

POINTS of MEASURE, **WOVEN**   (GIRTH MEASUREMENTS ARE WHOLE MEASURE)

code	TOP SPECS	Tol (+)	Tol (-)	Spec
T-A	Shoulder Point to Point	1/4	1/4	21
T-B	Shoulder Drop	1/4	1/4	2
T-C	Front Mid-armhole @ 8" fm HPS	1/4	1/4	19
T-D	Back Mid-Armhole @ 8" fm HPS	1/4	1/4	20
T-G	Armhole Drop from HPS	1/4	1/4	13
T-H	Chest @ 1" fm seam	1/2	1/2	50
T-I-2	Waist (across)	1/2	1/2	48
T-I	Waist position fm HPS	1/2	1/2	18
T-J	Bottom Opening	1/2	1/2	49
T-K	Front Length fm HPS	1/2	1/2	31
T-L	Back Length fm HPS	1/2	1/2	31
T-O	Center Back Sleeve Length (LS)	3/8	3/8	36
T-M	Bicep @ 1" fm Seam	1/2	1/2	19
T-N	Elbow	1/2	1/2	16
T-Z-1	Sleeve Opening, Bottom, unbuttoned and flat	1/4	1/4	9 1/2
T-P	Front Neck Drop, to seam	1/4	1/4	4
T-Q	Back Neck Drop, to seam	1/4	1/4	1/2
T-T	Collarband length, bttn to bttnhole	1/4	1/4	17 1/2
	STYLE SPECS			
T-W	Collar Point	1/8	1/8	2 3/4
T-S	Collar Spread	1/4	1/4	3
T-U	Neck Band Height at CB	1/8	1/8	1 1/8
T-V	Collar Height At CB	1/8	1/8	2 1/8
	Back yoke fm HPS	1/4	1/4	4
T-AA	Cuff height	1/4	1/4	2

SKETCH IS FOR REFERENCE ONLY, NOT FOR DETAIL

XYZ Product Development, Inc.

GRADE PAGE

PROTO# SWT 4343
STYLE#
SEASON:Fall 20XX
NAME:Woven Shirt
FIT TYPE: Standard Shirttail
BRAND:XYZ, SPORT
STATUS:Prototype-1

SIZE RANGE: Mens, S-XXL
SAMPLE SIZE: L
DESIGNER: Rita Wilson
DATE FIRST SENT: 1/11/20XX
DATE REVISED:
FABRICATION: YD2w3,stripe

POINTS of MEASURE, WOVEN (GIRTH MEASUREMENTS and tolerances ARE TOTAL CIRCUMFERENCE)

code	TOP SPECS	Tol (+)	Tol (-)	S	M	L-sample size	XL	XXL
T-A	Shoulder Point to Point	1/4	1/4	20	20 1/2	21	21 3/4	22 1/2
T-B	Shoulder Drop	1/4	1/4	2	2	2	2	2
T-C	Front Mid-armhole @ 8" fm HPS	1/4	1/4	18	18 1/2	19	19 3/4	20 1/2
T-D	Back Mid-Armhole @ 8" fm HPS	1/4	1/4	19	19 1/2	20	20 3/4	21 1/2
T-G	Armhole Drop from HPS	1/4	1/4	12 1/2	12 3/4	13	13 3/8	13 3/4
T-H	Chest @ 1" fm seam	1/2	1/2	46	48	50	53	56
T-I-2	Waist (across)	1/2	1/2	44	46	48	51	54
T-I	Waist position fm HPS	1/2	1/2	17	17 1/2	18	18 1/2	19
T-J	Bottom Opening	1/2	1/2	45	47	49	52	55
T-K	Front Length fm HPS	1/2	1/2	29	30	31	32	33
T-L	Back Length fm HPS	1/2	1/2	29	30	31	32	33
T-O	Center Back Sleeve Length (LS)	3/8	3/8	34	35	36	37	37
T-M	Bicep @ 1" fm Seam	1/2	1/2	18 1/4	18 5/8	19	19 1/2	20
T-N	Elbow	1/2	1/2	15 1/2	15 3/4	16	16 3/8	16 3/4
T-Z-1	Sleeve Opening, Bottom, unbuttoned and flat	1/4	1/4	9	9 1/4	9 1/2	9 3/4	10
T-P	Front Neck Drop, to seam	1/4	1/4	3 1/2	3 3/4	4	4 1/4	4 1/2
T-Q	Back Neck Drop, to seam	1/4	1/4	1/2	1/2	1/2	1/2	1/2
T-T	Collarband length, bttn to bttnhole	1/4	1/4	16 1/2	17	17 1/2	18 1/4	19
	STYLE SPECS							
T-W	Collar Point	1/8	1/8	2 3/4	2 3/4	2 3/4	2 3/4	2 3/4
T-S	Collar Spread	1/4	1/4	3	3	3	3	3
T-U	Neck Band Height at CB	1/8	1/8	1 1/8	1 1/8	1 1/8	1 1/8	1 1/8
T-V	Collar Height At CB	1/8	1/8	2 1/8	2 1/8	2 1/8	2 1/8	2 1/8
	Back yoke fm HPS	1/4	1/4	4	4	4	4	4
T-AA	Cuff height	1/8	1/8	2	2	2	2	2

XYZ Product Development, Inc.
Bill Of Materials

PROTO# SWT 4343	SIZE RANGE: Mens, S-XXL
STYLE#	SAMPLE SIZE: L
SEASON: Fall 20XX	DESIGNER: Rita Wilson
NAME: Woven Shirt	DATE FIRST SENT: 1/11/20XX
FIT TYPE: Standard Shirttail	DATE REVISED:
BRAND: XYZ, SPORT	FABRICATION: YD2w3,stripe
STATUS: Prototype-1	

ITEM / description	CONTENT	PLACEMENT	SUPPLIER	WIDTH / WEIGHT	FINISH	QTY
Yarn-dye stripe, 150/1 x 44/1 , 34 x 23	100% cotton	body	Metro Ltd	44" cuttable/ 165 gm / m2	peach, washable	
interlining, non-woven, fusible	--	collar, cuffs, CF plkt	factory sourced	--	--	
Button, horn , 4-hole rimmed		CF placket and cuffs	Parma Supply	18L	semi-dull	12+1
Button, horn, 4-hole rimmed		slv placket	Parma Supply	14L	semi-dull	2+1
thread-DTM body	100% polyester	join and overlock	A & E	60's x 3 (tex 30)		
woven loop label, #IDC12		CB neck	Standard Label, factory sourced			1
woven loop label, #CCO14		left side seam	Standard Label, factory sourced			1
hang tag-sport		right underarm				1
retail ticket						1
poly bag, and bag sticker (Flatpack)		see label page	factory sourced	H X W = 18 X 15	self stick, closes at bottom	1
safety pin--brass --with string, for hangtags		see label instructions for placement	factory sourced			1

XYZ Product Development, Inc.
CONSTRUCTION PAGE

PROTO# SWT 4343		SIZE RANGE: Mens, S-XXL	
STYLE#		SAMPLE SIZE: L	
SEASON: Fall 20XX		DESIGNER: Rita Wilson	
NAME: Woven Shirt		DATE FIRST SENT: 1/11/20XX	
FIT TYPE: Standard Shirttail		DATE REVISED:	
BRAND: XYZ, SPORT		FABRICATION: YD2w3,stripe	
STATUS: Prototype-1			

Cutting information: see sketch on details page

Matching: match center of CF placket vertically, to dominant stripe

Stitches per inch (SPI) 12 +/- 1

AREA	DESCRIPTION	JOIN STITCH	SEAM FINISH	TOP STITCH	FUSIBLE	CLOSURES
collar	join and TS	SN-L	clean finish	SN-L	PCC 243, nonwoven	
collarband	join and TS	SN-L	clean finish		PCC 243, nonwoven	B/H zz, horizontal
CF placket	join and TS	SN-L	clean finish		PCC 243, nonwoven	B/H zz, vertical
back yoke	join and TS, sandwich bottom	SN-L	clean finish			
armhole	join and TS	SN-L	mock flat fell			
shoulder	join and TS	SN-L				
side/underarm seam	FLFL	FLFL	FLFL	FLFL		
cuff		SN-L	clean finish			B/H zz, horizontal
sleeve placket	join and TS	SN-L	clean finish	E/S		B/H zz, vertical
bottom opening		SN-L	clean finish- twice turned			

XYZ Product Development, Inc.
LABEL and PACKAGING PAGE

PROTO# SWT 4343

STYLE#

SEASON: Fall 20XX

NAME: Woven Shirt

FIT TYPE: Standard Shirttail

BRAND: XYZ, SPORT

STATUS: Prototype-1

SIZE RANGE:Mens, S-XXL

SAMPLE SIZE: L

DESIGNER: Rita Wilson

DATE FIRST SENT: 1/11/20XX

DATE REVISED:

FABRICATION: YD2w3,stripe

LABELS

LABEL PLACEMENT

XYZ SPORT

IDS15 (ENDFOLD)

CENTER BACK, INSIDE

FOLDING INSTRUCTIONS

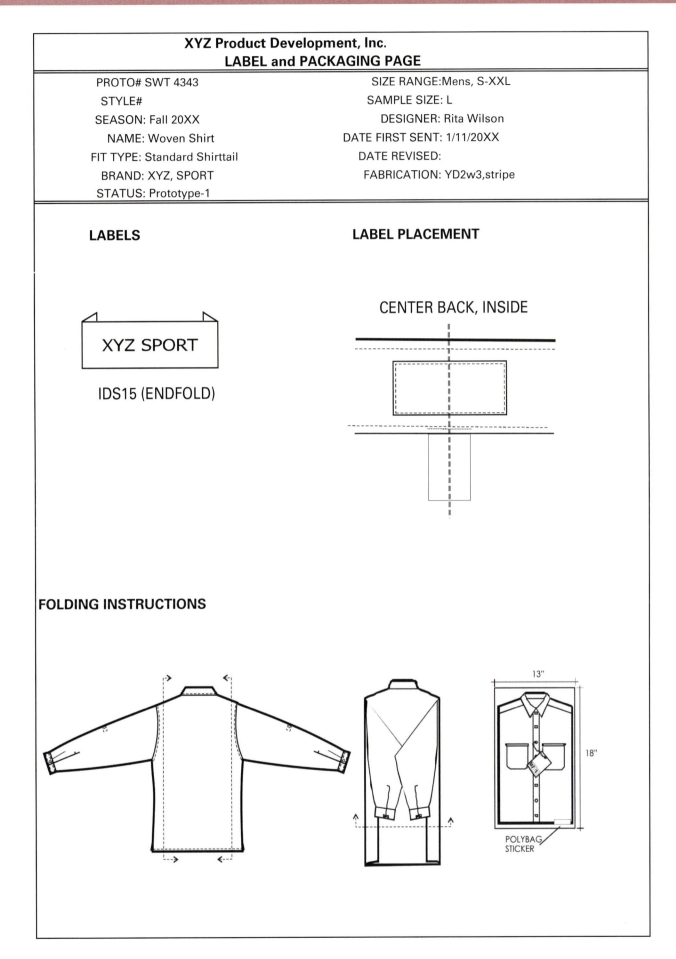

13"

18"

POLYBAG
STICKER

Skiwear

XYZ Product Development, Inc.
FRONT VIEW

PROTO# O-3LS 772

STYLE#

SEASON: Fall 20XX

NAME: Outerwear

FIT TYPE: Third layer

BRAND: XYZ SPORT

STATUS: Prototype-1

SIZE RANGE: Womens, XS-XL

SAMPLE SIZE: M

DESIGNER: Glinda

DATE FIRST SENT: 1/3/20XX

DATE REVISED:

FABRICATION: Waterproof-Breathable

XYZ Product Development, Inc.
BACK VIEW

PROTO# O-3LS 772

STYLE# 0

SEASON: Fall 20XX

NAME: Outerwear

FIT TYPE: Third layer

BRAND: XYZ SPORT

STATUS: Prototype-1

SIZE RANGE: Womens, XS-XL

SAMPLE SIZE: M

DESIGNER: Glinda

DATE FIRST SENT: 1/3/20XX

DATE REVISED: 0

FABRICATION: Waterproof-Breathable

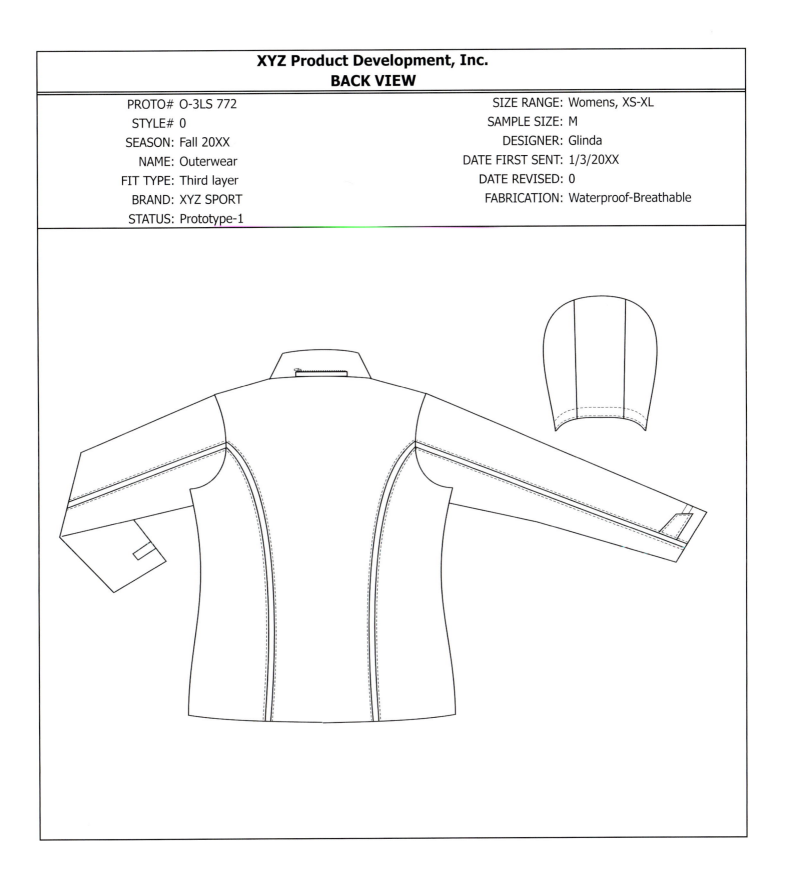

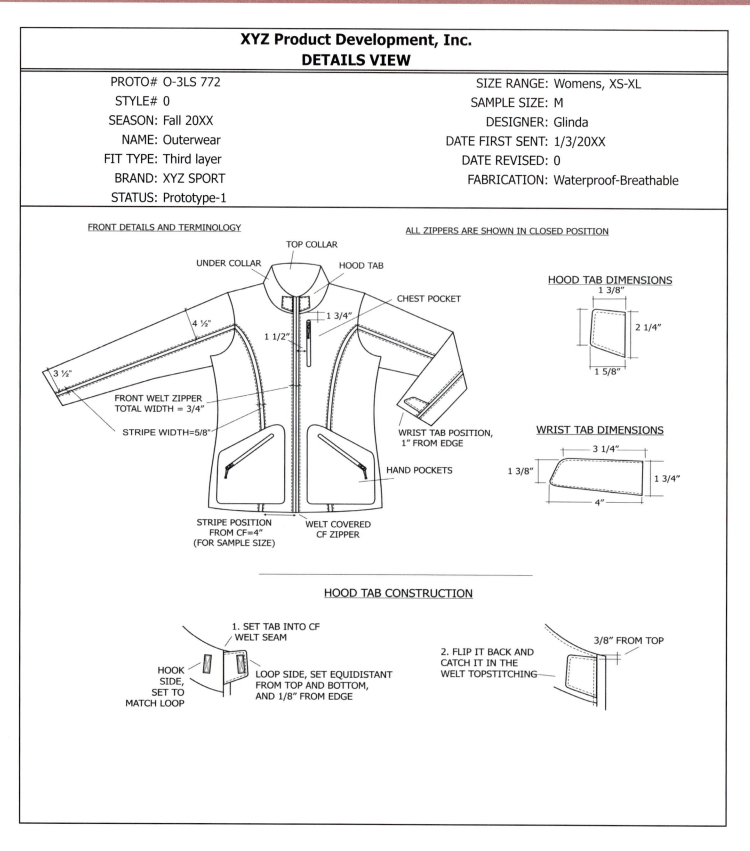

XYZ Product Development, Inc.
DETAILS VIEW

PROTO# O-3LS 772
STYLE# 0
SEASON: Fall 20XX
NAME: Outerwear
FIT TYPE: Third layer
BRAND: XYZ SPORT
STATUS: Prototype-1

SIZE RANGE: Womens, XS-XL
SAMPLE SIZE: M
DESIGNER: Glinda
DATE FIRST SENT: 1/3/20XX
DATE REVISED: 0
FABRICATION: Waterproof-Breathable

FRONT DETAILS AND TERMINOLOGY

ALL ZIPPERS ARE SHOWN IN CLOSED POSITION

TOP COLLAR
UNDER COLLAR
HOOD TAB
CHEST POCKET
4 ½"
1 3/4"
1 1/2"
3 ½"
FRONT WELT ZIPPER
TOTAL WIDTH = 3/4"
STRIPE WIDTH=5/8"
WRIST TAB POSITION,
1" FROM EDGE
HAND POCKETS
STRIPE POSITION
FROM CF=4"
(FOR SAMPLE SIZE)
WELT COVERED
CF ZIPPER

HOOD TAB DIMENSIONS
1 3/8"
2 1/4"
1 5/8"

WRIST TAB DIMENSIONS
3 1/4"
1 3/8"
1 3/4"
4"

HOOD TAB CONSTRUCTION

1. SET TAB INTO CF
WELT SEAM
HOOK
SIDE,
SET TO
MATCH LOOP
LOOP SIDE, SET EQUIDISTANT
FROM TOP AND BOTTOM,
AND 1/8" FROM EDGE

2. FLIP IT BACK AND
CATCH IT IN THE
WELT TOPSTITCHING
3/8" FROM TOP

XYZ Product Development, Inc.
POCKET DETAILS

PROTO# O-3LS 772

STYLE# 0

SEASON: Fall 20XX

NAME: Outerwear

FIT TYPE: Third layer

BRAND: XYZ SPORT

STATUS: Prototype-1

SIZE RANGE: Womens, XS-XL

SAMPLE SIZE: M

DESIGNER: Glinda

DATE FIRST SENT: 1/3/20XX

DATE REVISED: 0

FABRICATION: Waterproof-Breathable

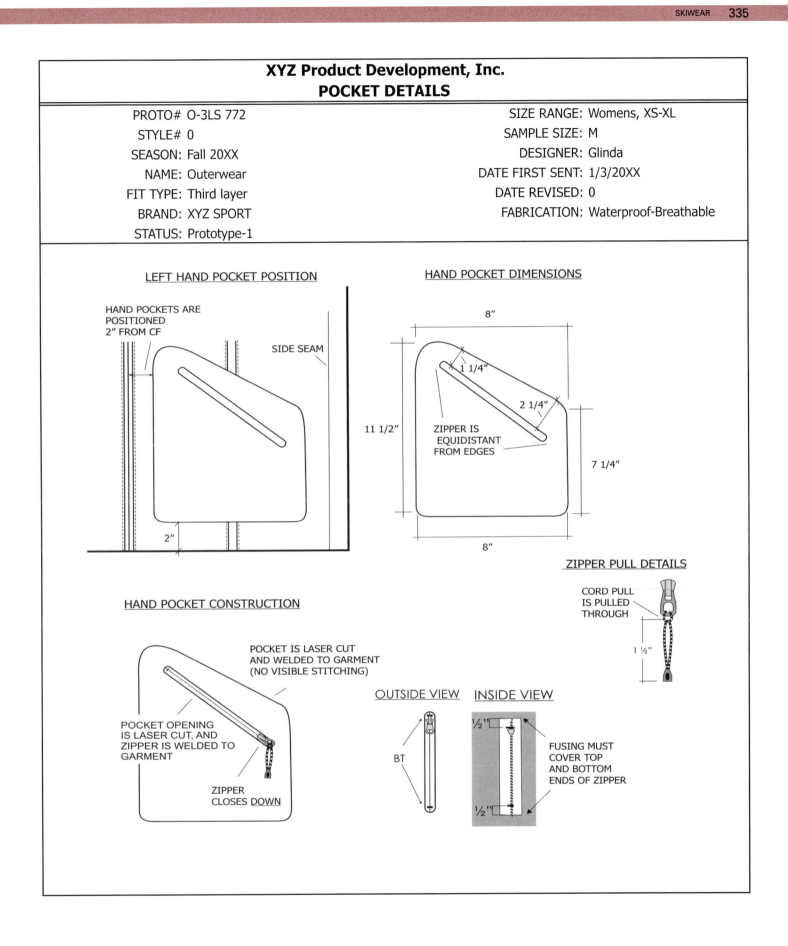

LEFT HAND POCKET POSITION

HAND POCKETS ARE POSITIONED 2" FROM CF

SIDE SEAM

2"

HAND POCKET DIMENSIONS

8"

1 1/4"

2 1/4"

ZIPPER IS EQUIDISTANT FROM EDGES

11 1/2"

7 1/4"

8"

ZIPPER PULL DETAILS

CORD PULL IS PULLED THROUGH

1 ½"

HAND POCKET CONSTRUCTION

POCKET IS LASER CUT AND WELDED TO GARMENT (NO VISIBLE STITCHING)

POCKET OPENING IS LASER CUT, AND ZIPPER IS WELDED TO GARMENT

ZIPPER CLOSES DOWN

OUTSIDE VIEW

BT

INSIDE VIEW

½"

½"

FUSING MUST COVER TOP AND BOTTOM ENDS OF ZIPPER

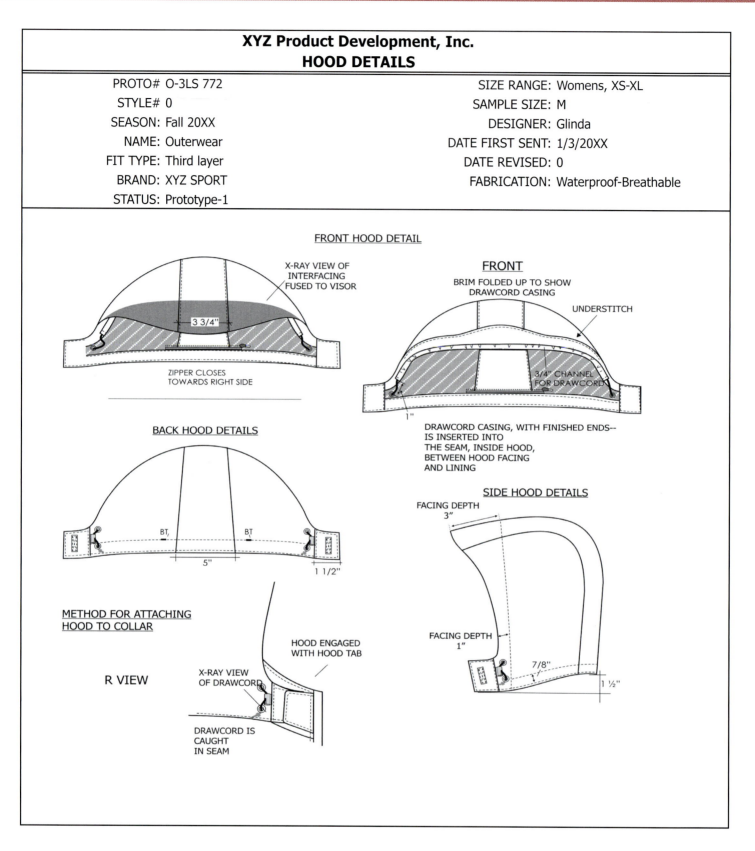

XYZ Product Development, Inc.
HOOD DETAILS

PROTO# O-3LS 772
STYLE# 0
SEASON: Fall 20XX
NAME: Outerwear
FIT TYPE: Third layer
BRAND: XYZ SPORT
STATUS: Prototype-1

SIZE RANGE: Womens, XS-XL
SAMPLE SIZE: M
DESIGNER: Glinda
DATE FIRST SENT: 1/3/20XX
DATE REVISED: 0
FABRICATION: Waterproof-Breathable

FRONT HOOD DETAIL

X-RAY VIEW OF
INTERFACING
FUSED TO VISOR

3 3/4"

ZIPPER CLOSES
TOWARDS RIGHT SIDE

FRONT

BRIM FOLDED UP TO SHOW
DRAWCORD CASING

UNDERSTITCH

3/4" CHANNEL
FOR DRAWCORD

1"

DRAWCORD CASING, WITH FINISHED ENDS--
IS INSERTED INTO
THE SEAM, INSIDE HOOD,
BETWEEN HOOD FACING
AND LINING

BACK HOOD DETAILS

BT   BT

5"

1 1/2"

SIDE HOOD DETAILS

FACING DEPTH
3"

FACING DEPTH
1"

7/8"

1 ½"

METHOD FOR ATTACHING
HOOD TO COLLAR

R VIEW

HOOD ENGAGED
WITH HOOD TAB

X-RAY VIEW
OF DRAWCORD

DRAWCORD IS
CAUGHT
IN SEAM

Skiwear, page 5 of 16

XYZ Product Development, Inc.
LINING DETAILS

PROTO# O-3LS 772
STYLE# 0
SEASON: Fall 20XX
NAME: Outerwear
FIT TYPE: Third layer
BRAND: XYZ SPORT
STATUS: Prototype-1

SIZE RANGE: Womens, XS-XL
SAMPLE SIZE: M
DESIGNER: Glinda
DATE FIRST SENT: 1/3/20XX
DATE REVISED: 0
FABRICATION: Waterproof-Breathable

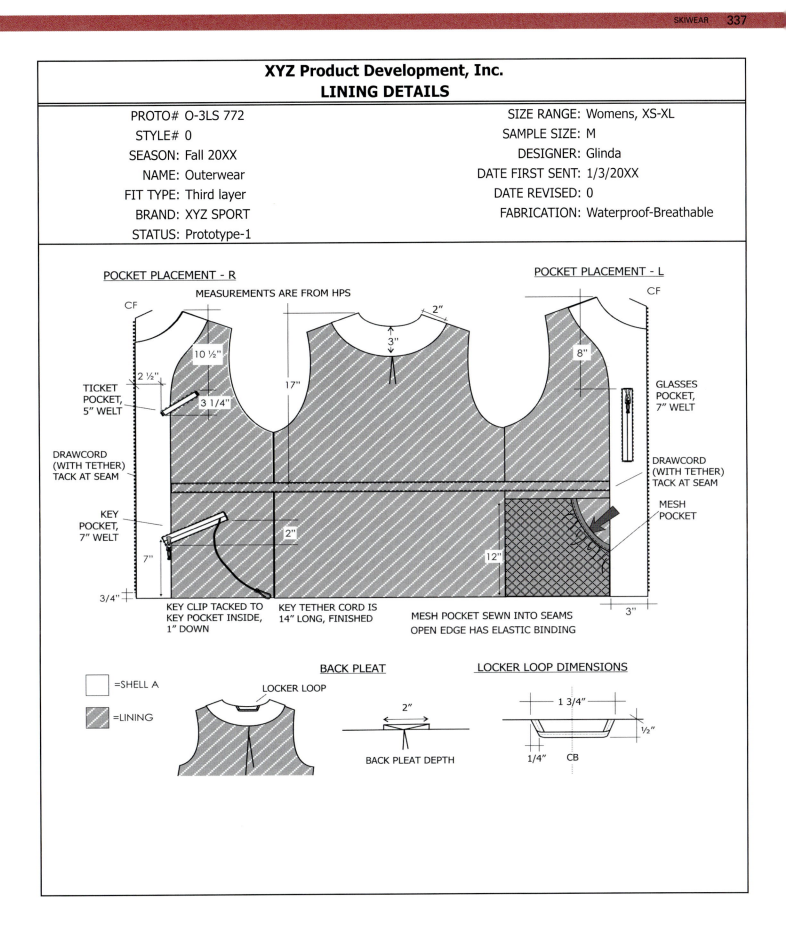

POCKET PLACEMENT - R
MEASUREMENTS ARE FROM HPS

POCKET PLACEMENT - L

CF

CF

2"

3"

10 ½"

8"

2 ½"

TICKET POCKET, 5" WELT

3 1/4"

17"

GLASSES POCKET, 7" WELT

DRAWCORD (WITH TETHER) TACK AT SEAM

DRAWCORD (WITH TETHER) TACK AT SEAM

KEY POCKET, 7" WELT

2"

MESH POCKET

7"

12"

3/4"

3"

KEY CLIP TACKED TO KEY POCKET INSIDE, 1" DOWN

KEY TETHER CORD IS 14" LONG, FINISHED

MESH POCKET SEWN INTO SEAMS OPEN EDGE HAS ELASTIC BINDING

=SHELL A

=LINING

BACK PLEAT

LOCKER LOOP

2"

BACK PLEAT DEPTH

LOCKER LOOP DIMENSIONS

1 3/4"

½"

1/4"   CB

XYZ Product Development, Inc.
BACK VIEW

PROTO# O-3LS 772
STYLE# 0
SEASON: Fall 20XX
NAME: Outerwear
FIT TYPE: Third layer
BRAND: XYZ SPORT
STATUS: Prototype-1

SIZE RANGE: Womens, XS-XL
SAMPLE SIZE: M
DESIGNER: Glinda
DATE FIRST SENT: 1/3/20XX
DATE REVISED: 0
FABRICATION: Waterproof-Breathable

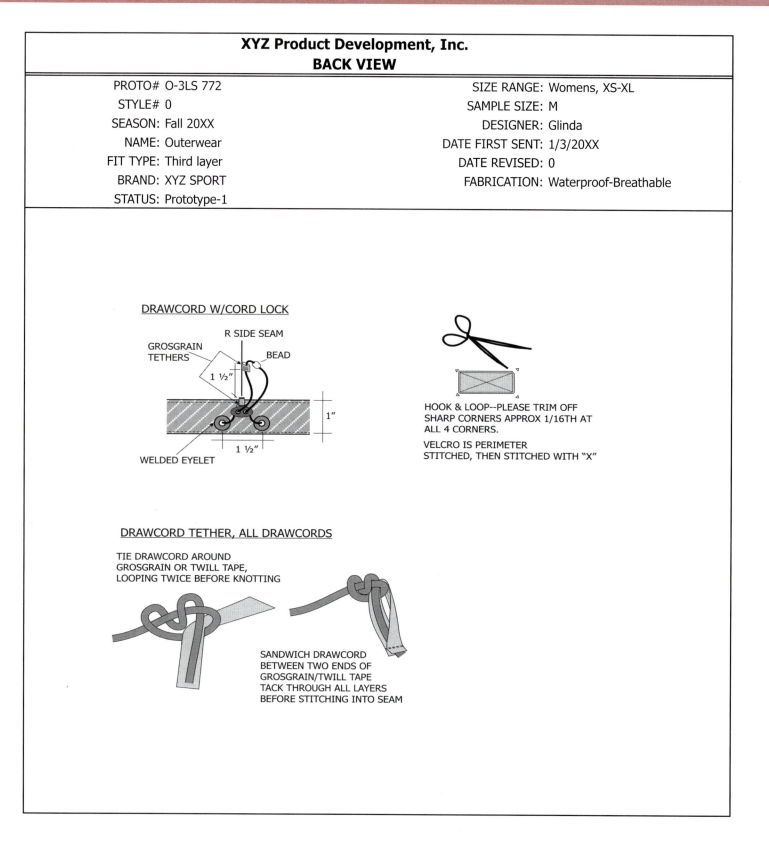

DRAWCORD W/CORD LOCK

GROSGRAIN TETHERS
R SIDE SEAM
BEAD
1 ½"
1"
1 ½"
WELDED EYELET

HOOK & LOOP--PLEASE TRIM OFF SHARP CORNERS APPROX 1/16TH AT ALL 4 CORNERS.

VELCRO IS PERIMETER STITCHED, THEN STITCHED WITH "X"

DRAWCORD TETHER, ALL DRAWCORDS

TIE DRAWCORD AROUND GROSGRAIN OR TWILL TAPE, LOOPING TWICE BEFORE KNOTTING

SANDWICH DRAWCORD BETWEEN TWO ENDS OF GROSGRAIN/TWILL TAPE TACK THROUGH ALL LAYERS BEFORE STITCHING INTO SEAM

XYZ Product Development, Inc.
BACK VIEW

PROTO# O-3LS 772
STYLE# 0
SEASON: Fall 20XX
NAME: Outerwear
FIT TYPE: Third layer
BRAND: XYZ SPORT
STATUS: Prototype-1

SIZE RANGE: Womens, XS-XL
SAMPLE SIZE: M
DESIGNER: Glinda
DATE FIRST SENT: 1/3/20XX
DATE REVISED: 0
FABRICATION: Waterproof-Breathable

WELDED AREAS MARKED IN BLUE

(ZIPPERS, HAND POCKETS AND
HEM FOR BOTTOM AND FOR SLEEVES)

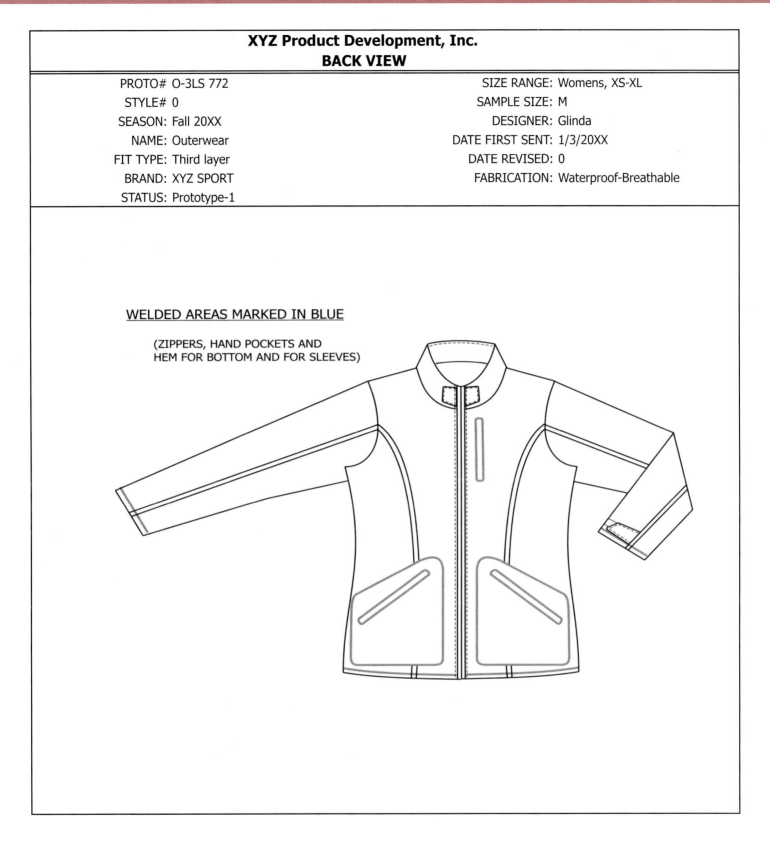

XYZ Product Development, Inc.
BACK VIEW

PROTO# O-3LS 772

STYLE# 0

SEASON: Fall 20XX

NAME: Outerwear

FIT TYPE: Third layer

BRAND: XYZ SPORT

STATUS: Prototype-1

SIZE RANGE: Womens, XS-XL

SAMPLE SIZE: M

DESIGNER: Glinda

DATE FIRST SENT: 1/3/20XX

DATE REVISED: 0

FABRICATION: Waterproof-Breathable

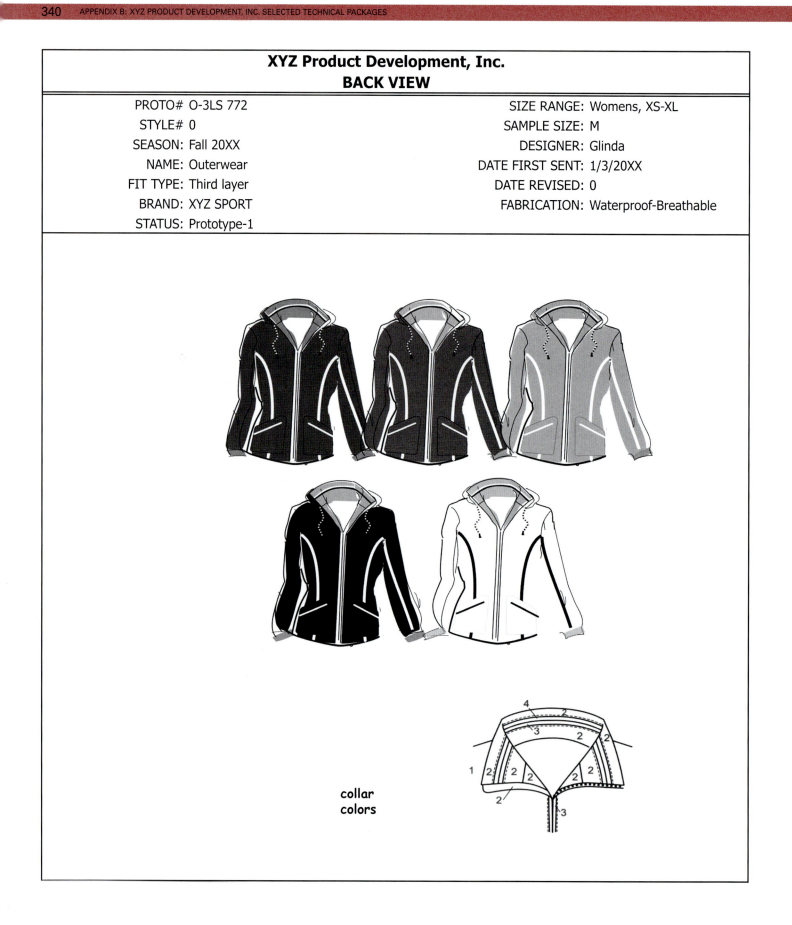

collar
colors

XYZ Product Development, Inc.
BACK VIEW

PROTO# O-3LS 772

STYLE# 0

SEASON: Fall 20XX

NAME: Outerwear

FIT TYPE: Third layer

BRAND: XYZ SPORT

STATUS: Prototype-1

SIZE RANGE: Womens, XS-XL

SAMPLE SIZE: M

DESIGNER: Glinda

DATE FIRST SENT: 1/3/20XX

DATE REVISED: 0

FABRICATION: Waterproof-Breathable

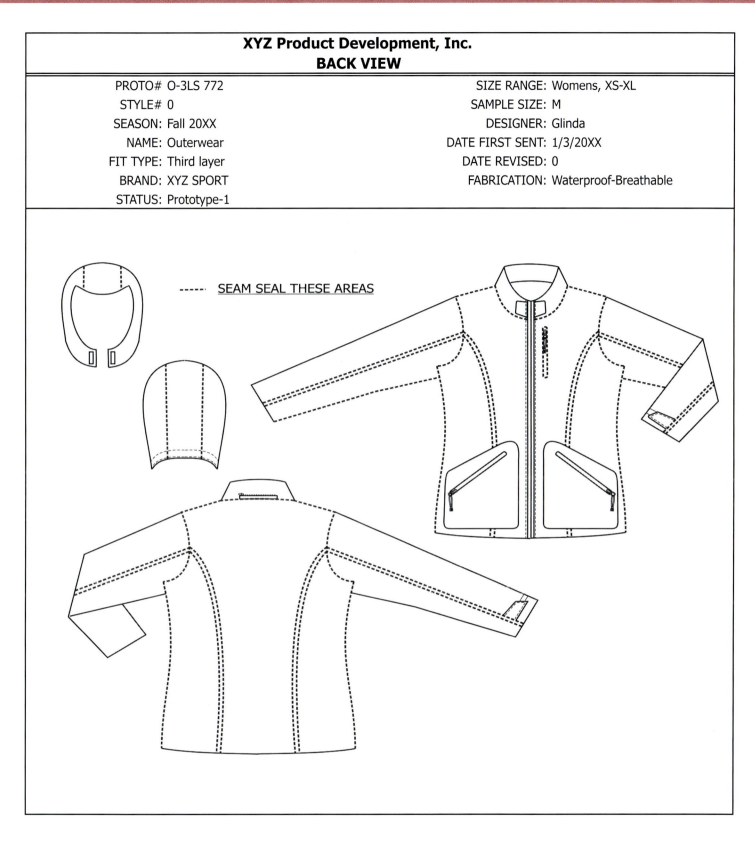

- - - - SEAM SEAL THESE AREAS

XYZ Product Development, Inc.
POINTS OF MEASURE

PROTO# O-3LS 772	SIZE RANGE: Womens, XS-XL
STYLE# 0	SAMPLE SIZE: M
SEASON: Fall 20XX	DESIGNER: Glinda
NAME: Outerwear	DATE FIRST SENT: 1/3/20XX
FIT TYPE: Third layer	DATE REVISED: 0
BRAND: XYZ SPORT	FABRICATION: Waterproof-Breathable
STATUS: Prototype-1	

POINTS of MEASURE, W's SWEATER

(GIRTH MEASUREMENTS ARE FULL MEASURE--numbers in **Boldface**)

meas code	**BODY SPECS**	Spec	+ tolerance	− tolerance
T-A	Shoulder Point to Point	16 1/2	1/2	1/2
T-B	Shoulder Drop	1 1/2	1/4	1/4
T-C	Front Mid Armhole	14 1/2	1/2	1/2
T-D	Back Mid Armhole	16	1/2	1/2
T-E	Armhole Drop from HPS	9 1/2	1/4	1/4
T-F	**Chest** @ 1" fm seam	42	1	1
T-G	**Waist**	38	1	1
T-G2	Waist position fm HPS	15 1/2	1/2	1/2
T-H	**Bottom** Opening	46	1	1
T-I	Front Length fm HPS	32	1/2	1/2
T-J	Back Length fm HPS	32	1/2	1/2
T-K	Center Back Sleeve Length (LS)	33	3/8	3/8
T-L	**Bicep** @ 1" fm Seam	18	1/4	1/4
T-Q	**Elbow**	13	1/4	1/4
T-M	**Sleeve Opening,** Bottom	10	1/4	1/4
T-N	Front Neck Drop, to seam	4	1/4	1/4
T-O	Back Neck Drop, to seam	3/4	1/4	1/4
	Collar at Top, closed (1/2 measure)	8 3/4	1/2	1/2
T-P	Neck Width, seam to seam	8	1/4	1/4
H-1	Hood Height, HPS to top	14	1/4	1/4
H-2	Hood Width at peripheral vision draw cord	10	1/4	1/4
H-3	Hood at CF	6	1/4	1/4
H-4	Hood Face opening, top to bottom	11 1/2	1/4	1/4
H-5	Hood front to back	19 1/2	1/4	1/4

STYLE SPECS

	Spec	+ tolerance	− tolerance	
Collar Point (Collar height at CF)	3	1/8	1/8	SKETCH IS FOR REFERENCE ONLY,
Collar height at CB	2 3/4	1/8	1/8	NOT FOR DETAIL

ABBREVIATIONS

CF=center front   HPS=High Point Shoulder
CB=center back   LS=Long Sleeve

XYZ Product Development, Inc.
POINTS OF MEASURE

PROTO# O-3LS 772
STYLE# 0
SEASON: Fall 20XX
NAME: Outerwear
FIT TYPE: Third layer
BRAND: XYZ SPORT
STATUS: Prototype-1

SIZE RANGE: Womens, XS-XL
SAMPLE SIZE: M
DESIGNER: Glinda
DATE FIRST SENT: 1/3/20XX
DATE REVISED: 0
FABRICATION: Waterproof-Breathable

STANDARD POMs

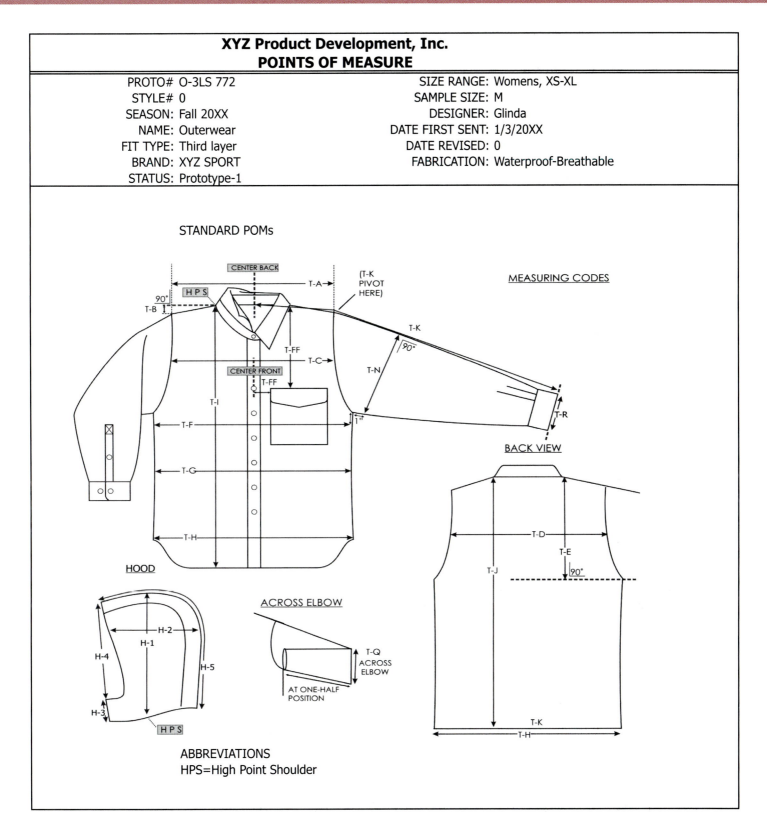

MEASURING CODES

BACK VIEW

HOOD

ACROSS ELBOW

ABBREVIATIONS
HPS=High Point Shoulder

XYZ Product Development, Inc.
Grade Page, WOMENS ALPHA

PROTO# O-3LS 772
STYLE# 0
SEASON: Fall 20XX
NAME: Outerwear
FIT TYPE: Third layer
BRAND: XYZ SPORT
STATUS: Prototype-1

SIZE RANGE: Womens, XS-XL
SAMPLE SIZE: M
DESIGNER: Glinda
DATE FIRST SENT: 1/3/20XX
DATE REVISED: 0
FABRICATION: Waterproof-Breathable

POINTS of MEASURE, **WOVEN** (GIRTH MEASUREMENTS ARE TOTAL CIRCUMFERENCE)

meas code	BODY SPECS	XS (0-2)	<2">	S (4-6)	<2">	MED-sample size(8-10)	<3">	L (12-14)	<3">	XL (16-18)	+ tolerance	- tolerance
T-A	Shoulder Point to Point	15 1/2		16		16 1/2		17 1/4		18	1/4	1/4
T-B	Shoulder Drop	1 1/2		1 1/2		1 1/2		1 1/2		1 1/2	1/4	1/4
T-C	Front Mid Armhole	13 1/2		14		14 1/2		15 1/4		16	1/4	1/4
T-D	Back Mid Armhole	15		15 1/2		16		16 3/4		17 1/2	1/4	1/4
T-E	Armhole Drop from HPS	9		9 1/4		9 1/2		9 7/8		10 1/4	1/4	1/4
T-F	Chest @ 1" fm seam	38		40		42		45		48	1/2	1/2
T-G	Waist	34		36		38		41		44	1/2	1/2
T-G2	Waist position fm HPS	14 1/2		15		15 1/2		16		16 1/2	1/2	1/2
T-H	Bottom Opening	42		44		46		49		52	1/2	1/2
T-I	Front Length fm HPS	30		31		32		33		34	1/2	1/2
T-J	Back Length fm HPS	30		31		32		33		34	1/2	1/2
T-K	Center Back Sleeve Length (LS)	31		32		33		34		34	1/2	1/2
T-L	Bicep @ 1" fm Seam	17 1/4		17 5/8		18		18 1/2		19	1/2	1/2
T-M	Sleeve Opening, Bottom	9		9 1/2		10		10 3/4		11 1/2	1/2	1/2
T-N	Front Neck Drop, to seam	3 3/4		3 7/8		4		4 1/4		4 1/2	1/4	1/4
T-O	Back Neck Drop, to seam	3/4		3/4		3/4		3/4		3/4	1/4	1/4
T-P	Collar at Top, closed (1/2 measure)	7 3/4		8 1/4		8 3/4		9 1/2		10 1/4	--	--
	Neck Width, seam to seam											
	STYLE SPECS											
	Collar Point (Collar height at CF)	2 3/4		2 3/4		2 3/4		2 3/4		2 3/4	1/4	1/4
	Collar height at CB	3		3		3		3		3	1/8	1/8
0		3		3		3		3		3	1/8	1/8

The tolerance for left side different than right side is 1/4"

XYZ Product Development, Inc.
Bill Of Materials

PROTO# O-3LS 772		SIZE RANGE: Womens, XS-XL
STYLE# 0		SAMPLE SIZE: M
SEASON: Fall 20XX		DESIGNER: Glinda
NAME: Outerwear		DATE FIRST SENT: 1/3/20XX
FIT TYPE: Third layer		DATE REVISED: 0
BRAND: XYZ SPORT		FABRICATION: Waterproof-Breathable
STATUS: Prototype-1		

ROLL GOODS

ITEM	CONTENT	LOCATION on garment	SUPPLIER	WIDTH / WEIGHT	FINISH / COLOR	QTY, UOM	Description	Unit of Meas
Fabric A (Color 1)	100% polyester	Main body	SiemonTex	58" cuttable	DWR	2.2 yd		yard
Fabric B (Color 2)	100% polyester	Collar	SiemonTex	58" cuttable	DWR	0.25 yd		yard
Fabric C (Color 3)	100% polyester	Sleeve, body stripe	SiemonTex	58" cuttable	DWR	0.05 yd		yard
Fabric D (Color 4)	100% polyester	Stripe on collar	SiemonTex	58" cuttable	DWR	0.02 yd		yard
Taffeta	100% nylon	Lining	Formosa Taffeta	48" cuttable	n/a	2.4 yd		yard
Mesh	100% nylon	Inside pocket	Champion	54" cuttable	Black for all	0.2 yd		yard
Brushed tricot	100% nylon	Glasses pocket bags	factory sourced		Black for all	0.22 yd		yard

FINDINGS

ITEM	CONTENT	LOCATION	SUPPLIER	WIDTH / WEIGHT/ STYLE #	FINISH / COLOR	QTY, UOM	Description	Unit of Meas
Zipper, CF	n/a		YKK	#5 Vislon, DA8LH1		1 pc.	One way separating, left hand insert	pc
Zipper, pocket	n/a	Hand pockets	YKK	7" reverse coil		2 pc.		pc
Zipper, pocket	n/a	Chest pocket	YKK	5" reverse coil		1 pc.		pc
Zipper, pocket	n/a	Key clip pocket	YKK	7" Vislon		1 pc.		pc
Zipper pull, slider	n/a				Antique Nickel	7 pc.	DFL	pc
Zipper pull cord	n/a	all exterior pulls	Ing-Tron		b/w for all	6 pc.	XYZ-104873	pc
Hook and loop	n/a			3/4"	Black for all	0.47 yd		yd
Seam seal tape	n/a			5/8"				yd
Drawcord	n/a	Waist				1		yd
Cordlock	n/a	Waist				1		pc
Bead	n/a	Waist				1		pc
Welded eyelet	n/a	Waist, hood				6		pc
Elastic binding	n/a	Top of mesh pkt.			Black for all	0.3		yd
Key Clip	n/a	key pocket			Black for all	1		pc
Key tether	n/a	key pocket				0.5		pc
Grosgrain	100% nylon	tethers				0.2		yd
Hang tag-sport	n/a	right underarm				1		pc
Retail ticket	n/a	right underarm				1		pc
Poly bag, and bag sticker (Flatpack)	n/a	see label page	Factory sourced	H X W = 18 X 13	self stick, closes at bottom	1		pc
string, for hangtags	n/a	see label instructions for placement	Factory sourced			1		pc

COLORWAY SUMMARY

color 1 Shell	color number	color 2, Collar	color 3, Stripe: body, sleeve, collar	color 4, Stripe--collar	color 3, pkt zippers	color 4, CF zipper	drawcord	color 1, lining
Royal	4473	Lt. royal	white	black	501	580	b/w	Royal
Siren	2677	Dawn	white	black	501	580	b/w	Siren
Dawn	0672	Lt. royal	white	black	501	580	b/w	Dawn
Black	6037	Lt. royal	white	black	501	501	b/w	Black
White	2880	Dawn	white	black	580	580	b/w	White

14. Bill of Materials

XYZ Product Development, Inc.
CONSTRUCTION PAGE

PROTO# O-3LS 772	SIZE RANGE: Womens, XS-XL
STYLE# 0	SAMPLE SIZE: M
SEASON: Fall 20XX	DESIGNER: Glinda
NAME: Outerwear	DATE FIRST SENT: 1/3/20XX
FIT TYPE: Third layer	DATE REVISED: 0
BRAND: XYZ SPORT	FABRICATION: Waterproof-Breathable
STATUS: Prototype-1	

Cutting information: see sketch on details page

Matching: match center of CF placket vertically, to dominant stripe

Stitches per inch (SPI) 12 +/- 1

AREA	DESCRIPTION	JOIN STITCH	SEAM FINISH	TOP STITCH	FUSIBLE	CLOSURES
collar	join	SN-L	seam seal		PCC 243, nonwoven	
collarband	join	SN-L	seam seal		PCC 243, nonwoven	
CF placket	join	SN-L	seam seal		PCC 243, nonwoven	
back yoke	join	SN-L	seam seal			
armhole	join	SN-L	seam seal			
shoulder	join	SN-L	seam seal			
side/underarm seam	join	SN-L	seam seal			
tabs	join and TS	SN-L	clean finish	Edge		
sleeve placket		SN-L	clean finish	E/S		
bottom opening						

XYZ Product Development, Inc.
LABEL and PACKAGING PAGE

PROTO# O-3LS 772

STYLE# 0

SEASON: Fall 20XX

NAME: Outerwear

FIT TYPE: Third layer

BRAND: XYZ SPORT

STATUS: Prototype-1

SIZE RANGE: Womens, XS-XL

SAMPLE SIZE: M

DESIGNER: Glinda

DATE FIRST SENT: 1/3/20XX

DATE REVISED: 0

FABRICATION: Waterproof-Breathable

LABELS

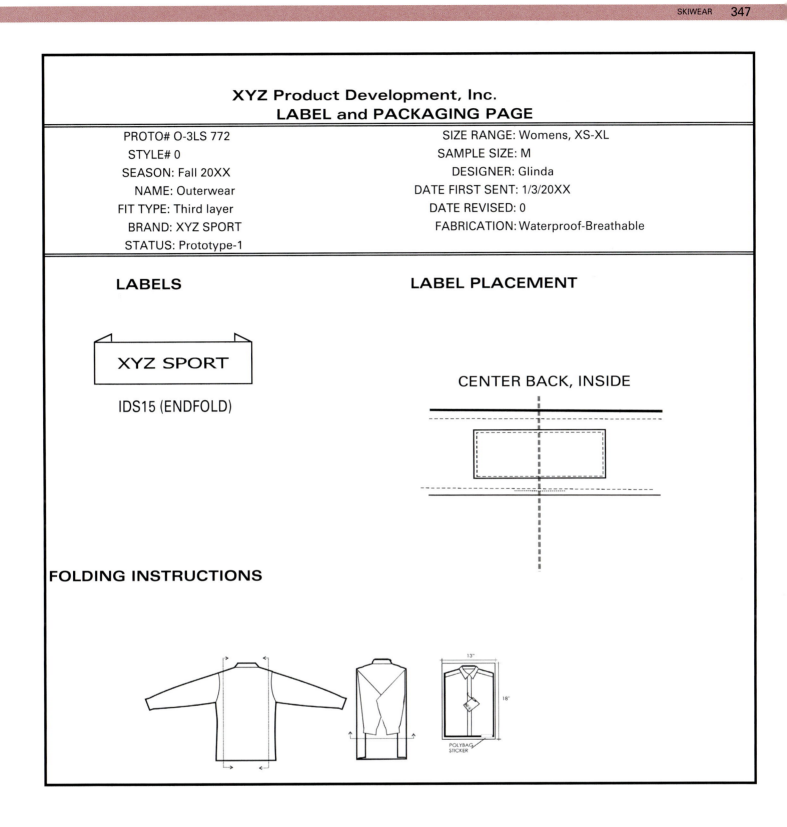

XYZ SPORT

IDS15 (ENDFOLD)

LABEL PLACEMENT

CENTER BACK, INSIDE

FOLDING INSTRUCTIONS

Thumbnail Clip Art

These pages contain thumbnails for clip art, representing a library of editable style flats and pocket details in two different digital formats. All these files can be accessed in the *Technical Sourcebook for Apparel Designers* Studio. This library of images can be used for developing new styles and new product development tech packs.

Dresses

1 TRAPEZE OR TENT · 2 TUNIC AND SKIRT · 3 JUMPER · 4 PRINCESS · 5 BABY DOLL · 6 SURPLICE · 7 SHIRTWAIST · 8 COATDRESS · 9 SLIPDRESS · 10 PEASANT · 11 CHEONGSAM · 12 CAFTAN · 13 T-SHIRT DRESS (POLO) · 14 SUN DRESS · 15 STRAPLESS

Additional Basic Dress Silhouettes

16 FITTED SHEATH · 17 A-LINE SHEATH · 18 EMPIRE WAIST · 19 HIGH WAIST · 20 DROPPED WAIST · 21 CHEMISE

Skirts

1 BASIC SKIRT · 2 WRAP · 3 KILT · 4 4-GORE A-LINE · 5 JEAN SKIRT · 6 DIRNDL · 7 SARONG · 8 PEGGED · 9 POUF · 10 A-LINE CULOTTE · 11 TRUMPET · 12 PEASANT, 3-TIERED · 13 HOBBLE SKIRT · 14 GATHERED FROM SCALLOPED YOKE

Pants

1 BELL BOTTOMS · 2 CROPPED · 3 ACTIVE · 4 TROUSER, HOLLYWOOD WAISTBAND · 5 KNICKERS · 6 BIB OVERALLS · 7 PEGGED · 8 PAPERBAG WAIST · 9 PALAZZO · 10 HAREM · 11 JODHPUR · 12 DHOTI · 13 GAUCHO · 14 JUMPSUIT · 15 LEGGINGS · 16 ROMPER

Shirts and Tops

1 CAMP SHIRT · 2 POLO · 3 TUXEDO · 4 TIE BLOUSE · 5 WESTERN · 6 SHELL · 7 PEASANT · 8 DOLMAN, 3/4 SLEEVE VERSION · 9 TAILORED SHIRT · 10 SMOCK · 11 PENDLETON SHIRT JACKET

Sweaters

1 CREW NECK · 2 TURTLE-NECK · 3 MOCK TURTLE · 4 FUNNEL NECK · 5 CARDIGAN · 6 ARGYLE · 7 FAIR ISLE · 8 RIB · 9 ARAN CABLE · 10 COWICHAN · 11 TWIN SET · 12 SHRUG

Women's Jackets

1 JACKET WITH 2-PIECE SLEEVE · 2 JACKET WITH CONTRAST TRIM · 3 FITTED JACKET, SHAWL COLLAR · 4 JACKET WITH HIDDEN PLACKET · 5 DOUBLE BREASTED BLAZER, PEAK LAPELS · 6 SWING COAT · 7 SPENCER · 8 RIDING JACKET · 9 BOMBER JACKET · 10 HOODY · 11 30s INSPIRED, a · 12 30s INSPIRED, b · 13 30s INSPIRED, c · 14 30s INSPIRED, d · 15 40s INSPIRED, DOUBLE PEPLUM · 16 40s INSPIRED, SWAGGER COAT · 17 50s INSPIRED, PORTRAIT COLLAR · 18 50s INSPIRED, A-LINE · 19 60s INSPIRED, BOLERO

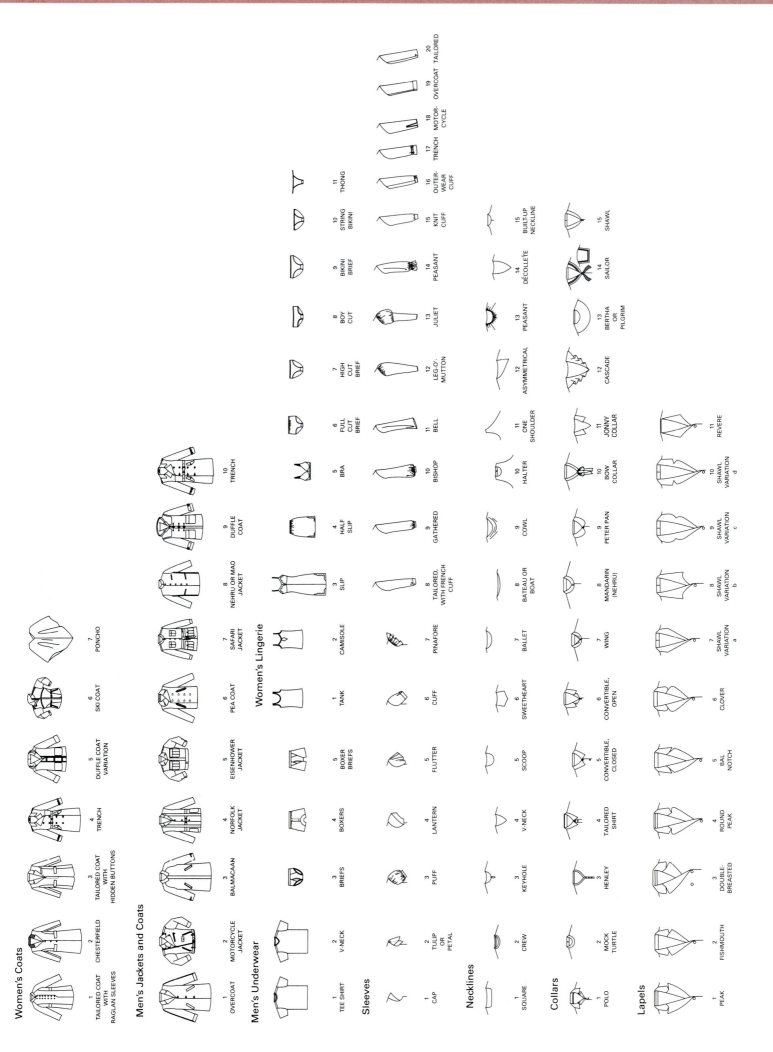

101 Pockets

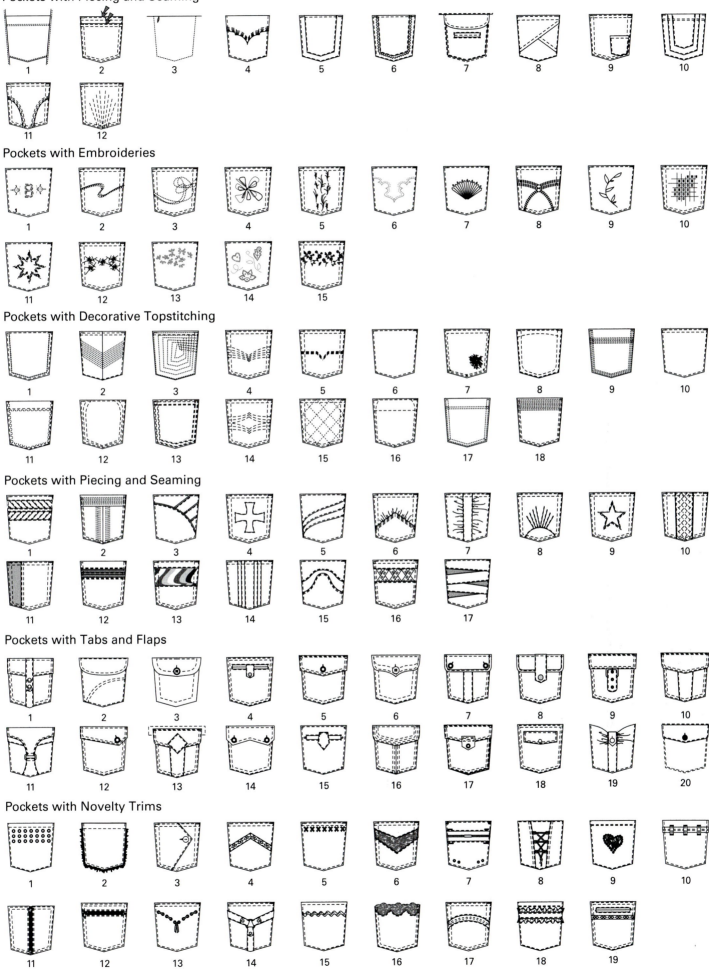

Pockets with Piecing and Seaming

1 2 3 4 5 6 7 8 9 10

11 12

Pockets with Embroideries

1 2 3 4 5 6 7 8 9 10

11 12 13 14 15

Pockets with Decorative Topstitching

1 2 3 4 5 6 7 8 9 10

11 12 13 14 15 16 17 18

Pockets with Piecing and Seaming

1 2 3 4 5 6 7 8 9 10

11 12 13 14 15 16 17

Pockets with Tabs and Flaps

1 2 3 4 5 6 7 8 9 10

11 12 13 14 15 16 17 18 19 20

Pockets with Novelty Trims

1 2 3 4 5 6 7 8 9 10

11 12 13 14 15 16 17 18 19

Glossary

accordion pleating Narrow pleats that fit close to the body, similar to the shape of the musical instrument the accordion.

active pant Pant style used for running, bicycling, and other active sports.

agent Individual who works between apparel companies and factories as a middle man. The design team in an apparel company provides the completed tech pack for a new design; the agent studies it, chooses the factory best suited to produce it, negotiates prices, and is paid a percentage of the price as a commission after the goods are completed and delivered to the port for shipping.

alpha sizing Sizing designated by letters, such as S-M-L (small, medium, and large).

argyle Sweater term for a multicolored diamond pattern with diagonal lines overlaid; a form of intarsia knitting.

armscye (or armseye) The armhole seam.

baby doll dress A short dress or top style with pleats or gathers hanging from a yoke, for girls' or women's style. The term refers to styles used for children's and infants' clothes in the early 20th century.

balance A symmetrical quality to a garment that occurs when it is cut on grain and the right and left sides match.

band An edge treatment consisting of fabric in a double-ply cylindrical construction, sewn to the raw edge of a garment to extend and finish the edge. A band can be used as a collar, at the hem edge of a skirt, pant, or sleeve, or the waist of a skirt or pant.

bartack Zigzag reinforcement stitches used for the areas where extra strength is needed, such as belt loops and the edges of pocket openings.

basket weave A variation of plain weave that has two warp threads woven over two weft threads. Sometimes called mat weave because it is used in floor matting.

bell bottoms Pants that flare from the knee down; popular in the 1960s. The style is adapted from a traditional navy uniform.

bell sleeve (also called angel sleeve) Sleeve flared between the elbow area and the bottom opening.

belting A type of stiff interfacing used inside a belt or strap.

bertha collar A type of oversize collar, round at the outside edge, sometimes made of lace. When made in an oversize version extending past the shoulders, it is called a *cape collar*.

binding An edge finish to one or more plies of fabric where a separate piece of fabric encases the raw edges. Part of the classification bound seam (BS).

binding off Sweater knitting term for finishing the final edge, such as the top edge of a turtleneck collar.

boat neck (also called bateau neck**)** A high, wide shape adapted from a French sailor's sweater.

bodice Portion of a woman's garment between the shoulders and the waist.

booked seam A seam in which the edge finish method is a blindstitch and the seam join method is a plain seam. The seams are then busted.

bottom weight Fabric heavy enough for pants or a skirt.

bound seam (BS) A seam category in which the raw edges are covered with a narrow piece of fabric.

bow collar A popular collar style introduced in the 1920s. Band collar with ends that extend into ties, often tied into a bow.

bowed Fabric grain distortion in which, during the finishing process, the center of the fabric feeds faster or slower than the selvage edges.

box pleats Pleats evenly spaced and pressed in alternate directions. The reverse side of inverted pleats is similar to box pleats. Inverted pleats are reversed so that the fullness is turned inward.

bra strap keeper The loop that holds a bra or camisole strap in place.

braid A type of trim formed in a bias construction of a woven trim; used where a more flexible and curved application is needed.

braid binding A kind of woven bias used for facings and edgings.

break point Place where the lapel folds back from the edge of the garment.

busted seam A seam that is pressed open. Also called a butterfly seam.

cable stitch Sweater knitting term for a pattern of crossed stitches creating a raised, rope-like design.

caftan Long, loose-fitting garment with origins in the Middle East, often with embroidered trim at the neckline.

callout Description or explanation notes accompanying a garment or detail sketch, used for floats and technical flats.

carding A process to disentangle fibers and remove small bits of debris and align the fibers, usually done for cotton yarns.

care label A label that describes how to clean the garment and what restriction there may be, if any, on the processing.

cargo pocket Patch pocket with bellows or pleats to add capacity.

carry-over styles Styles that are repeated in a line from one season to the next.

cascade collar A type of circular flounce attached at the neck seam.

casing A tunnel of fabric, usually made to enclose a drawcord.

cast off A horizontal area that is finished clean at the underarm and improves the shape and fit of the armhole.

chain off The operator continues to sew after finishing the seam, creating a chain of thread to secure the stitch.

chainstitch A stitch created by a machine that uses a needle thread interlooped with a bottom looper thread (401 multi-thread chainstitch).

cheongsam A slim garment, originally Chinese, with a Mandarin collar, side closure, and slit skirt.

child labor The employment of children under an age determined by law or custom. Each country has different standards in terms of its minimum age. Under the child labor laws in the United States, the minimum age to work in an establishment without parents' consent is 16.

Chinese collar See Mandarin collar.

clean finished seam A seam in which the edge finish method is a turned and stitched hem, and the seam join method is a plain seam. The seam is then busted.

cluster pleats Pleats arranged in groups, usually made by a combination of a large box pleat and several small knife pleats on either side.

coatdress A style of dress that has one or more details borrowed from a coat or trenchcoat (epaulets, belt, and so on).

collar stay The plastic stick inserted inside men's shirt collars. It shapes the edge of the shirt collar points and keeps the edges from curling.

color story A palette of related colors that follows a theme; used to color a line of coordinating apparel products.

colorist The member of the design team who works with the forecasting companies, researches color trends, and develops storyboards to present color direction to the rest of the group at the beginning of each season.

colorway For solid garments, the colors in which a style is offered. For garments of more than one color, all of the components that make up a certain color combination. For fabric prints, the specific color combination for each print.

combing A process that removes shorter fibers in order to create yarns of finer denier, smoother feel, and more uniform diameter.

commercialization process Process in which a concept is turned into an actual product and brought to market.

concept board Presentation boards incorporating sketches, swatches, and other inspiration. A preliminary presentation concept board usually includes illustrations on figures, colors, fabric swatches, print ideas, and trim examples.

construction detail Specific information in the tech pack about how each area of a garment is sewn and assembled. Construction details in sketch form are found in the detail pages of the tech pack and written notations are found in the construction notes area.

contour waist style A pant or skirt style without a straight waistband, wherein the top waist is shaped to fit the contour of the body.

convertible collar (also called a pajama collar or Hawaiian shirt collar) Style with no stand that has more or less roll depending on the collar pattern.

courses The horizontal rows of stitches in a weft knit.

covering power Measure of yarn to occupy an area. In knits, covering power is related to tension; the higher the tension, the greater the covering power. Yarns with good covering power produce thicker fabrics.

coverstitch (sometimes called interlock stitch) Type of stitch used to cover a raw edge or seam; used for seaming knit underwear, activewear, and intimate wear.

croquis Outline of a figure used as a master sketch for tracing over.

crosswise grain (also crossgrain, weft, fill, and width) The yarns that are interwoven with the warp.

crowd sourcing A new way of creating products by soliciting contributions from people who are not related to the company rather than from traditional employees or suppliers. Internet technology has made it possible for companies to solicit ideas from the online community.

crystal pleats A series of very narrow parallel pleats, used to create a slim, straight silhouette. Similar to but narrower than accordion pleats.

cuff An applied band or finished turnback at the bottom opening of a sleeve or pant leg.

culotte Type of bifurcated skirt that is a blend of skirt and pant; a longer version is called a gaucho.

cut-and-sew Apparel products produced with flat patterns, which are then cut and joined on sewing machines.

dart A method used to take up excess fabric to incorporate the shape of the body.

dart depth The total height of the dart fold, which is measured at the seam line (not at the cut edge).

dart folding Dart is created by folding the fabric to take up excess fabric. The direction of folding is differentiated based on where the darts are located.

dart length Total length of a dart, measured from the seam to the point of the dart.

design ease Certain areas of a given style that are tighter or looser according to the current silhouette.

development window Timeframe given to complete the development of the styles from the line plan.

dhoti [doe' tee] A kind of draped pant; an ethnic style from India. It has come to refer to a type of pant with a low draped rise; may be gathered at waist and tight at the lower legs.

dirndl skirt A straight skirt with ease or gathers going into a straight waistband. The origin of this style comes from Tyrolean peasant costume.

dobby A small geometric pattern woven by means of a dobby attachment to a loom.

dolman sleeve (also called batwing sleeve) A variation of kimono sleeve but with no gusset.

double-face fabric In sweater terms, a knit that looks the same on both the technical face and technical back, such as 1 × 1 rib.

double jacquard A jacquard method that achieves more complex patterns than the single jacquard method, as it does not have the two-color-per-row restriction. It requires a machine with two beds with no floats on the back.

double knit A knitted fabric made to produce a double thickness with each thickness joined by interlocking stitches; also, an article of clothing made of such fabric.

down The soft undercoating of waterfowl, most commonly ducks and geese.

drag line Fold of fabric that occurs on the body when there is not quite sufficient fabric, or too much fabric, for the distance required; fabric is pulled off grain in an unattractive way.

drawcord A string inserted inside a casing in garments where shaping is needed, usually found in the waistline, sleeve hem, or neckline.

drawing conventions Standardized ways for drawing different elements, such as seams, topstitching, and so on; used to make technical sketches consistent and easy to understand.

drawn to scale Visual interpretation of a set of measurements, in this case of a garment.

drawstring pant A style of pant with waist finished with a cord threaded though a casing at the top edge.

dual distribution Companies that sell their products wholesale, as well as through their own retail stores. This allows them to access more consumers, as well as present their brand message more completely in their own stores.

dyed to match (DTM) Often used to describe color matching, as for knit trims, buttons, and other matching details. The term is used on the BOM (bill of materials) page of the tech pack.

easing Shaping method similar to gathering, but very subtle with no visible folds. Usually used in a sleeve head and princess line.

edge finishes A classification of seams that incorporates the methods for finishing the edge of a single ply, including finishing the raw edges before seaming.

enclosed seam A seam type in which the fabric plies are sewn face sides together, then opened out and turned back wrong sides together. Topstitching is usually applied to encase the seam allowances.

engineered print Specially designed print in which the pattern is intended to end up in a particular place on the garment.

eyed buttons (also called sew-through buttons) Buttons that have holes to sew through. Two-hole and four-hole varieties are most common.

fabric layout Fabric plan for cutting, with the goal to use the least amount of fabric.

facings A way of finishing a raw edge of a garment with a separate piece of fabric; considered an enclosed seam.

fallout The fabric in between the pattern pieces in a lay-up that ends up as scrap.

fashion sketch (also called fashion illustration) Sketches that incorporate a garment on a figure, usually of idealized proportions.

fastener Buttons, zippers, lacing, ties, hook-and-loop (most commonly known as Velcro), hooks, and snaps are among the methods used to fasten the openings of apparel products for the wearers' ease in dressing and undressing.

Federal Trade Commission (FTC) An independent agency of the U.S. government established to promote consumer protection.

filament yarns Yarns formed by twisting together multiple, long, continuous fibers.

findings All the smaller items and trimmings that are used for sewing and garments construction; everything that is not the fabric or packaging. The list of findings to be used is found on the BOM (bill of materials) page of the tech pack.

fit ease Areas of a garment that are just enough larger than the body to allow for comfort and movement.

fit history Page of the tech pack that is the record of reviewing each sample against the points of measure.

flap A part of a pocket that covers the opening edge.

flat (also called technical flats or tech sketches) Specialized two-dimensional drawing, drawn to scale, that may also include sewing and construction information.

flat seam (FS) A seam formed by joining panels along the cut edges, butting them together or overlapping them slightly. Certain specialized machines are used for this; the most common is the 600 series flatlock machine.

float (or portfolio flat) A simplified fashion drawing without a figure. Floats are often used in conjunction with fashion illustrations.

float thread In a single jacquard, for the color not used, the color is carried along the back as a "float."

FOB (Free on Board) The garment price quote including cutting, sewing, finishing, folding and bagging, boxing, and sending the goods to the port for shipping. It does not include ocean freight, duty, and transportation to the destination warehouse.

folder A special device to keep binding precisely folded and set while sewing and for various other operations.

forecast companies Companies that specialize in researching colors and trends and creating books that predict the direction of fashion from 18 to 24 months in advance.

French darts Diagonal darts set at the side seam that start a couple inches above the waist and end near the apex of the bust.

French seam (SSae) A plain seam formed with two steps: seam is sewn wrong sides together, then a slightly wider seam is sewn right sides together encasing the first seam.

frog Usually made of cord or of bias-covered cord or wire. This style originated in China and first appeared on traditional Chinese garments. In this type of closure the button shank is made from the same cord as the button.

full-fashioning A method of widening or narrowing a knit panel.

garment bias Angles other than true bias (45 degrees).

gathered flared skirt A type of skirt with exaggerated fullness; a silhouette used by Christian Dior and popular after World War II.

gathering Method of controlling the predetermined amount of fullness drawn up to correspond to a smaller adjoining seam line or measurement. It means the fullness on one side of a seam is gathered into the smaller side on the other.

gathering ratio Ratio between the length of the longer fabric and that of the shorter fabric.

gaucho A type of pant with a wide below-knee length, typically worn with boots, with no bare leg showing.

gauge (or cut) Sweater term for the needles per inch on a given knitting machine; gauge is also a sewing term for the distance between topstitching rows.

gimp Cord added to a buttonhole that adds stability.

globalization Working as one unit with different sectors of production, marketing, and distribution channels in different regions in the world.

godet A triangular piece of fabric usually set into the hem of a garment to help facilitate the movement of the wearer or to add fullness to the silhouette.

gored skirt A skirt with flared, shaped panels rather than dart shaping.

gores Vertical divisions within a garment, usually tapered panels seamed together for shaping.

gorge A seam where the collar meets the lapel in tailored garments.

go-see The visit a potential fit model makes to be measured for suitability to the sample size.

grade rules Amounts and locations of proportionate growth or reduction for sample-size pattern pieces to achieve the different sizes needed for production. The grade rules are applied, for example, to a size 8 sample-size pattern to produce all the other sizes in the offering. The grade rules are incorporated into the grade page of the tech pack.

grading The process of proportionately increasing the perfected sample size pattern for the larger sizes and decreasing it for the smaller sizes.

graphic designer Designers who create graphics for apparel products, packaging, labels, hangtags, logos, embroideries, and signage of the product.

greige (also called loom state) A commercial run of fabric which is yet undyed and unfinished.

gusset A diamond-shaped, triangular, or sometimes tapering piece of cloth, designed to ease restriction in an armhole or crotch.

gypsy skirt See peasant skirt.

hair canvas Used in classic tailored jacket construction; made of a special very springy fabric.

hand The feel of the fabric when it is handled; the properties of a textile that help predict how it will make up into a garment.

handloom A small woven swatch created by a fabric mill, representing a plaid colorway.

hand-loom machines Sweater term for knitting machine powered by hand.

hand pin knitting Term used by scholars for the type of knitting most similar to hand-knitting of today, to distinguish it from other ancient techniques: knotting, twisting, circular peg frames, and crossed loop fabrics.

hand sample A swatch sent for approval with the interfacing applied to the shell fabric.

hanger Swatches of fabric attached to a cardboard strip along the top edge.

harem pant A pant with gathers set at the ankle.

hat ring A spring device used to measure the inside of a hat. It looks similar to a pair of scissors, and when set inside a hatband and squeezed, it expands to the inside diameter, and the size can be taken from the calibrated numbers.

haute couture Literally "high sewing" in French. The design of high-end apparel collections, in special fabrics, with high-quality hand-finishing work, custom fit to the client's figure. In most cases it is produced in small quantities for an exclusive clientele by high-fashion design houses such as Christian Dior, Chanel, and Givenchy.

heading A technique used in combination with a casing to create a ruffle.

hem A finish at the edge of a garment, the most common of which is the turned-back hem.

hemline The bottom edge, or foldline, of a dress or skirt that will be the finished length.

herringbone twill A twill weave fabric reversing from right- to left-hand twill at regular intervals.

high point shoulder (HPS) Point on a top at the neck edge or seam where the garment folds when laid flat.

hobble skirt A skirt cut and draped in such a way as to narrow at the bottom. Paul Poiret made this design popular in the late 1910s. The original version was so restrictive at the bottom opening that it allowed only the smallest steps to be taken.

hook and loop (also called Velcro) A fastener that consists of two tapes one of woven hook-tape and the other of woven or knitted loop-tape.

horizontal integration Production process in which each part is owned and operated separately. For example, a garment where the trims and fabric are from different companies and the cutting, assembly, and packing are done by separate parties working in different places.

hourglass A women's silhouette associated with the late 19th and early 20th centuries in which corsets were worn to pull in the waist and push out the hips and bust. Revived in Dior's New Look of 1947.

inset corner A seam usually with a 90 degree corner that requires close clipping.

intarsia Sweater term for a color technique that enables designs of many colors. A crossover of yarns is made at the point of the color change, and there are no yarns carried behind. The separate colors are often wound onto bobbins to help keep the yarns from getting tangled.

interfacing A supportive fabric placed between the layer of garment and facing; adds weight and body to a garment and is used on edge parts such as collars, cuffs, flaps, and waistbands.

interlining An insulation layer placed between lining and shell fabric; used for additional warmth and also for quilted effects.

interlock Weft knit fabrics consisting of two separate 1 1 rib fabrics interknitted to form one cloth. The fabric is relatively stable, reversible, and has a smooth surface.

interlock stitches See coverstitches.

intersecting seams Seams formed at the point where two or more seams meet and cross each other; the seams must meet exactly on a quality garment.

inverted pleats Folds of fabric that meet each other at a central point on the face side of a garment.

jacquard A patterned fabric produced with an attachment to the loom that enables it to produce complicated patterns such as brocade; also, sweater term for color technique. Sweater jacquard incorporates single, double, and ladder-back.

jodhpurs Type of pant used for horseback riding; flared at the hip and tight from knee to ankle.

jonny collar (also called Italian collar) A collar set into a V-neckline.

J-stitch A type of topstitching used for a trouser fly closure.

Juliet sleeve A long sleeve with a puffed top, seamed to a slim lower arm.

jumper A sleeveless dress usually worn over a sleeved blouse, shirt, or sweater.

kick pleats An inverted or side pleat often found at the bottom of slim skirts to provide ease in walking.

kilt A pleated wrap-around skirt, traditionally plaid.

kimono sleeve A sleeve cut-in-one with the bodice, with a seam at underarm and overarm.

knickers A loose gathered or pleated pant with a buckled band at the knee, often seen as a part of a man's golfing outfit in the late 19th and early 20th centuries.

knife pleats (also called flat pleats or side pleats) Single pleats, with folds 1 inch or narrower, turned in the same direction.

knit A fabric formed by interlooping adjacent yarns on a fixed bed of latch-hook needles.

knitdowns Sweater swatches furnished by the mill or agent to assist the designer in determining the appropriate gauge, tension, and yarn weight.

knock-off Close facsimile of the original, usually in cheaper fabrics and trims; offered at a much lower cost to the mass market.

lab dip A small swatch of the fabric that has been dyed to match a standard (for example, a specific Pantone color). The colorist manages this process.

lacing A closure in which cord, braid, or ribbon is threaded through eyelets, grommets, hooks, or buttonholes.

ladder-back jacquard Hybrid of single and double jacquard. Ladder-back jacquard has short floats and creates a fabric that is lighter in weight than double jacquard.

landed price The price of a garment including duty, ocean freight, and shipping to the warehouse in the destination country.

lapped seam (LS) A seam category in which all layers are joined from the face of the garment by overlapping the seam allowances of two or more fabric plies and sewing them together, with the fabrics extending in opposite directions.

latch-hook needle Patented in the 19th century and still used on weft knitting machines today. This holds the yarns in place while the loops are being formed, then releases them to form the next stitch.

lay-up Plies of fabric rolled out to be cut. The marker is subsequently placed on top prior to cutting.

lead time The time frame of production from designing to finished manufacturing and delivery to the retail store. It can also refer to the time required to order textiles or other trims.

lengthwise grain (also called warp) The yarns that are attached to the loom before weaving begins.

lettuce-edge hem A type of hem formed on a stretch knit fabric in which the fabric is extended during the hemming process; when released, this creates a ruffled effect.

lignes A special measuring unit used for sizing buttons. A 40-ligne button is one inch.

line plan A spreadsheet of all the styles to be produced for the season, including the estimated quantities, colorways, import costs, and pricing information.

lining A fabric, usually lighter weight than the shell fabric, used for all or part of the inside of the garment, finishing the interior, and covering the seam allowances.

linking One of the construction methods of sweaters. It is created by the use of a specific knitting machine called a linker.

links-links A stitch created by an automated specialty machine with two needle beds that share one set of double-ended latch needles. This enables both knit and purl stitches to be knit on the same wale.

lockstitch The stitch is formed by an interlocking needle thread as a top thread and a bobbin thread as an underthread.

looper A stitch-forming device used in tandem with a needle or needles.

looper thread The bottom thread on a chainstitch, or threads that cover the edge of an overedge seam.

Mandarin collar (also called Chinese collar) A standing band collar whose ends do not meet at center front.

mark Sweater term for the stitch formed when narrowing occurs on a sweater panel. A stitch is transferred to an adjacent needle and creates a distinctive stitch called a mark.

marker Layer of paper with all the pieces drawn onto it in the most efficient arrangement possible to maximize fabric usage; to be placed atop the layup before cutting.

merchandiser Person who often heads up the design team and whose job it is to analyze the market, review the best-selling styles from the previous season, and provide direction to the design staff. Acts as a bridge between the buyers and the designers and also monitors the sales and retail performance of each item.

minimum stretched A particular type of extended measurement used for knits, which is often used for neck openings such as on the neck of a T-shirt. It is used to make sure that the neck can extend enough to comfortably get over the head.

miss stitch Sweater term for a stitch in which the machine needles deactivate at patterned intervals and do not move into position to accept a yarn. A float thread is formed when a needle stays back.

miter Lines in patterns or stripes that meet at an angle at a seamline.

mock neck A close-fitting collar, usually a pullover knit, but sometimes in woven fabric with a back closure.

moda pronto See ready-to-wear.

monofilament A single strand of man-made fiber such as fishing line.

multi-channel retailing A company provides numerous means for customers to purchase goods and services. This marketing strategy could include selling through traditional retailing options such as catalogs, brick-and-mortar stores, mail, and telephone, as well as e-tailing options such as Internet and mobile.

NAHM board A type of flattened foot form, developed to ensure consistency in sock fit and available in standardized sizes.

National Association of Hosiery Manufacturers (NAHM) Device developed to ensure consistency in sock fit; available in standardized sizes from 3 to 16.

national brands The brands distributed nationally, well known and to which consumers attach specific images, quality levels, and prices.

numeric sizing Size range designated with numbers, such as 4, 6, 8, 10, 12, and so on.

omni-channel retailing A new trend of the fashion retailing. *Omni* means "all" in Latin and *channel* means a route of distribution and retailing of products. Omni-channel retailing is a strategy combining the consumer experience online and offline, centered on providing a seamless and satisfying retail experience to customers.

one-way direction Indicating that the top of all the pattern pieces will be placed in the same direction.

on-seam pocket A type of pocket set into a seam.

ornamentation Any fibers, yarn, or trims imparting a visibly discernible pattern or design to a yarn or fabric.

overall A one-piece garment with bib top and suspenders derived from the workwear of farmers.

overedge A stitch formed by a triangle of thread encircling the edge of the seam; generally incorporating a knife to trim the seam to a compatible width.

overedger The machine which creates overedge, also called a serger.

padded hem A hem with an additional piece of thick, soft fabric or bias inserted between the hem and garment to prevent a sharp crease or to eliminate a ridge on a heavy fabric.

palazzo pant A wide, soft, divided skirt, or long culotte, popular in the late 1960s and early 1970s.

pant (trouser) A bifurcated garment covering the body from waist to ankle, in two parts, one for each leg.

paperbag waist High gathered waist on pants (and skirts); the name comes from the appearance of the gathers.

patch pocket A type of pocket that is a piece of fabric appliquéd onto the outside of a garment.

pattern maker Person in the sample department who will create patterns so samples can be produced for fitting and review.

peasant dress A style with a gathered neckline and raglan sleeves ending in a ruffle, and a skirt with two or more gathered tiers.

peasant skirt (also called gypsy skirt) A long skirt with gathered tiers, as is seen in the rural costumes worn in many countries, especially Eastern Europe.

pegged pant Pant silhouette with fullness at the top and a tapered leg.

pegged (or peg-top) skirt A skirt cut to be full at the hipline and narrow at the bottom.

personal sketch Hand sketch for design inspiration or design journal.

piece-dyed fabric Fabric that is woven as greige goods, then dyed.

pile Fabric structure with three sets of yarn: warp, weft, and a set of loops on the surface. Velvet and corduroy are examples. Knit fabric can also be pile; in that case, the pile yarns are looped through the knit structure.

pilgrim collar (also called puritan collar) Wide, round collar with front opening.

pinked seam An edge finish made with a zigzag cut, done with a shaped blade.

pin tucks Narrow folds of fabric, 1/8 inch or less, often used as inserts.

piping A type of trim or embellishment consisting of a strip of folded fabric, cut on the bias, and inserted into a seam to define the edges and/or seams of a garment.

placket A finished opening such as is found at the cuff of a sleeve or the center front finishing of a shirt. Plackets are used at the front or back neckline and are planned in such a way as to accommodate buttons, snaps, or other fasteners.

plain seam The most common of the superimposed seams. The panels are sewn face sides together.

plain weave (also called tabby weave or taffeta weave) Weave that consists of the warp and weft that are aligned and form a simple crisscross pattern.

plating Sweater term for employing two different colored yarns knit together using a special feeder. Plating is also used to introduce spandex yarns for shape retention.

pleat depth The distance from the outside fold to the inside fold of a pleat.

pleats Various folds of fabric that are formed by doubling the fabric back on itself, fixed at one end by pressing, stitching, or anchoring in a seam and released at the other.

plumules The element of down used for the finest fill.

pointelle Sweater term for a type of stitch transfer lace in which single jersey stitches are transferred to the needle to the left or right. Repeated in an overall pattern, it creates an openwork effect.

points of measure (POM) Points on a garment where each spec is defined, and where measurements are taken, such as "across chest at 1" below armhole."

polo dress A casual knit style often with a flat-knit collar.

pouf skirt A full, short skirt, gathered in at the bottom; a type of exaggerated silhouette generally reserved for evening and special occasions.

preproduction sample A sample produced right before the stage of main production, sewn in the actual factory doing the production to confirm all the fit specs and details are correct. When accepted, production can begin.

prêt-á-porter See ready-to-wear.

princess-seamed dress A dress fitted with seams rather than darts, often without a waistline seam.

princess seaming Seams that extend from the bodice to the hemline, creating a slenderizing silhouette.

private label (also called retail store brand) A line of products created by a retailer and sold only in their own stores.

product lifecycle management Computer software that integrates information about the entire lifecycle of products from concept through design, development, sourcing, and manufacturing.

prototype sample The original sample garment produced according to the instructions in the tech pack.

punch-card Guide for a hand-loom knitting machine that adds colors or patterns and shapes the dimensions of each panel.

purl stitch Sweater term for the technical back of jersey stitch.

quality assurance professional The quality assurance (QA) department helps to maintain fabric and trims standards through testing, and also deals with finished garment quality issues. Quality assurance personnel work closely with the design teams to help deliver the highest quality products.

raglan sleeve (also called saddle sleeve) A sleeve style cut partly in-one with the body and which ends at the neckline. A very simple shape that has a straight underarm-to-neckline seam.

ready-to-wear Off the rack, ready to be worn, as is most apparel produced and sold. Apparel products that are mass produced based on standardized sizing are ready-to-wear garments.

reece welt See welt pocket.

registration number (RN) A registered identification number issued by the Federal Trade Commission. The number is assigned upon request to a business residing in the United States that is engaged in the manufacture, importing, distribution, or sale of textile, wool, or fur products.

rep (representative) Company sales representatives, either in-house (employed by the company and paid by salary) or independent (self-employed, paid by commission), generally with a regional territory. They travel their territory to introduce the new line, then attend regional trade shows where the retailers come to place their wholesale orders.

repeat Printed pattern that is repeated at regular intervals.

reshoring The trend of bringing back manufacturing of a broad range of products to the company's own country (e.g., the United States) rather than having the work done elsewhere to save on labor costs. It results in a faster and smoother production process, and can also streamline the product development process by shortening the turnaround time of prototypes and sample approval.

retail store brand See private label.

rib knit structure Sweater term for a fabric created by alternating wales of knit and purl in the same course. This requires a double bed machine. A common example is one knit and one purl alternating, which creates a rib called 1×1.

running style A fabric, readily available from a mill, that has been sold to previous customers, is repeated continuously, and for which greige is available.

saddle sleeve See raglan sleeve.

safari dress Styled after an African bush jacket with belted and multiple pleated patch pockets; was restyled by Yves St. Laurent in 1967.

safety stitches A combination stitch that creates a 401 chainstitch plus 500 serged edges in one operation.

sailor collar A style derived from a traditional navy uniform, with a collar that is cut square in the back and tapers to a V in front. Often worn with a bow tie and used for children's styles, school uniforms, and costumes.

sample evaluation comments The notes, instructions, revisions, and updates on a sample, including fit history, which are added to the tech pack before the next sample is requested.

sample maker Sews the first prototype samples for a given style, and is employed either in-house by the apparel company or at the factory that will be doing the manufacturing. A sample maker has a high degree of sewing skill and familiarity with production sewing techniques as well as all the machines used in manufacturing.

sample status Stage of sample development, such as second proto or top of production sample.

sarong skirt (also called pareo) Derived from a simple piece of fabric that wraps and ties to one side; modern sarong styles are usually adaptations that give a similar look, but without needing to be adjusted.

satin weave Fabric with long floats across the surface, characterized by a shiny surface.

Schiffli lace A kind of embroidered eyelet with a finished scalloped border.

seam The stitched joint between two or more pieces of fabric, or the line of stitching that joins the edges in a single piece of fabric (as in a dart).

seam allowance The distance between the seam line and the cut edge of the garment.

seam grin A faulty seam wherein threads show on the exterior side when the seamlines are stretched.

seamline The place marked on the pattern to designate where the seams will be joined.

selvedge The self edge of the fabric that is lengthwise in the direction of the warp; formed as the weft is interlaced with the warp during weaving.

serger See overedger.

set A smooth fit of garment without drag lines or wrinkles.

set-in sleeve A sleeve style that is the basic standard and is the one included on the sloper pattern. It is attached to the body of the garment around the arm socket.

shank button Created with a premade attached shank or thread shank. Shanks raise buttons above the garment surface, allowing the button to sit sufficiently higher than the buttonhole to avoid distorting the garment.

shawl collar A collar, seamed in the back, without separate lapels, that follows the front neckline of garment.

shelf bra A stretchy second layer of fabric inside a top or dress with thin straps. This provides very light but very comfortable support.

shirring Method of shaping a garment to control fullness, similar to gathering. Shirring consists of two or more rows of gathered fabric. Shirring can be a pretty and feminine alternative to darts in small areas of a garment such as the cuffs.

shirtwaist A classic style based on a tailored shirt, with details such as a collar with collar band, cuffs, and front placket. It is usually made from woven fabric and is often belted.

silhouette The outline or shape of a garment.

single jacquard Method of adding color and pattern in which there are no more than two colors in a single row. It is called single because it is made on a single-bed machine. Compared to double jacquard, it has floats on the back as the color not being used is carried on the backside.

size set sample A graded set of samples such as 4, 6, 8, 10, 12, 14, and 16 for missy, or a representative set such as 4, 8, 12, 16, produced to prove out the grade.

skewed (or torqued) Fabric grain distortion in woven fabrics when crosswise yarns slant from one selvage to the other.

sleeve cap The area of a sleeve, or sleeve pattern, above the bicep.

slipdress A style for evening wear that incorporates details from lingerie, such as spaghetti straps, lace trim, lightweight silky fabric, and so on. It is often cut on the bias.

slit A long, straight opening, usually perpendicular to a hemline, used to provide easy movement for the wearer. A slit has the edges touching. A vent is a slit with an underlay.

sloper Basic pattern with fit ease built in, from which all other patterns are developed. Also called block pattern or foundation pattern.

social responsibility Ethical decision making of an individual or organization. It can be applied to any decision making related to product development and retailing processes.

soutache A narrow flexible braid.

specification buying (also called private label manufacturing) Retailers that have their own product development departments and styles exclusively for their company.

specifications (specs) Written guidelines for a style that include all the specific information related to producing a certain garment. The written specifications are called a "technical package."

staple fibers Term for yarns created from relatively short lengths twisted together, which may be a mix of natural and synthetic.

stitches per inch (SPI) Total stitches contained in 1 inch; one of the quality indicators for sewn products.

stitch-in-the-ditch (also called crack stitch) A finish in which the stitch line is sewn on top of the previous join seam; the crevice between the garment and binding.

stocking frame A device in which the operator would add rows of knitting quickly in a back-and-forth motion. Invented in 1589 by Reverend William Lee, the device would be described nowadays as a flatbed weft knitting machine.

stock-keeping unit (SKU) The identification of a product for inventory purposes. In planning an apparel line, the SKUs for a given item are calculated by multiplying the colors available by the sizes offered. For example, a blouse in three sizes and three colors has nine SKUs per style.

strikeoff Sample of a print design.

style number Numbers and/or letters that make up the unique identification of each garment. Some systems are "smart" systems in which the numbers and letters signify fabric, season, gender, or other information; some are simply sequential according to when a new tech pack is begun.

style summary Appears at the top of each page of the tech pack and includes important information including style number, season, fabric, size information, fit type, the dates first begun and last revised, and the sample status or stage of development.

sunburst pleating Pleats that widen from one edge to the other, meaning pleats are smaller at the top but larger at the bottom hem.

sundress A sleeveless style with a full skirt often worn with matching short-sleeved jacket.

superimposed seam (SS) A seam type created by stacking two or more fabric plies on top of the other; the raw edges are lined up and sewn together near the edges.

surplice (also called wrap dress) A style usually with overlapping layers, occasionally pleated at shoulders and waist.

sweat shop A working condition with unhealthy, difficult, or hazardous situations, or in which workers are not protected by labor laws. Workers may be forced to work long hours for little pay. Sweatshops are also often related to child labor.

swing tack A tack used to connect the lining to the shell at the bottom edge of the garment, usually at the seam allowances.

tailored knot A knot used to secure darts after sewing is done.

technical back Reverse side of a jersey stitch (i.e., purl side).

technical designer Contributes to the tech packs (manuals of each style) initiated by the design department, conducts fit meetings, revises the garment sketch CAD drawings as needed, writes fit comments, and directs the production process closely.

technical face Front side of a jersey stitch (i.e., knit side).

technical flat Proportionally correct, accurate sketches of a style viewed flat. These appear on the first pages of the tech pack, and include the front and back views and side view, if needed.

technical package (also called tech pack) A specification package, style file, or dossier. The blueprint or guideline of apparel production. It includes every detail needed for the development of apparel prototypes.

tech pack See technical package.

tent dress An exaggerated A-line shape. Introduced by Cristobal Balenciaga as a coat, and used for both dresses and coats in the 1950s.

tenter A frame used to move fabric through processing that secures the fabric at the edges with pins, forming tenter holes at the selvage.

tentering process A process used for pulling out wrinkles, shrinking, stretching, or straightening the grain, and many other finishing applications.

textile designer Designs new fabrics for apparel products. Knowledge about various colors, design motifs, printing techniques, fibers, and fabric structure, as well as CAD skills, are important for a textile designer, as is a knowledge of the technology of printing.

Textile Fiber Products Identification Act (TFPIA) Requires that labels disclose three different pieces of information: fiber content, manufacturer or importer, and country of origin. It should be permanently affixed to all garments sold in the United States.

textile lab technician Part of the quality assurance department, the textile lab technician tests the fabric against the textile requirements for apparel products.

tolerance The amount that the garment can be off specification, plus or minus, noted on the grade page.

top of production sample (TOP) A small sampling of the first garments coming off the production line. One or more are sent to the QA department, who will measure, check, and compare them to the preproduction (red-tag) sample and decide whether the shipment is approved to ship.

topstitching A line of stitching on the visible side of the garment, parallel to a seam.

top weight A blouse or shirt weight fabric.

torqued Fabric grain or seamline distortion in woven or knitted fabrics. In woven fabric, for example, it is what happens when crosswise yarns slant from one selvage to the other.

trade show A showcase of the newest products by companies who want to promote to prospective buyers under one roof. Trade shows are sponsored by apparel marts, promotional companies, and/or trade associations.

trapeze dress As introduced by Yves St. Laurent in 1958, a knee-length full-tent shape; an unfitted dress made with narrow shoulders that gradually widens to a very wide hem.

trims External decorative features that are added on to the basic garment, such as buttons, lace, ribbon, and bows.

trouser style A tailored pant with a waistband and relaxed fit.

true bias A 45-degree angle to the lengthwise or crosswise grain; the direction of maximum stretchability from a woven fabric.

trueing Process of checking the shapes and connections of a pattern to achieve smooth transitions.

trumpet skirt A longer skirt, fitted at the hip area, then flaring below the knee; commonly seen in ballerina length.

tuck depth The fold size of the tuck, measured on the face side of the completed garment.

tucks The take-up of fabric by stitching through parallel folds, usually evenly placed. Tucks are used to create a controlled amount of fullness.

tuck seam A type of lapped seam in which the stitching is farther from the folded edge, creating a tuck effect.

tuck stitch Sweater term for a stitch formed when the latch needle picks up a new stitch without dropping off the previous one.

tunic dress A straight, loose, unfitted garment of ancient origin, worn belted or unbelted. A shorter version is sometimes paired with a separate narrow skirt.

turned-back hem A common way to finish the edge of a garment by turning back the raw edge to the inside and securing it.

twill tape A type of firmly woven ribbon, used to stabilize seams and edges.

twill weave A woven pattern of diagonal parallel ribs, consisting of weft threads passing over one warp thread and then under two or more warp threads repeatedly.

underlining (also called backing) A layer of fabric placed behind the shell; used to stabilize fabrics and conceal construction details.

underpressing A pressing that is done during the sewing process.

understitching A stitch often added to help the seams roll to the inside and prevent the facing layer from slipping out and showing.

U.S. federal standard Originally set up as a foundation for increasing uniformity in sewn products such as military uniforms for the contractors who produced them, and later was adopted for the apparel industry for its usefulness.

vendor manual A notebook of company policies sent to each agent; may include some or all of the following: quality assurance standards, auditing procedures, shipping and carton standards, fair labor rules, how to measure standards, common terms and definitions, packaging and tagging methods, and sample timeline expectations.

vent See slit.

vertical integration When a company owns all production process facilities, including making the fabrics.

wales The vertical rows in knits.

warp See lengthwise grain.

warp knitting The knitting is performed with a variety of machines in which the yarn zigzags along the length of the fabric. The types of fabric produced by warp knit machines include tricot, raschel, and Milanese.

wearer's right or left Term to indicate apparel details in the right or left side, based on the wearer's perspective (rather than the viewers).

weft See crosswise grain.

weft knit Knit fabric and sweater loop structure, with the yarns applied horizontally; created by use of a fixed bed of latch hook needles. Common knit constructions are jersey, ribbed knits, and interlock.

welding When heat and pressure are applied to the seams to weld them, rather than sew them. There are no stitches or thread used, and the result is a watertight seal. The operator carefully monitors heat, pressure, and dwell time to assure the quality of bonding.

welt pocket (also bound or slashed pocket) A type of pocket for which the opening edge is a kind of finished hole or opening into the interior of the garment. Often made with an automatic machine called a reece machine.

wet process A special finishing such as softening, pre-shrinking, or a special dye or rinse.

wicking Any yarn or fabric finish that pulls moisture from one area and distributes it, letting it evaporate more efficiently.

wing collar A high, stiff, tailored shirt or blouse collar with spread points that turn down in front. Style worn by Eton College upperclassmen, and sometimes worn for daytime formal wear in the late 19th and early 20th centuries.

woolen yarns A yarn that is carded but not combed, and as a result the fibers are shorter and more "hairy." Woolen yarns are often preferred for sweaters and tend to be softer and warmer.

woven A fabric formed with warp yarns that are attached to harnesses and weft yarns interwoven on a loom by the use of one or more shuttles to form fabric.

yarn count Yarn thickness designated by weight and many other factors selected based on different kinds of fibers.

yarn dye Yarns that are dyed before they go onto the loom for weaving. Plaid fabrics are generally yarn dyed.

yoke A panel of fabric with a horizontal seam, used for shaping, style, or both.

zigzag stitch A variation of the lockstitch, the needle thread and bobbin thread meet in the center of the seam to form a symmetrical zigzag pattern stitch.

zoot suit A flashy suit style of extreme cut, including a thigh- or knee-length jacket with wide padded shoulders and baggy pleated trousers tapering to a narrow cuff. Popular in the United States in the 1940s, originating in Los Angeles.

Image Credits

All illustrations by Camille Steen unless otherwise indicated.

1.0 Venturelli/WireImage/Getty Images
1.2 Iannaccone / WWD / © Conde Nast
1.4 WWD / © Conde Nast
1.6 WWD / © Conde Nast
1.11 Courtesy of CLO
2.0 Victor VIRGILE/Gamma-Rapho via Getty Images
3.0 Pietro D'aprano/Getty Images
4.0 Estrop/Getty Images
5.0 Victor VIRGILE/Gamma-Rapho via Getty Images
6.0 Estrop/Getty Images
7.0 Victor VIRGILE/Gamma-Rapho via Getty Images
8.0 Victor VIRGILE/Gamma-Rapho via Getty Images
8.1 Ingrid Schneider
8.19 Ingrid Schneider
9.0 Estrop/Getty Images
10.0 Victor VIRGILE/Gamma-Rapho via Getty Images
11.0 Claudio Lavenia/Getty Images
12.0 Federico Magi/Mondadori Portfolio via Getty Images
13.0 Federico Magi/Mondadori Portfolio via Getty Images
14.0 AnthonyRosenberg/iStock.com
15.0 Fernanda Calfat/Getty Images
15.30a ASTM
15.30b Alvanon
16.0 Catwalking/Getty Images

Index